RIGHTEOUSNESS BY FAITH;

OR THE

Nature and Means of our Justification before God;

ILLUSTRATED BY A COMPARISON OF THE DOCTRINE OF THE
OXFORD TRACTS

WITH THAT OF THE

ROMISH AND ANGLICAN CHURCHES.

A NEW AND REVISED EDITION OF "OXFORD DIVINITY."

BY

CHARLES PETTIT M'ILVAINE, D.D., D.C.L.

BISHOP OF THE PROTESTANT EPISCOPAL CHURCH IN THE DIOCESE OF OHIO.

Second Edition.

WIPF & STOCK · Eugene, Oregon

Wipf and Stock Publishers
199 W 8th Ave, Suite 3
Eugene, OR 97401

Righteousness By Faith
Nature and Means of our Justification before God
By M'ILvaine, Charles Pettit
ISBN 13: 978-1-55635-708-4
ISBN 10: 1-55635-708-7
Publication date 11/8/2007
Previously published by Protestant Episcopal Book Society, 1864

	PAGE
PREFACE TO THE PRESENT EDITION,	5
PREFACE,	24
CONTENTS,	31
RIGHTEOUSNESS BY FAITH,	37
CHIEF DANGER OF THE CHURCH IN THESE TIMES, EPISCOPAL CHARGE IN 1843,	395
REASONS FOR REFUSING TO CONSECRATE A CHURCH HAVING AN ALTAR INSTEAD OF A COMMUNION TABLE,	425
THE WORK OF PREACHING CHRIST, EPISCOPAL CHARGE IN 1863,	451
INDEX OF SUBJECTS,	483
INDEX OF AUTHORS,	493

PREFACE TO THE PRESENT EDITION.

It will be seen by the Title-page that this volume is only a revised and improved edition of what has heretofore been known under the name of "Oxford Divinity." At this period in the history of a controversy which that name suggests, it is not supposed that, though the previous editions in this country and England are exhausted, there is any such demand for another as would justify the expense as a book-selling enterprise. There *is* a demand however, which has induced many zealous advocates of the great truths which the book maintains to desire its reprint, and which has prevailed with one of them to provide the means of perpetuating it in stereotype.

The author has been much more richly rewarded for his pains than ever he had expected to be. Instances in England and at home, in which God has graciously used it as the means of arresting a dangerous progress towards the full embracing of Romanism, under the teaching of the Oxford Tracts, or of kindred works; many more instances in which it has been honored in the promotion of a greatly increased clearness, decision, and spiritual discrimination, in the holding and teaching of those great central doctrines of the way of salvation, the denial of which is the parent of all Romish corruptions of Gospel truth, have come to his knowledge, and have been subjects of great thankfulness on his part to Him who puts his treasure "in earthen vessels that the excellency of the power may be of God and not of us."

But is not the work of this volume finished? Is not the controversy which gave it birth ended, or so fast expiring, and so nearly dead, that there need be no further fear of its influence? Has not its place been taken by a far more portentous evil, another Oxford Divinity, and another school of Tractarians, of a perfectly opposite character, and which, instead of promulgating only a corruption of Christianity, proclaims its virtual denial, even a vaunting and sceptical Rationalism, that stalks abroad on the high places of preferment in Church and university, a striking imitation of those primitive adversaries of the Gospel, to whose philosophic wisdom its central distinguishing facts and truths were "foolishness?"

We have not failed to take due notice of the rise and progress of this new school—new in certain respects; but still nothing more, in substance, that what the "evil heart of unbelief" has often raised up before, and "the power and wisdom of God" in Christ have often overcome. It is nothing more than a fresh, aspiring shoot from the decayed stock of that German rationalism, which having flourished at one time on the continent, in such pride, is now fast yielding to the revival of the Gospel. It is but an insidious form of that very Deism which, with more honest avowal of its nature and aims, sought to uproot Christianity in the times of Hobbes and Collins and Herbert and Tindal. We yield to none in our estimate of the unmixed evil, and the great danger of this new form of opposition to the Gospel; especially its barefaced dishonesty, in having for its leaders men who profess to be Christian ministers and occupy the places and enjoy the emoluments of clergymen of the Church of England. We trust that our venerable mother Church, by her righteous discipline, will cleanse herself of such dishonor. Shall indeed infidelity be allowed to speak from the pulpits of her Churches and the chairs of her universities? Shall men be allowed to preside over her great schools and venerable colleges, and live on endowments consecrated to the education of her youth in the ways of the Gospel, while they conspire together to bring into contempt and rejection all that she holds most vital and precious in the scriptures? Shall Unitarians have cause to taunt us with the boast, not only that what they call "eminent divines" of the Church of England, are avowing and propagating just *their* worst doctrines, but that in doing so, they have the sanction of Church-authorities and the patronage of their great University, since no decree silences—nor discipline ejects them? For the honor of the Gospel—the honor of the Church of England among whose children the Gospel is now having such precious fruit—for the interests of true religion, wherever her influence is felt, we trust not.

But because this school of rationalistic scepticism has thus arisen in the very halls where the Tractarian first appeared, and is now attracting so much attention that the remaining representatives of the latter are likely to be lost sight of, let it not be supposed that Tractarianism has no representation which need be watched, nor strength still to do great harm; that its evil doctrines are not by dangerous and zealous teachers still busily propagated; or that there are not classes and conditions of mind, wherever we go, in which its seed would find congenial soil and rapidly take root.

Because it has been signally defeated on the field of argument, it is too much taken for granted that its powers of mischief have been subdued. But had the Canaanites no power to trouble Israel and lead the victorious people into idolatry, after their strongholds had been taken and their land was in possession of the tribes? "The Canaanite was yet in the land;" defeated, but not slain; restrained, but not changed.

One thing is certain. The present advocates of the Tractarian system, do not think it defunct or likely soon to be so. They work it and glory in it, as a leaven that is spreading its influence; a tree that is multiplying its fruit. In a measure, we agree with them. It may be perfectly true that it has lost its first positions; that in the defection of so many of its chief leaders to avowed Popery, in spite of their strong anti-papal protestations, it has suffered great disgrace; that now we hear little of new converts to it, or by it to Rome; that the press has ceased to teem with its publications, and the magazines to make battle, in its favor or against it; that what it does, is done far more noiselessly, and secretly than formerly, far more as the sapper underground, than as a combatant in open field. And yet it may be just as true that it is still doing a very evil work; leading many souls astray; spreading a vast deal of false religion; preparing a great breadth of ground for a future harvest of popery; educating numbers of aspirants for the ministry whose preaching will be that of "another Gospel;" yea, and planting trees of which even Rationalism, just such as we now deplore, will be the genuine fruit. The old Upas tree may be standing no longer on its original roots; the old trunk may have perished; but its branches have taken root and become trees, and are sending out *their* branches to become, in their turn, a spreading contamination.

In our estimate of the present condition of Tractarianism, we must not mistake change of policy for decrease of zeal, or of influence. When at first the system had need to be strongly inaugurated in the public view, it came forth with an array of high pretending publications, bold in assumption, reckless in argument, promising wonders. Volume followed volume. A great flourish of trumpets announced the entrance of a great Reformation of the Reformed. Controversy was challenged to give notoriety. Controversy arose, at least as much as was desired. But now there is a marked change in the bearing of the system so introduced. Of a great deal that was first professed, we hear no more. It had its day and its use. Of many denials of what it was charged with and many strong professions of being the only safe ground of real Protestantism in distinction from "*Ultra* Protestantism," we hear no more. Of elaborate self-vindication the press now furnishes exceeding little. The silence of the *mine* has succeeded to the noise of the assault. The sower quietly sowing his seed, has succeeded to the soldiery storming a fortress. The latter gained a field and the former is now tilling it. Bustle had once its day. Quietness has it now. It was once desirable to draw the public gaze. It is better now to work away from it. The strategy has changed—not the enemy; the policy, not the cause.

The present plan is to promote a taste for a *ceremonial* sensuous religion; for Church ornament, pomp, symbolism, mystery and ritual, multiplied into the details of Church furniture, ministerial vestments, Clerical postures, and the like; under such fascinations, quietly to introduce and make fast the whole Sacerdotal system of Priesthood, Sacrifice, Altar, and the *opus operatum* of Baptismal efficacy. That system teaches the Church as the depository of saving grace; Sacraments as the only channels of that grace to the soul; Ministers of Sacraments as the only dispensers of that grace by those channels;

those Ministers real Priests, offerers of real sacrifice—of sacrifice by which comes remission of sins; those Priests officiating at a real *altar*, and in so doing, performing the office of *mediators* from man to God—by whom the people, through Christ, draw nigh to God, and without whose priestly mediation the approach of the people is at least imperfect and doubtful. The *Priest* at the altar offering sacrifice for the people, is represented as the prime and essential aspect of the Gospel Minister. *The Preacher* in the pulpit, teaching and preaching Jesus Christ to the people, is studiously, though stealthily, represented as in a position and work quite subordinate and incidental. All this, of course, is of the very essence of Popery. Against it, every nerve in the heart of true Protestantism is braced. Get it once inaugurated, and Popery has all its way prepared. It will argue and prove and branch out its whole array of doctrine and service from that central instalment. It is a sort of thing that may grow up among a people not preoccupied with decided and intelligent views of a contrary sort, without any very observable effort to convince them of it. It is insinuated, rather than enforced. It is asserted in the habitual language as if a thing of course. The people lose sight of the fact that any in our Church, of any just pretense to true Churchmanship, ever think otherwise. All that their eyes see, in the arrangement and furniture of the place of worship, and in the ways of the officiating minister is intended to train their minds in that one direction. In certain quarters, and under certain ministers, the people hear no more of the *communion table*. It is now "*the Altar.*" One sees no more, in such quarters, of any thing for the Lord's Supper that looks like a *table*, and that conveys the idea of a feast; but in place of it what is studiously fashioned to look like an *altar*, that it may convey the idea of priesthood and sacrifice. That this altar, as such, with its associated ideas, may be the one object in the sight of the people, the pulpit is often placed in a very inferior position, without reference to the convenience of speaking or hearing. The reading-desk is put on one side—and the reader is made to read side-ways, as regards the people, lest by facing them he should turn his back to the chancel and to the eminent sacredness of what has no right to be there, *the altar*. The minister's private prayer before beginning the service or sermon, which he used to offer in the desk and pulpit, is now offered at the chancel before *the altar*. There is, in all such things, and in divers other more minute things, a constant, silent, impressive and insinuating teaching, under which the people are gradually educated to the idea that in the chancel there is a presence of the Lord such as is no where else in the Church or in the earth; that grace is thence specially dispensed and thither the worshipper is specially to look, because there stands the Priest at the Altar, offering sacrifice for the sins of the people, (through the offering of the body of Jesus,) by whose priestly mediation the sacrifice of Jesus becomes efficacious for remission of their sins.

Need we tell any careful observer, how much of all this is going on among us in various parts; how successfully it is advancing from general impression to positive belief; how many have got so far as to suppose it the very essence of Churchmanship, almost regarding the rubrics of the communion office, which so pertinaciously adhere to the word *table*, and do not so much as indicate the possibility of an altar in a Protestant Church, as behind the age and of a Churchmanship decidedly too low? It is no unimportant indication of the progress thus being made, that with so many of the clergy of this country, when a new Church is built, or an old one repaired, if in the latter there used to be a *table*, (what good Bishop Ridley in his Injunctions for the removal of altars calls "an *honest table*,") it is seen no more. "Old things are passed away," and the thing placed in the chancel is studiously made to look as little like a table and as much like an altar as possible. Nothing else would express their doctrine of the Sacrament or satisfy their sacerdotal aspirations. Sometimes we would fain believe there is no very special design in it, but only a sort of sentimentalism which pleads no excuse but that of architectural gratification. But the direction is the same, and so the influence. We are told that the *form* is of little account. Very well. But then why so eager to change the old, time honored form, which certainly accords with the reiterated name, *table*, in the rubrics of the communion office, far better than its recently introduced and obnoxious substitute? We are told that what is *used* as a table, *is* a table no matter what its form, and why complain because it has not the form of a table?

Try the question upon a surplice. Any outer garment *used* as a surplice *is* a surplice, no matter what the form or color. Why then if some of our clergy should choose to wear some tastily contrived vestment, (tastily we mean in the tailor's eye) but as unlike as possible what is meant when we speak of a surplice, why take any exception? The form is indifferent. The use makes the thing. We venture to say there would be some sense of the value in some things, of a certain form, among those who plead the above excuse, should they witness such a garment under the profession and use of a surplice. But we have no hesitation in asserting that there could be no wrong in the use of the most inappropriate form of vestment for a surplice, in celebrating the Lord's Supper, comparable with that of substituting the form of a Romish altar for that of a proper table. That outlandish surplice, however repulsive to all right views of the fitness of things, would be only inappropriate. It would teach symbolically no false doctrine. It would contradict no great truth contained and taught in the Lord's Supper. It would be an offense, but not a heresy. But to cast out the table and substitute the shape of a Romish altar does teach symbolically a most unscriptural and pernicious doctrine, directly contradicting the true nature of the Lord's Supper and all the teaching of our Church concerning it and the office of the ministry connected with it. Romanists well understand how *table* and *altar* represent respectively the Protestant and Romish faith concerning the Lord's Supper. One of their learned men, a chief hand in their Rhemish translation of the New Testament (Gregory Martin) says: "The name of *altar*, both in the Hebrew and Greek, and by the consent of all peoples, both Jews and Pagans, implying and importing *sacrifice*, therefore we, in respect of the sacrifice of Christ's body and blood, say *altar* rather than *table*. But the Protestants because they make it a *supper* and no *sacrifice* therefore they call it a *table* only—to take away the holy sacrifice of the mass, they take away both altar and priest; because they know right well that these three, priest, sacrifice and altar, are *dependents and consequents, so that they cannot be separated.*"*

Nothing can be more out of place, in this question, than to speak of the indifference of the *form;* especially when such speech comes from those who are so zealous to get rid of the old form and, the almost universal form till recently, in our Churches, and to substitute that very form which in the English Church, after the reformation, was by authority every where cast out, the very name of it being erased from the Prayer Book. There is intended to be a symbolic expression of important truth in the table which wholly depends on its having a table-*form.* The form is the whole of it. Indifference to that, is indifference to the truth. Put an altar-form in its place, and you teach by a striking and well understood expression a most opposing and important error.

Now the extent to which that substitution is made in our Churches; the zeal in many clergymen to have it done, not as a mere matter of architectural taste, but of symbolical teaching; the degree to which it is regarded as the legitimate expression of a true Church spirit, by those who favor it; and the little notice now taken, among those who object in principle to the whole system with which it is connected, of a studied purpose to extend in our Church the whole theory and practice of Priest, Sacrifice and Altar—so that what a few years ago would have excited a general indignation as evidence of tendencies to be sternly resisted, is now so familiar that it passes without rebuke and almost without remark; all this should surely teach us that Tractarianism in its main evil and tendency, whatever may have become of the Oxford Tracts, is living yet; a leaven at work and too successful to be unheeded.

This Preface was begun with some remarks on the recent outbreak of Rationalism in the Church of England. The new school of Oxford divines, seems to many not only to have no affinity to its immediate predecessor, but as its opposite extreme, just as to such minds Italian Popery and German Neology seem antipodes,

---

* Fulke's Defence of the English Translation of the Bible. Park. Soc. Ed. pp. 515, &c.

the latter degrading reason into slavish subjection to the authority of Church decrees, the former exalting it above the authority of inspired scripture. In many respects, undoubtedly, the Tractarian and the Rationalist are in opposition. But as extremes sometimes meet; so have they sometimes the same beginning.

We are far from supposing that the offensive Rationalism of the famous "Essays and Reviews," by seven Members of the University of Oxford, is not strongly condemned by those who have succeeded to the authors of the Oxford Tracts, as leaders in the system they set up. We do not know, nor do we care to enquire whether any of the seven Rationalist Captains, or any of their recruits, were ever enlisted under the banner of Tractarianism.

But we maintain that there is ground common to the two schools and so fundamental in each, that it is perfectly intelligible how the teaching of the first Oxford school should have prepared the way for, and laid the foundations of, the second. We maintain that the former, in educating minds for its own conclusions, created a state of opinion which, if it failed to mature into Tractarianism, most naturally developed itself in Rationalism. We maintain that the Tractarians are logically connected, as cause and effect, with the seven Essayists—or rather with the preparedness of many to adopt their views; precisely as the Popery of Italy is accountable for the infidelity of Italy; or as the infidel school of France, in the last century, was a re-action from the whole dominion of ultramontane Romanism.

One thing is certain that when the Tract-school was in its first years, there were not wanting those who so read its tendencies as to predict a rise of Rationalism from the soil it would prepare. The present author so predicted, from its depreciation of the Inspiration of the Scriptures in its attempt, like the Church of Rome, to elevate a so called inspiration, abiding in the Church, into equal authority with that of the Bible; especially from its dishonoring the Scriptures as the only Rule of Faith by uniting with them, as of equal inspiration and authority, the traditions of the Church. It was not difficult to see how minds might easily be led so far by such teaching as to place the inspiration and authority of the Scriptures upon the level of traditions and councils, and yet deny that in the confusion and contradictions of the latter there is any real inspiration or authority at all.

Sixteen years ago Archbishop Whately compared the Tractarian system with the Rationalism of Germany, and wrote as follows: "Among those who express the greatest dread and detestation of 'German Neology,' 'German Philosophy,' 'the daring speculations of the German,' &c., are to be found some of that class of Anglican Divines, whose doctrines apparently correspond the most closely (as far as we can judge respecting two confessedly mystic schools,) with those of that very Neology. The very circumstance itself that both are schools of Mysticism; that both parties have one system for the mass of mankind, and another, whether expressed in different language, or in the same words, understood in a different sense, for the initiated, affords a presumption when there are some points of coincidence in the doctrine *divulged*, that a still further agreement may be expected in the *reserved* doctrines.

"As the advocates of Reserve among us speak of not intending to inculcate *generally* such conclusions as a logical reasoner will correctly deduce by following out their principles, and speak of an ordinary reader being likely 'to miss their real meaning by not being aware of the peculiar sense in which they employ terms,' so those German Transcendentalists whom I allude to, whose system of Theology, or rather of Atheology, is little else than a new edition of the Pantheism of the ancient Heathen Philosophers, of the Brahmans and the Buddhists, use similar double-meaning language. They profess Christianity, and employ profusely such terms as a 'God,' 'Faith,' 'Incarnation,' 'Miracle,' 'Immortality,' &c., attaching to these words, a meaning quite remote from what is commonly understood by them.

"Both parties, decry the historical evidence of Christianity, and discourage all appeal to evidence; and both disparage Miracles considered as a proof of the divine origin of Christianity; alleging that *every* event that occurs is equally a miracle: meaning therefore exactly what in ordinary language would be expressed by saying that *nothing* is miraculous.

"Other coincidences may be observed; such as the strong desire manifested by both parties to explain away or soften down the line of demarcation between what ordinary Christians call the *scriptures*, and every thing subsequent; between what we call the Christian Revelation, considered as an historical transaction recorded in the New Testament, and any pretended after-revelation or improvement or completion or perfect development of 'the system of true Religion.' To Christianity, as a *Revelation* completed in our sacred *books*, both parties, more or less openly, according to circumstances, confess their objection. And it is remarkable that even the vehement censures pronounced by one of these schools, on the speculations of the other, is far from being inconsistent with their fundamental agreement in principles."*

About the year 1850 appeared "The Nemesis of Faith," by F. A. Froude, Fellow of Exeter College, Oxford; a near relative, and if we mistake not, a brother of the Froude who once figured so prominently as a Tractarian leader.† The London Christian Observer, for March 1850, speaking of that book said: "Rumors had long been rife of a re-action at both the Universities, but more particularly at Oxford, against the principles and doctrines of the Tractarian self-styled Anglo-Catholic school. This new movement was understood to be Rationalistic, if not decidedly sceptical. And not a few of the immediate disciples of the most eminent Tract writers were said to be the chief oracles of coteries, in which, to use an expression reported to be current amog them, *the historic truth of Christianity was considered an open question.* When therefore a volume was announced from the pen of a Fellow of a college in Oxford, of a name signalized in the university by the history of his near relative, and bearing in its ominous title, evident allusion to *a reactionary movement* of a retributive character, the expecta-

* Kingdom of Christ. App. to Essay II., Note P. See the tendency to Infidelity in the Tractarian doctrine of *Reserve*, most forcibly shown in the Archbishop's "Cautions for the Times." Nos. XII., and XIII.

† It is not unworthy of Note, that of the two Froudes, one became an extreme Tractarian, the other an extreme Rationalist; and that of the two Newmans, the brothers Henry and Francis, the former became a Romish Priest—the latter a confirmed sceptic.

tion was very natural that it would turn out to be the exponent of Oxford scepticism, *disclosing its origin,* its present state, its observed results, its probable tendencies. The perusal of the book satisfied most of its readers, of the correctness of their 'foregone conclusion,' that such an exposition was intended by the author."

The book thus exhibiting the reaction of Tractarianism, was in 1850 substantially, in point of scepticism, what the "Essays and Reviews," are to-day. The following succinct account answers as well for the latter, as the former. "Let our readers imagine a work, evidently written for the purpose of showing the reasonableness of modern infidelity, in which the most prominent objections to the inspiration of the Old Testament, are borrowed from Thomas Paine; the great argument of Butler mentioned only to be dismissed as insufficient and irrelevant; Paley, treated with unmitigated contempt, and the sophistries of Hume and the slander of Gibbon, with corrallative respect; and to crown the whole, the vast mass of internal evidences, accumulated principally in our times, and still rapidly increasing, absolutly ignored,—and he has the work of Mr. Froude before him."* We add, he has the general character of the Rationalism of the "Essays and Reviews." It is to be much desired that some such expression may be witnessed at Oxford concerning the latter, as was seen in connection with the former. The "Nemesis of Faith," was treated with an Auto da Fé in the Lecture room of its author's own college, and he found it necessary to resign his fellowship.

If it had been the settled purpose of the Tractarian writers, covertly to prepare the way for, and ultimately to introduce and educate, a school of just such Rationalism as that now attracting the attention of all England, they could not have acted more wisely for their object, than they did in some of the chief positions they assumed and much of the policy they used.

To make Faith in the Inspiration of the Scriptures rest on evidence merely, or to believe in a doctrine as divine, only in proportion to the evidence that it is found in Scripture; to make Christianity depend on what are called "the Evidences;" to make the

* London Christian Observer.

study of the latter in any way, a road to belief, is treated with derision and represented as exceedingly dangerous to faith. The reply of "the uninstructed peasant," who to the question *why he believes* answered " because I have been told so by persons wiser and better than myself" is espoused by one of the writers as so very wise, that "there is nothing to be compared with its logic, either intellectually or morally or religiously in all the elaborate defenses and evidences which could be produced from Paley and Grotius and Sumner and Chalmers."* Another says that "Nature certainly does give sentence against a habit of enquiry, in that by the confession of all, happiness is attached to confiding *unreasoning faith.*"† It is very instructive, in view of the reasonings, and doubtings and unbeliefs of the seven Essays, to read the 85th of the Oxford Tracts. It would seem as if it were written for the express purpose of breaking up ground, clearing away obstacles, undermining beliefs, insinuating doubts, and by a general unsettling of peoples' minds, to make all ready for the bolder and more unmasked entrance of Rationalism. Difficulties to faith are stated at least in full strength; evidences for faith to rest on, are most unjustly depreciated; objections to various parts of Scripture, the very parts to which the objections of the Essays are made, are broadly stated, and either not attempted to be set aside, or so feebly answered, as to be really strengthened. The Tract proceeds throughout on the abominable assumption that all parts and particulars of what it calls "the Church-system," namely its own doctrines of Apostolic Succession, of the presence of Christ in the Eucharist, of Church Union, Absolution, Ministerial Power, &c.,—*as well as the doctrine of the Trinity, of the Atonement, Original Sin, the Inspiration of the New Testament*, are so on a level in point of Scriptural evidence—all so "*latent*" in the Scriptures; none "on the surface;" so few texts for any—and those so indirect and circuitous in their application—their proof so "*oblique*"—and the conclusion in favor of all alike being at best only "*a balance*" on their side, that if we conclude against the one we must, to be consistent, conclude against all. Thus the Atonement must be rejected, if you

* British Critic. † Tract 85.

will not believe in the divine warrant for what the Tractarian means by Absolution; the Trinity, if you reject his Apostolical Succession.

What, we ask, is the tendency of such a sentence as the following: "Consider whether the doctrine of the Atonement may not be explained away, by those who explain away the doctrine of the Eucharist,"—the Tractarian doctrine of the Eucharist. What is the tendency of the following? "If we will not content ourselves with mere probable, or (what we may be disposed to call) insufficient proofs of matters of faith and worship, we must become either Latitudinarians," that is, as before defined, we must believe that the Scriptures contain "nothing that can be made the subject of belief at all,"—"or else Papists." Thus the necessity is plainly given, either to believe the great matters of faith without what we should call sufficient evidence of Scripture, or become Papists, getting our convictions outside of the Scriptures, or else just what so many who used to read those Tracts have become, Rationalists—Sceptics.

Again; what is the tendency of such passages as the following? "If it be a good argument against the truth of the Apostolical Succession and similar doctrines, that so little is said about them in Scripture, this is quite as good an argument against nearly all the doctrines which are held by any who is called a Christian, in any sense of the word." Or thus, "God has given us doctrines which are but obscurely gathered from Scripture and a Scripture which is but obscurely gathered from history," a *Revelation* obscure in its *substance*, obscure in its *evidences!* All the great doctrines of eternal life are here included in the obscurity. Again; "Doubt and difficulty as regards evidence, seem our lot. The simple question is what is our duty under it? Difficulty is our lot, as far as we take on ourselves to enquire." "If we will not allow evidence to be sufficient which merely results in a balance on the side of revelation—if we will not go by evidence in which there are (so to say,) *three chances for revelation, and only two against, we cannot be Christians.*"

Most worthy of all this playing into the hands of scepticism is the conclusion of the Tract. "Why should not the Church be divine? The burden of proof surely is on the other side. I will accept her doctrines, her rites and *her* Bible; not one, and not the other, but all—till I have a clear proof that she is mistaken. I love *her* Bible, *her* doctrines and *her* rites, and *therefore* I BELIEVE." These last emphatic marks are those of the Tract. And herein is the conclusion of the whole matter and the key to all the Tract. *The Church!* her Bible, *her* doctrines, &c. Our ground of faith is not evidence; not because such and such doctrines are to our eyes contained in Scripture; not because we see conclusive evidence that the Scriptures are inspired, but *we love* and therefore we *believe*. But we love what? Why first the Church, and because the Bible is *her* Bible we love the Bible and the doctrines are *her* doctrines, therefore we love them, and loving we believe. To bring us thus to the Church as the Warrant and Determiner of faith; to make us feel that if we look to evidence we must launch to sea in open boat without chart, compass, or star, and be always driven to and fro by currents of doubt and winds of doctrine, in constant danger of being stranded on shoals and reefs of difficulty; that we can have refuge or quiet of mind only by sitting down under the shadow of the Church's authority, in the obedience of an unreasoning, implicit, uninquiring faith, taking all things, doctrine and rite, the Trinity, the Atonement, Absolution, Church Unity, (meaning of course Papal Unity,) Apostolical Succession, &c., on precisely the same warrant, namely, *the Church says so*, (meaning *what Church*, let the reader consider,) such was the single object of this insidious Tract. But what if its readers should be willing to be led just so far as to take in all its suggested doubts and be perplexed by all its suggested difficulties, and believe the doctrines of the Gospel to be so doubtfully contained in Scripture and Scripture so doubtfully proved by historical or internal evidence, and there stop and refuse to be guided any further by this *ductor dubitantium?* What if the doubter should have no mind to believe the Church till he can first believe the Scriptures on which all its being depends and which he has already learned to doubt? He is landed in Rationalism or Infidelity. The whole remedy proposed for the doubts attempted to be raised is exactly what the Tract calls it "a *kill or cure remedy*." If taken at all it must make Tractarians Romanists or it must make Rationalistic Sceptics. We do not wonder that the Tract writer should have said, "I predict as a coming event that minds are to be unsettled as to what is Scripture and what is not." The prediction is now abundantly fulfilled. But it was the calculator of causes and effects, not the eye of a prophet that made it. That such a seed bed should have produced such growths, is certainly not surprising. If, while some ripened into a concealed or avowed Romanism, others went to seed before they got that far, and in another generation have come forth an indigenous crop of well marked Rationalism, where is the wonder?

But let us take another view. The doctrine of *Development* belongs to the Tractarian system, as well as to the Romish. To justify belief in a certain doctrine as of divine authority, as *contained* in Scripture and properly an article of Faith *to us*, it is not necessary (we read,) that it be capable of proof from the Scriptures, nor that to any eye there should be even the appearance of it in the Scriptures. It is not necessary that it should have had any place in the creed of the early Church. Nay, it may have been expressly condemned in the early Church as unscriptural. The invisible germ of it may be in the Scriptures, and yet concealed under apparently opposite forms. The Church, as possessing the inspiration of the Spirit of Truth and Life has power to develope that germ into form and assign it a place in Christian faith. It may be a process of many centuries. The very condemnation of the doctrine in the early Church may have been part of the process. Thus the creed may grow; thus Christianity is progressive. What it is to-day, may be very unlike what it was at first. To be a believer in the nineteenth century, may be a very different matter from what it was to be a believer in the second. Such is the theory on which the Church of Rome defends her infallibility in paying to the Virgin Mary a worship which Councils, whose authority she owns, condemned. Thus the Pope's new article of Faith, that of the Immaculate conception of Mary, makes necessary to salvation a belief which it is not pretended that any eye can detect in the Scriptures or in the teaching of the early centuries of the Church. Out of the Christianity of the Apostolic age, was developed that of the Nicene; out of the Nicene, the Mediæval; out of the last, the creed and decrees of the Council of Trent; out of the Romanism of Trent, the Ultra Montanism of the Italian Church in the days of Pius the ninth.

Such is the doctrine of Development, advocated in substance by Tractarians. If only Mr. Newman brought it out in fulness and by name, the whole doctrine of *Reserve*, so notoriously belonging to the Tract School, involves it in principle, and Tract No. 85, insinuates it continually. What is the teaching of the following extract? "The early Church always *did* consider Scripture to be what I have been arguing from the structure of it, viz., a book with *very recondite* meanings—not merely with reference to its teaching the particular class of doctrines in question," (including the Atonement, the Trinity, &c.,) "but as regards *its entire teaching*. They considered that it was *full of mysteries*, that the Church doctrines are *not on its surface*. It is also certain that the early Church did herself conceal these same doctrines. Viewing that early period as a whole, there is on the whole *a great secrecy* observed in it concerning such doctrines as the Trinity and the Eucharist, that is, the early Church did the very thing which I have been supposing Scripture does, *conceal high truths*. If the early Church had reasons for concealment, perchance Scripture has the same; especially if we suppose, what at the very least is no very improbable idea, that the system of the early Church is a *continuation* of the system of those inspired men who wrote the New Testament."

Mark well the last sentence of this half concealing and cautiously developing exhibition of the Tractarian doctrine of Reserve. What is meant by *"continuation?"* If merely that the system of the early Church was a *preservation* of, or an adherence to that of the inspired writers, why say that it is "no very improbable idea?" Then in what other sense was it a *continuation?* Why, of course, as *development* is a continuation; as the tree is a *continuation* of the sapling; as something so recondite as not to be recognised is *continued* when you see a complex system of doctrine imposed upon the belief of men and are told it is that once recondite invisible something. Mr. Newman's full expansion of the doctrine of Development, in his book on that subject, was just such a *continuation* of the more hidden and recondite attempt to insinuate the same doctrine in the Tract from which the above is taken.

Now what is this whole doctrine but just the fundamental idea of the Rationalism of the seven Essays and Reviews, changing only the Church, as the *incubator*, for human reason? What else is the idea of one of the Essayists that " the human race is a colossal man?" The creeds of the Church, they say were "*evolved*" by the Church, which occupied six centuries "in the creation of a theology," a number of the decisions of which are now "*practically obsolete*." It is indicated "that there was a Bible before our Bible, and that some of our present books are expanded (developed) from simpler elements." An implied antagonism in Christianity to the intellectual convictions of mankind, one of the writers hopes may be removed, when it is considered whether the intellectual forms under which Christianity is described may not also be in a state of transition and revolution.

Now with this development doctrine thus in common to the Tract, the Romish and the Rationalistic systems, what is to hinder the last from taking the ground that the religion of the Scriptures is a development from some previous religion or combination of previous religions and philosophies, as unlike it, as Buddhism is unlike Christianity? Why not if the Christianity of the New Testament has been legitimately developed into the present Pio Nono Romanism? Or what is to hinder the Rationalist of Oxford from legitimately holding that his whole system is a veritable development of the religion of the New Testament, going on to a further development of, he knows not what extent of positive infidelity, if Pio Nono, on the throne of universal supremacy, the center of unity, infallible oracle of truth, Vicar of Christ, "sitting as God in the Temple of God," creating, at will, Articles of Faith, and conditions of salvation, is only a development of the office of Peter, the Apostle, as exhibited in the Scriptures? Or, in fine, what hinders the conclusion that the present school of Rationalism is a legitimate development of its predecessor, the Tractarian, if the latter be a true development of the doctrine of the Apostles? Whither this Rationalistic growth is to attain we know not. One thing we know that the Gospel truth has fought and conquered in battles as hard as these *septem contra Christum* can make. The Greeks, seeking after wisdom, and therefore treating the Gospel as foolishness, were in their day an adversary at least as strong as their followers in our day. When the powers of death could not hold the crucified Jesus—but HE ROSE; assurance was given to all ages that no enmity can finally prevail over Him or His Gospel. Through Him, and like Him, it is "*the Power of God.*"

PREFACE.

WHOEVER may honor this work with their attention will soon perceive that the author is deeply impressed with the grave importance of the errors, and the probable evil consequences to the Church, of that system of doctrine which in Tracts and other writings has recently appeared under the names of certain learned divines of the University of Oxford. In his view, the vital principle of that Divinity, so far as the system is peculiar, is precisely the same as that to which are to be traced all the various and gross departures from truth and godliness in the Church of Rome. It was well advised by "the principal Theologues" of the Council of Trent, that the Fathers and Divines of that body should be "assiduous and exact in their studies" concerning the doctrine of Justification, "because all the errors of Martin (of the Reformation) were resolved into that point. For (said they) having undertaken from the beginning to oppugn the Indulgences, he saw he could not obtain his purpose, except he destroyed the works of repentance, (*expiatory penances*) in defect whereof, Indulgences do succeed. And Justification by faith only, seemed to him a good means to effect this—from whence he hath denied efficacy in the Sacraments, authority of Priests, Purgatory, Sacrifice of the Mass, and all other remedies for remission of sins."

Such was the just view entertained in the Council of Trent, of that on which the whole work of the Reformation was built, and by which the whole structure of Romanism was cast down. The doctrine of Justification by Faith was the master-principle of the Reformation. "Therefore by a contrary way (said the chief Theologians of the Council) he that will establish the body of the Catholic doctrine (in other words, he that would re-instate Indulgences, Penances, Purgatory, the *opus operatum* of the Sacraments, the authority of the Priest's absolutions, the Sacrifice of the Mass, &c.) must overthrow the heresy of Justification by faith only."* In all this, there was the soundest view of the relation of cause and effect. And therefore have we no question, that now, while Oxford Divinity is fast developing its real character, in divers ramifications of overt

---

* Paul's Hist. Council of Trent, p. 190.

Romanism, and exhibiting the strongest tendencies to do so, more and more; the only explanation needed is to be found in its entire defection from the Scriptural doctrine of how a sinner can be "just with God;" and the only antidote required is the clear understanding, the faithful teaching, the full carrying out of that same great doctrine, so mighty in the war of the Reformation, so feared and hated and libelled in the Councils of the Church of Rome,—Justification, by the Imputed Righteousness of Christ, through the alone agency of a living faith.

Clearly as the strength of Romanism was known, by the English Reformers, to lie in her errors concerning Justification, there were not wanting, even in their times, those who, for lack of a right view of the relative bearing of this subject on all other parts of divinity, were disproportionately occupied with manifestations of Romanism, which, however evil, should have been regarded only as the poisonous issues of that one central source of error in religion "where Satan's seat is." To such mistakes, the celebrated Reformer Foxe, referred, when, in his discourse, entitled "Christ Triumphant,' he said, "It is necessary that this doctrine (Justification) should be retained and preached in the Church; which, being of long time hidden from Christians and almost extinguished, the heroical, and mighty spirit of Christ, by the ministry and preaching of Martin Luther* hath kindled and raised up again in the Church. Yet such is the mischief and misery of these wicked days, through the subtle practicing of Satan, that all Christendom is in an uproar by matters of contentions; and in the mean time, all regard of that which is the most principal point of our salvation is set at nought, and almost brought again to utter decay."

The Reformer is evidently referring to contentions about the more superficial parts of Romanism; as if the symptoms were the disease, while its "evil heart of unbelief" was overlooked. Such has been far too much the case, in what has been said and written concerning the system of doctrine which is considered in this volume.

Had it been always tried by such an eye as that which searched the heart of Romanism at the Reformation; or as that with which our Andrews and Hall and Usher and Davenant detected the mainspring of all Romish corruptions, in the controversies of their day, we should not have heard less indeed of the tendencies of this

---

* Elsewhere, this Reformer speaks, as all English Reformers were wont to speak, of "the grave and excellent judgment of Martin Luther, that most singular and chosen instrument of setting forth the gospel of Christ."

new divinity to the more manifest heresies of Popery; but we should have heard much more of its identity with Popery in that grand defection from the truth concerning the sinner's justification before God, from which, as from a root, all these evil branches spring.

Few evidences of that sad decline in the Church of England from the spirit and doctrine of her martyred Reformers, which the eighteenth and latter part of the seventeenth century exhibited, are more striking than that which appears in the almost entire exclusion from the controversies carried on in those days, with Rome, of the doctrine of justification. In the days of the Reformation, who would have written upon Popery and not spoken of the doctrine of justification by inherent righteousness, as its main and vital principle? Read the solemn confessions of the Anglican Martyrs! They are full of protests against this chief corruption. What pains does the venerable Latimer take to be distinct and continual on this head! How does Hooper labor it! The controversial work of Haddon, in the reign of Elizabeth, against the Portuguese divine, Osorius,—written as a sort of State-Book, as Strype calls it, in defense of the English Reformation, and completed by Foxe,—is occupied, in a very large part of its pages, with the single subject of justification. How much the judicious Hooker made of it, whoever has read his Discourse of Justification cannot but know. Such views of the eminent prominence of this subject in all controversies with Rome continued unabated up to the seventeenth century. The works of Perkins, a great light at Cambridge, and a strong adversary of Rome, who died in the beginning of that century, are stored with it. In Usher's writings it is the grand topic. Bishop Downame devoted a whole folio volume of controversy with Rome to this one point. The same sense of the great importance of the difference between the faith of the Anglican Church, and that of the Church of Rome, on this head, appears in the works of Andrews, Hall, Davenant, Hopkins, Jackson, &c. But as we approach the latter periods of that century, when it is acknowledged that true religion was greatly on the wane in the Church of England, we find this great subject more and more excluded from the controversies with Rome, as if the greater number of Protestant writers were either agreed with her doctrine in that particular, or considered the objections of Protestants of no great importance. When however we have reached the eighteenth century, wherein it is universally conceded that the spiritual character of the Church of England was at its lowest depression, we take leave of Justification by Faith, as occupying any conspicuous place in the differences between Popery and Protestantism. The axe is laid no more at the root of the tree. The great effort against Popery is to trim off some of its branches.

This lamentable change in the doctrinal character of the divines of the Church of England, must be considered as having received one of its earliest impulses from the writings of that learned continental writer Hugo Grotius. His peculiar views on justification, met with favor from Archbishop Laud. Sheldon, after the Restoration, renewed their influence. They were rescued from the disgrace of being associated with the rapidly growing irreligion of that age, by finding in the main, a most learned and vigorous champion in that truly excellent Prelate, Bishop Bull. This eminent divine had commenced his studies in divinity under a Puritan and Non-Conformist, named Thomas. Recoiling from the Antinomianism which he perceived to be rapidly growing up under the extremes of doctrine to which many of that school had gone, he became a devoted reader of Grotius and Episcopius, associating with those writers the works of Hammond and Jeremy Taylor, wherein he perceived no little sympathy with the views of the former, on the subject of justification. In the year 1669 was first published his Harmonia Apostolica, for the reconciliation of the Epistle of St. James with those of St. Paul, in reference to that matter. By this work, far more than any other, was the standard of Orthodoxy, among the Divines of the Church of England, on Justification and its kindred subjects, reduced to that low degree which afterwards reigned so widely in the times of the Non-Jurors, and which went on debilitating and exanimating the religion of the Anglican Church; till, in the latter part of the last century, by "the renewing of the Holy Ghost," there took place the contemporaneous and connected blessings of the revival of true spiritual piety, and the return of the teaching and preaching of the doctrine of the Reformers, as to the sinner's justification before God.

But greatly as the Antinomian abuses during the time of the Commonwealth, followed by the general languor in regard to religious doctrine which the excitements of that stormy period had left upon the public mind, and the flood of licentiousness which ensued, had prepared the way for the gradual reception of such doctrines as were taught by the disciples of Bull, often going beyond their teacher; the famous work of that great Master did not appear without arousing the strongest opposition to its doctrines, as an abandonment of the principles of the Reformation, inconsistent with the Articles and Homilies of the Church of England, and essentially in agreement with the vital principle of Romanism. "There was presently (says Nelson, in his Life of Bull,) no small alarm both *in* the Church and *out* of it, from Mr. Bull's performance; as if the Church of England and the whole Protestant religion were, by it, in danger. For his departing herein from the private opinions of some doctors of our Church, was, by several, interpreted for no less than a departing from the faith by her delivered; hence there arose in the Church no small contention whether this interpretation of Scripture were conformable to the Articles of Religion, and the Homily of Justification therein referred to: some maintained with our author that it was; some doubted about it, and others downright denied it, and condemned it as heretical. There was many a hard censure passed upon the book—yea, there were not wanting *then*, even men of some eminence in our Church, who, with all their might, opposed him, probably out of a well-meant zeal, and would certainly have overwhelmed him and his doctrine, had it been possible."

Thus much is acknowledged by the non-juring Nelson, who fully embraced the views of Bull. Among the Bishops who resisted the influence of those views, the one who proceeded much farther than any of his brethren, was Morley, Bishop of Winchester. Lectures were read against them, before the University of Oxford, by Dr. Barlow, then Margaret Professor of Divinity, afterwards Bishop of Lincoln.* But the most conspicuous writer in the Church of England, against the doctrines of Bull, was Dr. Tully, Principal of St. Edmund's Hall, Oxford, a divine of high standing in the University for learning, eloquence, piety, zeal, and usefulness. This writer was amazed at the indifference or insensibility to the interests of religion, of many who endeavored to persuade him to decline the controversy, on the ground that the points in dispute were matters of comparative unimportance, not worth the risking of the peace of the Church, while to him they seemed to involve "the most noble and momentous of all controversies," and to put in jeopardy "the very palladium of the Reformation." Under this conviction he published, in 1674, a Latin Treatise, entitled "*Justification, as delivered by St. Paul, without works, asserted and illustrated according to the sense of the Church of England, and of all the rest of the Re-*

---

* The present Margaret Professor, Dr. Fausset, has followed the example of his learned Predecessor, in having published strongly against the new and enlarged edition of Bull's doctrines, as exhibited in the new divinity of Oxford; while the Regius Professor of Divinity, Dr. Hampden, has borne a noble testimony to the truth, against the same errors, in a late Sermon on Justification by faith.

formed Churches, against the late innovators." In the publication of that work, the author was encouraged by Bishop Morley, who read it in manuscript, with approbation. Therein, it was charged that the doctrine of Justification, as expounded by the author of the Harmonia, "was properly heretical, as being contrary, in a fundamental point, to the testimony of Scripture, and against the opinion of the Catholic fathers, the judgment of the Church of England, and the determinations of all the foreign reformed Churches."

The grand question in dispute, "the τὸ Κρινομενον" according to Dr. Tully, was expressed precisely as in the ensuing volume we have stated the main question between Popery and the new Divinity, on the one hand, and the doctrine of the Anglican Church, on the other, viz. "what is that, for the sake of which God may receive a sinner to grace, may acquit him from the curse of the law, and make him an heir of everlasting life."* The side espoused by Dr. Tully, which was precisely that of justification through faith only, by the imputed righteousness of Christ, was maintained by reference to the Ancient Fathers, the literal and grammatical sense of the Articles and Homilies of the Church of England, and the testimony of her most famous divines, such as Andrews and Hooker.

The feeble attempt of Bishop Bull, in his Apologia, to answer the appeal of Dr. Tully to the standard divines of the Church, and the anxiety of his biographer to claim for him that he should be judged, not by the Anglican Reformers, but by the Ancient Fathers, and the Holy Scriptures, are strong evidences how futile was considered in that day, the pretense that such doctrine as that of the Harmonia had received the suffrages of those divines whom the Church then looked to, as her standard writers.

If it shall be the honor of this volume, in any degree, to revive the attention of the members of the Church, especially of her clergy, and candidates for orders, to the works of the elder divines of the seventeenth century, such as Usher, Hall, Hopkins, Andrews, &c., as well as to those of the age preceding them, up to the period of the Reformation, so that the nervous and clear displays of divine truth, as therein abounding, and as distinguished from that feeble, confused, mode of representing the way of salvation which characterises the majority of the more modern Anglican divines, shall become more thoroughly studied and appreciated, then, whatever becomes of the doctrine herein opposed, this book will be amply rewarded.

It may perhaps be considered a great defect of this volume, that

* Apologia pro Harmonia, Sect. 3. § 7.

it does not institute a comparison of the system reviewed, directly with the Scriptures. The author must not be understood as countenancing, by this omission, the idea that there can be any approach to a final settlement of Christian truth, short of a direct appeal to the Inspired Word. But all objects cannot be embraced at once. Sometimes, the recalling of the doctrine of the Church, at some particular period, may be of more benefit, for a special purpose, that even the exposition of the Scriptures. To recal the great principles of the Reformation, as illustrated by a comparison with those of the Church of Rome, and the Romanising Divinity here considered, seemed to the author to be the precise desideratum at the present juncture, and of dimensions sufficient to occupy a volume by itself. He is fully persuaded that with a truly Protestant communion the most direct refutation of this system is *itself*. Only let it be displayed "*without reserve*," let that which has been brought before the public so skilfully and reservedly, so by heterogeneous parts, that it required the skill of a professional anatomist to find out their several places in the body, and to form, from them, any accurate idea of the whole frame-work, only let it be set up and seen in its own proper aspect; its several members and joints, and dependencies, and connections, and humors, and issues, and appetencies—all presented! Its work then is done. Its day is ended. The Protestant Church is too much alive to the truth that Popery is the Antichrist, "that Man of Sin," revealed in the Scriptures, "who opposeth and exalteth himself above all that is called God, or that is worshipped," and that "there is no society of Christians in the world, where Antinomianism and Libertinism more reign, than among the Papists, with whose very faith they are interwoven,"[*] not to be turned away, in entire rejection, from a system which, as will be shown in this volume, is nothing else than *Popery restrained*.

[*] Bull's Works, by Nelson, Sermon I.

CONTENTS.

	Page
PREFACE TO THE PRESENT EDITION,	v
PREFACE,	xxiv

CHAPTER I.

Introductory Remarks—The Tracts for the Times before the publication of Dr. Pusey's Letter—Effect of that Letter—Convictions of the present Author—Reasons for this publication—The doctrine of Justification selected, as that by which the Romanism of the new Oxford Divinity may be most thoroughly tried—That this was the great point with the Reformers, shown from Hooker, &c.—Three presumptive objections to the charge of Romanism, from the character of Oxford Divines, removed—The views of the writer as to the designs and snares of Satan, - - - - - - - - - - - - 37

CHAPTER II.

STATEMENTS PREPARATORY TO THE RIGHT ESTIMATION OF THIS SYSTEM AS TO THE DOCTRINE OF JUSTIFICATION.

Professions of Oxford Divines concerning the conformity of their doctrine with that of the Church of England—Their account of Ultra-Protestantism—The identity of their system with that of Alexander Knox—The condemnation of the latter, as Romish and dangerous, by certain eminent divines, of diverse schools in the Church of England, before its development, at Oxford, had excited any special notice, - - - - - - - - - - - 53

CHAPTER III.

THE DOCTRINE OF THIS DIVINITY AS TO THE RIGHTEOUSNESS OF JUSTIFICATION, EXHIBITED.

To set forth the precise doctrine of this divinity, as to the way of Justification, the object of this chapter.—The main question of Hooker, as to the Romish doctrine, adopted here—The great point of enquiry stated—The Scriptural use of the word Justification—Two kinds of righteousness, asserted by Hooker, Beveridge, Andrews—Only one by this system—This opens the door to the divinity of Oxford, as well as that of Rome—That one righteousness, made identical with Sanctification—What is meant in this divinity by Imputation, Accounted, &c.—Extended proof that it makes Sanctification the same as Justification—The position in which it puts the cross of Christ—The use it makes of the merits and passion of Christ—Its effect upon the consolations of the believer—Singular effort to escape from being identified with Romanism, by denying what was before asserted as to Sanctification and Justification being essentially one—The same in Mr. Knox—This doctrine shown in Osiander—Concluding observations, 66

CHAPTER IV.

THE DOCTRINE OF THIS DIVINITY, AS TO THE RIGHTEOUSNESS OF JUSTIFICATION, COMPARED WITH THAT OF THE SCHOOLMEN.

Origin of the Romish doctrine of Justification in the self-righteousness of the human heart—Advance until the age of the schoolmen—The origin of Scholastic Theology—Character of the Schoolmen—Fitness of the age for the rapid growth of error—The corruptions of Romanism which were matured in that age. The seven sacraments—Sacramental Confession—Transubstantiation—Half Communion—Image worship—Purgatory—Indulgences—The same age, as was to be expected, gave birth to the Romish doctrine of Justification—Connection between the Schoolmen and the divines of Trent—Three propositions to show the identity of the doctrine of this system with that of the Schoolmen—Similar tendencies—Concluding remarks—Note, showing the resemblance between this doctrine and that of the early Quakers. - - - - - - 98

CHAPTER V.

THE DOCTRINE OF THIS DIVINITY, AS TO THE RIGHTEOUSNESS OF JUSTIFICATION, COMPARED WITH THAT OF THE COUNCIL OF TRENT.

Recapitulation—Language of the Council of Trent—State of the Question at the Reformation, and now, from Chemnitz, Jackson, Hall, Usher, Hooker—Holiness required at least as much by Protestants as Romanists—Tractarian interpretation of single passages of Scripture, compared with those of Romish divines—Three particulars in which Oxford divines claim to be regarded as not conformed to Romanism—These considered, and shown, to make such conformity only the more obvious—The vindication drawn from the Romish claim of merit, answered—Hooker's argument against the Romish doctrine of merit shown to be applicable, in the same way, to this system—Concluding remarks. - - - - - - - - - - - 117

CHAPTER VI.

THE DOCTRINE OF THIS DIVINITY, AS TO THE NATURE AND OFFICE OF JUSTIFYING FAITH, EXHIBITED, AND COMPARED WITH THAT OF THE ROMISH CHURCH.

The influence of the doctrine of Justification, whether true or false, upon the body of divinity in general—The sameness of the Oxford Doctrine and that of Rome, tested by the sameness of influence upon connected and subordinate doctrines—This, first exhibited as to the doctrine of Justifying Faith—The doctrine of Faith, as held in the Romish Church, stated in six propositions—The doctrine of this system stated in comparison, under the same propositions, showing the nature and office of Faith, before Baptism, in Baptism, and after Baptism—The profession of making Faith the sole internal instrument of Justification examined and shown to be without any reality—Justification by Faith, in this system, nothing but Justification by Christianity—A rebuke from Bishop Beveridge. - - - - - - - - - - - 142

CHAPTER VII.

THE DOCTRINE OF THIS DIVINITY, AS TO THE OFFICE AND EFFICACY OF THE SACRAMENTS, ESPECIALLY OF BAPTISM, COMPARED WITH THAT OF THE ROMISH CHURCH.

Tendency of all such principles as that of Justification in this divinity, to magnify external ceremonies, and ultimately to make all religion consist in them—This tendency prominent in regard to the Sacraments—Baptismal Justification similarly held by the Romish Church and the divines of Oxford—The *opus operatum* of Baptism held alike by both—Effect of this, the same in both, in keeping out of view the truth, that the Sacraments are *signs*, and identifying the visible sign with the invisible grace—The tendency of transubstantiation in this divinity, explained from the same cause—The false and injurious comparison between the spiritual nature of the Sacraments of the Old and New Testaments, resulting alike from Romish and Tractarian divinity,—Extract from Jeremy Taylor—Limbus Patrum—Bishop Burnet on Sacramental Justification.   163

CHAPTER VIII.

THE DOCTRINE OF THIS DIVINITY FURTHER EXHIBITED BY ITS EFFECTS UPON OTHER DOCTRINES AND PARTS OF CHRISTIANITY.

Effects upon the doctrine of Original Sin; Testimony of Jackson to the Peculiar Romanism of these results—Sin after Baptism—Mortal and Venial Sins—Tendencies of Oxford Divinity to the doctrine of Purgatory—to Prayers for the Dead—Invocation of Saints—Transubstantiation—Working of Miracles—Aricular Confession—Extreme Unction—Anointing at Baptism and Confirmation—Additional matters of *Restoration* contemplated—Sacramental character of Marriage countenanced—Use of Romish Prayer Books and Rules of Fasting—Favor to Image-Worship—Christian Holiness—Tradition; Why this topic reserved to the last—Extracts from the late Charge of Bishop Wilson.   180

CHAPTER IX.

THE DOCTRINE OF THIS DIVINITY, AS TO THE RIGHTEOUSNESS OF JUSTIFICATION, AND THE NATURE AND OFFICE OF FAITH, COMPARED WITH THAT OF THE ANGLICAN CHURCH.

Matter of mortification that such comparison is necessary—A general account of the doctrinal standards of the Anglican Church—Statement of the questions investigated in this Chapter—Arguments from the assertion of Dr. Pusey that the Article, of Justification says nothing of what Justification consists in—The Articles xi., xii., and xiii.—Exposition of the xi. from the language of its Authors —elsewhere—From its own peculiar precision as to the office of faith—Homilies quoted and expounded—Seven difficulties into which the Oxford doctrines are brought by the language of the Articles and Homilies—Each made use of as an evidence against the consistency of that Divinity with that of the Anglican Church. - - - - - - - - - - - - - 237

CHAPTER X.

THE DOCTRINE OF THIS DIVINITY, AS TO BAPTISMAL JUSTIFICATION, COMPARED WITH THAT OF THE ANGLICAN CHURCH.

Recapitulation of Tractarian and Romish Doctrines—Difference between remission of Original Sin as held by the Anglican Church, and by the Oxford Divines—Testimony of Jackson—Baptismal Justification of Adults—*A priori* reason for believing that the Anglican and Oxford doctrine are diverse on this head—Silence of the Articles and Homilies unaccountable if the Oxford doctrine were that of the Church. Language of the Articles and Homilies irreconcileable with the Oxford doctrine—Language of Scripture, Fathers, English divines needs explanation—Evidence of necessity of other interpretation than this system gives—Barrow—Beveridge—Hooper—Frith—Hooker—Hall—Homilies—Usher—Beveridge—Inconsistencies in English divines, according to the Oxford Interpretation—Barrow—Hooker—St. Bernard—Jewel. Inconsistencies of Augustine and other Fathers according to the Oxford doctrine—True doctrine shown from Bishops Hooper, Beveridge, and Taylor—Mode of Interpreting the strong language of the old divines, &c.—Bishop Bethell's mode rejected as too low—Strange inconsistencies of Oxford divines—Mode of interpretation illustrated from Augustine, Jewel, from language of Hooker, &c.—Concerning the membership of infants in the Church before baptism; common language concerning a call to the ministry, and language of Scripture as to the baptism of Christ—further illustration from common law-terms—application to language of Nowell's Catechism—Passages from Whitgift, and Dr. Haddon—Concluding Observations. - - - - - - - - - - - - - - - 271

CHAPTER XI.

THE DOCTRINE OF THIS DIVINITY AS TO THE RIGHTEOUSNESS OF JUSTIFICATION AND THE OFFICE OF FAITH, COMPARED WITH THAT OF STANDARD DIVINES OF THE ANGLICAN CHURCH.

Majorities in such a question of no avail—Laud's testimony—Divines of the 17th Century especially relied on by the Oxford writers.—The same mainly employed in this Chapter—Testimony of Oxford writers to the eminent authority of Hooker—His views acknowledged to be in entire opposition to those of this divinity on Justification—Force of the confession—Singular attempt to escape its force—Citations from Hooker—Tyndale—Barnes—Cranmer—Bishop Hooper—Bishop Latimer—Edward VI. Catechism—Confession of Martyrs and

Divines in Prison—Nowell's Catechism—Haddon and Foxe against Osorius—Perkins—Bishop Downame—Bishop Andrews—Mede—Bishop Hall—Bishop Nicholson—Archbishop Usher—Bishop Hopkins—Bishop Beveridge. - - 326

CHAPTER XII.

CONCLUDING OBSERVATIONS, - - 370

THE CHIEF DANGER OF THE CHURCH IN THESE TIMES: A CHARGE DELIVERED TO THE CLERGY OF THE PROTESTANT EPISCOPAL CHURCH IN THE DIOCESE OF OHIO, AT THE TWENTY-SIXTH ANNUAL CONVENTION OF THE SAME, IN ROSSE CHAPEL, GAMBIER, SEPTEMBER 8TH, 1843, BY THE RT. REV. CHARLES PETTIT M'ILVAINE, D.D. - - 395

REASONS FOR REFUSING TO CONSECRATE A CHURCH HAVING AN ALTAR INSTEAD OF A COMMUNION TABLE: OR, THE DOCTRINE OF SCRIPTURE, AND OF THE PROTESTANT EPISCOPAL CHURCH, AS TO A SACRIFICE IN THE LORD'S SUPPER AND A PRIESTHOOD IN THE CHRISTIAN MINISTRY, BY CHARLES PETTIT M'ILVAINE, D. D., BISHOP OF THE PROTESTANT EPISCOPAL CHURCH IN OHIO. - - - - - - 425

A CHARGE: DELIVERED TO THE CLERGY OF THE DIOCESE OF OHIO, AT ITS FORTY-SIXTH ANNUAL CONVENTION, IN ST. PAUL'S CHURCH, AKRON, ON THE 3D OF JUNE, 1863. BY CHARLES PETTIT M'ILVAINE, D.D., D.C.L., BISHOP OF THE DIOCESE. - - - 451

RIGHTEOUSNESS BY FAITH.

CHAPTER I.

Introductory Remarks—The Tracts for the Times before the publication of Dr. Pusey's Letter—Effect of that Letter—Convictions of the present Author—Reasons for this publication—The doctrine of Justification selected, as that by which the Romanism of the new Oxford Divinity may be most thoroughly tried—That this was the great point with the Reformers, shown from Hooker, &c.—Three presumptive objections to the charge of Romanism, from the character of Oxford Divines, removed—The views of the writer as to the designs and snares of Satan.

FEW observers of what is passing in the Christian Church, can fail to be aware that what is called for the sake of convenience, Oxford Divinity,—meaning, by that term, not the dominant theological system of the University of Oxford, but that which is far from holding a rank so distinguished, the peculiar doctrines of certain scholars and divines of high standing in that institution,—has reached a position of prominence, in the public view, of great importance, for evil or good to the vital interests of religion. It is also a matter of notoriety that this divinity, zealously urged as the true doctrine of the English Church, and of the Scriptures, sustained by singular industry of the pen and press, and certainly with great vigor of mind, and diligence of research, is confidently accused, by writers of no less repute for all soundness of mind and adornment of learning and piety, of a lamentable departure from the true doctrines of the Gospel and of the Church of England; as also of a correspondent approximation to those doctrinal corruptions of the Church of Rome of which the Temple of God, in England, was cleansed, at the blessed era of the Protestant Reformation.

Between the two sides of the accusers and accused, thus arrayed, the controversy was carried on for some time, abroad, before the friends of Christian truth in America were called to take any part; except as spectators, deeply interested in the animated disputations of their transatlantic brethren. At length, however it was thought expedient by some of those spectators, that the controversy should commence in the Church of this land, and that the publications on *one side*, viz. that of the Oxford divines, should have a reprint here. Hence the far-famed "*Tracts for the Times*" were issued from the press of New York, preceded by the promise of the reprint of a large selection of other English publications on the same side of the question. During the progress of these works, the most zealous efforts have been made to commend the peculiarities of these writings to the diligent reading, and confidential reception, of the clergy and laity of this country. Thus has the controversy been forced upon those who, while the publications were confined to a transatlantic Church, and only introduced among us by scanty importations, would have been content to leave it with those to whom it especially belonged, however deeply convinced themselves, that the divinity in question, was most justly accused.

As yet, however, the name, *Oxford Divinity*, seemed to very many readers, like its famous aversion, *Ultra-Protestantism*, a something indeed of no unportentous mien, but exceedingly difficult to reduce into distinct expression and shape. The Tracts were by no means a full, systematic, or satisfactory development of this divinity. They displayed its peculiarities only here and there; in many of their earlier portions, scarcely at all, except to a practiced eye; while they contained so much that was unquestionably good; so much, in a somewhat new relation, of what we had always held to be true and necessary, especially as to points of defect in the outward being of the Church of England as she is oppressed and disfranchised by the State, that scarcely any unprofessional reader would discover in the Tracts alone the several distinctive doctrines of the system. Indeed it is questionable whether any reader having no other aids, would be able, without much care, and familiarity with the precise bearings of the Romish controversy, as it was waged by the Reformers, to construct in his own mind, the whole edifice of that system. The difficulty would be, not in discovering divers places in the Tracts to which a mind well instructed in the Gospel, and thoroughly protesting against Romanism, would most seriously except. It would be rather in the gradual manner in which these developments are brought before the reader, in proportion as his mind may be expected to become prepared to bear them. It would lie also in the disjointed scattering of such parts over the whole surface of the Tracts, the intervals being filled in with an attractive display of original matter, or of selections from approved writers, to which none could except.

But the new Divinity is by no means confined to Oxford *Tracts*, technically so called. Some of them indeed are sufficiently objectionable. Many, however, contain a sort of material which, when read by itself, insulated from the more direct manifestations of *the system*, may be, not only innocent, but useful. It would be singular indeed, if works so voluminous, abounding in extracts from so many of the best divines of the Church of England, and composed throughout by learned and estimable men, should not contain a great deal of useful knowledge, of sound and valuable discussion, and of practical principle important to be had in remembrance. Read Cardinal Bellarmine's defense of Popery! May not as much be said of the works of that learned champion of the decrees of Trent? Read the works of Socinus! May not as much be said of the writings of that learned, acute, zealous originator of the modern school of Unitarian divinity? Surely it is but a poor voucher for the *system* inculcated in any work of theology, to say that many of its parts, taken in separation from each other, are sound and useful. Many a man is slowly dying of disease at the vitals, whose hands or feet are still capable of useful service.

The system is represented partly in the Tracts, but in other writings also of various authors, some of whom are known as leaders, others as followers, all disclaiming the name of being connected together as a school or a party, or in any way to be associated but as having been raised up, in the same age, under the same providence and teaching, to testify against the same departures from primitive truth, and in favor of the restoration of Catholic verity from the supposed disintegrating influences of what they have united in branding as *Ultra Protestantism*. In this concert of action and purpose, and of real system, it would not unfrequently occur, so long as there was no common symbol or confession marking out their common peculiarities, that an attempt to designate the doctrines of the school by the teaching of individuals, would be met by the answer, that the former was not responsible for whatever might appear in the writings of all who professed to be of it.

This difficult diffusiveness of essence, without corporate responsibility, has been, in some wise, removed by the publication in England, and the reprint in this country, of "A Letter by the Rev. E. B. Pusey, D. D., Regius Professor of Hebrew, in the University of Oxford," addressed to the Bishop of Oxford;—a work of more than two hundred well-filled pages, and purporting to contain, in behalf of the author and his fellow-laborers, a declaration of faith on the points whereon they have been accused, with a special view to a vindication of their doctrines from the charge of a tendency to Romanism. The object of the author of that Letter is, in his own words, to lay before the Bishop "*An explicit confession.*"

How far the confession is *explicit* on all points, professedly exhibited, may hereafter appear. How far it tends to remove the imputation of a dangerous tendency to Romanism, need not yet be said. It certainly places the question of *what this doctrine is, what it is responsible for, and where it is to be found*, in a much more satisfactory position for investigation. Its distinct mention of other vouchers beside itself, particularly the Lectures of Mr. Newman on Justification, as containing an exhibition of the system, equally authentic and responsible with itself, enables the inquirer to embrace a wider field of reference, without fear of depending upon authorities which might afterwards be called in question.

The present writer has devoted a long time and a great deal of pains to the study of the *system*, as exhibited in the several sources to which the Letter of Dr. Pusey has opened the way. With great truth he can say that he has diligently STUDIED the system, and that too with every effort to judge it fairly, kindly, conscientiously, and with frequent prayer to know the truth with regard to a movement which promises so much influence, good or evil, upon the state of Religion in the Protestant Churches.

He is constrained to say that every further step of insight into what is indeed a throroughly wrought, highly complex, and deep-laid scheme or system of doctrine, has produced but a deeper and deeper conviction, that, whatever may be the intention of its advocates—it is a systematic abandonment of the vital and distinguishing principles of the Protestant faith, and a systematic adoption of that very root and heart of Romanism, whence has issued the life of all its ramified corruptions and deformities. He does not mean that all the divers particulars—all the extremities of error and corruption into which Romanism has branched, and by which, far more than by its deep-rooted principles, it is known in modern controversy, are manifested in this system. Far from it. Romanism did not grow into its present stature and wide extension of limb and shade in an age. But in its essential and characteristic life, it existed nevertheless, and was no less Romanism when modestly sending out its feelers, and quietly widening its under-ground roots and shooting forth its branches, as the *times* allowed,—than it is Romanism now, in all its maturity and boastfulness. And so may this Divinity be essentially Romish, built on the same foundations, squared with reference to the same cardinal points, and by the law of its own nature, necessarily proceeding, in proportion as room is given, and the "Times" will bear, to make itself known in all those evils to the Gospel of Christ, by which the sway of Romanism has been so lamentably distinguished; while as yet, being truly a system *"for the times,"* it may not be Romanism in such overt self-confession and unreserved manifestation, before an unprepared community, or even in the unprepared minds of its immature, but growing disciples, as to strike the common eye, or be generally recognized, as of the house and lineage of Popery.

The present writer is fully convinced that such is the precise character and such are the certain results of this Divinity, in proportion as tendencies shall have time and room to develop themselves. Every additional examination, as additional documents have appeared from its advocates, or a closer dissection of those long in hand, has been made, has only rendered this conviction more and more immoveable. Instead of its being in any degree impaired by the consideration that sundry branches of Romanism have not yet been avowed, or have been really opposed by the advocates of this system; the fact only shows that, if their doctrine be Romanism, in essential character and influence, by making it less observable as such, it is only the more dangerous. "Surely in vain the net is spread in the *sight* of any bird."

Under the serious and painful conviction thus expressed, and in consideration of the many internal attractions of learning, and of bold pretension to primitive simplicity and purity under which this system appears; accompanied, as it is, by the influence of distinguished scholars and divines, and emanating from one of the two great Universities of our Mother Church of England; it has seemed to the present writer to be a duty arising out of his relation to the Church Catholic, and his more immediate relation to the clergy, candidates for orders, and laity of his own Diocese, to lay it before the public, in its essential principles, as compared with the doctrines common to the Protestant Episcopal Churches of England and America, on the one side, and those of the Church of Rome on the other. And this he conceives to be the more necessary, because of the manner in which it has been presented, the attractive but defective raiment in which it is put forth, the unexplained phraseology it sometimes uses, but especially because the main positions and fundamental interests of the Romish controversy as carried on by the Reformers of England and the Continent, in common, have passed so much out of mind. Protestants in these days are accustomed to contemplate Romanism, rather in its extremities, than its roots, and to aim only at cutting off its limbs, instead of taking away its heart, and thus are not ready to compare with it a system which, though it may have put out comparatively but few of the branches, has yet all the root and life of Romanism, ready to ramify just as fast as the "Times" shall be prepared. One may be charged with great presumption in attempting to discover in the writings under consideration, what their own authors, so learned and acute, and their friends, so learned and acute, seem not to have discovered; and in attempting to arraign on the charge of such serious error, the opinions of authors at whose feet it would be no evidence of humility that one should be ready and glad to sit, as well for examples of personal excellence, as for the benefit of deep thought and various and matured erudition. But in the words of one of them, *"By-standers see our minds."* It may be added, *By-standers of very inferior capacity* may see their minds, when they do not. A very skilful physician may be blind to his own malady; while to one of very inferior skill it may be quite evident. With no profession, then, but of an honest, single, prayerful desire, by the grace and mercy of God, to discharge his solemn responsibility as "a watchman over the House of Israel," feeling at the same time that many others in the Church might discharge the duty far more efficiently, the author must request, at least, his brethren in his own diocese, to accompany him in the examination of this widely circulated and high-pretending theology.

But to go over the whole system, in all its members, for the sake of estimating its dominant character, were an endless task. We must select some fundamental question, which, as viewed in one aspect, constitutes the ruling doctrinal feature of the Protestant faith; and viewed in an opposite aspect, the ruling doctrinal feature of Romanism; and to which, as held in the two opposite systems, may be traced their chief distinguishing peculiarities of teaching and practice. Then we must inquire to which of the two contrasted views of that main question, the essential features of this system before us are most conformed. If we find them conformed to that of Rome, and opposed to that of the Church of England, then we have essential Romanism, even though not a single branch of Romanism, such as Purgatory, Image-worship, Transubstantiation, &c., may have been developed. But if we shall find, moreover, that it is not only thus conformed in the main principle, but is going on to shoot out more and more, however slowly and cautiously, into just the same growth of bud and branch; then we shall be the more confirmed in the conviction, not only that it is Romanism in essence, but that, in proportion as the times allow, and room be given, it will become Romanism in full manifestation.

Now what is that fundamental question which will thus serve as a position whence we may command the whole field of inquiry before us? We need go no further than the judicious Hooker for an answer. "*That grand question*," he says "that hangeth in controversy between us and Rome, is *about the matter of justifying righteousness.* We disagree about *the nature and essence of the medicine whereby Christ cureth our disease;* about *the manner of applying it;* about *the number and the power of means,* which God requireth in us for the effectual applying thereof to our soul's comfort. When they are required to show what the righteousness is whereby a Christian man is justified, they answer that it is a divine spiritual *quality;* which quality received into the soul, doth first make it to be one of them who are born of God; and secondly, endue it with power to bring forth such works as they do that are born of Him; even as the soul of man, being joined to his body, doth first make him to be of the number of reasonable creatures; and, secondly, enable him to perform the natural functions which are proper to his kind: that it maketh the soul amiable and gracious in the sight of God, in regard whereof it is termed Grace; that it purgeth, purifieth, and washeth out, all the stains and pollutions of sins; that, by it, through the merit of Christ, we are delivered, as from sin, so from eternal death and condemnation the reward of sin. This Grace they will have to be applied by infusion; to the end that, as the body is warm by the heat which is in the body, so the soul might be made righteous by inherent Grace; which Grace they make capable of increase; as the body may be more warm, so the soul more and more justified, according as Grace should be augmented; the augmentation whereof is merited by good works, as good works are made meritorious by it. Wherefore, the first receipt of Grace, in their divinity, is the first Justification: the increase thereof, the second Justification. As Grace may be increased by the merit of good works: so it may be diminished by the demerit of sins venial; it may be lost by mortal sin. Inasmuch, therefore, as it is needful, in the one case to repair, in the other to recover, the loss which is made, the infusion of Grace hath her sundry after-meals: for the which cause, they make many ways to apply the infusion of Grace. It is applied to infants through baptism, without either faith or works; and, in them, really it taketh away original sin, and the punishment due unto it: it is applied to infidels and wicked men in the first Justification, through baptism, without works, yet not without faith; and it taketh away sins both actual and original together, with all whatsoever punishment, eternal or temporal, thereby deserved. Unto such as have attained the first Justification; that is to say, this first receipt of Grace,—it is applied farther by good works to the increase of former Grace: which is the second Justification. If they work more and more, Grace doth more increase: and they are more and more justified. To such as diminish it by venial sins, it is applied by holy water, Ave Marias, crossings, papal salutations, and such like: which serve for reparations of Grace decayed. To such as have lost it through mortal sin, it is applied by the sacrament (as they term it) of Penance: which sacrament hath force to confer Grace anew; yet in such sort, that, being so conferred, it hath not altogether so much power as at the first. For it only cleanseth out the stain or guilt of sin committed: and changeth the punishment eternal, into a temporal satisfactory punishment here, if time do serve, if not, hereafter to be endured; except it be lightened by masses, works of charity, pilgrimages, fasts, and such like; or else shortened, by pardon, for term, or by plenary pardon quite removed and taken away. This is *the mystery of the Man of Sin. This maze, the Church of Rome doth cause her followers to tread, when they ask her the way to Justification.* Whether they speak of the first or second Justification, they make the essence of a divine quality inherent; they make it righteousness which is in us. If it be in us, then it is ours; as our souls are ours, though we have them from God, and can hold them no longer than pleaseth him; for, if he withdraw the breath of our nostrils, we fall to dust. But the righteousness, wherein we must be found, if we will be justified, is not our own. Therefore we cannot be justified by any inherent quality. The Church of Rome, in teaching Justification by inherent Grace, doth *pervert the truth of Christ:* and, by the hands of the Apostles, we have received otherwise than she teacheth. Now, concerning the Righteousness of *Sanctification*, we deny it not to be inherent: we grant, that, unless we work, we have it not: only we distinguish it, as a thing different in nature from the Righteousness of *Justification*. By the one, we are interested in the *right of inheriting:* by the other, we are *brought to the actual possession* of eternal bliss. And so the end of both is everlasting life."*

Now here we have a regular pedigree of the most injurious corruptions of the Romish Church, and all traced to the *parent cause* in her doctrine of Justification. All together make up "*the mystery of*

* Hooker's Disc. of Justif. § 5, 6.

the man of sin"—"*the maze which the Church of Rome doth lead her followers to tread, when they ask her the way to Justification;*"—all constitute that "building" of manifold error which Hooker believed *must* fall "in the presence of the building of God," "as Dagon, before the Ark." But the *corner stone* on which that building rests; the *clue* to that maze; *the secret* of that mystery, is the DOCTRINE OF JUSTIFICATION BY INHERENT RIGHTEOUSNESS—the answer given to a sinner inquiring what he must do to be saved, instead of that plain answer of St. Paul, "*Believe on the Lord Jesus Christ and thou shalt be saved.*" Embrace the answer of Rome, and you have *essential* Romanism; carry out the principle, and you will have *developed* Romanism, in the whole of its maze and mystery. Embrace the answer of St. Paul, and you strike Romanism to the heart; so that, whatever its ramifications, they must all die and pass away. It is this Romish doctrine of Justification that gives value to indulgences; need to purgatory; use to the sacrament of penance; motive to the invocation of saints; credit to the Papal treasury of supererogatory merits; that makes auricular confession tolerable, and all the vain inventions of meritorious will-worship, precious. Next come devices for the defense of these, and hence the Romish doctrine of tradition and of infallibility and of implicit faith. Such precisely was the view of the judicious Hooker, as furnished in the extract above given; a writer whose authority will not be denied, as to what was the fundamental question in the days of the reformation of the Church of England, in her controversy with Rome. In this prominence of Justification, there was a perfect agreement among the Protestant Divines, as well of England, as of the continent. It was in precise accordance with the view of Hooker, that Luther spake of the doctrine of Justification as "*the article of a standing or a falling Church;*" that Calvin maintained that "*if this one head were yielded safe and entire, it would not pay the cost to make any great quarrel about other matters in controversy with Rome;*"* that Melancthon said he and his brethren were brought into danger for the only reason that they denied the Romish doctrine of Justification;† that divines in the Council of Trent opposed the Protestant doctrine of Justification because it "*abolished the punishment together with the guilt, and left no place remaining for satisfaction,*"‡ that is, it made all the devices of sacramental penance, propitiatory masses, yea, the whole "maze and mystery of the man of sin," unnecessary. Such was the view universally taken by the earlier divines of the Church of England.

---

* Bp. Hall's Works, ix. p. 44, 5.   † Ep. i. 120.
‡ Paul's Hist. Counc. of Trent. p. 200.

With such men as Usher, Hall, Andrews, Beveridge, as well as a host before them the Romish Justification was always that one essential departure from Gospel truth from which the whole brood of Romish corruptions in doctrine and practice originated.

In this work, the author goes back to the essential test of the Romanism of any system of divinity. *Is this conformed essentially to the doctrine of Rome, on the question of Justification; or to the opposite doctrine of the standards common to the Church of England, and her daughter-Church in America?* To arrive at the right answer to this question, will be the object of the following pages.

But here it will be asked how can we suspect such men as the advocates of this system, men of a reputation so unimpeached, and under such solemn vows of conformity to the doctrines of the English Church, of a *design* to bring in Romanism, or to bring over the Church of England to that of Rome?

It is answered that we suspect no such thing. That they consider themselves as laboring to introduce what *they* call Romanism; that they have any desire to make the Church of England subject to that of Rome; or to make her similar, in *all* those peculiar features which most strike the eye and excite the general aversion, and some of which their own writings have opposed; that they do not consider themselves special lovers of the mother-Church, we by no means assert.* The very fact, that their personal reputation is so unimpeachable, and their conviction of the propriety of what they are doing, is apparently so sincere, must make their teaching, if erroneous, the more dangerous. Men are often half persuaded already of a doctrine, when its advocate adds to learning evident sincerity, and zeal. We should little fear much evil result from the writings of these divines, did they stand disclosed as *knowing* their doctrines to be inconsistent with those of the Church of which they profess to be devoted sons, and promotive of a system against which that Church so earnestly protests. In such a case, we might trust in a great degree, the evil, for its remedy; the criminal, for his halter.

But some of the worst corruptions of religion have had their origin with its best and sincerest friends. Among those who most disturbed the Churches of Rome and Carthage in the days of Cornelius and Cyprian, were Confessors, with maimed and mangled bodies, from the torture, in which they had borne a noble testimony

---

* What might have been asserted, had this book been written a few years later as to the motives of some of the chief movers in the Tractarian effort, it now requires but little acquaintance with the history of the movement to say. (1860.)

to their Master. What is now a full-grown idolatry in the Church of Rome, had its beginnings in the bosoms of men ready to die for Christ, and was nursed by some of the purest piety of the early Church. The *ovum* of saint-worship was laid, by the Serpent, in the ashes of the martyrs; and in the assemblies of devout men, around their tombs, met together out of just veneration for their holy example and noble death, the embryo was cherished. The whole history of the Church warns us against forgetting that very good and sincere men may set on foot great errors—and thus inflict an injury upon the cause of Gospel truth of which worse men would not be capable.*

Again: it is asked whether the *eminent learning* united to the religious character of these Divines, is not such protection against serious error, that we may feel assured they have not fallen into doctrines approximating in any evil or dangerous degree to Romanism? The idea has weight practically, but it is only necessary to ask the question, to answer it. "Let him that thinketh he standeth, take heed lest he fall." "The depths of Satan" are deeper than any man's learning. His wiles are stronger than any man's goodness. His great enmity is against the redemption of man by Jesus Christ, and consequently against the true way of Justification through his righteousness. And to cut off the supplies of the Church, by choking up, if he cannot wholly cut off, that new and living way to the Father, was his grand device in Romanism, and will ever be among all people. No human learning and goodness can be trusted for security against his "principalities and powers." "We wrestle not with flesh and blood." The war which began when it was said to the Serpent, "thou shalt bruise his heel," is still waged without ceasing against that "Seed of the woman," "the second Man," "the Lord from Heaven." His mystical body, on earth, is compassed with stratagems which often elude the most careful search. Many a learned, many a zealous, many a sincere man has been unwittingly harnessed to the work of that "Ruler of the darkness of this world," who never succeeded in constructing such an Antichrist as when he invented Romanism, and has no device so dear as that of sustaining the same in all its integrity, and of reducing the whole kingdom of Christ, on earth, to its dominion.

* "The founders of almost all heresies, as Arius, Pelagius, Nestorius, &c., have been famed for external piety and sanctity." Palmer on the Church. v. 1. p. 102. In Dr. Pusey's Scriptural Views of Holy Baptism we are warned against the "delusive criterion" of allowing ourselves to be influenced in the enquiry whether any doctrine be a scriptural truth, by *the supposed religious character of those* who hold or deny it.—p. 11. *Am. El.*

But, again, it is asked, how can the writers in question be charged with a dangerous tendency to Romanism, when it is well known that they have frequently expressed themselves, and even written treatises directly against certain conspicuous features of the Roman Church?

That these divines have so written, we have no disposition to deny. Whether they have not confined themselves, in their arguments against what *they* call Romanism, to a very meager selection of topics; expressly excluding what our Reformers and ancient divines considered to be the great cardinal matters of the controversy; whether, in the points embraced, they have not taken ground exceedingly low and tame, using language which often betrays a disposition, rather to apologize for the Church of Rome, than to expose her heresies; whether they have not confined themselves to such a selection of the weapons of argument, especially in the exclusion of the authority of Scripture, and the substitution of a single reliance upon that of tradition, as in reality to dishonor and betray the very cause of which they are the professed defenders; whether they be not precisely such advocates of Protestantism, as the Church of Rome, in her steady effort to re-establish her dominion in England would select, had she the choosing of her adversaries; whether, by the very nature and mode of their restrained and tame and apologetic controversy, so wholly unlike the vigorous onsets of England's Reformers and greatest divines, they are not really doing Rome's work, in England, far more advantageously, *for the present Times*, than any of her own professed sons could do it, and that simply because they call themselves consistent clergymen of the Church of England, and because many cry out loudly against the uncharitableness of supposing they are not; whether, if they were citizens of a country in which Romanism was the established faith, they would not find themselves bound by their present principles, and but little forbidden by their present sympathies, to fall in submissively, with the ways, and bow to the authority of, the Romish Church, it would be premature, in this place, to consider.*

Let it, however, for the present, be granted that these divines have written well and faithfully against such features of Romanism, as the Papal Supremacy; the schismatic position of the Church of

---

* It was not long after the above was published before one of the chief, perhaps *the* chief leader in the movement, and he who was most referred to as a strong writer against Rome, had become openly a Romanist, and it became apparent that he had even been a conceded Romanist when the strong language cited in proof of his anti-Romish views was written.

Rome within the Dioceses of the Church of England; the denial of the cup to the laity, &c., &c., so as to prove that so far as these and similar matters constitute Romanism, they desire none of its ways. But surely it is not uncommon for persons to be opposing the overt manifestations of deadly disorder, while unwarily, but constantly, cherishing its vital principle. The seat of ruinous evil may as easily be mistaken in the mystical body of "the Man of Sin," as in the natural body of any of its individual members. It is indeed a singular mode of argument to contend that because certain writers oppose some things in the Church of Rome, they may not be charged with the vital essence of Romanism, and with maintaining those very principles which, above all others, have made her Apostate, and us Protestants. The fact that these divines have written with learning and sincerity against some of the more offensive and *inconvenient* developments of Popery, (for the claim of Papal Supremacy would certainly be quite *inconvenient* to the clergy of England, if allowed,) puts them in the precise position from which, if they be wrong in the one radical matter of justification, the publication of their doctrines, on that, will operate the more covertly and dangerously upon the Protestant community around them. Men will be the less awake to the maintenance of the more abstract and impalpable error, because they are witnesses to the resistance presented to the more superficial, but impressive. Let a school of divines appear among us who, under the profession of Protestants, instead of appearing as advocates of only some of the more interior and least familiar, but head sources, of Roman corruptions, shall come out also full handed with arguments for the supremacy, and transubstantiation, and divers other matters of equal note: We shall little fear their influence. Ten years of open attack around the walls of Troy, effected nothing. But one day of delusion amongst the wardens of her gates; the not examining what lay concealed under an apparent *act of religion*, betrayed the city. So it is, says Usher, "They who kept continual watch and ward against the more direct introduction of evil, might sleep while the seed of an iniquity, cloaked with the name of piety, were a sowing; yea, peradventure might, at unawares themselves, have some hand in bringing in their Trojan horse, commended thus unto them under the name of religion and semblance of devotion."*

"We do not hold, (says the same admirable prelate) that Rome was built in a day; or that the great dunghill of errors, which we now see in it, was raised in an age;" neither do *we* hold that Rome

---

* Answer to a Jesuit, p. 4.

could be rebuilt in any country where she has been cast down, in a generation; nor that the re-construction must necessarily be called *Rome*, and have all the forms and outward and visible signs of that inward and spiritual departure from grace which is usually denominated Popery. Should we conceive of the grand enemy, actually employing a band of men, concealed under the garb of Protestants (and we may do so for the sake of illustration, without offense) to lay open a secret road for Popery, into the very citadel of the Protestantism of England, we could readily understand that they would select the most *gradual* means, as the most *effectual;* the most *noiseless* and *unseen*, as the most *ensnaring*; that they would seem to be great opposers of Romanism, in some points, while insinuating it in others; would break ground at a distance, where they would be least feared and remarked; get their position fixed in peace, "while men slept;" then cautiously commence approaches, gradually familiarizing the watchers upon the walls with the sound of their working, and never putting forth a new approach, till the novelty of the former was forgotten. We can readily conceive that the weapon of such a siege would not be as the Roman Catapult, hurling, in open day, its bolts and fiery darts. Some Christian Archimedes, with the bright mirror of the word, would soon burn up the engine, and put the workers to confusion. But the weapon would be the pick of the sapper, digging at the base; and the foundation selected would be that of the bastion, which, while in reality the key of the fortress, *is least known in that importance to the multitude*, and therefore the least watched; and their object would be, like that of the gun-powder plot, under the Senate-House and Throne, to subjugate the whole, in the ruin of the head; and could they only persuade some honored and trusted men of the city, under the sincere supposition, on their part, that they were only searching after *hid treasures of Antiquity*, or endeavoring to effect some useful *restoration* in the old walls of a venerable monument of ancient prowess, *to do the digging for them*, till they themselves could work unseen in the mine, it would indeed be great gain. By and by, it would be seen that a portion of the wall was fallen—then another, but each with such interval, that all lookers-on had grown familiar with the sight of the first dilapidation, before the second was permitted. By and by, that bastion is in ruins, and the city at the mercy of the enemy, but all has gone on so gradually and imperceptibly, that it excites but little apprehension. Now because there is little change to the eye; no change of accustomed names; no overt invasion of old attachments and usages; no hoisting of the flag of the Pope, men may be saying, where is the fear of his coming—for all things continue as they were from the beginning. But, like Samson asleep, their strength is departed, and the Philistine is upon them. That strong bastion of our Reformed Church is *Justification by Faith;* erected "upon the foundation of the Apostles and Prophets—Jesus Christ himself being the chief corner-stone." *That* gone, the temple is taken, the ark is in captivity; "from the daughter of Zion, all her beauty is departed." What then if there never grow up over the desolate courts of the Lord's House, the thorns and thistles, and all those rank growths, whose names are in the Breviary of abominations indigenous to Romanism? Satan is well content. The land is desolate. The work is done. A greater display of ruin, might make it only less permanent.*

To some readers it may occur that, in the above remarks, the writer has made insinuations disrespectful to the honesty and sincerity of the writers whose works we are now considering. But not so. *They* are in no wise intended, but as they may be *unconsciously* instrumental in the process described. But so is the writer impressed with the Scripture-warnings as to the enmity of Satan against the Lord our Redeemer, who being personally out of reach, in heaven, can only be assailed through his mystical body—the Church, on earth;—so fully does he believe that in these last times, Satan has come down, having great wrath, because he knoweth he hath but a short time;† so does he feel the importance of that petition, "*That it may please thee to beat down Satan under our feet;*" and so do the signs of the times seem to indicate that the Church of England, as it has been always the strong-hold of the truth, is now the grand object of a special effort in these last days of the "Ruler of the darkness of this world;" and so deeply is the writer impressed, by the history of all ages, that it is the good men and strong—the Peters of the Church, whom Satan intensely *desires to have, that he may sift them as wheat*—and that out of these he may yet succeed, as he did with Peter, and has often since succeeded, in causing some to fall into his snare, and drag in his traces, and make a stand against the truth, while they know not what they do; that the writer could not adventure on this subject, without expressing these habitual and solemn thoughts of his mind: however liable he might make himself to the false imputation of an unkind, un-

---

* *Amisso Articulo Justificationis, simul amissa est tota doctrina Christiana—*Luther.

† Rev. xii. 12.

brotherly, disrespectful meaning towards the authors particularly referred to in his pages. It is nothing more, however, than these authors not unfrequently say, in substance, of those, their brethren in the Church of England, whom they are fond of distinguishing as Ultra-Protestants, and to whom they unequivocally attribute, not only essential Rationalism, but a direct tendency to Socinianism, and ultimate Infidelity. Now since such features of the system of these unhappy Ultra-Protestants, must in the judgment of their accusers, be "*not of the light, but of the darkness,*" and consequently of "*the Ruler of the darkness of this world,*" however unconscious the instruments, the present writer may be excused in expressing a similar opinion of the secret instigation of what he considers to be Romanism at Oxford.

Mr. Newman expresses precisely the writer's mind when he says that "Satan ever acts on a system, various, manifold and intricate, with parts and instruments of different qualities, some almost purely evil, *others so unexceptionable, that in themselves, and detached from the end to which all is subservient, they are really 'Angels of Light,'* and may be found so to be at the last day."*

---

* Newman on the Prophetical Office of the Church, p. 102. "Taking it for granted," says a writer now of great note at Oxford, "that the Devil had as great a longing since Christ triumphed over him, as he had before, to work the bane of men's souls throughout Europe—it were a brutish simplicity to think he could not, and a preposterous charity to think he would not, minister his receipts in a cunninger fashion, since the promulgation of the Gospel, than he did before; although the poison be still the same. To eat figs, or other more cordial food, with the infusion of subtle and deadly poison, exempts not men's bodies from danger. Much less can speculative orthodoxal opinions of the Godhead free men's souls from the poison of idolatrous practices, wherewith (in the Romish Church,) they are mingled." "Were rats-bane as simply and grossly ministered to men, as it is to rats, few would take harm by it."—*Jackson's Works*, book v. chap. xxii.

CHAPTER II.

STATEMENTS PREPARATORY TO THE RIGHT ESTIMATION OF THIS SYSTEM AS TO THE DOCTRINE OF JUSTIFICATION.

Professions of Oxford Divines concerning the conformity of their doctrine with that of the Church of England—Their account of Ultra-Protestantism—The identity of their system with that of Alexander Knox—The condemnation of the latter, as Romish and dangerous, by certain eminent divines, of diverse schools in the Church of England, before its development, at Oxford, had excited any special notice.

BEFORE proceeding further, it is proper to state that the system of divinity which we propose to examine, is loudly claimed by its advocates to be the middle path, the *Via Media*, of the Church of England; "distinct from the by-ways of Ultra-Protestantism on one side, and neither verging towards, nor losing itself in, Romanism on the other."* The formularies of the Church of England, and the writings of her standard Divines are often and confidently appealed to as exhibiting the precise doctrines of the system. Now it is the simple question how far these pretensions are true, which we propose to institute. But in order to estimate this Via Media aright, the first thing is to get a view of the opposing sides between which it professes to pass. Of the one side, viz., of Romanism, we are to speak particularly hereafter. Of the other—ULTRA-PROTESTANTISM, a something which occurs with singular frequency in the works of these writers, what shall we say? What is Ultra-Protestantism? We have seen no definition. But according to the use of Dr. Pusey, and others, the name seems to be applied to whatever is *in* religion, or *relating* to it, negatively, or positively, for, or against, *only excepting Romanism and their teaching;* embracing all varieties of cause and effect, doctrine and inference; from the views of those who, though in the main, orthodox and sound, in spite of the natural tendency of their principles are not of this way, through all Lutheranism and Calvinism, and every grade of

---

* Pusey's Letter to the Bishop of Oxford. Let it be noted that all our quotations from the Tracts or any of the writings of Dr. Pusey will be from the American Editions, unless otherwise stated. p. 14.

unromish dissent down to what is considered *the result of a tendency common to the whole group*—an entire Rationalism, and Socinianism; *ut nec pes, nec caput uni reddatur formæ.* One would suppose that a coast so undefined would afford but little guidance in keeping the middle way, except as when mariners, under fear of hidden shoals and currents, on an unseen shore, keep as far at sea as possible.

Some specimens will help us to judge how far this Via Media is really *a middle way*.

Dr. Pusey describes "*a large portion*" of the clergy of the Church of England as holding "that Justification is not the gift of God through his sacraments, but the result of a certain frame of mind, of a going forth of themselves, and resting themselves upon their Saviour; that this is the *act* whereby they think themselves to have been justified; and so as another would revert to his "baptism and ingrafting into Christ, and his thus being in Christ, so do *they* this act whereby they were justified." "They sever Justification from Baptism, and make it consist in the *act* of reliance upon the merits of Christ only; sin, according to them, is forgiven, *at once*, upon each renewal of this act: and in that, they thus virtually substitute this act for Baptism; a man has no more to do with his past sins, than he has with those remitted by baptism. According to them, when men have been once brought in repentance to renounce their sins, and seek reconciliation through the free mercy of Christ, then their sins are done away, they are covered, they can appear no more; the hand-writing is blotted out." This "apprehension of Christ's merits is to them a full remission of sins, completely effacing them." "To revert to past sin is to doubt of Christ's mercy; to bear a painful recollection of it is to be under the bondage of the law; to seek to efface it by repentance is weakness of faith; to do acts of mercy or self-denial, or self-abasement, or to fast with reference to it, is to interfere with 'the freeness and fullness of the Gospel:' to insist upon them 'is to place repentance in stead of Christ.'"*

It is impossible not to see in this strange caricature, which really applies, in all respects to no class of the clergy of England, that "*the large portion*" intended is that of the class best known in this country by such names as Robinson, Scott, Venn, the two Milners, Simeon; of whose mode of exhibiting the way of salvation, the writings of such living divines as the present Bishop Wilson, of Calcutta, the two Bishops Sumner, one of Winchester, the other

---

* Pusey's Letter, pp. 74, 8, 54, 5.

of Chester, the Rev. G. S. Faber, &c., are fair examples.* True, indeed, the views of this most honorable and useful body of the English Clergy are very singularly overdrawn; one can hardly recognize them under the strained and warped features for which they are made to be accountable. But without doubt, the Ultra Protestantism referred to in the above extracts is intended to be understood as being displayed in the general mode of that class of English divines in representing *the nature and essence of the medicine whereby Christ cureth our disease, the manner of applying it, and the number and power of the means."* Of such views, does Dr. Pusey write as follows: "This abuse of the doctrine of Justification by faith sears men's consciences now, *as much as the indulgences of the Romish system did before.* It used to be said that 'the Romish was an easy religion to die in,' but even the Romish, in its corruptions, scarcely offered terms so easy, at all events made not a boast of the easiness of its terms." Then follows an evident preference of the Romish system on the ground that if it have only "*the dregs* of the system of the ancient Church," *it has the dregs—* "*something of the bitterness of the ancient medicine;*" it still teaches men "*to make sacrifices for the good of their souls;*" "*to accuse and condemn themselves, that so they might find mercy*" through Christ—to be "*punished in this world, that their souls might be saved in the day of the Lord.*" We are given distinctly to understand that the system of "*a large portion*" of the English clergy, is worse than even these stale dregs of the medicine of the ancient Church; because it "stifles continually the strong emotions of terror and amazement which God has wrought upon the soul, and by an artificial wrought-up peace, checks the deep and searching agony, whereby God as in a furnace, purifies the whole man, by the spirit of judgment, and the spirit of burning." It is "a spurious system, misapplying the promises of the Gospel, usurping the privileges of baptism, which it has not to confer, giving peace which it has not to bestow, and going counter to the whole tenor of Scripture, that every man shall be judged according to his works."†

The same singularly extravagant and most painful strain of condemnation is found every where in Mr. Newman's Lectures on Justification. The following is a specimen. He calls the righteousness of Christ imputed to us for Justification, as held by the "large

---

* Bishop Wilson died in 1857. His Memoir is one of the most valuable in all the range of Christian biography. The Bishop of Chester, mentioned above, is the present most venerable and excellent Archbishop of Canterbury, Dr. Sumner. (1860.)

† Pusey's Letters, pp. 56—59.

portion " of the English Clergy above referred to, " *an unreal righteousness and a real corruption*," "bringing us *into bondage to shadows*"— " *another Gospel*." " *Away then* (he says) *with this modern, this private, this arbitrary, this tyrannical* system, which promising liberty, conspires against it; which abolishes sacraments, to introduce dead ordinances; and for the real participation of Christ, and justification through his Spirit, would at the very marriage feast, feed us on shells and husks, who hunger and thirst after righteousness.*

It is not my purpose here to say a word, in argument, concerning these wonderful and most melancholy exhibitions of morbid mind and perverted spiritual discernment. Whoever has paid any serious attention to the writings of the Clergy, thus *professedly* displayed, will need no help in estimating the gross injustice of the condemnation. But where there is no need of argument, there may be propriety in assertion; and sometimes there is a solemn duty in assertion, if only for the purpose of bearing our testimony, whatever it may be worth, to some precious, but despised and reviled portion of the truth as it is in Jesus. Such testimony, the writer feels constrained to give, in this place, after such an afflicting reprobation of what he most solemnly believes to be nothing else than "the glorious Gospel of the blessed God," our Saviour. Denying entirely that the doctrine of the class of divines described, is given with any correctness in the above representations; but perceiving just enough of truth therein to mark distinctly who compose " the large portion " of Clergy thus caricatured; the author of these pages does earnestly hope that his name may be counted worthy to take part in their condemnation. If the way here called another Gospel, even that of Justification through the obedience and death of Christ, accounted unto us for righteousness, through the instrumental agency of a living faith, be not the only hope of the sinner, then he, for one, has no hope. He knows of no other "*anchor of the soul sure and stedfast, which entereth to that within the veil.*" He does hope he may be ever identified with that way of preaching Christ Jesus the Lord, which instead of a "*reserve*," in making known the precious doctrine of his Atonement, instead of treating *salvation by grace, through faith,* as "*a great secret,*" keeping *it* out of the sight of the ungodly, for fear of " an *indelicate exposure of the sacred mystery,*"† lifts up the voice to the perishing and penitent, like the Master and Lord, when he cried, "*If any man thirst, let him come unto me, and drink* ;" a mode

---

* Lectures on Justification. p. 61. Extremes meet. Socinus calls the same doctrine, *fœda, execranda, pernitiosa, detestanda*.

† See No. 80 of Tracts for the Times.

of preaching Christ, that delights to proclaim to all people, a full, perfect and ready salvation to the vilest sinner, truly repenting and believing in Jesus—a salvation which justifies *perfectly and immediately*, on the act of a living faith, and which sanctifies *perfectly, but progressively*, as the necessary fruit of the same faith; a salvation so perfect and free, that, in the words of Hooker, "although in ourselves, we be altogether sinful and unrighteous, yet even the man which is impious in himself, *full of iniquity, full of sin*, him being found in Christ, through faith, and having his sins remitted through repentance, him God beholdeth with a gracious eye, putteth away his sin by not imputing it, taketh quite away the punishment due thereto by pardoning it, and accepteth him in Jesus Christ; *as perfectly righteous as if he had fulfilled all that is commanded him in the Law.* Let it be counted folly or frenzy, or fury, whatsoever, it is our comfort and our wisdom."* So testifies our admirable Hooker—most surely an Ultra-Protestant, in the matter of Justification, according to these divines. One can scarcely open the works of such writers as Beveridge, Usher, Reynolds, Andrews, Hopkins, and Hooker, without meeting the very teaching, and often the very words, which have received such condemnation from this divinity.

Having now obtained some general idea of the system in question, by a brief view of one of the opposite sides which it professes to avoid, and of the *extreme antipathy* with which its advocates recoil therefrom; we are ready to proceed to a more direct investigation.

Our single object will be to enquire *whether this divinity does preserve, as it professes, the* MIDDLE WAY *between the extremes of Protestantism, on the one side, and of Romanism on the other*—the way of the Protestant Church of England as indicated in her standards of doctrine, and in the writings of her standard divines; *whether in reality it does not substantially renounce the doctrines of the Church of England, as thus expressed and expounded, in regard to the way of a sinner's justification before God, and its connected truths; and substantially identify itself with those very doctrines of the Church of Rome, on these points*, against which the Church of England, in common with all the Protestant Churches of Europe, in the days of the Reformation most solemnly protested.

But how great would be the advantage, in favor of a correct conclusion, could this question be pursued entirely aloof from the various temptations to bias, arising out of the present wide-spread

* Discourse of Justification. § 6.

feeling in reference to the system under consideration. This cannot be. But then, as the next thing, how great would be our aid could we obtain the deliberate judgment of learned and good men upon the same divinity, expressed *before it came to be identified with Oxford Tracts;* before the peculiar views of Mr. Newman on Justification, and which are now avowed by Dr. Pusey, as those of the Oxford school, had excited any general attention, or drawn any party lines. But the advantage of the opinions of learned and good men, in such circumstances, would be greatly enhanced, should they come from those two schools of doctrine in the Church of England, which would be the most likely to differ on such a subject; so that while on one side there would be all ability, candor and fairness, on the other there would be also a special inclination to see matters in a favorable light. Then if the opinions of such men should be essentially the same, the probability that their judgment was right would be exceedingly strong.

The opinions of such men, in such circumstances, and thus concurring, can be produced.

The reader is, perhaps, acquainted with the name and character of the late Alexander Knox, a member of the United Church of England and Ireland; a gentleman of secluded life and high excellence of character; an author of meditative habits of mind, and of extensive research. He was known, while living, to be possessed of some peculiar views on several subjects of divinity, especially those of Providence and Justification. His "Remains," of which the first volumes appeared in 1834, excited no little attention. The notions put forth therein, on the doctrine of Justification, "would appear to have come across the path of our Protestant Divinity (says the British Critic) with a disturbing influence similar to that of a comet upon the orbit of our globe." Many greatly feared their influence. Others apprehended little from the "meditations of a recluse and solitary thinker, whose life exhibited the pattern of every Christian grace."

But whatever were the peculiar views of Mr. Knox, and though they were published long before those of Oxford, on Justification, had excited any attention, it is distinctly intimated in a late number of the British Critic, under its now well-known, though recent character, as *an organ of the new divinity*, that between the views of Mr. Knox, and those of its own *present* school, there is so great an identity that the former was but *"an instance in rudiment"* of what the latter has since developed. Let us cite the words. *"His writings* (says the Reviewer) *are no slight evidence of the intellectual* *and moral movement under consideration."* Again: *"He is an instance in rudiment of those great restorations which he foresaw in development. He shares with the eminent writers of the day in the work of advancing what he anticipated."**

Now let us see what were those anticipations of Mr. Knox, which are thus spoken of, as being now advancing to development at Oxford. "Of Mr. Knox's more conspicuous peculiarities, none (says the Critic) are more remarkable than those on the subject of *Justification by faith,* and his speculations relative to divine Providence." But peculiarities concerning the doctrine of Providence certainly are not referred to as *rudiments* of the present developments at Oxford. It follows that those concerning Justification are. What then were the peculiar views—what the anticipations of Mr. Knox on this subject, by which he came into such acknowledged identity with the "restorations" at Oxford?

Mr. Knox has declared that *"no writer on this earth is more misunderstood and misrepresented than St. Paul"* upon the subject of Justification.† " I greatly suspect, (he writes) that the time is not very distant when even Theological Creeds will be brought to a PHILOSOPHICAL TEST, and be discarded, should they not stand the trial. At such a season, I have little hope for those who are only acquainted with St. Paul, through the interpreting medium of Luther or Calvin, Dr. Owen or Mr. Romaine. Confident I am, they will awake and wonder how they could have dreamed of MAN's CHIEF HOPE resting on any ground but that MORAL ONE upon which our omniscient Lord himself has placed it,—'*Blessed are the pure in heart,*' &c., or of a state of favor with God existing, for one moment, independently of moral qualification. They will, I doubt not, at length, discover this strange defect in the present favorite system."‡ This then is the sum of Mr. Knox's anticipations on this head;—viz., 1st. "The application of a *philosophical test* to the Scripture doctrine of Justification, and the discarding of whatever abides not that fire. 2d. The passing away, as a dream, of the doctrine of Justification by the *extrinsic righteousness* of Christ, *accounted to us by faith, only,* and the substitution of a Justification resting exclusively upon the *moral* basis of an *inherent personal righteousness.*

These then are the views which Mr. Knox *"shares with the eminent writers of the day in advancing,"* which constitute a part of *"these great restorations which he foresaw in development,"* and of which he himself was *"an instance in rudiment."* So then by the

---

* British Critic, No. 56, pp. 40, 41, 42.
† Remains, vol. i. p. 284, 285.   ‡ Ibid. p. 315.

volunteer-profession of the Oxford school itself, as declared by its present organ, the British Critic, the theology of Mr. Knox on the subject of Justification was *essentially their own.* Further proof of this identity will appear by and by. At present we have enough to warrant the introduction of some account of Mr. Knox's doctrine, with a view to the opinions upon it which we have promised.

His system is thus expressed in his own words: In St. Paul's sense, *to be justified* is not simply, to be accounted righteous; but also *and in the first instance, to be made righteous by the implantation of a radical principle of righteousness.*"* "What I am impressed with is, that our being reckoned righteous before God, always and essentially implies a *substance* of righteousness *previously* implanted in us; and that Reputative Justification is the *strict and inseparable result of this previous efficient Moral Justification.* I mean: that the reckoning us righteous *indispensably presupposes an inward reality of righteousness* ON WHICH THIS RECKONING IS FOUNDED." This Justified state, Mr. Knox says, "is simply and essentially a state of *Spiritual Vitality*"—that is: to be Justified is nothing more, nor less, than to be *spiritually alive,* a state which, he says, "*when duly cultivated, thrives and advances, when neglected withers and dies.*"† In common words, to be justified is just to be in a state of *sanctification,* "simply and essentially." They who are in this Justification, he says, "derive all their comfort *not from abstract reliance on what Christ did for them in the days of his flesh,* but from *consciousness of his effectual grace within them.*"‡ "How completely this system (says Mr. Knox, with serious truth) sweeps away the *merely forensic system,* leaving it neither root nor branch, I need not say more to illustrate." He assures us that never, till the Reformation, was the theory in vogue, "of a *doctrinal faith, giving ease to the conscience, through reliance on what Christ has done to satisfy divine Justice.*"

The sum of the doctrine is this:—We are justified not by what Christ has done for us *externally,* when in the days of his flesh he offered himself a sacrifice for our sins, which would be to be justified by a righteousness *extrinsic and accounted to us;* but by what Christ works in us *internally,* by his Spirit, a righteousness *infused,* instead of *accounted; internal and inherent, a personal* righteousness, an effectual, inwrought grace *on which our Justification is exclusively founded. This inherent righteousness however is not acquired except through faith and the merits of Christ.*

---

* Treatise on Redemption and Salvation in Remains, Vol. II. p. 60.
† Treatise on Justification in Remains. Vol. I. p. 306, 311.
‡ Treatise on Bap. in Rem. Vol. I. p. 516, 517.

Now there are few living writers in the present day whose opinion as to how far this doctrine partakes essentially of Popery, would command more attention in the Church of this country, than the Rev. George Stanley Faber, whose well-known learning is accompanied by an unquestioned and single love of the truth, and a spirit of moderation in all things.* From his able pen we have been favored with a lucid and learned volume on "the Primitive doctrine of Justification;" a work highly to be commended for its clear and vigorous setting forth of the doctrine of the Scriptures, and of the Church, on that head. Its main object is to exhibit the divinity of Mr. Knox in comparison with that of Rome, of the Church of England, and of the Scriptures. In that work, Mr. Faber writes as follows: "so far as I can perceive, THERE IS NO DIFFERENCE BETWEEN THE DOCTRINE ADVOCATED BY HIM (Mr. Knox) and THE DOCTRINE OF THE COUNCIL OF TRENT—*that Man is justified before God, not by the extrinsic righteousness of Christ, but by an intrinsic righteousness, which really as much belongs to him, as his soul or his body belongs to him, being inherently infused into him by God through faith* in our Lord Jesus Christ.

"Mr. Knox and the Tridentine Fathers and the Schoolmen, with whatever subtle distinctions and explanations, make the *Procuring Cause of Justification* to be *our own infused, and therefore inherent and internal righteousness.*

"The Church of England, on the contrary, and all the other Reformed Churches, make the *Procuring Cause* to be *the extrinsic righteousness of Christ apprehended and appropriated by the instrumental hand of Faith.*

"With respect to the necessity of holiness, both in thought, and in word and in work, as AN INDISPENSABLE QUALIFICATION for the kingdom of heaven, all parties are agreed.

"But when they come to treat of the place, which in the economy of Justification, is occupied by Holiness, they differ considerably, and INDEED ESSENTIALLY; for this in truth is the hinge upon which the controversy turns."† "I think it is indisputable both that the Church of Rome teaches the doctrine of Justification *by the merit of our own inherent righteousness;* and that Mr. Knox, without any perceptible difference, has adopted the *very same system.* In other words, the Church of Rome and Mr. Knox have alike confounded

---

* Mr. Faber died a few years after this work was first published; but not till he had written strongly and earnestly against what he did not hesitate to call the Popery of these Tractarian doctrines.

† Faber's Primitive Doctrine of Justification. Preface xviii., xx.

together, *the Righteousness of Justification, which is perfect, but not inherent; and the righteousness of Sanctification, which is inherent, but not perfect.* Whence, overlooking the theological fact that the *one is consequential to, and distinct from, the other,* they have, in truth, made the two altogether identical; and the natural, or rather the inevitable result has been, that the office of the former they have ascribed to the latter." "It is painful to say that I cannot but deem the views of Mr. Knox, in regard to the doctrine of Justification, HIGHLY DANGEROUS, AND ESSENTIALLY UNSCRIPTURAL."*

We have now exhibited the opinion of a writer, who, however learned, and excellent, and moderate, and of good report for fairness and candor, is not of that class in the Church of England, with which (the Oxford school excluded) the peculiarities of Mr. Knox would be likely to find the nearest sympathy. The work of Mr. Faber was published in 1837. The Lectures of Mr. Newman on Justification were not then before the public, and his peculiar views on that subject had excited but little attention.

The class of English theologians most likely to sympathise with Mr. Knox, from a general similarity of tastes, and aversions, and modes of viewing matters in the Church, is that which was represented by the British Critic, till such time as that Review, having changed hands, was transformed into a decided advocate of that very system of which the views of Mr. Knox were the rudiment. In several numbers of that work, in the years 1835 and 1838, we have Reviews at large of his Remains. From no quarter could a more favorable judgment have been expected. It is the very source from which we should desire an opinion for comparison with that of Mr. Faber. The Critic writes as follows:—" Closely connected with Mr. Knox's speculations on the ways of God in justifying the believer, was his mode of contemplating the one great Sacrifice once offered for the redemption of the human race. According to the notions usually entertained by Protestant divines, *the cross of Christ is the grand and central object in their system of theology.* Thus it is we believe for the most part, *with those who profess the truth for which our martyr Bishops poured out their souls unto death.* But this, it must be acknowledged, *was not precisely the view of redemption which presented itself to the meditations of Alexander Knox.* THE CROSS WAS NOT THE CENTRAL OBJECT OF HIS DIVINITY. It held a somewhat remote and subordinate position. *His chief reliance was not so much on what Christ had, once for all, effected for the whole human race,* as upon that which Christ stands

* Primitive Doctrine of Justification. pp. 36, and xxiii.

pledged to accomplish within the heart of every true believer. The *blood of sprinkling* is supposed to have done little more than to satisfy him that the destroyer had once been averted from his dwelling; and to have given him no distinct assurance that a preservative and healing power was continually present with him." The Reviewer supposes himself asking Mr. Knox such questions as the following: "Has the remission of sins passed away with the waters of baptism? Is it no more than a mere transitory absolution? Is every lapse and failure, in the subsequent life of the Christian, to be engraven on the rock? Has the Saviour's blood no healing or absolving virtue for them who may still appear to be more or less afflicted with the taint of our original distemper?" To these questions the Reviewer says—and coming from such a source, we would mark it with special emphasis: "Were we to answer *according to the spirit of Mr. Knox's theology,* we do not see how we could do otherwise, than answer them in a manner which might send *despair into many a contrite and broken spirit,* and lead to the apprehension that all but a very minute and insignificant remnant of mankind were indeed LEFT WITHOUT A SAVIOUR." In agreement with Mr. Faber, the Critic says, "*On the whole matter he does seem to us somewhat unwarrantably to identify the remission of sin, with deliverance from the bondage (the inherent corruption)* of sin. He affirms, or at least he plainly and pointedly intimates, that they *are one and the same thing.* The whole tenor of his speculations seems to imply *a denial of the Christian's right to fly to the cross, when troubled with the conscience of sin.* According to him the blood of Christ has, once for all, given us access to the Father. Having done this, *its propitiatory virtue passes away. We have nothing more to do with it,* than as we find the office of the Sanctifier, which it has purchased for us, realized in our hearts, &c. NOW THIS WE CONFESS, (continues the Critic,) DOES APPEAR TO US TO BE SOMEWHAT FEARFUL SOUND OF DOCTRINE. It nullifies at once the dying words of Hooker, which are constantly in the thoughts of every humble Christian, 'Lord, I plead not mine own righteousness, but the forgiveness of my unrighteousness, for the sake of Him who came to purchase a pardon for penitent sinners.' It almost deprives the word *pardon* of any meaning, except in its application to those who are taking their first step from death to life. In short, it does appear to us, to have been conceived *in strange forgetfulness of the office and character of Him who will neither crush the broken reed, nor tread out the smoking flax.*"* Again, in another number of the

* Review of the Remains of Alexander Knox. *British Critic* for July, 1838.

Critic; "Mr. Knox professed himself utterly unable to imagine that the Deity would ever confer upon us a title to which there was nothing actually corresponding in ourselves—declare any one to be righteous, or account him to be righteous, or deal with him as righteous, *otherwise than with reference to some moral quality inherent in that individual.*"

After all this we are not surprised that the Reviewer is prepared to avow a conclusion so similar to that of Mr. Faber, as that the above difficulty "drove Mr. Knox into a theory which, IT CANNOT BE DENIED, APPROXIMATES VERY CLOSELY TO THE EXPLODED THEOLOGY OF ROME."

But, adds the Reviewer, "the approximation did not much discompose him. His greatest embarrassment arose from the *manifestly imputative or forensic* language of certain of our formularies. But he extricated himself from the objection, by affirming that God PRONOUNCES *us to be righteous simply because* He *has* MADE *us so.*"*

Now from the concurrent judgments of two writers, so diverse as to their respective schools, and each so prominent, as Mr. Faber and the recent editor of the British Critic, the reader may see what is *Romanism*, as to this main doctrine of salvation, and great point of the English Reformation; what it is for a distinguished member of a Protestant Church to be *identical* with Romanism, or to *approximate very nearly thereto*, in his most important published opinions; how it is that a man, very eminent for reading and thought, of very pure motives, serious spirit, and high elevation of character, as Mr. Knox certainly was, may be "beguiled by philosophy" (so called) into a singular departure from the simplicity of the Scriptures, as well as the plainest declarations of his own Church, into a singular abandonment of the very life-vein of our redemption, and a distinct adoption of that by which the whole gigantic system of anti-christian error, in the Church of Rome, has always had its being; that very thing, in which, says Hooker, that Church *differs from ours in the nature and essence, and manner and means of applying the medicine whereby Christ cureth our disease;* and lastly, how it is, that a writer may *be* and may *do* all this, and yet be, as Mr. Knox doubtless was, an opposer of Rome in several of those particulars which to the common eye are the most offensive.

Having now seen the character of Mr. Knox's doctrines and anticipations, we recur to the claim put forth by the School at Oxford, to the connection between him and them; his views and their

* *British Critic*, No. lxvii. p. 89.

views; his rudiment and their development; his anticipations and their fulfillment; his hopes of restorations, and the concurrence of his writings with their writings in the bringing of them about; and we ask, what inference is to be drawn? What else can be inferred, than that the doctrine of Justification in the Oxford School, is precisely that which, in the judgment of Mr. Faber, is *identical with that of Rome;*—"*highly dangerous and essentially unscriptural,*" and in the judgment of the British Critic, under its former management, is "*a fearful sound of doctrine;*" "*approximates very closely to the exploded theology* of Rome;" a form of doctrine which, in the words of the Critic, does away with almost the whole substance of pardon, except in the initial step of a Christian; removes the cross of Christ from its central position in the system of Christian verity; sends despair into many a contrite spirit; deprives all but a precious few of the consolations of a Saviour; nullifies the only refuge of the dying Hooker; a doctrine "conceived in strange forgetfulness of the office and character of the blessed Redeemer." Alas! what would such men as Beveridge and Usher and Hall and Andrews and Hooker and Cranmer, men who were never awakened from that "DREAM" of a hope based *exclusively upon the perfect righteousness of Christ, imputed through faith,* till they awoke in the white raiment of a personal righteousness, made perfect, in heaven; what would they say to such restorations?

Old English Churches, erected in times of dominant Romanism, and for the superstitious purposes of old Romish worship, but long since reformed, have sometimes presented examples of similar restorations. Under the process of repair, when some later erection has been removed, there has sometimes been suddenly revealed, to the great delight of the *antiquary,* an ancient "*rood-loft*"—the old "chamber of imagery" and *conservatory of idols,* the symbol of "the mystery of the man of sin," *an instance in rudiment of the exploded theology of Rome.** From similar restorations in doctrine, it behoves the whole Church most earnestly to pray, " *Good Lord, deliver us!* "

---

* Of the rood-lofts of the Old English Churches, prior to the Reformation, some extended along the whole width of the nave and aisles; smaller ones extended merely across the chancel-arch and over the screen, and were used for the purpose of setting up the rood with its attendant images. The present organ-lofts of the cathedrals were once the rood-lofts. Where in many small churches, there was no loft or gallery for such purposes, a beam extended across the chancel-arch, to which the rood and other images were affixed.

CHAPTER III.

THE DOCTRINE OF THIS DIVINITY AS TO THE RIGHTEOUSNESS OF JUSTIFICATION, EXHIBITED.

To set forth the precise doctrine of this divinity, as to the way of Justification, the object of this chapter.—The main question of Hooker, as to the Romish doctrine, adopted here—The great point of inquiry stated—The Scriptural use of the word Justification—Two kinds of righteousness, asserted by Hooker, Beveridge, Andrews—Only one by this system—This opens the door to the divinity of Oxford, as well as that of Rome—That one righteousness, made identical with Sanctification—What is meant in this divinity by Imputation, Accounted, &c.—Extended proof that it makes Sanctification the same as Justification—The position in which it puts the cross of Christ—The use it makes of the merits and passion of Christ—Its effect upon the consolations of the believer—Singular effort to escape from being identified with Romanism, by denying what was before asserted as to Sanctification and Justification being essentially one—The same in Mr. Knox—This doctrine shown in Osiander—Concluding observations.

IN the last chapter, the acknowledged "*rudiment*" of this divinity, as exhibited in the writings of Alexander Knox, was shown to have been pronounced by two eminent writers of high authority in their respective schools, to be "*highly dangerous*," and "a very near *approximation*" to, if not essentially identical with, Romanism. The chief importance of the opinions thus adduced, independently of the standing of their authors, arises from the consideration that they are derived from those two classes of Clergy in the Church of England, whose diversities of opinion in other matters are just such as should make their concurrence in these, the more impressive. They were published, moreover, at a time when the peculiarities of this system on the subject of Justification, had excited but little attention, and consequently, when they were wholly free from all suspicion of such party-bias, as the present excitement, may be supposed to produce. The concurrence of such opinions, in the one point of attributing to the "*Rudiment*" a decided character of Romanism, as to some of the most vital parts and applications of Gospel truths, justifies us in entering upon our further investigations of the "*Developments*" with the expectation that, if Romanism be apparent in the germ, much more will it be seen in the half-grown tree.

We now address ourselves to the work of setting forth the precise doctrine of this divinity, as to *Justification before God.*

The manner of Hooker in commencing the same work with Romanism will answer in the present case.

He begins with a statement of the precise points of agreement and disagreement between the doctrine of the Church of Rome and that of the Church of England.

"Wherein do we disagree? We disagree about *the nature and essence of the medicine whereby Christ cureth our disease; about the manner of applying it; about the number and power of means which God requireth in us for the effectual applying thereof to our souls' comfort.*"*

These assuredly are most grave matters of disagreement. But they are precisely those on which we charge the divinity under consideration with being essentially opposed to the doctrine of the Church of England, and identically Romish.

The present chapter will be occupied with an exhibition of what this system teaches as to "THE NATURE AND ESSENCE OF THE MEDICINE WHEREBY CHRIST CURETH OUR DISEASE."

Now Justification, according to our eleventh Article, is the being "*accounted* RIGHTEOUS *before God.*" Hence it presupposes some *righteousness,* as its essential basis. "The nature and essence of the medicine," is simply the nature and essence of that righteousness. Hence the great question has always been, as Hooker gives it:—"*What is the righteousness whereby a Christian man is justified?*" or as Mr. Newman, in the name of this divinity, states it: "*What is that which constitutes a man righteous in God's sight?*"† or, as the learned Chemnitz, representing the Reformers in their controversy with the Divines of the Council of Trent, states it:—"*What is that which we are to interpose between the anger of God, and our sins, so that on account thereof, we may be absolved from the sentence of condemnation; received into the favor of God, adopted as sons, and accepted to everlasting life.*"‡

It will materially assist in the development of the answer, given, in this system, to this fundamental question, if we first occupy a few moments in considering the Scriptural use of the word *Justification,* as bearing upon the nature of the *righteousness* by which we must be justified.

The Justification of a sinner must be in one of two ways. It must be either by a *personal change in a man's moral nature,* or by

---

* Hooker's Discourse on Justification. § 4, 5.   † Lectures on Justification, p. 144.
‡ Examen. Dec. Conc. Trid. p. 144.

a relative change in his state, as regards the sentence of the law of God. The former justification is opposed to unholiness; the latter, to condemnation; the one takes away the indwelling of moral pollution; the other, imputation of judicial guilt. If we understand Justification, in the first sense, as expressing the making a man righteous, "*by an infusion of righteousness*," as Romanism expresses it, we make it identical with *Sanctification*. It is as gradual as the progress of personal holiness, and never complete till we are perfected in heaven. But how will that sense appear in such a passage as that wherein it is said: "He that justifieth the wicked and he that condemneth the just, even they both are an abomination to the Lord?" Not to speak of the evident opposition between the words *justify* and *condemn*, implying in both a *judicial*, and not a *moral* change: how could it be *an abomination* to the Lord to justify the wicked, by *making* him personally holy? But if we take Justification in the latter sense, as indicating a relative change, it is then a term of law, used judicially, and expresses the act of God, as the Judge, acquitting the accused, accounting him righteous; so that he becomes the man "unto whom the Lord imputeth no sin."

In relation to the former sense, there is not a place in Scripture wherein the word Justify, in any of its forms, having reference to remission of sins, can be so interpreted. As to the latter, the judicial sense, there are passages, very many, in which with no appearance of reason, can it be understood in any other.* This is specially manifest where *Justification* is spoken of as the opposite of *condemnation*. Take Rom. v. 18. "As by the offense of one, judgment came upon all men to condemnation; even so by the righteousness of one, the free gift came upon all men unto justification of life." Here, most evidently, Justification imports a judicial clearing from the imputation of guilt, in the precise sense and degree in which condemnation imports a judicial ascertaining of guilt. The same appears in Rom. viii. 23. "Who shall lay any thing to the charge of God's elect? It is God that *justifieth;* who is he that *condemneth?*" Here is the idea of a judicial process, a tribunal, a person arraigned. Now, if by the condemnation spoken of, we may understand an act of the Judge making the accused guilty by the infusion of unrighteousness; then also by the Justification spoken of, we may understand an act of the Judge making the accused righteous, by an infusion of righteousness, and so justifying him. But if this would be absurd in the former case, so must it be in the latter.

* Psalm cxliii. 2.   Rom. iii. 28.   Acts xiii. 39.

But it is not necessary to go very particularly into the proof of the judicial sense of the word Justification in the Scriptures. The great matter is to keep clear the essential difference between Justification and Sanctification; between the former, as opposed to the imputation of guilt, and the latter, to the indwelling of unholiness; the former as a restoration to favor; the latter, to purity; this, as the act of God within us, changing *our moral character;* the other, as the act of God without us, changing our *relative state;* blessings inseparable indeed, but essentially distinct. "There be two kinds of Christian righteousness; (says Hooker) the one without us, which we have by imputation; the other in us, which consisteth of Faith, Hope, Charity, and other Christian virtues—God giveth us both the one justice and the other; the one by accepting us for righteous in Christ; the other by working Christian righteousness in us."

In Bishop Beveridge, of most venerable memory, we thus read:—

"It is evident that the Holy Ghost useth this word Justification, to signify a man's being accounted, or declared, not guilty of the faults he is charged with, but in that respect a just and righteous person, and that too before some Judge, who in our case is the supreme Judge of the world. And this is plainly the sense wherein our Church also useth the word in her articles: for the title of the XIth Article runs thus: '*Of the Justification of Man.*' but the Article itself begins thus: 'We are accounted righteous before God,' &c.—which clearly shows that in her sense, to be justified is the same with being *accounted* righteous before God; which I therefore observe, that you may not be mistaken in the sense of the word as it is used by the Church and by the Holy Ghost Himself in the Holy Scriptures, like those who confound Justification and Sanctification together, as if they were one and the same thing: although the Scriptures plainly distinguish them; Sanctification being God's act in us, whereby we are made righteous in ourselves; but Justification is God's act in Himself, whereby we are accounted righteous by him, and shall be declared so at the judgment of the great day." *

Such then being the *judicial* or *forensic* sense in which man is said to be justified before God, a sense so essentially important to be kept distinctly in mind, that, as Bishop Andrews says, "we shall never take the state of the question aright unless we consider it in

* Beveridge's Sermons, No. 74.

this view;"* and since a judicial process implies *a law*, according to which it is conducted, and a law requires, of course, *a perfect fulfillment* of its precepts; in other words, *a perfect righteousness*, before any can be justified by sentence of the Judge; the question occurs, *where is that righteousness to be found by which a sinner may be justified before God?*

The reader is requested to mark particularly "the two kinds of Christian righteousness" spoken of by Hooker as above—the one NOT IN US, which we have by imputation," whereon Justification, which Beveridge calls "the act of God, IN HIMSELF" is based; the other IN US, a personal, inwrought righteousness, which constitutes our sanctification, and which Beveridge calls "God's act" not in *himself*, like the other, but "in *us*, whereby we are made righteous in ourselves." "That both these there are, (says Bishop Andrews,) there is no question." But let us quote this great divine more fully.

"In the Scripture, there is a *double* Righteousness set down, both in the Old and in the New Testament. In the Old, and in the very first place that Righteousness is named in the Bible; 'Abraham believed, and it was *accounted* unto him for righteousness.' A Righteousness *accounted!* And again, (in the very next line) it is mentioned, 'Abraham will teach his house *to do Righteousness.*' A righteousness *done!* In the New Testament, likewise. The former, in one chapter, (Rom. iv.) no fewer than *eleven* times; *Reputatum est illi ad justitiam*—'*It is accounted to him for righteousness*'— a *Reputed* Righteousness! The latter in St. John—'He that *doeth* righteousness, is righteous'—a Righteousness *done!* Of these, the latter, Philosophers themselves conceived, and acknowledged; the other is proper to Christians only, and altogether unknown in Philosophy. The one is a quality of the party. The other an act of the Judge declaring or pronouncing righteous. The one, ours by influence *or infusion;* the other, by *account*, or *imputation*. That both these there are, THERE IS NO QUESTION."†

The reader is requested to mark the words of Bishop Andrews, that, of the existence of these two kinds of righteousness, so distinct in nature and office, and yet equally necessary, *he knew of no question*. This fundamental distinction between the righteousness of Justification, and that of Sanctification, so universal in Protestant Divinity, is found by Hooker, as in other places of Scripture, so especially in that notable passage of St. Paul, (1 Cor. i. 30.) where

---

* Sermons (Justification) fol. 725. † Sermon on Justification.

the Apostle says, "Of him are ye in Christ Jesus, who of God is made unto us wisdom, righteousness, sanctification and redemption." Here most evidently there is a righteousness spoken of, which is as much distinguished from sanctification, as wisdom is made distinct from righteousness. Hence, says Hooker, Christ is made "Righteousness, because he hath offered up himself a sacrifice for sin; Sanctification, because he hath given us his Spirit."* And this very distinction he considers the key to the whole controversy on the subject of Justification, with the Church of Rome. "It openeth the way (he says) to the understanding of that *grand question*, which hangeth yet in controversy between us and the Church of Rome, about the matter of Justifying righteousness."† It is a distinction which the Church of Rome entirely denies; and which the Church of England, with all the Churches of the Reformation, has most earnestly maintained, as fundamental in the Gospel plan of our salvation.

Now it is precisely that same distinction which opens the way to the understanding of the whole controversy between the doctrines of the Church of England, and the derived Church in America, on the one hand, and those of this divinity on the other, as to *the matter of Justifying Righteousness*. The whole of the latter is founded upon *the denial* of that distinction. The whole of the former is founded upon its assertion. It teaches a righteousness *external*, and *imputed*, and also a righteousness *internal and inwrought* by the Spirit; the two inseparably connected indeed, but of very different natures and offices. The other acknowledges that only which is *internal and inwrought*. And that distinction is the key to all the interior of this system; precisely as to all the sinuosities of Romanism.‡

Mr. Newman, in his Lectures on Justification, writes as follows:—

"It is usual at the present day to lay great stress on the *distinction* between deliverance from guilt, and deliverance from sin; to lay down as a first principle, that these are two coincident indeed, and contemporary, but *altogether* independent benefits; to call them *justification and renewal*, and to consider that any confusion between them argues serious and alarming ignorance of Christian truth."

---

* Discourse of Justification, § 2. † Ibid. § 3.

‡ "In all doctrinal discussions, the undeveloped germs of many diversities of practice and moral character lie thick together, and in small compass, and as if promiscuously and without essential differences. The highest truths differ from the most miserable delusions, by what appears to be a few words or letters."— Tracts for the Times, No. 79, Am. Ed. vol. iii. p. 513.

This distinction, Mr. Newman says, IS NOT SCRIPTURAL. "In truth, Scripture speaks of but one gift, which it sometimes calls *renewal*, sometimes *justification*, according as it views it, passing to and fro, from one to the other, so rapidly, so abruptly, as to force upon us irresistibly the inference that they are *really one*." *

Some fifteen or twenty pages are occupied by Mr. Newman in making good this position, so directly in the teeth of the doctrines given above, from Hooker, &c., as the very corner-stone of his system.

Then, since in the view of these divines, there is but one righteousness, and that is the righteousness of renewal or sanctification, and called the righteousness of Justification, only because viewed sometimes in a different aspect or relation; it is of course to be inferred that when we ask the great question of the Reformation, "what is that on account of which we may be absolved from the sentence of condemnation, received into the favor of God, adopted as sons, and accepted to everlasting life;" their answer can point to nothing else than the righteousness of *renewal or sanctification*.

This is expressly stated by Mr. Newman as follows:

"One side says that the righteousness in which God accepts us is *inherent*, wrought in us by the grace flowing from Christ's atonement; the other says it is *external, reputed*, being Christ's own sacred and most perfect obedience on earth, viewed by a merciful God, as if it were ours. And issue is joined on the following question, whether Justification means in Scripture, *counting* us righteous or *making* us righteous." †

Of these two sides, Mr. Newman selects the latter most decidedly. That the mere *word* Justification, means *counting* us righteous, or *imputing* to us righteousness, he is obliged to admit somehow or other, since he grants that "but one passage can be produced where justification is used for *making* righteous, and there the reading is doubtful." ‡ Indeed no one can assert more strongly the exclusively forensic or judicial use of the *word* "Justify," in the Scriptures.

"Justification extends to the present, as well as the past; yet, if so, still it must mean an *imputation* or *declaration;* or it would cease to have respect to the past. And if it be once granted to mean an imputation, it cannot mean any thing else: for it cannot have two meanings at once." §

* Lectures. pp. 42, 43; also pp. 120, 129. † Lectures, p. 67.
‡ Ibid. p. 75. § Ibid. p. 72.

But while the *name* is thus confessed to be forensic and imputative, the *thing* (he says) is moral and effective. Justification is, nominally, *accounting* us righteous; really, *making* us righteous.—

"I would thus explain myself. To justify *means* counting righteous; but includes *under* its meaning making righteous; in other words the sense of the *term* is counting righteous, and the sense of the *thing* denoted by it is making righteous. In the *abstract*, it is a counting righteous; in the *concrete*, a making righteous."*

Thus, while the Scriptures, as this writer, one of the standard bearers of the system, till he openly declared himself, what he had some time been in secret, a Romanist, so distinctly grants, never mean by the *word*, Justification, the *making* us personally righteous, and always mean by it the *accounting* us righteous; they always mean by the *thing* the precise reverse.

Then what can this writer mean by the imputation or accounting of righteousness, on the part of God, to the sinner? To this, attention is especially requested, because it is the free use of such familiar words, which has made so many readers suppose that the difference between these writers and those who object to them cannot be of much importance. The sense of the Church of England, as to *imputation*, is thus given by Bishop Beveridge.

Having quoted the text which speaks of Christ, as made *sin for us, that we might be made the righteousness of God in him*, he says:—

"How was Christ made sin for us? Not by our sins *inherent* in him; that is horrid blasphemy; but by our sins imputed to him, that is true divinity. And as he was made sin for us, not by the inhesion of our sins in him; but by the imputation of our sins to him; so we are made the righteousness of God in him, by the imputation of his righteousness to us, not by the inhesion of his righteousness in us. He was accounted as a sinner, and therefore punished for us; we are accounted as righteous, and therefore glorified in him. He was accounted as a sinner, for us, and therefore he was condemned: we are accounted as righteous in him, and so we are justified. And this is the right notion of Justification, as distinguished from Sanctification. Not as if these two were ever severed or divided in their subjects: no, every one that is justified, is also sanctified; and every one that is sanctified is also justified. But yet, the acts of sanctification and justification are two distinct things; for the one denotes the imputation of

* Lectures, p. 70.

righteousness to us; the other, the implantation of righteousness in us. And, therefore though they be both the acts of God, yet the one is the act of God *towards* us; the other is the act of God *in* us. By our sanctification, we are made righteous in ourselves, but not accounted righteous by God; by our justification we are accounted righteous by God, but not made righteous in ourselves."*

Let not the reader suppose that it is any such sense as this, (which is no other than the ordinary) in which these writers speak of righteousness being accounted or imputed to the sinner: What then?

"It is *a sort of prophecy*, (says Mr. Newman,) announcing God's purposes before the event, and working towards their fulfillment." This he illustrates by the prophecies. As the chosen people were accounted as being already formed, when as yet they were only promised, because God intended to form them; "such is justification as regards an individual," so far as he is accounted just.† God intends to make him righteous, and therefore declares him to be righteous, and with the declaration, sends forth the power that begins the work. Thus,

"In justification the whole course of sanctification is *anticipated*, *reckoned*, or *imputed* to us, in its very beginning." "It is a pronouncing holy, while it proceeds to make holy. As Almighty God in the beginning created the world augustly and in form; speaking the word not to exclude, but to proclaim the deed—so does he now (in Justification,) create the soul by the breath of his mouth, by the sacrament of his voice."‡

Just as far then as you could, with any propriety, call the creation of the world a *forensic* or *judicial* act, because it was preceded by God's word, so far, is the justification of the soul forensic or judicial, being, (according to Mr. N.) a new-creating act, preceded by "the voice of the Lord." Precisely so far as the world may be said to have been *accounted* as created, before it was created, because God *intended* to create it, and because, with His word, indicating his will, He sent out his power to affect it, so far, according to Mr. N., is the sinner *accounted* righteous in the sight of God, before he *is* righteous, because God *intends* to make him righteous, and, with the will declared, sends forth grace to renew his heart and accomplish his sanctification. Thus we read that:

* Beveridge on the Articles. † Lectures p. 89. ‡ Ibid. pp. 79, 80.

"*Imputed righteousness is the coming in of actual righteousness.* They whom God's sovereign voice *pronounces* just, forthwith *become* just. He declares a fact, and makes it a fact by declaring it. He imputes, not a name, but a *substantial word*, which, being ingrafted in our hearts, is able to save our souls. God's word *effects* what it *announces.*"*

And this is all that in this system is meant by the *forensic* sense of the word Justification. It never means *making* righteous, and yet it differs from that sense only so far as the *command,* " let there be light," differed from *causing* light to be. What egregious trifling! What irreverent forcing of the plain meaning of Scripture into subjection to the demands of a predetermined system!

Now, since Justification is accounting us righteous "in the sense of the *term*" only, and *making* us righteous "in the sense of the *thing* denoted by it;" and as we are seeking *a thing*, when we ask what is the righteousness by which we are justified, and care for terms only as they lead to things; we must be allowed to lay aside the above distinctions, and conclude that Justification, according to this divinity, is neither more nor less than *making* us righteous, by "a righteousness *inherent,* wrought in us by the grace flowing

---

* Lectures pp. 86, 87, and the whole of Lecture III.

Should a physician having full intention and full ability to heal a sick man say to him "I will heal you," and instantly begin to effect a change in his health, which if continued, would result in entire restoration, and should that man be already, by that physician, *accounted* well, or be said to have *imputed* health, the case would be precisely parallel to what Mr. N. understands by *accounting* righteous as distinct from *making* righteous. In other words, imputed righteousness is simply a *promised, declared and imperfectly-accomplished Sanctification.*

Mr. Newman, in a note, refers to Mr. Knox, as illustrating his view of *accounting* righteous, by precisely the same reference to the creation, and in the same sense— (see note on p. 87 of Lectures.) The following is Mr. Knox's idea according to the British Critic: " In the creation God said, *Let there be Light, and there was Light;* and then he saw *that the Light was good.* So in the work of redemption, God says to the chaos of our fallen nature, Let there be light, and there is light, even the light of faith, the grand *vitalizing* principle. And when once this light is actually given, he pronounces the individual to be a child of light. In other words, he *accounts* him to be righteous. So that according to this scheme, God justifies man, first by *making* him righteous; and then again by pronouncing him *to be* righteous when he is actually made so. And the whole of this process is implied in the term Justification." Brit. Critic, No. 34, p. 264. Mr. Newman's idea seems to be a little worse than this. His accounting is a declaration of what *is* to be, and now, by the force of the declaration, *begins* to be. Mr. Knox makes it a declaration of what *is.* With the former we are *accounted* righteous, because God intends, promises and begins to effect our righteousness; with the latter, because we are actually made righteous. " *Vain jangling !*"

from Christ's atonement;"* it is neither less, nor more, than SANCTIFICATION. This, Mr. N., in so many words declares. A large part of his second Lecture is occupied with the proof that Justification and Sanctification are "*really one;*" that to distinguish them as "two kinds of righteousness," is "not Scriptural." He considers himself as having "proved that Justification and Sanctification are *substantially the same thing;*—parts of one gift; properties, qualities or aspects of one." He maintains their "*identity, in matter of fact,* however we may vary our terms, or classify our ideas"—

This then is the righteousness by which we are justified before God, according to this system; that same inwrought, inherent righteousness, which, in all true divinity, is *sanctification.*

Such then is the fundamental doctrine, the grand distinguishing feature of this new divinity, asserted, with so much assurance, to be no other than the doctrine of the Church of England and of her standard divines, as well as of Primitive Christians, and inspired Apostles. As the very corner-stone of the whole system, Mr. Newman has devoted a whole octavo volume to its setting forth, and Dr. Pusey another, besides the article on that subject in his letter to the Bishop of Oxford, so that on no one part of their doctrinal reformation, have this school bestowed near so much of the labor of their diligent press. They have used such a variety of illustrations as to leave no possibility of doubt as to their meaning on this head.

Some of these various illustrations may be here exhibited.

Our Justification is made to consist in OBEDIENCE. "Cleanliness of heart and spirit, obedience by word and deed, this alone can constitute our Justification." "The gift of righteousness (for Justification) is not an imputation, but an inward work.†"

The righteousness whereby we are justified before God, is made to consist in the fulfilling of the Law *by us.* Because love, in the abstract, is said by the Apostles, to be "the fulfilling of the law;" therefore the love of Christ abiding in us, such love as Christians have implanted in them by the Spirit of God, is said to be "imputed to us for our justification." ‡

"We needed a justification or making righteous, and this might become ours in two ways, either by dispensing with that exact obedience which the law required, or by enabling us to fulfill it. Now the remedy lies in the latter alternative only; not in lowering the law, much less in abolishing it; but in bringing up our

* Newman's Lectures, pp. 67, 68.   † Ib. pp. 34. 39.   ‡ Ib. p. 101.

hearts to refashioning them, and, as it were, attuning them to its high harmonies." "If he (God) counts righteous, it is by *making righteous*; if He justifies, it is by *renewing*; if He reconciles us to him, it is not by annihilating the Law, but by creating in us new wills and new powers for the observance of it."*

Again, we learn, that those who are regenerate in Baptism, can and do so fulfill the divine law, that their indwelling righteousness has in it a SATISFYING AND JUSTIFYING QUALITY, and does justify them in the sight of God.

That indwelling righteousness "the indwelling of our glorious Lord," as says Mr. Newman, is "the propitiation for our sins in God's sight." †

Again, "Justification consists in God's *inward* presence." "It is the act of God imparting His divine presence to the soul, through baptism, and so making us the temples of the Holy Ghost."

"It is the habitation in us of God the Father, and the word Incarnate, through the Holy Ghost." "Christ is our Righteousness by dwelling in us by his Spirit, justifies by entering into us, con-

---

* Ib. pp. 35. 36. "That in our natural state, and by our *own* strength, (says Mr. N.,) we are not, and cannot be justified by obedience, is admitted on all hands. But it is a distinct question altogether, whether, with the presence of God the Holy Ghost, we can obey unto Justification; and while the received doctrine in all ages of the Church has been that through the largeness and peculiarity of the gift of grace, *we can*, it is the distinguishing doctrine of the first Protestants, that we cannot." (pp. 66. 67.) "In the same sense in which we are unrighteous or displeasing to God, by nature, we are actually righteous and pleasing to Him in a state of grace. Not that there is not abundant evil still remaining in us, but that justification coming to us in the power and inspiration of the Spirit, so far dries up the fountain of bitterness and impurity, that we are forthwith released from God's wrath and damnation, and are enabled in our better deeds to please Him. It places us above the line in the same sense in which we were below it." "By grace we are gifted, not with perfection, but with a principle hallowing and sweetening all that we are, all that we do religiously; sustaining, abiding, and (in a sense) pleading for what remains of sin in us, making intercession for us according to the will of God." "And here we see in what sense Christians are enabled to fulfill the Law. Christians then fulfil the Law in the very sense of pleasing God. Not that we are able to please Him simply and entirely, (for in many things we offend all;) but that the presence of the Spirit is a sanctifying virtue in our hearts, changing the character of our services, making our obedience new in kind, not merely fuller in degree, and in this sense a *satisfying obedience*, rising up, answering to the kind of obedience which is due from us, to the nature of the *claims* which our Creator, Reedeemer, and Sanctifier has upon us." "It seems then that a Christian's life is *available, justifying*; not of course the origin, or well-spring of our acceptableness" (God forbid,) &c. (Lect. pp. 93, 99, 100, 101.)

"Works done in faith, though mixed with evil, are good *in themselves*, as being the fruits of the Spirit."—(Note to p. 351.)

† Lectures p. 252.

tinues to justify us by remaining in us." This divine gift, or indwelling, is "an angelic glory which Prophets and Apostles exult in as the great gift of Divine mercy, as the rich garment of salvation, and the enjeweled robe of righteousness; as linen *clean* and *white*." This is "the glorious Shekinah of the word Incarnate, the true wedding garment in which the soul must be dressed." This doctrine "buries self in the absorbing vision of a present, *an indwelling* God." *

Again, Justification is made to consist in "the *inward application of the atonement.*"

Let it not be supposed that in this language there is intended the least resemblance to what is usually meant when we speak *of the appropriation of the atonement to our souls by the instrumental act of faith*. It simply means that Justification consists in our being crucified unto sin—or, as before, our sanctification. "It is *the setting up of the Cross within us*." We have been accustomed to suppose that the Israelite's looking upon the brazen serpent, was, according to our Saviour's words, (John iii. 14, 15,) a clear illustration of how we are to look unto the great atoning sacrifice for sin, on the cross, and be justified through the obedience and death of Christ. But such is far from being the teaching we are now to learn. On the contrary, had that serpent been set up *within each Israelite*, so that precisely as the poison wherewith he was dying was within him, so should have been the remedy,—then would have been typified the true way in which we are now to be justified, viz: *by a Christ crucified within us.*†

---

* Newman's Lectures, pp. 318, 160, 167, 184, 220. The above quotations from Mr. Newman are declared by Dr. Pusey to express truly the doctrine of his own system. *Letter to Bp. of Oxford.*

† "You hear men speak of glorying in the cross of Christ, who are utter strangers to the nature of the cross as actually applied to them, *in water and blood, in holiness and pain*. They think individuals are justified immediately by the great atonement—justified by Christ's death—justified by what they consider *looking* at his death. Because the brazen serpent healed by being looked at, they consider that Christ's sacrifice saves by the mind's contemplating it.—Gazing on the brazen serpent did not heal; but God's giving invisibly the gift of health to those who gazed. * * * So Justification is a power exerted on our souls by Him, as the healing of the Israelites was a power exerted on their bodies. * * * Christ's cross does not justify by being gazed at IN FAITH, but by being actually set up within us, and that not by our act, but by God's invisible grace. Men sit and gaze and speak of the great Atonement, and think this is appropriating it. * * * Men say that *faith is an apprehending and applying;* FAITH CANNOT REALLY APPLY IT; man cannot make the Saviour of the world his own; the cross must be brought home to us not in word, but in power; and this is the work of the Spirit—*This is Justification.*"—Newman's Lect. pp. 202, 203.

These passages, (and similar ones occur every where,) will suffice to show how earnestly and entirely it is the fundamental principle of this divinity, that Justifying righteousness has no *external* character at all; is not in any true sense a righteousness *accounted* unto us; is identical with Sanctification, a righteousness *in us* and not *in Christ;* *personal,* as opposed to *imputed;* a righteousness infused and inherent, and therefore *our own* righteousness, as much as our souls, our intellect, our affections are our own.

We proceed. Justification according to this Divinity is PROGRESSIVE, increasing as sanctification increases. This is expressed by Dr. Pusey as follows:—

"We are by baptism brought into a state of salvation or justification, (for the words are thus far equivalent,) a state into which we were brought of God's free mercy alone, without works, but in which having been placed, we are to work out our salvation with fear and trembling, through the indwelling Spirit of God, working in us to will and to do of his good pleasure; *a state admitting of degrees according to the degree of sanctification*—(although the first *act* whereby we were brought into it did not;) a state admitting of relapses and recoveries, but which is weakened by every relapse, injured by lesser, destroyed for the time by grievous sin; and after such sin, recovered with difficulty, in proportion to the greatness of the sin and the degree of its willfulness, and of the grace withstood."*

The meaning of all this is, that when a sinner comes to Baptism, he comes without any of that indwelling righteousness in which Justification consists. He is therefore brought into a state of Justification without antecedent works, of God's free mercy alone, for Christ's sake—that is, his past sins are pardoned and he is justified by having an indwelling righteousness then implanted in him by the Holy Spirit, in virtue of the passion of Christ. This takes place only at Baptism. This first act of Justifying, does not admit of degrees; but after that, Justification is greater or less, increases or diminishes, precisely according to the degree, of Sanctification.†

---

* Letter to Bp. of Oxford. pp. 54, 55.

† *Justificatio impii*, says Aquinas, *fit a Deo in instanti*—P. 12. Q. 113. a. 7. "Justification of the ungodly takes place instantaneously." This from the Romish Saint, refers to what takes place in Baptism, the first Justification.

"Christians are justified by the communication of an inward, most sacred, and most mysterious gift. From the very time of Baptism, they are temples of the Holy Ghost. This is what is common to all. * * * The fact that we are the Temple

The reader will now be good enough to mark the position occupied in this scheme by that which St. Paul so exclusively gloried in; which he so exclusively preached; which stands so conspicuously in the creeds and hopes of Christians; which so fills the petitions of our Liturgy, and the hearts of all who devoutly take up its hallowed strains—THE CROSS OF CHRIST, *the Atonement of our blessed Lord.*

Read in our Homilies and great writers, of the righteousness of Christ, as constituting our justification. For example, the Homily on Salvation says, that what the Apostle calls the Justice, (Righteousness) of God in our Justification, is that righteousness of Christ "which consisteth in paying our ransom and fulfilling of the Law."* Thus Hooker says, "the external righteousness of Jesus Christ, which is imputed," is that by which we are justified, distinguishing it from "the habitual righteousness of the Spirit, which is ingrafted."† But "it appears (we use the language of the British Critic) from the whole tenor of his work, that Mr. Newman recoils with something approaching to a positive antipathy, from the thought of a justification *external* to ourselves. He seems to derive but meager satisfaction from the contemplation of what was done for us eighteen hundred years ago." In truth, what Hooker and the Homily in the above passages, mean by the righteousness of Christ, a Mediatorial righteousness, wrought out for us by his obedience and death, and made ours by imputation only, through the *instrumental* agency of faith alone, has no place in this divinity. Its very existence is denied. When St. Paul, in the Epistle to the Philippians, says: "that I might win Christ and be found in him; not having mine own righteousness which is of the law, but that which is through

---

of God does not admit of more or less. Righteousness then, considered as the state of being God's temple, cannot be increased; but considered as the divine glory which that state implies, it can be increased, as the pillar of cloud which guided the Israelites could become more or less bright. Justification being acceptableness with God, all beings who are justified differ from all who are not, in their very condition. In this sense, it is as absurd to speak of our being more justified, as of life, or color, or any other abstract idea, increasing. But when we compare the various orders of just and acceptable beings with one another, we see that though they all are in God's favor, some may be more pleasant, acceptable, righteous than others; that is, may have more of the light of God's countenance shed on them; in this sense their Justification does admit of increase and degrees, and whether we say justification depends on faith or on obedience, in the same degree that faith or obedience grows, so does justification. And again, as Holy Communion conveys a more *awful* presence of God, than Holy Baptism, so must it be the instrument of a higher justification."—*Newman's Lect.* 167—169.

* Homily of Salvation, Part I. † Discourse of Justification, § 21.

the faith of Christ, the righteousness which is of God through faith;" it is denied that he speaks of two kinds of righteousness, the one *his own, of works;* the other, *of Christ* and *of faith;* the former of the law, the latter not of the law; it is maintained that he speaks throughout only of a righteousness *of the law,* of obedience, of works; a righteousness of *his own,* and that the only difference intended is that between obedience in a natural state, by one's own strength, and obedience in a converted state, by grace helping, obedience inwrought by the grace of God, in Christ, and therefore called "the Righteousness of God by faith." *

But does this scheme entirely exclude the *Merits* of Christ? We answer in the words of Mr. Knox, which perfectly express the sense of that doctrine of which his was the acknowledged "rudiment." "Doubtless the Church never loses sight of the merits of our blessed Saviour; but she confides in them, *not as a substitute for internal grace,* (in Justification,) but as an infallible security that this grace shall be freely communicated to all who cordially ask it." †

Then the doctrine is; "The merits of Christ have purchased for us the grace of Sanctification, by which we are made righteous for Christ's sake. When a sinner first turns to God, his past sins are pardoned freely, through the merits of Christ; after that, his acceptableness depends upon his fulfilling the law. He fulfills the law by having a righteousness implanted in his heart at Baptism, for Christ's sake. By that he works out his salvation. His works are now "*good in themselves.*" "Love is imputed to him for righteousness." "His life is *available, justifying.*" He looks *unto himself,* to a "*cross within,*" for acceptableness and peace. He can, he does, fulfill the law for righteousness, unto salvation. Justification, at its commencement, was chiefly pardon; as it advances it loses that aspect more and more and becomes more simply sanctification. It ends in being not pardon, but all sanctification, so that "the righteousness wherein we must stand at the last day, is not Christ's own imputed obedience, but *our good works.*" ‡

Now see what is done with the cross of Christ, in this system, and what it means by preaching, and glorying in the same.

"The cross in which St. Paul gloried, was not (what persons among ourselves would take it to be, without even the plea of being literal, as the Romanists have,) the actual *sacrifice* on the cross; but it is that sacrifice coming in power to him who has faith in it, and

---

* Newman's Lectures, p. 128.   † Knox's Remains, vol. i. p. 517.
‡ Newman's Lectures, p. 60.

converting his body and soul into a sacrifice. It is the cross realized, present, living in him, sealing him, separating him from the world, sanctifying him, afflicting him." *

Such is "the inward application of the Atonement." "A cross erected within, made *ours* by our being marked with it." To glory in the cross of Christ then is to glory *in our own cross*, in our own crucifixion, our own sanctification. To preach Christ crucified, is not to preach Christ on the cross of Calvary, making propitiation for our sins; but Christ *within* us, crucifying our flesh, "with its affections and lusts." To look unto Jesus, as the Israelites looked upon the brazen serpent, we must behold the Lamb of God not lifted up on the cross "*without the gate*," but *within our hearts;* not crucified, but crucifying; not suffering for us, but causing us to suffer for him; not satisfying the law for us, but enabling us to satisfy the law for ourselves. Alas! alas! if this be true, we must turn our creeds, and hopes, and sermons, and books, and homilies, inside out; old things indeed must pass away, and *all* things become new. †

The reader may now understand in what sense the merits of Christ have any share in our Justification. He reads in Oxford writings that while it is a righteousness within us, by which we are justified, *all, nevertheless is through the merits of Christ,—the passion of Christ.* Now if he supposes that by this is meant any thing like what is usually meant by such language, viz., that a sinner *looks* to the atoning sacrifice of Christ as his only hope, and *pleads*, and in his heart *relies* upon, and glories only in the merits of that sacrifice for all peace with God, he is exceedingly mistaken. And yet undoubtedly such is the meaning in which this theology is taken by the many who suppose it to differ from the common faith, chiefly in the use of words. That we are not misrepresenting this matter is evident from the fact that one large Tract, by these divines, is expressly devoted to the inculcation of "*Reserve in communicating*

---

* Newman's Lectures. p. 206.

† The same doctrine is pressed, by the same Author, in the Tract on Reserve, No. 80. For example—"It is a great mistake to suppose that by preaching the Atonement, we are preaching what St. Paul meant when he said, "*we preach Christ crucified.*" It is the opposite of this modern notion which St. Paul always intends by it. It is the necessity of our being crucified to the world, it is our humiliation together with him, mortification of the flesh," &c. (p. 75.) It is difficult to see how the Apostles could have been charged with *making void the law through faith*, and encouraging *a continuance in sin that grace might abound*, if this was all they meant by preaching *Christ crucified*. Our Oxford divines do not seem to be much in danger of sharing in that reproach of the Apostles.

religious knowledge," in which the "*Necessity of bringing forward the doctrine of the Atonement,*" without reserve, of teaching it to the impenitent at all, or even to any but those who have made progress in grace, is denied. In that Tract, we read that:—

"Fully to know that we are saved by faith in Christ only, and not by any works of our own, and that we can do nothing, excepting by the grace of God, is *a great secret,* the knowledge of which can only be obtained by obedience—as the crown and end of great holiness of life." * "In all things it would appear that this doctrine (the Atonement) instead of its being what is supposed,† is in fact the very secret 'of the Lord' which Solomon says is with the righteous," &c.—'the hidden manna' which he will give to those who overcome the world. To require, as is sometimes done, from both grown persons and children, an *explicit* declaration of a belief in the Atonement, and the full assurance of its power, appears untenable. If a poor woman, ignorant and superstitious, as might be supposed, was received by our Lord, by so instant a blessing, for

---

* Tract on Reserve, (No. 80.) p. 49.

† The supposed idea is learned from Tract No. 73, where it is mentioned as a very objectionable feature of "the popular theology of the day," that it considers "that the Atonement is the chief doctrine of the Gospel—that on this, as on the horizontal line in a picture, all the portions of the Gospel system are placed and made to converge; as if it might be fearlessly used to regulate, adjust, correct, complete every thing else." The author of the Tract No. 80, considers that in the days of the Puritans great evils arose from the putting forward of divine truths "without that sacred reserve" which he has been urging. "The consequence of this *indelicate exposure* of religion was the perpetration of crimes almost unequalled in the annals of the world." That is, the making known of the Gospel—the preaching of the death of Christ as an atonement for the sins of the whole world; the calling of sinners to flee to that refuge by repentance and faith, to seek rest only in the Cross of Christ, was productive of all this ruin. What will it be when the Gospel is preached to *every creature?* A writer of the same school, reviewing the Tract on Reserve, in the British Critic, now an organ of this school, carries on the strain as follows; "How very different this sacred reserve from the manner in which the sacred mystery (the Atonement) is in the present day, pressed forward by a peculiar school, whether for the conversion of unbelievers, or for winning back stray souls to their duty and allegiance. It is held forth and touchingly depicted to all men indiscriminately. The characteristics of its full reception into the heart of any individual, seem to be an entire disclaiming of any merit or desert in himself, a watchful jealousy of any worth or importance in any thing he can do—a casting himself upon Christ," &c. Again: "It is notorious how popular books of the day bring forward the doctrine of the Atonement, and press it in every rhetorical form, as the great instrument for the conversion of the careless and ill-living."—*British Critic for April,* 1839. If Paul did not preach it to unconverted Jews and Greeks, how could it have been to the one *a stumbling block, to the other foolishness?*

touching the border of his clothes," (what a perversion! Was it for touching his clothes, or for *knowing* and *believing* in him?) "may it not have been the case that in times, which are now considered dark and lost to Gospel truth, there might have been many such? That there might have been many a helpless person, who knelt to a crucifix in a Churchyard, who might have done so under a more true sense of that faith which is unto life, than those who are able to express the most enlightened knowledge." *

From the above it is manifest that according to this divinity there may be *a true sense of a living faith,* where an *explicit* belief in the Atonement of Christ is not to be required or expected; that an adult is supposed to be a true Christian, a true believer, feeling, enjoying, displaying the power of a living, justifying faith, to whom the Atonement is not only not the prominent object of his faith, the single foundation of his hope, the great argument with God in his prayers, the only source whence he expects any *merit* before his Judge, but to whom that great propitiation, once for all, is so unknown, that to expect of him as much knowledge of it as would enable him to profess explicit belief in it, would be too great a trial of his faith—to bow down before a crucifix, *ignorant* of the great sacrifice of which it is the symbol, is evidence of knowledge enough to be the basis of a saving faith. Who now are hastening to the very gulf of Unitarianism? It is not the divinity of Christ that Unitarians chiefly aim at, but his vicarious Atonement. Suffer them to be possessors of a saving faith in Christ while they have no reliance in his sacrifice, and their zeal against his Divinity, as essentially involved therein, will die away.

Now let the reader judge, how much is meant by the expressions of these divines, as to all Justification, &c., coming through the *passion* of Christ. The *knowledge* of his atonement, a *looking* to that atonement, a *reliance* upon that atonement, as all one's hope and peace, has nothing to do with it. It is like the Romish sacrifice of the Mass, which is effectual for all the faithful, whether any but the sacrificing Priest unite in it, or not. The merits of Christ are applied to the sinner, according to this new way, without any knowledge or act on his part, except as he comes to the sacraments, or uses other "sacred symbols," and "effectual signs of grace." And this application of Christ's merits consists in the communication of inherent righteousness which constitutes his justification. All this explains the manifest favor with which

* Tract on Reserve, p. 76, 78.

these writers look upon the superstitious profaneness of administering the Lord's Supper "*to infants, or to the dying and apparently insensible,*" which we read is "not without the sanction of primitive usage," * and of course, therefore, claims their reverent submission. If a person can believe in Christ crucified, with a living, justifying faith, without an explicit belief in his atonement; then he can take the Lord's Supper in *remembrance* of the death of Christ, while incapable of remembering any thing about it.

An explanation of *explicit* faith, as distinguished from *implicit*, in the Church of Rome, will help the reader here. In Aquinas we read, that some things are objects of belief, *per se, essentially,* and these, therefore, are Articles of Faith, and must be believed with an *explicit* faith. Others are objects of faith only *per accidens*, or in a *secondary* sense; as, for instance, that *Abraham had two sons*. Such need be believed only *implicitly;* that is in a preparation of mind to receive what Scripture contains. Such faith requires no knowledge of that which is said to be believed, but only a readiness to receive it when made known.

All are not bound equally to have an explicit faith. Teachers of religion are bound to have more than others—*ad quos pertinet alios erudire, tenentur magis explicite credere.*†

The Incarnation and the Trinity are the only doctrines which Aquinas speaks of as requiring *explicit faith.*

Now, as *explicit faith*, in the *atonement*, according to this Divinity, is not to be required of an adult, but one may have a strong influential faith, who believes therein only inasmuch as believing the Scriptures or the Church in general, he believes whatever they teach, though he be wholly ignorant what it is; it follows that the Atonement is an article of *faith*, (*de fide*,) only in a secondary sense; not *per se*, but *per accidens;* or like such a secondary truth as Aquinas brings to illustrate the difference, viz., that *Abraham had two sons,* a truth indeed, but certainly not an article of *faith.* Thus we see how indeed, the true cross, the sacrifice of Christ, is taken out of sight. And this, they call the Gospel!!

Again, let the reader distinctly observe and estimate the uncertainty into which this new way necessarily casts the dearest hope of the penitent and believing sinner.

According to the Scriptures, when one is "justified by faith," he has "peace with God." "In this grace, (of justification) he *rejoices* in hope of the glory of God." It is manifest, that the Scripture not only represents a very joyful assurance of salvation as attain-

---

* Pusey's Views of Baptism, p. 5.   † Aquinas Summa P. I. Q. 2. A. 5.

able by all Christians, but as the bounden duty of all, when it tells us so frequently that the saints in this life, *have known* their justification and future salvation; when it declares, that whosoever believeth in Christ, "*hath* everlasting life;" which it would be vain to declare, if we cannot know whether we be believers or not; when it bids us examine ourselves, prove, know ourselves, whether we be in the faith; when it speaks of the happiness of the man unto whom the Lord imputeth no sin; when it makes the knowledge of peace, in the shape of hope, the anchor of the soul, the helmet of the head in storm and battle; when it requires us to rejoice in the Lord always; to love and haste unto the appearing of our Lord.

But where is the possibility of this, if, according to this scheme, our Justification be dependent on our own inwrought righteousness. Let us see! *Justification* and *peace* with God are essentially connected in Rom. v. 1. "*Being justified—we have peace with God.*" But, Justification, we are told, consists in a righteousness dwelling in us, and that righteousness may be more or less. Of course, then, we may be more or less justified, and so more or less at peace with God. "In the same degree, that faith or obedience grows, so does Justification. * * * On the other hand, those who are declining in their obedience—as they are quenching the light within, so are they diminishing their justification,"* and, of course, *so are they decreasing in peace with God.*

Now in what way is a poor sinner, working out his salvation, ever to know whether he has peace with God, and may rejoice in hope? He has peace so far only as he is justified. And according to this doctrine, some are more justified than others; the same person, at various periods, may be in various stages of justification. One asks for some mark in the alleged degrees of justification, by which he may know when he is justified enough to have peace with God. None can be pointed out. Whether he is at peace, or under wrath, (for there is no medium,) he can never know. Where then is that "confidence and rejoicing of hope," which we are to "hold firm unto the end?"

Now what is the natural consequence of such a comfortless doctrine—this "*feeding on husks and shells?*" "A man who can never know whether his amount of inherent Righteousness is sufficient, will always be excogitating some device or other by which God may be the more effectually propitiated and satisfied. A gloomy, or a poverty-stricken aspirant resorts to those unbidden austerities and severe bodily macerations, by which it is fully hoped that sins

* Newman, pp. 168, 169.

may be expiated and heaven meritoriously attained." In such righteousness there is something that seems tangible, measurable, appreciable. One may count his penances, measure his pilgrimages, weigh his gifts, and thus keep account of his fancied righteousness, and at last account himself sufficiently righteous to be at peace with God. Sinners of various minds will resort to various modes of establishing such a righteousness; the rich will purchase what they are not willing to work out. The prayers of priests, the merits of saints, the virtue of indulgences, bought with money will save them the pain of personal austerities. Thus arises the monster of Supererogatory Merit. And so there grows out of the effort of a troubled conscience to cure the awful uncertainty of a scheme of justification, which knows nothing better for righteousness, than our own works and personal holiness,—that whole retinue of vain devices for the manufacture of a righteousness of our own, by which the Church of Rome is so defiled and degraded.*

The direct tendency, to precisely such results, is manifest already in the system before us. Nothing is more evident, than that precisely this state of uncertainty about one's actual peace with God, is inculcated there as a matter of duty. Any thing like a "rejoicing of hope," a "strong consolation," is sternly repudiated as presumption and Ultra-Protestantism.

Thus Dr. Pusey condemns, with all severity, the views of those who believe that, "when men have once been brought to lay hold of Christ's saving merits, then their sins are done away; they are covered; they can appear no more; the hand-writing is blotted out; that this apprehension of Christ's merits is a full remission of sins; and that, after they have laid hold on Christ by faith, and so have their sins forgiven, "to *seek to efface past sin* by repentance, is weakness of faith; to do acts of mercy, or self-denial, or self-abasement, or to fast *with reference to it,* is to place repentance instead of Christ." This he considers worse than Romish indulgences; just because it does give what the Gospel calls us to, "a strong consolation," instead of "the bitterness of the ancient medicine," (of penance and austerity,) and because, by what he calls "an artificial, wrought-up peace, it checks the deep and searching agony, whereby God, as in a furnace of fire, purifies the whole man by the Spirit of judgment, and the Spirit of burning—going counter to the whole tenor of Scripture, that every man shall be judged according to his works."†

We cannot leave this painful uncertainty under which the doc-

---
* See Faber's Primitive Doctrine of Justification. c. v.
† Letter to the Bishop of Oxford, pp. 55, 6, 8, 9.

trine under consideration shrouds in gloom the dearest hopes of the humble believer, without refreshing the devout reader with the following from Mr. Faber.

"If we adopt the system recommended to us by these authorities, ancient and modern, (the ancient Fathers and the standards of the Church of England,) the modern being swelled by the assent of the various Reformed Churches of the Continent, we shall encounter no imperious and perplexing requisition to draw a line between *sufficiency* and *insufficiency;* for in that case we shall build our Justification, not upon the ever-shifting sands of man's Imperfect and Inherent Righteousness, but upon the immovable rock and absolute, cubical unity of the Perfect and Finished Righteousness of Christ. Thus freely justified through an imputation to us of faith, (the righteousness of Christ by faith,) instead of any righteousness of our own; henceforth, by the Sanctification of the Spirit, we sedulously work and abound, not FOR Justification, but FROM Justification. Our efforts therefore, through grace, to advance in every good thought and word and work, perfecting holiness in the fear of God, are the willing and grateful exertions of sons anxiously desirous to please a reconciled and most merciful father; not the reluctant and constrained and grudging labors of slaves, fearful lest any slackness in their hated task should call forth the lash of an exacting and unrelenting master. Erecting our edifice on this sure foundation of Christ's Righteousness; and knowing that there is therefore no condemnation to them who are in Christ Jesus, who walk not after the flesh but after the Spirit; perfect confiding love, casting out all that slavish fear, which in the very nature of things, cannot but attend upon the Romish system, (the Oxford system,) we have peace with God, being justified through faith—and we thankfully experience the blessedness of those, to whom the Lord will not impute sin, inasmuch as their iniquities are forgiven, and their sins are covered."*

Before we conclude the Chapter and proceed to the comparison of Romanism, there is one main point which must be set out with special distinctness.

We have treated this doctrine of Justification by a righteousness within us, as contradistinguished from a righteousness external and imputed, as being neither more nor less than Justification by inherent righteousness, or *Sanctification*. And we suppose that, to the reader whose only knowledge of the writings from which we have

---

* Faber's Prim. Doc. of Justif. p. 211.

taken it, has been derived from the citations we have given, the idea has not occurred that such identity could gravely be questioned. But let him remember that if this be granted, the essential Romanism of their Divinity, on this main doctrine of the Reformaation, is also granted. Justification by inherent righteousness, or *Sanctification*, is the grand distinguishing feature of Romanism, in regard to "the nature and essence of the medicine whereby Christ cureth our disease." Can it then be expected that a point of resemblance between them and Rome, so essential, could be allowed to appear without some attempt, at least, to give it a different aspect? Would it not be silly indeed for Dr. Pusey to publish a volume for the very purpose of showing that his system is not Romanism in its chief features, and yet tacitly acknowledge or not expressly deny its identity with that doctrine which by our great Anglican authorities is treated as the very soul of Romanism? Of course he denies it, and attempts to make out such distinctions between the indwelling righteousness that justifies and what, in all theology is called Sanctification, as will enable him to hold to the former, without feeling convicted of that very essential Romanism from which he labors to vindicate his system. Doubtless he thinks his distinctions good, but whether they be real or fictitious, it is our duty to judge for ourselves. A man may teach Socinianism and honestly deny that it is Socinianism. We must not take his word, except for the fact that such is his opinion. A man may concoct a poison and sincerely deny that it is poison, and by mixing it with ingredients foreign to, and contradictive of, its natural properties, may take it himself, without death; but we must judge of its legitimate tendency, neither by his assertion, nor his foreign admixture, nor its effects upon him, but by its own properties. We have a good example of this in these divines themselves. They will by no means receive the assertions of those whom they call "Ultra Protestants" as to whether *their* system involves this or that evil consequence. What is good in them personally, or their ministry, they say is *in spite of their system*. We must be excused, then, for maintaining that, if there be any expressions or inferences, or practical effects, in the works of these writers or in their Christian views and hopes, which are better than the natural and direct effect of their doctrine, (and we know there is much, and strange would it be were there not) it only proves that the teachers are better than their system: that the seed of truth within them which is in spite of their system, has its growth, as well as the seed of error belonging to their system, the wheat as well as the tare. To use their words: "The tendencies are doubtless checked in individuals; but whatever checks there are, are the results of past duty, of an implanted integrity, of God's law within them, in despite of their system. Their tendency is to act upon a theory, not upon Scripture."* The same language we may use of many Romanists, Socinians, Antinomians, as well as many who are less astray.

Now for the distinction contended for by these writers as the line of demarcation between the Romish doctrine of Justification and their own.

Dr. Pusey expressly declares that he and those who bear him company do "*exclude Sanctification from having any place in our Justification.*" Where the line runs between it and the righteousness within us which they say *is* our justification, he does not say. But he does tell us with singular contradiction, that "the state of Justification admits of degrees according to the degree of *Sanctification.*"†

Mr. Newman attempts a distinction.

"This is really and truly our Justification, *not faith, not holiness,* not (much less) a mere imputation; but the very presence of Christ,"‡ "not faith, not renovation, not obedience, not any thing cognizable by man, but a certain *divine* gift in which all these qualifications are included." § "Scripture expressly declares that righteousness is a definite inward gift, while at the same time it teaches that it is not any mere quality of mind, whether faith or holiness." Justification is "not *renewal* or the *principle* of renewal." "The Apostle goes on to say that the only true Justification is the being *made* holy or renewed; does not this imply from the very nature of the case that renewal was not just the same thing as Justification but that *in* which God justifies." (The implication is beyond our ken. But again): "If the justifying word be attended by the spiritual entrance of Christ into the soul, justification is perfectly distinct from renewal, with which Romanists identify it."

The astonished reader asks in the name of common sense, what is the distinction aimed at—a distinction between Justification, as *being made holy or renewed,* and Justification as being *holiness and renewal?* between righteousness as being *in* us and being a *quality of* us? All the answer of Mr. Newman is found in the following extracts, which the reader may understand if he can.

"If we say that Justification consists in a supernatural quality im-

---

* Dr. Pusey's Letter p. 48. † Ib. p. 54. ‡ Lectures p. 167. § Ib. p. 159.

parted to the soul by God's grace, as the Romanists say, then in like manner the question arises, is this quality *all that is in us of heaven?* Does not the grace itself, as an immediate divine power or presence, dwell in the hearts which are gifted with this renovating principle? It may or it may not; but if it does, then surely its *possession* is really our Justification; and not renewal or the principle of renewal." *

Here then is the attempted distinction. Something there is, called "grace," which is supposed to dwell in the heart, and which *works* holiness, but is not holiness; it is holy, but not holiness. It is "the *presence* of the Holy Ghost shed abroad in our hearts, the Author both of faith and of renewal. This is really that which makes us righteous (or justifies us) and our righteousness is *the possession of that presence.*" †

So then the possession of the *presence* of the Holy Ghost—the *simple presence*, irrespective of the effect upon our hearts, is our Justification while the effects of that presence are our Sanctification. But as living faith is said to be one of the "*fruits* of that presence," ‡ if Justification be that presence, faith must *follow after* Justification, while St. Paul says we are " Justified *by* faith."

But we have the distinction still more remarkably expressed.

"The righteousness on which we are called righteous, or are justified, that in which justification results or *consists*—this *justifying principle*, though *within* us as it must be, if it is to separate us from the world, yet is not *of* us, or *in* us, not any quality or act of our minds, not faith, not renovation, not obedience, not any thing cognizable by man, but a certain *divine gift* in which all these qualifications are included." §

Now let us mark! This "divine *presence*" by which we are justified, viz., "the habitation in us of God the Father, and the Word incarnate through the Holy Ghost," is a "*righteousness;*" it is also a "*principle;*" (the divine presence a *principle!*) It is also a

---

* Lectures, pp. 154, 151, 76, 179. Mr. Newman is wrong if he means that it is part of the *established and enjoined creed* of Romanism that it " consists in a *supernatural quality* imparted to the soul." Romanists are as subtle and wary in distinctions as our Oxford divines. *Mr. Newman got his distinction from them,* as we shall see. We read in Tract No. 71, that in Romanism " It is *de fide* that man is justified by inherent righteousness; it is not *de fide* that justifying righteousness is *a habit or quality,*" see p. 22 of American Edition. What the author of the Tract means by saying that *he does not deny the reality of the distinction and that it may be properly insisted on,* but does deny *that it exists in the particular case,* (p. 21) passes understanding.

† Lectures, p. 151.   ‡ p. 151.   § p. 159.

"*gift.*" This righteousness, or principle, or gift, is WITHIN US, WITHIN our hearts, our minds, our affections, yet is not OF us; it is not IN us; is not IN our hearts and minds and affections. It is *our* righteousness; it is a principle, a possession and gift of our minds, and yet "not *any quality of our minds.*" It is not the qualities of faith, renovation, holiness; but something which includes them all.

Such is the strongest exhibition of the whole middle wall of partition on which this divinity relies for the separation of its doctrine of Justification from that *by inherent righteousness* or Sanctification.

We have no intention of spending any time to show that this laborious and intangible distinction is unscriptural, and unreal; that in so serious a matter, it is mere trifling, and to all pretense of sober, biblical, theology, disgraceful. It speaks for itself. Flimsy as it is, however, it shows to what straits these divines are driven if they would even seem to keep clear of the charge of essential identity with Popery. In our next chapter, it will be shown how entirely, by the very using of this distinction, which is no other than an old device of scholastic Romanism, the charge of Popery becomes the more fixed. We need no stronger proof of how near these writers have gone to Popery than that the only separation from it they can find, in regard to the great subject before us, is in this wall of interposing mistiness. Mr. Knox, with a similiar approximation, was sensible of the necessity, of some such vindication. With less scholastic subtlety, if he has not used precisely the same he has at least expressed himself more intelligibly. In reply to the objection that to suppose Justification to have an *efficient*, as well as *reputative* sense, is to confound it with Sanctification, he says "This is a wonderfully common idea. But I apprehend that it rests on this pure mistake—that Sanctification is a general term for all inherent goodness wrought in us by the grace of Christ. On the contrary, I am persuaded it is a *distinctive* term for goodness *grown into*, or *growing into maturity*. And I apprehend, that among all the preliminary knowledge necessary to the beneficial reading of the Scriptures, none is more important than an accurate idea of this distinction and of the weight attached to it." The substance of it is that grace *in infancy* is Justification; *grace-adult, or approximating thereto*, is Sanctification.

We may be the more easily acquitted of presumption in rejecting all this distinction between the righteousness in which Justification, according to this divinity, consists, and Sanctification, when it is remembered that in so doing we only conform to what Mr. Newman in several parts of his Lectures asserts. He expressly declares, and considers himself to have proved, that the distinction ordinarily made between "two kinds of righteousness," that of Justification and that of Renewal or Sanctification, is "*not Scriptural*"—that these two are "*really one;*" that there is but one righteousness. He expressly says that "Justification and Sanctification are substantially the same thing"—described, in Scripture, as parts of *one gift*, properties, *qualities* or aspects of one."*

Thus we see that Justification is sometimes called a *quality*, sometimes denied to be a *quality;* sometimes the *property* of a "divine gift," and then the gift itself and none of its properties, but including them all. The reader must unravel the maze for himself.

Again, the "*real identity*, in matter of fact, between Sanctification and Justification, *however we may vary our terms, or classify our ideas*," is positively asserted.† Justification is described as "coming to us through our *sanctified wills and doings;* as *wrought out* for us by the power of God, actively employed within us," ‡ and "may be viewed as consisting in *evangelical obedience*," § and "will stand either for imputation or for *Sanctification*." ‖ Perhaps no stronger expression of the real identity of these two terms, in this divinity, could be given, than its assertion that "we become inwardly just or righteous in God's sight (i. e. justified) *upon our regeneration*, in the same sense in which we are utterly reprobate and abominable by *nature*." ¶ As it will not be denied that our natural unrighteousness is a *quality* of our minds, inherent *in* us and *of* us, as well as *within* us; our supernatural righteousness according to the above assertion, must be equally a quality of our minds inherent, &c.**

* Lectures, p. 42, 67.   † P. 68.   ‡ P. 59.
§ Lectures, p. 104.   ‖ P. 107.   ¶ P. 96.

** This very doctrine of justification with the same distinction between the righteousness of a divine presence within us, and that of a personal sanctification, was broached by Osiander, a Protestant in the 16th century. That continental theologian, whose niece Archbishop Cranmer married, excited much controversy among the reformed, after the death of Luther, by his peculiar views of Justification. So far as the present writer can see, Osiander's views and expressions were just those now re-edited at Oxford. Mr. Newman indeed disclaims connection with Osiander, because the latter maintained that "the Christian's justifying righteousness is the essential righteousness of the divine nature infused." True, there is much language in Osiander that bears this interpretation, but so there is in Mr. Newman. And if in Mr. N. there is much opposite language, as if our justifying righteousness were *regeneration, renewal, sanctification*, or the personal holiness wrought in us by the Holy Ghost, there is quite as much in Osiander. The great aversion of the latter is to a "gratuitous imputation;" his great principle is that we are justified by *being made* personally righteous; he confounded "that gift of acceptance *with regeneration*," that inward, justifying sanctity, he

But we are heartily wearied with the handling of such aerial forms. Can it be necessary to say that our Church, in her standards, knows but one internal righteousness—and that, *Sanctification*—that her standard divines know no more, and never dreamed of any more? Barrow, on Justification, has a passage which looks as if it had been made for our present use. "That which is by some termed *making a person just, infusion into his soul of righteousness,* of grace, of virtuous habits, is in the Scripture style called *acting by the Spirit, bestowing the gift of the Holy Ghost, renovation of the Holy Ghost, creation to good works,* SANCTIFICATION *by the Spirit.*" * It need not be declared that all such divines as Beveridge, Hall, Andrews, Hooker,

speaks of as consisting of "the inhabitation of Christ," in respect to his divine nature, and he maintained a difference between that indwelling righteousness and our personal holiness, at the same time that he often spoke of them as convertible terms. The Reformers indeed understood him as teaching justification by the *communication to us of the essential righteousness of the divine nature*, and so he did, and so we think they would have understood Mr. Newman as teaching. But Osiander did not teach this alone. He contradicted himself, just as mariners, in a mist, often turn around insensibly and go precisely an opposite course. He taught also justification by our own personal holiness. So precisely does Mr. N. contradict himself. The latter, when he says that our justifying principle is "the *inhabitation of God through the Spirit*," is involved in this predicament,—he must either mean, that it is the *personal holiness* which that blessed Spirit works in us, which is *Sanctification*; or else that it is a *communication of the divine, essential holiness*, to us; or else, that it is simply a *presence* of God within us, without respect to any communication, influence, effects. But what shall we say of *justification by a presence!* What is "unreal, abstract, visionary righteousness," if this be not? Mr. Newman is sometimes upon one of these alternates, sometimes another—sometimes all three are mixed up together, literally in an inextricable fog, the *mistified* mariner turning round and round, and all the while rowing with all his might for the haven. So much for losing sight of the true cross. So much for being guided by a cross within us instead of a cross on Calvary. The latter is always fixed. The former wanders as we wander. There is all the difference in the world between steering by an object *on shore*, and an object *in the boat*.

The writer could devise no better refutation of Mr. Newman than what Calvin, in his Institutes, has in refutation of Osiander. B. iii. c. xi. § v. to xiii. Said Melancthon, "I regard Osiander's dogma as no mere logomachy or strife of words. He differs from our Churches in a very essential point, and obscures, or rather destroys the only consolation provided for distressed consciences, seeing he leads us, not to the promise of mercy, through the obedience of the Mediator, but directs us to another object." "Osiander holds that we are justified by the divinity dwelling in us. This differs little from the doctrine of the heathen philosophers, who taught that man attains not to virtue but by a divine influence. Osiander, in effect, says that we are justified by our renovation to holiness. We, on the other hand, while we admit the necessity of renovation, hold that the renewed man is justified or accepted of God for the sake of Christ's obedience."—*Scott's Continuation of Milner's Ch. Hist.* vol. II. pp. 115, 116.

* Barrow's Works, 8vo. vol. iv. p. 120.

&c., continually use the words Sanctification, Inherent Righteousness, Indwelling Righteousness, as identical expressions; that the only other Righeousness they know is the *external* and *imputed* Righteousness of Christ; and a *tertium quid*, a *something between*, under the name of Righteousness, they have no acquaintance with. *

We fear that "philosophy falsely so called," has had far too much to do with this Divinity; philosophy such as Mr. Knox was thinking of when he said, "I greatly suspect that the time is not very distant when even Theological Creeds will be brought to a Philosophical test and be discarded should they not stand the trial." † "The philosophers themselves conceived and acknowledged that righteousness *which is a quality of the party.*" We need no revelation to teach us that. But "*the other* (righteousness by imputation and external) is proper, *to Christians only, and altogether unknown in Philosophy*." ‡ "Philosophy," said Clement of Alexandria, "should submit itself to theology, as Agar to Sarah; should allow itself to be advised but if it be unwilling to become obedient, *cast out the handmaid.*" "All heresies," said Tertullian, "have drawn existence from the brains of philosophers. They affect truth, and in affecting, they mar it."

We have now seen that great improvement in "the popular theology of the day;" that grand reform of Ultra-Protestantism; that high tower from which to defend the truth, against Rationalism, on the one hand, and Romanism on other; that Via Media, which, is now, we are told being rapidly restored from the sad dilapidations under which, through a Reformation that needs reforming, it has long been suffering; *the old path* from which those who are 'dreaming" of the opposite, hoping to be justified by "the unreal righteousness," the "abstract, visionary, tyrannical, usurping system" of Hooker, Andrews, Beveridge, &c., have been wandering in

---

* Hooker makes a distinction between what he calls "two kinds of sanctifying righteousness, habitual and actual. *Habitual*, that holiness wherewith our souls are inwardly endued, the same instant when first we begin to be the Temples of the Holy Ghost; *actual*, that holiness which afterwards beautifieth all the parts and actions of our life." But these two kinds are *one Sanctification*, in Hooker's view—not sanctification and *something else also*, which is its essence, and yet not sanctification. "The virtue of the Spirit, the habitual justice which is *ingrafted*," he opposes to the "*external justice of Jesus Christ*, which is *imputed*." The former, however divided into parts, he makes to be neither more nor less than Inherent Righteousness, or Sanctification. To neither does he assign any part in Justification. See Discourse of Justification, § 21. For Hooker's and Beveridge's account of the "two kinds of righteousness" see the beginning of this chapter.

† Remains, vol. I. p. 315. ‡ Andrew's Sermons, p 474.

a path "as ruinous to men's consciences, as the indulgences of Romanism."*

We must be excused indeed. We are far behind this new march of intellect. We are not yet prepared for this Reformation. We have been believers too long in a path washed with the tears and crimsoned with the blood of the Saints, to be easily moved away from that hope of the Gospel, which we have heard from a long line of noble witnesses, reaching up to the first day of the Protest of the Church, against the Roman Anti-Christ: "that blessed hope" preached in the beginning to every creature, "whereof Paul was made a minister."

If, as these modern, retrograde Reformers *declare*, the way of Justification by the external, imputed righteousness of Christ be "*another Gospel*" to them, then it follows that their way of Justification by a righteousness, not *external*, but *within us;* not *Christ's* but ours; not imputed or accounted to us by faith; but wrought in us by the Spirit, is another Gospel to us. We are bound, therefore, with regard to it, by that Apostolic charge: "Though an angel, from heaven, preach unto you any other Gospel than that ye have received, let him be anathema."†

We must take heed. There may be much restoration of what is old, in this system; but it may be old error, wearing a venerable aspect to some, because antiquated, and seeming full of piety just as prayers in an unknown tongue seem very devout. We must "try the spirits." Even "angels of light" must not be received as Reformers, without their credentials. The Canaanite is yet in the land. Romanism is working hard to renew its strength. The Church was once reformed away from Rome by powers of light. The next thing attempted will be to reform her back to Rome, by powers of darkness. Our Protestant Reformers, were at first Romish Priests; and when they began their work, were led by ways they knew not of, and to an extent of reformation which they did not at first contemplate, and would not at first have dared to attempt. Our next Reformers may be Protestant Presbyters, reversing the work of the others; led as they, though by another hand, in ways they know not of, to an extent of change, which in

* Pusey's Letter. p. 56.

‡ Oxford divines have led the way in the application of this text. In a late British Critic, (No. 53.) we find it said, that while the changes in the Latin Church, from the truth, have been only "objective and external;" that made by "common Protestantism involves a radical change of inward principle, sufficiently startling, to recall with unpleasant sensations, those awful words, 'Though we or an angel preach,'" &c.

the beginning, they may have no idea of seeking, and have not conscience to undertake. Reformation, as other things, *vires acquirit eundo*. Reformers learn new ends, by attempting to revive old paths; changes, once begun, have a wonderful tendency to make more advanced ones expedient, practicable, and at last obligatory. From imputed righteousness to *inherent* for Justification, is a great step; but once accomplished, it makes many others easy. It would be a wonderful leap, to cross at once, from *imputed* righteousness to *purgatory;* but the middle ground of *inherent* righteousness as our justification once gained, the rest is soon accomplished. From the righteousness of *Christ* imputed to me, to the righteousness of Saints imputed to me, is indeed a great gulf, which no leap of reforming agility could cross at a bound; but the half-way position of *man's* righteousness, for Justification, takes half the difficulty away, so that under a sense of the need of some better righteousness than his own, the leap of the sinner for salvation into the midst of the righteousness of "All Saints," living and dead, deposited under the keys of St. Peter, for the convenience of the Church, *and the benefit of the system of Indulgences* ceases to be difficult.

"Consider your ways." "Ponder the path of thy feet." This *Via Media* (*qu.* Via Appia?) may be an old path, worn deep with the steps of pilgrims, who have traveled far and toiled hard, and dropped many a scalding tear over the doubtfulness of a salvation which laid the foundation of hope in their own righteousness, and yet it may not be so old as that *Via Stricta*,* that narrow way that leadeth unto life, in which we walk by faith, the way of peace, to the world "foolishness," of which it is written : " Few there be that find it."

That narrow way is an *old path* indeed. Patriarchs, Prophets, Apostles, Martyrs, and Saints of all ages have walked therein and found it "a way of holiness," as well as of "joy unspeakable." It is the "new and living way consecrated for us through the blood of Jesus ;" by which we draw near to God, "in full assurance of faith ;" not fearing lest our sins should be too great or our own indwelling righteousness too little for a plenary Justification; but honoring the infinite riches of divine grace, by the full assurance that whosoever believeth in Jesus hath everlasting life, and there is no condemnation for him.

* Matt. vii. 14.

CHAPTER IV.

THE DOCTRINE OF THIS DIVINITY, AS TO THE RIGHTEOUSNESS OF JUSTIFICATION, COMPARED WITH THAT OF THE SCHOOLMEN.

Origin of the Romish doctrine of Justification in the self-righteousness of the human heart—Advance until the age of the schoolmen—The origin of Scholastic Theology—Character of the Schoolmen—Fitness of the age for the rapid growth of error—The corruptions of Romanism which were matured in that age. The seven sacraments—Sacramental Confession—Transubstantiation—Half Communion—Image worship—Purgatory—Indulgences—The same age, as was to be expected, gave birth to the Romish doctrine of Justification—Connection between the Schoolmen and the divines of Trent—Three propositions to show the identity of the doctrine of this system with that of the Schoolmen—Similar tendencies—Concluding remarks—Note, showing the resemblance between this doctrine and that of the early Quakers.

BEFORE proceeding to a direct exhibition of the doctrine of the Romish Church, as set forth in mature growth, and in solemn, didactic, array, by the Decrees of the Council of Trent; we will pursue a course similar to that by which we arrived at the doctrine of the Oxford divines. We first contemplated that doctrine "*in rudiment,*" as contained in Mr. Knox; and then the same in "*larger development,*" in the writings of its present chief representatives at Oxford.

The real origin of the Romish error of Justification, by inherent righteousness, may be dated as far back as when men first began to go *about establishing their own righteousness, not submitting themselves to the righteousness* of God. Like the system of the Gospel, which it has been the unceasing aim of the Adversary, by this heresy, to subvert; it has had its various dispensations. Before the era of Christianity, it was a counterfeit Judaism, professing the righteousness of God, under the forms of the Mosaic ritual, but relying upon the righteousness of the Scribes and Pharisees, under a yoke of traditions which taught for doctrines the commandments of men, and changed the truth of God into a lie, and lost the power of godliness in devotion to the form thereof; full of pretense without, but within, of all uncleanness.

The proneness of the human heart to depart from the righteousness of God was not eradicated, nor was the malice of the devil satiated, when the Church arose out of the shadows of the Jewish dispensation, and into the clearer light of the Christian. To make the cross of Christ of none effect; first, by making it foolishness to the Greek, and a stumbling-block to the Jew; and then, when men would embrace it, by turning it into an idol, like the brazen serpent of a former age; so that men, retaining the name of Christ upon their lips, and making the sign of the cross upon their foreheads, might be substituting a foundation of self-righteousness, for "Jesus Christ and him crucified;" their own cross, for his; their sacrifice, for the one oblation once offered for the whole world; such has been the grand effort of Satan, to which the errors and heresies of every century of Christianity bear most impressive testimony. It was a circumstance favorable to the covert introduction of great practical error, in regard to the justification of the sinner before God, that for many centuries the chief points of controversy raised in the Church, while connected, in a very important sense, with whatever related to salvation, were calculated rather to keep the eye of careful guardianship away from the precise question of justification, by the excitement they created around others which seemed to be more immediately endangered. While men thus slept, came the Adversary, and found an open field and many a propitious soil, in which to sow those prolific seeds of self-righteous doctrine, which early sprang up in the Platonic soil of the Alexandrian divinity, and afterwards ripened so abundantly during what are most truly called the "*dark ages*" of Christianity.

But as yet, there was no publicly professed and general creed, *embodying* what was already the widely diffused *spirit* of departure from "the righteousness of God by faith." It was active, vigorous, practical, appearing under a thousand forms, speaking all languages, giving life to a rapidly increasing and multiplying burden of formal observances; resisted indeed by some faithful confessors of the truth, and not yet introduced to the formal dignity of theological profession, nor honored with any scholastic degree.*

But a new dispensation was now about to arise. About the year 1140, the form of doctrine within the bounds of the Latin

---

* "When all good learning, and lessons of the holy Scripture, were drowned by the Goths and Vandals in Europe, Asia, and Africa, and yet somewhat rescued and taught again by Charles the Great, A. D. 800, men, not acquainted with the phrases and vein of Scripture, accustomed themselves to *the reading of doctors, and left the word of God.*"—Hooper's Fifth Sermon on Justification.

Church, began to be greatly changed by the profuse admixture of human traditions and philosophy.

At the head of that movement was the chief Schoolman of that century,—Peter Lombard, known, after the name of his chief work as *The Master of the Sentences*. Around that work, composed of sentences from the Fathers, was soon assembled a busy tribe of lesser Schoolmen, as bees around a cluster of flowers, whose whole business was to make Commentaries upon the Sentences of the Master. But, in the next century, arose a disciple whose fame eclipsed that of the Master, and to whom were given the high names of the Universal and the Angelic Doctor, the celebrated Thomas Aquinas. Cotemporary with him was Bonaventura, a Schoolman of almost equal renown, particularly noted for *mystic* theology and the worship of the Virgin Mary. Of these and the whole constellation of Doctors of inferior magnitude, belonging to the scholastic age, the learned Mosheim gives the following description:

"The greatest part of these Doctors followed Aristotle as their model, and made use of the logical and metaphysical principles of that subtle philosopher in illustrating the doctrines of Christianity. Yet notwithstanding all the subtlety of these Irrefragable and Seraphic and Angelic Doctors, as they are called, they often appeared wiser in their own conceit, then they were in reality, and frequently did little more than involve in greater obscurity, the doctrines which they pretended to place in the clearest light. The method of illustrating divine truth by *reason and philosophy*, prevailed universally: and was followed with such ardor that the number of those who, in conformity with the example of the ancient Doctors, drew their systems of Theology *from the Holy Scriptures and the writings of the Fathers*, and who acquired on that account the name of *Biblicists*, diminished from day to day."*
John of Salisbury, one of the most discreet writers of the twelfth century, testifies of the divines of his day, that "they collected auditors solely for the ostentation of science, and designedly rendered their discourses obscure, that they might appear loaded with the mysteries of wisdom; and that though all professed to follow Aristotle, they were so ignorant of his true doctrine, that in attempting to explain his meaning, they often advanced a Platonic notion, or some erroneous tenet, equally distant from the true system of Aristotle and of Plato." † The learning even of the Universal and Angelic Doctor, was confined to the Scholastic The-

---

* Mosheim's Eccl. Hist. Cent. xiii. p. ii. c. 3.   † Enfield's Hist. of Phil. 8vo. p. 502.

ology. Unable to read Greek, he was confined in his study of Aristotle, to some miserable Arabian translations, till a better version was made by an unknown hand. The leading characteristic of the Schoolmen, was that they employed themselves " in an ostentatious display of ingenuity, in which axioms, assumed without examination, *distinctions, without any real difference, and terms without any precise meaning*, were made use of, as weapons of assault and defense, in controversies about abstruse questions, which after endless skirmishes, it was imposible to bring to any issue, and which, notwithstanding all the violence of the contest, it was of no importance to determine." *

" The opinions which these philosophical divines instilled into the minds of youth, appeared, even in that day, to the remaining votaries of the ancient fathers, highly dangerous and even pernicious. When it was objected to several of their tenets that they were in direct contradiction to the genius of Christianity, and to the express doctrines of Scripture, these scholastic quibblers had recourse for a reply, or rather for a method of escape to that perfidious distinction, which has been frequently employed by modern Deists,—that these tenets were *philosophically true* and conformable to right reason, but that they were indeed *theologically false*, and contrary to the orthodox faith."†

Such a dispensation of divinity coming after many centuries of extreme spiritual and intellectual darkness, and characterized by such neglect of the Scriptures and idolatry of Aristotle; by such emptiness of the mind, and yet such sharpening of its powers of disputation; by such pride of reason, and yet such poverty of knowledge, when the Church was literally *spoiled* "*through philosophy and vain deceit*"—when the Masters in Israel did literally "*strive about words to no profit, but to the subverting of the hearers*," continually starting "*foolish and unlearned questions, which did but gender strifes;*" so that, as Dr. Jackson describes them, " they delighted to draw all doubts and queries, about the most solid points of divinity, or matters most capable of philosophical expressions, into *second notions*, or terms of art, or artificial fabrics of words; as if they meant to rend or resolve strong and well-woven stuff, into small and raveled threads, to entangle themselves and their readers, in perpetual fallacies, *a rebus ad voces*": ‡—such a dispensation was a most favorable opportunity for the maturing of the divers growths of heresies, which had long been silently, but vigorously, spreading

---

* Enfield's Hist. of Phil. 8vo. p. 509.   † Mosheim, Cent. xi. c. iii. § 8.
‡ Jackson's Works, iii. p. 19.

their poisonous roots through the wasted vineyard of the Church. It is the precise period from which we should naturally expect the springing up of heresies which would afterward be received into the rank of doctrines of Faith. The history of that period most abundantly confirms that idea. The age of the Schoolmen was singularly an age of superstitions and heresies; the age of the installation of those several peculiar features of Romanism, which had long been growing into prominence, and were afterwards ecclesiastically robed, and more authoritatively proclaimed by the Council of Trent.

"The most received Tenets of the Romish Church, were first hatched by the Schoolmen, which never saw the light of heaven, but through the dark painted glasses of the cells wherein they were imprisoned; and hence imagined our Saviour's form of doctrine to be of the same hue with midnight duncery, or grossest ignorance of sacred dialects." *

Let us briefly advert to some of the inventions of that ingenious age.

THE SEVEN SACRAMENTS.

Cassander, a learned Romish divine, says: "You shall not easily find any man *before Peter Lombard,* (twelfth century,) which had set down *any certain and definite number of Sacraments."* †

SACRAMENTAL CONFESSION.

This bird, (says Bishop Hall,) was hatched in the Council of Lateran, 1215, and fully plumed in the Council of Trent." ‡

TRANSUBSTANTIATION.

"Scotus says that before the Council of Lateran, 1215, Transubstantiation was no point of faith; as Bellarmine confesses." § The name was first used by Peter de Celles, and Stephen Bishop of Autun, in the twelfth century. ‖

HALF COMMUNION.

"We cannot deny, (says Vasquez,) that in the Latin Church, there was the use of *both* kinds, and that it so continued until the days of St. Thomas, which was about the year of God, 1260." ¶ In the previous century, Lombard "gives an account why the body and blood are administered under *two kinds,*" and Pope Paschal II., orders that in the communion they should give *the bread and wine*

---

* Jackson's Works, i. p. 678.   † Cassand. Consult. Art. 13, de Numero Sac.
‡ Works, ix. p. 275.   § Bp. Taylor's Dissuasive from Popery, c. i. § 5.
‖ Dupin's Eccl. Hist. v. ix. p. 156.   ¶ Quoted by Bp. Hall.

apart, which was contrary to the custom of Cluny, where sometimes they dipped the host in the wine. Infants and the Infirm were excepted from this order.*

IMAGE WORSHIP.

Aquinas (13th cent.) held, "that the Image is to be worshiped with the same adoration which is due to the thing represented by it;" an opinion which sounder Schoolmen refused. A writer of the previous century, Guibert, had gone no further than to say: "We fix our wandering mind on the contemplation of spiritual things, by looking upon pictures, which serve as it were to admonish us of our duty."† This was the doctrine of Durandus and other Schoolmen. But that of Aquinas became the doctrine not only of all his disciples but also of "all the old Schoolmen almost," and has since been, says Azorius the Jesuit, "the constant judgment of divines." ‡

PURGATORY.

"For extinguishing the imaginary flames of Popish Purgatory, we need not go far, (says Archbishop Usher,) to fetch water. And if we need the assistance of the ancient Fathers, behold they be here ready with full buckets in their hands." The silence of antiquity concerning it is avowed by Fisher (Romish) Archbishop of Rochester, Alphonsus de Castro and Polydore Virgil. Fisher says: "For a while it was unknown to the Church Universal. Then it was believed by some, by little and little." Oxford Tracts. No. 79. Usher shows, from Otto Frisingensis, that in the *twelfth century*, "the doctrine of purgatory was esteemed only a private assertion, held by some, and not an article of faith." To Thomas Aquinas, and other Schoolmen of the next century, Usher ascribes "the *bringing of the frame of this new building towards perfection.*" §

INDULGENCES.

These follow Purgatory of course. "Bishop Fisher, the Romish Prelate, says, that in the beginning of the Church, there was no use of indulgences; that they began after the people were awhile affrighted with the torments of purgatory; and many of the Schoolmen confess that their use began in time of Pope Alexander III., towards the end of the twelfth century.∥ Chemnitz challenges the production of evidence to the existence of Indulgences, according to the Trent doctrine, prior to the age of Thomas Aquinas.

---

* Dupin's Eccl. Hist. cent. xii. pp. 198 and 35.
† Ibid. cent. xii. p. 141   ‡ Usher's Answer to a Jesuit, pp. 432, 3.
§ Ibid. pp. 164—166.   ∥ Bishop Taylor's Disuasive from Popery, c. 1. § 3.

DISUSE OF THE SCRPITURES.

Cotemporaneous with the coming in of the above corruptions and the multiplication of subordinate branches, was the removal in a great measure of the Scriptures from the daily services of the Church, as they had been already from the studies of the leading divines and Schoolmen, and the substitution of legends and tales of saints. To this we have the testimony of the Oxford Tracts. "It would seem as if the eleventh, or at least the twelfth century, *a time fertile in other* false steps in religion, must be charged also, as far as concerns Rome and its more intimate dependencies, with a partial removal of the light of the written word from the sanctuary." In the year 1278—grave and sounder matter being excluded, apocryphal legends of saints were used to stimulate and occupy the popular mind; and a way was made for the use of those invocations to the Virgin and other saints, which heretofore were unknown in public worship.*

Thus it is impressively evident that the age of the elder sohoolmen, particularly that of Thomas Aquinas, was productive of all the most odious of the overt deformities of Romanism. Then it was that, as from a forcing bed, long seeded and fermenting, they sprang up together, suddenly, vigorously, and rank. Now in all the corruptions that have been mentioned, there is an important connection with the question of Justification; while in Confession, Image Worship, Purgatory, and Indulgences, there is so direct and near a connection that they could not have gained acceptance but in consequence of a gross departure from the truth on that vital point. With a confident expectation, threfore, we look to the Schoolmen of that age for an advance of corruption in the doctrine of Justification, corresponding with, and accounting for, that great advance of corruption in all those parts of religion which depend on this as their head and heart. We are not disappointed. The age of Peter Lombard and Thomas Aquinas was emphatically that of the introduction into the high places of school and Church-doctrine of the present Romish dogma of Justification. They were the men who, when the widely-diffused and spreading *spirit* of self-righteousness, as yet without a fixed doctrinal form in the Church was fast gathering itself up, like the fabled genii of oriental tales, into shape, and demanding "a local habitation and a name," *they* were the men who clothed it first in solemn didactic raiment, invested it with the dignity of formal theology, ushered it before the Church under high

---

* Tract on the Roman Breviary, No. 75. American Edition. pp. 180, 182.

scholastic sanction, and recorded, for coming generations, that *doctrine* of self-righteousness, under shape of a righteousness implanted and inherent, for justification, which the Council of Trent subsequently adopted as the model of its decree, and which has been ever since a most lamentable evidence of how the Church of Rome was beguiled "by the rudiments of the world, and the traditions of men," into the substitution of another Gospel for that of God. The history of the debates of Trent is continual proof that the Schoolmen, especially Aquinas, were the Masters of *those sentences* which issued from that Council. Andrada, a famous defender of the Council, is cited, by Chemnitz, as acknowledging that the decree of Trent "was only a *paraphrase* of the doctrine which had been taught by these Schoolmen, and that the *single purpose in constructing that decree was to repeat and confirm their opinion;*" * while another learned member of the council, Pighius, said it could not be denied that this great doctrine of Christianity had been "rather obscured than illustrated by the thorny questions and disputations of the Schoolmen." †

Andreas Vega, another prominent divine of the Council, has left us the following account of the origin of its doctrine. "Some ages since, there was a great concertation among divines what should be the formal cause of our Justification. Some thought it to be no created justice infused into man; but only the favor and merciful acceptation of God: Others, whose opinion is more common and probable, held it to be some *created quality,* informing the souls of the just." "This opinion was allowed in the Council of Vienna; and the *School Doctors, after the Master of the Sentences,* delivered this *not as probable only, but as certain.* Afterwards, when some defended the opposite part to be more probable, it seemed good to the holy Synod of Trent thus to determine it." ‡

* Chemnitz Examen. Dec. Con. Trident, p. 146. † p. 126.
‡ Vega, quoted by Bishop Hall—Works, 8vo. ix. p. 239.

The theology of the Schoolmen retained undisputed sway till the era of the Reformation, when Erasmus, Ludovicus Vives, James Faber, &c., not having the fear of heresy before their eyes, boldly charged, with solid learning and cutting ridicule, upon the follies of the prevailing systems of *theologizing,* as well as *philosophizing.* But the *Malleus Scholasticorum* was Luther, and the swelling tide that rent asunder, and cast off, and sent to oblivion, the chains of ice in which the mind of all Europe had been so long bound down under darkness, was that of the Reformation throwing off Romanism, and with it the whole dominion of Aristotelian and Scholastic subtlety. "The study of ancient languages being now revived, and the arts of eloquence and criticism having now resumed their ancient station, the Reformers were soon convinced that ignorance and barbarism had been among the principal causes of the corruption of doctrine and discipline

Now, if it may not be shown that the divines at Oxford have gone, like the holy Synod of Trent, among the *spinosas quæstiones et definitiones Scholasticorum,* to get their doctrine of Justification, it will at least be made to appear that they have arrived at a singular agreement with the doctrines of the Schoolmen.

in the Church." "Luther saw much reason to consider the scholastic philosophy as the foundation of the principal errors which had been introduced into theology, and the chief support of that oppressive dominion which the See of Rome exercised over the consciences of men; he regarded the logical and metaphysical parts of Aristotle as the immediate grounds of those disputes which had given rise to the factions of the Thomists, Scotists, Occamists and others." But in order to retain this Palladium of the Church of Rome, the advocates of established forms pleaded that the evils complained of had arisen, not from the Scholastic method, but its abuse. Under this futile pretense, the friends of the Romish hierarchy retained in their hands an instrument, which had been found so useful in establishing and perpetuating the reign of ignorance and superstition. Hence the Scholastic philosophy was still studied and professed in the colleges and monasteries belonging to the Church of Rome. The generality of the Romish Clergy still retained so much of the Scholastic spirit that, instead of promoting, they only retarded, the progress of true philosophy.

Their writings chiefly consisted of systems of philosophy, summaries of logic, theses upon Scholastic topics, and commentaries upon the works of Aristotle, and Thomas Aquinas.[1] ([1] Enfield's History of Phil. b. viii. c. 3.)

Platonism and the Middle Ages are quite hobbies in the Oxford School. The Republic of Plato is to Mr. Newman almost an inspired type of the Church. He cannot account for "the close parallelism" between the "Republic" and the Church, without adverting to the idea of "a species of inspiration from the same Being who formed the Church." He considers Plato as having foreseen with an almost "prophetic eye" "the phases through which the Church would pass, having supplied the best outline ever yet given, not only of the civil, but of the ecclesiastical history of man."—British Critic, No. 53.

Much of the peculiar mysticism of the Oxford School, and its fondness for the Alexandrian, may be accounted for by its love of Plato. "Enthusiasm, *mysticism,* and fanaticism, have been the extravagances of Platonism." The school of Alexandria, in the second century, was miserably unevangelized by that Philosophy, many of its divines remaining devout Platonics after they became Christians. The school of Oxford is most reverently following their steps, *under the guidance of the Schoolmen.*

It may here be remembered that in England "the study of the Greek philosophy has been chiefly confined to the University of Oxford, which providentially (says the British Critic) has been saved from setting the seal of its sanction either to Paley or to Locke; and has adhered firmly to Aristotle as the text-book in her plan of education." "Precisely the reverse is the case at the University of Cambridge, where Locke and Paley have long held a prominent place in instruction."—See British Critic for July, 1838, p. 2.—and Sedgwicke on the studies of the University of Cambridge. p. 40.

It may also be noted, that, *pari passu,* with the coming out of Oxford Divinity, there was a decided effort, by a series of elaborate papers in the British Magazine, (a work sympathizing entirely with that way,) *to write up* the Middle ages; to call attention to their *stores;* to vindicate them from that character

From the extract from Vega, just given, we learn the following important particulars.—1. That prior to the Council of Trent, the doctrine of the Church of Rome was *not determined* on this great point of all vital religion,—whether justification consists in an *infused, personal righteousness,* or in an *external and imputed.* 2. That, on this subject there had been a *great controversy among divines, some ages prior to the Council.* No doubt he refers to the age of the elder Schoolmen.* 3. That while the doctrine of *infused* righteousness for justification, was "*allowed*" in the Council of Vienna, (*tolerated,*) it was reserved for the School Doctors, after their great leader, Peter Lombard, the Master of the Sentences, to propound this growing doctrine, "*not as probable only, but as certain.*" 4. That still there were those in the Church of Rome who maintained the opposite doctrine. And those continued of that side till the Council of Trent. Some in the Council, we know, from other sources, were of that side, and openly maintained it. But this was to countenance Lutheranism. Therefore it seemed good to the Council to determine that justifying righteousness is

of "*Dark Ages;*" by which it has been the universal opinion of Protestants they ought to be known. As a specimen of such effort, we have in a late British Critic the following passage, found in an article which decries the study of the evidences of Christianity as inimical to the right sort of faith, and advocates the receiving of our doctrines from *the traditionary Creed of the Church,* prior to any reference to Scripture, *and just because it is what the Church believes.* "There is a certain era of the Church (says the Review) of which our enlightened generation seldom deigns to speak with respect; holding it to have been *dark;* not only in arts and sciences, not only in its manners and laws; but also, and that above all, *in its religion.* Any one who has passed a few hours in a college library, will remember vast rows of gigantic volumes, which, heavy and sombre as they frown on the modern student, look like the sepulchral monuments of an obsolete literature. These are the works of the Schoolmen, great men in their day, heard and read and admired, and imitated by thousands. Taken, as a whole, it was a vast school of learning, vast in its duration and extent; in the powers and labors of its chief masters, and in the multitudes of those they led. Yet the judgment of the moderns (we are not inquiring whether true or false) their deliberate judgment is, that all this learning was but a cloud of darkness, obscuring both Gospel truth and the natural light of human reason; that it was all labor lost, a mere shadow of knowledge."—See British Critic for July, 1839, p. 22. How these hints are intended to operate, cannot be doubted.

* That this controversy originated in comparatively modern times is thus granted by Vasquez, another distinguished Trent divine. "Ea quæ pertinent ad formalem causam nostræ justificationis—difficillima eorum quæ de justificatione nostra tractari solent, neque præteritis sœculis tam exacte a patribus discussa, quam ea quæ de necessitate auxillii gratiæ ad operandum et recte vivendum hactenus a nobis sunt disputata." Quest. 112, Disp. 202. Barrow has a similar observation.—See on Justific.

infused and inherent righteousness, and to curse all who, like those of whom Vega speaks, should presume to hold any different opinion.*

Since it thus appears from one of the chief divines and defenders of the Council of Trent, and from other sources previously mentioned, that the doctrine established at Trent, was there considered as having been drawn directly from the Schoolmen, and to have been first propounded, for a sure doctrine, by those "Irrefragable" Doctors; it follows that the Romanism of Trent, and the Romanism of the Schoolmen, on the present subject, are one, in all important respects. Hence it will tend not a little toward a right estimate of the Romanistic character of the Divinity under consideration if we shall make good the three following propositions.

1. That the Schoolmen described the righteousness of Justification, precisely as do the Oxford Divines.

* Mr. Faber believes that "the system of human, justifying righteousness, infused and therefore inherent," derived its origin from the early Schoolmen, especially Peter Lombard and Thomas Aquinas. After showing that the doctrine of the famous St. Bernard, of Clairval, the head of the Biblicists, in opposition to the speculative philosophico-theology of the Schoolmen, in the middle of the twelfth century, was directly the reverse; and after declaring that he can find in the writings of St. Bernard, no evidence that he had ever heard of such a doctrine, sums up his thoughts on the point of derivation, as follows: "Scripture rejects it: The Ancient Church disowns it: Bernard, the last of the Fathers, apparently knows nothing of it. But the Schoolmen who immediately followed Bernard, and whose characteristic was a desertion both of Scripture and of Ecclesiastical Antiquity, for Human Reason and Human Philosophy, give it, as the fruit of their novel mode of illustrating divine things, with the utmost precision and intelligibility. Furthermore, though the speculations of the Schoolmen were strongly opposed by the Biblicists of the Old Theology, they rapidly became so fashionable, as to be received even by acclamation, and thence to form henceforth, the basis of the accredited system of Orthodox Divinity."—Primitive Doc. of Justific. p. 276.

The following is an example of St. Bernard's doctrine. "What can all our righteousness be before God? Shall it not, according to the Prophet, be viewed as a filthy rag; and if it be strictly judged, shall not all our righteousness turn out to be mere unrighteousness and deficiency? Yet who shall bring any accusation against the elect of God? To me, it is sufficient for all righteousness only to have him propitiated, against whom only I have sinned. Every thing which he shall have decreed not to impute to me, is thus, as if it had never been. Freedom from all sin, is the righteousness of God. The pure indulgence of God is the righteousness of man. Since the Apostle, if one died for all, then were all dead; meaning that the satisfaction made by one, should be imputed to all, even as one bare the sins of all; so that there should not be found one distinct person who incurred the forfeit, and another who made satisfaction; because truly the head and the body are one Christ. The head satisfied for its members: Christ for his own bowels."—See St. Bernard as quoted by Faber, in Prim. Doc. of Just. pp. 155, 158.

2. That they felt the same necessity, as do the latter, of finding out a distinction between an indwelling righteousness that justifies, and an indwelling righteousness that sanctifies, and that they fell upon precisely the same subtle and shadowy expedient.

3. That this very distiction of the ancient Schoolmen, which equally characterizes the divinity of our Oxford Schoolmen, is used by our ancient writers as one distinctive characteristic of Popery.

1. As to the first of these propositions, there is no need of argument—Mr. Newman declares it. "Great divines, (he says) as Lombard and Thomas Aquinas, (*the two chiefs of Schoolmen*) declare that the Holy Spirit indwelling, is the *formal cause of Justification.* Justification by *inherent righteousness*, in other words;—or to use the words of St. Thomas himself, 'Justifying Grace is something real and positive in the soul, a supernatural quality."*

2. The second proposition may be as readily established. It will be remembered that while in this system it is most directly asserted that there is but one righteousness; that Justification and Sanctification are substantially the same; that the usual distinction between them is unscriptural; that they are really one, the terms Renewal and Justification being *identical;* a distinction is attempted on which Dr. Pusey positively asserts, that he and his fellows " *exclude* Sanctification from having any place in our Justification," and on which Mr. Newman asserts, that Justification is "not renewal, nor the principle of renewal, but perfectly distinct from renewal, *with which Romanists identify it*." The idea then is, that between "the divine gift," or "the justifying principle," or "the inward reality, of righteousness," or "the indwelling of the Holy Ghost," (whichever expression we choose for justification) and personal holiness, there is such a difference, that while the latter is the *complex* of the several virtues of the renewed mind, the *other includes them all but is not any of them.* Hence that curious description of the Justifying Righteousness, as a something "*within* us, yet not *of* us, nor *in* us, not any quality or act of our minds; not faith, not renovation, not obedience, not any thing cognizable by man, but a certain divine gift in which all these are included."

Now on what ground can Mr. Newman assert that the Romanists "*identify Justification with renewal*," one whit more than he does; how rest, as he does, his grand claim of distinction between his doctrine and that of Rome on the fact that *they* make that identifi-

---

* Gratia gratum faciens, id est justificans, est in anima, quiddam reale et positivum, qualitas quædam supernaturalis. Aquinas, p. 1, 2, q. 110.

cation and he does not, when we find him saying, that "the *real* distinction already alluded to, (his own,) *is allowed in the Church of Rome, and held by Romanists*, both before the Council of Trent and after?"

"St. Thomas contends that the *gratia justificans*, (the justifying righteousness,) is not the same as the habit of love; the latter belonging to the will, and the former to the essence of the soul. In which opinion he is followed by Cajetan, Conradus, Soto and others. Bonaventura" (one of the most mystical and superstitious, and idolatrous of the Schoolmen,) "assents, so far as to consider there is a real distinction between them. This alleged distinction was a subject of dispute at the Council of Trent between the Franciscans and Dominicans, on all which accounts it was left unsettled by the Fathers there assembled."*

We add to the above, the extract from Annati, a Romish writer in Tracts for the Times, No. 71. "It is *de fide* that man is justified by inherent righteousness; it is not *de fide* (not an established article of faith,) that justifying righteousness *is a habit or quality*."

Now, with all this before him, how could Mr. Newman say, as he does on page 150 of his Lectures, that Romanists make Justifying righteousness "consist in a supernatural *quality*," as if that word *quality* were decided upon any more, among them, than it is with him; and as if in the use of that word lay the great difference between his doctrine and theirs?

* Lectures, p. 159, 397. "There was a sharp disputation between those two orders (says Father Paul,) whether the habit of grace be the same with the habit of charity, as Scotus would; or distinct, as St. Thomas." Hist. p. 198.

Whoever will take the trouble to read what Thomas Aquinas has left us under his 110th question of the second—first page of his Summa, as well as under question 113th—will perceive an exact resemblance between Mr. N. and him on the subject in hand. Does Mr. N. sometimes treat the Grace of Justification as the same with infused righteousness? so does St. Thomas. "Idem est gratiæ infusio, et culpæ remissio, sicut idem est illuminatio et tenebrarum expulsio. Q. 113. Does Mr. Newman make them diverse in certain respects?—so does St. Thomas. He mentions certain respects in which Justifying grace is not a quality of the soul—and one in which it is. As to the latter he says: Quædam est qualitas supernaturalis, non eadem cum virtute infusa; sed aliquid præter infusas virtutes, quædam habitudo, quæ præsupponitur in istis virtutibus sicut earum principium et radix, &c. The same difference is expressed elsewhere, as follows:—Aliter est in anima gratia, et aliter character. He says, Character importat quandam potentiam spiritualem ordinatam ad ea quæ sunt divinæ cultus. Anima est subjectum characteris, secundum intellectuam partem, in qua est fides. And the difference between this character and grace is thus given. Gratia est in anima sicut quædam forma habens esse completam in ea; character autem est in anima sicut quædam virtus instrumentalis.

Enough has now been said for our second proposition, viz., that the Schoolmen and our Oxford Divines, not only are agreed as to inherent righteousness for justification, but are characterized by precisely the same vain device to prevent its being considered exactly the same thing as Sanctification.

3. For our third proposition, that our ancient writers have used that very distinction as a distinctive characteristic of Popery; Hooker will suffice as an example. In the commencement of his famous discourse on Justification, he sets out with that admirable account of the doctrine of the Church of Rome, which we have laid before the reader already. The only authority which he quotes for the account there given of what justifying righteousness consists in, according to Rome, is in the words of Thomas Aquinas, containing the precise distinction in question, and that which Mr. Newman refers to above, as agreeing with his own.

"Justifying grace is something real and positive in the soul— not the same with infused virtue as the Master (Lombard) maintains; but something beside the infused virtues, faith, hope, charity; a certain habitude which is presupposed in those virtues, as their principle and root: it occupies, as its subject, the essence of the soul, *not its powers;* yet from it flow virtues into the powers of the soul by which the powers themselves are formed into actions."*

This is precisely Mr. Newman's idea; a "*Quodlibet* of the Schools," (as Bishop Andrew's says,") a *habitude* distinct from any *habit;* an *essence* in the soul distinct from any *quality* of the soul; righteousness distinct from the righteous affections of faith, hope, and charity. And this is the Romanism of the Schoolmen, which Hooker selects as the best expression of the very essence of all Romanism. And this too is Oxford Divinity—and this also is what the Council of Trent referred to as the source and model of theirs—the new divinity of the dark ages, engendered of Pagan

---

* Thom. Aquin. 1, 2. quæst. 110. Gratia faciens gratum id est justificans, est in anima quiddam reale et positivum, qualitas quædam (art. ii. concl.) supernaturalis, non eadem cum virtute infusa, ut magister; sed aliquid (art. ii.) præter virtutes infusas, fidem, spem, charitatem, habitudo quædam (art. ii. ad. 3.) quæ præ-supponitur in virtutibus istis, sicut earum principium et radix; essentiam animæ tanquam subjectum occupat, non potentias, sed ab ipsa (art iv. ad. 1.) effluunt virtutes in potentias animæ, per quas potentiæ moventur ad actus— Hooker's Disc. Justif. § 5.

It may be of use to remark that, in all editions of Hooker, which the author has seen, the above quotation is referred to quest. 100 of § ii.—first part of Aquinas It should be as above, viz. 110.

philosophy and Papal superstition, married together under the bans of the Schoolmen.

It is manifest from the above, that the question which the Trent doctors left unsettled, and therefore an open question, was one on which Aquinas differed from his Master, Peter Lombard; the latter making justifying righteousness precisely the same as Sanctification; the former attempting the distinction which Mr. Newman and Dr. Pusey would now use as evidence that their doctrine differs from that of Rome.

We are indebted to Mr. Keble, in his Appendix to Book v. of his learned edition of Hooker, for the following additional evidence, that Hooker considered that very distinction as a striking *characteristic* of the Romanism of the Schoolmen. Hooker writes as follows:

"The Schoolmen, which follow Thomas, do not only comprise in the name of grace, the favor of God, his Spirit, and effects of His Spirit; but over and besides these three, a *fourth kind of formal habit or inherent quality*, which maketh the person of man acceptable, perfecteth the substance of his mind, and causeth the virtuous actions thereof to be meritorious. This grace they will have, (as we shall see our Oxford divines will have,) to be the principal effect of *sacraments*; a grace which neither Christ nor any apostle of Christ did ever mention. The fathers have it not in their writings, although they often speak of *sacraments*, and of the grace we receive by them. Yea, they which have found it out, are as doubtful as any other, *what name or nature* they should give unto it."*

They could not have been more puzzled about its name and nature than their present successors seem to be, as we have already seen in the assertion, that it is the same as Sanctification; and then the flat denial that it is any such thing.

Such then is the doctrine at once of Oxford Divines, and of a race of theologians eminently distinguished in their day, for the preference of heathen dialectics to Holy Scripture; the words of Aristotle to the writings of the Christian Fathers; so that those who made the Bible their guide, were called in distinction from them, by a name rendered opprobrious by the general neglect of the Bible—*Biblicists*.

The question is forced upon us;—Since the age that was distinguished by the bringing in of this doctrine of inherent righteousness for Justification, was also so remarkable for the introduction of all the other chief corruptions of Romanism, such as the full

---

* Keble's Ed. of Hooker, vol. ii. p. 702.

doctrine of *image-worship*, as now established, that of *transuostantiation*, of *purgatory*, of *indulgences*, &c.; and since the very men who were foremost in the former, were also eminently distinguished as patrons of the latter, as Aquinas and Bonaventura, (the latter, the chief devotee of the Virgin Mary,) what are we to anticipate from the introduction of precisely the same doctrine of Justification among Protestants? Is its natural strength abated? Call it by a Protestant, or a Romish name, set it up at Oxford, or at Trent, is it not the same; the old righteousness of the Scribes and Pharisees, and as able as ever, to lead men to go about "establishing their own righteousness, not submitting themselves to the righteousness of God?" The light abroad may face it down; the barrier around, of better principles, may hedge it in. But can it live now in a Protestant land, without having, and exerting, and manifesting those same old tendencies, especially upon such as shall receive it at second or third hand, from its original propagators?—The present aspect of the Oxford system, so far as its practical developments have had room and time to appear, answer impressively, *No*. There is enough in what has been already exhibited, as will appear more fully by and by, to show that the strong tendency is now precisely as it was in the days of the Schoolmen; more restrained indeed by circumstances—more refined in its tastes, by higher intellectual culture; but strongly bent, as of old, upon the taking of its doctrine from man's wisdom, to the serious disparagement of the authority of Scripture; and to the introduction, though under better pretensions, and a more attractive type, of divers overt corruptions of Romanism. This tendency seems to be at present quite as strong and active, and is doing its work quite as fast, *considering the differences of age and circumstances*, as in the days of Aquinas.

We are very far from meaning that the leaders of this new school are conscious of all this tendency, or see *all* the way in which they are being led in the wilderness they have entered upon. We have no expectation that they will ever get to the full advocating of Image-worship, Purgatory, &c. We speak of the tendency of their *system*. It has weaker minds, and more unfixed hearts, and incautious heads, and reckless hands than theirs to work on. A generation of unfledged disciples is to swarm around the Master of the Sentences, and suck honey and poison out of his flowers, choosing which they please; unfolding principles which the Master left in bud; applying principles which the Master left in abstract; marching boldly and proudly, where he feared to tread but slowly and humbly; mounting upon his shoulders, and therefore reaching higher, and seeing further into reserved mysteries, than he. *They may see by his aid a need and a reason and a fitness in Image-worship, and Purgatory, &c., which he did not dream of.* What the Master would revolt at, the School may boast of. There is such a thing as *growing wiser than our Teachers*. "Transubstantiation (says Dr. Pusey) was at first connected with high and reverential feeling for our Lord, and no one could have anticipated beforehand that this one error would have had effects so tremendous." True—and this error of Justification may be connected with reverential feeling of no little depth; and yet who knows what desolating consequences may ensue therefrom? "Let us fear!"

As we have found a striking resemblance in this divinity to the mystic and subtle doctrine of Romanism in the 13th Century, it may not be out of place, before closing this chapter, to point out its resemblance to what is much supposed, we think without reason, to have been the opposite extreme to Romanism, viz., *the mysticism of the early Quakers.* Few things would seem, at first sight, more unnatural than to associate Mr. Newman and Thomas Aquinas with Robert Barclay and William Penn; but mysticism is a feature common to them all—the fog in which, unknowing and unknown, they all row one way, and meet at last at the very *Ostia Tiberina*, from which Barclay supposed he was so distant and Mr. Newman is so confident he has turned his back. Strange meetings often occur in a mist. Besides, there is no knowing in what company a man may find himself who goes much abroad. A disciple of Penn once went to Rome to convert the Pope. But the Pope converted the disciple of Penn. "*The light within,*" of the latter, was no *new* light to Romanism. In that great monastery, are many cells, furnishing accommodations for any sort of *idiosyncracy.* But to the likeness between Oxfordism and the Quakerism of Penn and Barclay.

"By this holy birth, *to wit,* Jesus Christ *formed within us,* (says Barclay) and working his work in us, as we are sanctified, *so are we justified in the sight of God.*" *

"By the light which they call the Spirit, the Grace, the Word of God, Christ within, the flesh and blood of Christ which came down from heaven, they do not mean 'the Essence and Nature of *God* precisely taken.' They make it a distinct and separate thing from man's soul and all its faculties." Mr. Barclay says, with Mr. Knox, 'we know it to be a substance;" with Mr. Newman, "by this seed,

* *Apol. prop.* 7. *p.* 364.

(the Christ within) we understand a spiritual, heavenly, and invisible principle, a real spiritual substance, in which God, as Father, Son and Spirit dwells." *

"Though the light within, is by them supposed to be the immediate efficient cause of Justification; yet they believe the sacrifice of our Saviour, through whose obedience and sufferings the Light is purchased, that thereby this birth, (by which we become regenerate, sanctified, justified, &c.) might be brought forth in us; I say, they believe the sacrifice of Christ to be (what we may call) the meritorious cause thereof." But, says Mr. Barclay, "not so as to exclude the real worth of the work and sufferings of Christ IN US." "They do therefore (says Bennet) attribute a real worth, 1, to the work of the Light shining in them, and bringing forth righteousness.—2, to the sufferings of Christ in them;—for he being united to such as resist not the Light, is said to suffer, when any evil is inflicted, on them.—3, to the Intercession of Christ, that is, to his intercession within them, by the Light's stirring, moving, and enabling them to pray unto God. For my Author (Barclay) distinguishes this intercession of the Saviour, from his intercession without us in heaven." †

The *cross set up within* was a favorite expression of the Quakers. To this, they ascribed the formal cause of Justification as well as of Sanctification. "It is by this inward birth of Christ in man (said Barclay) that man is made just, and therefore so accounted by God. Wherefore, to be plain, we are thereby, and not till that be brought forth in us, *formally* (if we must use that word) justified in the sight of God. Because Justification is both more properly and frequently in Scripture taken in its signification for *making one just*, and not reputing one merely such, and is all one with Sanctification." ‡

William Penn maintained, just as Romish and Oxford Divines, that the remission of sins, in the case of a sinner first turning to God, is only for the merits of Christ; but like them also he made the ground of *subsequent acceptance* to be *an inherent righteousness*, and like Oxford Divines he was charged with Popery for it, and he vindicates himself precisely as they do. "We would provide (he says) against the malice of those who rank us among the *Papists* as pleading for the merit of Good Works. For we lay not this *second* sort of Justification (precisely what is called *second* in Romanism) and much less the first, upon any exterior works—as merely exterior, be they acts of Justice, Mercy, Charity or such

---

* Bennet on Quakerism, pp. 111, 112, 113.
† Ib. pp. 125, 126.   ‡ Ib. p. 168.

like; but upon the holy working of God's power and Spirit in the heart, and the creature's believing it and resigning himself up unto God, to be by him renewed, ordered, &c. So our wills thus daily submitted to the holy will of God, which is Sanctification, is the ground of our daily acceptance with God, and being received (not as just by the non-imputation of sins formerly committed, for that alone depends on Repentance and Faith in God's free love to remit; but) as just by *being actually and really made so through the participation of the Just and Righteous Nature of Christ.*" *

The mysticism of the early Quakers, of the ancient Schoolmen, and of the present Schoolmen of Oxford, is the same thing, allowing for modifications arising out of varieties of learning, and of general circumstances.

* Penn's Quakerism a new nick-name for Old Christianity, 1672, pp. 152, 153.

CHAPTER V.

THE DOCTRINE OF THIS DIVINITY, AS TO THE RIGHTEOUSNESS OF JUSTIFICATION, COMPARED WITH THAT OF THE COUNCIL OF TRENT.

Recapitulation—Language of the Council of Trent—State of the Question at the Reformation, and now, from Chemnitz, Jackson, Hall, Usher, Hooker—Holiness required at least as much by Protestants as Romanists—Tractarian interpretation of single passages of Scripture, compared with those of Romish divines—Three particulars in which Oxford divines claim to be regarded as not conformed to Romanism—These considered, and shown, to make such conformity only the more obvious—The vindication drawn from the Romish claim of merit, answered—Hooker's argument against the Romish doctrine of merit shown to be applicable, in the same way, to this system—Concluding remarks.

BEFORE proceeding to an exhibition of the doctrine of the Church of Rome, as at present established, the reader is requested to bear in mind, that in making out the doctrine of our Oxford divines, the following prominent features were made to appear—viz:

1. That the righteousness by which we are justified before God, is exclusively internal and infused, a righteousness *within* us, inwrought, by the Holy Ghost.

2. That by the acknowledgment and strong assertion of Mr. Newman, this justifying righteousness is "*really one*" with *Inherent* righteousness, or *Sanctification,* so that the terms are convertible;—the distinction afterwards attempted, instead of showing any difference, only making the identity the more certain, by its purely imaginary character, and rendering the sameness of the whole doctrine with that of Romanism only the more certain.

3. That the regenerate can, and do, so fulfill the Law, that their indwelling righteousness has in it a satisfying and justifying quality, and does satisfy and justify them before God.

4. That this Justification is progressive, increasing and decreasing according to the degree of Sanctification.

We now proceed to show that such are precisely those characteristic features of *the present established doctrine of Rome*, against which the Reformation was directed, and which our ancient and standard writers considered, without question, as constituting the middle wall of partition, so far as Justification is concerned, between Protestants and Romanists.

For the present doctrine of Rome, the decisions of Trent must be considered as sure authority. The decrees of that Council, it is true, so far as they relate to *Discipline*, have not, in all countries, been implicitly obeyed by Romanists. In France, for instance, the Gallican Church has been opposed to the decrees on Discipline. But not so as to those relating to *Doctrine*, which are universally received by such as profess the Romish faith.*

From Session vi., Canons vii. and xvi., we make the following extracts.

"Justification is not merely the remission of sins, but also *Sanctification and renewal* of the inward man, by his voluntary reception of grace and gifts. Whence a man becomes righteous from unrighteous, a friend of God for an enemy, so as to be an heir according to the hope of eternal life."

After saying that the *meritorious* cause of Justification is Christ, the Council proceed to declare that

"The only *formal* cause is God's justice, not by which he himself is just, but by which he makes us just, wherewith being endowed by him, we are renewed in the spirit of our minds, and are not only reputed, but *are truly just*."

"Thus, neither our own proper righteousness is so determined to be our own, as if it were from ourselves; nor is the righteousness of God either unknown or rejected. For that which is called our righteousness, because, through its being inherent in us, we are justified; that same is the Righteousness of God, because it is infused into us by God, through the merit of Christ." ‡

* See Marsh's Comparative View of the churches of England and Rome, c. ii. § iv.

† Justificatio non est sola peccatorum remissio sed et Sanctificatio et Renovatio interioris hominis per voluntariam susceptionem gratiæ et donorum: unde homo ex injusto fit justus, et ex inimico amicus, ut sit hæres secundum spem vitæ æternæ.

‡ Unica formalis causa est justitia Dei, non qua ipse justus est, sed qua nos justos facit, qua videlicet ab eo donati, renovamur spiritumentis nostri, et non modo reputamur, sed vere justi nominamur, et sumus, justitiam in nobis recipientes.

Ita, neque propria nostra justitia, tanquam ex nobis, propria statuitur; neque ignoratur aut repudiatur justitia Dei. Quæ enim justitia nostra dicitur, quia per eam nobis inhærentem justificamur: illa eadem Dei est, quia a Deo nobis infunditur per Christi meritum.

Now what was the interpretation which the Reformers, soon after the issuing of these decrees, put upon them? Chemnitz, a Lutheran divine, who lived in the time of the Council, and wrote a refutation of its doctrines, which all Protestants, as well in the Church of England, as on the Continent, regarded as of eminent value, and whom Bellarmine treats as high authority on the Protestant side, thus states the great question between Protestants and Romanists, and how the Council answered it. "What is that which we are to interpose between the anger of God and our sins, so that on account thereof we may be absolved from condemnation, and received to everlasting life. The decrees of Trent respond in two ways. 1, They deny that Justification is merely the Remission of Sins; and they anathematize any that shall say that a man is justified by the imputation of Christ's righteousness only, or only by the remission of sins, or by the mere favor of God. 2, They affirm that Justification before God, to eternal life, is not remission of sins alone, but the *sanctification of the inner man;* and affirm that *the only formal cause* of Justification, is that righteousness given to us, of God, by *which we are renewed in the spirit of our mind*, and are not only *reputed*, but *are made truly* righteous; this righteousness in us, they say is charity, inherent in us, which, by the Holy Spirit, is wrought in us, through the merit of the passion of Christ."*

Dr. Jackson, an eminent divine of Oxford, in the seventeenth century, states the issue as follows, viz: "The point then in which, with him, (the Romanist) we must join issue is; What should be the true, immediate, and next cause of this final absolution from the sentence of death? AUGHT WITHIN US, OR SOMEWHAT WITHOUT US? We deny, and he affirms, righteousness inherent to be such an absolute cause of absolution or remission of sins, of *Justification, howsoever taken.* Christ's righteousness they grant to be the *efficient or meritorious* cause *for* which, not the *formal* cause *by* which our sins are remitted, or we are justified. He alone is *formally* just, which hath that form inherent in himself, by which he is denominated just, and so accepted with God; as Philosophers deny the sun to be formally hot, because it hath no form of heat inherent in it, but only produceth heat in other bodies. To be formally just, we, for these reasons, attribute *only unto Christ*, who alone hath such righteousness in himself, as by the interposition of it

---

* Chemnitz's Examen. Dec. Conc. Trid. p. 144. Bishop Hall speaks of him "our learned Chemnitius."

between God's Justice and sinful flesh, doth stop the proceedings of his Judgment."*

How the judicious Hooker delineates what he calls that grand question which hangeth yet in controversy between us and the Church of Rome, the reader is requested to review in our first Chapter.

Bishop Hall describes the difference between us and Rome, as follows:

"What can be more contrary than these opinions to each other. The Papists make this inherent righteousness the *cause* of our Justification: the Protestants, the effect thereof. The Protestants require it as the companion or page: the Papists, as the usher, yea, rather as the parent of Justification." †

"The question, (says Usher,) between us and them is, whether there be any Justification besides Sanctification; that is, whether there be any Justification at all? We say Sanctification is wrought by the Kingly office of Christ. He is a King who rules in our hearts, subdues our corruptions, by the scepter of his word and Spirit; but it is the point of his Priestly Office, which the Church of Rome strikes at; that is, whether Christ hath reserved another righteousness for us, besides that which as a King, he works in our hearts; whether he hath wrought forgiveness of sins for us? We say he hath, and so said all the Church, till the spawn of the Jesuits arose." ‡

From the high authority of the Authors we have now cited, it is unquestionable that, whatever other points may be connected subordinately with the controversy between the Church of Rome, and the Reformed Church of England, as to Justification,—the main question, and that, therefore, with reference to which our Article of Justification and its explicating Homilies were framed, was simply whether we are justified before God, by a righteousness *external* and *made ours only by imputation*, or by a righteousness *in us*, and ours because *in us*; by *infusion*, and not by *imputation*. The Reformed Church of England, like all other Reformed Churches, stood fast upon the former ground, maintaining, as Hooker says, that the Church of Rome, "in teaching Justification by inherent Grace, *doth pervert the truth of Christ.*"

"The righteousness of Sanctification, we deny not to be inherent, only we distinguish it as a thing different *in nature*, from the

* Jackson's Works, vol. i. pp. 754, 755.
† Hall's Works, vol. ix. p. 46. ‡ Usher's Sermons, No. xvi

righteousness of Justification." "That whereby we are justified, is perfect, but not inherent. That whereby we are sanctified, is inherent but not perfect."*

Between Romanists and us, there is no difference as to the *necessity of Holiness*, for the kingdom of heaven. We preach Sanctification at least as much as they, a more real sanctification, and upon a much higher and more effective ground. But the *relation* of that holiness to the justification of the sinner, is the precise point of disagreement, the hinge of the whole controversy. By the standards of our Church, it is made to *follow after* Justification, as its fruits, and as evidences of a Justifying Faith. By the Church of Rome, It is *Justification itself;* or at least the *ground of* it.

In the last chapter of the decrees of the Sixth session of Trent, we read as follows:

"Since Jesus Christ himself as the head into the members, and as the vine into the branches, perpetually causes his virtue to flow into the justified; which virtue always precedes and accompanies and follows their good works, and without which they would in no wise be acceptable to God and meritorious; we must believe, that nothing more is wanting to the justified themselves by which they may consider themselves to have satisfied *the divine law*, according to the state of this life, by those works which are performed in God; and in their own time *truly to merit the attainment of eternal life* provided they depart in grace."†

Where is the difference between this doctrine, and that shown in the last chapter as pertaining to the system under review, from Mr. Newman?

Does this divinity neutralize the distinction of two kinds of righteousness, and confound Justification and Sanctification? So does Romanism. The following, from Bishop Downame, of the 17th Century, shows how this feature of Popery was regarded in his day.

* Disc. of Justif. § 6 and 3.
† Cum ille ipse Christus Jesus, tanquam caput in membra, et tanquam vitis in palmites, in ipsos justificatos. jugiter virtutem influat ; quæ virtus bona eorum opera semper antecedit et comitatur et subsequitur, et sine qua nullo pacto Deo grata et meritoria esse possent ; nihil ipsis justificatis amplius deesse credendum est. quo minus plene illis quidem operibus, quæ in Deo sunt facta, divinæ legi pro hujus vitæ statu satisfecisse, et vitam eternam suo etiam tempore, si tamen in gratia decesserint, consequendam, vere promeruisse censeantur.

"The first capital error of the Papists is, that they confound Justification and Sanctification, and by confounding of them, and of two benefits making but one, they utterly abolish the benefit of Justification; which notwithstanding is the principle benefit which we have by Christ in this life, by which we are freed from hell, and entitled to the kingdom of heaven. And this they do in two respects: first, they hold, that to justify in this question signifieth to make righteous by righteousness inherent, or by infusion of righteousness, that is, to sanctify. Secondly, they make remission of sin, to be not the pardoning and forgiving of sin, but the utter deletion or expulsion of sin by infusion of righteousness. Thus they make Justification wholly to consist in the parts of Sanctification."*

Do these writers declare that the regenerate or baptized can, and do fulfill the law; that their obedience has a justifying and sanctifying quality or virtue; that divine love, in the Christian, is imputed to him for righteousness?† The Council of Trent declares that the justified, that is, the baptized, "can satisfy the divine law, according to the state of this life, by those works which are performed in God." Cardinal Bellarmine, in defending this doctrine of the Council, contends that "they that are able to love God and their neighbor, are also able to fulfill the law; that notwithstanding our charity in this life is imperfect, because it may be increased, yet that it is so perfect as may suffice for the fulfillment of the Law."

The following comparison between the Papists and Pelagians, by Bishop Downame, as to the keeping of the Law, will show, not only the Romish doctrine on this head, but also in what light it was regarded by the great divines of the English Church before the middle of the 17th Century.

"The difference between the Pelagians and Papists is not in respect of possibility or impossibility, but in respect of greater or less difficulty. For the Papists do not acknowledge that men by nature are dead in sin, and utterly deprived of the spiritual life: but that they are fickle and weak, and tied with the bands of sin, so that they cannot fulfill the Law of God, unless they be holpen and loosed by grace; but being holpen by grace, then the fulfilling of the Commandments is easy to them. The Pelagians likewise confess, that by the Grace of God, which they call *bonum naturæ*, or the power or possibility of nature, they were enabled; by the grace of God vouchsafed in his word and law, guided and

---

* Downame on Justif. p. 50. † Newman's Lectures, pp. 34, 39, 101

directed; by the justifying grace of God freed from the bond of their sins; and by the sanctifying grace of God holpen with more ease to fulfill the Commandments of God.

"So that the Papists, although they do not with the Pelagians deny original sin, or the necessity of saving grace: yet they do extenuate the original corruption, and so magnify the strength of nature, that they differ not much from them.

"And as touching the other difference; though the Papists hold that a man cannot be without sin for any long time, though for some short time, (in which short time, if he shall say he hath no sin, he shall make St. John, and not himself, a liar, 1 John i. 8.) yet they say they may be without all sins excepting those which they call venial; which they do so extenuate, that indeed they make them no sins, as being no *anomies* or transgressions of the Law, committed against the Law, or repugnant to charity, but only besides the Law; such as may well stand together with perfect, inherent righteousness. For they say he only is a righteous man in whom there is no sin, and yet that there is no man so righteous, as that he liveth without these venial ones. But if they be besides and contrary to the Law, then they are neither commanded nor forbidden, and so no sins at all but things indifferent."*

On the subject of the increase and decrease of Justification, according to the degree of Sanctification, the Council of Trent pronounces thus:

"If any one shall say that Justification once obtained, is not increased by good works, but that these are only the fruits and signs of Justification, let him be accursed."—c. xxiv. sess. vi.

But Hooker's statement of this point of Romanism will answer best.

"The grace of Justification (he says) they make capable of increase; that as the body may be made more and more warm, so the soul, more and more justified, according as grace should be augmented; the augmentation whereof is merited by good works, as good works are made meritorious by it. Wherefore the first receipt of grace, in their divinity, is the first justification; the increase thereof the second justification. As grace may be increased by the merit of good works; so it may be diminished by the demerit of sins venial; it may be lost by mortal sin. If they work more and more, grace doth more and more increase, and they

* Downame on Justification, pp. 503, 504.

are more and more justified." This is one of the characteristic features of what Hooker calls *"the maze* which the Church of Rome doth cause her followers to tread, when they ask her the way to Justification."

The reader may compare for himself the Oxford Doctrine as stated in our second chapter.

We now give a specimen or two of Mr. Newman's interpretation of Scripture, in comparison with the Romish.

"By the deeds of the Law there shall no flesh be justified in his sight, for by the law is the knowledge of sin." That is, says Mr. N., "by a conformity to the *external* law," not an internal, shall none be justified.

"But now the righteousness of God without the law is manifested— even the righteousness of God, which is by faith of Jesus Christ unto all and upon all them that believe." "That is, (says Mr. N.) the *new righteousness* introduced and wrought upon the heart by the ministration of the Spirit," *new* as distinguished from that of the unconverted heart.

Again: "By grace ye are saved through faith, and that not of yourselves, it is the gift of God,—not of works, lest any man should boast." "'Not of works,' means, not, of *all* your works, but only works done in *your own unaided strength, in conformity to the natural law.* Here the difference is marked between the works of the Spirit, which are good," (for justification,) "and those of the Law, which are worthless." *

Again: "That I may win Christ and be found in him, not having mine own righteousness, which is of the law, but that which is through the faith of Christ, the righteousness which is of God by faith." † It is maintained by Mr. Newman that the righteousness of the Law, which Paul renounced, is the righteousness or obedience "done in his own strength before faith, and without grace;" and the righteousness which he desired to have in its place was "a new righteousness, consisting in obedience and in faith, and by the grace of Christ," p. 128. "If legal righteousness is of a *moral* nature, (he asks,) why should not the righteousness of faith be moral also?" ‡

It will be shown, that all this is directly the reverse and in entire denial of the interpretation, most confidently and solemnly put upon these and the like passages, by such standard writers of our Church as Hall, Beveridge, Usher, Reynolds, Andrews, Hooker, &c.

---

* Rom. iii. 20., iii. 21, 22. Eph. ii. 8—10. † Phil. iii. 8, 9.
‡ Lectures, pp. 54, and 55.

But the present point is here, viz., that while in entire departure from the doctrine of those great divines,—they are also identical with the interpretation of leading Romanists.

Chemnitz sums up the interpretation given by Andrada, a distinguished member and defender of the Council of Trent, as follows:

"Andrada contends that both kinds of righteousness spoken of by St. Paul,—the righteousness of the law and of faith,—consist in our obedience to the law, and that they differ not in office, but only in the manner of their office; so that when one is rendered by the unregenerate, then it is the righteousness of the law; but the righteousness of faith consists in this, that it leads the regenerate to the obedience of those things which are written in the law—so that the righteousness is the obedience itself, of the regenerate to the law; when love, which embraces the whole law, is poured into those who believe by the Holy Ghost." *

Now, after all this marvellous conformity of this divinity, to that of Rome, the reader is doubtless ready to enquire with amazement, what defense do its teachers set up? Dr. Pusey publishes a work purposely in answer to the charge of a *"Tendency to Romanism;"* he draws his answer, in a great degree, from Mr. Newman. What is the defense?

After searching again and again, the writer can discover nothing but the three following allegations.

1. That Romanists make the infused and indwelling righteousness by which we are justified, a *quality or habit of the mind*, and thus the same as Sanctification; while in this divinity, it is not a quality, but that which includes in it all the qualities and virtues of holiness; a righteousness "*within* us, but not *of* us or *in* us," "a divine gift," "a principle," but not a quality of our minds.

But it has been abundantly showed, that these writers do positively assert, though not without afterwards contradicting themselves, that justifying righteousness is a *quality* of the mind and *identical with sanctification;* that when it attempts a distinction, a mere scholastic figment is adopted, which, as it is precisely the same as that invented by the Schoolmen, to whom the Council of Trent resorted for its doctrine, only shows more perfectly the identity between Romanism, and the divinity in question; and again, that whether the distinction be good or bad, it is just as admissible in one as the other; the Council of Trent having, by

* Chemnitz Examen. Doc. Conc. Tred. p. 148.

Mr. Newman's own showing, forborne to decide the point, and therefore it is not *de fide* in the Church of Rome.

So much for one of the three lines of demarcation.

2. Another is found in this, that in one of the Canons of Trent, it is declared, that "Inherent righteousness is the only *formal cause of Justification*"—*Unica Formalis causa Justificationis*.* This we are told is a doctrine of "high" Romanism, from which this divinity dissents. Mr. Newman maintains *two* formal causes, *proper* and *improper*. "The *proper* formal cause, *with the Romanists*, I would consider, (he says) as *an inward gift*, yet with the Protestants, *not a quality of the mind.*" †

But what is the other formal cause; The *Improper?* The difference of this latter, from the former is thus expressed:—"We are made absolutely acceptable to God through the propitiatory indwelling of His Son," "yet are not without the beginnings of *inherent acceptableness wrought in us by that indwelling.*" ‡ The indwelling of Christ, elsewhere called the justifying "principle" and "gift," is here the *proper formal* cause; the "acceptableness" or holiness wrought in us by that divine gift, is the *improper formal* cause; both uniting in the completion of our Justification?

Now where is the difference between these two? Nothing more than the shadowy figment by which, as we have before seen, these divines, like the Schoolmen of old, try to distinguish between an indwelling divine gift of righteousness, and Sanctification. As we cannot admit the distinction, we must deny that these two formal causes are else than one and the same; and must maintain their doctrine and *the unica formalis causa* of Trent, to be one and the same.§

---

* That is called a *formal* cause of Justification, in Romish Divinity, which contains that, in itself, which causes the person to be denominated just or righteous. "He alone is *formally* just which hath that inherent in himself, by which he is denominated just, and so accepted of God; as Philosophers deny the sun to be *formally* hot, because it hath no form of heat inherent in it, but only produceth heat in other bodies."—Jackson's Works, vol. i. p. 755.

† Lect. p. 426. Here again it is indicated, that the Romanists differ from the Protestants in that they do not make it a quality, whereas by his own showing they have left the point unsettled so that should they agree with the Protestants, they would not contradict any article of *faith*.

‡ Lectures, p. 428.

§ The decree of Trent says: "The only formal cause (of Justification) is the righteousness of God; not that by which he himself is righteous, but that by which he makes us righteous; that is to say, by which we being endowed by him, are renewed in the spirit of our mind, and are not only *reputed* righteous, but are truly righteous." The Council proceeds: Quanquam nemo possit esse justus nisi cui merita passionis Jesu Christi communicanter, id tamen in hac justificatione

But strange! While maintaining that Romanism is distinguished by the doctrine that inherent righteousness is the ONLY formal cause, he expressly refers to Romanists as admitting *two*, precisely as he does. "It would seem, (he writes) as if there were two formal causes of justification admitted by Romanists, *love or inherent righteousness,* and *grace* or *the presence of the Holy Spirit's indwelling.*" *

We conclude then that here, as elsewhere, there is no difference at all between the Oxford doctrine, and that of Rome. The attempted distinction between two formal causes is just as admissible on one side as the other, and is a mere scholastic figment at any rate. Let us hear, then, Dr. Jackson, whom we like to quote on such matters, because of his high name at Oxford.† His words are quite as applicable to one party as the other.

"Our adversaries in that they acknowledge inherent righteousness to be *the sole formal cause* of Justification, do, by the same assertion, necessarily grant it to be the true immediate cause of remission of sins, of absolution from death, and admission to life. *This is the only point from which they cannot start;* at which, nevertheless, while they stand, they may acknowledge Christ born in flesh, crucified, dead and buried, or perhaps ascended into heaven, but deny, they do, the power of his sitting at the right hand of God, the virtue of his mediation or intercession, and more than half evacuate the eternity of his Priesthood." ‡

---

impii fit dum, ejusdem sanctissimæ passionis merito, per Spiritum Sanctum, charitas Dei diffunditur in cordibus eorum, qui justificantur. "Since none can be justified but those to whom the merits of the passion of Christ are communicated, yet that communication takes place in this justification of the ungodly, when, by the merit of that most holy passion, the love of God is shed abroad by the Holy Ghost, in the hearts of the justified:"—Concil. Trident, Sess. vi. c. vii.

In these expressions is contained the whole of Mr. Newman's *formal causation.* Whether he be the more accurate in making *two* formal causes, or the Council in making both *one,* the learned in disputes of words, may determine.

* "Nor does Vasques take any objection to thus viewing the subject; on the contrary he says, 'Neque enim incommodum aliquod est, constituere *duas* formas per quas homo justificari possit apud Deum, nempe duos habitus.'" Lectures, p. 399.

† We have before quoted this truly learned divine—an Oxford man, of great eminence in his day—but that day was the day of the giants in the controversy with Rome. Usher, Hall, Andrews, &c., were his cotemporaries. It was said (by the British Critic,) that his works rose wonderfully in the Oxford market after the new divinity began, showing that his authority is acknowledged *by that side* **to** be of great weight. We shall find use for him hereafter.

‡ Jackson's Works, vol. i. pp. 755, 756.

The reader is requested to compare the last sentence with the extract from Usher, near the beginning of this chapter.

3. The last of the three particulars, in which the advocates of this system attempt to show a difference between their doctrine and that of Rome, is in the matter of *imputation*, as follows:

"In this I conceive to lie the unity of Catholic doctrine, that we are saved by Christ's imputed righteousness, and by our own inchoate righteousness at once." But more at large as follows. "Our divines, though of very different schools, have, with a few exceptions, agreed in this, that justification is gained by obedience in the shape of faith; that is, an obedience which confesses it is not sufficient, and trusts solely in Christ's merits, for acceptance; which is in other words the doctrine of two righteousnesses, a perfect and imperfect; *not the Roman*, that obedience justifies without a continual imputation of Christ's merits: nor the Protestant, that imputation justifies distinct from obedience; but a middle way, that obedience justifies *in*, or *under* Christ's covenant, or sprinkled with Christ's meritorious sacrifice."*

At first sight, there is here an appearance of something like the Gospel. Here are "*two* righteousness," whereas Mr. Newman has before expressly said, that such a distinction is unscriptural. But, on examination, it will appear that a change of *language* is the only difference from all that has gone before, and that still the doctrine is in no sense distinct from that of Rome.

We have before shown, that because these writers can manage to screw the word *imputed* into their system, we are not to suppose that it means, in their use, any thing like what it stands for in common Anglican divinity. It would have been too great a leap to have arrived, all at once, at a doctrine so glaringly unscriptural, that a word which St. Paul employs so often in the fourth Chapter of Romans, (*eleven* times, in its several forms of *impute, account,* and *reckon*) could not, by any possibility, find room therein. To save appearances it must be got in somehow or other.

But in what sense do these writers now speak of *two righteousnesses* and one *imputed*? Hooker, in the common use of words, says, "There be two kinds of Christian righteousness; the one *without us,* which we have by *imputation;* the other *within us,* which consisteth of Faith, Hope, and Charity, and other Christian virtues."

But that righteousness "without us," which is here said to be by *imputation* for the very purpose of distinguishing it from that

* Newman's Lectures, pp. 414, 420.

which is *indwelling* and *inwrought*, is precisely what this system stigmatizes "*as a mere abstract title of righteousness*," a mere name—"the gift of the Law," in distinction from the Grace and truth which came by Jesus Christ."

"When divines who seem to be pillars, come to me with their visionary system, an unreal righteousness, and a real corruption, I answer, that the law is past, and that I will not be brought into bondage by shadows. Reputed Justification was the gift of the law; but grace and truth came by Jesus Christ. Away then with this modern, this private, this arbitrary, this tyrannical system, which promising liberty, conspires against it, and for the real participation of Christ, and justification through his Spirit, would at the very marriage feast feed us on shells and husks. It is a *new Gospel*. * * * It is surely too bold an attempt to take from our hearts the power, the fulness, the mysterious presence of Christ's most holy death and resurrection, and to soothe us for our loss with the name of having it." *

Of course then we must so far obey this peremptory injunction, that though we may not be quite willing to "*away*' with the "two kinds of righteousness," which such authorities as Hooker find, we must at least away with the idea that, in this divinity, the expression, "*two righteousnesses, perfect and imperfect,*" participates in the least of a righteousness "*without* us, which we have by imputation," or really means any other than that one righteousness "which consisteth of Faith, Hope, Charity,"—and is wrought in us by the Spirit, through the merits of the Passion of Christ. We cannot forget that it has been elsewhere said in this divinity that "*Imputed righteousness is the coming in of actual righteousness,*" actual, or personal, as distinguished from external. And further that "Christ is our righteousness, *by dwelling in us by the Spirit.*" The sanctifying indwelling of the Spirit is therefore all that is meant by "the imputed righteousness of Christ," in the speech of these divines. Then since the phrases "*righteousness of Christ,*" "*merits of Christ,*" "*meritorious sacrifice of Christ,*" have all the same use, it follows that when in the extract above given, Mr. Newman seems, after all that has gone before, of such exceedingly diverse aspect, to speak at length a little like the Gospel, of our being justified by "obedience which trusts only *in Christ's merits* for acceptance," in "the *sprinkling of Christ's meritorious*

---

* Newman's Lectures, pp. 61, 62.

sacrifice," we are to understand only a trust in the indwelling of the Spirit, or that righteousness of Sanctification, which the Spirit works in us, for Christ's sake; and thus the cross which we are referred to for merit is that of our own obedience, is "the cross *within*"—"the mysterious presence of Christ's death and resurrection;" and so Mr. Newman is, after all, no better than he was before, when he said that "the cross in which St. Paul gloried," (and of course, "the sprinkling" we are to trust in,) "was not the actual *sacrifice* on the cross, but that sacrifice coming in power to him who has faith in it, *and converting body and soul into a sacrifice—* the cross realized, present, living in him, sealing him, separating him from the world, *sanctifying, afflicting* him." *

We have now reached the precise meaning of the declaration "that we are saved by *Christ's imputed righteousness, and by our own inchoate righteousness at once.*" It is simply the doctrine of the *two formal causes* of Justification, of which we have already spoken, the proper and the improper—the former consisting of "the indwelling of the Spirit," or Christ's "propitiatory indwelling;" the latter of our own sanctification; of which two, we learn moreover from Mr. Newman that both are "*admitted by Romanists.*" † So that after all this work about *imputed Righteousness*, as if at last our Oxford gentlemen were getting back to something like the Gospel and Protestantism, the whole distinction between what they call by that name, and our own righteousness with which they associate it, is that old Scholastic *Quodlibet* of Thomas Aquinas, the distinction between "that divine *gift*," or "*principle*" of indwelling righteousness which is *within* us, but not *in* us, or *of* us; which includes all holy virtues, but is not any, or all of them, and on the other hand that "*quality*" of holiness which is *in* us as well as *within* us, and which Mr. Newman says elsewhere, is nevertheless "*substantially the same as the other.*"

But this distinction, instead of being a dissent from Romanism, is of Romish origin. Mr. N. himself assures us that it was a subject of debate in the Council of Trent, and was left undecided, and is therefore perfectly consistent with its established creed. Here then is the whole result. The imputed righteousness of Christ, in this Divinity, is nothing else than our own Sanctification, com-

---

* Newman's Lectures, p. 206.

† Lectures, 399. Bishop Hall also shows this. "Who can abide, (he says,) that noted speech of Bellarmine, 'A just man hath by a double title, right to the same glory: one by the merits of Christ, imparted to him by grace, another by his own merits.'" Hall's "No Peace with Rome." Works, ix. p. 51.

municated by the Spirit, for Christ's sake; to be saved by that and our own inchoate righteousness at once, means simply to be saved by our own inceptive holiness, wrought in us in virtue of the death of Christ. So much for the only three particulars in which these divines profess to distinguish between their doctrine and that of Rome, viz. 1. That Romanists make the indwelling righteousness of Justification *a quality of the mind*, and they do not. 2. That Romanism admits but "*one formal cause of Justification*, (inherent righteousness,) while they have *two*. 3. That Romanism teaches we are justified by obedience, without the continual imputation of Christ's merits, while they teach that we are justified by both at once.

But these three, though treated separately, really amount to but one, as they all unite in the merits of the first, and must stand or fall with the validity of the distinction attempted therein.

The reader is now prepared to set the true value upon the declaration of Dr. Pusey, that what *he conceives* to be the true Anglican doctrine differs "from the Roman, in that it *excludes Sanctification from having any place in our Justification*." * Mr. Newman knows better, and grants it to be one of the "two *formal* causes." The Romanists know best of all, and interpret the Justification of this system as an entire return to theirs.

As to the use of the word *impute*, in the sense of these writers, there never has been any objection among Romanists.

The anathema of Trent is not against those who hold Justification by imputed righteousness *in part*, or *in any sense;* but precisely according to the *procul este profani* of Mr. Newman; it is against those who hold "that we are justified by the *mere* imputation of Christ's righteousness *to the exclusion of grace and charity*, which by the Holy Spirit is shed abroad in our hearts"—in other words, to the exclusion of "inchoate righteousness." †

The merits of Christ come into the Romish doctrine quite as much as into the Tractarian. "They teach as we do, (says Hooker) that unto Justice (righteousness) no man ever attained, but by the merits of Jesus Christ. They teach as we do that although Christ, as God, be the *efficient*, *as man* he is the *meritorious* cause of our Justice, and without the *application* of the merit of Christ, there can

---

* Letter, to Bp. of Oxford. p. 46.

† Si quis dixerit hominem justificari, vel sola imputatione justitiæ Christi, vel sola peccatorum remissione, exclusa gratia et charitate, quæ in cordibus eorum per Spiritum Sanctum diffunditur—anathema sit.—*Sess.* vi. c. **xi**.

be no Justification."* Now this is quite as strong, as to the merits of Christ, as any thing in this divinity. The Romanist cannot deny, (says Chemnitz) that Paul often uses the word *impute* in reference to Justification; but Andrada maintains that the *imputation of Christ's righteousness* signifies nothing more than the infusion of inherent righteousness into the regenerate for Christ's sake. As if to impute *iniquity* were, in St. Paul's sense, to *infuse iniquity* into any one.†

* Hooker on Justification, § 4.
† Chemnitz Examen. Dec. Trid. p. 149.

This put Chemnitz in mind that during the Osiandrian controversy, he had heard, not without laughter, of some who philosophized on the word *putare*, and its compounds, as *verbum hortense*, a word pertaining to *horticulture;* so that, as *amputare* signifies to *take away* something, so *imputare* must signify to *insert, implant, pour in* new qualities into a man. And this *wisdom*, he says, viz., "that imputation signifies only to infuse righteousness, was introduced in the Council of Trent." (p. 149.) Father Paul gives us some of the debate on this subject. Vega, a leader, maintained "that it is a most proper Latin word to say that *the righteousness of Christ is imputed for satisfaction and merit*, and that it is *continually* imputed to *all that be justified*, and do *satisfy for their own sins;* but he would not have it said that it was imputed *as if it were* ours." This is better doctrine than that of Oxford. The Eremite General held "that in Baptism the justice of Christ is imputed, because it is communicated wholly and entirely, *but not in penance, when our satisfactions are also required*." But Soto, who thoroughly held to the *effective* sense of Justification, said "the word *Imputation* was most popular and plausible, because it signified, at the first sight, that all should be acknowledged from Christ, but yet that he did ever suspect it, in regard of the bad consequences which the Lutherans did draw from thence"—that is, that this only is sufficient (for Justification) without inherent righteousness; "that the punishment is abolished, together with the guilt; that there remaineth no place for satisfaction. This admonition begat such a suspicion in the hearers, that there appeared a manifest disposition to condemn the word for heretical, *though reasons were effectually applied to the contrary*."—Paul's Hist. Conc. Trent, pp. 199, 200.

Much was said against the Lutherans, who grounded their doctrine of Imputation upon the Hebrew *Tsadak* and the Greek δικαιουϛθαι signifying to be *pronounced*, not *made* just. This leads us to some amusing features of the debate on the Scriptures, in which great care was taken against being troubled with the interpreting of the Bible in its original tongues.

Soon after the opening, "there was much difference about the Latin Translation, between some few who had good knowledge of Latin, and some taste of Greek, and others who were ignorant in the tongues." Friar Aloisius urged much, on the authority of Cajetan, a reference to the Hebrew and Greek Texts, the latter having said that "to understand the Latin Text was not to understand the infallible word of God," and that if "the Doctors of the former age had gone to the original texts, the Lutheran heresy never would have found place." But "the major part of the divines (knowing better where their strength lay,) said, it was necessary to account that Translation which formerly had been read in the Churches, and used in the Schools, divine and authentical; otherwise they should yield the cause to the Lutherans—that the doctrine of the Church of Rome is in a great part founded by the Popes and by *School Divines*, upon some passage of the

A vindication of this divinity may be attempted on the ground that whereas it is a prominent feature of Romanism, that it positively attributes a degree of merit to the good works of the Justified, so that by them they truly deserve an increase of grace, and eternal life; the Oxford divines, on the contrary, expressly ascribe all merit in Justification to the Cross and Passion of Christ.

To those who are familiar with the position of the doctrine of merits, in the decrees of Trent, it is needless to answer this plea. But for others, a little may not be uselessly given it.

Now it is true that in the decrees of Trent, we find this most appalling language:

"If any man shall say that the good works of a Justified Person are the gifts of God, in such a manner that they are not also the Justified person's merits; or that the Justified person does not truly deserve increase of grace, eternal life, and (upon condition that he die in the grace of God,) the obtaining of eternal life, and also an increase of grace, by those good works which he does by the grace of God, and the merit of Jesus Christ, of whom he is a living member,—let him be accursed." *

It is true also that Dr. Pusey interprets the Article of the Church of England on Justification, as putting "in strong contrast the merits of Christ and the merits of man," and as saying, "that we are justified solely for the sake of his merit, and not for our own works or deservings." "The Article opposes, the merit of Christ, to any thing which we have of our own, to our own works and deservings, as the MERITORIOUS cause of our salvation." "It is so plain a truth, (he says,) and has been so often inculcated by us, that every sin of man which is remitted, is remitted only for the sake of His meritorious Cross and Passion, every good and acceptable

---

Scripture, which if every one had liberty to examine whether it were well translated, running to other translations, or seeking how it was in the Greek or Hebrew, these new Grammarians would confound all, and instead of Divines and Canonists, Pedants should be preferred to Bishops and Cardinals. The Inquisitors would not be able to proceed against the Lutherans, in case they knew not Greek and Hebrew." To this, some, as Isidorus Clarus, a Benedictine Abbot, were directly opposed. Vega proposed middle ground—but Richard of Mans, a Franciscan, said that "the doctrines of faith were now so cleared, (viz., by Popes and Schoolmen) that we ought no more to learn them out of Scripture; that the studying of the Scripture should be prohibited to every one that is not *first confirmed in School divinity; neither do the Lutherans gain upon any but those that study the Scripture.*"— Paul's Hist. pp. 155—159.

* Concil. Trident, Sess. vii. c. 32.

work is such through his power working in us, that little, I believe has thus far been objected." *

To a superficial reader, it may seem that between these words and those of the Council of Trent, there is a vast discrepancy. But in sober truth, there is not the least disagreement. They refer to different matters entirely. Dr. Pusey speaks of merit for the obtaining of that *Justification* whereby an *ungodly* man becomes a *righteous* man in God's sight,—what the Romanists call the *first* Justification. But the words cited from the decrees of Trent, as do all pretenses of merit in the Romish Justification, refer only to "*the increase of that grace*," the progression of that Justified state, or what Romanists call the *second* Justification.† When the Church of Rome speaks of that Justification, on which we are writing, and of which Dr. Pusey wrote, the only one indeed of which the Scriptures speak, namely, when a sinner, hitherto abiding under condemnation, *repents and turns to God, and seeks remission of sin, and peace through Jesus Christ*, the claim of merit is scrupulously avoided, and the language of Dr. Pusey is fully paralleled, if not word for word employed.

The doctrine of this divinity and that of Rome, as to what Justification consists in, being precisely the same, it is quite as much the declaration of the Council of Trent, as of the school of Oxford, that whether the infusion of righteousness, by Baptism, be in the case of infants, or of "wicked men," it is in either case "*without works.*' ‡ We are then said to be justified *freely*, in the sense of Trent, "*because nothing which precedes justification, whether faith or works, deserves the grace of Justification.*" § Does Dr. Pusey ascribe the "*meritorious* cause" only to Christ? So does Rome precisely in the same words. "This first Justification, they say, is by faith, the obedience and satisfaction of Christ being *the only meritorious cause thereof.*" The Council *warily avoided the name of merit*, with respect unto the first justification." ∥ How could we

---

* Letter, p. 41.

† They call that the *First* Justification, when a man, not before regenerate, first receives the infusion of inherent righteousness. And this infusion of grace, they say, is what no works going before deserve, as a due reward, *tanquam, debitam mercedem*. They call that the *Second* Justification, when infused grace exercises its proper operations, bringing forth good works. And this, they say, is obtained and deserved by good works, but still through the merits of Christ.

‡ Hooker's Discourse of Justification, § 5.

§ Quia Nihil eorum quæ justificationem præcedent, sive fides, sive opera, ipsam justificationis gratiam promeretur. Sess. vi. c. 7.

∥ Owen on Justification, c. v. pp. 170, 171

expect any thing else? The *substance* of doctrine, may involve a glaring departure from the Scriptural way of justification by the righteousness of Christ; but it would be to charge men professing to teach the Gospel, not only with tremendous heresy, but singular futuity, to suppose them capable of maintaining in *words*, yea of not denying in *words*, that when an ungodly man, yesterday at enmity with God, repents to-day and is baptized and justified, his justification is by any merit of his own. There are no passages in these Oxford writings in assertion of salvation only through Christ's merits, stronger than those which Hooker has given to the same point, from the writings of leading divines of Rome.

"Can any man, that hath read their books, be ignorant how they draw all their answers unto these heads? That the remission of all our sins, the pardon of all whatsoever punishments thereby deserved, the rewards which God hath laid up in heaven, are by the blood of our Lord Jesus Christ purchased, and obtained sufficiently for all men; but for no man effectually for his benefit, in particular, except the blood of Christ be applied particularly to him, by such means as God hath appointed that to work by. That those means of themselves, being but dead things, only the blood of Christ is that which putteth life, force, and efficacy, in them to work, and to be available each in its kind, to our salvation." *

Where in these Oxford writings, is more thorough-going language than this? But even this does not save the Church of Rome from Hooker's charge of being "*an adversary to Christ's merits*," and a maintainer of a heresy, on this particular point, "*which overthroweth the foundation of faith.*"

"If any think, (he says,) that I seek to varnish their opinions, let him know, that since I began thoroughly to understand their meaning, I have found their halting greater than perhaps it seemeth to them which know not the "depths of Satan," as the blessed Divine speaketh. For although this be proof sufficient, that they do not *directly deny* the foundation of Faith, yet, if there were no other leaven in the lump of their doctrine, but this (merit,) this were sufficient to prove that their doctrine is not agreeable to the foundation of Christian faith. The Pelagians, being over-great friends unto Nature, made themselves enemies unto Grace, for all their confessing, that men have their souls, and all the faculties thereof, their wills and all the abilities of their wills from God."

* Discourse on Justification § 33.

And so, after all the protestations of Romanists, Hooker taking their *doctrine* of Justification, and choosing to judge *for himself*, how far its essential nature referred all to the merits of Christ, sums up the whole in this one sentence of entire condemnation.

"Whether they speak of the *first* or *second* Justification, they make the *essence of a divine quality inherent*; they make it *righteousness which is* IN US. If it be righteousness *in us*, then it is OURS, as our souls are ours, though we have them from God, and can hold them no longer than pleaseth him; for if He withdraw the breath of our nostrils, we fall to dust; but the righteousness wherein we must be found, if we will be justified is *not our own;* therefore we cannot be justified, by any inherent quality."

Now let the force of this exceedingly pregnant passage be well understood. Hooker has just been displaying the whole "maze which the Church of Rome doth cause her followers to tread when they ask her the way to Justification." He has spoken of the second Justification by professedly *meritorious* works, as well as of the first by baptism, without. works He says he cannot take time "to unrip this building and sift it piece by piece;" he will, however, pass it with a few words, "that that may befal BABYLON, in the presence of that which God hath builded which happened unto Dagon before the Ark." Such is his idea of Romish Justification— emphatically *Babylon*. Then he selects for an example of "that which God hath builded," those blessed words of St. Paul, "*Doubtless, I have counted all things but loss, and do count them but dung, that I may win Christ and be found in him, not having my own righteousness, but that which is through the faith of Christ, the righteousness which is of God through Faith.*" Before this building of God, he unravels the maze of Rome, in the passage we have quoted; in which, as thus connected, let the reader well observe,

1. That, though the Church of Rome *disclaims* merit in the first Justification, and *pretends* to it in the second, and *in both ascribes all to the merits of Christ;* in Hooker's judgment, the *foundation in both* is really neither more nor less than *our own merits of righteousness;* precisely that "own righteousness" which St. Paul rejected as opposed to righteousness of faith, and which he counted as dung.

2. He considers the foundation of both Justifications to be simply *our own merits of righteousness*, not because, in either case, merits are *claimed*, but because in both, whether claimed or denied, the "*essence*," or "*justifying principle*," is a "divine quality," or a

righteousness in us." Its being a righteousness in us, and not "the external righteousness of Jesus Christ, which is imputed, is the sole ground on which he rests the charge of Justification by our "*own* righteousness" or merits. That Romanists do actually *pretend* to merits in the second Justification, is, in Hooker's view, the advancing of no claim not substantially professed before, but only the further development in words, of what existed before in reality, the bolder carrying out of the principle of Justification by a righteousness WITHIN US.

3. In Hooker's view no righteousness can be *within us*, whether called "*the presence of God by His Spirit*," or "*a divine glory*," or "*light*," or "*gift*," or "*Shekinah*," without being *inherent*, in the same sense as *our souls* are inherent; or without being our *own*, in the same sense in which *our souls are our own;* so that, in his view, to say that the righteousness within us is a "*divine* gift needing continually a divine renewal," and therefore, to be justified thereby, is not to be justified by our own merits, is just the same as to say that as the faculties of our souls are a divine gift, continually sustained in us of God, therefore, to be justified by them or their works, would not be a justification by our own merits.

Thus, in Hooker's view, however odious and awful the Romish positive claim of merit, in the second Justification, the doctrine involves it, whether they make it, in so many words, or not. There is, indeed, a revolting extent of abomination in the overtness and barefacedness with which the Council of Trent, and sundry Romish writers, since, have evolved the rudiment of merit into daring expressions of anti-christian presumption;* as if Satan's right hand had forgot its cunning. But in planting the doctrine of a *righteousness in us*, as the *justifying* principle, they planted the tree, which must ramify into such boasting, if allowed its natural spread, whether planted at Trent, or at Oxford.

Now let us see how all this applies to the system of our Oxford divines. Like Rome, they ascribe the "*meritorious* cause" of Justification, only to Christ; the *efficient*, to the Holy Spirit; the *instrumental*, to Baptism, and the "*formal*," only to a righteousness in *us*. Then, we say of them, according to the words of Hooker; "Whether they speak of the first or second Justification, they make it consist in a righteousness which is *ours*, as our souls are ours;" *inherent* as our souls are inherent; they make it the righteousness which St. Paul *renounced* that he might win Christ, and not the righteousness for which he counted that as worthless and

* See Usher's Answer to a Jesuit; Chapter on Merits.

loathsome; precisely because they make it our *"own."* Then, if it be said that it is infused of God and sustained of God, without our desert; so we say of our souls and all their faculties. Let them deny that they ascribe any merit to such righteousness, or to any works proceeding therefrom; let them maintain that in making Justification thus to consist in a righteousness in them, instead of an *external* righteousness only in Christ and only *accounted* unto them, they attribute all to the merits of Christ, and nothing to their own works or deservings; it is nothing more than Romish writers have often done; nothing more than the Council of Trent itself has done."* They teach, (says Hooker,) that our good works do not these things *as they come from us*, but as they come from *grace in us;* which grace in us, is another thing in their divinity, than is the mere goodness of God's mercy towards us, in Christ Jesus.†

To deny, in the *development*, what is substantially contained in the acknowledged *rudiment*, is an inconsistency by which many, we hope, very many, professed Romanists, as well as our brethren of Oxford, have held on, in their hearts and words, to that only foundation of a sinner's hope before God, which their more formal doctrine has substantially denied; and have rejected, in their devout affections, the very righteousness of works which their written creed has embraced. Thus says Bishop Andrews, "the very Schoolmen themselves, take them from their questions, quodlibets, and comments on the *Sentences*, let them be in their *meditations or devotions*, and especially in directing how to deal with men in their last agony—then take Anselm, take Bonaventura, take Gerson, you would not wish to find *'Jehovah our Righteousness'* more pregnantly acknowledged."

The same venerable bishop shows the same happy inconsistency in Gregory of Valentia, in Stapleton, in Cardinal Bellarmine. We earnestly hope there is the same to be found in their followers at Oxford. With their personal, private, practical reliance for salvation, whether it be consistent or inconsistent with their great error of Justification, we have nothing to do. God grant their piety

---

* "Thus neither our own proper righteousness is so determined to be our own, as if it were from ourselves; nor is the righteousness of God either unknown or rejected. For that which is called *our* righteousness, because through it being inherent in us we are justified; that same is the righteousness of God, because it is infused into us of God, *through the merits of Christ*. Far however be it from a Christian man, that he should either trust or glory in himself and not in the Lord; whose goodness to all men is so great, that what are truly his gifts, he willeth to be estimated as their merits."—Concil. Trident. Sess. vi. c. 16.

† Discourse of Justification, § 33.

may be better than their theology. We are dealing only with their doctrine, which we maintain, is that of our own righteousness, or works, or merits, in rejection of what St. Paul calls the Righteousness of God by faith."* Their denial of such rejection only proves that such is not the inference *they* make from their doctrine. We must draw our own inference. Their doctrine is now public property, doing its good or evil independently of its authors; just as a poison, or a medicine, works its health or death in those who take it, independently of the apothecary who compounded it. The public must judge of the compound, as to its nature and consequences, without being bound by the opinion of the apothecary. And so the public will, and can, draw the true inference as to whether this Divinity is essentially a system of human merits, as much as that of Rome, without being governed by the deductions of its advocates. And as sometimes the public voice adjudges to be poisonous in its operation upon the human body, what the son of Æsculapius has issued under the name universal cure; so may it most justly determine that what has thus issued from Oxford as the Grand Restorative, "the Salve to heal the Church's Wounds," is mere Popery disguised; rats-bane in figs: fraught with the most baneful consequences to truth and piety; certain to intoxicate the Church with the spiritual pride of a full system of Pharisaic observances, and that just in proportion as it shall pass out of the hands of its authors, away from the antidotes which in spite of

* Our own righteousness and that of God by faith are always set in opposition by the inspired writers. Is one called "*the righteousness of law?*" the other is "*the righteousness of faith;*" is the one called by St. Paul, our "*own righteousness?*" the other he calls "*the righteousness of God.*" Is one described as "*by the law?*" the other is "*without the law.*" Is one "reckoned *to him that worketh?*" the other is "*to him that worketh not.*" Is the one "*of debt?*" the other is "*of grace.*" Does the one give man "*whereof to glory*" because it is "*of works?*" the other "*excludes boasting,*" because it is "*of faith.*" Does St. Paul "count all things but loss that he may win Christ and be found in him?" He has no hope of succeeding till he has first laid aside *his own righteousness*, as worthless, and put on, in *its stead*, "the righteousness which is by the faith of Christ." In his view, these two cannot coalesce; cannot unite into one vesture; they are essentially inconsistent in the office of Justification; so that if we trust in the one, we cannot have the other; if we "go about to establish our own righteousness," it implies that we *have not submitted to, but rejected the righteousness of God*. Our justification must be either of grace exclusively, or of works exclusively. It cannot be of both. "*Not of works lest any man should boast. If by grace*, (says St. Paul) *then is it no more of works, otherwise grace is no more grace*. But *if it be of works, then it is no more grace; otherwise work is no more work.*" "It is not grace any way, (says Augustine) if it be not free every way."

Now between one or the other of these rival hopes must every sinner choose. His choice of one is necessarily the rejection of the other.

their theory, it meets with in them, and shall be adopted into the practice of disciples of equal zeal, but less restraint. The Rudiment of Merit, now unprofessed, will soon expand into its development, boldly declared. The march of Restoration will look back to the present outset at Oxford, as a propitious beginning indeed, and good *for the times;* timid indeed, and slow and *reserved,* but well suited to a Church which, as they say of the Church of England, is not privileged with the "richer banquet" out of the "depth and richness" of the ancient services," such as are found in the Roman and Parisian Breviaries; but must, as yet, put up with "the homelier fare which a merciful Providence has set before her," because she has "sullied her baptismal robe of purity, and is not permitted to come into the Divine Presence till she has done *penance*—nor to raise her voice in the language of joy and confidence, without many a faltering note of fear and self-reproach." She is now, they tell us "in a degraded condition." "She seemed to say at the Reformation, 'Make me as one of thy hired servants;' and she has been graciously taken at her word; lowered from her ancient and proper place, as the king's daughter, into the condition of a *slave* at the table where she should preside. Lower strains befit her depressed condition; and with such, in the English Liturgy, she is actually provided."*

How long will it be before the disciples of this school will consider the march of Restoration to have proceeded far enough to warrant the taking off of that *penance;* the advancement of the present *slave,* to the daughter's seat; the elevation of her now faltering and depressed notes, to the higher strains of the Roman and Parisian Breviaries; the breaking off of the degrading fetters put on at the Reformation, for the glorious liberty of that yoke of ceremonial service under which all piety, all morality, all knowledge, all improvement, all civilization groaned and travailed in pain until Luther arose, a man of God, and sounded the trump of Jubilee, and, in the name of the Lord, opened the prison-doors to them that were bound?

We doubt not "the Tracts for the Times" are fast hastening on this second Reformation. The *disciples* of the first Restorationists are evidently too much elated with present success, to be patient much longer under the degradation of their penance-stricken Church. We fear the time is fast drawing on, when what is now being prepared for, and of which the large importations into Oxford of Roman and Parisian Breviaries, "for *private devotion,*" as well as literary study,

* British Critic for Apr. 1840.

are a sign, will be ready to take its stand in the gates, and proclaim itself upon the housetops.* We must in deep solemnity remind the Church of our parent land, standard-bearer of the Reformation, object of hatred for her firm stand on the side of religious and civil liberty, to all who would bind the fetters of despotic power, of bigot intolerance, of priestly domination, of popish superstition, upon the minds and souls of men; set upon and surrounded by a combination, for her abasement, in which the money, craft, learning, power of all the popery of Europe is leagued, in alliance with all that radicalism and infidelity can do to help them; we must in deepest sympathy, and with earnest prayer for our mother Church of England, beseech her to remember the word of the Lord:—"*Satan hath desired to have you that he may sift you as wheat.*" "Watch and pray, lest ye enter into temptation!"

* How sadly the above anticipations have been fulfilled, every body knows. The Article in the British Critic, from which we have taken the extracts above given, is a Review of the latest "Tract for the Times," No. 86, on the Church Service; and its expressions are just an echo of that Tract. In that Review we read that whereas "the Liturgies of Rome and Paris were, till very recently, sealed books to the Protestant world,"—"now, Mr. Parker, of Oxford, finds it worth his while to import a considerable number of copies, both of the Roman and Parisian Breviaries, every year; whence we infer (says the Reviewer) and with great satisfaction, that the ancient services are coming to be studied, not merely as a matter of literature—but for purposes of private devotion." If the selections from the Roman Breviary, occupying one hundred pages of the Tracts, are favourable specimens of its "hid treasures," we must confess that, except as it contains what is also in our own Bible and Prayer Book, its treasures are sufficiently *hid*. What our Oxford Divines mean by the richness of the ancient services, as displayed in these Breviaries, is clearly seen in the fact that they have not only constructed "*for social or private devotion,*" a full Matin service for the commemoration of Bishop Ken's Day," and also a Matin, Vesper and Laud Service for "THE COMMEMORATION OF THE DEAD IN CHRIST;" but have followed most strictly the model and peculiarities of the Roman Breviary as to Nocturns, Antiphons, and every other minute feature of order and mode, with as little reference to the peculiarities of the English Liturgy, as if it were not in existence. Because the Romish Breviary introduces here and there little scraps of a Homily by St. Ambrose, &c., therefore the service for Bishop Ken, does the same with a scrap of a sermon from Bishop Taylor. Because in the Romish services are legends of the Saints, therefore in the Oxford service is a legend of Bishop Ken, which tells where he was born and educated, ordained, &c.—how he brought Anabaptists to baptism, was self-denied, charitable, faithful, &c., that he died in the Holy Catholic and Apostolic Faith, &c., but has not one word by which may be learned any one *distinctive* doctrine or precept of the Gospel of Christ.

CHAPTER VI.

THE DOCTRINE OF THIS DIVINITY, AS TO THE NATURE AND OFFICE OF JUSTIFYING FAITH, EXHIBITED, AND COMPARED WITH THAT OF THE ROMISH CHURCH.

The influence of the doctrine of Justification, whether true or false, upon the body of divinity in general—The sameness of the Oxford Doctrine and that of Rome, tested by the sameness of influence upon connected and subordinate doctrines—This, first exhibited as to the doctrine of Justifying Faith—The doctrine of Faith, as held in the Romish Church, stated in six propositions—The doctrine of this system stated in comparison, under the same propositions, showing the nature and office of Faith, before Baptism, in Baptism, and after Baptism—The profession of making Faith the sole internal instrument of Justification examined and shown to be without any reality—Justification by Faith, in this system, nothing but Justification by Christianity—A rebuke from Bishop Beveridge.

THE great error that Justification consists in a *Righteousness Inherent*, as the basis on which alone "we are accounted righteous before God," is so fundamental as to require for conformity thereto an essential change in all parts of the Gospel plan of salvation, especially in those connected most intimately with the nature of sin, and the way of deliverance from its defilement and condemnation. Of this subordinating influence, all the peculiarities of Romish divinity are conspicuous evidences.

If we shall succeed in showing that the fundamental doctrine of the system before us, as to the righteousness of Justification, is of such similar influence, that it affects precisely the same subordinate doctrines, in substantially the same way, and with reference to the same accommodation; so that the tree is not only Romish in *root* and *trunk*, but, so far as it has spread out doctrinally, is Romish in *ramification* also; it will then be the more manifest that the difference between this divinity and that for which our Reformers gave themselves to death, is no mere *logomachy, a rebus ad voces;* but a difference of vital importance to the integrity of the Christian faith, involving not one doctrine merely, but the whole system of doctrine, from corner-stone to roof, so that according to

Oxford Divines themselves, it makes the one side or the other, "*another Gospel.*"

In proceeding to this showing, we begin with *the Nature and Office of Justifying Faith.* Next to an inquiry as to the righteousness by which the sinner is justified, is the question, *by what means he becomes possessed of that righteousness.* The plain answer of the Scriptures is, "*by faith.*" No doctrine then may be expected to participate more directly in any essential peculiarity in regard to justifying righteousness, than that of justifying faith. "Hence it comes to pass (says Chemnitz,) that the devil is so angry at the doctrine of faith. When he could not hinder the divine decree concerning the redemption of the human race, he brought all his arts to bear upon the destruction or corruption of the appointed means of its application; knowing what was written, that the word preached does not profit except it be mixed with faith in them that hear it."

The doctrine of the nature and office of Justifying faith, as held by the Church of Rome, is squared in entire consistency with her doctrine of Justification by Inherent righteousness. We shall see the same squaring, for the same reason, and with reference to the same cardinal points in the system before us.

As in both systems, the nature of Faith is accommodated to the position assigned to Baptism, as *the sole instrument* of Justification; so in both there is a distinction assumed as to the nature and efficacy of faith *before*, and *after*, Baptism. And this distinction is the key to the whole doctrine of faith as well in the one system as the other.

What then is the teaching of the Church of Rome concerning faith *before* Baptism; the faith required of Adults *in order to* Baptism? It cannot be properly a *justifying* faith, because Baptism is made "*the only instrument* of Justification." It cannot, therefore, be the faith of a *justified* or righteous person, and so must be the faith of the unrighteous. Hence it cannot be "a *lively* faith," the "faith that worketh by love." What then does the Church of Rome pronounce? She anathematizes in Canon xii., those who understand by justifying faith such a trust in the divine mercy as apprehends and accepts, in the promises of the Gospel, the remission of sins, through the mediation of Christ; and who hold that, by such trust alone, we are justified before God unto eternal life. And she moreover pronounces that "we are said by the Apostle to be justified by faith, because faith *is the initiatory step in human salvation, the foundation and root of all justification.*"

And just how we are to understand these words, we learn from the interpretation of Andrada, professedly expounding and defending the doctrines of Trent. He says that the power of justifying is ascribed to faith, because it *prepares* the mind for the receiving of justification. "The wicked (he says) are said to be justified by faith, and faith is the beginning and foundation of justification in this sense, viz., *that it opens the door to hope and charity*, which works are necessary to the obtaining of Justification." Faith, therefore, according to the Trent decree, is the *beginning and preparation* for Justification, not because it apprehends the remission of sins through Christ, but because it excites the will to such motions, or acts, as are necessary to the obtaining of Justification. Consequently, it is in no sense a direct *instrument of obtaining* Justification; but only a *sine-qua-non;* a preparation, as the Trent-Council says, "without which, it is impossible to please God, and obtain the adoption of sons."

By faith, therefore, as a preparation for Justification, the Church of Rome understands, (says Chemnitz,) *a mere historical knowledge and naked assent*, by which, in general, we acknowledge that those things are true which are revealed concerning God and his word, not only in Scripture, but also in those things which are proposed under the title of traditions. This general assent, says the Priest Gandolphy, is called "a *divine* faith," because it is based on the testimony of God, in distinction from *human* faith, based on the testimony of men. "It essentially excludes the existence of doubt," "and consists in believing, without doubting, truths revealed by the Deity."

Such then is the *fides informata* according to Rome, or unformed faith, required in Adults for Baptism, and which until Baptism give it some additional quality, is described as a *mere naked assent, a mere preparative for hope and charity, and all good works;* not a *living* faith, but still "*divine*" because "founded on the testimony of God." And yet it is not necessary that such testimony be drawn directly from God's word. "*The testimony of the Church*, derived from God, is a motive sufficient to command the soul to render a full, perfect and steady faith. Now this motive being supernatural and divine the assent of the soul becomes a supernatural and divine act, for which the special grace is necessary, and forms what is termed a supernatural and divine faith. It is even an act of the soul, as distinct, and as much above a moral or human act, as God himself is raised above all created objects."* Thus a mere naked assent to the

* Gandolphy's Defence, vol. II. p. 490.

testimony of God, or of the Church, which the wicked as well as righteous have; *which even devils have,* for on the testimony of God they "believe and tremble," is exalted into a divine, supernatural act, requiring for its exercise a special grace. But when asked how such naked faith can justify the soul before God, they answer that in justification there is something added to it; to wit, *charity,* which gives it greater weight and merit. Andrada, for instance, says that, "not by faith only, but by faith together with hope and charity, we apprehend Christ for righteousness—that in the Epistle to the Hebrews, the Justification of many is attributed to faith, because faith excited those illustrious men to the good works of hope and charity." Now since it is declared in chap. vii. of Trent, that no Justification can take place *until Baptism;* that in that sacrament, "the love of God is shed abroad in the heart by the Holy Ghost, by which we are renewed in the Spirit of our minds," it follows that it is in Baptism that the *unformed* faith which preceded it, becomes *fides formata,* that is, becomes joined with hope and charity, so as to be no longer *a mere assent,* of the mind, preparing the way for justification, but a *living principle,* an inherent righteousness, by which, in its degree, the justification first infused in Baptism is continued. So that *before* Baptism, the faith of the Adult coming to that scacrament is a naked *unvivified* assent, justifying only as preparing the way for Justification; a "*divine* faith," however dead, because resting like that of devils on the testimony of God. *After* Baptism, it is the same faith, but with a new heart given to it, a regenerate faith, having the spiritual qualities of hope and love infused, or superadded; in virtue of which, and not because of any special agency in itself, it justifies before God. What utter ruin all this makes in the Scriptural doctrine of Justifying Faith, we will not stop to show.

Its main points to be kept in view, for the comparison now to be made with the system before us, are

1. That Faith before Baptism is not and cannot be a living faith.

2. That Faith before Baptism is said to Justify, or to be an instrument of Justification, only as a *sine-qua-non,* a necessary preparation for, and that which leads to, Baptism, the latter being the only real instrument of the first Justification.

3. This faith, so dead, is nevertheless a *divine, supernatural* gift, based on the testimony of God, through the Creeds and traditionary doctrines of the Church, independently of a direct application to the Scriptures, as the Primary and only Authoritative Rule of Faith.

4. That this faith, before Baptism, instead of being in any sense Justifying, until after the sinner becomes Justified *in Baptism*, must itself be first justified, or made *living* by justification in Baptism.

5. That Faith when regenerate and justified in Baptism, is not such a *trust* in the divine mercy as *apprehends* and *accepts* remission of sins through the mediation of Christ, and justifies the soul through his righteousness accounted to the believer.

6. That Faith after it has become a living faith by baptism, so that it is now joined with hope and love, only *continues* or *sustains* the Justification already received, in Baptism; and even this, not in any proper sense, as an *instrument* applying by itself the righteousness of Christ, but only as acting in common with all other Christian virtues and works.

We proceed to show that all these several propositions are strongly asserted in the system we are considering.

1. That the faith of the adult coming to Baptism, is not and cannot be a *living* faith.

The Catechism of our Protestant Church, requires of those who come to be baptized, "*repentance*, whereby they forsake sin, and *faith*, whereby they stedfastly believe the promises of God made to them in that Sacrament." Precisely the same are required for the Lord's Supper. We have been accustomed to suppose that by these were intended a *godly sorrow*, and a *godly* or *living* faith: that as there is no true repentance without love to God, so there can be no truly penitent *faith*, without it. We must be pardoned this grievous error, since our great Dr. Barrow, in the same darkness, not to mention a thousand others, has told us concerning this repentance and faith, required for baptism, that " each importeth a *being renewed in mind, in judgment, in will, in affection;* a *serious* embracing of Christ's doctrine, and a stedfast resolution to adhere thereto in practice; *that death to sin, and resurrection to righteousness, that being buried with Christ and rising again with him, so as to walk in newness of life, which the baptismal action signifies.*" * But unhappily, Dr. Pusey and Doctor Barrow are not agreed. " Faith and repentance in adults, (says the former) are necessary to the new birth; but they are *not the new birth*." †

What then is Faith *before* Baptism and required *for* Baptism? We answer by first stating, according to Mr. Newman, that "what faith was in the days of the Son of Man for temporal

---

* Barrow on the Doctrine of the Sacrament.
† Views of Holy Baptism, p. 178.

blessings, such surely it is now under the ministration of the Spirit for heavenly." This seems a promising beginning. One hopes for something clear and sound from such premises. Again—"Faith is substantially the same habit of mind under all circumstances, or it would not be called faith; and so far it has always the same office." Hence we hope to see that faith before Baptism, and after Baptism, are substantially the same, and of one office—both Justifying, and in the same sense. But now our encouragement is at an end—for says Mr. N., "*Faith, as gaining its virtue from Baptism, is one thing before that sacred ordinance; another, after.** Baptism raises it from a *condition* into the *instrument* of Justification—from a mere *forerunner*, into its accredited *representative*." This we should suppose to be a very substantial difference both of nature and office. To be a *condition* and *forerunner* only, and to be an *instrument* we should think was not very "*substantially the same thing.*" But the view opens. "Justifying faith may be considered in two main points of view, either as it is in itself, and as it exists in *fact*, in those who *are under grace*," (that is before Baptism and after Baptism.) "In the former point of view, it is not necessarily *even a moral virtue;* but when illuminated by love, and ennobled by the Spirit, (which only takes place in Baptism, according to this divinity,) it is a name for all graces together." So then, when our Church requires faith as a preparation for Baptism, she does not require what is *necessarily a moral virtue!* Hence we read that "nothing is said of it before Baptism, that is not said of *restitution*, as a necessary condition in order to Baptism." Before Baptism, "it is without availing power, *without life*, in the sight of God, as regards our Justification," that is, as regards "the indwelling of the Spirit," which is Justification according to this system. This view is expounded in a passage in which faith before Baptism is called a "*moral virtue*," as its highest possible condition; after Baptism "*a grace.*" The latter as "*lively;* the former as "*willing without performing;*" being only "full of

---

* Lectures pp. 268. 278. Aquinas furnishes us with all this in equal plainness. He states a variety of opinions as to whether faith before Baptism, *fides informis*, dead faith, is the same essentially with that after Baptism, *fides formata*, living faith, or not. Some thought that God, in the infusion of the latter, expelled the former—but that would not do; because, as both were made to be gifts of God, it did not seem right to suppose that he would expel his own gift. The conclusion of Aquinas is precisely that of Mr. N., that the dead and living faith are substantially the same faith. Fides informis et fides formata unus et idem habitus est, his diversis nominibus appellatus, ab ipsa charitate, quæ est illius forma. P. 1, 2, Q. 4, A. 4.

terror and disquiet, VAGUE, and dull-minded, feeble, sickly, wayward, fitful, INOPERATIVE," "nothing till Christ regenerate it" in Baptism. Such faith must be baptized before it can be alive. "When it comes *for Baptism*, it is on the point of being rid of itself and hid in Christ. It comes to the Fount of Life to be *made alive*, as the dry bones in the Prophet's vision were brought together in preparation for the Breath of God to quicken them; and He who makes all things new, as he makes *sinners righteous*, &c., so also by His presence *converts* what is a condition of obtaining favour, into the means of holding and enjoying it." One would now suppose that a dead faith and a living, were not "*substantially the same*," or "*of one office.*" *

Such then in this divinity is faith before Baptism, though called by Doctor Barrow, &c., &c., "*the inward grace which Baptism signifies.*" Such, according to this system, was the faith of Paul, the converted, before he was baptized; such the faith of Cornelius, before he was baptized, although he was already "*a devout man*" and "feared God, and prayed to God always," and "his prayers came up for a memorial before God," and the Holy Ghost had come upon him. His faith must have been *dead, vague, inoperative, unregenerate, needing to be converted*, because it was *before Baptism*. Hence we are told that, "Cornelius had not *Christian* faith, nor love, nor prayer, for as yet he knew not Christ; he could not call God Father, (*to whom he prayed always,*) because he knew not the Son. Faith and repentance are necessary in adults to the new birth, but they are not the new birth." †

This may suffice for our first proposition, and one would suppose should suffice for the whole system, with all who know the Scriptures and are willing to walk by their light.

2. That faith before Baptism is said to Justify, or to be an instrument of Justification, only as a *sine-qua-non*, a necessary *preparation* for, and that which leads to, Baptism; the latter being the only instrument of the first Justification.

This proposition requires but few citations out of the many which might be adduced. "What (we read) does the Scripture say of faith before Baptism, *except as a necessary step* to Baptism? Its highest praise before Baptism is that it *leads to it;* as its highest efficacy after it is that it comes from it. Nothing is said of it before Baptism, that is not said of Repentance or of *Restitution*, which are also necessary conditions in order to Baptism. Upon these, not *in*

---

* Newman Lectures pp. 295, 277, 278.
† Pusey's Views of Holy Baptism, pp. 177, 178.

and *through* them, comes Gospel grace, meeting, not co-operating with them." * "We are saved by faith *bringing* us to Baptism, and by Baptism, God saves us"—"faith being but the *sine-qua-non*, the necessary condition on our parts for duly receiving the grace of Christ." "This may be set down as the essence of sectarian doctrine, to consider faith, and not the sacraments, as *the proper instrument of Justification* and other Gospel gifts, instead of holding that the grace of Christ comes to us altogether *from without.*" And it was to correct this undue elevation of faith, in other words, to degrade that which the Scriptures every where speak of as the only instrument of Justification into a dead, in-operative, unmeaning nothing, for the sake of elevating the sacrament of Baptism into "*Salvation, the Cross and the Resurrection,*" asserting that in Christianity, there is no two fold baptism, no separation, except in thought, between the outward form and the inward substance," denying even the language of our Article that Baptism is "a sign," saying it is "*not a sign, but the putting on of Christ ;*" it was for this, we are told, that Dr. Pusey's labored work on Holy Baptism was written.†

Here the reader will perhaps remember such passages as the following in Dr. Pusey's Letter to the Bishop of Oxford, viz., "Justification comes through the Sacraments, is received *by faith,*" &c. "The merits of Christ applied in Baptism *by the Spirit,* and *received by a lively faith,* complete our Justification for the time being."

Again—"The instrumental power of Faith cannot interfere with

---

* Newman's Lectures, p. 275.

† Views of H. Bap. pp. 49, and 5,—142 ; 206 and 102.

That faith which Mr. Newman can hardly call a *moral virtue*, and which he says is not *necessarily* one, he in one place, denies even the name of faith, so dead is it and of no account in his sight. "Faith (he says) does not *precede* Justification, (that is Baptism), but Justification precedes faith and makes it Justifying, so that the faith required for baptism is not faith." Truly the zeal of his system hath eaten him up. This entire degradation, into a mere name, of the spiritual qualification for Adult baptism is a most impressive comment upon the *real* spirituality, both in essence and tendency, of what in language, so mysterious and mystical, seems so spiritual. It is just the full *opus operatum* of Rome. We must fear, when the repentance and faith required alike for Baptism and the Lord's Supper, are degraded into dead things hardly worth mentioning in the matter of salvation, for the sake of elevating an outward sign into the highest seat of spiritual dignity and efficacy. Spiritual *words* do not always express spiritual *views*. Mysticism and spirituality are as much alike as the foolish and wise virgins in the parable—both have lamps—both shine—but mysticism has no oil in its vessel with its lamp. When the Bridegroom cometh, its light is gone out in darkness.

the instrumental power of Baptism; because faith is the *sole* justifier, not in contrast to all means and agencies whatever—but to all other *graces*. When then Faith is called the sole instrument, this means the *sole internal* instrument of any kind."*

It is exceedingly probable, that most readers of these passages, as they stand thus unqualified, have supposed that they referred to faith, *preceding* Justification,—that which one has who repents and believes, before he is baptized as well as that which remains with him after baptism; and they have supposed probably that such faith was indeed made an *internal and the sole instrument* of justification while an *external* instrumentality only was given to Baptism. But they are deceived. Faith *before* Baptism is not in the least referred to in these passages. If they will read them again, they will see it is " a *lively* faith " that is spoken of. But this cometh only by Baptism. All before is dead and inoperative and unregenerate—a mere *sine-qua-non*, no more instrumental in Justification than is *restitution*. So that, whenever faith, in these writers is spoken of as in any other sense justifying, let the reader remember that it is faith *after Baptism*, a *justified* faith. There is too much " *reserve*," in Dr. Pusey's statements on this subject. A reader, not otherwise informed, would hardly suspect the real restriction of his meaning. There is not a line in all his professed confession of faith, to the Bishop of Oxford, by which a reader, unenlightened by other means, can get an idea of the distinction so fundamental in this system, between faith before, and faith after Baptism; or that by the faith taken as the *sole internal instrument*, is not meant that by which in our usual Protestant understanding of things, the penitent sinner coming to Christ prepares for baptism. In reality that faith is not mentioned, and not a line is devoted to the great question what a penitent soul, just awakened and turned to God, must do to be saved; whether he must *believe*, or *how* he must believe, or *what sort of faith* he must have, or *how it operates*; nothing but that he must be *Baptized*. The whole account of Justifying Faith, has reference to its influence *after* a Justification already obtained by baptism, after the faith required for baptism has itself been *converted, regenerated, justified, raised from death,* made *operative* by being baptized. We do not like this " *Reserve in communicating religious knowledge.*"

3. That this Faith which precedes Baptism and is dead, is nevertheless *a divine supernatural gift,* and based on the testimony of God, *through the creeds and traditionary doctrine of the Church,*

* Letter, pp. 42, 3, 4. These passages are quoted by Dr. P. from Mr. Newman.

independently of any direct application to the Scriptures as the *primary and only authoritative Rule of Faith.*

"By faith," as we read in this divinity, "is meant the mind's perception of knowledge of heavenly things, arising from an *instinctive* trust in the divinity or truth of the external words, informing it concerning them." This *instinctive trust,* is "a *moral* instinct, *supernaturally* implanted and independent of experience;" it is a moral *instinct* just as the trust of the mind to the testimony of sense is a natural instinct. Of this *instinctive* faith, "*the inward grace of God is the first cause;*" yet it is "*mere faith,*" unregenerate faith until love be afterward imparted in Baptism. Though "supernatural," and the gift of the inward grace of God, it "is not a practical principle, nor peculiar to religious men," "*not a virtue or grace,* else *evil spirits could not possess it.*" "Devils believe and tremble.—Thus dread and despair are the essential properties of the devil's faith; hope or trust of religious" (or baptized) "faith; but both are in their nature *one and the same faith, as being simply the acceptance of God's word about the future and unseen.*" *

Thus the faith required for baptism in connection with repentance, the faith of a repenting sinner seeking mercy through Christ, is identified with the faith of devils, equally dead, and equally without moral virtue or excellence, while each, the faith of the devil, and the faith of the penitent catechumen, is called a *moral, supernatural instinct,* implanted by *the inward grace of God!!* Was ever truth like this?

Now we are prepared to understand that *such* faith should be

---

* Newman's Letures, pp. 287, 289, 290 and 291.

All these points are given in Aquinas, as in Mr N., except that the former attempts a distinction between the faith of devils and that of unbaptized persons, which the latter gives up. That the dead faith of the unbaptized is the supernatural gift of God, Aquinas asserts. Fides informis est donum Dei. That it is destitute of moral excellence, because not a grace, and without love, he also maintains; Fides et opus sine charitate possunt esse; sed sine charitate, proprie loquendo, virtutes non sunt. But he cannot venture to say that it is no better than that of the devils. Its peculiarity, in his view, is that it is based on the testimony of God, and therefore is a gift from grace; but he denies that devils believe on such testimony. Vident enim multa manifesta indicia, ex quibus percipiunt doctrinam ecclesiæ a Deo esse; quamvis ipsas res quas Ecclesia docet non videant—P. 1, 2; Q. A. 1.—Fides in dæmonibus coacta est, non laudabilis, nec donum a gratia. Q. 6. A. 2.

But Mr. N. considers that devils do believe on the testimony of God. "They believe in a Judgment to come; and on what, but God's infallible word announcing it?" Hence, he makes, of necessity, their faith to be the same as that of all the unbaptized, no more dead essentially than theirs.

rested on the testimony of God, *through the creeds of the Church,* independently of all consultation of the Scriptures, as the Primary and only Rule of Faith. Such is the doctrine of this system. Mr. Newman contends that "the sacred volume was never intended, and is not adapted to teach our creed, however certain it is that we can *prove* our creed from it, when it has once been taught us." He contends for "the insufficiency of the mere private study of Holy Scripture (i. e. without the precomposed creed of the Church as a guide) for the arriving at the exact and entire truth which it really contains." "From the very first (he says) the rule has been, as a matter of fact, *for the Church to teach the truth,* and then appeal to Scripture in vindication of its own teaching," while the way of heretics from the first has been "to elicit a systematic doctrine FROM THE SCATTERED NOTICES OF THE TRUTH *which Scripture contains.*" Therefore the creeds of the Church are said to be "*divinely provided;*"* "*a gift equally from God*" with Holy Scripture. The Bible is the "*record,*" Church tradition the "*interpreter,*" of necessary truth;† and so it is contended that in primitive times "the great duty of the Christian teacher was to unfold the sacred truths in due order, and not to insist prematurely on the difficulties," (that is, the spiritual doctrines) "OR TO APPLY THE PROMISES." ‡ Among our Oxford teachers the matters to be sacredly reserved from the catechumen, are such as the Atonement, because says their Tract No. 80, "fully to know that we are saved by faith in Christ only, *is a great secret, the knowledge of which can only be obtained by obedience, as the crown and end of holiness of life.*" But this Reserve can only be used, now that the Scriptures are in all hands, by discountenancing the free use of them among the uninitiated, the *neophytes;* and shutting up the people virtually, to such teaching of the Church, as her ministers may choose to communicate. Hence the stern war of Oxford divines against the study of the Evidences of Christianity as a way of becoming established in the truth, instead of *hearing the Church,* and trusting by an "*instinctive* faith" in her testimony. Hence the complaint that "Protestants dispense with the Church,

---

* Newman's Hist. of the Arians, pp. 55, 56.

† Tract, No. 71, p. 5. Whatever is the *final* interpreter of Scripture must be the final Arbiter of Faith. If one goes among people of a strange language, his interpreter is his only guide to the knowledge of their words. It is one thing to call Tradition the *Interpreter,* another to call it a *help* in interpretation of Scripture. In the former sense it would be to us in place of the Scriptures. In the latter it is a witness and handmaid to them.

‡ Hist. of the Arians, p. 57.

by basing the *genuineness and authenticity of the Scriptures on history and criticism.*" Paley's Evidences are as much an object of aversion to these writers, as substituted for the testimony of the Church to the truth of Christianity as his Moral Philsophy is in comparison with that of Plato. Hence we read that because the Church of Rome requires this implicit faith in the Church, not sending her sons to the Scriptures, but requiring them to hear what they contain *by and on her testimony,* it "must be allowed the praise, *that it was ever distinguished as a pillar of the truth,*" so that "the Romanist cannot fail to think it a great defect in the English Church, that she has no *authoritative voice of her own,* and cannot put *forth the Bible in the name of the English Church;* and therefore is driven to make the Bible stand by itself, by a cumbrous apparatus of evidences." Hence it is maintained that "young men," catechumens, "though they may not be able formally to state the ground of their faith, yet they do receive it, whether they would say so or not, *on the authority of the Church.*" Hence also it is said to be "natural and proper that youth should have a *comparatively external* knowledge of religion. Do what we will, we cannot make its knowledge other than *external*—the opinions of youth are not so much *in* religion, as *about* religion."* When therefore youth, in due season make a *right* religious choice, it is not owing to clearness of intellect, &c., but to the possession of certain habitual ways of thinking and feeling, which we are not ashamed to call *wholesome predjudice,* constituting our notion of the believing temper." †
Thus we come round again to the "*instinctive faith*" which precedes baptism, faith in the Church, faith without distinct knowledge; engaged only upon the externals of religion, the *naked assent* of the catechumen of the Church of Rome. And this is all the faith required of a sinner prior to being baptized! What then is the repentance?

4. That Faith, before Baptism instead of being in any sense an instrument of Justification *in* Baptism, is itself first *Justified, made Regenerate,* and *living, by Baptism.*

"Faith being the appointed *representative* of Baptism, derives its authority and virtue from that which it represents. It is justifying because of Baptism; it is the faith of the baptized—of the regenerate; that is, of the Justified. Faith does not precede Justification; but justification precedes it, and makes it justifying. Baptism is the

---

* British Critic, No. 51.   † British Critic, No. 41.

primary instrument, and creates faith to be what it is, and otherwise is not, giving it power and rank, and constituting it as its own successor. Each has its own office, Baptism at the time, Faith ever after—the Sacraments, the *instrumental*, Faith the *sustaining* cause."*

5. That Faith when regenerate and justified in Baptism, is not such a *trust* in the divine mercy as *apprehends, embraces,* or *lays hold on* the righteousness of Christ for remission of sins, and thus obtains justification before God.

We have not been accustomed to such language. In the Catechism framed in the reign of Edward VI., faith is said to be "*trust alone*, that doth *lay hand* upon" the righteousness of God. The Homilies say that faith is "a *sure trust* of the mercy of God through Christ," and *sends* us to Christ;" *joins us* to Christ," "makes him *our own, and applies his merits,*" that by faith we "*embrace* Christ;" "we touch him with our mind and receive him with the *hand* of the heart;" Hooker says, "This is the *only hand which putteth on* Christ for Justification." So precisely says Usher. Beveridge says it consists in "a *fiducial* reliance or dependence upon Christ for the pardon of our sins, in a particular manner;" it is "to *trust, depend and confidently rely upon Christ for salvation.*† Bishop Andrews says, "By faith Abraham *took hold* of Christ, and that faith was accounted to him for righteousness, and to us shall be, if we be, in like sort, *apprehensive* of him. There is a double *apprehension;* one of St. Paul, the other of St. James; work for *both hands to apprehend;* both love which is by faith, and faith which worketh by love, (Sanctification and Justification.) ‡ In divers places, Bishop Andrews, as do the Homilies, Bishop Hooper, and all the Reformers, illustrates the faith justifying, by the looking of the Israelites upon the brazen serpent; for example: "Forasmuch as it is Christ, his own self, that resembling his passion on the cross to the Brazen Serpent, maketh a correspondence between their *beholding* and our *believing*, we cannot avoid, but must needs make that an effect," &c. § Thus that good Bishop calls faith "*the eye of our hope;*" Leighton, "*the seeing faculty of the soul,* which, as it is that which discerns Christ, so it alone *appropriates Christ or makes him our own;*"∥ and Andrews again: "As from the Brazen Serpent no virtue issued to heal, but unto them that steadily *beheld* it, so neither doth there

---

* Newman's Lect. p. 260.   † Sermons, No. 134.
‡ Andrews' Sermons, p. 3.   § Andrews' Sermons, p. 224.
∥ On 1 Peter ii. 7, 8.

from Christ, but upon those that with the eye of Faith *have their contemplation on this object, who thereby draw life* from him."*

But all this is directly denied of faith, in this divinity. "It would seem (it says) that Luther's doctrine, now so popular, that Justifying faith is *trust*, comes first, justifies by itself, and then gives birth to all graces, is not *tenable;* such a faith *cannot be, and if it could, would not justify.*"† It treats as Ultra Protestant, the view "that Justifying Faith is nothing else than a reliance (fiducia) on the divine mercy, remitting sins for Christ's sake." ‡ Mr. Newman writes: "Because the Brazen Serpent healed by being looked at, they consider that Christ's sacrifice saves by *the mind's contemplating* it: (the very words of Bp. Andrews.) This is what they call *casting themselves* upon Christ, *coming* before him *simply*, and without *self-trust, and being saved by faith*." "Christ's cross does not justify by *being looked at*, but by being applied; not by *being gazed at in faith*, but by being actually set up within us. * * Men sit and gaze and speak of the great atonement, and think this is the appropriating it not more truly than kneeling to the material cross itself is appropriating it. Men say that faith is an *apprehending and applying;* faith *cannot really apply it.* * * Man cannot make the Saviour of the world his own." §

Such is asserted by these divines to be the doctrine of our Homilies and standard divines. We shall see hereafter more clearly how far this is true.

6. That Faith, after it has become *regenerate* and living, by being baptized, so as to be joined and dignified with hope and love, only *continues* or *sustains* the Justification, already received in Baptism; but this, not in any proper sense, as an instrument applying by itself the righteousness of Christ, but only as joined with and the complex of all other Christian virtues and works.

It is to this faith, *after Baptism*, that all instrumentality in Justification is ascribed by these divines, so far as it is ascribed to Faith in any sense. It is said to be the "*sole internal* instrument" of Justification. "The merits of Christ applied in Baptism by *the Spirit*, and *received* by a *living* faith, complete our justification for the time being." "Justification *comes* through the Sacraments; is *received* by Faith and *lives* in obedience." ‖ "On all accounts, from the

---

* Sermons, p. 222. † Newman's Lectures p. 293.
‡ Pusey's Letter to Bp. of Oxford, p.46. § Lectures, pp. 202, 203.

‖ Pusey's Letter, pp. 42, 43. The reader will naturally ask how faith, even after Baptism, can be "*the sole internal instrument of Justification*," when Justification must precede, in order to make it a lively faith? how the merits of Christ,

instances, statements and analogy of Scripture we may safely conclude that there is a *certain extraordinary and singular sympathy* between faith and the grant of Gospel privileges, such as to constitute it, *in a true sense, an instrument of Justification.*" Now then after such passages, who would not expect to find that faith becomes at last really and peculiarly an Instrument, "*in a true sense,*" and as such, having had no hand in Justification *before Baptism,* except as restitution has, is now honored with some peculiar instrumentality after Baptism, which other gifts and graces and works have not? But we are doomed to entire disappoinment.

First we ask in what sense is faith justifying *after* Baptism? "Such (we read,) is justifying faith, justifying not the ungodly, *but the just, whom God has justified when ungodly; justifying the just,* as being the faith of the Justified, who through baptism first became so, when as yet they were unjust." What an honor is here conferred on faith, that it makes those righteous *who are righteous already!* This language is explained as far as it *can be* by the following: "Justification needs a perpetual instrument, such as Faith can, and Baptism cannot be.—Faith *secures* to the soul continually those gifts which Baptism *primarily* conveys.—The Sacraments are the immediate, faith is the *secondary, subordinate, or representative* instrument of Justification. Or we may say, varying our mode of expression, that the Sacraments are its *instrumental,* and Faith its *sustaining cause.*"* Thus we get to the point.—Faith is only *representatively* justifying; only as it acts in the name, by the authority, and as the instrument, or servant, of *Baptism,* and thus *sustaining* what Baptism alone begun; so that on the principle *qui facit per alium, facit per se,* it is only Baptism justifying still.

Now here arises a very grave question for this system to answer. According to its advocates, in full agreement with the Church of Rome on this head, Sin after Baptism, or as they make it, Mortal Sin, necessarily destroys the virtue of Baptism, removes its Justication, makes it unjustification. Faith now has lost its power to sustain what Baptism gave, can no more act as its representative,

---

applied in Baptism, can be received by a *lively* faith, when faith is not, and cannot, according to this divinity, be lively till *after, and in consequence of* the prior application of those merits; how Justification coming by the sacraments, "*is received by faith,*" when faith before Justification, has no hand wherewith to receive, but that which is dead, and must, in baptismal justification, be itself raised from the dead. These are questions without answer.

* Newman's Lectures, pp. 271, and 272, 220.

because it is dead again, and needs again to be justified before it can be again an instrument in any way of Justification. Such Dr. Pusey supposes may have been the case of Simon Magus. In his zeal to support the *opus operatum* of Baptism, in every case in which the recipient may not be supposed to have been an infidel or a hypocrite, he supposes that Simon may have been indeed *regenerated and justified* in his Baptism, though, so soon afterwards, he was declared by St. Peter to be "in the gall of bitterness and in the bonds of iniquity." His faith did not sustain his Justification; it proved an *unfaithful representative;* such is the explanation.*

But the question is, how, in the case of Sin after Baptism, which is no other than the universal case of those who have been baptized in infancy, *how is Justification to be renewed?*

The answer must be, *not by faith,* for that, by the supposition, is now dead again, and incapable of acting as the Representative of Baptism. And Baptism cannot be repeated. So that faith seems out of the question. Some other instrument must be ascertained, if possible, for the renewal of Justification.

Mr. Newman meets the difficulty by making both Sacraments instruments of Justification, so that sin after Baptism is remitted in the Eucharist. But here is the difficulty in such a scheme: How is the poor sinner to come to the Eucharist? By Faith, of course. But, alas, his faith is now dead, and there is no more Baptism to revive it—so that if he come to the Lord's Supper, and does truly and spiritually receive the body and blood of Christ to his soul's health—to his renewal in justification, it must be with a *dead* faith, such as, according to Mr. N., is not even necessarily a moral virtue, has no moral excellence. From this result there is no escape.† But possibly Mr. N. does not desire an escape; for why is a *dead* faith any the less meet preparation for the Lord's Supper, than for Baptism, when in both we receive the body and blood of Christ, *by putting on Christ,* in one, and *feeding on him,* in the other? It is sufficiently revolting as to either. But what more revolting than *"to administer the Lord's Supper to infants, or to the dying and apparently insensible?"* And yet, say the Oxford Tracts, "neither practice is *without the sanction of primitive usage:"* ‡ of course, then, not without the sanction of their Divinity; for primitive usage is its

---

* Views of Holy Baptism, p. 185.

† "For as the benefit is great, if with a true penitent heart, and lively faith, we receive that holy Sacrament, so is the danger great if we receive the same unworthily."—*Communion Office.*

‡ Views of Holy Baptism, p. 5.

law. If these writers are prepared to give the Eucharist to infants and the insensible, it is probably no objection in their view, to a system, that it requires, in certain cases, that the same be administered to a dead faith. Mr. Palmer, however, though of this school, seems not to be quite ready for such an extreme, and yet cannot very positively go against it. On the question, whether those who have not a living faith can receive the Eucharist to their soul's health, he cautiously remarks that, since we read in the Scriptures, "*he that eateth my flesh, &c., hath everlasting life,*" therefore the Church regards it as *the more pious and probable opinion* that those who are totally devoid of true *and lively faith*, do not partake of the holy flesh of Christ, in the Eucharist, God withdrawing from them so divine a gift." * This, indeed, is a most cautious opinion. But it cuts off Mr. Newman's mode of escape from the difficulty in which Sin after Baptism involves the system. It forbids the use of the Eucharist as a remedial ordinance, in the case of one whose faith by such sin has relapsed into death.

The necessity of this Dr. Pusey well understands; so that *he* does not think the Eucharist can justify in such a case, nor does he at all shrink from the consequence; but, more boldly carrying out the system to its results, than his chief co-worker is ready for, he freely acknowledges, as well in the Tracts, as in his lettter to the Bishop of Oxford, that "there are but two periods of absolute cleansing—Baptism, and the Day of Judgment,"—and as the Church "*has no second Baptism to give*"—so in the case of the sinner supposed, "*she cannot pronounce him altogether free from his past sins*—she therefore teaches him continually to repent, that so his sins *may* be blotted out, though she has no commission to tell him absolutely that they *are.*" †

Thus of the two standard bearers in this divinity, one has no way of Justification in this life for sin after Baptism; the other doubtfully thinks *he* has, in the Eucharist—unless, however, we are mistaken in his use of words, when he calls the Eucharist a *justifying* Sacrament. He may mean, with the Romanist, only that it takes away *venial* sins not *mortal.*

Now let us see how Romanism surmounts the difficulty. According to the system of Rome and that of Oxford, sin after Baptism, destroys Justification, and makes a living faith to be *dead*. Rome agrees with Dr. Pusey in denying that Justification from such sin can be obtained in the Eucharist, on the ground that he who is

---

* Treatise on the Church, vol. i. p. 529.
† Letter, p. 62. Tract No. 79. pp. 7 and 32. No. 80. p. 47.

spiritually dead ought not to receive that spiritual food which is only for the living, and cannot be united to Christ.* Still, however, the Eucharist is called in Romish language a *justifying* Sacrament, as is also Extreme Unction, and as sprinkling with holy water, and the Episcopal Benediction, are called in Romish Divinity justifying ordinances; but it must be remembered their efficacy is only for the remission of *venial* sins, such as the Church of Rome says "*have not properly the nature of sin.*"

How then does the Church of Rome provide for sin after Baptism? She invents a new Sacrament for its remission—viz.: that of *Penance* which is composed of contrition, confession and satisfaction, with the absolution of the Priest. Without this, the sin is absolutely unpardonable. The tendency of the Oxford system to the same contrivance will be more manifest as we proceed.

Now let us return, and since we have seen that Faith is considered as being justifying *after* Baptism, as "the *sole internal instrument,* of Justification," and as doing this however only as *the secondary subordinate, representative* instrument of *Baptism,* let us inquire how far it is really an instrument in any sense other than that in which all other graces are instruments. Mr. Newman says "It is a *symbol* of the nature and mode of our Justification, or of its history; and hence is said by Protestant divines to justify only, that our minds may be *affected* with a due sense of their own inability to do any good thing of themselves." The Representative we perceive, is now exhibited as a *symbol* of Baptism, sustaining justification *symbolically;* an *inward* and *spiritual grace,*" the symbol of "*an outward* and visible sign." This is at least new. "This symbol, (we read) is *said* to justify, not that it really justifies more than other graces, but it has this peculiarity, that it signifies in its very nature, that nothing of ours justifies us; or it typifies the freeness of our justification. Faith *heralds* forth divine grace, and its name is a sort of representative of it, as opposed to works. Hence it may well be honored above the other graces, and placed nearer Christ than the rest, *as if it were* distinct from them, and before them, and above them, *though it be not.* It is suitably said to justify us, because it says itself *that it does not*—so

---

* Quicunque habet conscientiam mortalis peccati, habet in se impedimentum percipiendi effectum hujus Sacramenti, tum quia non vivit spiritualiter et ita non debet spirituale nutrimentum suscipere, quod non est nisi viventis; tum quia non potest uniri Christo dum est in effectu peccandi mortaliter.—Unde in illo qui ipsum percipit in conscientia peccati mortalis, non operatur remissionem peccati. Aquinas, P. 1, 2. Q. 78. A 3.

to speak, as a sort of reward to it." Thus we are gravely told that faith is rewarded for something, by *being said to justify, when it does not*—as if it were a little child to be amused with a name and honored by a bauble, and deceived by a fraud. "It is but *said,* (it is said again) to be the sole justifier, and that with a view to inculcate another doctrine, not said, viz.: that all is of grace." "It is plain that 'faith only' does not apprehend, apply, or appropriate Christ's merits; but it only *preaches* them." The symbol has now become a Preacher. Because our Homily has these words; "The very true meaning of this *proposition* or *saying,* we be justified by faith only, &c.;" Mr. N. concludes from thence that "Justification by faith only is here said to be a SAYING"—and then says, "Consider how astonished and pained we should be were the doctrine of the atonement, or Christ's divinity, said to be a *proposition* or *saying.*" * Alas! Alas! such a shift!

We have now reached this point, that the faith which is "the *sole internal* instrument" of justification, the Representative, and Symbol, and Preacher of Justification, does not really justify any more than other graces; but is only *said* to do so. Justification by faith only "*a saying.*" Thus we are prepared for further light. Mr. N. asks, "why faith should cease to be justifying faith, if called *love or obedience?*" "It justifies *as including all other graces and works in and under it.*" "Works viewed as one with faith, which is the appointed instrument of justification after Baptism, are in one sense instruments too, as being connatural with faith and indivisible from it, organs through which it acts and which it hallows— instruments with faith of the continuance of Justification or of the remission of sin after Baptism." † Thus, "Justification by *obedience*" and by faith, only as a part of and the representative of all obedience, is the *distinguishing tenet* of this divinity. Mr. N. speaks therefore of "*love being imputed for righteousness.*"

We are now ready to interpret the select definition furnished by Dr. Pusey in his Letter, (App. p. 20,) that "we are justified *by obedience in the shape of faith:*" that is, *really* by obedience, *apparently* by faith; faith, the *saying;* obedience, the *doing;* faith, the *symbol;* obedience, the *thing.* And thus also of that other account, that "Justification is *received* by faith—*lives* in obedience;" in which the *sustaining* instrumentality of faith is taken away from the symbol, and ascribed to the substance. The whole is summed up

---

* Neuman's Lectures, pp. 278, 281, 2, 3, and 285.
‡ Ib. pp. 300, 346, 349.

in these words—"Justification by faith is Justification by God's free grace in the Gospel, as opposed to every thing out of the Gospel;"* not by faith as distinguished from works, but as opposed to whatever is "out of the Gospel."

Such honor then has Faith in this divinity. The grace which stands out so conspicuously in the language of the Saviour and of his Apostles, connected by them with every thing in salvation, so that we "live by faith," "stand by faith," "walk by faith," are "kept by the power of God, through faith, unto salvation;" condemned if we have it not; not condemned if we have it; faith, that is spoken of in the Scriptures a hundred times where Baptism is once; which fills whole series of discourses of our great divines, when Baptism is not mentioned; acknowledged by Mr. N. to be represented in the Scripture as having "*a certain extraordinary and singular sympathy with the grant of Gospel privileges;*" this distinguishing grace is first degraded to a dead, inoperative thing, before Baptism, such as even devils have; into a mere symbol of Baptism, after Baptism; a justifying instrument, in nothing more than its being *said* to be, what it is not—obedience being after all, the real and only internal instrument. We invoke Bishop Beveridge to deliver his testimony against such doctrine.

"Although Faith be always accompanied with obedience and good works, so as that it can never be without them, yet *in the matter of our Justification, it is always opposed to them by St. Paul.* And indeed to look to be justified by such a faith, which is the same with obedience, or which is all one, to be justified by our obedience, is to take all our hopes and expectations from Christ, and to place them upon ourselves—and therefore this notion of Faith overthrows the very basis and foundation of the Christian Religion."

The Bishop ascribes the doctrine we have exhibited, to *Socinians*, who hold, he says, that

"Justifying or Saving Faith is nothing else but obedience sincerely performed to the Law of God; so that Good Works are not the Fruit of Faith, but constitute the very form and essence of it." "This contradicts the whole tenor of the Gospel and the grand design of Christ's coming into the world, and of all that he hath done or suffered for us." †

---

* Newman's views of Holy Baptism, p. 22. † Beveridge's Sermons, No. 134.

Socinians and Romanists are not wide apart on the subject of Justification and Faith. A veil of mystical words, and the *opus operatum* of Sacraments, is nearly all that separates them. It is quite refreshing to dip into such doctrine as that of Beveridge, after all the shadows and symbols, and vain show with which we have been so long dealing. But it is with far other feelings that we recur to what we cannot but consider the improperly *reserved* language of Dr. Pusey, quoted from Mr. Newman, and adopted as his own, viz.,

"The instrumental power of Faith cannot interfere with the instrumental power of Baptism; because Faith in the *sole* justifier, not in contrast to all means and agencies whatever, (for it is not surely in contrast to our Lord's merits, or God's mercy,) but to all other *graces*. When then, Faith is called the *sole instrument*, this means *the sole internal instrument*, not the sole instrument of any kind." *

All this is evidently mere words. Faith *before* Baptism is, in this divinity, no instrument at all, because *dead*. *In* Baptism, it is no instrument at all, because not made alive till Baptism is completed. *After* Baptism it is an instrument of Justification, only as it *sustains* what Baptism has already effected, and which, when lost, it cannot renew. And even in that instrumentality, it is not a *sole* instrument, but is instrumental only as all other graces are also; and it is only *said* to be the sole instrument, as a reward for something peculiar to itself, which we do not pretend to understand. Such is the whole internal and sole instrumentality of that Faith which St. Paul speaks: "*Being justified by Faith*, we have peace with God, through our Lord Jesus Christ."

* Letter to Bp. of Oxford, pp. 43, 44.

CHAPTER VII.

THE DOCTRINE OF THIS DIVINITY, AS TO THE OFFICE AND EFFICACY OF THE SACRAMENTS, ESPECIALLY OF BAPTISM, COMPARED WITH THAT OF THE ROMISH CHURCH.

Tendency of all such principles as that of Justification in this divinity, to magnify external ceremonies, and ultimately to make all religion consist in them—This tendency prominent in regard to the Sacraments—Baptismal Justification similarly held by the Romish Church and the divines of Oxford—The *opus operatum* of Baptism held alike by both—Effect of this, the same in both, in keeping out of view the truth, that the Sacraments are *signs*, and identifying the visible sign with the invisible grace—The tendency of transubstantiation in this divinity, explained from the same cause—The false and injurious comparison between the spiritual nature of the Sacraments of the Old and New Testaments, resulting alike from Romish and Tractarian divinity,—Extract from Jeremy Taylor—Limbus Patrum—Bishop Burnet on Sacramental Justification.

IN proceeding further to show that the fundamental doctrine of the system before us, as to a righteousness inherent for Justification, is so identical with that of Rome, in ramification, as well as root, that it affects the same subordinate doctrines, in precisely the same way, and with reference to the same ends, we proceed from the doctrine of Faith, to that of the Sacraments, and especially of Baptism.

We have found that Justifying Faith, like Justifying Righteousness in this system, is a matter of works altogether; that the latter is identical with Sanctification, and that the former is justifying only as it is a name for all Christian virtues. Thus Justification by faith, is justification *by all the Christian's privileges and gifts*—since they are all a part of the faith bestowed on one who embraces the mercies of God, in Christ, and through the Sacraments is made a partaker of His life. "It is justification by God's free grace in the Gospel, *as opposed to every thing out of the Gospel.*" * The amount then is, that Justification by faith, through God's free grace, means nothing more nor less than *Justification by Christianity*.

* Pusey's Views of Baptism. p. 22.

Now the moment a system of religion gets thus to rest in works for justification before God, its strong tendency is to run into reliance on *external* works, because tangible, appreciable; they can be counted, measured and easily fled to for refuge. Hence, while all corrupt systems of Christianity have talked much of inherent righteousness, inward holiness, &c., their real working, in the long run, has been most grossly to neglect all inward religion, and make the whole of salvation consist in external observances; and the more they have resulted in this, the more has the outward show of devotion increased in bodily postures and gestures, and the power and efficacy of external symbols and gestures been magnified. All this is natural. We could make the whole aspect of our congregations at once as devout in bodily expression as that of a Romish Monastery, or a Mohammedan Mosque, or a Hindoo Temple, did we only make them thoroughly believe, like Papists, and Mohammedans, and Hindoos, that by works we are to be acceptable to God. But what, in such an experiment, we should gain in outward exhibitions of devotion, we should lose in that inward holiness, without which no man shall see the Lord. "*We are the circumcision,*" (we are God's true people) says St. Paul, "*which worship God in the Spirit, and rejoice in Christ Jesus, and have no confidence in the flesh.*"

The first indication of the tendency referred to, after adopting a righteousness of works, is the undue magnifying of *the office and efficacy of the Sacraments*.

How this appears in the present system, in comparison with its phases in that of Rome, we now proceed to show.

It is notoriously the doctrine of the Trent Decrees, that Baptism is "*the only instrumental cause*" of justification; so absolutely necessary thereto, that without it justification is obtained by none.* That this is precisely the doctrine, and a very distinguishing one of the Oxford School, there can be no need, after all our previous showing, of bringing any passages to prove. Justification in Baptism, and only there, is the sole subject of a whole volume of Oxford Tracts called "*Scriptural Views of Holy Baptism.*" The only exception to this absolute necessity which is granted to have occurred in ancient times, is considered as not applicable in our days. †

---

* Instrumentalis causa—Sacramentum Baptismi sine quo nulli unquam justificatio contingit.—Concil. Trident. Sess. vi.

† "Faith considered as an instrument is always secondary to the Sacraments. The most extreme case in which it seems to supersede them, IS NOT FOUND IN OUR

It is equally notorious that, in the view of the Church of Rome, Baptismal Justification consists in an infusing of righteousness, by which all original sin in Infants, and all actual sin, as well as original in adults, is entirely remitted. The remission of Original Sin, is held to be, not in the sense of its non imputation as a matter of guilt, but in that of *being entirely taken away* as a matter of indwelling corruption, EXTINCTION.

There is no necessity of occupying space with the showing that this is also the teaching of our Oxford divines. The advocates of this system do not pretend to any distinction on this point between their views and Romanism.

The reader is now requested to observe that what is called the OPUS OPERATUM, in the Romish doctrine of the Sacraments, is found in all its offensive substance in this divinity. This we proceed to show.

In the scholastic language of Romanism, there are two technical

own, but in the ancient Church; in which the faith of persons dying in the state of catechumens was held to avail to their reception, in death, into that kingdom of which Baptism is the ordinary gate."

In the absolute necessity of Baptism to Salvation, Mr. N. seems to exceed some Romanists. The latter deny not salvation to such as have desired Baptism, but died without it; but in strange inconsistency with their doctrine concerning the deadness of faith, and the necessary absence of love in all faith which precedes Baptism, they allow that such persons may have internal Sanctification, and such a desire of Baptism, as proceeds from *faith working by love*, and therefore living and justifying. First, Aquinas says that Baptism is necessary, simply and absolutely as food is to life; non, sine quo non habetur finis ita convenienter, sicut equus necessarius est ad iter; sed simpliciter sicut cibus est necessarius vitæ humanæ. He then cites Augustine as saying that invisible Sanctification might be possessed, and might be availing without the visible Sacrament: but that the visible Sanctification by the visible Sacrament, without the invisible Sanctification, though it might be possessed, could not profit. Invisibilem Sanctificationem quibusdam affuisse et profuisse, sine visibilibus Sacramentis; visibilem vero Sanctificationem, quæ fit Sacramento visibili, sine invisibili posse adesse, sed non posse prodesse. Hence St. Thomas concludes that a person may obtain Salvation by invisible Sanctification, who by a desire of Baptism has received it in wish, though not in form, which wish or desire proceeds from faith working by love, through which God, 'who is not tied to visible Sacraments,' internally sanctifies the interior of the man. Videtur sine Sacramento Baptismi aliquis possit salutem consequi per invisibilem sanctificationem—minime salvari possunt qui nec re, nec voto Sacramentum susceperint; qui vero salutem voto sacram—Baptismi susceperint, etsi non re, salvari possunt. Cum aliquis baptizari desiderat, sed aliquo casu prævenitur morte—talis sine Baptismo actuali salutem consequi potest, propter desiderium Baptismi quod procedit ex fide per dilectionem operante; per quam Deus interius hominis sanctificat, cujus potentia Sacramentis visibilibus non allegatur. But such a person must go to Purgatory, however. Talis decedens non statim pervenit ad vitam eternam, sed patietur pænam pro peccatis præteritis; ipse tamen salvus erit, sed quasi igne.—P. 1, 2. Q. 65. A. 4. 2.

expressions with regard to the efficacy of the Sacraments, viz., *opus operans* and *opus operatum*. The expression that the Sacraments confer grace *ex opere operante*, means that their efficacy requires in the recipient a preparatory state of inward piety; precisely what we are accustomed to understand by the Repentance and Faith required for the Baptism of Adults. Such was the efficacy of the Sacraments of the *Jewish Church*, according to the Church of Rome; Abraham having been justified by faith, while in uncircumcision. But the Sacraments of the Christian Church are exalted above those which went before, in this, viz., that they confer grace *ex opere operato;* by which is meant that no preparation of internal piety, such as that of a living faith, is required in the recipient to make them effectual. The Schoolmen made a general rule that in order to receive the grace of the Sacraments unto salvation, it is not necessary that you have faith, that is to say, a good internal affection of heart; but it is sufficient that you place no obstacle in the way. The *opus operatum* then is simply the efficacy of the Sacraments, without respect to the state of the recipient, except that he do not positively shut up his soul against them. He may be entirely negative as to all spiritual affection, and still the efficacy will remain. This does not mean that in the adult recipient of Baptism no faith is required, but that it need not be a *living* faith; it may be dead, inoperative, and yet be no hindrance to the sacramental efficacy. Neither is it contended in the Church of Rome, that the efficacy is not by the sole power of God, making the Sacraments thus mighty, for Christ's sake, and in application of his merits.*

* The whole preparation required in the Church of Rome for adult Baptism is thus expressed in the catechism of the Council of Trent—"If they have been born of infidel parents," (the children of Christians being supposed to have been baptized in infancy) "the Christian faith is to be proposed"—"If converted to the Lord," (that is if they renounce infidelity) "they are to be admonished not to defer Baptism beyond the time appointed by the Church; and they are to be taught that in their regard perfect conversion (that is the spiritual work) consists in regeneration *by Baptism*." "The Church must take particular care, that none approach this Sacrament whose hearts are *vitiated by hypocrisy and dissimulation*," (the *obex* or impediment of the schoolmen).—"The necessary dispositions for Baptism are, that in the first place, they *must desire and purpose to receive it;* for as in Baptism we die to sin, and engage to lead a new life, it is fit to be administered to those only who receive it of their own free will and accord, and is to be forced on none." Faith for the same reason is also necessary—(not a living faith, for that comes *by* Baptism.) "Another necessary condition is *compunction* for past sins and a fixed determination to refrain from their future commission." The reason of this is that when many on the day of Pentecost were "*compunct in heart,*" Peter said to them, "*do penance* and be Baptized." Thus we have a desire

This *opus operatum* has ever been considered, among Protestants, a dark and deadly plague-spot of Popery. But is not this precisely the doctrine of this divinity as to the efficacy of Baptism? The reader need but refer to what has been shown under the head of faith, to perceive, without a doubt, that Baptism is considered, in that scheme, as efficacious to justification in the adult recipient, without any faith except such as devils may have, as well as we. One is made *righteous* by Baptism, from being, up to the time of Baptism, *unrighteous*. A living faith, is begotten in Baptism, and is expressly said, not to precede, but to follow it. Further evidence cannot be needed than this, that in the *opus operatum* of Baptism, the two schemes of Rome and Oxford are one.

But further, in consequence of the doctrine of the Church of Rome, as to the *immediate* efficacy of the Sacraments, it is well known that nothing is more studiously kept out of view, as pertaining to Baptism and the Lord's Supper, than that they are

to be baptized, a dead faith and compunction *(not contrition)* for sins, composing all the requisites for Baptism. Devils have compunction as well as faith—for they "believe and *tremble*." For the Sacrament of Penance, which is for the remission of "sin *after* Baptism" *contrition, confession, and satisfaction* "are required; but for sin *before* Baptism only *compunction*."—See Catechism of Council of Trent, pp. 164, 167, 241.

Aquinas, defining the faith required for Baptism, says that though a person should not have a right faith as to other articles, he may have it as to Baptism; and thus he may have the *intention* to receive Baptism. But even though he should not think correctly concerning this Sacrament, *a general intention* is sufficient for its reception; because though he knew nothing correctly about it, he intends to receive it as Christ appointed, and the Church has handed it down. Etiam non habens rectam fidem circa alios articulos, potest habere rectam fidem circa Sacramentum Baptismi, et ita non impeditur quin possit habere intentionem suscipiendi Sacramentum Baptismi. Si tamen etiam circa hoc Sacramentum non recte sentiat, sufficit ad perceptionem Sacramenti generalis intentio, quia intendit suscipere Baptismum, sicut Christus instituit et Ecclesia tradit.—P. 1, 2, Q. 67, Q. 8.

Thus the most general assent, a mere profession of faith, in whatever may be asserted by the Church, without knowing anything about it, is the whole requirement for Baptism. Aquinas teaches no more concerning the repentance required. He says, Penitentia ante Baptismum est actus virtutis disponens ad Sacramentum Baptismi; it is an act of virtue *disposing* one to Baptism. This is precisely what he and Mr. Newman say of the *dead faith* before Baptism. Of course, if faith is dead, repentance must be also. Hence Romanists call it mere *attrition*, that is, a sort of penitence, resulting only from fear, having no love to God, which is the distinguishing feature of *contrition*. Thus Aquinas: Antequam gratia infundatur non est habitus a quo actus contritionis postea elicitur; et sic nullo modo attritio potest fieri contritio. "Before grace is poured into the heart (in Baptism) there is no habit from which the act of contrition may be elicited; and thus in no way can *attrition* become *contrition*."—Part 3. Supp. Q. 2, A. 3.

signs of grace; the one a *sign* of regeneration, instead of regeneration itself—the other a *sign* of the body and blood of Christ, instead of being the body and blood itself.

It is true, that in the defining of Sacraments in general, the definition of Augustine is adopted—that "a Sacrament is a visible *sign* of an invisible grace."* But when they come to the definition of Baptism, the word, sign, is omitted, and it is defined as the "*Sacrament of Regeneration.*" How essentially the idea of sign is dropped by *the doctrine of a substantial transubstantiation* in the Eucharist, need not be said. But the connection between their doctrine of justification and their view of the *substantial* presence of Christ in the Eucharist, may not be generally perceived. "They were not willing to conceive, (says Jackson) how Christ's body and blood could have any *real operation* upon our souls, unless they were so locally present, as that they might *agree per contactum*, that is to purge our souls by *Oral Manducation*, as physical medicines do," (which is the pretended use of Transubstantiation.) Now, is not this the explanation of that singular effort of this Divinity, to keep out of sight, as much as possible, and in a most subordinate position, that view of the Sacrament, which, in all our standards, is held out so prominently, viz., that it is not grace, but the "*sign*" of grace, and to fix all attention upon the real presence of the body of Christ, in and under the sacramental elements, as if there were some presence, not corporeal indeed, and local, as Romanists maintain, nor yet simply a presence by the operations of his Spirit conveying the spiritual benefits of his atonement to the believing communicant, as Protestants teach; but *some other presence*, which they do not pretend to define, but which they consider is intended by the words, "*This is my body?*"

Now when with this, we connect, what appears so conspicuously in the writings of Mr. Newman, an utter contempt of the idea of justification by a righteousness *external*, a something done for us 1800 years ago, and of a faith looking to the cross of Calvary for remission of sins, and his strong insisting upon an *inward* application of the atonement, *a cross within*, a *present substantial* righteousness, &c., &c., we may see the plain bearing of *his* doctrine of justification upon the exclusion of the idea of *signs* in the Sacrament, and the fixing of his whole mind upon a "*substantial*" presence (as the Oxford Tracts have not scrupled to say) of the body of Christ. In other words, his doctrine of Justification makes him unable to conceive "how Christ's body and blood can have

* Catechism of Trent.

any real operation, unless by *contact*." The idea by which Jackson, and Andrews, and the Catechism of Edward the Sixth, not to speak of others, explain the *real* presence of Christ, as distinguished from a *local* presence, viz., that he is *really* present, when present *effectively*, as he was to the woman who touched, *not him*, but *his garment;* while he was *locally*, but not *effectively*, present to the multitude that pressed and touched him, but who derived no benefit, because they had no faith; this idea, carried into application to the believer's faith, in the Eucharist, receiving the *signs* of the body and blood of Christ, and through them, ascending to heaven, and making Christ present to it, by its being present to him; this sort of real presence, which is just as applicable to Christ's imputed righteousness, as to his ascended body in heaven, is too distant, and abstract, and visionary for these writers, and therefore, though not denied perhaps, is kept out of view, and the impression sought to be produced is, that there is some mysterious presence of the body of Christ in some other sense, which is neither that of Romanists, nor Protestants, but (like their doctrine of an inherent righteousness "*within* us, but not *in us*,") a *substantial* presence, but not *corporeal;* a *real* presence of his *real* body, but not a *local* presence; a *substantial* presence, wherever the Eucharist is administered, but not the presence of *ubiquity*, not *transubstantiation;* but the next thing to it, and acknowledging itself to be a great deal more like transubstantiation, and evidently sympathizing with it far more, than with the anti-transubstantiation doctrine of Protestantism.*

* The following extract from Dr. Jackson, on the *Real* Presence of Christ in the Eucharist, will beautifully explain in what sense the Real Presence was understood by divines of the days of Bishop Andrews, &c. Precisely the same illustration is used by that Bishop.

"With whomsoever he is *virtually present*, that is, to whomsoever he communicates the influence of his body and blood by his Spirit, he is *really present* with them, though *locally* absent from them. Thus he was really present with the woman, which was cured of her bloody issue, by touching the hem of his garment. But not so *really* present with the multitude that did throng and press upon him, that were *locally* more present with him. She did not desire so much as to touch his *body* with her hand, for she said in herself, *If I may but touch the hem of his garment, I shall be whole.* And yet by our Saviour's interpretation, she did touch him more immediately than they which were nearer unto him, which thrust or thronged him. And the reason why she alone did more immediately touch him than any of the rest, was, because *virtue* of healing did go out from him to her alone. It is true, then, (for our Saviour saith it) her faith did make her whole, and yet she was made whole by the virtue which went out from him. This was the fruit or effect of her faith—or rather the reward or consequent of her faith. In like sort, as many as are healed from their sins, whether by the Sacrament of

This aversion to signs in the Sacrament, with its *opus operatum* is broadly declared by Dr. Pusey, in the very teeth of the most express language of his own Church. Baptism, says our 27th Article, "is a *sign* of regeneration or new birth—whereby the promises, &c., are visibly *signed and sealed*." But he says expressly, "Baptism *is not a sign, but the putting on of Christ*: wherefore Baptism is a thing *most powerful and efficacious*." * In other words, Baptism, instead of being the sign of regeneration, is *regeneration itself* It is in itself "most powerful and efficacious." The Church of Rome never exceeded this. The *opus operatum* was never more decidely and boldly expressed.

The reader may now appreciate a more singular passage in Dr. Pusey, to the Bishop of Oxford as to the Romish doctrine of Baptism, intended to produce the impression that, as to baptismal regeneration and justification, the Romish Church and the Oxford School are not quite agreed, the former falling below the mark, somewhat like Ultra Protestants.

The chief charge against Rome, as to the Sacrament of Baptism, is not that she has unduly exalted it, but on the contrary that she has depreciated it. She insists indeed on its necessity, and there

---

Baptism or the Eucharist, are healed by *faith relatively* or instrumentally. Faith is the mouth or organ, by which we receive the medicine; but it is the virtual influence derived from the body and blood of Christ which properly or efficiently doth cure our souls and dissolve the works of Satan in us.

"This woman, as St. Matthew relates the story, had said within herself, if I may but touch the hem of his garment I shall be whole. She wanted either the opportunity or boldness to touch the fore part of his garment, or to come into his sight or presence. Yet he then knew, not only, that she had touched the hem of his garment, but that she had said this within herself, and out of his knowledge of this her faith and humility, he did pronounce and make her whole. Now it is but one and the same act of one and the same Divine wisdom, to know the heart and secret thoughts of men afar off and near at hand. And therefore a matter as easy, for the Son of God, or for the Man Christ Jesus, in whom the Godhead dwelleth bodily, though still remaining at the right hand of God, to know the hearts of all such as present themselves at his Table here on earth, as well as he knew the secret thoughts of this woman which came behind him. What need then is there of his *Bodily Presence* in the Sacrament, or of any other presence than the influence of emission of virtue from his heavenly sanctuary unto our souls? He hath left us the consecrated elements of bread and wine, to be unto us more than the hem of his garment, if we do but touch and taste them with the same faith by which this woman touched the hem of his garment. This our faith shall make us whole, and staunch the running issues and cleanse or cure the leprous sores of our souls, as perfectly as it did this woman's issue of blood."—*Jackson's Works*, vol. iii. p. 307.

* Views of Baptism, p. 102.

leaves it. Her members are taught to look upon Baptism as a mere preliminary act, in the *back-ground* as it were of the Christian life; the foreground, upon which their eye is fixed, being taken up by their Sacrament of Penance and the Eucharist. As to Holy Baptism, Rome innovated not; and yet she has doubly lowered it."*

One would suppose that to lower Baptism, was to innovate. But the lowering consists not in any depreciation of Baptism, but in the undue raising of penance and the Eucharist. If the reference be, in any degree, to the position of Baptism, in its necessity and efficacy in regeneration or justification, according to the standard of our Oxford men, it is wholly unfounded. There is not a word in the latter, as to those points, which is not to be found in Romish writers. Thomas Aquinas is entirely an Oxford man, on this, as well as other matters. It would seem to be a singular depression of Baptism in comparison with the Eucharist, to assign to the former the power of remitting *mortal* sins, and to the latter only the remission of *venial* sins; a power given equally to holy water, the Bishop's blessing, &c.; to make Baptism the communication of life to the dead, and the Eucharist only the continuation of that life.

Another manifestation of the doctrine of the Sacraments, in which this divinity and Romanism singularly concur, is seen *in the wide difference made between the Sacraments of the Old and New Testaments, in regard to saving efficacy.*

Nothing is more notorious than the fact that the old, as well as the modern, divines, of the Church of England, have regarded the Sacraments of the two dispensations, as standing on essentially the same footing in regard to spiritual grace, that the only difference was in the sign; the inward and spiritual grace, signified, pledged, sealed, conveyed and confirmed, was precisely the same in both. On this identity it is well known that our divines have been accustomed confidently to argue the propriety of Infant Baptism, because the spiritual grace being the same, there could be no reason why infants under the Gospel should be excluded from what infants under the law enjoyed. But there is a great inconvenience in this identity of circumcision and Baptism, to those who hold the latter to be the *only instrument of Justification.* Abraham *was justified,*

---

* See the whole passage on p. 76, 77, of Dr. Pusey's Letter. Do not Oxford divines commit the very same thing with which they charge the Romish Church? Do they not say that "as Holy Communion conveys a more awful presence of God than Holy Baptism, so must it be the instrument of a higher justification?"—Newman on Justif. p. 169.

being *uncircumcised,* says St. Paul. Consequently, if circumcision and Baptism in point of the grace signified, be the same, a sinner may be justified being *unbaptized.* Again, the whole generation of Israel that were born in the wilderness continued *uncircumcised,* some of them nearly forty years; and this by divine command: nor was the Sacrament of circumcision given them till they had entered into Canaan. If justification was linked to circumcision, as we are now taught it is with Baptism, how could all that generation be required to remain so many years unjustified? Evidently it could not have been; and hence results a most inconvenient argument against baptismal justification; and how is it to be obviated? Very easily. Our Oxford divines deny that circumcision and Baptism do bear the spiritual resemblance mentioned above; and holding fast the *exclusive instrumentality of Baptism* in justification, they maintain that, since the Old Testament Saints were not baptized, they were not justified, but were in bondage, under the law and not under grace, and received not justification until Christ came, and with him, the grace and gift of Baptism. To this general rule Mr. Newman makes Abraham and Elijah exceptions.

The doctrine is not only that the Sacraments of the law did not confer grace; but that justification and regeneration were not conferred, except in special cases, before the Gospel.

" The law could not be the means of life, because life as yet was not; it was not created. The law could not justify, because whatever special favor might be shown *here and there by anticipation,* (as in Abraham's case) justification was not purchased as a free gift *to all who sought it.* God justified Abraham, and glorified Elijah; but he had not yet promised heaven to the obedient or acceptance to the believing. He wrought first in the few what he afterwards offered to all; and even in those extraordinary instances he acted immediately from himself, not through the Jewish law as his instrument. * * * The ceremonies of the Law were tokens not of the presence of grace *but of its absence*—(they were not so much as *means* of grace before grace was purchased.) They were attempts in a bad case towards what was needed—the humble and anxious representation of nature making *dumb signs* for the things it needed—the Jews were told to approach God with works, which could not justify, *as if they could,*" (we suppose this is on the plan of faith being rewarded with being *said* to justify when it does not) "what to the Jews then was impossible even to the last is imparted to us from the first. They might not even end where we begin. They wrought *towards* justification, and we from it. They came to God with *rites*, He comes to us in Sacraments."*

In the same strain, Dr. Pusey complains that we "take what is said of Baptism, as if it inculcated *the same as circumcision.*" "The new birth and renewal of the Holy Ghost imparted in Baptism are something different *in kind* from what had been before made known—the relation of Israel as the child of God could but shadow forth, not *realize,* the privilege of our sonship." The Flood and the Red Sea are put on a level, as ordinances, with circumcision, in point of grace. All are mere *types*—Sacraments they are none. "Circumcision was no means nor channel of spiritual grace." It was only "a type of Baptism"—a mere "symbol" or "shadow of a Christian Sacrament."†

From all this it is manifest not only that the sacramental character is denied to circumcision, which St. Paul says was a *"seal of the righteousness by faith, which Abraham had being uncircumcised;"* but that all those who lived before the Gospel, from Adam downwards, with two or three favored exceptions, were without *regeneration,* without *justification, without acceptance to heaven,* till Christ came.

Now Simon Magus, because he received Christian Baptism, is supposed by Dr. P. to have been regenerated and justified ; at least, that writer sees no reason to suppose the contrary in as much as he is said to have *believed,* though it is not pretended that he believed before Baptism, with a *living* faith, and though an apostle so soon after he was baptized pronounced him in the bonds of iniquity. ‡ So also Voltaire, Rousseau, and all other infidels and reprobates, who were baptized in infancy, *when they could place no impediment of infidelity or hypocrisy* to the efficacy of Baptism, were once according to this system regenerate and justified, entirely cleansed from the stain of sin, and had, as Tract No. 82, says, all thus baptized do receive, " so super-abounding and awful a grace tabernacled in them, that no other words describe it more nearly than to call it an Angel's nature," "a Divine presence in the soul, abiding, abundant, and efficacious," distinguished from the greatest gift of the Spirit to the saints of the Old Testament. § This most distinguishing grace of Baptism, which Dr. Pusey says, "gives a depth to our Christian existence an actualness to our union to Christ, a reality to our sonship to God,

---

* Newman's Lectures, p. 325—7. † Views of Baptism, pp. 103, 49, 254.
‡ Views of Holy Baptism, p. 185. § No. 82, pp. 13 and 14.

an *overwhelmingness* (for this system makes words, as well as doctrines,) to the dignity conferred on human nature—a substantiality to the indwelling of Christ:"* all this Simon Magus, for aught Dr. P. sees, may have had by Baptism, though immediately after he was in the very depth of wickedness; and all this every reprobate and Atheist, baptized in infancy, certainly once possessed. But none of this, was possessed by those noble men of God, Moses, Samuel, and all that "cloud of witnesses" who "through faith subdued kingdoms, wrought righteousness;" "obtained a good report through faith," "died in faith," except in a few especially favored instances, because, says St. Paul, "they received not the promise, God having provided some better thing for us, that they without us should not be made perfect." That *better thing* says this divinity, is the *baptismal* grace which Simon Magus may have received though holy men of old did not. One would think no system could endure such condemnation.

Dr. Pusey assigns as a reason for the usual teaching among Protestants of the sameness of the Sacraments of circumcision and Baptism, as to the spiritual grace consignated, "an over-anxious seeking for some Scriptural justification of infant Baptism, since they debarred themselves from appealing to *the authority of the Church.*" Now if the reader will consult Bishop Taylor (whom we cite because he is a great favorite with these writers,) he will find not only that *he* was not disposed to rest the Baptism of infants on the *authority of the Church,* but that in appealing to Scripture in its favor, he places his argument upon *the entire identity of circumcision and Baptism in all spiritual respects.*

"That which is of the greatest persuasion is that the children of the Church are as capable of the *same covenant* as the children of the Jews, for it was the *same covenant* that circumcision did consign, a *spiritual* covenant, under a veil; and now it is the *same spiritual covenant without a veil.*" Circumcision "principally related to an effect and a blessing greater than was afterwards expressed in the temporal promise, which effect was forgiveness of sins, justification by faith." "The promises which circumcision did seal, were the same promises which are consigned in Baptism." "To as many persons, and in as many capacities, and in the same dispositions as the promises were applied, and did relate, in circumcision, to the same do they belong, and may be applied in Baptism"

---

* Views of Baptism, p. 16.

—"the covenant which circumcision did sign, was a covenant of *grace* and faith; the promises, were of the Spirit, or spiritual."*

But what does our Church, in her Homilies, say? We adduce the following passage, not to show the truth, for it needs no showing, but to show the miserable shifts to which this system is driven.

"And although they were not named Christian men, yet was it a Christian faith that they had: *for they looked for all benefits of God the Father, through the merits of his Son Jesus Christ, as we now do. This difference is between them and us—that they looked when Christ should come, and we be in the time when he is come. Therefore, saith St. Augustine, the time is altered and changed, but not the faith. For we have both one faith, in one Christ. The same Holy Ghost also that we have, had they,* (2 Corin. iv. 13,) *saith St. Paul. For as the Holy Ghost doth teach us to trust in God, and to call upon him as our Father; so did he teach them to say, as it is written, 'Thou, Lord, art our Father and Redeemer; and thy name is without beginning, and everlasting.'* (Isa. lxiii. 16.) God gave them then grace to be his children, as he doth us now. But now, by the coming of our Saviour Christ, we have received more abundantly the Spirit of God in our hearts; whereby we may conceive a greater faith, and a surer trust, than many of them had. But in effect they and we be all one: we have the same faith that they had in God, and they the same that we have." †

Now is it credible that such a passage could be produced by our Oxford writers as evidence that the English Church teaches nothing opposed to their doctrine? It is extracted in Tract No. 82, a tract in express defense of their teaching on Baptismal Regeneration; and the remarks succeeding it are a fair specimen of the treatment, which the standards of the Church, as well as the Scriptures, receive from those scholars, and logicians. Thus writes the Tractarian immediately after the above extract from the Homilies:

"Though man's duties were the same, his gifts were greater after Christ came. Whatever spiritual aid was vouchsafed before,

---

* Bp. Taylor's Life of Christ, p. i. § ix. Bp. Jewel's Works. v. iii. p. 497. See also Cranmer's Works vol i. p. 75. Bp. Hooper's Works, vol. ii. pp. 89 and 50. Becon's Works, vol. ii. p 216.—Here let it be stated once for all, that our references to the English Reformers, unless otherwise noted, are from the Parker's Society Edition.

† Homily of Faith, P. ii.

yet *afterwards it was a Divine presence in the soul*, abiding, abundant and efficacious. In a word, it was the Holy Ghost himself, who influenced indeed the heart before, but is not revealed *as residing in it*." *

But the reader will ask, in astonishment, how can men thus write under pretense of not being inconsistent with the standards of the Church, when the Homily says expressly, that as we have the Holy Ghost, so had the Old Testament Fathers, " God gave them grace to be his children as he doth us now." If he will look at the extract from the Homily as given above, he will see how such things are done. The Tract-writer quotes the first sentence of that extract. Then all that follows, distinguished above by italics, is *omitted;* The very pith of the passage, just what asserts the very opposite of his doctrine—*all omitted*. But does he give us notice of an omission? So far from it that the two sentences, next before and after the Italics, are joined by a *colon*, precisely as if they were members of the same sentence. Nothing indicates that a word of the passage has been left out. Comment upon such shifts to hide the glaring departure of this wretched coveting of Popery, from the doctrines of that Church, which these writers profess to love and follow, is needless.

The same views of the Sacraments and privileges of the Old Testament saints which we have given from the Homilies may be found everywhere in the divines of the English Church. Scarcely any argument have they written on the Scriptural warrant for infant Baptism, in which those views have not been presented. Thus are our Oxford Restorationists constrained by their doctrine of baptismal justification into a consequence directly at war with the most common and notorious verities of Protestant divinity. But precisely where they thus differ from our Protestant divines, they agree with those of Rome.

The Schoolmen described the difference between the Sacraments of the two Testaments, by making the efficacy of those of the New, to proceed *ex opere operato*, that is without an internal piety in the recipient; while that of the Old, proceeded *ex opere operante*, that is from a living faith, or a pious affection of the recipient. And the Council of Florence, confirming the opinion of the schoolmen, said that the Sacraments of the Old Testament did not confer grace: but as types or figures, they signified that it was to be afterwards

---

* No. 82, p. xiii. Eng. Ed.

given through the passion of Christ; while our Sacraments both contain grace, and confer it on those who worthily receive them.*

The reader may very reasonably inquire here, what, in the view of those who think thus concerning the Old Testament Saints, was the state of their souls after death—did they go to Heaven? Romish divinity answers *nay*—and consistently, because they were not *regenerated* nor *justified*, since Christ had not died, and therefore Baptism was not given. Where then? To *Limbus Patrum*, answers Romanism.

The Jesuit, whom Usher answered, undertook to prove, not only that there is a Limbus Patrum, but that our Saviour descended into hell to deliver the ancient Fathers of the Old Testament; because before his passion, none ever entered into heaven. Whether that Limbus were distinct from that in which infants that die without Baptism, are now believed by the Romish Church to be received, the divines do doubt, says Maldonat. The Dominicans in 1252, answered in the affirmative. "The more common opinion, (says Usher,) is that these be two distinct places,"—that of the Fathers "now being emptied of its old inhabitants."† That our Oxford

---

* Chemnitz. Examen. Dec. Conc. Trid. p. 207.

The doctrine of Aquinas as to the relations between the Sacraments of the Old Testament and the inward grace signified, is almost precisely what our Articles express concerning that relation in the Sacraments of the Gospel. He says the Sacraments of the Old Testament were professions of faith, *signifying* the passion of Christ and its benefits, but they had not any virtue in themselves by which *they* conferred grace, but were only *signs of that faith* by which the saints were justified. They differed from the Sacraments of the New Testament in this, that the latter contain grace, as in a *vessel* which is thus made an instrument of grace—while in the former grace was conferred only as they were *signs* of the passion of Christ. Sacramenta veteris legis erant quædam illius fidei protestationes, in quantum significabant passionem Christi et effectus ejus. Sic ergo patet quod non habebant in se aliquam virtutem, qua operarentur ad conferendam gratiam justificationis, sed solum *signa erant fidei per quam justificabantur.*

After giving various opinions in his day as to the efficacy of circumcision, showing that this doctrine was by no means then well settled, for instance one of Peter Lombard, that circumcision *took away sin, though it did not confer grace,* and another, that it conferred grace so as to make one worthy of eternal life, but not to repress concupiscence tempting him to sin, Aquinas concludes that it *is best to say* that circumcision, as other Sacraments of the Old Law was "*only a sign* of Justifying faith," and therefore in it grace was conferred, inasmuch as it was a *sign* of the future passion of Christ. *In circumcisione conferebatur gratia, in quantum erat signum passionis Christi futuræ*—P. 1. 2. Q. 62. A. 6. & Q. 70, A. 4.

† Usher's Answer to a Jesuit, c. viii.

The Romish doctrine of the Limbus Patrum, or the absence of the Old Testament Saints from the vision of God, and their enduring *in limbo* a certain negative evil, consisting in the want of what, since the New Testament blessedness, the dead in Christ and all departed saints have inherited, arose entirely out of this

Divines have said any thing directly on this subject, we know not; but how they can escape a Limbus Patrum, substantially the same as that which has been set apart for the accommodation of the Romish doctrine of baptismal justification, we cannot conceive. If nothing under the Jewish dispensation did confer grace, if regeneration and justification were not promised, nor given, till Christ came; if heaven, nor acceptance, was promised to obedience then, as is maintained; then, though "in some favored cases," God may have given justification, *directly, and not through the Jewish dispensation;* yet, as to the multitude of them that believed, all those, for instance, who are mentioned by St. Paul, that "great cloud of witnesses," who "*all died in faith,*" it must follow that they did not enter into heaven. But certainly they did not go into a place of torment. It remains that they must have gone to some place intermediate between that of the *impenitent*, and that of the *justified*, waiting the coming of Christ, and from which they were

figment of the difference between the spiritual efficacy of the Sacraments of the two dispensations; and in its essential character, it is a necessary consequence of that doctrine of the Sacraments in which this Divinity and the Romish so well agree.

The doctrine of Romanism, as to the state of the dead, is given, in all its fulness, in the "Angelic Doctor." Aquinas enumerates five *receptacula* for disembodied souls, according to their several states, viz.: *Paradise, Limbus Patrum,* (for the Old Testament Saints) *Limbus Puerum,* (for children unbaptized,) Purgatory, and Hell. The Limbus Patrum, and Puerum, and the place of positive punishment of the wicked, are all considered, as to location, essentially one. Quantum ad situm loci, sunt loca, continua; though they differ as to quality—that of children, being an upper apartment to that of the damned, that of the Old Testament Saints, before the advent of Christ, superior *(pars superiors)* to all. Supremum et minus tenebrosum locum habuerunt omnibus puniendis. The Limbus Patrum, and "Abraham's bosom," are supposed to have been the same before the advent of Christ. Since the descent of Christ ad *inferos*, the bliss of the Old Testament Saints has been rendered as complete as that of the departed saints under the Christian Dispensation. But before that, they endured the pain of *hope deferred*, dolor de delatione seperatæ gloriæ, privatio gloriæ separatæ; et secundum hoc habet rationem inferni, et doloris. This *dolor* is called "an exclusion from the life of glory," and the reason given for the incarceration of the Old Testament Saints in that Limbus, is that although they had been liberated by the faith of Christ from all sin, as well original as actual, and from all liability to punishment for *actual* sin, they had not been from liability to punishment *(for original sin,)* a reatu pœnæ originalis peccati; and the reason for this is just the reason given by Oxford divines, as shown above, viz., that the price of redemption was not yet paid, Christ had not died,—nondum soluto pretio redemptionis. And therefore Christ descending *ad inferos*, by virtue of his passion, absolved those Saints from this liability— *ab hoc reatu*, that they might see God, *per essentiam*.—Aquinas, P. 3. Q. 52, & Suppl. Q. 69.

delivered when he had accomplished that of which all their religion had been, in the view of this system, but an inoperative, inefficacious shadow.

The comparison of this Divinity, with that of our Church and standard divines, on the main topics now brought into comparison with Romanism, viz: the *constituent principle of Justification*, the *Nature and Office of Justifying Faith*, and *Sacramental Justification*, will be reserved for other Chapters. We finish the present subject by quoting the testimony of Bishop Burnet, on Sacramental Justification.

"It is a tenet of the Church of Rome, that the use of the Sacraments, if men *do not put a bar to them*, and if they have only *imperfect acts of sorrow*, accompanying them, does so far complete those weak acts, as to *justify* us. This we do utterly deny, as a doctrine that tends to enervate all religion; and to make the Sacraments, that were appointed to be the solemn acts of religion for quickening and exciting our piety, and for conveying grace to us, upon our coming devoutly to them, become *means to flatten and deaden us*, as if they were of the nature of charms, which, if they could be come at with ever so slight a preparation, would make up all defects. The doctrine of *Sacramental Justification* is justly to be reckoned among the most mischievous of all those practical errors that are in the Church of Rome. Since, therefore, this is no where mentioned in all those large discourses, that are in the New Testament, concerning Justification, we have just reason to reject it: since also the natural consequence of this doctrine is to make men rest contented in low imperfect acts, when they can be so easily made up by a Sacrament, we have just reason to detest it *as one of the depths of Satan.*" " And thus we object, not without great zeal, against the fatal effects of this error, all that is said of the *opus operatum;* the very doing of the Sacrament; we think it looks more like the incantations of Heathenism, than the purity and simplicity of the Christian Religion." *

* Burnet on Art. XI., and XXV.

CHAPTER VIII.

THE DOCTRINE OF THIS DIVINITY FURTHER EXHIBITED BY ITS EFFECTS UPON OTHER DOCTRINES AND PARTS OF CHRISTIANITY.

Effects upon the doctrine of Original Sin; Testimony of Jackson to the Peculiar Romanism of these results—Sin after Baptism—Mortal and Venial Sins—Tendencies of Oxford Divinity to the doctrine of Purgatory—to Prayers for the Dead—Invocation of Saints—Transubstantiation—Working of Miracles—Aricular Confession—Extreme Unction—Anointing at Baptism and Confirmation—Additional matters of *Restoration* contemplated—Sacramental character of Marriage countenanced—Use of Romish Prayer Books and Rules of Fasting—Favor to Image-Worship—Christian Holiness—Tradition; Why this topic reserved to the last—Extracts from the late Charge of Bishop Wilson.

IN the two preceding chapters we have exhibited the developments of the grand principle of the system before us, as already seen in its effects upon the doctrine of faith and of the Sacraments. We proceed to further ramifications, in evidence that the tree of Romanism, planted in the classic soil of Oxford, is bringing forth Romish fruit, and going on to do so more and more, and may thus be known, according to the Scriptural test, to be good or evil, according as we consider the spreading shade of Popery to be good or bad. *Tendimus in Latium.*

We begin with the doctrine of *Original Sin.*

As we are not arguing with Romanists, a protestant authority may answer for a view of their doctrine; and as we are dealing with Oxford men, no protestant authority could be more in place than that of the learned Dr. Jackson, whom we have several times quoted already, and whose authority, we have said, is now of great price in the new school of Oxford theology.

This author, in the beginning of his third volume, is writing on Original Sin.

He begins by stating, that many Divines (Schoolmen) have peremptorily determined that "*the righteousness of the First Man did formally consist in* A PECULIAR GRACE, SUPERNATURAL, *even to him;*" consequently, that Adam's justification, or his being accounted

Righteous, before he sinned, was not on account of his being created in the Image and Likeness of God, but on account of something *superadded* to his constitution, as he was the work of God, and without sin, viz., a Grace *Supernatural*, in which was his Justifying Righteousness; so that, in the creation of the first man, there were two distinct works of God; one of which consisted in making him in God's own Image; the second, in endowing him with a certain supernatural grace or righteousness, *over and above* that perfect Image; as if in making a round body, there were two distinct works, the one, in making the round body, the other, in giving it *rotundity;* so that Original Sin consists not in the loss of any thing *natural* to Adam, as he was the work of God, but only in the loss of a righteousness *supernatural;* not in any positive effect, any " infection of nature," as our Article has it; not "in the coming in of a multiplicity of wounds or diseases in our nature," but only in a *" privation of that supernatural grace."* *

"To maintain this opinion, (says Jackson,) the Romish Church, (especially since the publishing of the Canons of the Trent Council,) is deeply engaged: For unless this supposition be granted, many dogmatical resolutions which the whole Christian world is by the Romish Church bound to believe, *sub pæna Anathematis*, cannot possibly, or with any mediocrity of possibility, be maintained."

Among the consequences from this Romish dogma, which Jackson deduces, are the two following:

1. That if Original Sin be only the *privation* of a supernatural grace or righteousness, superadded to the original image of God in man, then the restoration of that supernatural gift, will be both the removal of original sin, and justification from it; consequently, "the satisfaction of our Lord Jesus Christ had been superfluous; and the opinion of the Socinians would be more tolerable and more justifiable, than the doctrine of the Romish Church, so far as it concerns the value or efficacy of Christ's sufferings, or *satisfaction*

---

* Whoever will take the trouble to consult the Schoolmen of the 13th and 14th Centuries, will find them full of this doctrine. Thomas Aquinas treats of it in Quest. 95 of Part 1. In answer to the question, "whether the first man was created in grace," he says: Primus homo non fuit creatus in gratia. Illa prima subjectio qua ratio suadebatur Deo, non erat solum secundum naturam, sed secundum *supernaturale donum gratiæ*. "The first man was not created in grace. The subjection of his mind to God was not only according to nature, but the result of a supernatural gift of grace." Instead of the illustration given by Jackson of the difference between a *round body and rotundity*, Aquinas instanced the difference between a *white body* and *whiteness*—so important are the distinctions of a scholastic theology.

by *his Merits*, or *justification by works*, rather than by *faith*, especially works of the Moral Law."

2. The second consequence (and that to which we ask a special attention) is that, if this dogma be true, "we of the Reformed Churches should be concluded to yield, that Adam's posterity were to be *formally* justified by *inherent righteousness*." The deduction is thus made by our author:

"It is *in confesso*, and more than so, an undoubted *maxim* of the Church of Rome, that the grace which is *infused* by, and from, our Lord Jesus Christ, is a *supernatural* quality, or a qualification more sovereign than the first grace which God bestowed on the first Man. Now if that grace were a super-addition to his *Nature*, or constitution, as he was the work of God, the loss of that grace could not have made any wound in the human Nature, which the least drop of that grace, which daily distilleth from the second Adam, might not more than fully cure. In respect of these and other reasons which might be alleged, *all such congregations or assemblies of Christian men as have departed, or have been extruded out of the Romish Church, stand deeply engaged to deny, that* THE RIGHTEOUSNESS OF THE FIRST MAN WAS A GRACE OR QUALITY SUPERNATURAL."*

Evidently it was the adoption of justification by an *inherent righteousness* that led, in self-defense, to this strange perversion of the doctrine of original righteousness, and consequently of Original Sin. The idea is, that as what Adam lost by sin, we gain by grace; then if it was a SUPERNATURALLY *infused* grace or gift that he lost, and thus came under condemnation, it is a SUPERNATURALLY *infused grace* whereby we are to be delivered from condemnation, or justified.

But this is precisely the doctrine of the present divinity. The way of justification taught therein has wrought precisely the same change upon the doctrine of Original Righteousness and Sin, and for the same reasons.

The ground is taken that such strong expressions of Scripture as being "*clothed with the garments of salvation*," "*bring forth the best robe and put it on him,*" &c., having "*put on Christ*," "cannot very well be taken to mean newness of life, holiness and obedience, for this reason—that no one is all at once holy and renewed in that full sense which must be implied, if these terms be interpreted of holiness." "Thus there is a call for some more adequate interpre-

* Jackson's Works, vol. iii. pp. 4, 5, 6.

tation of such passages than is supplied by the Roman or Protestant creed."

Now the unwary reader will suppose that Mr. Newman is going to furnish something indeed in which Romanism is *defective*. He will be amazed to find that his interpretation is nothing but the very *Romanism* given by Jackson as above; found, not indeed in the *formal* creed of Rome, as contained in the Canons of Trent, but in those "Doctors" of the Church of Rome, to whom, it is maintained in No. 71 of the Tracts, we have a right to go, for "*the legitimate comment*" upon, and elucidation of, "*the actual system* represented in the Tridentine decrees."* In Mr. Newman's particular friends, the Schoolmen, and others, who maintained a sort of *tertium quid* distinction, between *inherent righteousness* for justification, and common *holiness*, and therefore had the same reason, with himself, to desire the "adequate interpretation" he is looking for, we find the very light he furnishes.

But what is the interpretation? Why "*the robe of righteousness*," in those strong passages, means "*the inward presence of Christ, ministered to us by the Holy Ghost*." Then, to set out this inherent righteousness, we are taken to Adam, thus:—

"*Whereas we have gained under the Gospel what we lost in Adam, and justification is a reversing of our forfeiture, and a robe of righteousness is what Christ gives,* PERCHANCE A ROBE IS WHAT ADAM LOST. If so, what is told us of what he lost, will explain what it is we gain. Now the peculiar gift which Adam lost certainly seems to have been a *supernatural* clothing—Christ clothes us in God's sight with something *over and above nature;* which Adam forfeited." †

Mr. N. then declares that this "*supernatural* clothing" of Adam, was not "*actual inherent holiness*," (the Image of God) but "agreeably with the view of justification already taken, nothing less than the inward presence either of the Divine Word or of the Holy Ghost." Of this "he was *stripped by sinning, as of a covering, and shrank from the sight of himself.*"

Thus have we, in completeness, the Romish doctrine of original sin, consisting in a mere "*privation* of original righteousness," instead of a positive "*infection of nature*," as our Article teaches. ‡ The Romish doctrine of original righteousness consisting in a *supernatural* gift, *superadded* to the holiness of the Image of God;

---

* See 71 of Tracts, p. 12 and 13.   † Mr. Newman's Lectures, pp. 179, 180.
‡ See the Article on Original Sin.

and all this for the purpose of maintaining justification by inherent righteousness, and that vain distinction of the Schoolmen, between such righteousness, as *a supernatural gift*, and what is usually understood by holiness, or sanctification in a sinner's heart, as if this were not supernatural also. And thus have we, in a system of divinity which feels exceedingly injured in being called Romish, a doctrine which, while Mr. Newman is propounding it *professedly as a remedy for what is defective in the creed of the Church of Rome*, is precisely the doctrine which one of his own *professedly* standard writers declares "the Romish Church, especially since the Council of Trent, is *deeply engaged to maintain*," and "all congregations of Christian men out of the Romish Church stand deeply engaged to deny."

But a little more Romish illumination may be let in here. Bishop Burnet says, "Those of the Church of Rome, as they believe that original sin is quite taken away by Baptism, so finding that this corrupt disposition ('*infection of nature*') still remains in us, they do from thence conclude that it is *no part of original sin;* but that this is the natural state in which man was made at first, only it is in us now without the restraint or bridle of *supernatural* assistances, which was given to him, but lost by sin, and is restored to us in Baptism." *

Here we see this divinity again. According to its system, Baptism takes away, or justifies us from, Original Sin. It does this, by the infusion of a *supernatural gift of righteousness*, which is the restoration of what Adam lost. But this cannot be the same as the *holiness* of the regenerate, because, as Mr. N. says, that is so *imperfect*. Therefore what Adam lost could not have been mere holiness, the Image of God, in which he was created, but a *supernatural grace, superadded.*

Here then we have the concurrence of two eminent Protestant divines, the one, a writer whom our Oxford men specially praise, the other, a writer whom they seem absolutely to hate, both setting down, as characteristic of Romanism, that precise doctrine of original righteousness and sin, to which they are driven by their peculiar views of justification; and the first considering it a feature of Romanism so inwrought into its very system, that Romish divines, ever since the Council of Trent, have felt deeply bound to maintain it; so utterly subversive of the fundamental doctrine of justification, that all Reformed Churches "stand deeply engaged to deny it;" and so absolutely ruinous that "it would render the

* Burnet on Art. ix.

opinion of the Socinians as to the value or efficacy of Christ's sufferings more tolerable and justifiable!"

SIN AFTER BAPTISM.

It was well known to be a prominent doctrine of the Romish Church, that *sin committed after Baptism,* cannot be forgiven, except through what they call, "the Sacrament of Penance." The doctrine is expressed as follows, by the Priest, Gandolphy. "As God has chosen men to be his instruments and agents in purifying his creatures from *original* and *actual* sin, by the spiritual regeneration of Baptism; so has he likewise commissioned men to pardon and restore those to grace who might afterwards relapse. He has instituted for the latter a *form* of repentance, a tribunal of contrition and penance." "If the grace of Baptism be forfeited by sin, the subsequent pardon and renewal, though gratuitous on the part of God, are to be accompanied and secured by the criminal's own humiliation and repentance. Hence in the Catholic Church, it is called the Sacrament of *penance.*" "No individual can obtain the remission of sins after Baptism without submitting to penance either in effect or desire." "Jesus Christ has instituted the Sacrament of penance for the ordinary remission of all sin committed after Baptism." *

This is consistent ground. Sins before Baptism are remitted or taken away by the *infusion* of grace at Baptism. But sin after Baptism, how shall it be remitted? The true Protestant says, "Repent and believe in the Lord Jesus Christ." No, says the Romanist, remission can come now only through some Sacrament, as it came at first. But what Sacrament? The Romish church invents one, comprising *contrition, confession, satisfaction and absolution.* When the Priest says "*I absolve thee in the name of the Father,*" &c., then sin after Baptism is remitted, so far as that their persons are accepted though their sin as to penalty in purgatory has not been canceled.

Now it will be made to appear that Dr. Pusey is precisely in the difficulty for which this Sacrament of Penance was invented.

He too considers that only in Baptism are sins absolutely forgiven. But what of him who sins after Baptism? *He knows no way of absolute forgiveness in this life.* "The Church (he says) has no second Baptism to give, and so she cannot pronounce him altogether free from his past sins. *There are but two periods of absolute cleansing,* Baptism and the day of Judgment." * Here is

* Gandolphy's Defence, vol. iii. pp. 384—391.
† Letter to Bishop of Oxford, p. 62.

the precise doctrine of the Romish Church. But we proceed.—
Dr. Pusey informs us that there are some points connected with
this head, on which he and his fellows in doctrine "differ more or
less from each other." One is this—"Whether or not, Baptism,
besides washing away past sins, admits into a state in which for
sins henceforth committed, *repentance stands in place of a Sacrament*,
so as to ensure forgiveness without specific ordinance; or whether
the full and explicit absolution of sin after Baptism is *altogether put
off till the day of Judgment*." * Grave questions indeed for Protestant divines, with the Articles and Homilies of the Church of
England, and the Word of God in their hands, to be divided about!

* But whatever their differences on this head, Dr. Pusey, who is evidently the
Magister, the Master of the Sentences, and more ready than others to run the
system to all its consequences, has taken good care that his doctrine shall be the
doctrine of the Tracts, and characterize the school. He gets it in wherever there
is a door. In the Tract on Purgatory, p. 7, we read that penitents for sin after
Baptism, "from this time to the day of Judgment may be considered in that double
state of which the Romanists speak—their *persons* accepted, *but certain sins uncanceled.* Such a state is plainly revealed to us in Scripture as a real one, in various
passages, *to which we appeal as well as the Romanists.*" See also p. 32 of No. 79,
and p. 46 of Tract on Reserve, No. 80. The miserable doctrine is defended and
re-asserted in No. 82, p. xxiii. The same appears in Dr. Pusey's Scriptural Views
of Baptism.

If "after having been washed once for all, in Christ's blood, i. e. in Baptism,
we again sin, there is no more such complete absolution in this life: no restoration
to the same state of undisturbed security, in which God had by Baptism placed us."

The difficulty into which the advocates of this system are thrown, as to the forgiveness of post-baptismal sins, when they dare not be consistent, as Dr. Pusey
is, with their principles, is seen in the following strange passage from the book of
Bishop Bethel on Regeneration, referred to by Dr. Pusey as a "valuable work,"
and by Dr. Hook as "a standard." "As to those persons who, after having been
baptized in a state of hypocrisy and wilful sin, afterwards become *true penitents
and believers*, I for my part, entertain no doubt of their forgiveness and salvation.
But by what *physical process* they are brought into a state of salvation and acceptance with God, whether by the infusion or resuscitation of the incorruptible seed,
or by what other mysterious means, I neither know, nor do I wish to enquire.
*It is a case not mentioned in the covenant, nor supposed and provided for in the word of
God.*" Here then is the case of *a true penitent believer, not provided for in the word
of God!* How one who was baptised in hypocrisy and therefore received not the
grace of justification, but has since become penitent and believing, can be accepted
of God through the merits of Christ, is a mystery neither to be understood nor
inquired into by this divinity. As he did not receive Justification at his Baptism,
how can he ever get it, seeing Baptism cannot be repeated!—There is the difficulty—and one which this system cannot solve. Nothing need show more completely how the system opposes the first principles of the Gospel, than that while
Bishop Bethel cannot find it in his heart to believe that one possessing true repentance and faith in Christ will fail of salvation, he can find nevertheless no explanation in his system of *how* such a person can be saved, the covenant of grace
having no revealed remedy for such a case.

Go and learn the alphabet of the Gospel! Spell the name of Jesus! "He shall save his people from their sins." Behold what miserable perplexity of mind in the following dark and doubtful questionings! The writer is trying to get round the plain meaning of our 16th Article on this subject which says, "*Not every deadly sin* willingly committed after Baptism is unpardonable, wherefore they are to be condemned that deny the place of forgiveness to such as truly repent.*" On this Dr. Pusey says:

"But who *truly* repent; what are helps to true repentance; when a man who has been guilty of deadly sin willfully committed after Baptism may be satisfied that he is truly repentant for it; whether and to *what degree* he should all his life continue his repentance for it—wherein his penitence should consist; whether continued repentance would *efface the traces of sin in himself;* whether he might ever in this life look upon himself as restored to the state in which he had been had he not committed it; whether it affect the degree of his future bliss, or its effects be effaced by his repentance, but their extinction depend upon the continued greatness of his repentance; whether cessation of his *active repentance (qu. penance)* may not bring back degrees of the sin upon him; whether it shall appear again in the day of Judgment: these and the like are questions upon which the Article does not speak." †

What! when that Article expressly says, "*they are to be condemned who deny the place of forgiveness,* to those who truly repent" for such sin? But does not the Homily speak to such points, when it says:

"We do not without a just cause *detest and abhor the damnable opinion of them which do most wickedly go about to persuade the simple and ignorant people,* that if we chance, after we be once come to God, and grafted into His Son, to fall into some horrible sin, repentance shall be unprofitable to us; there is no more hope of reconciliation, or to be received again into the favor and mercy of God." "If (after such sin) we rise again by repentance, and with full purpose of amendment of life, do flee unto the 'mercy of God, taking sure hold thereupon through faith in his Son Jesus Christ, there is *an assured and infallible* pardon and remission of the same, and that we shall be received again into the favor of our heavenly Father."

* Bishop Beveridge, on this Article interprets "*deadly sin*" as meaning "*every sin*"—"for every sin (he says) is deadly." Beveridge on the Articles, p. 358.
† Letter to the Bishop of Oxford, p. 55.

This, the Homily illustrates by the case of St. Peter.* What havoc does this indignant declaration of the truth of the Gospel make amidst the miserable doubtings and questionings we have quoted! We cannot but feel indignation in every vein as we write. Allow this darkness about sin after Baptism, and we take leave of all the consolation in Christ. Grant it! Then welcome Popery! We must have all the substitutes Popery can give us, in such affliction. One thing or other—the Sacrament of penance for relief, or else to be all our lives, through fear of death, subject to bondage waiting the Judgment to know whether our repentance and faith and prayers, have availed, to secure a justifying interest in Christ.

The reader is particularly requested to mark the buds, which lie in almost every one of the above questions, waiting the auspicious time to expand into full blown Romanism. " Who TRULY *repent?*" "*When a man may be satisfied that he is* TRULY *repentant*" for sin after Baptism? Of course the implication is that there is a different *kind* of repentance, to be known by different *marks* after Baptism, from that for sins before. It means that he who understands all about repentance in the usual sense, may not understand it when it is for sin after Baptism. "*Wherein his repentance should consist?*" One asks with amazement, what can it consist in but *true sorrow of heart and turning unto God?* but Dr. Pusey means something else. *Whether,* and TO WHAT DEGREE, *he should all his life continue his repentance for it.*" What means this? to what degree! With *all his heart*, we answer of course—let his turning to God be perpetual. But Dr. Pusey means something else. His eye is upon *degrees and continuance of external bodily penances*—what he calls elsewhere "*the bitterness of the ancient medicine,*" *when men made sacrifices for the good of their souls,—practiced self-discipline, accused and condemned themselves,*—sought to bring forth fruit worthy of '*penance,*'—and were punished with open penance, *that their souls might be saved in the days of the Lord.*" †
A broken heart, with faith in the blood of Christ, is not enough. The grand question, in Dr. Pusey's sight, is how much *penance,* as distinct from *repentance,* is necessary for pardon. "*Whether one might ever in this life look upon himself as restored to the state in which he had been, had he not committed the sin.*" Compare this with the precious language of our Communion Office, just after we have been confessing, and professing to bewail and repent of, sin upon sin, after Baptism. "Hear what comfortable words our Saviour

---

* Homily of Repentance, Part I. See also Homily of Salvation, Part I.
† Letter to the Bp. of Oxford p. 56.

Christ saith to all who truly turn to him. Come unto me, all ye, &c., and I will give you rest. If any man sin, we have an advocate with the Father, &c. Lift up your hearts." Oh! calumniated Church, that one of thine own children and pastors should teach such doctrine as thine own! But again—"*whether it* (the sin repented of) *affect the degree of his future bliss, whether it shall appear again in the day of Judgment.*" No leaning towards Purgatory in the other world, discoverable in these words! If we depart this life with sin not entirely effaced and pardoned—if it is to meet us in the day of Judgment, then what can be our hope? Nothing at the day of Judgment, for that is the day of *trial*, not "a day of salvation," when we may supply any deficiencies in our hope. Where then except in the interval between death and the Judgment? Here, if any where after death, must the *remaining traces of sin be effaced.* How? By the efficacy of *purgatorial discipline,* of course. Can any eye help seeing what all this is driving at; what fruit such buds must bring? But Dr. Pusey is perfectly consistent. He is only following out his doctrine of justification to its legitimate results. Justification is by infused righteousness. This infusion takes place at Baptism. Baptism cannot be repeated. But sin after Baptism destroys the grace of Baptism; that is, the justifying efficacy of the infused righteousness. The light is quenched. The bright mirror is marred. What shall remedy the loss? The Eucharist is only for the increase and brightening of the righteousness infused at Baptism and still retained; and if any say otherwise, they differ from Dr. Pusey, and are inconsistent with their own principles. Faith will not answer, for it is "*subordinate to Baptism,*" and has lost its life by sin after Baptism. A new Sacrament, such as that of penance with a purgation between death and Judgment, for what penance leaves uncanceled is absolutely necessary to such a scheme. "O my soul, come not into their secret!" Who can fail to see in these dark passages, in this shadow of death, just that state of dependence on our own works for Justification, that very blindness to the fullness and glory of Christ, as "the Lord our Righteousness," from which proceeded all that "maze" of inventions for the putting on of the polluted rags of our own righteousness, "which the Church of Rome doth cause her followers to tread, when they ask her the way to justification." The rudiments of *expiatory* penances, pilgrimages, masses, offerings, &c.; yea, all the elements of purgatorial burnings in the future world, for the souls of those who have sinned after their Baptism, are contained in, and scarcely veiled under, those ominous and melancholy questionings. The mind that fully sympathizes with such views, is penetrated with the essential virus of Romanism, and only needs, like some latent bodily diseases, an exciting cause, a favorable atmospheric influence, to be made to break out all over with a full eruption of Romanism in active development. To cross over to an entire acceptance of the doctrine of Purgatory, without some Romish terms perhaps, but with the whole Romish substance, would be but a natural and easy transition from such views.

Now we beg the reader to compare the extract we have made from Dr. Pusey, with the following, from a modern Romish writer, on the very same subject. The ideas and the language are so much alike that it looks as if a *Popish defense of penance* had furnished our Oxford divines with ideas and words.

"As repentance, according to the Protestant, is absolutely necessary for the sinner (who has sinned after Baptism) to attain salvation, let him say what is the quality and nature of this repentance; let him determine the *degree* in which it will avail; let him say if the interior moral act of the soul is to be accompanied or unaccompanied by any *outward corresponding act*, (penance.) In short, let him positively state *how much* repentance is necessary to appease the anger of the Almighty, otherwise he must find himself in the awful and singularly distressing condition of being left in ignorance of the condition so severely enjoined, and which alone is to entitle him to the forgiveness of heaven."*

How singular the resemblance of this passage to that of Dr. Pusey! It may be accounted for by the precisely similar states of mind of the two writers. The Protestant writes the more Popishly of the two. He is on ground which leaves him entirely exposed to the raking fire of the next paragraph of the Romanist, which is as follows:

"Nothing can more evidently prove the divine superiority of the Catholic religion over every other—nothing more plainly declare its high origin, than the circumstance of every point being definitely settled therein, concerning this interesting question of salvation. While the reformer is ever insecure, the Catholic is enjoying a moral repose—and while the repentant Protestant" (*of the Oxford School*) "looks back upon his crimes with anxious

* Gandolphy's Defense, vol. iii. pp. 388, 389.

trepidation, uncertain of what is demanded of him by the justice of God, the penitent Catholic retraces his past sins in the sorrow of his heart, but in humble composure of mind, builds his hope of forgiveness on the solid ground of a faithful compliance with every condition, that Jesus Christ and his Church have specially marked out for him;—I mean *contrition* before God—*confession before his minister,* and *satisfaction imposed by his Church.*" *

The coincidence between the questions of Dr. Pusey, and those of Father Gandolphy, may be explained by the supposition that both minds were formed as to this subject, under the same Master. Whoever will consult the Schoolmen will find precisely the questions both have asked—and not only so, but answered precisely as it is manifest both would answer them, except as Dr. P. flies only to a purgation after death, and the Schoolman adds the Sacrament of penance. A few specimens of questions proposed and answered at large in the *Summa* of Aquinas, the great *thesaurus* of the divinity of Trent, will show with whom the latter has been taking counsel.

Dr. Pusey asks, "whether a man should all his life continue his repentance" for sin after Baptism—"whether cessation of his *active* repentance (Penance) may not bring back degrees of the sin upon him." Aquinas asks, *Utrum tota hæc vita sit contritionis tempus,*—whether the whole of this life is the time for such repentance.

Whoever understands the Gospel, as to the nature of godly sorrow, will say *yes;* we are to be penitents, of a contrite heart, for *all* sin, unto death. But the answer is not so easy to those who take Dr. Pusey's distinction between *active* repentance and *passive*—the former meaning *the doing of penance,* for the remission of sins.

Again Dr. P. asks: whether he who truly repents for sin after Baptism "be altogether pardoned; or whether only so long as he continue in a state of penitence." Aquinas also asks: *Utrum peccata dimissa redeant per sequens peccatum,*—whether sins remitted may return by subsequent sin—which is the same thing as to ask whether they be *altogether* remitted. Dupin cites "the Master of the Sentences" as treating the same question.

Again, Dr. Pusey asks: "Whether continued repentance would efface the traces of sin in himself." Aquinas—*Utrum remissa culpa mortali, tollantur omnes reliquiæ peccati*—whether when the guilt of mortal sin is remitted, all traces of the sin are effaced.

Again Dr. Pusey—"Whether one might ever in this life look

* Gandolphy, iii. p. 389, 390.

upon himself as restored to the state in which he had been, had he not committed it?" Aquinas—*Utrum post pænitentiam, resurgat homo in equali virtute;* Whether after penance, the man attains the same virtue he had before—*Utrum per pænitentiam restituitur homo in pristinam dignitatem*—whether after penance a man is restored to his former dignity.

Again, it is a question among the Oxford writers, whether "the change in the soul made by Baptism is indelible for good or for evil."* Aquinas asks, *Utrum character insit animæ indelibiliter.* What is here called *character,* and which is conferred only in Baptism, according to Romanism, is *in anima sicut quædam virtus instrumentalis et importat quandam potentiam spiritualem.* The questions of the Tract and the Schoolman are precisely alike.

Again, Dr. Pusey—"Whether it (sin after Baptism repented of) affect the degree of his future bliss—whether it shall appear again in the day of Judgment." Aquinas—*Utrum remissa culpa per pænitentiam remaneat reatus pænæ*—whether the guilt being remitted, by penance, there remains any liability to penalty. The answer of Aquinas, is that although by virtue of penance the guilt is remitted, and with it *eternal* punishment, nevertheless there may remain a liability to punishment of a temporal kind—in other words *purgatory.* And this is precisely that "double state," viz: that of one's person being "accepted," but his having sins yet "*uncanceled,*" after death, till the day of Judgment, in which, Dr. Pusey says, the divinity of Oxford agrees with the Romanists, and which he asserts, is plainly revealed in the Scriptures.†

Blessed be God, who has spared us such bondage, and showed unto us a more excellent way—even that "new and living way," whereby we have "boldness of access" to his mercy-seat, and are "brought nigh by the blood of Christ," and are commanded to "draw near with full assurance of faith," and to rejoice in the certainty that "the blood of Jesus Christ cleanseth us from *all sin,*" so that nothing can separate us from his love.

The following extract from the late charge of the Bishop of Exeter, derives very serious additional weight from all that we have now seen as to the Oxford doctrine, of which we have been writing.

"I lament to see the reason for which they (the Oxford divines) enumerate the necessity of *confession* in their list of those 'practical grievances'! to which Christians are exposed in the Romish communion, viz: *because without it no one can be partaker of the*

---

* Tract, No. 76. † Tract, No. 79, p. 7.

Holy Communion." The Bishop means that it is a lamentation that they could give no stronger reason against that "abomination of desolation," *Auricular Confession,* than that in the Church of Rome it is made necessary to the communion. But he proceeds as follows:

"They thus seem studiously to decline including in the same list the pretended Sacrament of *penance* generally; (of which confession is but a part;) though Penance, as taught by the Church of Rome, is the greatest, because the most soul-destroying, of all those 'grievances'—we might rather say, the foulest perversion of God's saving Truth, which the cunning of Satan ever put into the heart of man to conceive. For this unhallowed device, by abusing the gracious promise of Christ given to the Church, in his Apostles, by making the *Absolution of the Priest* not only effectual, but also necessary, for the pardon of all sin committed after Baptism—while it bows the souls and consciences of the people, to a state of slavish fear of the Priest, practically releases them from all other fear, and gives the rein to every corrupt affection of unregenerate nature. Yet, this is not, it seems, one of 'the subjects, which,' in the opinion of these writers, 'may be profitably brought into controversy with Romanists of the present day.'"

MORTAL AND VENIAL SINS.

It is a well known doctrine of the Romish Church that sins are divisible into *Mortal* and *Venial.* Mortal sins are those "which are either done willingly, or are of any magnitude. To these eternal punishment is due." Venial Sins are such as may not properly be called sins; those that may not be considered *willful,* and are of no magnitude, or so light that they do not avail to destroy grace, or to render one worthy of death eternal. "Venial sin differs from Mortal in *kind* and *degree*—Anger is a venial sin when slight and undesigned; but when indulged, interferes with love, and is mortal; *a theft of a large sum may be mortal, of a small venial.*" * In the Romish Church Sin *after Baptism,* which is ordinarily remitted only through the Sacrament of Penance, means only mortal sin never venial. But *venial* sins may be taken away by lighter appliances. Romish writers say that this sort of sin "deserves pardon of itself"—that "venial sins are not *against* but *besides* the law—that while all sin is a transgression of the law, all

---

* Tract, No. 59.

transgression of the law is not sin," meaning *mortal* or *deadly sin*. Hence Franciscus a Victoria writes that a Bishop's blessing, or a repetition of the Lord's Prayer, or a *tunsio pectoris*, a knock on the breast, or a little holy water, is sufficient to remit venial sin.*

This doctrine has an important connection with that of indulgences and supererogation; but the reader is requested to note well how directly and necessarily it arises out of the Romish doctrines of justification and Original Sin. For instance; justification is *the infusion of righteousness*, by which we are made acceptable in the sight of God. This infusion takes place at Baptism. Baptism entirely takes away both *Original and Actual Sin*. But it is granted on all hands that, in the baptized and regenerate, there remains, what the decree of Trent and our ninth Article call *concupiscence*, (the lust of the flesh, the φρόνημα σαρκὸς of St. Paul.) This our Article declares "*hath of itself the nature of sin*," and "though there is no condemnation for them that believe and are baptized," nevertheless it "*deserves* God's wrath and damnation." This concupiscence therefore, in the judgment of our Church, is a *mortal* sin, as all sins truly are. But the Church of Rome cannot hold this, and at the same time hold that justification is by inherent righteousness, infused by Baptism, which takes away *all original and actual* sin; for if the concupiscence remaining be a mortal sin, then is that infused righteousness no justification; it has not taken away all sin; our Baptism has not done what is ascribed to it. She must and does maintain not only that the guilt of original sin, is all taken away in Baptism, but pronounces, "If any one shall assert, that all that which has in it the *true and proper nature of sin* is not taken away, let him be accursed." "In the regenerate or

---

* Aquinas considers venial sin to be referred to in 1 John i. "If we say we have no sin, we deceive ourselves, &c." This kind of sin, he says, is remitted in the Eucharist. But not only there. Unus actus charitatis potest delere omnia venialia sine actuali cogitatione eorum. One deed of charity can blot out *all* venial sins, even without the least positive thought about them. Nor only this, but many other ways there are to the same remission. Manifestum est generali confessione, pectoris tunsione et oratione Dominica, quatenus cum detestatione peccati sunt, peccata venialia remitti; episcopali etiam benedictione, aquæ benedictæ aspersione, aliisque hujusmodi actionibus, quatenus cum Dei reverentia exercentur.

"Venial Sin, has not simply and perfectly the nature of sin, but is a sort of disposition towards sin"—sed est quasi dispositio ad illud. "It causes properly no spot in the soul, but impedes the actions of virtue,"—nullam proprie maculam causat in anima, sed impedit actus virtutum. "No act without the consent of the reason, is a mortal sin"—nullus actus sine consensu rationis est peccatum mortale.

baptized," continues the Decree of Trent, "*there is nothing which God hates.*" "They are "*innocent, immaculate, pure.*" But still there remains this "*concupiscence,*" this lust of the flesh. Consequently, it cannot have, what our Article declares it has, of itself, *the true and proper nature of sin.* It cannot be *hateful to God.* It cannot be inconsistent with strict purity before Him, and with the perfectly justifying virtue of inherent righteousness. The Holy Synod of Trent, therefore, decreed "that this concupiscence, though *sometimes called sin* (it acknowledged) *by the Apostle*, the Catholic Church had never understood to be so called, because *truly* and *properly* sin in the regenerate, *but only because it comes from sin, and inclines to sin.*" * Concupiscence, therefore, is *venial sin*, which a little holy water or a Pater Noster will suffice to remit. Thus the sufficiency of inherent righteousness for justification, and the entire taking away of original sin, by making concupiscence to be no sin at all, are preserved.

But how do they get at the doctrine that concupiscence is no sin, not even a part of *original sin?* This is answered by a reference to what we have said of the Romish doctrine of original sin. Original sin in the Church of Rome, is not, what our Article says it is, a *positive "fault and corruption,"* or "*infection* of nature," so that man "of his own nature is inclined to evil," &c.; but it is simply a "*privation* of original righteousness." But that righteousness, according to Rome, was a *supernatural grace, superadded* to the constitution of man's nature, as he was already the work of God, and made in God's Image. Now, if the mere loss of that was original sin, then as it was only the loss of what was *superadded* to man's original nature, and not the loss of any thing essential to that nature, it follows that "an infection of *nature,*" has nothing to do with it, or that concupiscence, which is an infection of nature, is no part of original sin, and not being, in Romish divinity, *actual* sin, has not properly, in any way, the true nature of sin.

Then, since justification, through Baptism, is the restoration, in the shape of infused righteousness, of that "*supernatural grace*" which Adam lost, it is in no way hindered or abridged or rendered imperfect by this infection of nature remaining in the regenerate.

Such is the Romish doctrine of *venial* sins, and its essential connection with that of original sin and hence of justification. The reader is now requested to consider wherein lies any substantial difference between this doctrine and that of the system before us. Precisely, as is taught in Romanism, this new divinity teaches

* Dec. Trident. Sess. 5.

that the justifying righteousness infused at Baptism takes away all *original and actual sin.* Nevertheless it is granted that there does remain in the unregenerate and baptized, that *concupiscence* or lust of the flesh of which speaks our Article. How then is inherent righteousness not rendered insufficient for justification? How does it appear that Baptism, in justifying, takes away all our original sin, since it is granted that it does not take away this remaining concupiscence? Of course by denying that such remnant is original sin. How? Why by teaching, as has before been showed, precisely the Romish doctrine, that original sin consists only in the loss of a *supernatural* grace; of "*a robe of righteousness superadded*" to man's original nature; and that justification, or regeneration, for as we have seen, they are the same thing in this divinity, is simply the restoration, not of what may have been lost of man's original nature, but only of that supernatural grace. So that we come to this, that concupiscence not being *original sin,* and certainly not, in the view of these divines, *actual sin,* and its existence not being inconsistent with an inherent justifying righteousness, it has not what our Article says it has, "*of itself the nature of sin,*" nor "*deserves God's wrath and damnation;*" but is only what the Church of Rome has pronounced concerning it, viz: "though sometimes called sin by the Apostle, it is not sin *truly* and *properly,* but only because, *ex peccato est, et ad peccatum inclinat,* it comes of sin, and inclines to sin." In other words, it is *venial sin.*

Now let us show this from some passages of these writers. "*Baptized persons do not so put on Christ as to be forthwith altogether different men from what they were before.*"* This can only mean, what our article says, that "*this infection of nature* (or *concupiscence*) doth remain even in them that are regenerate;*" in other words, that the change in Baptism is not the entire putting off of "*the old man.*" But still Baptism does take away all original sin. Consequently, to retain any portion of "the old man," or "carnal mind," is not to retain any original sin. In other words, this remnant of the carnal man is only *improperly* sin—or, as Rome says, *non habet veram et propriam rationem peccati.* It needs not Justification; it is therefore not mortal, but venial. †

---

* Newman's Lectures, p. 177.

† In one very important sense, it is true that from him who believeth in Jesus, all Original and Actual Sin is taken away. But the wide difference between the doctrine of our Chuch on this subject, and that taught above, is that, in the view of the Oxford divines and the Romish, both descriptions of sin are taken away by *the infusion of a substance of righteousness;* which is equivalent to saying that they

Now see how entirely Dr. Pusey's doctrine of sin after Baptism, confirms all this.

He says "the Church has no second baptism to give, and *therefore cannot pronounce the person who has sinned after Baptism altogether free from his past sins,*"—"*there are but two periods of absolute cleansing—baptism and the day of Judgment.*" *

Let the reader consider, that in a country such as England, where infant Baptism is almost universal, there are hundreds of thousands of persons, baptized in infancy who have been living, some years, in willful sin. Does this writer mean that there is no way for the pardon, on repentance, of any of these, until the day of Judgment? How then, when they repent and come to be confirmed, can the Bishop say over them that prayer of the Confirmation office which begins, "Almighty God, who hast vouchsafed to regenerate these thy servants, &c., and *hast given unto them forgiveness of all their sins?*" But again; We open our Morning and Evening Service with the words—"*If we say that we have no sin we deceive ourselves,*" &c.— We then fall down and confess that "*We have erred and strayed like lost sheep.*" The Bible says "*There is not a just man on earth that*

---

are taken away by a righteousness, which, because it is *in* us, is our own righteousness, as much as our souls are our own ; according to what, we shall have no difficulty in showing, is the plain doctrine of our Protestant Church, they are taken away by the mere imputation of the external righteousness of Christ, fulfilling the law and paying its penalty for us, that righteousness being simply accounted unto us, through the instrumental agency of our faith. In the former case, the taking away of sin has reference to its indwelling ; in the latter to its condemnation—the one is remission by *expulsion*, the other by *forgiveness*. The former is a moral change of personal character : the latter is forensically a change of relative state. In the doctrine of the one side, there is no direct reference to the Saviour ; the cross is almost out of sight. The righteousness of Christ, consisting in his obedience and death, as Mediator, has no part nor lot therein. In that of the other, Christ is all ; his Mediatorial righteousness, wrought out by his obedience, finished on the cross, apprehended by faith and imputed to the believer for Justification, is the only hope. With the latter view, there is no inconsistency in the fact that the moral nature of Original Sin, the infection, the concupiscence of which our Article speaks, in part remains even in the Regenerate and Justified, (though its power must be broken, and daily it is becoming weaker, through the progressive increase of personal holiness,) because, while Sanctification is always and essentially the companion of Justification, it is not Justification. The one is inherent, but not perfect. The other is perfect, but not inherent. The one is in us ; the other, in Christ "our Righteousness." But with the other view, the remaining of that infection is incompatible, because it has the nature of sin, and therefore conflicts essentially with the justifying efficacy of our inherent righteousness—so that in Oxford, as in Romish divinity, its having the nature of sin must be denied, and to this end, the nature of Original Sin must be changed.

* Letter, p. 62.

doeth good and sinneth not." Our fifteenth Article, on " Christ alone, without sin," says "all we, *although baptized and born again in Christ*, yet offend in many things: and if we say we have no sin, we deceive ourselves and the truth is not in us." Now is it credible that these Oxford writers mean to say that every man thus referred to is beyond Justification, till the day of Judgment? Incredible! Certainly not! What then? Why, when they speak of sin after Baptism, they mean not such sins as are thus mentioned, but MORTAL sins. Hence such as the Christian daily confesses must be only VENIAL sins. Here then is the precise conclusion we have been aiming at; viz., that it is essential to this system to make such a distinction between sins *mortal*, and sins venial as amounts to a destruction of all Scriptural views of the nature of sin; so that although the sins of the Christian's daily course are expressly called *sins* by the Scriptures, by the Church, and by her holiest divines, yet so little do they seem to these writers to have the "*true and proper nature of sin*," that when they use the expression "*Sin after Baptism*," they do not mean to include them under that denomination, and do not think it worth while to hint that they even exist.

But when the Homilies of our Church speak of sin after Baptism, they mean no distinction between sins *mortal* and *venial*. When our 21st Article speaks of "*deadly sin* after Baptism, it means no such distinction. Bishop Beveridge interpreting its language, says the expression "*every deadly sin*" in the Article, means "*every sin, for every sin is deadly.*" * Bishop Hall says "some offenses are more heinous than others, yet *all*, in the malignity of their nature, are *deadly*. If we have respect unto the infinite mercy of God, and to the object of his mercy, the penitent and faithful heart, there is no sin which is not *venial;* but in respect to the disorder, there is no sin which is not *worthy of eternal death.*" †

* Beveridge on the Articles.
† Bishop Hall's Works, ix. p. 57. The present Bishop of Exeter takes a similar view of the language of the Oxford writers, with that we have now exhibited.

"Nor may we forget (he says in his late Charge) the tendency of such language to encourage the pernicious and perilous habit of distinguishing between such sins as may destroy our state of grace, and such as we may think still leave that state secure. Let it never be absent from our minds, that every willful sin is deadly—and let us beware of hardening our own hearts, and corrupting the hearts of our brethren—by whispering to ourselves, or them, *which* sin is more or less deadly than others. That which we may deem the least will be deadly enough, if unrepented, to work our perdition: those which we deem the most deadly, will, if repented, have been thoroughly washed away in the blood of our Redeemer."

There is, indeed, *no condemnation to them that are in Christ Jesus;* but it is not because they do not sin; nor because their sin is not of its own nature deadly; but simply because they are 'in Christ Jesus,' and are 'justified by faith.' That application by faith to the justifying righteousness of Christ, is just as necessary to the taking away of the *one* sin of the holiest man on earth, as of the million sins of the most unholy. We glory, not that we have not sinned after our Baptism, but, confessing that we have sinned continually, we ' glory only in the cross of our Lord Jesus Christ,' and 'believing, we rejoice in hope of the glory of God.'

We have now exhibited ramifications of Romanism, from its doctrine of Justification, which may be proved to be actually well *grown* in this system already. We now proceed to show *tendencies* of no doubtful character, towards other and more overt developments; *buds* getting ready to burst into branches.

PURGATORY.

The decree of the council of Trent on this subject determines:

"That there is a Purgatory, and that souls there detained are aided by the suffrages of the living, and above all, by the acceptable sacrifice of the Altar." Bishops are enjoined to "provide that the suffrages of the believers living, that is, the sacrifices of masses, prayers, alms, and other works of piety, which believers living are wont to perform for other believers dead, be performed according to the rules of the Church, piously and religiously," &c.— Session 25.

Now, of this dire Romish corruption, as is expressed in the above very words, do the Oxford writers, say:

"Taken in the *mere letter* there is little in it against which we shall be able to sustain formal objections." *

This is consistent. The Oxford system must admit as much. And here follows the reason in its own words: "The Roman Church holds that the great majority of Christians die in God's favor, yet more or less under the bond of their sins. And so far we may unhesitatingly allow to them, or rather *we ourselves hold the same,* if we hold that after Baptism, there is no plenary pardon of sins in this life to the sinner, however penitent, *such* as in Baptism was once vouchsafed to him." †

Now the only difference pretended to between the Oxford and Romish doctrine, is that while both maintain a purification or

---

* Tract No. 79, p. 516, vol. iii.   † Ibid, pp. 517, 518.

purgation for believers from sin, or a *purgatory*, in the future world, the Romanist makes a definite *place* for it, and makes that place to be one of *pain*, and the pain to be meted out " in a certain fixed proportion," * so that "every sin of a certain kind has a definite penalty or price;" while the Oxford divine contents himself with saying that it is a *purification from sin*, not determining, but not denying, that there is *pain* in, and a place for, it, such as Romanists speak of. How near, however, the Oxford divine approximates to his neighbor of Rome, may be judged from the following comment upon 1 Cor. iii. 12, 15. "If any build," &c.

"Now it would seem plain, that in this passage, the *searching* process of final Judgment, assaying our works of righteousness, is described by the word *fire*. Not that we may presume to *limit* the word fire to that meaning, or on the other hand to say it is a merely *figurative* expression, denoting judgment; which seems a stretching somewhat beyond our measure. Doubtless there is a mystery in the word *fire*, as there is a mystery in the words *day of Judgment*. Yet it any how has reference to the *instrument* or *process* of Judgment. And in this way the Fathers seem to have understood the passage; referring it to the last judgment, as Scripture does, but at the same time religiously retaining the use of the word *fire*, as not affecting to interpret and dispense with what seems some mysterious economy, lest they should be wiser than what is written." †

To understand the approximation of this passage to Romish purgatory, the reader must bear in mind that the process of Judgment, spoken of, is not in regard to the *unrighteous*, but the righteous, and the "*some mysterious economy*," means an economy for the *purgation* of the righteous in the world to come. The Church of Rome could not desire a publication better suited to advance her doctrine of Purgatory, *in these days*, a better " Tract for the Times," going just as far as is expedient, *under the circumstances*, than Tract No. 79, from which the above extracts are taken.

Connecting all this with what has before been shown under the head of Sin after Baptism, one would suppose that the *flames* of Purgatory could hardly be prevented from soon bursting out in open day, from the "wood, hay, and stubble" of this divinity. Mr. Newman began to prepare the public mind for such maturer developments, when in his Parochial Sermons, he wrote as follows:

* Tract 79, pp. 517, 518.   † Ibid, p. 538.

"Who can tell, but in God's mercy, the time of waiting between death and Christ's coming, may be profitable to those who have been his true servants here, as a time of maturing that fruit of grace, but partly formed in them in this life; a school-time of contemplation, as this world is of discipline, of active service. Such surely is the force of the Apostle's words, that He that hath begun a good work in you, will perform it, *until* the day of Christ —not stopping at death, but carrying it into the Resurrection,— as if the interval between death and his coming, was by no means to be omitted in the process of our preparation for heaven."*

PRAYERS FOR THE DEAD.

We have seen, that in the injunction of the Trent decree, concerning "the suffrages of the living, such as sacrifices, masses, prayers, alms, and other works of piety, which the living (in the Church of Rome) are wont to perform for believers dead," "there is little *in the letter*" against which our Oxford writers think themselves "able to sustain a formal objection."

Hence Mr. Newman likens the intercession of the Christian to that of Christ, and calls it a *propitiation*. "The Christian (he says) is plainly in his fitting place when he intercedes. He is made after the pattern of Christ. *He is what Christ is. Christ intercedes above, and he intercedes below.*" Again, speaking of those whom infirmity prevents from attending on the public worship, he asks, "shall not their prayers unite in one before the Mercy Seat, sprinkled with the atoning blood, as a pure offering of incense unto the Father, and a *propitiation* both for the world of sinners, and for his purchased Church." † But the following extract from the late Charge of the Bishop of Exeter, will answer on this head of fast-developing Romanism.

"I lament the encouragement given by the same writers to the dangerous practice of prayer for the dead. They disclaim, indeed, the intention of giving such encouragement, and I doubt not the sincerity of their disclaimer. But to state that this practice 'is a matter of sacred consolation to those who feel themselves justified in entertaining it,'—(and all, they seem to suggest, may '*feel themselves* justified,' for it is 'warranted by the early Church,')—to say, further, that it is 'a solemn privilege to the mourner'—'a dictate of human nature'—nay, that it 'may be implanted by the God of Nature, may be the voice of God within us:'—to say all this, is

* Pp. 411, 412. † Parochial Sermons, No. xxi.

surely an 'encouragement' of the practice so characterized which is very feebly counterbalanced by their admitting that 'Our Church does not encourage it'—by their abstaining from in 'any way inculcating it'—or even by their thinking 'it inexpedient to bring forward such a topic in public discussion.'

"Nor do I assent to their opinion that 'our Church does not discourage' prayer for the dead; on the contrary, if, as they admit, the Church, having at first adopted such prayer, in the general words in which it was used in the ancient Liturgies, afterwards 'for the safety of her children relinquished the practice,' even in this sober and harmless form, 'in consequence of abuses connected with it in the Romish system'—abuses, of the least of which, she says, that they are 'grounded upon no warranty of Scripture, but rather repugnant to the Word of God;' while of others she declares, that they 'were blasphemous fables, and dangerous deceits;' —I can hardly propose to myself any more decisive mode of discouraging a practice, which, in itself, could not be condemned as absolutely contrary to God's word.

"I must go further: I must add, and I do so with unfeigned respect for the integrity and sincerity of these writers, as well as for their eminent ability and learning, that I cannot easily reconcile it with Christian discretion, for any member of the Church to speak with so much favor of a practice which was thus deliberately, and for such grave reasons, repudiated by the Church herself. Still less can I understand what justification can be offered for his saying of the Romanist, that in 'deciding that almost all souls undergo a painful purification after death, by which Infectum eluiter scelus, aut exuritur igni, he only follows *an instinct of human nature.*' Surely, if this be true, the Romanist is right in his decision: for an instinct of our nature could have come only from the Divine Author of that nature—it must be indeed 'the voice of God within us.'"

INVOCATION OF SAINTS.

On this head, we are content to let the Bishop of Exeter speak again:

"Next, of 'the invocation of Saints,' these writers say, that it 'is a dangerous practice, as tending to give, often actually giving, to creatures the honor and reliance due to the Creator alone.'

"But how does the good Bishop Hall, whom they profess to follow, speak of this same point? '*These foul superstitions,*' says he 'are not more *heinous* than new—and such as wherein we have justly *abhorred* to take part with the practicers of them. 'Again, 'This doctrine and practice of the Romish Invocation of Saints, both as new and erroneous, against Scripture and reason, we have justly rejected; and are thereupon ejected, as unjustly.'"

The Invocation of Saints in the Roman and Parisian Breviaries is called, in a late No. of the British Critic, by the modest name of an "*uncatholic peculiarity.*" In the 22nd Article of our Church it is grouped with the Romish doctrines of Purgatory, Pardon, Worshiping and Adoration, as well of Images, as of Reliques; and the whole doctrine is called "a fond thing vainly invented and repugnant to the word of God."

NEW SAINTS' DAYS.

We are content, under this head, with the words of the Bishop of Exeter, as follows:

"In connexion with this subject, I cannot but deplore the rashness which has prompted them to recommend to private Christians the dedication of particular days to the Religious Commemoration of deceased men—and even to furnish a special Service in honor of Bishop Ken, formed apparently on the model of an office in the Breviary to a Romish Saint. Would it be safe for the Church itself—and is it becoming in private individuals—to pronounce thus confidently on the characters of deceased Christians—in other words, to assume the gift of 'discerning of spirits?' To what must such a practice be expected to lead? The History of the Church of Rome has told us; and the Fathers of our Reformation, in compiling the Liturgy, have marked their sense of the danger by rejecting every portion of the Breviary which bears on such a practice, even while they adopted all that was really sound and edifying in it. Yet these writers scruple not to recommend this very practice, thus deliberately rejected by those wise and holy men—and, strange to say, recommend it as only completing what our Fathers have begun—a means of carrying out in private the spirit and principle of those inestimable forms of devotion, which are contained in our authorized Prayer Book."

A more barefaced insult to all decent consistency with the principles of the Church of England was never perpetrated than the "*Matin Service for Bishop Ken's Day*"—constructed and published by these devout admirers of the Roman and Parisian Breviaries—"for social or private devotion." How can they pronounce consistently with their doctrine of sin after Baptism, upon the present blessedness of Bishop Ken? How do *they* know that he has not to be subjected to their "mysterious economy" of purification by fire from "*uncanceled sins?*" Whence have they authority to canonize a Saint, and call upon Christians to commemorate his holiness? It is but a completing, (they say) a carrying out, in spirit and principle, of what is already begun in our Prayer Book. How is this? Has the Prayer Book appropriated days or services to the memory of any but a few distinguished personages *mentioned in the New Testament, and those almost all Apostles?* Has the Prayer Book any difficulty in pronouncing on the present beatitude of the dead in Christ arising out of such doctrine of sin after Baptism and of a purgation hereafter to believers, as these writers teach? But how is it a carrying out of the spirit of the Prayer Book, when the model of the Prayer Book, in the commemoration of Saints, is entirely deserted, and the whole service, in words, and form, and parts, and arrangement, and every single feature, is most studiously adjusted according to the Romish Breviary? Not a feature of the mode of the English Prayer Book appears: not one of the Romish Breviary is omitted, in this Matin service.

This edifying "Restoration;" this *tentative* effort to raise up the "degraded" Church of England from her present place as "a slave" at her Father's table, and set her in the condition of "the King's daughter," and enable her to enjoy "the depth and richness of the ancient services of the Universal Church," as contained in the Roman and Parisian Breviaries, must doubtless be considered but as a *feeler* to try how far the mind of English Protestants is able to bear such an increase of light and privilege. Should it appear that enough of the ancient spirit has returned, as no doubt it will seem to these very confident Restorers, we shall certainly be favored with additional Saints and commemoration days. For why should they stop at Bishop Ken? Cannot the principle be advantageously carried out much further? If one such Saint is good, would not two be better? Such is the principle on which these gentlemen proceed in other things; the sign of the Cross is used in Baptism, and why not at all other times? To bow at the name of Jesus in the Creed *once*, is considered well, (though the present writer does not think so) and why not therefore at any other time? So reasons Dr. Pusey, to the Bishop of Oxford.*
Then surely as it is so good to have a Matin Service for Bishop

* Letter, pp. 6 and 7.

Ken, and as among the Non Jurors were many men of great repute at Oxford for Catholic doctrine and spirit, such as Sancroft, and Hickes, and Kettlewell, there can be no reason, but the necessity of waiting for a proper preparedness in the "degraded" state of the Anglican Church, to prevent the further development of the riches of ancient Catholic services in the publication of Matins, with Nocturns and Antiphons, for other departed Saints. "Let the *keeping of holy days* become universal, Saints and Angels will be with us at all events," says the British Critic, reviewing the latest of the Tracts.* Are not these writers developing their system too fast for the times?

TRANSUBSTATIATION.

So much has been written to show how near this divinity approaches to the Romish doctrine of Transubstantiation, in its zealous maintenance that there is, not only a *real* presence of the body and blood of Christ, in the Eucharist, in the sense of *effective*, through the Holy Spirit applying the "benefits of his Passion," which is simply the sense of the Anglican Church; but that there is also a *real*, in the sense of a "*substantial* presence;" "an *immediate*, unseen Presence of that body, itself," that we need not here exhibit the language of Oxford divines any further on that head. The *tendency* at least of such views cannot be mistaken.

But connect with this the anxiety of these writers that the subject should not be discussed, expressed as follows:

"This consideration (the danger arising out of the sacredness of the subject) will lead us to put into the back-ground the controversy about the Holy Eucharist, which is almost certain to lead to profane and rationalistic thoughts in the minds of the many, and cannot well be discussed in words at all, without the sacrifice of 'godly fear,' while it is well nigh anticipated by the ancient statements, and the determinations of the Church concerning the Incarnation. It is true that learned men, such as Stillingfleet, have drawn lines of distinction between the doctrine of transubstantiation, and that high mystery; but the question is, whether they are so level to the intelligence of the many, as to secure the Anglican disputant from fostering irreverence, whether in himself or his hearers, if he ventures on such an argument. If transubstantiation *must* be opposed, it must be in another way; by showing, as may

* No. 54.

well be done, and as Stillingfleet himself has done, that, in matter of fact, it was not the doctrine of the early Church, but an innovation at such or such a time; *a line of discussion which requires learning both to receive and to appreciate*"*

On the above singular paragraph, first barring all discussion, and then, if the subject *must* be discussed, excluding all reference to Scripture, and confining us to the *clear type and simple page* of Tradition, the Bishop of Exeter thus writes:

"I lament to read their advice to those who are contending for the truth against the Romanists, that, 'the controversy about Transubstantiation be kept in the back ground; because it cannot well be discussed in words at all without the sacrifice of godly fear;'—as if that tenet were not the abundant source of enormous practical evils, which the faithful Advocate of the Truth is bound to expose: in particular of the extravagant exaltation of the Romish priesthood, which seems to have been its primary object —and, still worse, of that which is its legitimate and necessary consequence, the adoration of the Sacramental Bread and Wine, which our Church denounces as 'Idolatry to be abhorred of all faithful Christians.'"

But while discussion has thus been discouraged, advancement has been made towards Transubstantiation. Behold to what length the matter has come in the following passage from the last British Critic.

---

* Tract No. 71.

This keeping of certain matters in the back-ground, for the purpose of preventing an inconvenient discussion, by drawing a veil of awfulness or mystery over them, appears with singular frequency in these writers. For example: While the writer in the British Critic, on the Church Service, is saying all he desires to say on the comparative richness of the ancient services, and those of the Anglican Church, depreciating the latter exceedingly, he shuts up the question against less reverent critics by this remark: "To say that the depth and richness of the ancient services of the Universal Church have no parallel in modern times, were to bring into a painful comparison *what is far too sacred for human criticism.*" —British Critic, No. 54, 251. The same writer, reviewing the second part of Froude's Remains, on the subject of Rationalism in the interpretation of Scripture, says "the awful manner in which the author treats the subject positively cows us"—"it is more like that of a spirit speaking to us in a vision, than the tone of a theological treatise. All we can summon heart to do is to take the elementary *principles* of the essay," &c. The Reviewer leaves the work to those who will "come to it with *fasting and mortification.*" Is not this inconceivably foolish? A book on Rationalism only to be read with fasting and mortification! What next? How soon will the memory of Froude be enshrined in a Matin Service, with Nocturns and Antiphons, and all the richness of the Roman Breviary?

"Is the wonder wrought at the marriage of Cana, a miracle, and the change which the holy Elements undergo, as consecrated by the Priest, and received by the faithful, no miracle, simply because the one was perceptible to the natural eye, while the other is discerned by the spiritual alone? Protestants must take care what they are about when they speak at random against the Church of Rome, lest they pave the way for things as far worse than Popery, as irreligion is worse than superstition; first rationalism, and next infidelity."*

AGE OF MIRACLES.

It is a well known tenet of Romanism that the age of miracles has never ceased—that divers miracles are wrought at tombs of Saints, by the touch of relics, &c.,—and that miracles are a distinguishing mark of the true Church. This system is disposed to claim thus much also.

The last Tract as yet published, No. 86, asks why we should suppose that with respect to sudden and extraordinary cures, a broad line is drawn between primitive and later ages? On which the writer in the British Critic above quoted says:

"Surely—it is want of faith, which is the only hindrance to these gifts in later times. Why does St. James apply to Elias the epithet ὁμοιοπαθής, except to show that the question turns upon difference, not of privilege, but of faith, or of privilege as depending upon faith? What is the meaning of the popular phrase 'the Age of Miracles'? Is not every age of the Church an Age of Miracles? Is there *all* the difference, or, indeed, any thing more than the difference between things seen and unseen (a difference worth nothing in Faith's estimate,) between healing the sick and converting the soul: raising man's natural body, and raising him in Baptism from the death of sin?" †

AURICULAR CONFESSION.

How far we may go towards the Church of Rome without ceasing to be sound Protestants, in the judgment of these divines, appears, in part, from the following. In the British Critic, for January last, is a review of Brewer's Court of King James I., by Goodman, Bishop of Gloucester, who was a reputed Papist in the time of Archbishop Laud. The Reviewer praises the Editor for meeting Ultra Protestants "with their own weapons," and says that

* Br. Critic. No. 54, p. 260.   † British Critic, pp. 259, 260.

"he fairly argues that it does not *follow*, it is not *necessary*, it is not *certain* that because Bishop Goodman said this or that, therefore he was other than a '*sound Protestant.*'"

Now what did Bishop Goodman say? The Reviewer says he advocated *Auricular Confession*. The Editor says, that in his will was the following passage: "*I do acknowledge the Church of Rome to be the mother Church. And I do verily believe that no other Church hath any salvation in it, but only so far as it concurs with the faith of the Church of Rome.*" Then in the concurrent judgment of these writers, (we mark that of the British Critic, especially, because of its office as an organ of this system,) a Bishop may advocate Auricular Confession, as well as record his solemn belief that no Church has salvation but so far as it concurs with the Church of Rome, and still be "*a consistent Protestant.*" This is a stride indeed!

EXTREME UNCTION.

The British Critic in the review of the late Tract, No. 86, on Church Service, complains of the author "because he did not enter a more decided protest, than he has against the common Protestant objection to Extreme Unction." The Reviewer thinks the testimony of Scripture, unexplained and unguarded by Tradition, is in favor of it. The only reason against it is that it wants *Catholic consent*. But that may be discovered before long.

ANOINTING AT BAPTISM AND AT CONFIRMATION.

The absence of these in the Anglican Church is called "*the loss of a privilege.*" And the keeping up of the Coronation-Service, in which anointing is retained, is regarded for that reason, as an indication of special "Providential care over the Church"—thus keeping up a witness to both of the Catholic truths, of which the omission of anointing at Baptism and Confirmation might seem to betoken a disparagement.*

INCREASE OF SACRAMENTAL SIGNS AND EFFICACIOUS SYMBOLS.

The cross is called "*a sacramental sign,*" and memorial to the eyes of the faithful; "a holy *efficacious* emblem."† Now this is precisely the distinguishing description, given in our Article of the Sacramental character of Baptism and the Eucharist—"Sacraments be not only badges or tokens of Christian men's profession, but rather

---

* British Critic, No. 54, p. 259. † Ib. No. 54, p. 271.

they be sure witnesses and *effectual* signs of grace." Thus is the cross put on a level, as a sacramental sign, with Baptism and the Lord's Supper. The writer, now quoted, is not fond of the *Crucifix* in Churches. He would not object to it "as an object for *very* private contemplation under certain trying circumstances." But " openly exhibited, it produces the same sort of uncomfortabe feeling with certain Protestant exposures in preaching the Mystery which it represents." On the other hand, "the mere Cross embodies what no Christian should shrink from contemplating; while of the awful Mystery therewith connected, it is but suggestive.— We hope the time will come when no English Church will want, what many possess already, the Image of the Cross in some place sufficiently conspicuous to assist the devotions of the worshiper. — Let us multiply the same *holy, efficacious* emblem far and wide. There is no saying how many sins its awful form might scare, how many evils avert." * Truly efficacious indeed!

But the Cross is not the only sacred symbol which is soon to be erected in the Churches. The above zealous restorer of the depth and richness of the ancient services says :

" With the Cross should be associated other Catholic symbols still more than even itself φωνᾶντα συνέτοις, (*vocal to the spiritual discerners.*) For these, painted windows seem to furnish a suitable place. They should at all events be confined to *the most sacred portion of the building.* Such are the Lamb with the standard ; the descending Dove ; the Anchor ; the Triangle ; the Pelican ; the Ιχθύς, (fish) and others. Perhaps the two or three last mentioned, *as being of most recondite meaning, should be adopted later than the rest.*" †

Here we see *Symbols* "for the Times," as well as *Tracts.* The writer speaks of "others" besides those most *edifying and sacred* which he has thought the Times do not permit him to name. The other names will doubtless follow in good time. So then we shall soon need no preaching of the word by the Minister's voice. The lessons in the service, with the preaching of these symbols, which has the advantage over that of the sermon, in being audible only by the ear that is prepared for their awful and sacred meaning, will do a great deal better than the present Ultra-Protestant mode of dispensing the truth as it is in Jesus, without reserve.

* British Critic, No. 24, p. 271.   † Ib. No. 54, pp. 271, 272.

ADDITIONAL RESTORATIONS.

The writer of the Review of Tract No. 86, on the Church Services, in the British Critic, proceeding in his revival of ancient services with a degree of boldness which promises very much in the way of subsequent developments of what, like the fish and triangle, &c., may be "too recondite" yet for the state of the times, recommends as follows:

"There should be some special decoration on Festival-days; altar coverings and pulpit hangings of unusual richness; or the natural flowers of the season woven into wreaths, or placed (according to primitive custom) upon the Altar. These should be chosen with especial reference to the subject of the Festival. White flowers are most proper on the days consecrated to the Blessed Virgin, as emblematic of sinless purity; purple or crimson upon the several Saints' days (except St. John Evangelist, and perhaps St. Luke), to signify the blood of martyrdom; and on All Saints' Days and the Holy Innocents, white should be intermingled, as a memorial of virgin innocence. We deprecate forced flowers, which look artificial; but we believe with a little management natural flowers of the proper colors may be found nearly throughout the year. *It is difficult to conceive a more suitable occupation for the Christian poor, than that of cultivating flowers for such a purpose, and afterwards arranging them.* The decoration of the chancel, however, should be the especial privilege of the Minister himself. The Church bells should, according to Archbishop Laud's Injunctions, be rung on Festivals and their Eves. Two lights should be placed upon the Altar, according to Edward the 6th's order, ratified in our present Prayer Book. We think it plain that these candles were meant at the reformation to be lighted, as had been usual, during the celebration of the Holy Eucharist; otherwise they do not so well 'signify' (in the words of the Injunction) the truth—*Christus Lux mundi*. But such practices might give offense in these days, and we do not advise it, though inclined to regard it as strictly Anglican. For the same reason, we should be unwilling to press sudden changes in the ecclesiastical dress, though it is plain that these also might be reconciled with the order in our Prayer Book, which directs us to Edward 6th's time for the practice of our Church as respects both vestments and ornaments. Persons should be encouraged to make obeisance on entering Church, and the minister should never approach, or pass, the Altar without doing reverence, as is customary at this day in some of our cathedrals. We think it quite consistent with the Rubric of our Church to consecrate the Holy Elements at the center of the Altar and facing it. We should like to see all alms offered at the Altar, and in a kneeling posture. At least the alms and oblations of Bread and Wine, should be so offered; and the remnants after consecration should be received likewise kneeling."*

SACRAMENT OF MARRIAGE.

The germ of this Restoration is quite visible in the following mystic language:

"The ordinance of Marriage has an inward and spiritual meaning, contained in it and revealed through it—as if persons, to place themselves in that human relation, interested themselves, in some secret way, in the divine relation (that of Christ and the Church) of which it is a figure."—Tract, No. 71, p. 89.

USE OF ROMISH PRAYER BOOKS AND RULES OF FASTING, ETC.

An Ecclesiastical Almanac for 1840, has been published for the guidance of disciples of this school, amid the riches of the ancient services as found in Roman and Parisian Breviaries. In this is "a selection from the old Catholic Service Books, of Psalms and other passages of Holy Scripture, appropriate to the several classes of Saints' Days," while "*the minute rules of the Roman Catholic Church are quoted as a guide to individuals,*" in reference to days of fasting and abstinence.

We have already stated that the British Critic regards it as a very delightful sign of the growth of the Times that Parker, in Oxford, finds it his interest to import a large number of copies of the Roman and Paris Breviaries for "private devotion."

SERVICE IN AN UNKNOWN TONGUE—AND DISUSE OF PREACHING.

That these writers have said any thing positively in favor of service in an unknown tongue is not here asserted; but their whole system of Reserve, of sacred veils over "awful mysteries" to conceal them from the eye of the profane, and of the use of all those sacred Symbols which the initiated alone are supposed to be capable of reading, indicates the very principle on which the Service in an unknown tongue in the Romish Church is defended.

---

* See British Critic, No. 54, pp. 272, 273.—All surely very edifying. How much of the above has since been accomplished in certain of our American Episcopal Churches, and what zeal is expended on them and of what importance they are made, it is most painful to see. (1861.)

It is considered by these divines a great advantage in Hymns or Psalms for public worship, when they "not only open and disclose, but also *withdraw* and *conceal* the higher spiritual senses, according to the character of the persons who make use of them —serving as a religious veil to withhold from some what they impart to others"—lest it should "be profaned by a worldly eye." *

Why then should there be no such veil over the service for the Eucharist, to hide its awful mysteries from the profane, and so of Baptism, &c. Why, if a poor creature, ignorant of the Atonement and of every thing else but that the Cross is "a sacred symbol and efficacious sign of grace," standing or prostrating herself before it, with no *explicit* faith in what it signifies, may be supposed to have a strong sense of the power of a saving faith, as we have seen asserted; why may not a whole congregation of such persons be equally profited by the mere contemplation of the sacred "Catholic Symbols" above described, the Triangle, the Fish, the Anchor, the Pelican, added to the manipulations and genuflexions of the Priest, his divers bowings and incensings, accompanied with the aid of rich altar-cloths, symbolic candlesticks, splendid sacerdotal vestments, and enchanting choral music?

The same considerations teach how litttle use there is in frequent preaching, for all the purposes of the Oxford system. The Principle of Reserve requires a far more restrained method of preaching than is at present practiced, especially as to the Atonement and other such doctrines, which in this divinity are not among the matters which must be *explicitly* believed, in order to a saving faith. The "image of the cross," contemplated, is considered as so "efficacious," that one need know nothing more of the Atonement, to have the merits of Christ applied to his soul.

"The Church," says the British Critic, "is out of her place, converting in a Christian country." The present "degraded" state of the Church of England reconciles the Oxford Reviewer "in some measure to a more excited tone of preaching than is consistent with the perfect theory of the Catholic system." But says, the cautious writer:

"Not indeed to the prominent exhibition in preaching of the Christian Mysteries; for this were inadmissible under far more extreme circumstances and even upon the supposition of our con-

---

* See Review of a New Version of the Psalms in the British Critic, No. 53.

gregations being literally heathen; indeed the more inadmissible the farther the hearers receded from the perfect state," &c. *

IMAGE WORSHIP.

That these writers have advocated Image Worship, is not here pretended. But that they manifest a strange tenderness and tendency towards the abominable idolatry, we shall easily show. This is one of the subjects which they would exclude from discussion; but if it *must* be discussed, as with Transubstantiation, they would not rest the argument on Scripture, because there may be a difference of opinion as to its meaning; but on tradition. As if the simple command, "*Thou shalt not make to thyself any graven image,*" &c., which any one can read for himself, were of less plainness and solemn decision, than the confused libraries of tradition for which the million must depend on the reading of the few.

We quote again from the Charge of the Bishop of Exeter.

"I yet cannot but lament, that they sometimes deal with some of the worst corruptions of Rome, in terms not indicating so deep a sense of their pernicious tendency, as I doubt not that they feel.

"For instance: defending themselves against the charge of leaning towards Popery, they confidently affirm, that 'in the seventeenth century the theology of the body of the English Church was substantially the same as theirs;' and in proof of this, they profess, in stating the errors of Rome, to 'follow closely the order observed by Bishop Hall in his treatise on 'the Old Religion,' whose Protestantism, they add, 'is unquestionable,' and is claimed, therefore, as a voucher for their own. But, looking to particulars, I lament to see them 'following, indeed, the *order* of Bishop Hall,' but widely departing from his truly Protestant sentiments, on more than one important article.

"First, of 'the *worship* of images,' (for so that great Divine justly designates what they more delicately call 'the honor paid to images,') they say only, that it is 'dangerous in the case of the uneducated, that is, of the great part of Christians.' But Bishop Hall treats it as not merely 'dangerous' to some, but as sinful in all; as 'against Scripture;' 'the Book of God is full of indignation against this practice;' and 'against reason.' 'What a madness is it,' says he, 'for a living man to stoop unto a dead stock!'"

Of the singular tenderness of these writers towards the idolatry

* British Critic, No. 54, p. 261.

of the Romish Church, there is one example, which, as it comes incidentally into the mass of Oxford writings, may be considered as specially indicative of their habit of mind. The Reviewer in a late number of the British Critic is describing the Decorations of English Churches in Papal times. He has gone over the whole detail of pictures of St. George and the Dragon, of St. Thomas a Becket, &c., and "numerous other subjects from the Legends of the Saints"—he has told us of the various crucifixes, and roods, and images, and rood-lofts, and beams, for the display of roods and images; we look in vain for the least expression of sensibility or aversion at the thought of the idolatry of which those "*decorations*" were once the objects. At last it is mentioned that—

"To some particular images, peculiar honor was paid; sums were bequeathed to furnish lights to burn before them, and pilgrimages and vows were made to them. Those of the virgin, thus noted, were in the highest repute and very numerous. Amongst others, our Lady of Pity, our Lady of Grace, our Lady of Walsingham, &c."

But now we are told of a most famous image—our Lady of Bolton, once in Durham Cathedral, which in Romish times was connected with a monastery. A sickening account is drawn from an old writer, full of devout admiration of this most goodly spectacle.

"It was made to open with gems from the breast downwards. And within the said image was wrought the image of our Saviour, marvellously finely gilt, holding up his hands, and betwixt his hands, a large fair crucifix of Christ—the which crucifix was to be taken forth every Good Friday, and every man did creep unto it that was in the Church—and every principal day, the said image was opened, that every man might see pictured within her, the Father, the Son, and the Holy Ghost, most curiously and finely gilt; and both the sides within her were finely varnished with green and flowers of gold, which was a goodly sight for all the beholders thereof."

Such was "Our Lady of Bolton." A more profane enormity was never set up in the house of God. It was this very Image, with others, of which Cranmer speaks by *name*, and with zealous indignation:

"They kissed their feet devoutly; and to them they offered candles and images of wax, rings, beads, gold and silver abundantly. And because they that so taught them had thereby great commodity, they maintained the same with feigned miracles and erroneous doctrine, teaching the people that God would hear their prayers made before this image rather than before another image. Seeing therefore it is an horrible idolatry to worship the sun, which is a most goodly creature of God; let every man consider how *devilish idolatry* it is, to worship our own images, made by our own hands."*

Such is the language of one of those "our old martyrs who rather than they would once kneel or offer up one crumb of incense before an image, suffered most cruel and horrible deaths." †
But how speaks the organ of this Divinity of this hideous development of the genius of Romanism? Words of loathing, surely the heart of a Clergyman of the Church of England cannot smother. Let us hear!
"*Much there was* (in the ancient Churches of England) *which sober piety cannot sanction.*" ‡
But is this all? Yes—every syllable of the censure! Human ingenuity could not have invented less. Entire silence would have been more severe. But even this pin-mark is too severe a wound without some healing balm. "Much there was which sober piety cannot sanction; but (adds the indulgent apologist) let us not forget what was *holy and religious* on account of INCIDENTAL CORRUPTIONS." Here the subject is dropped, on the principle, it would seem, of "*least said, soonest mended;*" leaving us to the necessary conclusion, that all these hideous forms of Antichrist, these diversified tools of an abominable idolatry, uniting "Christ with Belial, the Temple of God with idols," were only *incidental*, nothing to be charged to the legitimate tendency or systematic patronage of Romanism; only *incidental*, and of little consequence, compared with "*all that was holy and religious*" in the essential working of the system. Where shall we find in these authors such kind apologies for that system of doctrine, and that way of preaching Christ—the way of "a large portion" of the most devoted, most spiritual, most useful Clergy of the Church of England—the way which this divinity calls Ultra-Protestant? We hear nothing of *incidental* evil in that connexion. Corruption there is in-bred, essential, systematic. To be "*holy and religious*" under that system is the *incidental.* While to worship

---

* Crammer's Catechism; on First Commandment.
† Homily against Peril of Idolatry.   ‡ British Critic, No. 50, p. 381.

profane representations of the Trinity and of the Virgin in images of wood, and paint, and gilding; images disgusting to delicacy, as well as odious to piety, is an incidental corruption, with which we should deal tenderly, because of so much that was holy and religious connected with it. To preach, as Hooker preached, *Imputed* righteousness for Justification before God—to teach that "*it is not by the inhesion of grace in us, but by the imputation of righteousness to us, that we are justified*"—that "*we cannot be accounted righteous but by Christ's righteousness imputed to us*"*—this, they brand as "a real corruption, a bondage to shadows—the gift of the law—a tyrannical system which promises liberty, but conspires against it—which feeds us on shells and husks," instead of upon Christ, "another Gospel." "*Away with it!*" exclaims the indignant reprobation of Mr. Newman. Alas! that we could see a little more in these writers of such indignation against the manifold and deep-seated corruptions of that Church, which our Homilies call emphatically "*the idolatrous Church*."† Do they feel constrained to cleanse from the Temple as a monstrous profanation, the preaching of justification by imputed righteousness only, and will they not with at least equal zeal, drive out with the knotted scourge of a Christian indignation, such teaching as would turn the House of Prayer into a den of idols? Will they not partake in the spirit of their own Church, "purged from dumb idols to serve the living God," when she exclaims against the Papacy to which she was once in that bondage: "O worldly and fleshly wisdom! ever bent to maintain the inventions and traditions of men by carnal reason, and by the same to disannul or deface the holy ordinances, laws and honor of the Eternal God." "Away for shame with these colored cloaks of idolatry, of images and pictures to teach idiots, nay, to make idiots and stark fools and beasts of Christians!" ‡

But why should we be unprepared for strange evidence of extreme tenderness in these writers towards corruptions, which filled our Cranmers and Hookers and Jewells with loathing, when in the " Remains " of one of the writers of the Oxford Tracts, edited by some of the others, "because of the *extreme importance* of the views to which the whole is meant to be subordinate " §—and edited too without the least hint of disapprobation of any part, we read such passages as the following: "I think people are injudicious to

---

* Beveridge on the Articles, pp. 307, 308.
† Against Peril of Idolatry, part III.
‡ Homily against Peril of Idolatry, **Part III.**
§ Preface to Froude's Remains.

talk against Roman Catholics for worshiping of Saints and honoring the Virgin and Images, &c. These things *may perhaps* be idolatrous, I cannot make up my mind about it." Again, "As for the Reformers, I think worse and worse of them. Jewell was what you would call in these days, an irreverent dissenter: his Defense of the Apology disgusted me more than almost any work I ever read." Again, "Really I hate the Reformation and the Reformers, more and more." *

Such is language out of a book, and characteristic of a book, which belongs, of right, to the documents in evidence of the nature of this Divinity, and of its influence in begetting a taste and sympathy and general character in accordance with the most odious features of the Church of Rome. We cannot leave it till we have invoked the spirit of the devout and faithful Bishop Hall, to come forth and rebuke it.

"Sooner may God create a new Rome, than reform the old. Yea, needs must that Church put off itself and cease to be what it is, ere it can begin to be what it once was. Rome may be sacked and battered, as it hath often been, by military forces; but purged by admonitions, convictions, censures, it will never be. Only this one thing which God hath promised we do verily expect; to see the day when the Lord Jesus, shall with the breath of his mouth, destroy this *lawless man*, long since revealed to his Church; and by the brightness of His glorious coming, discover and dispatch him. Not only in the means and way, but in the end also, is Rome opposite to Heaven. The Heaven shall pass away by a change of

---

* Remains, vol. i. pp. 294 and 377, 380.

It may perhaps explain some of Mr. Froude's disgust at Jewell's *irreverence*, &c., to remember that this able Apologist of the Reformation is supposed to have written the Homily against the Peril of Idolatry from which we have just quoted—and which tramples down in such just abhorrence the kind dubiety of Mr. Froude as to the worship of graven images. That "irreverent dissenter" was the Patron of Hooker. The Church would probably not have had her Hooker, had she not been blessed with a Jewell. The former, styled by Bishop Goodwin, *Theologicorum Oxonium*, the Oxford of Divines, as Athens was called "the Greece of Greece," was of a different opinion from Mr. Froude, as to his Patron's merits—even that "*he was the worthiest Divine that Christendom had bred for some hundreds of years.*"— Eccl. Pol. b. ii. § 6. It would perhaps have shaken, a little, Mr. Froude's confidence in his own judgment, had he remembered that the Biographer of Dr. Jackson counts it a high praise of that learned writer to compare him with "the invaluable Bishop Jewell." Le Bas, speaking of the Apology, says: "No man on earth was more consummately qualified than Jewell to render this good office to the Church."

quality, not an utter destruction of substance. Rome by destruction, not by change." *

CHRISTIAN HOLINESS.

It was well said by the divines in the Council of Trent, that when Luther wanted to destroy Indulgences, the Romish doctrine of Penances, of the justifying efficacy of the Sacraments, Authority of Priests, Purgatory, Sacrifice of the Mass, and all other Romish intrusions into, and perversions of, the Gospel way of salvation, "*Justification, by Faith only, seemed to him a good means to effect this.*" "Therefore, *by a contrary way,*" (it was argued in the Council) "he that will *establish* the body of the Catholic doctrine *must overthrow this heresy of justification by faith only.*" †

Both were right. It was justification by faith that went into the temple of the Lord, after Romish corruptions had turned it into a market-house of Masses, Indulgences, Relics and "souls of men," and overturning the tables of the money-changers and the shrines of images, drove out "the merchants of the earth," and said "make not my Father's house a house of merchandize." None of these profane intrusions into the sanctuary of God can stand the stern rebuke of that doctrine. Like Dagon before the Ark, they fall on their faces confounded, and their arms and heads are cut off. Justly then did the Fathers of Trent begin their work by casting out this, as the first step to the bringing

---

* Bishop Hall's Works (*No Peace with Rome*), 8vo. ix. pp. 73—75.

See a strong comparison between Romish and Heathen idolatry in Book V. vol. ii. of Jackson's Works—especially c. xxvi., in which it is maintained that "*the worship which Satan demanded of our Saviour was the very same wherewith the Romish Church worshipeth Saints.*"

The same strong writer, speaking of the covert devices by which Satan contrived to introduce idolatry into the Christian Church, says, "Now admitting a resolution in the great Professor of destructive arts, so as to refine or sublimate his wonted poisons, as they might the more secretly mingle with the food of life: where can we suspect this policy to have been practiced, if not in the Romish Church; whose idolatrous rites and service of Satan, in former ages, have been so gross, that if we had seen the temptation, unacquainted with the success, we should certainly have thought the great Tempter had mightily forgotten himself, or lost his wonted skill in going so palpably about the business; nor could any policy have so prevailed against God's Church, unless it had been first surprised with a lethargy, or brought into a relapse of heathenish ignorance. And what branch of implanted superstition can we imagine in any son of Adam which may not sufficiently feed itself with some part or other of the Romish Liturgy, or with some customs by that Church allowed, concerning the *Invocation of Saints*, the *Adoration of reliques*, or *Worship of Images.*"—Vol. i. 934.

† Father Paul's Hist. p. 190.

back of the whole host of their ejected "remedies for the remission of sins." All these must return, in substance, if not in name and form when, for the true Gospel doctrine of justification, that of Rome is preached. We have seen such results most impressively in the showing of this Chapter. With the return of Justification by Inherent Righteousness, has come back the Romish Doctrine of the Nature and Office of Faith; of the *opus operatum* of the Sacraments; of Baptismal Justification; of Original sin; of Mortal and Venial Sins; of Sin after Baptism; with most evident and lamentable leanings, to say the least, towards the whole array of Romish Purgatory, Invocation of Saints, Prayers for the Dead, Multiplication of Sacraments and of all external pomp and parade in Church services; Transubstantiation, Miracle-working, &c., &c.

"The tree is known by its fruits." We saw the tree first in its root and trunk; and we have now seen it more fully in its branches and products.

Now it is difficult to suppose that all this agreement with Romanism can exist without a corresponding effect upon *the general views and tastes and sympathies of those so conformed, in reference to the whole Christian walk and character*. All this we take to be strikingly indicated in the following passage of a Tract on Baptism.

" We should at once admit that whole bodies of men in the Church of Rome had arrived at a *height of holiness, and devotion, and self-denial and love of God*, which, in this our day, is rarely to be seen in our Apostolic Church; yet we should not for a moment doubt that our Church is the pure Church, although her sons seem of late but rarely to have grown up to that degree of Christian maturity which might have been hoped from the nurture of such a mother; we should not think the comparative holiness of these men, any test as to the truth of any one characteristic doctrine of the Church of Rome; we should rightly see that the holiness of these men was not owing to the distinctive doctrines of their Church; but that God had ripened the seed of holiness in their hearts, notwithstanding the corrupt mixture with which our Enemy had hoped to choke it; we should rightly attribute the apparent comparative failure among ourselves in these times, not to our not possessing the truth, but to our slothful use of the abundant treasures which God has bestowed on us. They held the great Catholic truths of our Creeds, and much of the self-discipline (as fasting) or means of grace (as more frequent prayer) which modern habits have relinquished: and these have brought their fruit." *

Thus is the holiness of the "pure" and "Apostolic Church" of England, whose doctrines and institutions these writers profess to regard as the old path, the Via Media, placed in such dishonorable, and assuredly most untrue comparison with that of a Hierarchy in which, according to the English Church, interpreting the Scriptures, "*Antichrist sitteth*" "that Man of Sin;" a Church which makes traditions of men paramount to the Word of God; which has dared to add uninspired books to the Canon of Holy Scripture; which destroys the Gospel doctrine of salvation by faith, and teaches human merits for the justification of sinners before God; which changes the nature of *Original* Sin, and makes a great part, and many of the worst, of *actual* sins, *venial;* which teaches that the mere fear of punishment, called "*attrition*," when united with the Sacrament of Penance, is a substitute for true *contrition* of heart; which preaches indulgences, works of supererogation, the intercession and invocation of Saints, and Purgatory; which sells Masses for the dead; dishonors the *one great sacrifice for sin* by making a propitiatory sacrifice of Christ in the daily Mass, offered by every Priest; which destroys the Sacrament of the Eucharist, by denying one half of its outward part to the laity, and, by paying it idolatrous worship, degrades the remainder; which teaches her people to be worshipers of Images, Relics, Pictures of Saints and Angels, elevating the Virgin Mary to a rivalship, in honor, with Christ; turning the Temple of the living God, into a den of idols, and filling it with "the abomination that maketh desolate."

This which our Reformers called, "*the Mother of Abominations*," the "Babylon" of the Revelations, and which that book declares "has become the hold of every foul spirit, and a cage of every unclean and hateful bird," so that "a voice from heaven" cries "come out of her my people, that ye be not partakers of her sins, and that ye receive not of her plagues;" † this, in the view of these modern Reformers, is the Church so far beyond comparison in the holiness of her people!

What kind of holiness then, we must ask? Turn back to the extract from our author and see—"*Whole bodies of men.*"—This of course can mean nothing else than *corporate religious bodies*, *Monastic* bodies. Then this eminent holiness of the Church of

---

* Scriptural Views of Baptism, p. 11, 12.—Am. Ed. † Rev. xviii. 2, 3, 4.

Rome is to be found in her Monasteries, among her Monks? Of course then, we are to look for it not where Romanism in its *developments* is modified by surrounding Protestantism; but in those countries where the Protestant Reformation has not reached it; where Monastic Bodies flourish in all the glory and holiness of those days of Monastic peace, when the sound of the trump of Luther had not yet broke upon the silence of the cell, or disturbed the quiet of the Litany of St. Mary. We must go then to the Monks of Italy, and Spain, and Portugal, and see them as they were before the Council of Trent, in order to find those "*bodies* of men in the Church of Rome who had "arrived at the height of holiness and devotion, and self-denial, and love to God, which in this our day is rarely to be seen in our Apostolic Church." And what caused this eminent superiority, in spite of all the false doctrines of Romanism? What corrected the tendency of that "maze in which the Church of Rome doth lead her followers when they ask her the way to Justification?" Dr. Pusey tells us, it was not any thing characteristic in doctrine, but, because, while the great doctrines of the Apostle's Creed are held alike in Rome and England, "much of the self-discipline (as *fasting*,) or means of grace, (*as more frequent prayer*,) which modern habits have relinquished," has been retained in the Church of Rome.

Now, let the reader observe that this eminent holiness is ascribed not merely to *fasting and more frequent prayer*, but to *other means of grace relinquished by Protestants*, of which these are only specimens. But what other? Do we not retain the Word, the Sacraments, Private and Public Prayer! Pray what are those other means of grace so productive of holiness? We know of none in the Scriptures. *What can they be?* Dr. Pusey speaks with Reserve. Why does he not enumerate them? Who can doubt what he means? What is there which Protestants have relinquished but Holy Water, Auricular Confession, Sacramental Penances, Extreme Unction, Anointing at Baptism and Confirmation, Praying for the dead, the use of Images, Pictures, Crosses, and other holy " Catholic and efficacious signs," the frequent Crossing and Genuflexions and Salutations, and Ave Marias, and Masses, and Pilgrimages, the hair-shirt and knotted whip of the Monastery? Some of these, at least, he must mean. The British Critic, as before shown, brings out his idea in reference to many of the above.

But, at any rate, Dr. Pusey ascribes the eminent holiness in the Church of Rome, to that more frequent praying and fasting which, he says, is relinquished among Protestants. What then is this more frequent praying?

Will he hear, on this subject, a writer for whom is professed among his fellows and disciples, a special regard?

"Rome, (says Jackson,) is so besotted with the grapes of her own planting, that she knows not what abominations she commits, nor with whom. Like a harlot drunk in a common Inn, she prostrates herself to every passenger, and sets open all the temples of God, whose keys have been committed to her custody, that they may serve as common stews for satiating the foul souls of infernal spirits; whom she thither invites by solemn enchantments, as by sacrificing and offering incense unto Images. And finding pleasure in the practice, dreams she embraceth her Lord and husband, whilst these unclean birds encage themselves in her's and her children's breasts." "The idolatry of Rome-Heathen agrees with the idolatry of Rome-Christian, as the type or shadow with the body or substance." "While I read these and other Litanies used by the Romish Church, I cannot but congratulate the wisdom and moderation of the Church wherein I was born and baptized, which hath so well extracted the spirit of primitive devotion from *the grossness of later and declining ages of superstition.* These admitted new Mediators unto their Liturgies, with as great facility as our Universities do students unto their Registers." "The Romish Church in her public Liturgy doth often give the reality of Christ's sovereign titles, sometimes the very titles themselves unto Saints; sometimes leaving not so great difference between the divine Majesty, or glorious Trinity, and other celestial inhabitants, as the heathens did between their greater and lesser gods." *

Of that part of the Romish Liturgy which is used for persons in the agony of death, the same writer says.

"To censure this part of their Liturgy as it deserves, it is no prayer but a charm, conceived out of the dregs and relics of Heathenish idolatry which cannot be brought forth without blasphemy, nor be applied to any sick soul without sorcery." "The Church of Rome," (continues this writer, one of those who fought side by side with, Andrews, and Hall, and Usher, not "*mincing* as they went,") "compasseth sea and land, and rangeth

* Jackson's Works, 1. pp. 990, 1001, 998 and 181.

through all the courts of the great King's dominion, with gift in her hand to entice, with the sacrifice of praise and hymns in her mouth to enchant, the chaste and loyal servants of their Lord unto her lust. And prostrates herself, *evening and morning, all the hours of day and night,* unto carved Images of both sexes; with whom her Lord and husband hath so strictly forbidden her familiarity. And yet, in her pride and cunning, she presumes she is able to blear that all-seeing eye—if she have but leisure to wipe her lips with this distinction *I did kiss* thy servants—only with kisses of *dulia,* not with *latria,"*—(p. 989.)

Bishop Beveridge gives us a view of the holiness of those "whole bodies in the Church of Rome," especially in connection with their many prayers and fastings:

"This hath been the ruin of many souls. As our Saviour plainly showeth; when speaking of the severe sect of the Pharisees, he saith that *when they had made any proselyte;* that is, turned a Publican, or an harlot, or some such wicked person, to their austere and superstitious way of living, they made him ten times more a child of wrath than themselves. Yet this is what is so much mistaken for conversion among us; yea, and amongst the Papists too, who speak and boast much of such kind of converts as these; who having lived many years in gross sins" (*sin after Baptism,*) "afterwards being weary of them, to make satisfaction as they think for their former lives, undertake some tedious pilgrimage, or else enter into a Monastery, and there spend the rest of their time in Whippings and Scourgings, in a constant repetition of so many *Pater Nosters* and *Ave Marias* every day. *And this is what the Papists call Religion.* And therefore these Houses (Dr. Pusey's "whole bodies") are called Religious Houses; these Orders, Religious Orders; and such persons, Religious Persons—whereas a man may do all this and yet be as far from God as ever. What cares He for the scourging of our bodies? It is the mortification of our lusts which he calls for. Neither doth he matter all the sacrifices and oblations that you can make him, so much as one sincere act of obedience to his laws." *

If the good Bishop thus characterizes the "*many prayers*" and other means of grace which Protestants have relinquished, but the Romish Church has retained, he also speaks of the *fasting* which

* Sermon No. 85, and 88.

Dr. Pusey mentions as accounting partly for her superior holiness. This Bishop is urging a true Fast in Lent, and explains his meaning by saying. "*Not as the Papists, who, abstaining from nothing but flesh, and using all sorts of other the most delicious food and wine, do rather feast than fast in Lent.*" Again, "*Not fasting on fish and wine and sweetmeats as the Papists do.*" *

But the Jesuit with whom Bishop Stillingfleet reasoned, had made precisely such an assertion of the eminently superior holiness of the Church of Rome, to which the learned Prelate thus replied:

"Doth it lie in the service of your Religious Votaries? For that is the great part of the conspicuous piety of your Church. But is this indeed the bright sunshine of your Church, that there are so *many thousands of both sexes who tie themselves by perpetual vows, never to be dissolved by their own seeking*, (and therefore doubtless pleasing to God, whether they are able to keep them or no,) *and these pray* (if they understand what they say,) *and sing Divine Hymns day and night, which you say is a strange and unheard of thing among Protestants?* What, that men and women (though not in Cloisters,) pray and sing Hymns to God? No, surely. For as the devotion of our *Churches* is more grave and solemn, so it is likewise more pious and intelligible. *You pray and sing*, but how? Let *Erasmus* speak, who understood your praying and singing well. *Cantiuncularum, clamorum, murmurum ac bomborum ubique plus satis est, si quid ista delectant Superos.* Do you think those prayers and hymns are pleasing to *God*, which lie more in the throat than the heart? And such as have been wise and devout men among yourselves have been the least admirers of your mimical, uncouth, and superstitious devotions; but have rather condemned them as vain, ludicrous things; and wondered (as Erasmus said) what they thought of Christ, who imagined he could be pleased with them. Are these then the glorious parts of your devotions, your *prayers and hymns?* If this be the only excellency of your devotion, how much are you out-done by the ancient *Psalliani* and *Euchitæ*, that spent all their time in prayer, and yet were accounted *heretics* for their pains? Still *you pray and sing;* but to whom? to *Saints* and *Angels* often, to the *Virgin Mary*, with great devotion, and most solemn invocations; but to *God* himself, very sparingly in comparison. If this then be the *warm sunshine* of your devotions, we had rather use such wherein we may be sure of God's blessing; which we cannot be in such Prayers and Hymns

* Sermons 87, and 88.

as attribute those honors to his creatures which belong wholly to himself.

"But you *not only sing and pray*, but can be very *idle* too; and the number of those men must be called *Religious Orders*, and *the Garment of the Church is said by you to be embroidered by the variety of them*. And are these indeed the ornaments of your *Church*, when those who had any modesty left were ashamed of them, and called loud for a *Reformation?* Those were indeed such *gardens* wherein it were more worth looking for *useful* or *odoriferous flowers*, (as you express it,) than for *Diogenes* to find out an honest man in his crowd of citizens. Therefore the main things we blame in the Monastic Institutions, are the great degeneracy of them in all respects from their Primitive *Institutions*, the great snares which the consciences of such as are engaged in them, are almost continually exposed to, the unusefulness of them in their multitudes to the *Christian* world, the general unserviceableness of the persons who live in them, the great debaucheries which they are subject to and often over-run with; and if these be the greatest ornaments of your *Church's Garments*, it is an easy matter to espy the *spots* which she hath upon her."—Stillingfleet's Grounds, p. 336.

Such then is the Church to which, say our Oxford writers, "there will ever be a number of *refined and affectionate minds*, who, disappointed in finding full matter for their devotional feelings in the English system, *as at present conducted*, will, through human frailty, betake themselves." *

We have seen that the horrible evils which our old Champions of Protestantism, whom we have just quoted, so strongly exhibit in the devotional character and personal holiness of the mass of Romanists, such as Invocation of Saints, and worship of Images, &c., are called, in Oxford writings, only "*uncatholic peculiarities*," "*incidental corruptions;*" "*practical grievances*." Now to these expressions, and all else that we have seen, put the following Oxford account of the comparative departure from primitive religion, in the Romish, and Protestant Churches.

"That a certain change in objective and external religion has come over the Latin Church, we consider to be a plain historical fact—a change indeed not so great as common Protestanism, for that involves a radical change of inward temper and principle as well, as indeed its adherents are sometimes not slow to remind us;

---

* No. 71, of Tracts, Am. Ed. vol. iii. p. 4.

but a change sufficiently startling to recall to our minds, with very unpleasant sensations, the awful words, 'Though we or an angel from heaven, preach any other Gospel unto you than that you have received, let him be accursed.'"*

So then the departure from primitive truth in the Church of Rome is only as to *external* matters—while that in common Protestantism, i. e. among the Ultra Protestants, who, they say, include a large portion of the clergy of the Church of England, is *radical*, a change of *principle*, a change which is most seriously threatened, at least, with the anathema pronounced by the apostle upon the preachers of a false Gospel—the very *anathema*, with which the Church of Rome has invested it.

Now what, according to these Divines themselves, are these certain *external* changes which religion has suffered in the Latin Church? We will take an account of some of them from their own words. The following specimens are given by the writer of No. 71, of the Tracts, as fair examples of Romanism.

Romanism teaches that "the Mass is a sacrifice *not only commemoratory of that of the Cross*, but also truly and properly propitiatory of the dead and the living," in which there is "a true and real death or destruction of the thing sacrificed;" that "the servants of the Blessed Virgin have an assurance, morally infallible, that they shall be saved;" that "she can, not only entreat her Son for the salvation of her servants, but, by her motherly authority command Him;" that her power, and that of her Son, "is all one, she being by Him, herself omnipotent;" that "she approaches the tribunal of divine Majesty, not asking, but commanding,—not a handmaid, but a Mistress,"—therefore the Church prays, '*Monstra te esse Matrem*,' as if saying to the Virgin, supplicate for us after the manner of a command, and with a mother's authority. Again, the Romish Church "promises salvation to mere *Attrition*, (that is, sorrow for sin arising from fear of punishment,) on the ground that real *Contrition*, that is, hearty sorrow for sin, proceeding from the love of God, above all things, and joined with a firm purpose of amendment, is to be found in very few; and hence deduces the necessity of an easier way for the salvation of men in general." And these are only objective, external changes!!

---

* British Critic, No. 53. Archbishop Laud, with all his tendencies to a Romish externalism in the Church, would have told these Apologists for Popery, that *there are not only doctrinal errors in that system, but such as most manifestly endanger salvation.* See "Relation of a Conference," &c., p. 147.

We have now seen the real value of the holiness prevalent in the Church of Rome, and of those means of grace for its promotion which she has been so wise as to retain, and Protestants are so foolish as to reject. We have seen especially the value of those means, and of their consequent fruits of holiness, in those "whole bodies," those monastic bodies in the Church of Rome, to which Dr. Pusey especially directs us. And to get a more correct view of the legitimate tendency of those means of grace, and of the unmodified character of that holiness, we have gone, where, of course, Romanism would have us go, to countries where Protestantism has not interfered with the entire carrying out, and the full working of what we are led to suppose is the genuine, ancient Catholic system. And there we have seen, what is called in this connection, "the ripening of the seed of life in the heart"—the sort of holiness, and that "height of holiness, devotion, self-denial, and love of God," which we are told "whole bodies of men in the Church of Rome have arrived at," and "which is rarely to be seen in the Apostolic Church of England." *

We may now form some idea of the holiness on which the minds of these writers are set, and which they would see introduced into the Anglican Church. We surely did not charge them with a desire to introduce the real depravity of morals and the debasing idolatry spoken of in the extracts we have given. Doubtless they would have purity of life and sincerity of heart.

---

* The following extravagant praise of Romish Monastic Institutions may well be noted here—taken from the British Critic, No. 51.

"If we find ourselves obliged to acknowledge that, as it is the literal, so it is the truest and highest form in which obedience to the precept of perfection, of selling all that we have and taking up our cross, can be expressed—then let us not sully with affected candor and faint praise, what we have not courage to imitate—rather let us be thankful that such an exemplar and encouragement of our puny striving has been vouchsafed to us." The same writer, by way of illustrating the meaning of the phrase, "*austere life*," and "how simple and unpretending *true Christian mortification is*" gives the following examples of austere life and true Christian mortification, from St. Francis Borgia. "One day when his broth had by accident been made with bitter herbs, he ate it cheerfully without saying a word. Being asked how he liked it, he said, 'I never eat any thing fitter for me!' When others found out the mistake, and the cook in great confusion asked his pardon: 'May God bless and reward you,' said he, 'you are the only person amongst all my brethren that knows what suits me best.' When one would have had a bed warmed for St. Charles Borremeo, he said, with a smile, 'The best way not to find the bed cold, is to go colder to bed than the bed is.' "—Br. Critic, No. 51, p. 156. We have no objection to these traits of humble and amiable temper, but such pin-scratches of mortification are miserable illustrations of what is meant by "*come, take up the cross and follow me.*"

But we do charge them with views, and tastes, and sympathies, in regard to the real nature of Christian holiness, and the practical duties of godliness, which lead them to feel that, amid all the mummeries of Romanism they are in a far more genial climate than that of a Protestant Church; and which lead them to look with such extenuating tenderness upon all the corruptions, all the idolatries, all the horrid leprosies of Romish monastic institutions, where Romanism is most unwashed, as so little incompatible with genuine holiness, that, in spite of them, and in consequence of such prayings and fastings as are practiced in connection with them, and of the *unctions,* the *bowings,* the *penances,* the *crossings, the reverence for Saints' Days,* the numerous *sacramental signs of grace,* of man's making, united with the great disuse of the preaching of the Gospel, and the substitution of the legends of Saints, there is in those monastic bodies a degree of eminent holiness rarely to be found in what, these writers believe to be, the most pure and apostolic of all Protestant Churches.

Let such views of holiness be spread; let them be propagated among weaker minds, and entrusted to less prudent advocates; let the irresponsible, those who are not specially interested to be circumspect, because not the heads of the school, be charged with the carrying out of such views; let the ignorant get hold of them, and the imaginative, the sentimental, then what sort of practical holiness will ensue! what leprosy will spread!

In the present leaders, the direct tendency of such views may be so restrained by better things, within and without, so hedged in by previous education, and associations, and antagonist views, and surrounding circumstances, as never to proceed to any such lengths; but with other hearts, another generation of disciples, under a more advanced state of this divinity, a more developed organ of veneration for "*the intrinsic majesty and truth* which remain in the Church of Rome, amid its corruptions;" with a greater heat from *without,* uniting with the present *bottom* heat, in the forcing-bed; what rank growths of zealous, unblushing Romanism must not be looked for? The earth is full of seeds which have never germinated. Give them air, and sun, and your garden will be over-run with weeds. Many a man professes entire renunciation of doctrines, to which his system directly tends, and of practices of which his principles and frame of mind contain already the ready germ and essence. Hazael said, with sincere indignation, "*Is thy servant a dog, that he should do this great thing!*" But the germ of the horrible thing was in him, nevertheless, and only waited the exciting cause to spring forth—and soon he *was* the dog, and *had done* it, and moreover *was well satisfied with the deed.* There was a time with the Church of Rome, when, had some Elisha " settled his countenance stedfastly until he was ashamed, and wept " at the foresight of her corruptions, and predicted what she would be guilty of, she would have exclaimed, with indignation and sincerity, *Am I a dog, that I should ever be so defiled?* But even then, the spirit and tendency were in her, and strong; and now she glories in her shame. *

TRADITION.

We have reserved what we have room to say about the Oxford error of Tradition for this place; because, though, *theoretically,* it would seem to be a starting point for all errors of doctrine, we regard it as in practice one of the last adopted. The sinner first says in his *heart* there is no God, and then he goes to hunt after arguments in support of his atheism. So the Romish Church first declined into great errors, and got upon a downward current to more and more, and then invented her doctrine of Tradition for defense. So it is with this system. Its doctrine of Tradition is

---

* When this Chapter was written in 1841, its apprehensions as to probable evil results from the extent of Romish tendency then exhibited in this system, were thought, by many, visionary, and to the writers concerned, very unjust. How could such men, with such professions, and such ecclesiastical relations be so zealous for a cause that could have such issues ! The result however exceeded very much the author's anticipations. He was thinking only of the generation following. He had no idea that the *introducers* of the system, full as they were of anti-papal professions ; eloquently as they eulogized their system as furnishing the only tenable ground against Rome and *the* ground on which impregnable bulwarks could be erected against her devices, that those men would ever be seen, tumbling as ripe fruit from the stem into the lap of " the Mother of Abominations." —But what have we seen ! Scarcely a man of any note, who belonged to the school when this Chapter was written, but has given in his submission to, and his adoption of, all that code of doctrine, a great part of which their writings, especially many of the Oxford Tracts, professed to reason against, and to labor to put down. They are now bound, hand and foot, to the whole Tridentine imposition, with all that has been added since by " *development* " under the Infallibility of the so called Vicar of Christ. They have bowed down to the sovereign authority of the Church and its pretended, Infallible head. *All* its revolting perversions of the truth, therefore, they must hold, under peril of *anathema.* That last brand of Antichrist and last and greatest provocation of the wrath of God—the making the Immaculate Conception of Mary, a matter of faith, *de fide,* to be universally believed, on pain of damnation, *that,* with all the loathsome idolatry of Mary, which the authorities of Rome naturally connect with it, they must believe. The author did not expect such issues of this divinity *so soon,* nor in those men.

not practically the source of its other peculiarities, but its wall of protection for them, against the Scriptures. The need was first felt, and then the *cordon sanitaire* was drawn. Into the argument against the views and uses of tradition, as developed in this divinity, we have no room, nor is it consistent with our plan, to enter. We are only showing developments. That these teachers are throwing themselves into the same defense as Romanism fled to, in maintenance of the same errors, we will be content with such evidence as may appear from the following extracts from the late Charge of the Bishop of Calcutta, the well-known and apostolic Daniel Wilson.* First, however, let a general idea of what was thought of the comparative authority of the Scriptures and the Fathers, by the Reformers of the Anglican Church, be taken from the following extract out of the Conferences between Bishops Ridley and Latimer, while in prison, "for the testimony of Jesus."

"But what (said Latimer,) is to be said of the Fathers? How are they to be esteemed? St. Augustine answers, giving this rule also, that we should not, therefore, think it true, because they say so, though they ever so much excel in holiness or learning; unless they are able to prove their saying by the Canonical Scriptures, or by a good probable reason; meaning that to be a probable reason, as I think, which orderly follows upon a right collection and gathering out of the Scriptures.

"Let the Papists go with their long faith, be you contented with the short faith of the saints, which is revealed unto us in the written word of God. Adieu to all Popish fantasies, Amen. For one man, having the Scripture and good reason for him, is more to be esteemed himself alone, than a thousand such as they either gathered together, or succeeding one another.

"The Fathers have both herbs and weeds, and papists commonly gather the weeds and leave the herbs. And the Fathers speak many times more vehemently—in sound of words, than they meant indeed, or than they would have done, if they had foreseen what sophistical wranglers would have succeeded them."

Bishop Wilson thus earnestly warned the clergy of his vast Diocese—

"It is to me, I confess, a matter of surprise and shame, that in the nineteenth century we should really have the fundamental position of the whole system of Popery re-asserted in the bosom of

---

* Now of most blessed memory, gone home to his Lord and rest. (1860.)

that very Church, which was reformed so determinately three centuries since from this self-same evil, by the doctrine, and labors and martyrdom of Cranmer and his noble fellow sufferers.

"What! are we to have all the fond tenets which formerly sprung from the traditions of men re-introduced, in however modified a form amongst us! Are we to have a refined transubstantiation—the Sacraments, and not faith the chief means of salvation—a confused and uncertain mixture of the merits of Christ and inherent grace in the matter of justification—remission of sins, and the new creation of Christ Jesus, confined, or almost confined, to Baptism—perpetual doubt of pardon to the penitent after that Sacrament—the duty and advantage of self-imposed austerities—the innocency of prayers for the dead, and similar tenets and usages which generate 'a spirit of bondage' *—again asserted amongst us ? And thus is the paramount authority of the inspired Scriptures, and the doctrine of the grace of God in our justification by the alone merits of Jesus Christ, which reposes on that authority, to be again weakened and obscured by such human super-additions; and a new edifice of 'will worship,' and 'voluntary humility,' and the 'rudiments of the world,' as the Apostle speaks, to be erected once more in the place of the simple Gospel of a crucified Saviour?

"My language is strong, my Reverend Brethren, but I think you will agree with me that it is not too strong for the occasion. You shall judge for yourselves. I select as a specimen of the whole system, and what forms its basis, so far as I can understand, a passage from the Sermon on Tradition, by the amiable, learned and accomplished Professor of Poetry in the University of Oxford.

"'With relation to the supreme authority of inspired Scripture,' says the Professor of Poetry, 'it stands thus—Catholic tradition teaches revealed truth, Scripture proves it; Scripture is the document of faith, Tradition the witness of it; the true creed is the Catholic interpretation of the Scripture, or Scripturally proved Tradition; Scripture by itself teaches mediately, and proves decisively; Scripture and Tradition taken together are the joint rule of faith.

"So then, Tradition is the primary, and Holy Scripture the secondary teacher of divine truth—so then, we are to search the

* "I confine myself to topics of which no dubious intimations have been given. I say nothing of what may possibly follow—the prohibition of the unfettered use of the Scriptures—purgatory—the veneration of relics—prayer to the Virgin Mary—the intercession of Saints—works of supererogation—monastic vows—the celibacy of the Clergy," &c., &c.

inspired Word of God, not as the one authoritative, adequate rule of faith, but as the document of what this Tradition teaches—we are to study the Scriptures, not in order to ascertain simply God's revealed will, but to prove Tradition by Scriptural evidence—and the standard of revelation is no longer the Bible alone, that is, the inspired Word of the Eternal God in its plain and obvious meaning, but 'Scripture and Tradition taken together are the joint rule of faith.'

"All this is surely sufficiently alarming; but it becomes incomparably more so, when we learn with what latitude the word Tradition is understood. It includes, as we gather from the other repeated statements of the learned author, 'unwritten, as well as written' traditions, 'certain remains or fragments of the treasure of Apostolical doctrines and Church rules;' in other words, an oral law, 'independent of, and distinct from the truths which are directly Scriptural;' which traditions are to be received 'apart from all Scripture evidence, as traditionary or common laws ecclesiastical.' So that it appears that SCRIPTURE AND UNWRITTEN, AS WELL AS WRITTEN TRADITION, TAKEN TOGETHER, ARE THE JOINT RULE OF FAITH.

"I appeal to you, Reverend Brethren, whether we have not here a totally FALSE PRINCIPLE asserted as to the Rule of Faith. I appeal to you, whether the very reading of this statement is not enough to condemn it. I appeal to you, whether the blessed and all-perfect Book of God, is not thus depressed into a kind of attendant and expositor of Tradition. I appeal to you, whether this is not to magnify the comments of men above the inspired words of the Holy Ghost. I appeal to you, whether this is not to make Tradition an integral part of the canon of faith, and so to undermine the whole fabric of the Reformation, or rather of 'the glorious Gospel of the blessed God,' which that Reformation vindicated and affirmed.

"I am as far as possible from supposing that the various pious and learned authors, to whose sentiments, and especially one of them, I am alluding, have any such intention. I am sure they have not. But the tendency of the system is not in my view the less dangerous. Such will and must be, I think, the general effect of its diffusion amongst a multitude of young divinity students, with comparatively little experience, and too apt to follow the new theories of popular and distinguished persons.

"And wherefore this deviation from our old Protestant doctrine and language; why this false principle; why this new school, as it were, of Divinity? Ancient testimony in its proper place, who had undervalued? The dignity and grace of the Sacraments, who had denied? The study of primitive antiquity, who had renounced? The witness of the early Fathers, who had disparaged? Wherefore weaken, then, by pushing beyond its due bearing, the argument which all writers of credit in our Church had delighted to acknowledge?

"The testimony of the Apostolical and primitive ages, for example, to the genuineness, and authenticity, and Divine inspiration of the Canonical Books of the New Testament, as of the Jewish Church to those of the Old, who had called in question? Or who had doubted the incalculable importance of the universal ancient Church at the Council of Nice, to the broad fact of the faith of the whole Christian world, from the days of the Apostles to that hour, in the mysteries of the adorable Trinity and of the Incarnation, as there rehearsed and recognized. Or who called in question the other matters of fact, which are strengthened by Christian antiquity, as the Divine authority and perpetual obligation of the Lord's Day—the institution and perpetuity of the two, and only two Christian Sacraments—the right of the infants of the faithful to the blessings of holy Baptism—the Apostolical usage of Confirmation—the permanent separation of a body of men for sacred services—the duty of willing reverence from the people for them—the threefold rank of Ministers in Christ's Church—the use of Liturgies—the observation of the festivals of our Lord's birth, resurrection, ascension, and gift of the Holy Ghost—with similar points; to which may be added, their important negative testimony to the non-existence of any one of the peculiar doctrines and claims of the modern Court and Church of Rome. These and similar facts we rejoice to acknowledge, as fortified by pure and uncorrupted primitive tradition or testimony.

"We rejoice also to receive, with our own Protestant Reformed Church, the universal witness of the Catholic Fathers and ancient Bishops, expressed in the three Creeds, as a most important method of guarding the words of revelation from the artful ambiguities of heretics, and as rules and terms of communion; just as we acknowledge our modern Articles, Liturgy, and Homilies for the same purpose. We rejoice again in tracing back almost the whole of our sublime and Scriptural Liturgy to a far higher period than the rise of Popery—to the Primitive ages of the Church in our own and every other Christian country. We thus admit, in its fullest sense, for its proper ends, the rule of Vincentius Lirinensis—Quod semper, quod ab omnibus, quod ubique traditum est.

"And we receive such tradition for this one reason—because it deserves the name of JUST AND PROPER EVIDENCE. It is authentic testimony. It is a part of the materials from which even the external evidences of Christianity itself are derived. It furnishes the most powerful historical arguments in support of our faith. It is amongst the proofs of our holy religion.

"But evidence is one thing; the rule of belief another. Not for one moment do we, on any or all these grounds, confound the history and evidences of the divinely inspired rule of faith, with that Rule itself. Not for one moment do we place Tradition on the same level with the all-perfect Word of God. Not for one moment do we allow it any share in the standard of revealed truth. Scripture and Tradition taken together are NOT—we venture to assert—'the joint rule of faith;' but 'Holy Scripture containeth all things necessary to salvation; so that whatever is not read therein, nor may be proved thereby, is not to be required of any man; that it should be believed as an article of faith.' And Tradition is so far from being of co-ordinate authority, that even the ecclesiastical writers who approach the nearest to them, and are read in our Churches—which not one of the Fathers is—'for example of life, and instruction of manners;' are still, as being uninspired, not to be applied to establish any one doctrine of our religion.

"Against this whole system, then, as proceeding upon a MOST FALSE AND DANGEROUS PRINCIPLE, and differing from the generally received Protestant doctrine, I beg, Reverend Brethren, most respectfully to caution you. I enter my most solemn protest against the testimony of the Fathers to any number of facts, being constituted a 'joint rule of faith.' I protest against their witness to the meaning of certain capital series of texts on the fundamental truths of the Gospel, being entitled to the reverence only due to the authoritative Revelation itself. I protest against the salutary use made of the testimony of primitive writers by our Church, as a safeguard against heresy and an expression of her view of the sense of the Holy Scriptures, being placed on a level with the blessed Scriptures themselves—that is, I PROTEST AGAINST A MERE RULE OF COMMUNION BEING MADE A RULE OF FAITH.*

* In the Appendix to his charge, Bishop Wilson thus accurately and succinctly states the precise question between this Divinity and its opposers, on the subject of Tradition:

"Yes, you may rely upon it, Reverend Brethren, that this 'joint rule of faith' will never long consist with the simplicity of the Gospel. I speak with fear and apprehension, lest I should in the least degree overstate the case. I suspect not—I repeat, I suspect not—the Reverend and learned Leaders of the least intention or idea of forwarding the process which I think is in fact going on. But the plague is begun. A FALSE PRINCIPLE IS ADMITTED IN THE RULE OF FAITH, AND IS ALREADY AT WORK.

"Already an amplitude is given, as we have seen, to the word Tradition, which may include any thing and every thing, and therefore justly awakens our increased alarm. Already texts of inspired Scripture are weakened or contracted to the narrowest and most doubtful sense. Already are appeals made to documents which were superseded by the more purely evangelical formularies of our present Book of Common Prayer, with its Articles and Homilies, at the definite settlement of our reformed Church; and a desire not obscurely expressed that our Reformation had retained more of the Traditionary model.

"All this is but too natural. The false principle will go on 'eating as doth a canker,' if things proceed as they now do. The inspired Word of God will be imperceptibly neglected; and the Traditions of men will take its place. The Church will supersede the Bible. The Sacraments will hide the glory of Christ. Self-righteousness will conceal the righteousness of God. Traditions and Fathers will occupy the first place, as we see in the sermons of the chief Roman Catholic authors of every age, and Christ come

" The question to be determined, is not whether the witness of the early Fathers to the facts of Christianity, is of the greatest importance—this is admitted. Nor is it the question, whether their testimony to the broad matter of fact, as to the faith of the universal Church at the Council of Nice, in the doctrines of the Holy Trinity and the Incarnation of our Lord, strengthens and sustains the interpretation of the orthordox Church in subsequent ages—all this we admit. Nor is it the question, whether our Church in her authorized formularies, especially in the three Creeds, makes this testimony a rule and term of Communion—this is most fully conceded. Nor is it the question, whether all the weight and influence which a sound criticism will ever give to writers situated like the Fathers, should be constantly granted them, especially where a consent of them can be shown—that is, where the Quod semper, quod ubique, quod ab omnibus traditum est, applies—this is cheerfully allowed.

" But the question is, Whether Scripture and Tradition, written and unwritten, taken together, are the joint rule of faith ?—Whether Catholic Tradition comes first as the teacher of revealed truth, and Scripture comes next, to prove it ?—Whether the true Creed is Scripturally-proved Tradition, or Catholic tradition supported by the Scriptures ?"

next or not at all; and a lowered tone of practical religion will come in.

"The whole system, indeed, goes to generate, as I cannot but think, an inadequate and superficial, and superstitious religion. The mere admissions of the inspiration and paramount authority of holy Scripture will soon become a dead letter; due humiliation before God under a sense of the unutterable evil of sin, will be less and less understood; a conviction of the need of the meritorious righteousness of the incarnate Saviour, as the alone ground of justification, will be only faintly inculcated; the operations of the Holy Ghost in creating man anew will be more and more forgotten; the nature of those good works, which are acceptable to God in Christ, will be lost sight of; and 'another Gospel' framed on the traditions of men, will make way for an apostasy in our own Church, as in that of Rome—unless, indeed, the evangelical piety, the reverence for Holy Scripture, the theological learning, and the forethought and fidelity of our Divines of dignified station and established repute at home INTERPOSE BY DISTINCT CAUTIONS TO PREVENT IT—as they are beginning to interpose, and as I humbly trust they will still more decisively do." Bishop Wilson's Charge, 1838, pp. 58—76.

CHAPTER IX.

THE DOCTRINE OF THIS DIVINITY, AS TO THE RIGHTEOUSNESS OF JUSTIFICATION, AND THE NATURE AND OFFICE OF FAITH, COMPARED WITH THAT OF THE ANGLICAN CHURCH.

Matter of mortification that such comparison is necessary—A general account of the doctrinal standards of the Anglican Church—Statement of the questions investigated in this Chapter—Arguments from the assertion of Dr. Pusey that the Article, of Justification says nothing of what Justification consists in—The Articles xi., xii., and xiii.—Exposition of the xi. from the language of its Authors elsewhere—From its own peculiar precision as to the office of faith—Homilies quoted and expounded—Seven difficulties into which the Oxford doctrines are brought by the language of the Articles and Homilies—Each made use of as an evidence against the consistency of that Divinity with that of the Anglican Church.

It is indeed a matter of deep mortification that, at this late age of the Reformed Church of England, we are called upon to show that her doctrine of justification, so prominent in the controversies waged in the time of her emancipation from Romanism, so carefully defined and guarded against all possibility of mistake in her standard writings, is not substantially the same with the main doctrine of that very system of Romish error against which she so earnestly protests.

But so it is. The doctrine of this divinity, which we have seen to be just the Romish, boldly claims to be also the Anglican; the very doctrine of the standards and standard divines, of the Anglican Church.

On this singular pretension, issue is now joined.

On no point of doctrinal confession are the declarations of our Church more full, more reiterated, or more earnest, than on that of Justification.

There is first, an Article entitled "*Of the Justification of Man,*" in which the doctrine is summarily declared in these words: "*We are accounted righteous before God, only for the merit of our Lord and Saviour Jesus Christ, by faith, and not for our own works and deservings.*"

And then on the subject of "*our own works and deservings*," as rejected from justification, we have two more; the one entitled, "*Of Works done* BEFORE *Justification*," which excludes them from all efficacy to make men meet to receive grace, or deserve it "*of congruity*," because "*not pleasant to God, forasmuch as they spring not of faith in Jesus Christ, and have the nature of sin;*" the other, of "*Works which are the Fruits of Faith, and* FOLLOW AFTER *Justification;*" declaring that though the necessary results of a lively faith, and pleasing to God in Christ, they "*cannot put away our sins.*"

Thus have three distinct Articles been expended on this subject.

But the Framers of our Confession were not content with this. They regarded the doctrine of "Justification, by which, of unjust, we are made just before God," as "*the strong rock and foundation of Christian religion.*" * The history of all the subtle devices by which Satan had in every age endeavored to undermine that "rock," was before them. The war, then at its height, with the corruptions of Romanism; the Council of Trent, then sitting and fulminating its Anathemas against the holders of the truth, secured their due remembrance of that history. It taught them the necessity of greater minuteness of declaration than was contained in the Articles above named. Homilies were therefore used for larger exposition. The Article on Justification refers the reader for a fuller view of the faith of the Church, to "*the Homily of Justification.*" The Homily entitled "*On the salvation of mankind, by only Christ our Saviour,*" is, by universal acknowledgment, the one referred to; though it is not known by what means, or when, its title was changed from that given in the Article. But this is not the only homiletic exposition bearing upon the subject. The doctrine of the Church on *Faith*, and also on *Good Works*, is essentially connected with that of Justification. We have therefore a standard Homily on each; so that there are three Homilies or Sermons, each in three parts, all asserted in our 35th Article to "*contain a godly and wholesome doctrine;*" and all of which together compose and make a treatise on Justification, and all of which are to be referred to for explaining the sense of the Church in her Article on that subject.

Now, with these combined and minute expositions so remarkable for precision of language and perspicuity of illustration, formed too with particular reference to the very points on which errors have arisen, it would seem impossible that the sense of the Church should be mistaken.

---

* Homily of Salvation, Part ii.

But a recollection of the particular *models* and *men*, most referred to in the construction of these formularies, as well as of those particular *corruptions* of the truth against which they were aimed, if it may not make their meaning more obvious, will at least render it more emphatic and impressive.

Of the Articles which were framed in 1551, and which, on the subjects involved in this discussion, the changes in the reign of Elizabeth did not materially affect, "Archbishop Cranmer must be considered as the sole compiler."* Of the first book of Homilies, with which chiefly we are concerned in this work, the same Reformer is believed by the best authorities to have been the chief composer, as well as was Jewell of the second. But the Homilies on Salvation, Faith, and Good works, to which the Article of Justification is especially related, are without a question ascribed exclusively to Cranmer. † Now it is well known that a frequent correspondence on the most important matters of the Reformation was kept up between him and the continental Divines, especially Melancthon. The latter was particularly consulted on the subject of the Articles, and is known to have urged, for a model, the Confession of Augsburgh. ‡ Hence the Articles of the English Church "chiefly derive their origin from Lutheran Formularies. Some of them are drawn from the Confession of Augsburgh, others from that of Wittemberg, known as the Saxon Confession, and professedly drawn up in strict accordance with that of Augsburgh." §
"The truth of the matter is, (says Le Bas,) that the English Reformers framed Articles not as a wall of partition between Protestant and Protestant, but as a bulwark against the perversions with which the scholastic theology had disfigured the simplicity of the Gospel. The only key therefore which can readily unlock the true sense of the Articles, is a knowledge, not of the opinions which afterwards rent the Protestant community into fragments,— but of the Papal doctrines against which the main struggle of the reformers had been carried on from the very first." "If any person could but sit down to the perusal of our Articles, in utter

---

* Soames's Hist. of the Reformation, vol. iii. 648. Strype's Life of Cranmer, b. ii. c. xxvii.

† Tomline's Elements of Theology, ii. 535. Soames, iii. 63. Todd on the 39th Art. pref. p. xi. Strype's Cranmer, b. ii. c. iii.

‡ Strype's Life of Cranmer, b. iii. c. xxiv. A son of Justus Jonas, the friend and fellow-laborer of Luther and Melancthon, resided with Cranmer and seems to have been his chief medium of correspondence with the Lutherans.—*Laurence's Bampton Lectures*, p. 210.

§ Soames, p. iii. 652.

forgetfulness that Europe had ever been seriously agitated by the Calvinistic dispute, and with nothing in his mind but the controversy between the Reformed Churches and the Church of Rome, he would then clearly perceive that those Articles were constructed for the most part on the Lutheran system, and principally as a rampart against the almost unchristian theology of the schools." *
This was emphatically the case as respects the doctrine now under consideration. Thus we have two very important auxiliaries, in case of any difficulty in understanding the precise meaning of our standard compositions on this subject. The writings of Luther and his associates, especially of Melancthon, together with the Augsburgh Confession, which the latter composed from materials prepared by Luther, are one of them. The doctrines of the Church of Rome, on the subject of justification, are another, and not the least to be relied on.

Now there is no necessity of going into an investigation of the doctrine of the Church in reference to all, or many, of the particular points which, as we have showed, are embraced in Oxford Divinity. All depend upon two main questions, viz.,

1. What is the righteousness whereby we are to be justified or made acceptable before God?

2. What is the mode or means by which that righteousness is applied?

On the settlement of these hangs all the controversy.

The first is resolved into the following: Is the righteousness by which we are justified an *external* or *internal* righteousness? If the former, then it must be what is ordinarily called the righteousness of Christ's obedience unto death, accounted unto us, through faith: If the latter, then it must be the righteousness of a personal holiness, wrought in us by the Spirit of God. Oxford Divines assert the latter, and so does the Church of Rome. We assert the former, and so we contend (and till recently we did not suppose it could be doubted,) do the Articles and Homilies of the Anglican Church. So that the first question comes to this—viz.,

Do the Articles and Homilies teach justification by a righteousness *external*, as distinguished from such as is *in* the believer; in other words, the righteousness which consists, not, in *our* obedience to the Law, through the aid of the Spirit; but exclusively in the obedience of Christ, as our surety, and in his death upon the cross?

---

* Le Bas' Life of Cranmer. See also Laurence's Bampton Lectures; Blunt's Reformation in England.

The second question, as to *the mode or means of applying the righteousness of justification*, may be divided into these two, viz.,

1. Is faith represented as an *instrument*, and the *only* instrument, on the part of man, in his justification before God?

2. While, as a living faith, it must work by love, and be productive of fruits of holiness, does it justify *on account* of these, its fruits and attendants, or through them, as instrumental, with itself; or does it renounce them all, in its office as justifying, and renounce even itself, so far as it is a virtue, or work, operating simply as the instrument or hand by which we embrace the righteousness of Christ?

The need of these questions will be easily perceived, if the reader will keep in mind what we have shown to be the doctrine of this divinity, as to the nature and office of faith, viz.—that, before Baptism, it cannot justify, but is necessarily a dead faith and must itself be brought to Baptism to be made alive thereby and justified; that it can be instrumental to justification, only as bringing us to Baptism, having no more concern in our first justification, than restitution, or any other similar moral act done before Baptism; that we are first justified by Baptism, and without a living faith; that in consequence of such justification, our faith becomes living and justifying; that even now, after Baptism, it is justifying only as a *symbol and representative* of Baptism, "*sustaining*" what has already been accomplished without its agency; and that in this mere sustaining office, its *peculiar* character as an *instrument* is only nominal, all other fruits of the Spirit having just as much instrumentality, and faith being mentioned above the rest, merely because all others are included under it; so that it is a name for the whole complex of Christianity, as carried out in practical piety. *

* It is not uncommon for those who would shrink from participation in the general system of this Divinity, as to faith, and the constituent principle of Justification, to maintain nevertheless the same doctrine substantially, as to the union of all fruits of faith with itself, in its relative office of Justification. We refer to the representation of the office of faith, as if it were efficacious unto Justification, *not as a single act of the soul, by which we embrace Christ*, operating merely as the appointed *instrument* of participation in his righteousness, and justifying only because it lays hold on that righteousness; but as efficacious, because it is "*the root of all Christian virtues*," "the originating principle of love and every good work," and thus, in root and branch, the "*complex of Christianity.*"

If this representation be correct, there is no propriety in saying that we are justified by *faith*, which there would not be also in saying that we are justified by "love, joy, peace, long-suffering," &c., by all those virtues of godly living which are "the *fruits* of faith," and which "*follow after* Justification."

To prove that it is the doctrine of our Articles and Homilies, not only that we are justified only by the *external* righteousness of Christ, accounted unto us; but that faith is the only instrumental means, on man's part, of his partaking in that righteousness; and that, in its agency, *as the only instrument*, it acts not as including, but as renouncing, the co-operating instrumentality of all those fruits of holiness within us, with which it is essentially connected in all practical piety; to make good these positions will sufficiently command the whole field of the present controversy.

In referring to the authorities, now to be cited, the passages bearing on all these points are so interwoven one with another, that it would be impossible to make separate citations for each, without too much repetition. We will therefore have them all in view together.

Now that the word faith is sometimes used in the Scriptures for the sum of Christianity, we freely grant; that justifying Faith is indeed the root of all Christian virtues, so that they "do all spring out *necessarily* of a true and lively faith," we consider a most necessary truth, exceedingly to be insisted on with every soul to whom the Gospel is preached. But that faith derives any of its justifying virtue from these fruits, which are not its life, but its evidences of life, we hold it of great importance to deny, and on the contrary, to maintain that, though *working by love*, as it must if living, faith is effectual for justification, simply as an act of embracing Christ, in all his offices, and benefits, and requirements, whereby the sinner lays hold of his promises and puts on the garment of his justifying righteousness. To some it may seem that the difference between these divergent views is too slight to be made of any importance. We apprehend, however, that it is the point of divergency where lies the unseen origin of those very errors which have for their legitimate issue, *when carried out*, nothing less than justification by *inherent*, and therefore by *our own*, righteousness.

Two ways may separate at so small an angle, that to some it may seem of little consequence which you choose; and for a long while, you may go on in one, without being very far separated from the other—but still they are getting wider apart, and if the lines be carried out, they will become separated by the breadth of the earth. So we think concerning the divergency above described. These two views of faith seem to begin their separation at an angle scarcely measurable. Many an eye would not detect it. But the angle is there, nevertheless, and the minister, though he may never trouble his people with its measurement, should know the importance of accuracy there, and govern his views and language accordingly. Two minds, taking the two ways from this point, may long continue very near one another in doctrine, and spirit, and fellowship; and because the tendencies of the way that leads erroneously may never be carried out, they may never be parted any further asunder. But evil tendencies are not always in such good hands. Let the wrong way be *carried out*. The issue will be, as appeared at the Reformation, and as now appears in the true Protestant and the consistent Romanist,—the two poles of doctrine, as far asunder as the North and South,—Justification by the *righteousness of Christ imputed*—Justification *by our own righteousness inherent*.

The first question, viz: as to whether justification consists in a righteousness *external,* or in one that is *inherent,* we consider to be settled by a singular assertion on the part of Dr. Pusey in his Confession of Faith.

In his Article on Justification, contained in his letter to the Bishop of Oxford, we find the declaration that the eleventh Article of the Anglican Church entitled, " *Of the Justification of Man,*" SAYS NOTHING AS TO WHEREIN OUR JUSTIFICATION CONSISTS.*

Now let the reader look back to what we have said, from Le Bas, &c., as to the Articles being framed simply " as a bulwark against the perversions with which the *scholastic theology* had disfigured the simplicity of the Gospel ;" that " the only key to their true sense is a knowledge of the *papal doctrines,* against which the main struggle of the Reformers was carried on ;" that the Articles " were constructed, for the most part, *on the Lutheran system,* and as a rampart against the almost unchristian theology of the schools ;" let the reader also consider that all this is granted, by Dr. Pusey, with regard to the intention of this particular Article of Justification, in these very words, viz : " *The eleventh Article bears the appearance, on its very face, of being a protest against Romish error ;*" † let it be remembered that " the almost unchristian theology of the Schools " and of the Romish creed, as founded on that theology, entirely excludes all *external* righteousness from that by which a sinner is justified, making justification to consist entirely of a righteousness *inherent ;* that this very doctrine it was, against which the Reformers leveled their most indignant protests ; that according to Hooker the " grand question which did then hang in controversy with the Romish Church, was about this very matter of justifying righteousness "—" *the nature and essence of the medicine whereby Christ cureth our disease ;*" that Mr. Newman states the fundamental question of justification in the same way, viz : *what does the righteousness of justification consist in ;* that when Dr. Pusey and Mr. Newman are engaged in setting forth, distinguishing and defending *their* own doctrine of justification, they feel it necessary to spend pages after pages, on this very question ; and yet when the Church of England, in the midst of the conflicts and jealousies and confusion and false accusations, of the era of the Reformation ; when the clouds of Romanism had only partially passed away from her parishes, and the Council of Trent was sitting and forging its decrees and anathemas on this very subject, and all

* Letter, p. 42.   * Letter, p. 41.

eyes, as well of the Reformed States of the Continent, as of the Romish hierarchy, were upon her, and precision and fullness of statement upon the chief matters in controversy with Rome, as well for the vindication of her own position, as for the guidance and protection of her people, were so specially demanded; then, her Archbishops and Bishops and great divines did solemnly frame and set forth a declaration of faith, on this great point of the Reformation, with express reference to the Romish error, calling it the Article of Justification, and yet, as Oxford Divines assure us, they say not a word as *to what justification consists in;* this they knew to be the great question, and yet they say nothing at all about it! Dr. Pusey and Mr. Newman could not possibly make such an omission, in *their* Articles and declarations; but the Anglican Reformers most singularly did. The very point on which their Article was most needed, for a rampart against the corruptions of the Schoolmen, and the decrees of Trent, is just that on which it is silent as the grave!

This of course is wholly incredible, utterly absurd. Not only does the face of the Article say so; but the whole condition of things in which, and the whole object for which, it was constructed. What then? How then shall we explain this assertion of Dr. Pusey? Most evidently, since it could not be pretended that the Article says any thing in favor of the Oxford doctrine of Justification; the only refuge was to deny that it said any thing against it; —hence the necessity of maintaining that on the main question it is utterly dumb. The desperateness of the refuge, the absurdity of the pretense, is the settlement of the question. It cannot be that the Article says nothing as to what Justification consists in. It must, it does, say something. What is it? Were it on the side of the Oxford doctrine, would it not be asserted? Nothing of the sort is claimed; and hence the plain conclusion, that its testimony is against that doctrine.

If all that our Oxford divines can pretend to is, that the Articles of the Church say nothing, one way or the other, then is there nothing but this assertion for us to answer. If we can show that the Articles do say *something*, it must be against their doctrines. If we can show that both Articles and Homilies speak strongly and earnestly to the point in question, it must be all strongly against them; it cannot be for them, or they would never have taken this tame, negative ground.

The Articles in question are the following:

"XI. *Of the Justification of Man.*

"We are accounted righteous before God, only for the merit of our Lord and Saviour Jesus Christ, by faith, and not for our own works or deservings. Wherefore, that we are justified by faith only is a most wholesome doctrine, and very full of comfort; as more largely is expressed in the Homily of Justification.

"XII. *Of Good Works.*

"Albeit that good works, which are the fruits of faith, and follow after Justification, cannot put away our sins, and endure the severity of God's Judgment; yet are they pleasing and acceptable to God in Christ, and do spring out necessarily of a true and living faith; insomuch that by them a lively faith may be as evidently known, as a tree discerned by the fruit.

"XIII. *Of Works before Justification.*

"Works done before the grace of Christ, and the inspiration of his Spirit, are not pleasant to God, forasmuch as they spring not of faith in Jesus Christ; neither do they make men meet to receive grace, or, as the School Authors say, deserve grace of congruity: yea rather, for that they are not done as God hath willed and commanded them to be done, we doubt not but they have the nature of sin."

Mark the precision of the first of these Articles. The righteousness which is by the faith of Christ, and *our own* righteousness, are here, according to the example of St. Paul,* set in direct opposition : the words "*only for the merits of Christ,*" being evidently the intended opposite of "*for our own works.*" The former excludes the latter. The two are incapable of standing together in this matter. Even faith, viewed as it is a work of personal grace, is excluded, and is considered only as an *instrument* of connection with Christ. † But such is the fullness of that *meritorious* cause, unto all who believe, that they are accounted *righteous;* in other words, righteousness is *accounted* or *imputed* to them; righteousness

---

* Phil. iii. 9.

† It is worthy of note how carefully, the merely instrumental office of faith is exhibited in the Article; as appears more plainly in the Latin form, which is of equal authority with the English. "Tantum PROPTER meritum domini ac servatoris nostri Jesu Christi, PER fidem, non PROPTER opera ét merita nostra, justi coram Deo reputamur. Quare sola fide nos justificari, doctrina est saluberrima," &c.

What is meant by *sola fide* is shown by the use of *per* with *fidem*, and *propter* with *meritum*, and its antithesis, *opera nostra*.

as perfect, as the merits of our Redeemer, because of those merits it consists; so that to believers God no more imputes sin, than if they had never sinned.

The reader will here inquire, by what device it can be made out, that the above eleventh Article does not state in what our justification consists. Does it not distinctly say, that we are accounted righteous before God only for the merits of our Lord and Saviour, &c.,—and is not this what justification consists in, even the accounting of the righteousness of Christ to the believer? No, says this divinity, God first *makes* us righteous, and then, and on that moral basis, *accounts* us righteous. The Article speaks of the latter, not of the former. But which is the more important of the two to be brought into a confession of faith—the *making* or the *accounting*, the *thing* or the *name*, the *reality* or its acknowledgment? Of course the *making* is the great matter. The *accounting*, on the part of God, follows of course. And yet, according to these writers, the Church, in her Article of Justification, has said not a word as to *how* that is to take place; but has spent the force of her solemn Confession upon the mere matter of course that when God has *made* a sinner righteous, however it may take place, then he *accounts*, or considers and deals with him, as righteous. This is incredible.

Now as the Article of Justification is known to have been written by Archbishop Cranmer, his other writings, when they speak on the same subject, must be considered the surest comment upon its meaning. We have then, in his Catechism, the following account of what ensues upon the exercise of a lively faith in Christ.

"Then God doth no more *impute* unto us our former sins; but he doth *impute* and *give* unto us the justice and righteousness of his Son Jesus Christ. And so we be *counted* righteous, forasmuch as no man dare accuse us for that sin for the which satisfaction is made by our Saviour Jesus Christ."*

From this passage it appears that Cranmer used the words *account* and *impute* for the same thing; that to be accounted righteous, and to have righteousness imputed to us, was one matter in his view. Then, if it be asked whether he does not use the phrase to *impute* or *account righteousness*, in the sense of the Oxford men, viz: as *making one righteous;* let it be asked if he used the

* Crammer's Catechism; (Redemption.)

analogous phrase—*imputing sin* in the sense of *making one sinful*. The absurdity of the last, is the key, if any be needed, to the whole phraseology. Imputing the righteousness of Christ must mean the *setting to the sinner's account* the righteousness of Christ, *as his own*, for justification. Then when the same writer uses the similar language of the Article, we must necessarily understand him in precisely the same sense. So that allowing the framer of the Article to explain his own words, we have the utmost clearness of evidence that the constituent righteousness of justification is, according to the Anglican Church, simply the external and imputed righteousness of Christ.

The office of faith, as the alone instrument of justification, is also clearly contained in the same Article,—its office of justifying, not as in itself a righteousness, but only as it is the appointed *instrumental* medium of obtaining the righteousness of Christ; not as that *on account* of which, but *through* which, we are justified. An inspection of the Latin wording of the Article, which is placed in the note, will make this still more plain.* We there learn, authoritatively, that when our Reformers say *by* faith, they mean *through* faith. And all doubt of the idea which they intended to convey is effectually removed by the import of the preposition which they employ to describe the efficacy and operation of Christ's merits. Their language is: "We are deemed righteous before God, only on account of the merits of our Lord and Saviour Jesus Christ *through* faith, and not on account of our own works and merits. Hence, from the very force of the two different prepositions employed, it is evidently the judgment of our Reformers that, in the sight of God, we are justified meritoriously, *on account* of the sole righteousness of Christ; while *through* faith, we are justified no futher than *instrumentally* or *mediately*." *

Let us now turn to the Homily to which this Article refers us for a larger explication of its doctrine. That singularly clear declaration of the way of salvation was evidently prepared with

---

* "Tantum propter meritum domini ac servatoris nostri Jesu Christi, *per* fidem, non *propter* opera et merita nostra, justi coram Deo reputamur. Quare sola fide, nos justificari, doctrina est saluberrima." &c.

Had the framer of this, confined himself to the expression *sola fide* (by faith only) which may mean either *by* faith, as *righteousness*, or *through* faith as only an *instrument*, he might have spoken obscurely. But all ambiguity is prevented by the expression *per fidem (through* faith,) in evident contradistinction from *propter meritum (on account* of the merits, &c.) *Through* faith and *on account* of faith are widely different ways.

† Faber's Prim. Doc. of Justification.

special reference to the peculiar errors of the Church of Rome, as to the Justifying Righteousness and the office of Faith. Let us cite the following passage.

"And of this justice and mercy of God knit together, speaketh St. Paul in the third chapter to the Romans (23—25): 'All have offended, and have need of the glory of God; but are justified freely by his grace by redemption which is in Jesus Christ; whom God has set forth to us for a reconciler and peace-maker through faith in his blood, *to show his righteousness,*' And in the tenth chapter (4); 'Christ is *the end of the Law unto righteousness, to every man that believeth.*' And in the eighth chapter (3, 4); 'That which was impossible by the Law, inasmuch as it was weak by the flesh, God sending his own Son in the similitude of sinful flesh, by sin condemned sin in the flesh; that *the righteousness of the Law might be fulfilled in us,* which walk not after the flesh, but after the Spirit.'

"In these foresaid places, the Apostle toucheth specially three things, which must go together in our justification. Upon God's part, his great mercy and grace: upon Christ's part, *justice;* that is, *the satisfaction of God's justice, or the price of our redemption, by the offering of his body, and shedding of his blood, with fulfilling of the Law perfectly and thoroughly:* and upon our part, true and lively faith in the merits of Jesus Christ; which yet is not our's, but by God's working in us. So that, in our justification, there is not only God's mercy and grace, but also his justice; which the Apostle calleth the justice of God: and *it consisteth in paying our ransom, and fulfilling of the Law:* and so the grace of God doth not shut out the justice of God, in our justification: but only shutteth out the justice of man: that is to say, the justice of our works, as to be merits of deserving our justification. And therefore St. Paul declareth here *nothing, upon the behalf of man,* concerning his justification, but *only a true and lively faith:* which nevertheless is the gift of God, and not man's only work without God.

"And yet that faith doth not shut out repentance, hope, love, dread, and the fear of God, to be joined with faith in every man that is justified: but it shutteth them out from the office of justifying. So that, although they be all present together in him that is justified, yet they justify not all together. Neither doth faith shut out the justice of our good works, necessarily to be done afterwards of duty towards God; for we are most bounden to serve God, in doing good deeds, commanded by him in his Holy Scripture, all the days of our life: *but it excludeth them, so that we may not do them to this intent—to be made just by doing of them.* For all the good works that we can do be imperfect, and therefore *not able to deserve our justification;* but our justification doth come freely by the mere mercy of God; and of so great and free mercy, that, whereas all the world was not able of themselves to pay any part towards their ransom, it pleased our heavenly Father, of his infinite mercy, without any our desert or deserving, to prepare for us the most precious jewels of Christ's body and blood; whereby our ransom might be fully paid, the Law fulfilled, and his justice fully satisfied.

"So that Christ is now *the righteousness of all them that truly do believe in him.* He for them paid their ransom by his death. He for them fulfilled the Law in his life. So that now, *in him, and by him, every true Christian man may be called a fulfiller of the Law; forasmuch as that, which their infirmity lacked, Christ's justice hath supplied.*" *

In this passage, the reader will notice an express commentary upon the passages quoted from St. Paul; especially upon the expression, "*his righteousness,*" or "*God's Justice;*" Christ "*the end of the Law for, or unto, righteousness;*" and "*the righteousness of the Law fulfilled in us.*" These being the texts, the object is to show what is meant by God's Justice, or Righteousness, in our Justification, and how Christ is the end of the Law, for righteousness, so that the Law is "fulfilled in us."

These are precisely the matters now in discussion. Mr. Newman expounds the passage, "*to show His righteousness,*" by these words, "*a righteousness of His own making,*" † as distinguished from a righteousness of *our* making; a righteousness wrought in us and by us, through the Holy Ghost, in distinction from that of our own unaided, unsanctified effort of obedience. The latter, he thinks, is what St. Paul calls, in Phil. iii., "the righteousness which is of the law;" the former, "the righteousness of God by faith." But let us see what the Homily calls this *righteousness of God.* It says that what St. Paul calls "the Justice," or righteousness "of God *consisteth in paying our ransom and in fulfilling of the Law.*" This same justice or righteousness is before called "the price of our redemption, by the offering of the body, and shedding of the blood of Christ, with fufilling of the Law perfectly and thoroughly,"—and this is said to be the justice or righteousness of Christ, or that

* Homily of Salvation, Part I. † Lectures on Justification, p. 54.

which is Christ's part in our justification. Now if there be any possible sense in which such righteousness can be *in us* instead of being *external* to us and *in Christ* only, we cannot perceive it.

This righteousness is said to consist in "the most precious jewels of Christ's body and blood." The only thing "on man's part" which the Homily considers as having any part in his justification, through that external righteousness of Christ, is "*a true and lively faith.*" But this, it takes great pains to show, has not its influence, as constituting any part of the justifying righteousness; for all good works, it says, (and faith is in, one sense, a *work,*) are excluded from that office and are not to be done for the purpose of our being justified by doing them; so that the office of faith is simply that of an instrument, whereby we embrace the righteousness of Christ. Thus the "justice" or righteousness "of man," that is to say, "the righteousness of our works," precisely that which we are told by these Divines has "*a satisfying and justifying quality,*" and does fulfill the Law and constitute the righteousness of our justification, this, the Homily says, *is shut out;* nothing in us being connected with our justification, but simply our faith. So, by the Ransom paid for us by Christ in his death, and the fulfillment of the Law in his life, He is "the end of the Law for righteousness," or he "is now the righteousness of them that do believe in him." Then if it be asked how "the Law is *fulfilled* in us," the Homily answers: "In him and by him, every true Christian man," i. e. every one who has "a true and lively faith in Christ," "*may be called a fulfiller of the Law, forasmuch as that which their infirmity hath lacked, Christ's righteousness hath supplied.*"

Here then is the external and accounted righteousness of Christ, in his Mediatorial office, asserted as the justification of the sinner, believing in him; to the entire exclusion of all other righteousness for that end.

To show how exceedingly careful is this Homily lest it should be supposed that anything *in us,* even our faith, can make up any part of the righteousness of our justification let the following extract be read.

"First, you shall understand that, in our justification by Christ, it is not all one thing, The office of God unto man, and the office of man unto God. Justification is not the office of man, but of God; for man cannot make himself righteous by his own works, neither in part nor in the whole: for that were the greatest arrogancy and presumption of man, that Antichrist could set up against

God, to affirm that a man might by his own works take away and purge his own sins, and so justify himself. But justification is the office of God only; and is not a thing which we render unto him, but which we receive of him; not which we give to him, but which we take of him by his free mercy, and by the only merits of his most dearly beloved Son, our only Redeemer, Saviour, and Justifier, Jesus Christ."

"So that the true understanding of this doctrine—We be justified freely by faith, without works, or that we be justified by faith in Christ only— is not, that this our own act, to believe in Christ, or this our faith in Christ, which is within us, doth justify us, and deserve our justification unto us—for that were to count ourselves to be justified by some act or virtue that is within ourselves—but the true understanding and meaning thereof is, that although we hear God's word, and believe it; although we have faith, hope, charity, repentance, dread, and fear of God within us, and do never so many good works thereunto: yet we must renounce the merit of all our said virtues, of faith, hope, charity, and all our other virtues and good deeds, which we either have done, shall do, or can do, as things that be far too weak and insufficient and imperfect, to deserve remission of our sins and our justification: and therefore we must trust only in God's mercy, and that sacrifice which our High Priest and Saviour Christ Jesus, the Son of God, once offered for us upon the cross, to obtain thereby God's grace and remission, as well of original sin in Baptism, as of all actual sin committed by us after our Baptism, if we truly repent and turn unfeignedly to him again"

"So that, as St. John Baptist, although he were never so virtuous and godly a man, yet in this matter of forgiving of sin, he did put the people from him, and appointed them unto Christ, saying thus unto them, " Behold," yonder is "the Lamb of God which taketh away the sin of the world " (John i. 29): even so, as great and as godly a virtue as the lively faith is, yet it putteth us from itself, and remitteth or appointeth us unto Christ, for to have only by him remission of our sins, or justification. So that our faith in Christ, as it were, saith unto us thus: It is not I that take away your sins, but it is Christ only, and to him only I send you for that purpose, forsaking therein all your good virtues, words, thoughts and works, and only putting your trust in Christ." *

Let it be remarked how carefully and strikingly the simply *instrumental* character of justifying faith is here exhibited; how, as a

* Homily of Salvation Part 2.

virtue, or work, its efficacy is excluded; so that we are made to consider faith, in the sinner's coming to Christ, to be justifying: only as the faith of Bartimeus was instrumental in opening his eyes—only as it leads us to Christ. Should we regard faith as in any other way concerned in this great office, we should then be counting ourselves, says the Homily, to be justified *"by some act or virtue that is within ourselves."* Any departure from the doctrine of the very simplest and merest instrumental office not of a faith that does not work by love, but of a faith that does not bring its love or other attendant graces into the work of Justification, is considered, by the Church, as inconsistent, with the putting of our trust *singly* in Christ, and as partaking of a reliance upon something inherent in ourselves.

That faith is not only the instrument, but the only instrument, is prominently asserted in the following extract.

"Truth it is, that our own works do not justify us, to speak properly of our justification: that is to say, our works do not merit or deserve remission of our sins, and make us, of unjust, just before God; but God of his mere mercy, through the only merits and deservings of his Son Jesus Christ, doth justify us. Nevertheless, because faith doth directly send us to Christ for remission of our sins; and that, by faith given us of God, we embrace the promise of God's mercy, and of the remission of our sins—which things none other of our virtues or works properly doth—therefore the Scripture useth to say, that faith without works doth justify. And forasmuch as it is all one sentence in effect to say, faith without works, and only faith, doth justify us; therefore the old ancient fathers of the Church, from time to time, have uttered our justification with this speech, Only faith justifieth us; meaning no other than St. Paul meant, when he said, 'Faith without works justifieth us."

"And because all this is brought to pass through the only merits and deservings of our Saviour Christ, and not through our merits, or through the merit of any virtue that we have within us, or of any work that cometh from us; therefore, in that respect of merit and deserving, we forsake, as it were, altogether again, faith, works, and all other virtues. For our own imperfection is so great, through the corruption of original sin, that all is imperfect that is within us—faith, charity, hope, dread, thought, words, and works—and therefore not apt to merit and deserve any part of our justification for us. And this form of speaking use we, in the humbling of ourselves to God, and give all the glory to our Saviour Christ, who is best worthy to have it."

"The right and true Christian faith is, not only to believe that Holy Scripture, and all the aforesaid articles of our faith, are true; but also to have a sure trust and confidence in God's merciful promises, to be saved from everlasting damnation by Christ; whereof doth follow a loving heart to obey his commandments. And this true Christian faith neither any devil hath; nor yet any man, which in the outward profession of his mouth, and in his outward receiving of the Sacraments, in coming to the Church, and in all other outward appearances, seemeth to be a Christian man, and yet in his living and deeds showeth the contrary."*

In the first of these paragraphs, there is an express distinction between the agency of faith and that of all other graces and works. The meaning of the expressions, "*only faith justifieth,*" "*faith without works justifieth,*" &c., is clearly declared to be, not that a faith which is not fruitful in good works, justifieth, but that a living faith does what "*none other of our virtues or works properly doth.*" "It doth directly send us to Christ for remission of our sins," and "by it, we embrace the promise of God's mercy, and of the remission of our sins." This no other virtues or works can do.

The nature and instrumental office of Justifying faith is expressed, if possible, more prominently in the following extracts from the Homily of the Passion.

"Now it remaineth that I show unto you, how to apply Christ's death and passion to our comfort, as a medicine to our wounds; so that it may work the same effect in us wherefore it was given, namely, the health and salvation of our souls. For as it profiteth a man nothing to have salve, unless it be well applied to the part affected; so the death of Christ shall stand us in no force, unless we apply it to ourselves in such sort as God hath appointed.

"Almighty God commonly worketh by means; and in this thing he hath also ordained a certain mean, whereby we may take fruit and profit to our souls' health. What mean is that? Forsooth it is faith. Not an inconstant or wavering faith: but a sure, stedfast, grounded, and unfeigned faith. "God sent his Son into the world," saith St. John. To what end? "That whosoever believeth in him should not perish, but have life everlasting." (John iii. 16.) Mark these words, "that whosoever believeth in him." Here is the

* Homily of Salvation, Part 3.

mean, whereby we must apply the fruits of Christ's death unto our deadly wound. Here is the mean, whereby we must obtain eternal life; namely, faith. 'For,' as Saint Paul teacheth in his Epistle to the Romans, 'with the heart man believeth unto righteousness, and with the mouth confession is made unto salvation." (x. 10.) Paul, being demanded of the keeper of the prison, 'what he should do to be saved,' made this answer: 'Believe in the Lord Jesus, so shalt thou and thine house both be saved.' (Acts xvi. 30, 31.) After the Evangelist had described, and set forth unto us at large, the life and death of the Lord Jesus, in the end he concludeth with these words: 'These things are written, that we may believe Jesus Christ to be the Son of God, and through faith obtain eternal life.' (John xx. 31.) To conclude with the words of St. Paul, which are these: 'Christ is the end of the law unto salvation, for every one that doth believe.' (Rom. x. 4.)

"By this then you may well perceive, that the only mean and instrument of Salvation, required of our parts, is faith.

"Therefore I say unto you, that we must apprehend the merits of Christ's death and passion by faith; and that with a strong and stedfast faith, nothing doubting but that Christ, by his one oblation and once offering of himself upon the cross, hath taken away our sins, and hath restored us again into God's favor, so fully and perfectly, that no other sacrifice for sin shall hereafter be requisite or needful in all the world.

"Thus have you heard, in few words, the mean whereby we must apply the fruits and merits of Christ's death unto us, so that it may work the salvation of our souls; namely, a sure, stedfast, perfect, and grounded faith. For, as all they which beheld stedfastly the brazen serpent were healed and delivered, at the very sight thereof, from their corporal diseases and bodily stings (Num. xxi. 9; John iii. 14;) even so all they, which behold Christ crucified with a true and lively faith, shall undoubtedly be delivered from the grievous wounds of the soul, be they never so deadly or many in number.

"Therefore, dearly beloved, if we chance at any time, through frailty of the flesh, to fall into sin—as it cannot be chosen but we must needs fall often—and if we feel the heavy burden thereof to press our souls, tormenting us with the fear of death, hell, and damnation; let us then use that mean which God hath appointed in his word; to wit, the mean of faith, which is the only instrument of salvation now left unto us. Let us stedfastly behold Christ crucified with the eyes of our heart. Let us only trust to be saved by his death and passion, and to have our sins clean washed away through his most precious blood; that, in the end of the world, when he shall come again to judge both the quick and the dead, he may receive us into his heavenly kingdom, and place us in the number of his elect and chosen people; there to be partakers of that immortal and everlasting life, which he hath purchased unto us by virtue of his bloody wounds: to him therefore, with the Father and the Holy Ghost, be all honor and glory, world without end. *Amen.*"*

Here we have faith distinctly called the "mean and instrument of our salvation;" "the *only* instrument of salvation now left unto us;" that "by which we apply Christ's death and passion to our comfort, and as a medicine to our wounds;" by which we "stedfastly behold Christ crucified with the eyes of our heart."

Now let us make a brief summary of the points which have been distinctly made from the Articles and Homilies. They are chiefly the following, viz., That the righteousness whereby we are justified, is exclusively the righteousness of Christ; that it consists in his obedience to the law for us, and his paying, by his death on the cross, the penalty of our sin; that this righteousness is what St. Paul calls the righteousness of God; that when accounted or imputed to the sinner, he is accounted *righteous* before God for Christ's sake; perfectly righteous, so that he is regarded and treated as, in Christ, a fulfiller of the Law; that the only mean or instrument by which we can apply or obtain the imputation of this righteousness is a living faith; that such faith acting thus, as the instrument of applying the righteousness of Christ, is not justifying because of any justifying efficacy in the love and other holy fruits with which it is attended, but solely as it leads the soul to Christ.

Let the reader compare these necessary conclusions from the standards of our Church, with the main features which have been exhibited of the Oxford doctrine on these heads. What the Articles and Homilies so distinctly teach, that system directly denies, most earnestly condemns, and most indignantly casts away. A more singular pretense was never penned, or conceived, than that such representations of Christian truth as those of this divinity, are capable of being squeezed, by any force of systematizing pressure, or any skill of critical management, into any thing but

---

* Second Homily of the Passion.

a perfect contradiction of the plainest and most repeated declarations of the Anglican Church.

But have not these writers some way of defending themselves against such charges of contradiction? Surely they have. How far they are sufficient, we will attempt to show. They first assert, as we have seen, that the Article of Justification says nothing of what Justification *consists in*. The absurdity of such an idea, considering the acknowledged object, and all the circumstances in and for which the Article was made, we have already shown, and turned against its advocates. Whether the Homily declares what Justification consists in, we are not told. But evidently the reader is intended by Dr. Pusey, in his Letter to the Bishop of Oxford, to take the impression that neither in the Article, nor in the Homily constructed expressly for its larger explication, has the Church pronounced upon "the nature and essence of the medicine with which Christ cureth our disease"—*the nature of the justifying righteousness*. Then what *does* the Church pronounce?

"The Article opposes the merit of Christ to any thing which we have of our own, to our own works and deservings, as the *meritorious* cause of our salvation; and thus far, we believe, little is imputed to us. It is so plain a truth, and has been so often inculcated by us, that every sin of man which is remitted, is remitted only for the sake of his meritorious Cross and Passion; every good and acceptable work is such through his power working in us, that little, I believe, has thus far been objected."*

And this is very plausible. But precisely such language is used by the Church of Rome, as was showed in the fifth chapter of this work. She makes the Lord Jesus Christ the only *meritorious* cause. She ascribes every good and acceptable work to the grace of God through the merits of Christ. She holds that the first justification, that of a sinner's first coming to God, and necessarily without any works, must be of the mere mercy of God remitting sins for Christ's sake. But the Church of Rome and the Oxford men agree that even in that case the remission consists, not in the accounting to that sinner of the righteousness of Christ, as the Homilies describe it; but in the expulsion of sin from his soul, and the *infusion* of righteousness for Christ's sake; so that when they speak of his receiving remission of sins for Christ's sake, their

---

* Pusey's Letter, p. 41.

meaning, and that of the Articles and Homilies, are entirely different.

When, however, they come to what constitutes the *subsequent* acceptableness of that sinner, in all his future course; while, with the Anglican Church, as above, that acceptableness is simply the being accounted righteous, through the imputation of the righteousness of Christ, from the first to the last of the Christian life; no virtue or work or grace of ours constituting any part of the ground of our acceptance, at the end, any more than at the beginning, of our race; with Oxford divines and Romanists, it is just the reverse. Acceptance, with them, is wholly founded upon our own righteousness. The Law is considered as fulfilled in our obedience. We are justified more and more as we grow in grace. The merits of Christ are only connected, as it is through them that any good work is wrought in us. But the whole process may go on without our ever looking to the atonement of Christ; or even knowing enough of what he did for us, to be capable of "an *explicit* belief in his atonement." With such a doctrine, the Papist and the Oxford writers may profess to ascribe all merit to Christ. The former may be sometimes more candid than the latter, in sometimes ascribing in terms a more modified merit to man's inherent righteousness, while, at the other times, he professes to give all merit to the Saviour. But the difference is only in words. Do any of this divinity employ stronger language than the following? "He that could reckon how many the virtues and merits of our Saviour have been, might likewise understand how many the benefits have been that are come to us by him; for so much as men are made partakers of them all by means of his passion; by him is given unto us remission of sins, grace, glory, liberty, praise, salvation, redemption, justification—merits and all other things which were behoveful for our salvation." Again: "All grace is given by Jesus Christ. True, but not except Jesus Christ be applied. He is the propitiation for our sins; by his stripes we are healed—all this is true, but apply it. We put all satisfaction in the blood of Jesus Christ; but we hold that the means which Christ hath appointed for us, in the case, to apply it, *are our penal works*." *

Beyond this language our Oxford men cannot go. Thus far they may go. But notwithstanding all this, the Council of Trent has decreed that "the Justified can and do *merit* eternal life." Bellarmine has labored to prove that good works are necessary to

---

* Lewis of Granada and Paulgarola, in Hooker on Justif. § 33.

eternal life, not only *neccesitate præsentiæ,* as the way to God's kingdom; which all confess; but also necessitate *efficentiæ,* as causes of eternal life. And " the most learned of the Papists hold that there is a due proportion between the works of the faithful proceeding from charity, and the heavenly reward; and that they *condignly* merit eternal life, not only in respect of God's promise, but also for the worthiness of the works, which are *dignified, they say, by the merit of Christ, that they become truly meritorious,* and do in Justice, according to their worth, deserve the heavenly reward." *

It is granted that precisely such language, the Oxford writers so far as we know, have not used. But they have used the *equivalent.* They constantly contend that our own righteousness has a justifying quality; does fulfill the law; is the basis of our acceptance with God. They call it the only wedding garment in which the soul can be invested. But that which constitutes our Justification is our *merit,* call it what else they please. "If it be a righteousness in us; (says Hooker,) it is as much *our* righteousness as our souls are ours." It is then a righteousness of works, as distinguished from the accounted righteousness of Christ. Differ as Romanists, and Oxford men may, as to the use of the word *merit,* in this application; when the former say that "*our works are so dignified by the merits of Christ that they become truly meritorious,*" they mean no more than Mr. Newman means, when he says "that, through the merits of Christ, our indwelling righteousness is our justification; that the righteousness in which we are to stand at the last day, *is not Christ's imputed obedience, but our good works.*"†

In this harmonizing, we do not diminish the excessive error of the Romanist; but we unveil the real error of the Oxford divines. Both are upon a system of human merit, under different language, because both look to *within themselves,* instead of to Christ, for righteousness before God; while both speak of ascribing all to the merit of the Saviour's passion, applied through the Sacraments, and by infusion of righteousness.

Thus it is obvious that the entireness of the contradiction between the doctrine of this divinity and that of the Articles and Homilies, concerning the basis of our acceptance, is not in any wise diminished by the profession of ascribing all *meritorious* causation to Christ.

But another effort to escape from the evident condemnation at the bar of the Articles and Homilies, is in reference to *the sole*

---

* Bishop Downame on Justif. b. 549.
† Lectures on Justification, p. 60.

instrumentality of faith, When accused of taking away from faith the office assigned to it in those standards as "the *only* instrument and mean of applying the death of Christ," as "the only thing upon the behalf of man, concerning his justification," we hear that the instrumentality of faith as the only *internal* instrument is not taken away. "When faith (they say) is called the sole instrument, this means the sole *internal* instrument; not the sole instrument of any kind."

"There is nothing inconsistent then, in faith being the sole instrument of justification, and yet Baptism also the sole instrument, and that at the same time, because in distinct senses; an inward instrument in no way interfering with an outward instrument." *

Now let us see how the language of the Homilies concerning this sole *internal* instrument will sound, according to the Oxford doctrine of the sole *external* instrument.

It will be remembered that this external instrument (Baptism) is made absolutely necessary to salvation by Oxford Divines—there is no regeneration, no justification, and therefore no entrance to Heaven, without it; before it is applied, faith is dead and incapable of any instrumentality, except as it prepares for, or leads to Baptism, or except as "restitution" of stolen goods, on the part of a thief, would be instrumental in justification. In Baptism, and by its sole instrumentality, while faith is in the act of being made alive and regenerate and justified, and therefore before it is capable of any justifying agency;—in and by Baptism, we are fully justified from all original and all actual sin. After Baptism, faith, which as yet has been no instrument at all, only "a forerunner," becomes "the symbol" and representative "of Baptism, *sustaining* only what, by that sole external instrument, has been already accomplished. But even now its instrumentality is "not that of conveying but only of symbolizing" the sole external instrument. Let the virtue of Baptism cease, and faith is dead. Thus its sole internal instrumentality is strictly "secondary and *subordinate*" to that of Baptism. It is a sole instrument so far as the tools of the apprentice, working for his master, are the sole instruments of that master. But the real instrument of the master, and the only one to be mentioned, is the apprentice. His instruments are his chisel, saw, plane, &c. And so, according to this Divinity, the sole

* Pusey's Letter, p. 44. Newman on Justification, p. 259.

instrument of God in our Justification is Baptism. The sole instrument of Baptism is faith. But the parallel is yet more complete. Faith, in this system, is no more the *sole* instrument of Baptism, than the saw or plane is the sole instrument of the carpenter's apprentice. He must use divers tools—one is no more the instrument of his trade than others; and so of faith in this system. It is expressly denied to have any distinction in the office of Justification, after Baptism, which all other graces have not. " We are saved by Christ's mercy, and that, not through faith, but through faith *and all graces.*" * Thus love may as well be called the *sole instrument*, as faith; and so of "joy, peace, long-suffering, gentleness," and every other of the fruits of the Spirit.

Such then being the amount of the sense in which Faith is considered, in this divinity, as *"the sole internal iustrument ;"* and such being the eminent superiority of Baptism, in every respect, as an instrument; what, supposing the same to be the doctrine of the Anglican Church, shall we say of the wisdom, sufficiency, propriety, common decency of the three Articles connected most nearly with this subject, viz: on *" Justification ;* on *" Good Works "* which are the fruits of faith, and on "Works before Justification," when they speak so particularly of " faith only " in justification, and do not so much as advert to the existence of any other instrument? What shall we think of the Homily to which we are referred, in the eleventh Article, for a fuller explanation of the subject of justification, when we find it so full of earnest preaching on the sole instrumentality of faith as the only thing which St. Paul " declareth, upon the behalf of man concerning his justification," and yet scarcely the least mention of Baptism, and that, not in any way as making it an instrument of justification ? How can we believe in the common sense, not to speak of the common truth and faithfulness of our Reformers, that, while professedly unfolding all that is necessary to the " Salvation of *all mankind*," whether baptized or unbaptized, in a heathen, or a Christian land ; especially when setting themselves particularly to the answering of the question " what is the mean whereby we must apply the fruits of Christ's death unto our deadly wound," the very question which lies at the beginning of the controversy with the Church of Rome, on the subject of Justification, and when they so earnestly and frequently repeat that *" the only mean and instrument of salvation requried of our parts is faith ;"* and when, if the representations of

* Newman on Justification, p. 281.

these writers be true, that same faith is no sole instrument at all, and Baptism is the only efficient instrument in any peculiar sense; what shall we think of our Reformers when all this language concerning faith is left entirely unchecked, unexplained; and Baptism, as in any sense an instrument of justification, is not mentioned? The utter absurdity of supposing them capable of such representations had they believed the doctrine of this divinity on this subject, is sufficient evidence that between this system and theirs, there is no reconciliation.

Another method of escape from the plain doctrine of the Church-standards concerning faith, is seen in the following extract from Mr. Newman on justification. Of the Homilies, he says:

"These are addressed, not to heathens but to Christians, they are practical and popular exhortations to Christians. They inform a baptized congregation, or, as they speak, 'dear Christians,' 'good Christian people,' how they may be saved, not how God will deal with the heathen. They are not missionary discourses, directing pagans how to proceed in order to be justified, but are composed for the edification of those who through God's mercy are already, 'dearly beloved in Christ.' And as regards the point before us, they lay down 'what the lively and true faith *of a Christian man* is.' Clear, however, as this is, at first sight, I will make some extracts from them, to impress it upon the mind. Take for instance the very passage I quoted in the opening, in which faith is called the sole instrument of justification; it will be found the writer is teaching a Christian congregation, what they must do. He does not, cannot say with St. Peter, 'Be baptized—every one of you, for the remission of sins;' that sacred remedy has been long ago applied and may not be repeated. What is left, then, after sinning, but, as it were, to renew their Baptism, or at least its virtue, by faith, as 'the only instrument of salvation *now left unto us*.' And this is why stress is laid upon a '*stedfast*, not a wavering faith;' he does not simply say lively, but stedfast, because faith is to be the abiding, sustaining means of justification, or in the words of the text, 'By faith we stand.' * * * All this shows that when the Homily speaks of faith as an instrument, it means a *sustaining* instrument; what the primary instrument is, being quite a separate question. Those who now speak of faith as the sole means of justification, too commonly consider the mass of Christians unregenerate, and call them out of their supposed heathen state, *through* faith as the sole *initiation* into Christ's kingdom. * * *

But it may be said there is nothing about Baptism here; let us then turn to the Homily on Salvation or Justification, to which the Article refers, where we shall find that doctrine clearly stated, though it does not enter into the scope of the Homily already cited. 'Infants, being baptized and dying in their infancy, are by this Sacrifice washed from their sins, brought to God's favor, and made His children, and inheritors of His kingdom of Heaven. And they, which in act or deed do sin *after their Baptism*, when they turn again to God unfeignedly,' that is, come to God in *faith*, as the Homily directly goes on to say, they are *likewise* washed by this Sacrifice from their sins.' Here is distinct mention of faith justifying *after* Baptism, but no mention of its justifying *before* Baptism; on the contrary, Baptism is expressly said to effect the first justification. The writer proceeds: *This* is that justification or righteousness which St. Paul speaks of, when he saith, 'No man is justified by the works of the Law, but freely by faith in Jesus Christ.' So it seems that St. Paul too, when he speaks of justification through faith, speaks of faith as subordinate to Baptism, not as the immediate initiation into a justified state." *

The meaning of this desperate leap from out of the difficulties with which the Homilies surround the doctrine of these gentlemen is this, viz., The Homilies are addressed to baptized persons, consequently to *justified* persons. The whole application therefore of all their strong language, as to faith being "the sole instrument" of Justification, applies exclusively to persons already justified, to whom therefore faith can only be justifying, as a *sustaining*, not as an *originating*, instrument. Such being its restricted application, we are forbidden to infer one word from the Homilies, as to faith having any sole justifying office, or any such office in any sense, but as "*repentance and restitution*" also have, in the case of persons repenting and believing, but as yet unbaptized. To them it is not the sole instrument, or any instrument: but Baptism is the only instrument of *their* justification. All this proceeds upon the assumption that the faith of the unbaptized is necessarily dead, not having the love of God shed abroad in the heart; while the faith of the baptized is *living;* that the first therefore is inoperative; the second justifying, and Baptism makes the infinite difference.

All this is encumbered and crushed by the weight of the following grave difficulties.

1. The Homilies know of but two kinds of faith, the one a living

---

* Newman on Justification, pp. 260—263.

faith, the other such as devils and ungodly men have in common. For example:

"That faith which bringeth forth, without repentance, either evil works, or no good works, is not a right, pure, and lively faith; but a dead, devilish, counterfeit, and feigned faith, as St. Paul and St. James call it. For even the devils know and believe that Christ was born of a virgin; that he fasted forty days and forty nights without meat and drink; that he wrought all kind of miracles, declaring himself very God; they believe also, that Christ for our sakes suffered a most painful death, to redeem us from everlasting death; and that he rose again from death the third day: they believe that he ascended into heaven; and that he sitteth on the right hand of the Father; and at the last end of this world shall come again, and judge both the quick and the dead. These articles of our faith the devils believe; and so they believe all things that be written in the New and Old Testament to be true: and yet for all this faith they be but devils, remaining still in their damnable estate, lacking the very true Christian faith.

"The right and true Christian faith is, not only to believe that Holy Scripture, and all the aforesaid articles of our faith, are true; but also to have a sure trust and confidence in God's merciful promises, to be saved from everlasting damnation by Christ; whereof doth follow a loving heart to obey his commandments. And this true Christian faith neither any devil hath; nor yet any man, which in the outward profession of his mouth, and in his outward receiving of the Sacraments, in coming to the Church, and in all other outward appearances, seemeth to be a Christian man, and yet in his living and deed showeth the contrary." *

Thus it follows that when a person comes to be baptized in adult years, as the Jailor of Philippi, the three thousand on the Pentecost, Cornelius and his household, who had already received the Holy Ghost; when according to the requisitions of the Church he has true "repentance whereby he forsakes sin, and faith whereby he stedfastly believes the promises of God," so that the officiating Minister can speak of him as "*truly repenting and coming unto God by faith,*" that, with all this, his faith is as dead as that of the devils, he hath not the love of God shed abroad in his heart; his repentance consequently is dead also, not the godly sorrow, which worketh repentance to salvation, since this cannot be where true love is not. No doctrine can bear such an absurdity as this.

* Homily of Salvation, p. 3.

Again. If all that is said about believing unto justification, or any thing else in the Homilies, has reference to those who are already justified, then we have the singular phenomenon of a whole volume of discourses upon all the great doctrines and duties of religion, especially a whole discourse on "the Salvation of *all* mankind," intended to teach of course how *all* mankind are to be saved, the baptized and the unbaptized being alike parts of all mankind; and yet not a word in this discourse, or any other of this volume, which teaches how any are to be saved but the baptized, who may be about one tenth of the whole population of the globe. We continually meet the unbaptized; we have them always in our congregations; we are commanded to go and preach the Gospel to all the hundreds of millions of the heathen, yet our Church has entirely omitted to say a word in her Homilies, as to how any of these are to be saved, on the principle, as it is expressed in a late British Critic, that "the Church is out of her place *converting* in a Christian country."

But again, another difficulty. The Homily of Salvation is referred to, by the Article of Justification, for a larger explication of its meaning, in these words: "*That we are justified by faith only, is a most wholesome doctrine, &c., as is more largely expressed in the Homily of Justification.*" Hence it is manifest that the Article and the Homily are on precisely the same doctrine, and of course must be addressed to the same persons, or the same condition of man, or else the one would not be an expression of the other. But the Oxford Divines are forced to apply them to precisely opposite conditions of persons, and make them teach entirely different doctrines. The Homily, as we have seen, they restrict to the baptized, teaching justification and faith, only as *they* are concerned. But as to the Article in question, Dr. Pusey says "*it does not speak of a state in which we ever actually were:*" "it does not apply to us" "who have been born within the Church, and who were never left to our mere natural powers, having been in infancy justified and cleansed from all sin, and had the grace of Christ given, and fresh supplies pledged to us." Mr. Newman also distinguishes between the faith of the Article as "*only the common belief of the Articles of our Faith*" and that of the Homilies as "*also a true trust and confidence of the mercy of God,*" &c.,—a justifying faith.* So then the Article refers only to the faith of the unbaptized; but its *expository* Homily to the baptized: the former to the unregenerated and unjustified, the latter to the regenerate and justified; the one teaches of faith in those

---

* Newman on Justification, p. 296.

who are yet in their sins; the other of faith in those who are children of God; and these two descriptions of faith are said to be as radically different as the faith of devils and the faith of true Christians, and yet the Homily is *a larger expression* of the doctrine of the Article, and both are on the Salvation of *all* Mankind, the Homily having the title in full, the Article, in the expression—"Justification of *Man*." How can these things be?

Again, another difficulty. In the Second Homily on the Passion of Christ, where the sole instrumentality of faith is so much insisted on (see the extracts before given therefrom,) the only example selected in illustration of the "*how* we are to apply Christ's death and passion" is the case of the *unbaptized* Jailor of Philippi. "Here is the mean, (says the Homily,) whereby we must attain eternal life; namely, faith. For as St. Paul, being demanded of the keeper of the prison 'what he should do to be saved,' made this answer, 'Believe in the Lord Jesus, so shalt thou and thy house be saved.'" Thus the instrumentality of faith, in an unbaptized jailor; a faith, which according to this system, was "dead," "vague," "inoperative," and "as different from that of the baptized, as that of devils is from a living faith," is taken, in a discourse, addressed, we are told, exclusively to the baptized and justified, and set up as an example of the faith by which, as with "a sole instrument," *they* are to apply the death of Christ.

It is of consequence to note that the Homily, in this reference to the direction of the Apostle, as to how the unbaptized Jailor was to apply the death of Christ, does not mention Baptism, either in this part or elsewhere, although the fact that the Jailor was afterward baptized is so immediately connected with the cited passage.

Again, another difficulty. Mr. Newman, in the extract from his pages, last given, dwells upon the use of the word, "*stedfast*," as designating the distinctive nature of the Faith of which the Homilies speak. "He, (the author of the Homily,) does not simply say lively, but *stedfast* faith, because faith is to be the abiding, sustaining means of Justification" to the baptized. Hence we are of course to infer that its stedfastness is an evidence and quality of its living and justifying nature. But does the Church speak of no other faith but that of the baptized as stedfast? What does she require of persons to be baptized? The Catechism answers: "Repentance, whereby they forsake sin, and *faith whereby they stedfastly believe the promises of God.*" To have a faith that stedfastly believes, and to have a stedfast faith, we suppose, are the same thing. So then, as the Jailor's faith is made, by the Homily, an illustration of the faith of the baptized, so does Mr. Newman, in making stedfastness the characteristic of justifying faith, identify such faith with that of the unbaptized.

We need not go into a proof, such as might easily be drawn from the Baptismal and Communion Offices, that our Church employs substantially the same language for the repentance and faith required for Baptism, and those required for the Eucharist; and consequently that she knows nothing of any difference between the sole instrument of justification to the unbaptized and the baptized. But it is making too much of such a refuge as this of our Oxford divines, to be spending so much time upon it. A greater condemnation they could not write upon their system than to show that it cannot be sustained without making this awful difference between the best faith before Baptism, and the weakest faith after Baptism; between what the unbaptized but penitent Jailor must do to be saved, and what the baptized infidel must do; on the mere ground that the latter, no matter what his present blasphemy, was once regenerate and justified, the possessor of "an angelic nature," the temple of God's presence, the wearer of the Shekinah, the wedding garment of God's in-dwelling glory; while the former, though repenting and believing, has not been baptized.

Again, another difficulty. When the plain meaning and application of the Homilies on the subject of faith cannot otherwise be escaped, we are told that our Homilies are *"popular discourses."* Thus, when it is said that they speak of Faith "as a mere *trust,* or a fiduciary apprehension of God's mercy," Mr. Newman answers: *"Certainly they do, but they are popular addresses.* It is quite another thing when statements which have a true and impressive *bearing,* are taken as adequate and accurate *definitions* of the matter in hand." * Mr. Knox was compelled by the same system to resort to the same expedient for protection against the plain dealing of the Homilies. "The Homily of Justification, (he says) whatever may be the case with the other Homilies, was written not to lay down theological definitions, but rather to furnish useful popular instruction." †

Now here is a singular position. The Article of Justification, being necessarily brief, refers for a more extended expression of its doctrine to the Homily on the same subject. The latter is popular in its cast; but still it is the larger explication of the Article. But what sort of explication is it, if when it expressly tells us, for example, that Faith is "*trust* in God's mercy," or "an apprehension

---

* Newman on Justification, p. 298.   † Remains, vol. i. pp. 293, 294.

of God's mercy," through Christ, and "the sole instrument on the behalf of man in his Justification," instead of receiving it as it is, we are to consider it only as having "a true and impressive BEARING;" and not as containing "adequate *definitions*" of the truth; *bearing* upon the truth indeed, but not declaring it plainly; so that instead of an explication, it needs itself to be so expounded as to show that, when it defines faith to be trust, and a fiduciary apprehension of God's mercy, and when it says that "faith is the only means of applying the merits of Christ," it is not to be taken in any such sense.

"I have always thought, that *Useful Popular Instruction*, in the matter of Christian Doctrine, was a faithful communication, in a familiar and popular form, of the Doctrinal System maintained by any particular given Church; so that the difference between such communication, and communication made in a scholastic form, should consist, not in a *departure* from the Doctrinal System in question, but merely in a *delivering* of it through the medium of familiar and popular and unscholastic language." *

What marvellous facility this consideration of the popular character of the Homilies affords, in making their declarations of doctrine *mere sayings*, and of no manner of weight, appears from the following most remarkable passage.

"Let us then now turn to the first book of Homilies; which will be found clearly to teach, that, whereas faith never is solitary, it is but *said* to be the sole justifier, and that with a view to inculcate another doctrine *not* said, viz., that all is of grace.

"This *sentence*, that we be justified by faith only, is not so meant by them, the Fathers 'that the said justifying faith is alone in man, without true repentance, hope, charity, dread and the fear of God, *at any time or season.*' Again in a passage which has been already cited, we are told, '*Faith doth not shut out repentance*, love, dread and the fear of God, to be joined with faith in every one that is justified, but it shutteth them out from the *office* of justifying.'

"What is the office here spoken of? Not the office of conveying, but of symbolizing justification. For instance, as great and godly a virtue as the lively faith is, yet it *putteth us from itself* and remitteth or *appointeth* us unto Christ, for to have *only by Him* remission of our sins or justification. So that our faith in Christ (as it were) *saith unto us* that, 'It is not I that take away your sins,

* Faber's Prim. Doc. of Justification, p. 68.

but it is Christ only, and to Him only *I send you* for that purpose, forsaking therein all your good virtues, words, thoughts, and works, and only putting your trust in Christ.' It is plain that 'faith only' does not apprehend, apply, or appropriate Christ's merits; but it only *preaches* them; and thus surely conveys a 'most wholesome doctrine, and very full of comfort.'

"The doctrine, then, on this interpretation, is not a practical rule but an abstract principle. Accordingly it will be observed, the Homilies do not attempt to *explain* its wording literally, but declare it to be a *sentence, saying,* or *form* of *speech,* one too, which, when drawn out, assumes quite a new shape, as far as its letter is concerned.

"For instance—'*This saying*, that we be justified by faith only, freely, and without works, is spoken *for to take away* clearly all merit of our works, as being unable to deserve our justification at God's hands;' the drift is given, not an *interpretation.* The writer proceeds, 'and *thereby most plainly to express* the weakness of man and the goodness of God; the great infirmity of ourselves, and the might and power of God; the imperfectness of our own works, and the most abundant grace of our Saviour Christ; and *thereby wholly to ascribe* the merit and deserving of our justification unto Christ only, and His most precious blood-shedding.' Can words be clearer to prove that faith is considered to justify not as an instrument, but as a symbol; it is to *do* nothing, but it is to '*say,*' to '*express,*' to '*ascribe,*' to '*glory,*' to '*warn,*' to '*bring good tidings.*'

'In like manner in the third part of the same Homily: 'The very true meaning of this *proposition or saying*, we be justified by faith only (according to the meaning of the old ancient authors,) is this, we put our faith in Christ, *that we be justified by Him only.* Justification by faith only is here said to be a *saying:* consider how astonished and pained we should be, were the doctrine of the Atonement, or of Christ's divinity said to be a proposition, saying, or form of speaking."*

In a note to some of these passages, we read that such an expression as *faith alone justifies*, is "the *emblem of a principle, not a literal statement*," that when faith is said to "*send us to Christ,*" it means only that it "*preaches* Christ," and again, that "the Homily does not so much affirm that faith only *does* justify, 'but is *said* to justify.'"

The following passage is still more curious.

* Newman on Justification, pp. 282—285.

"Faith is *said* to justify, not that it really justifies more than the other graces; but it has this peculiarity, that it signifies in its very nature, that nothing of ours justifies us, or it typifies the freeness of our justification. Faith heralds forth divine grace, and its name is a sort of representation of it, as opposed to works. Hence it may well be honored above the other graces, and placed nearer Christ than the rest, as if it were distinct from them, and before them, and above them, though it be not. It is suitably said to justify us, because it says itself that it does not, so to speak, as a sort of reward to it. In so determining, the Reformers are not laying down a practical direction how to proceed *in order* to be justified, what is required of us *for* justification, but a large principle or doctrine ever to be held and cherished, that in ourselves we deserve eternal ruin, and are saved by Christ's mercy, and that not through faith only, but through faith and all graces."*

What have we here, in illustration of the *popular* EXPLICATION given in the Homily of Salvation, of the Article to which it is attached? "The *drift* is given, not an *interpretation!*" There is no attempt "to *explain* literally the wording of the doctrine of faith in the Article." Singular explication then! That doctrine is declared to be only a "*sentence, saying, or form of speech*" which "*when drawn out assumes quite a new shape*" from that of its literal meaning. "Faith is but *said* to be the sole justifier." It "does not justify as an *instrument*, but as a *symbol*." Its whole office as the only mean and instrument, of applying the merits of Christ, consists in its *preaching* them; it is to *do* nothing, but it is to "*say*," to "*impress*" to "*ascribe*," to "*glory*," to "*warn*," to "*bring good tidings*." Faith is made to have about as much justifying efficacy as any preacher of the Gospel who tells the sinner of Christ and his salvation. "Justification by faith only" is treated as a mere "*saying*." More indeed than any other graces, faith is *said* to justify; but "not that it really justifies more than the other graces" Its only peculiarity is that "it *typifies* the freeness of our justification." "Its name is a sort of representation of divine grace." On this account, alone, is it so honored in the Scriptures, and the Articles, and Homilies above the other graces; *as if it were distinct from, before, and above them; though it be not*. It is *rewarded* for this single peculiarity of being in name a type or symbol of grace, by being "*said* to justify us," because "*it says it does not*."

* Newman, p. 281.

Thus all the labor and earnestness of the reiterated declarations of the Scriptures, and Articles, and Homilies, concerning the sole instrumentality of faith, are evaporated into a mere laudatory *saying;* a distinction of words; an ascription in terms of what exists not in reality. And thus is all sober, grave, dignified interpretation put to shame. Thus are the Standards of our Church brought into contempt. And thus is the common sense of every man, of the most ordinary understanding, outraged. The necessity of such refuges is condemation absolute.

CHAPTER X.

THE DOCTRINE OF THIS DIVINITY, AS TO BAPTISMAL JUSTIFICATION, COMPARED WITH THAT OF THE ANGLICAN CHURCH.

Recapitulation of Tractarian and Romish Doctrines—Difference between remission of Original Sin as held by the Anglican Church, and by the Oxford Divines—Testimony of Jackson—Baptismal Justification of Adults—*A priori* reason for believing that the Anglican and Oxford doctrine are diverse on this head—Silence of the Articles and Homilies unaccountable if the Oxford doctrine were that of the Church. Language of the Articles and Homilies irreconcilable with the Oxford doctrine—Language of Scripture, Fathers, English divines needs explanation—Evidence of necessity of other interpretation than this system gives—Barrow—Beveridge—Hooper—Frith—Hooker—Hall—Homilies—Usher—Beveridge—Inconsistencies in English divines, according to the Oxford Interpretation—Barrow—Hooker—St. Bernard—Jewel. Inconsistencies of Augustine and other Fathers according to the Oxford doctrine—True doctrine shown from Bishops Hooper, Beveridge, and Taylor—Mode of Interpreting the strong language of the old divines, &c.—Bishop Bethell's mode rejected as too low—Strange inconsistencies of Oxford divines—Mode of interpretation illustrated from Augustine, Jewel, from language of Hooker, &c.—Concerning the membership of infants in the Church before Baptism; common language concerning a call to the ministry, and language of Scripture as to the Baptism of Christ—further illustration from common law-terms—application to language of Nowell's Catechism—Passages from Whitgift, and Dr. Haddon—Concluding Observations.

It will be borne in mind that the doctrine of this divinity, on the subject of the present Chapter, embraces the following particulars, viz:

1. That justification is so inseparably connected with Baptism, as its instrumental cause, or means of conveyance, that before Baptism there can be no justification before God; and, by Baptism, whoever does not impede its efficacy by hypocrisy, or infidelity, is completely justified.

2. That this Baptismal Justification, consisting in the expulsion of sin, by the infusion of righteousness, takes *quite away all original and actual sin.*

In these propositions, the Church of Rome and the Divines of

Oxford entirely unite. We will consider the latter, first, because most readily disposed of.

First. Is it the doctrine of the Anglican Church, that justification takes away all *Original*, as well as *Actual* Sin?

We answer. *Yes, unquestionably!* "There is now *no condemnation* to them that are in Christ Jesus." But we shall find no evidence, but, on the contrary, express denial, in the standards of our Church, that justification is held to do this, in any degree, *according to the sense in which the proposition is used by our Oxford Divines and the Church of Rome.*

Only two passages are quoted by these writers in evidence of conformity on their part to the teaching of the Church, in this particular,—both from the Homily of Salvation. The first we here give. The Homily has been speaking of the fulfilling of the Law and the suffering of its penalty by Christ for us, and thus proceeds:

"Insomuch that infants being baptized and dying in their infancy, are by this sacrifice (of Christ) washed from their sins, brought to God's favor, &c. And they which in act or deed, do sin after their Baptism, when they turn again to God unfeignedly, they are likewise washed by this sacrifice from their sins, in such sort that there remaineth not any spot of sin that shall be imputed to their damnation. This is that justification which St. Paul speaketh of when he sayeth, No man is justified by the works of the Law, but freely by faith in Jesus Christ."*

Again, on the same subject of Justification the Homily says:

"We must trust only in God's mercy and that sacrifice which the Son of God once offered for us on the cross to obtain thereby God's grace and remission, as well of our original sin, in Baptism, as of all actual sin committed after Baptism, if we truly repent."

Now it is manifest that both of these passages are upon justification—they speak of justification from Original Sin and from Actual Sin in precisely the same language. But we have already showed that justification, in the sense of this Homily, consists in the *non-imputation* of sin, through the external and imputed righteousness of Christ embraced by faith; and not through a righteousness *infused* and *inherent*. It has also been seen that since Original

* Homily of Salvation, Part I.

Sin is defined by our Article to be an *"infection of nature,"* which is not *all* taken away, but *"remains even in the regenerate,"* and *"*in them has *the proper nature of sin,"* it is evident, that the remission, spoken of in the above extracts, is to be understood simply in reference to a *judicial pardon,* and cannot refer to its *actual removal.* In other words, that though it *remains,* even in the regenerate, it is not imputed to them for condemnation.

But very far from this is the sense in which these passages are quoted by our Oxford divines. Their doctrine is not that Original Sin is not imputed, but that it *does not exist* after Baptism. It is quite taken away *in fact,* as well as in *imputation.* It is remitted by *being expelled.* "There remaineth not any spot of sin," not merely that is *imputed,* but that can be said *to be.* How directly this contradicts the Article on Original Sin, and obliges them to imitate the refuge of Romanism, in changing the whole doctrine of Original Sin so as to suit their doctrine of justification, has been already shown.

Now that Original Sin, as an *"infection of nature,"* is not taken away in Baptism, our Oxford divines, if they will not hear the Article of the Church, will perhaps listen to the words of one whom they profess so highly to estimate, as the learned Dr. Jackson.

He says that the *Romish Church* and " SOME WHO HAVE PROFESSED THEMSELVES MEMBERS OF THE PRESENT ENGLISH CHURCH, teach that Original Sin *is utterly taken away,* or that our regeneration is instantly and fully wrought by the Sacrament of Baptism. That children (he replies) rightly baptized are truly regenerated by the Spirit of God, we deny not. And in case, being so baptized, *they die before they come to the use of reason,* yet ought we not to doubt of their salvation, because they have, by Baptism, been made partakers of regeneration *in such a measure as is requisite and sufficient for their salvation whilst they are infants.* But that Original Sin, the lust of the flesh, or the old man, should be *utterly extinguished* in them before their death, *we must deny.*" "If Original Sin, or the Old Man, with his members, be utterly extinguished in young infants by Baptism, I demand how possibly they could revive in the same parties, as soon as they come to the use of reason?" "*So that Baptism is rather a sacramental consecration of us to undertake the fight with the works of our flesh, or corruption of our nature, than an utter extinction or absolute drowning of those enemies.*" *

---

* Jackson's Works, iii. pp. 99, 100. Bishop Hopkins speaks of the origin of this notion of the removal of original sin by Baptism as a novelty among Pro-

Thus we see that a writer than whom none is more confidently claimed by the advocates of this divinity, not only condemns this, its doctrine, as untrue, and as not the doctrine of the Church of England, but sets it forth as *the peculiar property of the Church of Rome.*

The truth manifestly is, that our Church, in the Homilies above quoted, speaks of Original Sin being remitted in the Baptism of infants, precisely as it is remitted in that of penitent and believing adults and she speaks of its remission in both these cases, just as she speaks of the remission of the *actual sins* of adults. It is the removal, not of the *moral being*, but of the *judicial condemnation* of that which "has the nature of sin." In infants, Original Sin is thus remitted on account of the imputed righteousness of the "Second Adam," without their personal faith, just as they have been brought, without any act of theirs, under the curse of the sin of the first Adam. When baptized infants come to be capable of what is called *actual sin*, that is, *sin after Baptism*, then they must personally "repent and believe on the Lord Jesus Christ," or else they cannot be saved; but their Baptism, as to all participation in God's mercy, will be then as if they had not been baptized; just as the circumcision of the Jew was made, by unbelief, "*uncircumcision.*"

Secondly: Is it the doctrine of the Anglican Church that justification is so inseparably connected with Baptism, as its *only instrumental cause*, that without it no sinner can be justified before God? This we unequivocally deny—and on the contrary, we positively assert that it is the doctrine of our Church that *whenever a sinner repents and believes in the Lord Jesus Christ,* whether *before* Baptism

---

testants of his time—"Regeneration (he says) begins now to be decried by as great masters in Israel as ever Nicodemus was—they think, if they are but baptized, whereby *as they suppose, the guilt of original sin is washed away*," &c. The above extract from Jackson is of the greater force, because elsewhere, in divers places, he speaks strongly of "*the remission of* original sin in Baptism," as for instance—"Only original sin is remitted in such as are not guilty of actual sins, as in Infants," vol. iii. p. 297. Evidently then he distinguishes between the *remission* and the *extinction* of Original Sin in Baptism. The latter is the doctrine of this divinity and Popery, not only because their Justifying righteousness *is infused grace*, and to be justifying it must leave no original sin remaining, but because such are the express declarations of both. "The Council of Trent, to obviate the possibility of doubt on this subject, has added its own distinct declaration, by pronouncing anathema against those who should presume to think otherwise, or should dare to assert that 'although sin is forgiven in Baptism, it is not entirely removed or totally eradicated, but is cut away in such a manner, as to leave its roots still firmly fixed in the soil.'" Catechism of Council of Trent.

at Baptism or *after* Baptism, his sins are freely and perfectly remitted, he is freely and completely justified, through "the righteousness which is of God by faith."

The proof of this is already half made by the showing, in our preceding pages, of the entire opposition between the nature of justification as held in this system, and by our Church.

Since justification, in the judgment of our Church, consists in the imputation, or accounting, of the righteousness of Christ's Mediatorial obedience and death, to the believer, so that he is treated as if he had perfectly fulfilled the law; while in this, Divinity, it consists in no such thing, but in an infused and inherent righteousness, a *moral* righteousness abiding in us; it is not probable that the dependence of the former upon an external ordinance will be found to resemble that of the latter.

With these preliminary observations we proceed to a more direct inquiry.

If our Church does teach that Baptism is the only instrument of justification, so that no one, however penitent and believing before Baptism, can be justified; then surely we must expect to find so grave a doctrine asserted in those documents, in which she professes to state her doctrine as well of Baptism, as of justification. The Church of Rome does not publish her canon of Justification without declaring expressly that Baptism is *the only instrumental cause of justification, and that without it, justification can come to no one.* Dr. Pusey does not draw up his Article either of justification or of Baptism without being equally express. Mr. Newman can hardly write a page on justification without indicating his views as to its connection with Baptism. Now if our Church is of the same mind, surely her Articles on the Sacraments in General, and on Baptism in particular; her three Articles relating to justification and the catechism, in those parts relating to the Sacraments, might be expected to say something on this subject. It is the same question *essentially* whether a person, possessed of true repentance and a lively faith, may be considered as spiritually *born of God or regenerate*, though not yet baptized: for though justification as in Scripture-divinity is altogether a different matter from regeneration, yet as the two are inseparably connected, so that none are justified who are not also regenerate, and none are regenerate, who are not also justified, whichever way the question may be determined with regard to the one, it must be also as to the other.

But do the standard documents of the Anglican Church pronounce that no man, however penitent and believing, is either born of the Spirit, or justified, except he have been baptized?

The Article of Justification, which is applied by Oxford divines exclusively to the case in hand, viz., the justification of the unbaptized, contains *not a word about Baptism.* The only instrument it knows is *faith.* But that Article refers for a larger explication of its doctrine to the Homily of Salvation. That Homily enters at much length into the subject of justification by faith, and yet only in the two extracts given at the commencement of this chapter is *one word said about Baptism;* and in those passages, not a word about the penitent and believing, though unbaptized adult, but only about children incapable of believing, and persons repenting *after* Baptism. Now, this looks very strange indeed, if there be no justification without Baptism.

But what says the Article expressly given to Baptism?

"Baptism is—a SIGN of Regeneration or New Birth, whereby, as by an instrument, they that receive Baptism rightly are grafted into the Church: the promises of forgiveness of sins and of adoption to be the sons of God by the Holy Ghost are *visibly signed and sealed,* faith is confirmed, and grace increased by virtue of prayer to God."*

These words evidently refer to the Baptism of adults, or persons having what, the Catechism says, is necessary to a right receiving of Baptism viz., repentance and faith. The Article says that Baptism is the *sign* of regeneration. It goes no further. But the *sign* and the thing *signified* are not the same, or inseparable. The sign may be alone, as in Simon Magus; it may follow after, as in the Baptism of Cornelius and the Eunuch. To say that in Baptism "*the promises of forgiveness are visibly signed and sealed,*" is just as consistent with the idea that forgiveness has already taken place, as the signing, sealing, and delivering of a deed of conveyance of an estate is consistent with the estate having been for some time already in the actual possession and enjoyment of him, to whom the deed is made.

The same will hold with regard to the definition of a Sacrament in the Catechism, that it is "an outward and visible sign of an inward and spiritual grace, given to us, ordained by Christ himself as a means whereby we receive the same and a pledge to assure us thereof." The time of the giving of that "spiritual grace,"

---

* Article xxvii.

which is said to be "*a death unto sin* and *a new-birth unto righteousness*," is no more restricted to the time of the sign, than the time of entering on the use of an estate is restricted to the time of signing and sealing the title-deed. But Baptism is not only a sign and seal and pledge, but an *effective sign*. It is "a means whereby we receive," the grace signified, as well as "a *pledge* to assure us thereof." In the case of infants we doubt not it is a mean whereby they may, and do often receive the beginnings, of that grace; though even upon infants unbaptized, the prayer of faith may, and we doubt not does, sometimes bring down the grace of the Holy Ghost. But we are now on the case of *adults*. The language of the Catechism by no means teaches that the grace signified is *first* received by them when they receive its visible sign. The very nature of the repentance with which they are supposed to come, is "*a death unto sin and a new birth unto righteousness.*" The grace signified is therefore begun before. Baptism is the *means of receiving more* of it, and therefore the equivalent expression in the 27th Article is that, in Baptism, "*faith is confirmed and grace increased by virtue of prayer unto God*," both being already begun.

As we have said that neither in the Articles, Catechism, nor Homilies, is it ever hinted that justification is limited to Baptism, as its only instrument; we now add the assertion, that, in the Articles and Homilies *it is expressly limited to faith, as its only instrument of reception.*

For the illustration and support of this position, the reader must be referred to the evidence of faith being made the "*sole instrument,*" "*the only mean*" required "in behalf of man for his justification," as given in the review of Articles and Homilies, in the 9th Chapter of this work.

We cannot consider it necessary to go any further in vindicating the eminently evangelical doctrines of those standards from the charge of teaching that though a sinnner have truly repented, and is humbly believing in Jesus, and so has that very inward and spiritual grace of which Baptism is the sign, yet, if some cause, not involving a sinful disobedience, or neglect on his part, have prevented or delayed his Baptism, he cannot be now "justified by faith," and so *has not peace with God*. Yet this is the doctrine of this divinity—and this is the doctrine of Rome. If it be a good objection to the Romish doctrine of the necessity of the Priest's *intention* to the validity of the Sacraments, that thus, a poor penitent soul will be dependent for his dearest privileges upon the caprice of men who may be ungodly and caring nothing for his soul, why is it not just as much against this dependence of justification upon Baptism, that thus a sinner may be kept out of the peace of God, and out of heaven, by the indifference, indolence or absence of a Minister?

The plain testimony of the word of God is that "Whosoever believeth that Jesus is the Christ is born of God." "Every one that loveth, is born of God." "He that believeth in the Son hath everlasting life." Then as true repentance and faith are required for adult Baptism, and where there is true repentance towards God, there must be true love, it follows that the Church considers that whosoever is truly prepared for adult Baptism *is already born of God—and already justified.*

One would suppose that such truths could not be hid from any common reader of the Scriptures. And here we should drop the subject, but that passages occur in the Scriptures, in the service for adult Baptism, in the Homilies, and in standard writers of our Church on the subject of Baptism, which many minds, of correct views, find great difficulty in reconciling with the doctrine just exhibited. The passages in the Scriptures are such as that of Ananias to Saul, "*Arise and be baptized, and wash away thy sins:*" that concerning John's baptism, where it is called the "*Baptism of repentance for the remission of sins;*" that also of St. Peter on the day of Pentecost,—"Repent and be baptized, &c., *for the remission of sins.*" Those in the office for adult Baptism are similar. Baptism is called, in the Homilies, "*the fountain of our Regeneration*"—"*the Sacrament of our Regeneration or New Birth.*" We are said to be "*washed in our Baptism from the filthiness of sin.*" We say in the Nicene Creed, that we "believe in *one Baptism for the remission of sins.*" Such language appears abundantly in the ancient Fathers, and is found, every where, in the writings of the Old English Divines, as well as in those of Continental Reformers. A few examples will suffice for the whole.

Cranmer says: "The second birth is by the water of Baptism which Paul calleth the bath of Regeneration, because our sins be forgiven us in Baptism, and the Holy Ghost is poured into us as into God's beloved children, so that by the power and working of the Holy Ghost, *we be born again spiritually, and made new creatures.*"

Again: "By Baptism, the whole righteousness of Christ is given unto us, that we may claim the same as our own."*

Bradford says, that "*in Baptism is given to us the Holy Ghost*

---

* Sermon on Baptism.

and pardon of our sins—the old man is put off, the new man is put on." *

Such language is common in Hooker. For example; "This is the necessity of Sacraments. That saving grace which Christ originally is, or hath for the general good of His whole Church, by Sacraments he severally deriveth into every member thereof." Again, "We receive Christ Jesus in Baptism once, as the first beginner: in the Eucharist often, as being by continual degrees, the finisher of our life." Again, "Baptism is a Sacrament which God hath instituted in his Church, to the end that they which receive the same might thereby be incorporated into Christ, and so through his most precious merit obtain, as well that saving grace of imputation which taketh away all former guiltiness, as also that infused virtue of the Holy Ghost which giveth to the powers of the soul their first disposition towards newness of life." †

Such are faithful examples of the strongest language to be found on the subject—and without doubt, it need not be any stronger, to meet the meaning of Scripture.

But is it not manifest that the writers of such passages did believe that no man is made a new creature, spiritually regenerated by the Holy Ghost, justified by the imputation of Christ's righteousness, till he is baptized? Let us examine the case.

A few considerations will show that these expressions cannot be thus literally and strictly interpreted. Let it be premised that it is maintained by our Oxford Divines, and we have no disposition to dispute it, that, in the times of the Reformers, and of those men of strength who immediately succeeded them, there was no difference of opinion on this subject. Whatever therefore may appear in one, will be a valid explanation of the *general* doctrine of the rest.

Now if Cranmer did hold literally and strictly that justification cannot take place until we are baptized, how happens it that he writes the Homily on Justification which is referred to in the Article of Justification, for a full explication of the doctrine of Justification—a Homily in three parts, in which the connection of repentance and faith with Justification is fully treated, and faith is represented as the only means, and repentance as absolutely necessary to Salvation; and yet Baptism, as having any such relation, is not hinted at, and the only two places in which it is mentioned at all, are those already quoted, where the remission of

---

* Sermon on the Lord's Supper. † Eccl. Pol. 1. v. § 57 and 60.

Original Sin, in the Baptism of infants and of post-baptismal sin, in adults, is spoken of in a few lines.

Again, the same Reformer writes, or aids in writing, another Homily on Faith, which speaks largely of its nature and saving influence, and that whosoever *believeth* is born of God, but there is not a word about Baptism. Can it be supposed there could have been such an omission, had Cranmer believed that faith is always so "secondary and subordinate to Baptism," as to be dead till it has been administered; and repentance so defective that a sinner repenting and believing cannot be justified or at peace with God till he has been baptized? Could the Church of Rome, the great advocate of such doctrine, have made such an omission? Could Dr. Pusey or Mr. Newman have done so?

Again, Bishop Hooper (Reformer and Martyr) writes a Sermon on Justification, in which he speaks freely and very strongly of faith as the only means of justification, as in the following passage: "Though *sole* faith excludes not other virtues from being present at the conversion of every sinner, yet *sole and only* faith excludes the merits of other virtues and obtains *solely* remission of sin for Christ's sake *herself alone*." The good Bishop in this Sermon speaks of the Lord's Supper, and gets so near to Baptism as to speak of Nicodemus, whose case is so associated with baptismal regeneration, and yet not a word about Baptism occurs in the whole Sermon.

Again, Hooker has a long and learned Discourse of Justification, in which he is exceeding clear and pointed as to the office of faith, as well as divers other cognate subjects. He says "*Faith is the only hand which putteth on Christ unto justification,*" and "*by faith we are incorporated into Christ.*" In one place he expressly sets himself to show what is required in us, as absolutely necessary to salvation; he goes over divers particulars, yet in all the discourse, not a word is said of Baptism, except to mention, *as characteristic of Popery*, precisely what our Oxford divines so earnestly contend for, viz.: "that Romanists hold that the infusion of grace is applied to infants through Baptism, without either faith or works," and that "in them REALLY (*substantially,*) it taketh away Original Sin and the punishment due unto it"—that "it is applied to infidels and wicked men in the first justification, through Baptism without works, *yet not without faith*, and it taketh away both sins actual and original together."—

Certainly such omissions of Baptism in such discourses are very singular, if the authors held the doctrine which makes our Oxford writers so earnest and reiterated and emphatic for Baptism, whenever they speak of justification or faith.

Precisely the same might be said of many other standard authors. For example, Bishop Andrews, who writes a masterly discourse on Justification—full of *imputed righteousness and faith*, but not a word of Baptism. But the case of Bishop Beveridge is peculiarly strong. No writer employs the language which we have quoted above from Cranmer, Bradford and Hooker, concerning Baptism, with more fullness and force than Beveridge.* At first reading, one would suppose that without Baptism there could not possibly be either a new creature, the pardon of sin, or a hope of salvation. But the same admirable divine has a series of sermons on faith and repentance, *nine* in all, in one of which he treats of faith as *purifying the heart;* in another, as *overcoming the world;* in another, as *the only title to Sonship in Christ;* in a fourth, on *the profession of such faith,* which brings one Sacrament, the Lord's Supper, into prominent view; in a fifth, on the same; in a sixth, on *repentance;* in a seventh, on repentance as a *certain and the only method of obtaining pardon;* in an eighth, on repentance; in the last, on "*Repentance and Faith, the two great branches of the Evangelical Covenant*"—and yet in no part of these discourses is the subject of Baptism even mentioned, except, once or twice, in the most *incidental* manner.

But the case is stronger still in regard to two other discourses, expressly on the way of salvation, and entitled, "*Salvation wholly owing to Faith in Christ.*" The text is the answer to the Philippian jailor "*Believe in the Lord Jesus Christ,*" &c. † Here was a fine opportunity to show the dependence of faith on Baptism, and its entire subordination, for regeneration and salvation—because it immediately follows that the jailor "*was baptized, he and all his, straightway.*" How could Mr. Newman have handled the faith of the Jailor, without his Baptism; the *word* of faith from St. Paul, without the *Sacrament* of faith which he administered? But Bishop Beveridge, while he is full and glorious on the former, does

---

* See Sermon, No. 35.

† Such passages as the following occur continually in these Sermons. "It is to faith and faith only, under God, that all things relating to our future state are ascribed all the Bible over, not only our Pardon, Justification, Reconciliation," &c. "By the same faith whereby we are accounted righteous before God, through the Merits of his Son, by the same we are made sincerely righteous in ourselves, through the power of His Holy Spirit." "It is by Faith that we are ingrafted into Christ and made members of his body, and so partake of that Holy Spirit who proceeds from him."

not so much as mention the latter, except just to say, that doubtless the jailor received effectually the preaching of the Apostles because "it is expressly asserted that he and all his were presently baptized and *that " he believed in the Lord with all his house."* Such is the only mention of *Baptism*—all the rest is of *faith*. *

Certainly these omissions are singular, on the supposition that those venerable authors did agree with those of Oxford, as to our absolute dependence for our being born again of the Spirit, and justified, upon the receiving of Baptism.

But again, if the strong passages which we have quoted from Cranmer, Hooker, &c., are to be taken literally, *they will prove far too much for any system of divinity.*

For example. Cranmer says that in Baptism we are "*born spiritually,*" and made "*new creatures.*" Bradford, that "*the old man is put off, and the new man put on; yea, Christ is put on.*" But Mr. Newman on that very expression, "*put on Christ,*" which Bradford says is signified in Baptism, says that it "cannot be taken to mean newness of life, holiness, and obedience; for the reason that no one is all at once holy and renewed in that full sense which must be implied if the terms be interpreted of *holiness*.—Baptized persons (he contends) do not so put on Christ as to be forthwith altogether different men from what they were before," † that is in plainer words, they are not new creatures, by having been made holy, from unholy—Rome would agree with Mr. N. in that, as he, since he wrote it, has put himself in entire submission to Rome. The literal interpretation of all such passages as the above from the Reformers, would require the belief that all the baptized, adults as well as infants, are spiritually born again, have put off the old man and put on the new man; whereas it is not contended by Romish

---

* The contrast between this entire passing over of the Baptism of the Jailor, on the part of Beveridge, and the prominence assigned to it by Dr. Pusey, is very striking. Bishop Beveridge dwells exclusively upon the required faith. Dr. Pusey sees nothing scarcely in that faith but Baptism, as necessary to the very life of faith. Thus says the latter: " Paul says, '*believe on the Lord Jesus Christ,*' &c., *but a part of that belief was his Baptism without which his belief* HAD BEEN DEAD."
—Tract, No. 67. Am. Ed., p. 173. Now if Beveridge had believed, with Dr. Pusey, as is contended, that the jailor's faith was dead till Baptism gave it life, how was it possible that in expounding the way of salvation, as exhibited in the case of the jailor, he should have expended two whole discourses, the one on Salvation by faith in general, the other on Justifying Faith in particular, without even alluding to any dependence of Faith on Baptism, or any connection between them? and yet Beveridge is one of the examples given by the Oxford Tracts of those English Divines who teach their doctrine of baptismal justification.

† Newman's Lectures p. 177.

writers, or those who follow them so closely, that in adult Baptism there are not exceptions in the case of those who live in hypocrisy or infidelity.

Again, if the strong passages in question are to be taken literally, they are then in direct contradiction to others of the same Reformers and other Divines. For example, Hooker says that in Baptism, "We *are incorporated into Christ*, and obtain *that infused divine virtue of the Holy Ghost which giveth to the powers of the soul the first disposition towards newness of life.*"

Now since it is required of those who come to adult Baptism that they have *repentance and faith* before they come, a literal interpretation of that passage would teach that one may repent and believe not only without being a new creature, without putting off the old man, but even without "*the first disposition towards newness of life.*" But in another place, the same Hooker teaches precisely the opposite, for he says, " Repentance in the heart of man is God's handiwork, a fruit or effect of *God's grace,*" and of Faith, without distinction between that which is before Baptism, and that which is after Baptism—he says: "Faith is that which maketh us most holy in consideration whereof it is called our most holy faith." Does this look like Baptism giving *the first disposition towards newness of life?**

Again Bishop Beveridge in illustrating the Church's doctrine of Baptism quotes Augustine thus: " In the baptismal washing, not only the pardon of such sins as are committed, *but of such as shall afterwards be committed,* is granted to such as believe in Christ." Now that sins are forgiven before they are committed, is a doctrine which Oxford Divines are not prepared to hold. But the literal interpretation for which they are so strenuous, will make this, as well as that past sins are strictly remitted in Baptism, to have been the doctrine of Augustine. †

Again, while Hooker says that " by Baptism we are incorporated into Christ," and Cranmer, that in Baptism " the whole righteousness of Christ is given unto us;" both these divines ascribe, in other places, this same blessing as we have before abundantly showed, only to faith as the sole instrument of justification. "*By faith we are incorporated into Christ.*" It is impossible therefore to suppose that in the judgment of these writers, an adult in Baptism receives *spiritually* any new creation, any putting off of the old

---

* Eccl. Pol. b. vi. 800, p. 151. Second Sermon on Jude, § 27.
† Beveridge on Articles—Art. xxvii.

man, any death to sin, or new birth to righteousness, any union to Christ, which, as a penitent believer, he had not while unbaptized.

We therefore find in their writings and those of contemporaries, express declarations that all the inward and spiritual blessings signified and conveyed in Baptism, are effectually enjoyed before baptism by such as are prepared to be baptized. For example. Bishop Hooper says:

"Such as be baptized must remember that repentance and faith preceded this external sign; and in Christ the purgation was *inwardly* obtained BEFORE the external sign was given. So that there are two kinds of Baptism, and both necessary. The one interior, which is the cleansing of the heart—the operation of the Holy Ghost: and this baptism is in man, *when he believeth*."—" Then is the exterior sign added, not to purge the heart, but to confirm, manifest, and open to the world," &c. *

Hooker says: "We grant that those sentences of Holy Scripture which make Sacraments most necessary to eternal life are no prejudice to their salvation that want them by some inevitable necessity and without any fault of their own." But what does this amount to? A sinner repents and believes. He desires and determines to obey all God's will. That will includes Baptism. But by the appointment of his Minister, he is not to be baptized till the ensuing Sunday. The delay is no fault of his own. Does this delay cause him to be unjustified and unregenerate when both are necessary to peace with God? Would such delay on the part of the Church be excusable in such a case? But take a stronger case. The ancient Church for general Baptism made choice of two chief days in the year—Easter and Pentecost. Suppose a heathen soon after Pentecost becoming truly penitent and believing, and desiring to be baptized, as part of the will of God. His Baptism, according to the custom, would be deferred till the following Easter, "without any fault of his own." It is not possible that the Church believed that all that while, he was not born of the Spirit nor justified, and would not be till Easter. How could he have been left in such a state, not at peace with God, when a minister could at once have baptized him? So that Hooker's admission is simply this, that whenever a person professing repentance and faith remains unbaptized, out of a spirit of disobedience to the will of God, he is not justified, because that disobedience is evidence

* Hooper's Works, vol. i. p. 74.

that his repentance and faith are not genuine; and when his want of Baptism does not argue any thing against his repentance and faith, he is justified—or, in his own words, quoted from St. Bernard, "his religious desire of Baptism standeth him in the same stead;" which amounts to the admission that, when Baptism is said to incorporate us into Christ; to give us the Holy Spirit; to make us new creatures; to give us remission of sins, &c., the meaning is quite consistent with the belief, that whoso *truly* repents and believes is already spiritually incorporated into Christ, born of the Spirit, and has received remission of sins.—Hence is cited Augustine as saying: "He is not deprived from the *partaking* and *benefit* of the Sacrament (though he be not baptized) so long as he findeth in himself that thing, that the Sacrament signifieth:" which means that he who is already spiritually regenerate does not lack the virtue of the *Sacrament* of regeneration though he has not received it. And Ambrose also writing concerning Valentinian, a Christian Emperor, who died unbaptized, says: "I have heard that you are grieved because he took not the Sacrament of Baptism. Tell me what other thing is there in us but our will and our desire—*He which was endued with thy Spirit, O God, how might it be that he should be void of thy grace!*"

Hooker, in the Oxford *Catena Patrum* is cited as follows:

"As we are not naturally men without birth, so neither are we Christian men, in the eye of the Church of God, but by new birth; nor according to the manifest ordinary course of divine dispensation new born, but by that Baptism which both declareth and maketh us Christians. In which respect, we justly hold it to be the *door* of our actual entrance to God's house, the first *apparent beginning of life*, a seal perhaps to the grace of election before received; but to *our sanctification here, a step that hath not any before it.*" *

Now this will seem to many to be as strong as possible, on the side of Oxford doctrine. But a little reflection will show that we must look for some other sense of such words. If Hooker speaks here of Baptism as "the door of our entrance to God's house," "the first apparent beginning of life;" he elsewhere ascribes all this to faith. "By faith (he says) we are incorporated into Christ."

Besides, Hooker, as we have seen already, is acknowledged by Oxford Divines to have believed a doctrine of justification, and of faith as concerned therein, entirely different from theirs. Moreover

* Eccl. Pol. l. v. § 60.

to take him literally, would be to make him teach that when one repents and believes, before Baptism, he has not *"the first beginning of life,"* has not taken a single *step to sanctification;* which would be too much even for these writers, for they consider repentance and faith before Baptism to be a *step* at least to sanctification; and Bishop Bethell, whom they commend as a standard writer on this subject, expressly says, that *" Renovation"* the *being renewed by the Spirit* which we suppose is *"*a first beginning of life," and at least "a step to Sanctification," *does precede adult Baptism* Thus, should Hooker be strictly interpreted, he would be too strong even for this divinity.

Now let us compare him with himself. We are indebted to Mr. Keble's late Edition of Hooker for the following expressions of that standard writer.

"Let it therefore suffice us to receive *Sacraments* as sure pledges of God's favor; signs infallible that the hand of his saving mercy doth thereby reach forth itself towards us, sending the influences of his Spirit into men's hearts, which maketh them like to a rich soil, fertile with all kinds of heavenly virtues, purgeth, justifieth, restoreth, the very dead unto life; yea raiseth even from the bottomless pit, to place in thrones of everlasting joy.

"They pretend that to *Sacraments* we ascribe no efficacy, but make them bare signs of instruction or admonition, which is utterly false. *For Sacraments with us are signs effectual; they are the instruments of God, whereby to bestow grace, howbeit grace not proceeding from the visible sign, but from his invisible powers.* God by his Sacraments giveth grace (saith Bernard) even as honors and dignities are given—an abbot made by receiving a staff, a doctor by a book, a bishop by a ring; because he that giveth these pre-eminences declareth by such signs his meaning, nor doth the receiver take the same but with effect; for which cause he is said to have the one by the other; albeit that which is bestowed proceedeth wholly from the will of the giver, and not from the *efficacy* of the sign."*

This quotation from St. Bernard is directly in the face of the Oxford doctrine of the efficacy of Baptism. The idea evidently is that Baptism is said to convey the benefit of the Gospel precisely as an Abbot by receiving a staff. But an Abbot's staff is to his being made an Abbot, exactly as a King's crown so to his being made King. He is first made a King and then crowned; so a

---

* Keble's Hooker, vol. ii. p. 702.

sinner is first regenerate by the Holy Ghost, and then as such he receives the Sacrament of Regeneration, first the inward grace, then its sign, or profession before men.

But the following from St. Bernard carries out his meaning still further:

"The fashion is to deliver a ring, when seizin and possession of inheritance is given; the ring is a sign of possession, so that he which takes it may say, 'The ring is nothing, I care not for *it:* it is the inheritance that I sought for.' In like manner when Christ our Lord drew nigh to his passion, he thought good to give seizen and possession of his grace to his disciples, and that they might receive his invisible grace by some visible sign: for this end all Sacraments are instituted." *

Now here we have the visible mode of *conveying* an estate, produced by St. Bernard, as an illustration of the conveyance of remission of sins by Baptism. Does it follow, when a deed is signed, sealed and delivered, that the person to whom it is made, and who, in law, is said then to receive the "*conveyance*," was not before that in the real and equitable possession of the estate? Certainly not. Then, according to the above illustration of St. Bernard, it no more follows that, because remission is said to be "*conveyed*" or "*consigned*" by the sign and seal of Baptism, the person receiving it was not before in the actual possession before God, of remission of sins. Such is the sentiment which Hooker makes his own by quotation, and which must therefore explain the passages previously adduced from him.

But it will illustrate still further the sentiments of St. Bernard, thus adopted by Hooker, to see how they were understood by his contemporaries.

Aquinas, in the 13th century, quotes from St. Bernard the same passage concerning the book, staff, and ring, &c., and criticises it as conveying precisely the meaning which our Oxford divines so earnestly repudiate.

"Whoever (he says) rightly considers that passage will perceive that the mode of conveyance expressed does not transcend that of a mere *sign*. For the book is nothing but a certain sign by which the delivery of the office of Canon is designated. And according to this, therefore, the Sacraments of the new law would be *nothing more than signs of grace.*" †

* Sermon de Cœn Dom. † Aquin. Summa, P. iii. Q. 62. A. 1.

Here then we have an interpretation of St. Bernard, and of the expression which Hooker adopts from him, made by the great Schoolman of the 13th century, and the chief founder of Romanism. The fact that St. Bernard, who is styled the last of the Fathers, and head of the Biblicists in his day, one of the last champions in the Romish Church for the plain letter of the bible against the Schoolmen, did thus express himself, and was thus found fault with by Thomas Aquinas, of the following century, is a strong evidence what sort of doctrine of the Sacraments was then expiring, with all biblical theology, and when the present Romish and Oxford doctrine came in.

The views of St. Bernard are further seen by such passages as the following:

"A man may be saved *by faith*, without Baptism, when he has a pious desire of receiving it, if death or some other invincible cause should prevent." For this he quotes Ambrose, Augustine and Cyprian. He reads Mark xvi. 16, 'He that believeth and is baptized shall be saved,' &c., as teaching that "sometimes faith alone suffices for salvation, and without it nothing is sufficient. Although martyrdom, as is conceded, supplies the place of Baptism, it is plainly not the *pœna* (the suffering) that does this, but faith itself (*sed ipsa fides*). And the effusion of one's blood for Christ is a strong proof of a certain great faith, nevertheless not a proof to God, but to men."*

Thus we see by what opinions of the efficacy of Baptism, and the impossibility of justification and regeneration before Baptism, Hooker would have his own language explained.

Bishop Jewel having instanced the opinions of Augustine and Ambrose as before herein given, and having mentioned that Constantine, the first Christian Emperor, was not baptized until his death; that the thief on the cross was received into Paradise without Baptism, and that Jeremiah and John Baptist were sanctified, in their mother's womb, proceeds to say: "By these few it may appear that the Sacrament *maketh not a Christian*, but is a seal and assurance to all that receive it, of the grace of God, unless they make themselves unworthy thereof. The Church hath always received three sorts of Baptism—*the Baptism of the Spirit, or of blood,* (*martyrdom*) *or of water*. If any were prevented by death, or hindered by cruelty of persecution, so that they could not receive

* Epistles of St. Bernard.

the *sacrament* of Baptism at the hands of the minister, yet, *having the sanctification of the Holy Ghost*—they were *born anew and baptized."* Thus, according to Jewel, the Church has always held a Baptism of the Spirit independently of the outward Sacrament of Baptism by water.* Thus therefore writes Bishop Hall:

"No man that hath faith can be condemned; for Christ dwells in our hearts by faith, and he in whom Christ dwells cannot be reprobate. Now it is possible that a man may have a saving faith *before* Baptism. Abraham first believed to justification, then *after* received the sign of circumcision, as a seal of the righteousness of that faith which he had when he was uncircumcised. Neither was Abraham's case singular: he was the father of all them also which believe, not being circumcised. These, as they are his sons in faith, so in righteousness, so in salvation. Uncircumcision cannot hinder where faith admitteth. Baptism therefore without faith cannot save a man; and by faith doth save him. And faith *without Baptism*, where it cannot be had; not where it may be had and is contemned. That Spirit which works by means, will not be tied to means." †

Regeneration being thus, in the view of the Church and her standard divines, *a spiritual and inward birth*, which is not so inseparable from Baptism that it may not be without that Sacrament, or that Sacrament, without it; the Church in directing her members to examine themselves as to their having this grace, does not say, "*look to your Baptism, take that for evidence;*" but "here is now that glass wherein thou mayest discern, whether thou have the Holy Ghost within thee. If thou see that thy works be consonant to the prescript rule of God's word, savoring and tasting, not of the flesh, but of the Spirit; then assure thyself that thou art endued with the Holy Ghost; otherwise—thou dost nothing else but deceive thyself." ‡

But this is precisely what our Oxford Divines most pointedly ridicule, as Ultra-Protestant and vain. "Ultra-Protestants (they write) have been taught that Justification is not *the gift of God through his Sacraments*, but the result of a certain frame of mind, of a going forth of themselves and resting themselves upon their Saviour; this is the *act whereby they think themselves to have been justified;*" certainly,

---

* Bp. Jewel's Works, vol. ii. pp. 1107, 8.
† Bishop Hall's Works, vol. vii. pp, 236, 237.   ‡ Homily for Whitsunday.

we answer, that *act* is faith. "*He that believeth on Christ is justified from all his sins,*' saith the Scripture. "If, says our Church, we rise by repentance, and with a full purpose of amendment of life, do flee unto the mercy of God, *taking sure hold thereupon, through faith in his Son Jesus Christ,* there is an assured and infallible hope of pardon and remission" of our sins.* "Faith is the only hand that taketh hold upon Christ." † "In this, doubtless consists the very essence of Justifying faith, even in trusting and relying upon Christ alone for pardon and salvation, so as to expect it from him and from none but him." ‡

But continues this divinity, "So, as another would revert to his Baptism and his ingrafting into Christ (at his Baptism) and his thus being in Christ, so do they, to this act, whereby *they* were justified."§ Now here is indeed precisely the difference. The Oxford system, like Romanism, so identifies Baptism with regeneration and justification, that we are not, as the Homily, above quoted, directs, to look to our works, our walk, our conformity with God's will in His word, the *savor* and *taste* of our minds, as "the glass" in which we are to see whether we be in faith, in Christ, &c.; but we are to "*revert to our Baptism*"—*that* is the glass by which we are to examine ourselves whether we be in the faith—that is the evidence of our union to Christ by faith.

Nothing could more plainly or more impressively display the "*great gulph fixed*" between this divinity and that of the Scriptures, our Church, her standard divines, than simply this; that while the evidence of justification which the Scriptures and our Church refer to continually, is that of faith, and the evidence of faith is the *walk, the fruits, the being led by the Spirit, the purifying of the heart, overcoming the world, &c.*, and never *our having been baptized;* on the contrary, the evidence according to this system, and just like that of Romanism, is simply and exclusively our Baptism—our "being *thus* in Christ."

The general benefit of Baptism is thus stated by Archbishop Usher:

"It is "the same, (he says) as was the benefit to the Jew, outward;" (Rom. ii. 28; iii. 1, 2.) "there is a general grace of Baptism which all the baptized partake of as a common favor, and that is their admission into the visible body of the Church, their matriculation and outward incorporating into the number of the

---

* Homily of Repentance, P. 1.   † Hooker.   ‡ Beveridge's Sermons, No. 89.
§ Letter to Bp. of Oxford, pp. 47, 48.

worshipers of God by external communion. And so as circumcision was not only a seal of the righteousness which is by faith, but as an overplus, God appointeth it to be a wall of separation between the Jew and the Gentile; so is Baptism a badge of an outward member of the Church, a distinction from the common rout of heathen, and God thereby seals a right upon the party baptized to his ordinances. Yet this is but the porch, the shell, the outside. All that are outwardly received into the visible Church are not spiritually ingrafted into the mystical body of Christ. Baptism always is attended upon by that general grace, but not always by that special." Again: "Some have the outward sign and not the inward grace; some have the inward grace and not the outward sign; we must not commit idolatry by deifying the outward element."

"As Baptism, administered to those of years, is not effectual unless they believe; so we can make no comfortable use of our Baptism administered in our infancy until we believe. The righteousness of Christ, and all the promises of grace, were in my Baptism estated upon me, and sealed up unto me, on God's part; but then I come to have the profit and benefit of them, when I come to understand what grant, God in Baptism hath sealed unto me, and actually to lay hold upon it by faith."

Those excellent Bishops, Hopkins and Reynolds, would furnish us with abundant matter in point, but as Bishop Beveridge is especially strong, and is particularly referred to in the Oxford Tracts for the use of language which seems to indicate the inseparability of regeneration and justification from Baptism, we will now show that he ascribes all saving mercies to faith, without naming Baptism.

"When a man believes in Christ, the second Adam, and *so is made a member* of his *body*, he is quickened and anointed by his Spirit, which being the principle of a new life in him, he *thereby becomes a new creature*—another kind of creature from what he was before, and therefore is properly said *to be born again*, not of blood, &c., but *of God*. His whole nature is changed. He hath a new set of thoughts and affections,—and whereas other men are born only of the flesh, such a one is *regenerate or born again* of the Spirit. Hence all such are called the Sons of God, *and are really so*." These passages are from a sermon on *Regeneration*, in which Baptism is not mentioned.* The identity of the language with

* Beveridge's Sermons, No. 73. Whoever would see how little Bp. B. identifies

that of the Homily for Whitsunday is striking—*Such is the power of the Holy Ghost to regenerate men, and as it were to bring them forth anew, so that they shall be nothing like the men they were before.*"

Barrow is one of the Catena Patrum, furnished in the Oxford Tracts, in support of their doctrine of baptismal regeneration and justification. Their citation quotes him as saying:

"No man can enter into the kingdom of heaven (that is, become a Christian or subject of God's spiritual kingdom) without being regenerated by water, and by the Spirit; that is without Baptism, and the spiritual grace attending it, according as St. Peter doth imply that the reception of the Holy Spirit is annexed to Holy Baptism; 'Repent and be baptized every one of you for the remission of sins, and ye shall receive the gift of the Holy Ghost.'" *

"That the justification which St. Paul discourseth of seemeth, in his meaning, only or especially to be that act of grace which is dispensed to persons at their Baptism, or at their entrance into the Church; when they openly professing their faith, and undertaking the practice of Christian duty, God most solemnly and formally doth absolve them from all guilt, and accepteth them into a state of favor with him: that St. Paul only or chiefly respecteth this act, considering his design, I am inclined to think, and many passages in his discourse seem to imply." †

From all this, one would think that Barrow had no idea of such a thing as justification before Baptism. But how will this agree with the following passage in the same sermon?

"In Baptism, St. Paul saith, "we *die to sin* (by resolution and engagement to lead a new life in obedience to God's commandment,) and so dying we are said to be justified from sin (that which otherwise is expressed, or expounded, by being freed from sin :) now the freedom from sin obtained in Baptism is frequently declared to be the remission of sin then conferred, and solemnly conferred by a visible seal.

"Whereas also frequently we are said to be *justified by faith*, and according to the general tenor of Scripture, the *immediate consequent of faith is Baptism;* therefore dispensing the benefits consigned in Baptism is coincident with justification; and that

Spiritual Regeneration with its Sacrament let him read his sermon on the New Creature, No. 19.

* Sermon of the Holy Ghost. † Of Justification by Faith.

dispensation is frequently signified to be the cleansing us from sin by the entire remission thereof."

Now here is *justifying faith,* going *before* Baptism; Baptism made its *consequent.* But in Oxford doctrine, this order is directly reversed. Justifying faith is there the consequent of Baptism. The benefits of Baptism are said by Barrow to be "*co-incident* with justification," not productive of it. They come by faith, and are "*consigned*" by Baptism; "conferred, and solemnly confirmed" by it, as "a visible seal;" just as an estate, which has been long since purchased and possessed, is conferred by a deed of conveyance, and confirmed by a visible seal. The *death unto sin* which Paul speaks of as being contained in Baptism is here said to be "by resolution and engagement to lead a new life"—no "inward, spiritual" change. Dr. Barrow considers the latter as having been already wrought in repentance and faith. He expressly says, that repentance and faith, which are required as preparatory to adult Baptism, are "that death to sin and resurrection to righteousness, that being buried with Christ and rising again with him, so as to walk in newness of life, *which the baptismal action signifies.*" *

Here then if the interpretation put by these divines on the first passage from Barrow be correct, is a perfect contradiction, rendered the more manifest because Barrow considers the Oxford doctrine of justification by inherent righteousness an interpretation of St. Paul, "*arbitrarious and uncouth.*"

We will illustrate the difficulty in which the Oxford doctrine is placed, as to all consistent interpretation of ancient and standard divines, by further reference to Bishop Jewel.

That most eminent Bishop and Reformer is cited in the Catena Patrum of the Oxford Tracts as supporting their doctrine of sacramental justification. The following is a part of their extract:

"Such a change is made in the sacrament of Baptism. Through the power of God's working, the water is turned into blood. They that be washed in it receive the remission of sins; their robes are made clean in the blood of the Lamb. The water itself is nothing; but by the working of God's Spirit, the death and merits of our Lord and Saviour are thereby assured unto us." †

Jewel quotes and professes to adopt the very strongest language of the Fathers on this subject.

But in the second part of Froude's Remains, which is but a

---

* On the doctrine of the Sacraments. † Treatise on the Sacraments.

collection of what may be called Oxford Tracts, we have the following passage from Jewell given in evidence that he did not hold the right (the Oxford) doctrine of the Sacraments.

"Another fantasie Mr. Harding hath found, 'that the Sacraments of the New Law work the thing itself that they signify, through virtue (as he saith) given unto them, by God's ordinance, to special effects of grace.' This, as I said, is but a fantasie." "When Augustine saith 'Our Sacraments give salvation,' his meaning is, 'Our Sacraments teach us that salvation is already come into the world.'"*

Thus, in one Oxford publication, we have Jewell cited in favor, and in another against, their doctrine of sacramental justification.

How little Augustine agreed with our Oxford divines as to the inseparability of sanctification from Baptism may be judged from the following concerning the Baptism of Cornelius.

"In Cornelius there preceded a *spiritual sanctification* in the gift of the Holy Spirit, and the Sacrament of regeneration was *added in the washing* of Baptism."

Having instanced the pardoned thief as a case wherein Baptism had been of necessity dispensed with, he adds:

"Much more in Cornelius and his friends might it seem superfluous, that they should be bedewed with water, in whom the gift of the Holy Spirit had appeared conspicuously, by that sure token, viz., that they spake with tongues. Yet were they baptized, and in this event, we have apostolic sanction for the like. So surely ought no one, in *whatever advanced state of the inner man*, to despise the Sacrament which is administered IN THE BODY, by the work of the ministers, but God thereby spiritually operates the consecration of the man."

How is it possible to suppose that Augustine, writing such a passage, could have believed that sanctification and its commencement—Regeneration—did not, could not, precede Baptism! What is plainer than that he contemplated the case of adults, *unbaptized*, like Cornelius and his friends, as capable of being in *an advanced state of the inner man, or of sanctification!* What is plainer than that he considered the Sacrament of Baptism in such cases as the

---

* Froude's Remains, Part Second, vol. i. p. 408.

conferring of an *external sign*, by human ministers, of an *inward grace* which God had *already* wrought in the soul by the Holy Ghost? Miserable indeed is the shift by which Dr. Pusey evades the whole case of Cornelius, as well as this testimony of Augustine. One while he positively asserts that though Cornelius had "faith, love, self-denial and power to pray," and though the Scriptures tell us that *before he was baptized* he received *both the preaching of Christ* from St. Peter, and *the Holy Ghost* from God, yet "he had not Christian faith, nor love, nor self-denial, nor prayer; for as yet he knew not Christ." Afterwards, he seems to be sensible of the absurdity of maintaining that persons to whom Peter said, "the word which God sent unto the children of Israel, preaching peace by Jesus Christ—*that word ye know;*" that persons to whom he immediately preached that "through his name whosoever believeth in him shall receive remission of sins;" that such persons could not have *Christian faith before Baptism,* "*because they knew not Christ;*" that persons on whom immediately upon their receiving the words of Peter, concerning Christ, was poured out the Holy Ghost, "*could not* (even then) *call God the Father because they knew not the Son.*" He resorts therefore to the idea of the case being *miraculous* and *solitary,* and complains of its being drawn into precedent, and thus really acknowledges what before he had endeavored to escape, viz., that in the Baptism of Cornelius and his household and friends, that is, of the first congregation of believing Gentiles, the *Grace* of Regeneration preceded the *Sacrament* of Regeneration; which is virtually an acknowledgment that since Augustine, in the passage above quoted, alludes to the case of Cornelius and his friends, to show that *in similar cases,* Baptism ought not to be omitted, it was Augustine's opinion that the case of Cornelius was not *alone,* but was repeated, and not uncommonly in subsequent examples of believing, but unbaptized adults.* What that Father meant, then, by baptismal regeneration or justification, is plain by a comparison of the above quotation with the following on the same case of Cornelius and his friends. He says:

"They were accounted, (by St. Peter), as of those 'animals' pointed out in that vessel (the great sheet) whom yet *God had now cleansed* (before Baptism) in that he had 'accepted their alms.' They were then to be 'slain and eaten;' i. e. their forepassed life, wherein they had not known Christ, was to be destroyed, and they were to pass

* For the quotation from Augustine, and the treatment of the case of Cornelius by Dr. Pusey, see his Views of Holy Baptism, Amer. Edit. pp. 177—183.

into His body, *as it were* into *the new life of the society* of the Church." *

But did their "forepast life" remain *undestroyed* until they were baptized, when it is said they were previously *cleansed*, previously believers in Christ, and partakers of the Holy Ghost and of "spiritual sanctification?" What then could its destruction *in Baptism* have been, but the adding to it its outward *sign and seal*, the *sacramental* destruction accompanied by confirming and increasing grace? And what could the passing "*into the new life and society of the Church*," by Baptism have meant, but an incorporation into the *visible society and fellowship* of the Church, which is the mystical body of Christ?

Precisely according to Augustine is Cyprian's proof of the necessity of Baptism.

"We find (says he) in the Acts of the Apostles that this was carefully observed by the Apostles—so that when in the house of Cornelius the Centurion, the Holy Spirit had descended on the Gentiles who were there, *kindled with the glow of faith, and believing in the Lord with the whole heart*, filled with whom they blessed God with divers tongues," (*and yet Dr. Pusey says they knew not Christ, and had no Christian faith or love, because unbaptized*) "still nevertheless the blessed Apostle Peter, mindful of the Divine and evangelic command, commanded those same persons to be baptized, who had already been filled with the Holy Ghost, that nothing might seem to be omitted, or the Apostolic authorities to have failed of keeping universally the law of the divine command and of the Gospel." †

Now since the Baptism of Cornelius is thus employed by the Fathers for an example to us, it cannot be granted that it was, in any wise, so miraculous and singular as to furnish no general example on which the doctrine of the receiving of the Holy Ghost *before* Baptism, by those who come to it with repentance and faith, may be founded. Certainly there is nothing in it more miraculous, than in the conversion and baptizing of the three thousand on the day of Pentecost, or in the conversion and baptizing of Saul. But we apprehend it would be thought a great stretch of propriety to attempt to evade the reasoning of Dr. Pusey from the language

---

* Augustine quoted in Pusey's Views of Holy Baptism, p. 183.
† Cyprian quoted in Pusey's Views of Holy Baptism, p. 182.

of Scripture in connection with those cases, should we say they were too miraculous to be drawn into precedent.

But the language and doctrine of the Fathers is further illustrated in the case of Simon Magus, with which Dr. Pusey is exceedingly perplexed, not knowing whether to hold that Simon's faith was true, and that he was regenerate in Baptism, "*but in time of temptation fell away;*" or that he was hypocritical from the beginning, and received Baptism, without regeneration or justification. If the latter, then, he says:

"It gives *no disclosure as to God's general dealings in his Sacraments. It is an excepted case*, in which God restrains the overflowings of his goodness, and not to be stretched beyond the limits which He has pointed out. It is no proof that God withholds His grace from his Sacraments, *except when man disqualifies himself from receiving it—closes his own soul against God's gift.*" *

But let us hear some of the language of the Fathers concerning the case of Simon Magus. Augustine says, "he was baptized with Christ's Baptism"—that "*his sins were forgiven him;*" that he "*was born of water and of the Spirit;*" "that he "received *the gift of the Sacrament, in Baptism.*" "The Church BORE Simon Magus by Baptism." Jerome speaks of Simon as having been made by Baptism "*one of the faithful.*" † Now here the strongest language of *baptismal regeneration and justification*, is used by Augustine concerning a man who was "*in the gall of bitterness and the bonds of iniquity.*" Does it then mean that he was *spiritually*, or only *sacramentally* born, as he who partakes of the Lord's Supper, without faith, is *sacramentally*, a partaker, but not really, and *spiritually*, of the body and blood of Christ? If such language means no more than the latter, in the case of Simon, there is no reason to interpret it as meaning more in any other case.

Hear, then, St. Jerome. Speaking of those who receive not Baptism in full faith, he says:

"Of whom it must be said, that they received the water, *but received not the Spirit*, as that Simon Magus also, who was baptized indeed with water, and was not baptized to health."

Hear also St. Cyril:

"Even Simon Magus once came to the door of Baptism; he was baptized, *but not enlightened;* his body he dipped in water, but

* Pusey's Views of Baptism, Amer. Edit. p. 117. † Ibid. p. 186.

admitted not the Spirit to illuminate his heart—his soul was not buried with Christ, nor with him raised."

Hear also St. Augustine. Having just said that the Church *bore* him or brought him forth in Baptism, but that still he had no part in the inheritance of Christ, he asks:

"Was Baptism, was the Gospel, were the Sacraments wanting to him? But *since love was wanting,* he was born in vain, and perhaps *it had been better for him not to have been born.*" *

What can be more manifest than that the Fathers, in applying the strongest language of baptismal regeneration and justification to a case in which they acknowledge there was neither *spiritual health, enlightening, illumination, burial, nor resurrection with Christ, no love, a birth in vain,* did not intend to teach that spiritual regeneration and remission of sins are so tied to Baptism that they can neither precede nor follow it, but are exclusively and invariably conferred by it?

In reading the Fathers on Baptism, as on other subjects, it is necessary to remember, what even Bellarmine says of them, that "*they speak sometimes in a way of excess, less properly, less warily, so as to need benign exposition:*" that, according to Barrow they had their "*hyberbolical flashes*" and "did sometimes *overlash;*" that, according to Jackson, they "had a superfluity of rhetorical inventions or ejaculations of swelling affections in panegyrical passages."

"In all ages, (said Latimer) the devil has stirred up some light heads to esteem the Sacraments but lightly, as to be empty and bare signs; whom the Fathers have resisted so fiercely, that in their fervor they seem in sound of words to run too far the other way, and to give too much to the Sacraments, *when they, in truth, did think more measurably.* And therefore they are to be read *warily,* with sound judgment." †

Here it is reasonable to ask, what are we to understand to be the true doctrine of the Church of England on this subject. We answer by extracts from three writers, whose standing cannot be questioned; the first, Bishop Hooper, one of the Reformers and Martyrs of the days of our Articles, when as Dr. Pusey says, there was no difference of opinion on this subject; the second, Bishop

---

* Pusey's Views of Baptism, pp. 188—190. Amer. Edit.
† Conference with Ridley.

Beveridge, expressly expounding the Article on Baptism; the third, Bishop Taylor.

HOOPER—BISHOP, REFORMER AND MARTYR.

"And of Baptism, because it is a mark of our Christian Church, this I judge, after the doctrine of St. Paul, that it is a seal and *confirmation* of justice, (righteousness or justification) or of our acceptance into the Grace of God for Christ; for his innocency and justice, by faith, is ours, and our sins and injustice, by his obedience, are his; whereof Baptism is the *sign, seal,* and *confirmation.* For, although freely by the grace of God our sins are forgiven, yet the same is declared by the Gospel, received by faith, and *sealed* by the Sacraments, which are the seals of God's promises, as it is to be seen by the faith of faithful Abraham." *

"They (the Fathers) thought it best to name the Sacraments by the name of the thing that was represented by the Sacraments. Yet in many places of their writings, they so interpret themselves, that no man, except he will be willfully blind, can say but they understand the Sacrament *to signify,* and not to *be the thing signified:* to *confirm,* and not *exhibit* grace; to *help,* and not to *give* faith; to *seal,* and not to *win* the promise of God, (Rom. iv.); to show what we are *before the use of them,* and not *to make us the thing we declare to be after them;* to show we are Christ's; to show we are in grace, and not *by them to be received into grace;* to show we are saved, and yet *not to be saved by them;* to show *we are regenerated,* and not to *be regenerated by them;* thus the old doctors meant." †

BISHOP BEVERIDGE.

"As it was by circumcision that the Jews were distinguished from all other people in the world, so it is by Baptism that Christians are distinguished both from Jews and others; for all that are baptized are Christians, and none are Christians but such as are baptized, and so Baptism is a *mark of difference,* whereby Christians are discerned from such as be not Christened. But though this be one effect of Baptism, it is not all. For it is not only a sign of our profession, but also of our regeneration, and therefore it is called 'the washing of regeneration,' Tit. iii. 5. So that by it we are *grafted into the Church,* and made members of that body, whereof Christ is the head; for 'we are baptized into one body,' 1 Cor. xii. 13; have a promise from God of the forgiveness of those sins we have committed against him. And therefore Peter

---

* Hooper's Confession of Faith.   † Fifth Sermon on Jonah.

said unto them 'Repent and be baptized every one of you, in the name of Jesus Christ, for the remission of sins,' Acts ii. 28. That so 'being justified by his grace, we should be made (not only sons, but) heirs, according to the hope of eternal life,' Tit. iii. 7. And so in Baptism our faith is confirmed, and grace increased, by virtue of prayer to God; not by virtue of the water itself, but by virtue of prayer, whereby God is prevailed with to purify our souls by his Spirit, as our bodies are washed with the water; that as the water washeth off the pollutions of our bodies, so his Spirit purgeth away the corruptions of our souls."*

BISHOP TAYLOR.

No one is stronger in his impressions concerning Baptism than Bishop Taylor. He quotes the most panegyrical language of the Fathers as expressing his views—and yet, in concluding his account of its benefits, he uses this language:

"Because Baptism consigns it and admits us to a title to it (viz., resurrection with Christ,) we are said with St. Paul, to be risen with Christ *in Baptism:* buried with him in Baptism, &c. Which expression I desire to be remembered, that by it we may the better understand those other sayings of the Apostle, of '*putting on Christ in Baptism—putting on the new man,*' &c., for these only signify, επιχειρημα or *the design on God's part, and the endeavor and duty on man's*. We are then *consigned* to our duty and reward. We undertake one, and have a title to the other. And though men of ripeness and reason, enter instantly on their portion of work, and have present use of the assistances and something of their reward in hand, yet we cannot conclude that those who cannot do it presently, are not baptized rightly because they are not in capacity to 'put on the new man' in righteousness, that is in an actual holy life; for they may 'put on the new man' in Baptism, *just as they are risen with Christ;* (that is as he has before said, *prospectively, the 'real event in its due season'*) which BECAUSE IT MAY BE DONE BY FAITH, BEFORE IT IS DONE IN REAL EVENT, and it may be done *by Sacrament and design before it be done by a proper faith;* so also may *our putting on of the new* man be; it is done *sacramentally,* and that part which is wholly the work of God, *does only antedate the work of man, which is to succeed in its due time and is after the manner of preventing grace.* †

Now it is reasonably asked if such be all the doctrine of the

---

* Beveridge on the 27th Article. † Works, 8vo., vol. i. p. 127.

Church and the Divines whom we have quoted, viz., that Baptism is a *sign* of separation from the world, and consecration to God; a *seal* of the promises of God to those who truly repent and believe; an *effectual* sign and seal, whereby the grace of repentance and faith is confirmed and increased, how can such strong language as we have before quoted be explained and shown to be consistent with "truth and soberness?"

To this we proceed to direct our attention. But we cannot in conscience profess to get round the language, by such a device as that contained in the following extracts from Bishop Bethell on Regeneration a standard work with Dr. Pusey, Dr. Hook, &c.,— the device of making an entire distinction between *regeneration* and *renovation*, as if the latter were an *internal and spiritual* change, which *precedes* as well as follows adult Baptism, and is not necessarily implied in infant Baptism; while the former, after all the immense weight of strong language laid upon it by the Fathers and the Reformers, and in our Oxford Divines, *par excellence,* were only a relative change of *state,* including no change of *disposition, heart and temper.*

"*Regeneration,* (says Bishop Bethell, as quoted by Dr. Hook) is the joint work of water and the Spirit, or to speak more properly, of the Spirit only; *renovation* is the joint work of the Spirit and the man. *Regeneration* comes only once, in or through Baptism. *Renovation* exists *before, in* and *after* Baptism, and may often be repeated."—" This is what is meant by those divines who maintain that regeneration is in the strict sense of the word *the inward and spiritual grace of Baptism.* The *idenity,* if I may so express myself, of Baptism and regeneration, is a doctrine which manifestly pervades the writings of the Fathers. It is moreover evident that they did not imagine that Baptism produces *any saving effect in adults* without faith and repentance, or, in other words, without some *previous renewal* of the inward frame. Nor do they appear to have supposed *any positive or active renewal of the soul takes place in infants.* Hence it follows that they must have maintained this distinction between *regeneration* and *renovation* or *conversion*, which, in the present day, has been styled, by a strange fatality, a novel contrivance." *

Now here is a confession indeed—viz., that the Fathers did not imagine that Baptism *regenerated* without *previous renewal*, that is

---

* Bishop Bethell on Regeneration, p. 16, quoted in Hook's Call to Union.

without previous putting off the old man, and putting on of the new; a previous *new creation,* a conversion, or new birth, a sanctification of the Spirit; what others call a previous "*spiritual regeneration.*" *

Another confession—"*Nor do they* (the Fathers) *appear to have supposed any positive or active renewal of the soul takes place in infants.*" No "*positive renewal!*" no positive *creating anew;* no positive putting off of the old man. But still infant Baptism is regeneration and nothing else *is.* What then is regeneration? The doctrine of Bishop Bethell is that adults, before Baptism, are *converted and renewed,* but not *regenerated;* that infants, in Baptism, are *regenerated,* but not *renewed* or *converted.* What then is regeneration, according to this doctrine, but a mere outward work, a relative change not an inward sanctification.

Hence in the Sermon of Dr. Hook, to which the above extracts from Bishop Bethell are appended, we have the following summary of what he considers the difference between Regeneration and Renovation, which he charges the foreign Reformers with confounding. The former, he says, is "a change of *spiritual state and relations,* the latter is *an election of grace,* with a *subsequent change of disposition, heart and temper.*" This he says is taking the expressions of our Church services "in all the *simplicity* and *fullness* of their meaning." †

Thus, while Bishop Bethell says, "Regeneration is in the strict sense of the word *the inward and spiritual grace of Baptism;*" Dr. Hook interpreting him says, it is not "a change of disposition, heart, and temper," but only of "spiritual state, circumstances and relations," so that the doctrine of the Church Catechism that the "inward and spiritual grace" of Baptism is "*a death unto sin and a new birth unto righteousness,*" when taken "*in all the simplicity and fullness of its meaning,*" is nothing more than a change of *state, circumstances and relations,* no change of heart or disposition or temper. Now this we must style, "a *novel contrivance*" indeed. It is thus that our Oxford divines would arise above the low ration-

---

* Thus in one place, as we have seen, Hooker is quoted by these writers as saying that Baptism is "*the first apparent beginning of life,* and a step to our sanctification *which hath not any before it,*" and we are expected to take his words in the fullest and most literal meaning; and then we are recommended to a standard writer who tells us regeneration takes place in the Baptism of adults not *without some previous renewal of the inward frame,* &c. *Renewal* means a *making new.* So then there is no regeneration in Baptism that is not preceded by a spiritual new birth or new creation. And is this no beginning of life, no step to sanctification?

† Hook's Call to Union, pp. 22, 23.

alistic and poverty-stricken interpretations of modern theology, (as they speak,) and conduct us back to the fullness and depth and hidden mystery and awful grandeur of the Fathers concerning the relations of Baptism to regeneration and justification. That which, one while, they represent to be "the inwrapping and conveying of the whole soul of religion," "the sanctification, and the remission and the adoption and the life," they make at another time, a mere change of *relations and circumstances!* We cannot in any way reconcile such statements with those contained in Dr. Pusey's "Views of Baptism;" but nevertheless they are taken from a work which he pronounces a *standard* on this subject, and they go strongly to show that, after all the prodigious accumulation of spiritual and mystical and wondering *language*, which he and his school employ to express the change wrought in and by Baptism; they still mean a new birth which is *spiritual* in little else than that it is *mystical;* a change of which *repentance* and *faith* in the adult are no part, because they go before it; a something therefore which if it be *really* more than a relative change of state, must be a sort of *tertium quid*, a change neither of *inward* disposition nor *outward* relation, neither of *heart* nor of *circumstances*, worthy indeed of the *Quodlibets* of the Schoolmen, but wholly unworthy to be honored as embracing "the fullness" of the meaning of the Scriptures, the Fathers, the Reformers and the Offices of our Church.

In justice to these venerable authorities, we must reject a distinction so vital between renovation and regeneration. A glance at their works will show that by all such expressions as regeneration, renovation, conversion, new birth, putting off the old man, repentance, &c., they meant the same great inward and spiritual change, viz.: *a death unto sin and a new birth unto righteousness,*" the one grace of which Baptism is the sign and seal—while they certainly do speak of it as being effected, in *some sense*, in Baptism. If Hooker, in a passage above quoted, ascribes to Baptism "the infusion of that grace which giveth to the soul *the first disposition towards newness of life,*" then surely he ascribes to it *repentance, faith, renovation, conversion,* since none of these can take place without the first disposition towards newness of life. In the Homily for Whitsunday, to be *regenerate, born anew, new men in Christ Jesus, to have godly motions, agreeable to the will of God, stirred up by the Holy Ghost in our hearts,* are equivalent expressions. Cranmer, in his Sermon on Baptism, says that by the second birth we mean that which is *spiritual, whereby our inward man and mind are renewed* by the Holy Ghost, so that *our hearts and minds receive* *new desires*, &c.—that in this baptismal regeneration "*the love of God is shed abroad in our hearts*"—and "we are made *new creatures*"—and this is "a marvellous alteration and *renewing* of the inward man," so that "*new affections and spiritual motions* are in the souls of such as are born again by Baptism." Instances of the same use of terms might be multiplied indefinitely. One from Bishop Beveridge is at hand, and will suffice. He calls "*spiritual regeneration*, the *renewing* the Spirit of our minds, and so infusing into them a principle of new life, whereby they become *new creatures*,"* &c. In another sermon he says of repentance precisely the same, viz.: that it is that "whereby a man is quite changed from what he was, and therefore is called *a new man* and *a new creature*, because *old things are passed away and all things are become new* in him." † And this, which Beveridge says is repentance, the Homily for Whitsunday says is regeneration—"Such is the power of the Holy Ghost to REGENERATE *men, and, as it were, to bring them forth anew, so that they shall be nothing like the men that they were before*."

Such then being the evident convertibility of the terms regeneration, renovation, conversion, new-creation, repentance, &c., as connected with Baptism, in the use of those who speak of the effects of Baptism in the strongest terms, we must wholly reject the distinction between regeneration, as only "a change of *spiritual state, relations and circumstances*," and renovation as "*a change of heart, disposition, and temper*," which Bishop Bethell, and those who call his work a standard, would teach; we must speak of *spiritual* regeneration as being the "inward and spiritual grace" of which Baptism is "*a sign;*" ‡ and that spiritual grace or death unto sin and new birth unto righteousness, as being neither more nor less than a change of heart, disposition and temper, whereby men are so changed "*that they be nothing like the men they were before*." We must reject their doctrine, who contend that a sinner, repenting and believing in the Lord Jesus Christ, is not *spiritually* regenerate nor justified before God, until he receive the *Sacrament* of justification and regeneration, although confessedly *renewed*, and having that repentance which is a change of heart; in other words that he cannot with a renewed inward frame and a change of heart, be justified, until he receive the *outward sign;* cannot have peace from God, till he have the *seal* of that peace from man. The fact that this hard doctrine could not be maintained without doing such utter violence to all ideas of spiritual regeneration, robbing it of

* Sermon, No. 81.
† Sermon, No. 84.   ‡ Art. xxvii.

all real spirituality, giving all the real glory to renovation, as being quite another thing in its nature, is one of the strongest evidences that baptismal regeneration or justification, in their sense, cannot explain the language of our Church and of her standard Divines,—cannot be the doctrine of the Fathers, or the Scriptures.

What then is the explanation of the strong language of our old Divines, and of the Fathers before them, as to the benefits connected with Baptism? We answer, precisely that which the Homilies quote from St. Augustine.

"Writing to Bonifacius of the Baptism of Infants, he (Augustine) saith, 'If Sacraments had not a certain *similitude* of those things whereof they be Sacraments, they should be no Sacraments at all. *And of this similitude, they do for the most part receive the names of the self-same things they signify.*'"*

These words of Augustine, are thus applied by Bishop Jewel:

"Therefore *after a certain manner of speech (and not otherwise)* the *Sacrament* of the Body of Christ is called the Body of Christ; so the *Sacrament* of faith is faith."

And of course also, the Sacrament of regeneration, is, *after a certain manner of speech, and not otherwise,* called regeneration. Again in another place:

"We must consider that the learned Fathers, in their treatises of the Sacraments, sometimes use the outward sign instead of the thing signified; sometimes they use the thing signified instead of the sign. As for example, sometimes they name Christ's blood instead of the water. Sometimes they name the water instead of Christ's blood—this exchange of names is much used among the learned, specially speaking of the Sacraments. St. Augustine, using the water in place of the blood of Christ that is signified by the water, saith thus—'*It breaketh the bond of sin—it doth renew a man in one Christ.*'" He saith, "'Now ye are clean through the word that I have spoken to you.' But why saith he not—Now ye are clean, *because of the Baptism* wherewith ye are washed; saving that because in the water, it *is the word* that maketh clean? Therefore he saith, '*The water giveth us outwardly the Sacrament of grace.*'

* Homily on Common Prayer, &c.

And this (says Jewel) is the power and virtue of the Sacraments.'"*

Now then let us apply the language of Augustine. The Sacrament of Baptism, since it has a certain similitude of that which it signifies, does for the most part receive the *name of the self-same thing it signifies*. It is called the "Baptism for the remission of sins," because it *signifies* remission of sins; it is called "the washing of regeneration," because it signifies that washing; it is called by the Fathers and our Reformers, &c., the new birth, the new creation, because it is their sign. In Baptism we are said to receive remission of sins, the righteousness of Christ, and even the first motion of soul towards divine things; because in Baptism these are signified, and the promises of them are sealed,—the actual grace which is signified, being considered as already possessed in the required repentance and faith of the catechumen.

We have a similar mode of speech with regard to other matters in religion, where it is well understood, and occasions no difficulty or misunderstanding. For example, it is universal among divines to speak of Baptism as the admission of a person into the Church of Christ—and until baptized he is not considered a member of the Church. But it is also very common to speak of the children of believers being in the Church *from their birth*. Thus Usher speaks of children "*being born in the bosom of the Church*" † and Hooker says "*we are plainly taught of God that the seed of faithful parentage is holy from the very birth.*" ‡ And so Bishop Jewell: "Infants are a part of the Church of God. Why should they not bear the mark of Christ, why should they not partake of the Sacrament (Baptism) together with the faithful?" §

Here are children made members of the Church by Baptism, *who were members by birth*. How is this? The answer is plain. The birth-membership was not *sacramental*, not signed and sealed by visible ordinance, so as to be *professed* before men. When baptized their membership had a *sacramental sign and seal* upon it, which made it a matter of profession and vow; it was visible, and gave them access to other ordinances of the house of God.

Now precisely as the Baptism of adults is said to give a Regeneration which if they were truly prepared, in repentance and faith, was possessed spiritually before, so is the Baptism of infants

---

* Jewel's Works, vol. iii. pp. 462, 3.
† Body of Divinity, 391.   ‡ Eccl. Pol. v. § 60.
§ Jewel, quoted by Le Bas, in his Life of Jewel, p. 336.

said to give membership in the Church. *The sign, in both cases receives,* as Augustine says, *the name of the self-same thing which it signifies.*

The same language is common with regard to the Lord's Supper, which is called the Sacrament of the body and blood of Christ. In it, the true believer is said to receive the Body and Blood of Christ to his soul's health. Just as much as Regeneration is any where ascribed to Baptism, is this receiving of Christ ascribed to the Eucharist; and for the same reason that we should infer that regeneration is not received but in Baptism, must we infer that the body and blood of Christ are not received but in the Eucharist. But all our old divines and all the Fathers held that receiving the body and blood of Christ is not confined to the Eucharist. Bradford, for example, quotes Augustine and Jerome, &c., as follows:

"St. Augustine writes that Christ is received sometimes visibly, and sometimes invisibly. The visible receiving he calls that which is by the Sacrament: the invisible, that which is by the exercise of our faith with ourselves. And St. Jerome affirms that we are fed with the body of Christ and we drink his blood, not only in mystery (Sacrament), but also in the knowledge of Holy Scripture, wherein he plainly shows that the same meat is offered in the words of Scripture as in the Sacraments, so that Christ's body and blood is no less offered by the Scriptures than by the Sacraments."

Bradford also quotes Jerome as saying that where Christ says, "*He that eateth my flesh,* &c., it is more true to take Christ's body and blood for the word of the Scriptures and the doctrine of God." He denies that a man may ordinarily receive Christ's body by faith in the hearing of his word, with so much sensible assurance as by receiving the Sacraments; but adds, "Not that Christ is not so much present in his word preached, as he is in or with his Sacrament, but because there are in the reception more windows (more senses) open for Christ to enter into us, than by his word preached."[*]

The same is thus expressed by Dr. Jackson:

"They are said to eat Christ's flesh and drink his blood *spiritually* which rightly apprehend his death and passion, which by Faith meditate and ruminate upon them, &c. He which thus eateth Christ's flesh, and drinketh his blood by *faith,* although he do not (for the time present) eat his body or drink his blood

[*] Sermon on the Lord's Supper.

sacramentally, hath a true interest in this promise: (*He that eateth my flesh,* &c., *dwelleth in me, and I in him,*) so he do not neglect to eat his body and drink his blood *sacramentally* when occasion requires and opportunity serves. *So that spiritual eating and drinking Christ by faith is the true preparation for the worthy receiving of his body and blood sacramentally.*" *

Thus is expressed, by an authority which Oxford divines cannot but respect, the important distinction between receiving *really,* and *sacramentally; inwardly* by faith, *visibly* by ordinance: *savingly* by the former, *professedly* by the latter; the two united when the Sacrament is properly received; not so inseparable but that the true believer receives the *grace* signified in the Sacrament *before* the *sign,* while the unbeliever cannot receive the grace signified *with* the sign.

Let it be remembered that precisely the same definition is given by the Articles to *both* Sacraments. The relation of the *sign* to the *thing signified,* which is all that concerns us now, is defined in one precisely as in the other. We may therefore just change names and the above language of Dr. Jackson, which is none other than what is common elsewhere, will be equally suitable to Baptism and to the Eucharist. With such change it will thus read:

They that repent and believe are regenerated and justified spiritually, though (for the time present) they be not (by Baptism) regenerated and justified *sacramentally;* yet they have a true interest in the promise, *he that believeth shall be saved,* so they do not neglect to be regenerated, &c., *sacramentally,* when occasion requires and opportunity serves. So that *spiritual* Regeneration and Justification are the preparatives for the worthy receiving the *sacramental.*

Thus, as in the Lord's Supper, "the signs receive the name of the self-same thing which they signify," and we call the spiritual reception and the merely sacramental by the same name of "*eating and drinking the body and blood of Christ,*" and yet without confusion or misunderstanding no body supposing us to mean that all who receive the Sacrament receive also the grace it signifies; so taught our old Divines, and so may we in regard to Baptism. We may say that adults coming in repentance and faith receive remission of sins in Baptism; because they receive it as they have not before, viz.: *sacramentally;* under a form whereby the promises which they have *previously embraced by faith,* are "*visibly signed and sealed;*"

* Jackson's Works, iii. p. 334.

so that what they have been before *really before God*, they are now *professedly before men;* what before they had promised only in the sight of Him who searcheth the heart, they have now stipulated before his Church which can only look upon the outward vow; what before entitled them to the inheritance of the kingdom of heaven, being now sacramentally signed and sealed, entitles them also to the communion and fellowship of the Church on earth.

Whoever will now examine the 27th Article on Baptism, with the above explanation, will perceive that we have exactly expressed its meaning. *

We might carry this analogy further, and show that throughout the ordinances of the Gospel—this language, which seems so strong in regard to Baptism, is used, *mutatis mutandis*, without confusion or difficulty. The outward and visible call of the Church to the ministry, and its relation to the inward and spiritual call of the Holy Ghost, which is required to precede it; and the use of the same language for the outward, as for the inward, as if the former was not, till the latter be come, and as if the latter were always where the former is professed, would be a case in point.

The instance of our blessed Lord being anointed invisibly by the Holy Ghost, fully and perfectly for his ministry, but not being anointed in *one* sense, viz.: *outwardly and visibly* or *sacramentally*, till his Baptism, when the Holy Ghost descended in visible *sign* upon him, not conferring new powers, but only adding the outward sign of an unction which he had had from his birth, might well be used for illustration—seeing that when Jesus is said to have been anointed for his work on earth, as a Prophet, Priest, and King, that visible anointing in the river Jordan is referred to as if no other had preceded it.

But it is not merely in religious things that such language is common. It is of notorious use and clear comprehension in the most common transactions of life. For example. A man purchases an estate, pays the price, enters on the possession, but for some reason or other has not received the title-deed. When that deed is

---

* "Baptism is not only a sign of profession, and mark of difference, whereby Christian men are discerned from others that be not christened; but it is also a sign of Regeneration or New Birth; whereby, as by an instrument, they that receive Baptism rightly, are grafted into the Church; the promises of forgiveness of sin, and our adoption to be the sons of God by the Holy Ghost, are visibly signed and sealed; faith is confirmed; and grace increased, by virtue of prayer unto God. The Baptism of young children is in any wise to be retained in the Church, as most agreeable with the institution of Christ." Art. **xxvii.**

executed, signed, sealed and delivered, then the estate is said in law to be *conveyed*. The title is then said to become vested in him, precisely as if he had had none before; and this simply because, as the law knows no evidence of title but the *visible instrument*, it can recognize no title as existing without it. But shall we take this language of the law, and, in our private judgments, conclude from it that prior to the written instrument there can be no equitable title! We say No; that language refers only to the title *before a human tribunal*, which must depend on such visible warrant. A court of law can go into no investigation but that of the signed and sealed document. But before Him who searcheth the secrets of men, there may have been a true and rightful title long before that deed was executed. All this is familiar. Men, when they hear the law pronounce an estate, which long before was possessed, to be now first *conveyed*, when the deed is delivered, see nothing difficult to be explained. The difference between the real, and the visible, the reception truly, and the reception formally, the title before God, and the title before a human tribunal, is so notorious in the civil commonwealth, that it occasions no misunderstanding. Let it then be considered that the visible Church is a spiritual Commonwealth, with her laws and privileges of citizenship, and modes of ascertaining citizenship, precisely as secular Commonwealths; that all her administration is by men as incapable of looking beyond the outward appearance and the visible sign and seal and conveyance and profession, as those who sit in the high places of civil goverments —then the keeping in mind of the following simple principles, will render the language of the Church, as to the possession of grace, just as plain as the language of the State in regard to the title of earthly tenements, viz.:

That the Church pronouncing in her fixed formularies, on the spiritual state of her people, can know no private history, nor speak of any on the ground of his private experience; she knows him as a Christian only through his *public* profession of repentance and faith, and his *public* entering upon the vows of consecration to God: so that though an unbaptized person may have been a new creature for a long time, and affectionally treated as such by the individual members of the Church, yet can he not be known as such by the Church *collectively and formally* till the moment when he makes a credible profession of repentance and faith in the appointed Sacrament, and thus marks himself, visibly, as a Christian, and draws the open line of separation from the world. The time therefore of his doing this is properly called by the Church, the time of his repenting and believing, of his being regenerated and justified. This is precisely expressed by Bishop Jewell, when he says:—

"If any be not baptized, but lacketh the mark of God's fold, *we* cannot discern him to be one of the flock. If any take not the seal of regeneration, *we* cannot say he is born the child of God."

But he has just before said that "God knoweth who are his"—that is, He needs no seal of regeneration to distinguish them. But to the Church, Jewell says, "the Sacrament of Baptism *is the badge and recognizance of every Christian.*"

The Sacrament of Baptism being according to our Article, a "*sign* of regeneration or New Birth, whereby, *as by an Instrument*, they that receive Baptism rightly, are grafted into the Church, and the promise of the forgiveness of sin and of their adoption to be sons of God, by the Holy Ghost, *is visibly signed and sealed ;*" till that *instrument*, be executed, a man can no more be regarded by the Church in her corporate capacity, as *in possession* of forgiveness of sins and spiritual regeneration, however truly he may have been inwardly and spiritually regenerated and justified, than the State can regard him as owning a property, of which he can show no title-deed. He is rightly said by the Church not to have come to those blessings, until baptized, because till then she has no sacramental evidence; while, at the same time, he who judgeth not by the outward appearance, but looketh upon the heart, may say to him, "*Son be of good cheer, thy sins be forgiven thee.*"

There is one important difference indeed between the signing and sealing, in civil transactions, and the Sacraments of the Gospel. In the former the signs have no efficacy but as evidence of a certain fact. In the latter, the signs are said to be "not only badges or tokens, but rather they be *certain sure witnesses* and *effectual* signs of grace and of God's good will toward us, by the which *he doth work invisibly* in us, and *doth not only quicken, but also strengthen and confirm our faith in him.*" * In other words that good work which God hath begun in his believing people, he, by the Holy Spirit, through the Sacrament, doth carry on in them, so that "Faith is confirmed and grace increased by virtue of prayer unto God."

The application of this common-sense method of interpreting the Scriptures, the Fathers and Reformers, when they speak of the efficacy of Baptism, and also the absolute necessity of such method.

* Art. xxv.

unless we would charge them with numerous and glaring contradictions, may be illustrated by the language of Nowell's Catechism. The authority of that Catechism as representing the doctrines of the Church was of the highest grade in the age of the Reformers, as will be seen in the next Chapter, where its evidence will be adduced on the nature of justifying righteousness and faith. On the subject of the Sacraments, its definitions are only an enlargement upon the language used in our present Articles and Catechism. Take one set of expressions in that work, in relation to Baptism, and it would appear, just as we have shown of other writings, as if the highest degree of regenerating and justifying efficacy were ascribed to that Sacrament; as if those who come to it could not be spiritually regenerate or justified, till baptized; and as if all the baptized were, in the act of Baptism, spiritually both regenerated and justified. For example. Speaking of the two Sacraments, Baptism and the Holy Supper, the Catechism says " *by the former we are born again.*" "As in Baptism, God truly *delivereth us forgiveness of sins and newness of life*, so do we certainly receive them."

But this interpretation will not hold with other language of the same Catechism. In answer to the question "in what the use of Baptism consisteth," the Catechism answers: "*In faith and repentance.*" In other words, in faith and repentance consists the inward and spiritual grace of which the Sacrament is a sign and pledge and which it is effectual in promoting. Of course—a *godly sorrow* and a *living faith* are meant, or else they would not be benefits of Baptism. But immediately proceeds the Catechism, to speak of that *very repentance and faith,* as "*required in persons grown in years* before they be baptized." Now certainly such repentance and faith cannot exist where there is no "*newness of life.*" And yet "*newness of life*" was before said to be given us of God *in Baptism*, together with remission of sins. Here then is the apparent contradiction. Newness of life granted in Baptism, and yet required as a preparation for Baptism. But there can be no newness of life without being born again of the Holy Ghost—spiritually regenerate. Therefore we have it in substance stated that "by Baptism we are born again" and yet before Baptism, and for it, we are required to be born again. How can these things be? Certainly there is no real contradiction. But where lies the explanation? This divinity can furnish none, since it supposes the faith that precedes Baptism to be not *living* because unbaptized, and so of course without spiritual newness of life. It is therefore essentially contradictory to the language we are attempting to explain. Where then is the solution? We answer, in the difference between the *sacramental*, and the *spiritual;* between receiving the body and blood of Christ *sacramentally*, that is, merely by the *signs*, which the wicked do, to their condemnation; and receiving the same *spiritually*, by faith of the heart, as the righteous do, and are nourished to their soul's health; between receiving "the washing of Regeneration" *sacramentally*, in the outward emblem of Baptism, and *spiritually*, in the faith of a contrite heart. Thus, when we speak *sacramentally*, it is right to say of those in general who are baptized, that in Baptism they are *born of God*, because then the profession of newness of life is made; then, the seal of the Church is set upon that profession; then the promises of God to those who embrace them are visibly pledged and assured; then the man is received into visible fellowship of the household of faith, and communion with the people of God. Then, therefore, his Christian life, as one of the children of God, visibly and professedly begins. It could not be known, and recognized, and spoken of, by the Church, till then; even though, before God, it was indeed begun. Most properly, therefore, is he said by the Church, speaking in reference to her Sacraments, to have then, in Baptism, received of God "*remission of sins and newness of life*," precisely as in the delivery of a deed, a man is said to have received the *conveyance* of an estate, which he has been long enjoying, and of which, before God, he had long been the rightful owner.

That such is the meaning of the apparently contradictory language of the Church, as expressed by the Catechism now in review, will be manifest from a few citations.

In answer to the question: "Do all generally and without difference receive this grace?" (viz., of Baptism) it is answered:

"The only faithful receive this fruit; but the unbelieving in refusing the promises offered them by God, shut up the entry against themselves and go away empty. Yet do they not thereby make that the Sacraments lose their force and efficacy."

So then we see that Baptism loses not its force and efficacy even where the receiver goes away *empty*. Why? Because its force and efficacy, as a Sacrament, are those of a visible sign and seal. These the unbeliever can receive, as truly as a believer, though to his greater condemnation. If the "force and efficacy" consisted in a spiritual regeneration and justification, how could the language of the above citation be explained? But again "*the only faithful receive this fruit.*" What fruit? The context says, *regeneration and the forgiveness of sins.* But who are the faithful? This word is exclusively used in the Catechism for the possessors of a *living* faith, as for example: "The true faith goeth further. For thus far, not only *ungodly* men, but also the very devils do believe; and therefore neither are they indeed *faithful, nor are so called.*" So that only they who come to Baptism with a living faith, receive regeneration and remission of sins. But even Oxford Divines will not pretend that living faith can be where regeneration and justification are not. So that it comes to this, that only those do receive regeneration and remission in Baptism, who have received them before. What can be the meaning, but that while the unbaptized adult, who truly repents and believes, *is* before God, spiritually regenerate and justified, so that, were he to die in that state, without any sinful neglect of Baptism, he would enter into full communion with the Israel of God, in the Church on high; yet in regard to the fellowship of the visible Church on earth, he cannot be *treated* as regenerate and justified till he has received the *sacramental sign and seal*, and made the visible profession of regeneration and remission of sins. To him, receiving that sign and seal of God's favor to the true believer, there will be given the witnessing Spirit, and grace to deepen his repentance and confirm his faith, so as to make the visible Sacrament fruitful, in a sense in which the ungodly cannot partake; though to them the Sacraments, in respect to their nature as signs and pledges, "lose not their force and efficacy."

Now let us, with these thoughts in remembrance, quote a little more of the Catechism under review.

"*Ma.* Do we not obtain forgiveness of sins by the outward washing of water?

"*Schol.* No. For only Christ hath with his blood washed and clean washed away the spot of our souls. This honor therefore it is unlawful to give to the outward element. But the Holy Ghost, as it were, sprinkling our consciences with that holy blood, wiping away all the spots of sin, maketh us clean before God. *Of this cleansing of our sins we have a seal and pledge in the Sacrament.*"

Here the Sacrament has assigned to it no connection with the remission of sins but as "*a seal and pledge.*" Thus it is that, by seal and pledge, God, in that ordinance, "delivereth unto us forgiveness of sins and newness of life." And therefore, in answer to the question, why God would have us use sacramental signs, the highest efficacy assigned to the Sacraments is expressed in the following extract:

"By this means therefore God hath provided for our weakness, that we which are earthly and blind, should in outward elements and figures, as it were in certain glasses, behold the heavenly graces, which otherwise we were not able to see. And greatly for our behoof it is, that God's promises should be so presented to our senses, that they may be confirmed to our minds without doubting.

"The Lord did furthermore ordain his mysteries to this end, that they should be certain marks and tokens of our profession: whereby we should, as it were, bear witness of our faith before men, and should plainly show that we are partakers of God's benefits with the rest of the godly, and that we have all one concord and consent of religion with them, and should openly testify, that we are not ashamed of the name of Christians, and to be called the disciples of Christ.

"To lighten and give bright clearness to men's minds and souls, and to make their consciences quiet and in security, as they be indeed, so ought they to be accounted the proper work of the Holy Ghost alone, and to be imputed to him, and this praise not to be transferred to any other. But this is no impediment but that God may give to his mysteries the second place in quieting and stablishing our minds and consciences, but yet so that nothing be abated from the virtue of his Spirit; wherefore we must determine that the outward element hath neither of itself nor in itself inclosed the force and efficacy of the Sacrament, but that the same wholly floweth from the Spirit of God, as out of a spring head, and is by the divine mysteries which are ordained by the Lord for this end, conveyed unto us.

"Whereas by nature we are the children of wrath, that is, strangers from the Church, which is God's household, Baptism is as it were, a certain entry by which we are received into the Church, whereof we also receive a most substantial testimony, that we are now in the number of the household, and also of the children of God; yea, and that we are joined and grafted into the body of Christ, and become his members, and so grow into one body with him.

"As the uncleannesses of the body are washed away with water, so the spots of the soul are washed away by forgiveness of sins. The beginning of regeneration, that is, the mortifying of our nature, is expressed by dipping in the water or sprinkling of it. Finally, when we by and by rise up again out of the water, under which we be for a short time, the new life, which is the other part, and the end of our regeneration, is thereby represented."—*Nowell's Catechism.*

The Catechism above quoted appeared in the time of Archbishop Whitgift, under the approval of the Convocation, and the sanction of the Archbishops and Bishops. Whitgift, in particular, (see next chap.) commended it as of eminent value. In connection with it, therefore, we will give the opinions of that learned divine, expressed in circumstances which required unusual care and accuracy.

The following passages, from his Defense against Cartwright, contain evidence of the doctrine of the Sacraments, as held in the Church of England, in that age, the more conclusive against the views of the Oxford divines, because the Archbishop was defending the Church against the accusation of the Puritans, that *she made too much of the outward Sacraments.* Had it been the doctrine of the Church, as then held, that Baptism does, *ipso facto*, really, and substantially, regenerate and justify, how, as an honest man could he have avoided its plain declaration? He defines the Sacraments as follows:

"Sacraments in the proper signification be mystical signs whereby he keepeth in man's memory and sometimes reneweth his large benefits bestowed on his Church; whereby also he sealeth or assureth his promises, and showeth outwardly, and as it were layeth before our eyes, those things to behold, which inwardly he worketh in us."

What does he work in us?

"Yea, by them he strengtheneth and increaseth our faith, by the Holy Ghost working in our hearts."

Thus a true and living faith is supposed to be already begun in our hearts before the Sacrament.

"And to be short, by his Sacraments, he separateth us from all other people, consecrating us and binding us to him only, and signifieth what he requireth of us to be done."—p. 618.

Then when the opponent had said that the doctrine of the Church "*attributed to the sign that which is proper to the work of God in the blood of Christ,*" Whitgift being now called to a full declaration of sacramental doctrine, answers:

"You know very well that we teach far otherwise, and that it is a certain and true doctrine of all such as profess the Gospel, that the outward signs of the Sacrament do not contain in them grace, neither yet that the grace of God is of necessity tied unto them, but only that they be seals of God's promises, notes of Christianity, testimonies and effectual signs of the grace of God, and of our redemption in Christ Jesus, by the which the Spirit of God doth invisibly work in us, not only the increase of faith, but the confirmation also."

Here is no *regeneration* of faith, to make it *alive*, but only its increase, and confirmation.

"You have learned that there is such a similitude between the signs and the thing signified, that they are in Scripture usually called by the names of those things whereof they be Sacraments, as bread, the body of Christ, and water, regeneration—and therefore Christ saith, 'Except a man be born of water,' &c.

"These things being considered, it is no superstitious toy, but a godly and true saying that Christ hath sanctified all water used in Baptism to the *mystical* washing away of sin; not ascribing washing away of sin to external element any otherwise than instrumentally, or in any other respect than for the similitude that Sacraments have with the things whereof they be Sacraments: for we know that wicked men may receive these external signs, and yet remain the members of Satan."—p. 738.

Thus does Whitgift deliver the highest doctrine of the efficacy of the Sacraments in his day. He takes it for granted, all the while, that the adult coming to Baptism has the faith of the heart, or a justifying faith. He ascribes no further operation to the grace of Baptism, than the increase and confirmation of such faith. Oxford Divines could not have written thus, especially in answer to Puritans.

The book of Haddon, against Osorius, in the age of Elizabeth, is called by Strype *a State Book*, and said by him to have been, next to Jewell's Apology, an authentic vindication of the Anglican Reformation. See next chapter, under head of Haddon and Foxe against Osorius.

"*You say our divines do place naked images instead of Sacraments.* How naked, my lord, I pray you? We do agree with St. Augustine, that Sacraments are signs of holy things: or thus, that Sacraments are visible signs of invisible grace. I trust you will permit me the same liberty of words, which you use to take to yourself. We do grant, that we are by Baptism regenerate to eternal life; we do also yield, that in the holy communion our Lord Jesus is truly received of the faithful in Spirit by faith; whereby it appeareth, that our divines do not account the Sacraments as bare naked signs, but for things most effectual, most holy, and things most necessarily appertaining to our comfort; they be sacred mysteries of our religion; they be assured pledges of heavenly grace; and yet God the Father, which made us of clay, is not tied to his workmanship, nor bound to his creatures; 'but taketh mercy of whom he will have mercy, and forgiveth our sins for his own sake, (Exod. xxxii. Rom. ix.) not for the Sacrament's sake.

"Lastly, 'Life everlasting is the gift of God through Jesus Christ' (Rom. vi.), not through operation of the Sacraments. And therefore we do refuse and detest such naked and falsely-forged images, as dreams of your own drowsy brains, and use the true Sacraments as most sacred things, as pledges of our faith, and seals of our salvation; and yet we do not attribute so much unto them, as though by the means of them the grace of God must of necessity be poured out upon us, by the *works wrought*, as through conduit pipes. This impiety we turn over to your schoolmen, the very first springs of this poison. 'For inheritance is given of faith according to grace.' (Rom. iv.)

"The Sacraments are reverend signs of God's grace unto us, are excellent monuments of our religion, and most perfect witnesses of our salvation. If you cannot be satisfied with these commendations of the Sacraments, heap you up more unto them at your choice, we shall be well pleased withal, so that you bind not the grace of God to the signs of very necessity. For we are not saved by the receiving of these Sacraments: 'But if we confess with our mouth our Lord Jesus Christ, and with our hearts believe that God raised him again from death' (Rom. x.), this confession only will save us."*

The force of these passages from Nowell's Catechism, and the contemporaneous divines, Whitgift and Haddon, is greatly illustrated and strengthened by the following declaration of John

---

* Haddon against Osorius, in Fathers of the Eng. Ch. v. viii. p. 234, 435.

Frith, one of the most learned Reformers. They are taken from his Mirror of Baptism, and being written expressly against the sacramental doctrines of the Romish Church, are the more to our present purpose. On the Baptism of Cornelius and his friends he says:

"Here you may see, that as the Spirit of God lighteth where he will, neither is he bound to any thing. Yea, and this example doth well declare unto us, that the Sacraments are given to be an outward witness unto the congregation of *that grace which is given before privately unto every man.*" "Baptism to the adult is an outward sign of his invisible faith which was before given him of God." "It giveth not grace, but doth testify unto the congregation that he which is baptized had such grace given before." "He is not a Christian man which is washed with water; neither is that Baptism (*effectually*) which is outward in the flesh; but that is the very Baptism which God alloweth, to be baptized spiritually in the heart, that is to subdue and weed out the branches of sin, &c., of which our Baptism is but a sign. And there are many, I doubt not, which are thus spiritually baptized, although their bodies touch no water, as there were Gentiles thus spiritually circumcised." "Thus is St. Paul to be understood when he saith, 'All ye that are baptized into Christ, have put on Christ;' that is, you have *promised* to die with Christ as touching your sins and worldly desires past, and to become new men, or new creatures or members of Christ. This have we all promised unto the congregation, and it is represented in our Baptism; for this cause it is called of Paul the fountain of the new birth and regeneration, because it signifieth that we will indeed renounce and utterly forsake our whole life—yea, it is a common phrase to call the Holy Ghost water and fire, because these two elements express so lively his purging operation."

"If thou be baptized a thousand times with water, and have no faith, it availeth thee no more towards God, than it doth a goose when she ducketh herself under the water. Therefore if thou wilt obtain the profit of Baptism, thou must have faith; that is, thou must be surely persuaded that *thou art* new born again—and that thy sins be not imputed thee, but forgiven through the blood and passion of Christ. This faith have neither devils, neither yet the wicked."

"Besides that Baptism is an outward figure or witness unto the congregation of the invisible promise given *before* by grace unto every private man, and by it doth the congregation receive him openly, to be counted one of them, which was *first* received *by faith*, or through the grace of the promise; also it putteth in remembrance, &c.—otherwise it giveth no grace, neither hath it any secret virtue."—*John Frith's Declaration of Baptism, Russell's Ed. pp.* 285—292.

Precisely according to the doctrine of the above citations is that of the eminent Reformer and holy Martyr, Bishop Hooper. In his "Confession of Christian Faith," he speaks of "three principal signs and marks" of the true Church, viz: "the word, the Sacraments and discipline." As to the efficacy of the *word* and Sacraments he puts the former at least upon a level with the latter. Of the Word, meaning, he says, that which is "contained within the canonical books of the Old and New Testaments," he says:

"By the which word we are made clean, and thereby do receive the self same thing, and *as much as we do by the Sacraments;* that is to say, Jesus Christ by his word, which is the word of faith; who giveth and communicateth himself unto us, as well as by the Sacraments, albeit it be by another manner and fashion."

Then of the Sacraments, which he has already said do communicate Christ only as does the word, but *"in another manner and fashion,"* he writes:

"I believe the Holy Sacraments to be the *signs* of the reconciliation and great atonement made between God and us, through Jesus Christ. They are *seals* of the Lord's promises, and are outward and visible *pledges and guages* of the inward faith—not void and empty signs but full: that is to say, they are not only signs, whereby something is signified, but also they are such signs as do exhibit and give the thing that they signify indeed."

"I believe that Baptism is the sign of the new league and friendship between God and us, made by Jesus Christ; and it is the mark of Christians, now in the time of the Gospel, *as in time past, Circumcision was a mark unto the Jews which were under the law.* Yea Baptism is *an outward washing down with water*, thereby signifying an inward washing of the Holy Ghost wrought through the blood of Christ. * * * I believe also that Baptism is the entry of the Church, a washing unto a new birth, and a renewing of the Holy Ghost, whereby we do forsake ourselves, the devil, the flesh, sin and the world."*

* Hooper's Works, vol. ii. pp. 45, 46.

Also in Hooper's other Tract entitled "A Godly Confession and Protestation of the Christian Faith," and dedicated to Edward VI., we read:

"Of Baptism, because it is the mark of our Christian Church, this I judge, that it is a seal and confirmation of justice or of our acceptation into the grace of God. For Christ's innocency and justice, *by faith*" (not by Baptism) "is ours, and our sins and injustice by his obedience are his, whereof Baptism is the sign, seal and confirmation. For although freely by the grace of God our sins be forgiven yet the same is declared by the Gospel, *received by faith and sealed by the Sacraments.*" *

The Reader will compare these last words, "*received by faith and sealed by the Sacraments,*" with those of our Oxford divines; viz., "Justification comes *through* the Sacraments, is received by faith." What then Bishop Hooper considers to be only *signed, sealed and confirmed* by the Sacraments, Oxford Divinity makes to come *through* the Sacraments, and in no other way. In Bishop Hooper's "Declaration of Christ," we read again:

"Although Baptism be a Sacrament to be received and honorably used of all men, *yet it sanctifieth no man*. And such as attribute the remission of sins unto the external sign do offend. * * * This new life cometh not until such times as Christ be known and received. Now to put on Christ is to live a new life. Such as be baptized must remember that repentance and faith preceded this external sign, and in Christ, the purgation was inwardly obtained, before the external sign was given. So that there are *two kinds of Baptism*, and both necessary. The one *interior* which is the cleansing of the heart, the drawing of the Father, the operation of the Holy Ghost; and *this Baptism is in man, when he believeth and trusteth that Christ is the only author of his salvation*. Thus be infants examined concerning repentance and faith, before they be baptized with water, at the contemplation of which faith, God purgeth the soul. Then is the external sign added, *not to purge the heart*, but to confirm, manifest and open unto the world that this child is God's."

No words could more plainly express that the Baptism of the Holy Ghost, where there is the repentance and faith required of

---

* Hooper's Works, vol. ii. p. 80.

the catechumen, *precedes* the Baptism of water. Of the latter, says Hooper, immediately after: "Though it have *no power to purge from sin*, yet it confirmeth the purgation of sin, and the act of itself pleaseth God, because the receivers thereof obey the will of his commandment." Then, to illustrate how truly one who repents and believes before Baptism, is a child of God, born of the Spirit, and justified in Christ, and how the addition of the *sacramental* regeneration and remission is only the addition of the symbol, the giving of the ring to the Abbot or the staff to the Magistrate, according to St. Bernard before cited, Hooper proceeds:

"Like as the King's Majesty that now is, immediately after the death of his father, was the true and legitimate King of England, and received his *Coronation*, not to make himself thereby king, *but to manifest that the kingdom appertained unto him before*. He taketh the crown to confirm his right and title. * * * Though this ceremony confirm and manifest a king in his kingdom, yet it maketh not a King. * * * The babe in the cradle hath as good a right and claim, and is as true a king in his cradle *uncrowned*, as his father was, though he reigned a crowned king forty years. * * * So it is in the Church of Christ; man is made the brother of Christ and heir of eternal life by God's only mercy, *received by faith, before he receive any ceremony to confirm and manifest openly his right and title*. * * * Thus assured of God and cleansed from sin in Christ, he hath the livery of God given unto him, *Baptism*,—the which no Christian should neglect; and yet not attribute his sanctification unto the external sign." *

On the identity of the Sacraments of the old and New Testaments, as to all spiritual efficacy, Bishop Hooper says:

"As for those that say circumcision and Baptism be like, and yet attribute the remission of original sin to Baptism, which was never given to circumcision, they not only destroy the *similitude and equality that should be between them*, but also take from Christ remission of sin and translate it unto the water and element of Baptism." "I believe that the holy fathers, Patriarchs, Prophets, and all the faithful and good people that are gone before us, and have died in the faith, through the word and faith, saw Him beforehand, which was to come, and received *as much and the same thing that we receive by the Sacraments*. For they were of the self-same Church,

* Works, vol. i. p. 75.

faith, and law that we be of. They were as well Christians as we, and used the same Sacraments in figure, that we use in truth."*

The necessary *precedence* of spiritual regeneration, before Baptism, where the required preparation in the adult is complied with, is thus stated by Dr. Hammond, in his Practical Catechism, one of the writers whom Oxford Divines are specially fond of quoting. Of Repentance, required before Baptism, he says it is "A change of mind or a conversion from sin to God. Not some one bare act of change, but a lasting durable state of new life, which I told you was called also *regeneration.*" Then when the scholar asks: "But, is not regeneration an act of new birth?" he answers:

"Not only that, but it is also the state of new life, (called the new creature,) living a godly life, &c. For the Scripture phrase, to be *regenerate*, or born again, or from above, is all one with being a child of God."†

Thus does this great writer not only discard the distinction so insisted on by the advocates of baptismal regeneration in the most literal sense, between regeneration, and renovation, but expressly declares that spiritual regeneration, or new birth, goes before Baptism, is every case in which there is the preparation required before Baptism.

We conclude our view of the doctrine of our Anglican Fathers by a most pointed passage from Bp. Latimer, the cotemporary of Cranmer, Ridley and Hooper, and like them, a faithful witness, sealing his testimony by martyrdom at the stake. Let it be borne in mind that, by the acknowledgment of our Oxford writers, there was no difference of opinion among the Anglican Reformers on the question now before us—the connection of the Sacrament of Baptism with spiritual Regeneration and Justification. What one taught, all substantially taught. Latimer's teaching therefore stands for all. The passage selected from his writings is as follows:

"The preaching of the Gospel is the power of God to every man that doth believe. Paul means God's word *opened* is the instrument, and the thing, whereby ye are saved. Beware, beware, that ye diminish not this office; for if ye do ye delay God's power to them that believe. Christ saith, consonant to the same, '*Except a man be born again he cannot see the kingdom of God.*' He must have a Regeneration. And what is this Regeneration?

---

* Works, vol. ii. pp. 87 and 50. † Hammond's Works, vol. i. p. 19.

It is not to be christened in water, as those firebrands do expound it, and nothing else. How is it to be expounded then? St. Peter showeth that one place of Scripture declareth another. It is the circumstance and collocation of places that make Scripture plain. Saith St. Peter, '*we be born again.*' How? *Not by a mortal seed, but by an immortal.* What is this immortal seed? '*By the word of the living God;*' by the word of God preached and opened. THUS COMETH IN OUR NEW BIRTH." *

Plainer evidence that the Reformers held no doctrine of baptismal efficacy like that of this divinity, could not be. Latimer laid down the great principle that our new birth comes by *hearing the word preached and opened*. But infants cannot do so, therefore infants were not spiritually born again by Baptism. Nor was Baptism the instrumental cause of the spiritual regeneration of *adults*, as they might receive the word preached in their hearts *before* Baptism; so might they be born again, before Baptism. As they might not so receive the word till long *after* Baptism, so might they not be born again. Those who held the inseparable connection of spiritual regeneration with the Sacrament of Baptism, Latimer called "*fire-brands.*" We know to whom he applied that name. He certainly did not mean by it his fellow Reformers. They and he were agreed in doctrine. He meant their Romish antagonists. Thus is the doctrine of the divinity before us, as to Baptismal Regeneration and Justification, branded by Latimer, speaking for the whole Anglican Reformation, more especially for those who had the chief hand in framing our doctrinal formularies, as that of their Romish antagonists, and consequently that of antagonists to our Protestant faith at this time, and co-workers with Rome.

We have now showed that the Oxford doctrine of the *opus operatum*, the absolute tying of justification to Baptism, while it is precisely the doctrine of Rome, is not that of the Anglican Church, whose language in her standard documents, as well as that of her standard writers, must be otherwise interpreted.

It has appeared also that not only is there in every adult duly prepared for Baptism, the reality of spiritual regeneration and remission of sins before the administration; but that after it, if the preparation was not in true repentance and faith, though there would be a *sacramental*, there would be as the result of the Sacrament, no *spiritual*, regeneration.

* Works, vol. i. p, 202.

In having thus showed that *adult* Baptism is not always connected with spiritual regeneration, the same is showed concerning *infant* Baptism, since there is not a line in the Scriptures, nor in the articles or other standard documents of the Church in regard to the spiritual efficacy of the one, which does not alike apply to the other. And indeed the true way to get at the nature and benefits of infant Baptism is to begin with that of adults, since it is to them that all the Baptisms specifically mentioned in the Scriptures belong. The language of the New Testament therefore with reference to Baptism, belongs exclusively to that of adults.*

Were we writing a full account of Baptism, we should not cease till we had gone far into the great value of infant Baptism to families, to the Church, and to the children individually; we should speak strongly of the great need of a much higher and more solemn sense of the privileges and duties of parents, in regard to their children in this respect; we should urge more faith in God's blessing, in the Baptism of our children, and as a consequence of it, after their Baptism, if we duly wait upon him for it. We should urge that the remedy of the present lamentable deficiency would be, not in a higher sense of the efficacy of the Sacrament *itself*, but of its obligation and privilege as an appointed and precious divine mode of bringing little children to Christ, of putting them into his arms, of supplicating his blessing upon them, of consecrating them to his service, of expressing our determination to seek for them first the kingdom of God and his righteousness, and of sealing their covenant membership in the Commonwealth of Israel.

* For a complete view of the testimony of the Anglican Reformers and great divines on the subject of Baptismal Regeneration, the reader can look no where to such advantage as to the elaborate work of the Rev. William Goode, now Dean of Ripon, entitled " *The doctrine of the Church of England as to the effects of Baptism in the case of Infants,*" 1 vol. 8vo. The very best thing in smaller compass, and in a form obtainable by all, is a late work, of a hundred closely printed pages, by the Editor of the Southern Churchman, in answer to Bishop Whittingham, called "The Doctrine of Baptismal Regeneration as held by Cranmer, Latimer and Ridley, and as taught in the Book of Common Prayer ;" a most searching, discriminating, careful, accurate and able exhibition of the truth. It ought to be widely circulated. (1861.)

CHAPTER XI.

THE DOCTRINE OF THIS DIVINITY AS TO THE RIGHTEOUSNESS OF JUSTIFICATION AND THE OFFICE OF FAITH, COMPARED WITH THAT OF STANDARD DIVINES OF THE ANGLICAN CHURCH.

Majorities in such a question of no avail—Laud's testimony—Divines of the 17th Century especially relied on by the Oxford writers.—The same mainly employed in this Chapter—Testimony of Oxford writers to the eminent authority of Hooker—His views acknowledged to be in entire opposition to those of this divinity on Justification—Force of the confession—Singular attempt to escape its force—Citations from Hooker—Tyndale—Barnes—Cranmer—Bishop Hooper—Bishop Latimer—Edward VI. Catechism—Confession of Martyrs and Divines in Prison—Nowell's Catechism—Haddon and Foxe against Osorius—Perkins—Bishop Downame—Bishop Andrews—Mede—Bishop Hall—Bishop Nicholson—Archbishop Usher—Bishop Hopkins—Bishop Beveridge.

OUR Oxford writers, in appealing to the doctrines of the Anglican Divines, as agreeing with their own, speak of *majorities*. As for example: "The Anglican doctrine (of justification) or that which we conceive to have been the teaching of a *majority* of our Church."* Their own favorite, Archbishop Laud, would have taught them how little is gained in favor of a doctrine when it has gained a majority. Fisher the Jesuit pleaded *majority*. Laud answered: "As for the number and worth of men, they are no necessary concluders for truth. *Not number;* for who would be judged by the many? The time was when the Arians were too many for the orthodox." †

The time may be when there shall hardly be "found faith in the earth." The majority will be fearfully against it: but a faithful remnant will stand fast in their noble minority. Who does not know that one such name as that of Hooker is worth ten thousand of lesser note, in proof of the doctrines of the Church in his day, as handed down from the Reformers? Who knows not that in the question, what is the doctrine of the Articles and Homilies of the Anglican Church, one plain testimony from Cranmer and his colleagues, by whom those instruments were constructed, is worth

---

* Pusey's Letter, p. 46. † Conference with Fisher, p. 302.

all that could be collected from the writings of all the Non-jurors of 1688, and of those their contemporaries whom our Oxford Divines are so fond of quoting?

In citing the Anglican Divines, we shall proceed on the principle of selection furnished in Tract, No. 71, p. 29, where it is said that the Divines of the 17th century are considered as distinctly propounding and supporting the doctrines of the Fathers. "Nor could a more acceptable or important service be done to our Church at the present moment, than the publication of some systematic introduction to theology, embodying and illustrating the great and concordant principles and doctrines set forth" by those divines. We take for granted that this passage of the Tract is meant only to place the divines of the 17th Century in a place of preference as authorities, above those of the following Century. Certainly it could not have been intended that writers of the previous Century, cotemporaneous with the framers of the Articles and Homilies, and some of them those framers themselves, should not be considered as at least as good expounders of those documents as men of a subsequent period. If it be true that the Fathers who lived nearest the Apostolic age are worthy of special deference when they testify to the doctrine of the Apostles; for the same reason must we conclude that, in the question, what doctrines the Articles and Homilies were designed to teach; the most direct appeal is to the writings of those who lived nearest to the days of their composers. Beginning therefore with the Reformers, we shall not descend lower than those writers of the 17th Century, whom the Oxford Tracts have pronounced to be of such special value in ascertaining the doctrines of the Church.

But there is one writer whose testimony may be considered as of such final authority upon this question, by the acknowledgment of Oxford divines themselves, or of those who belong to that school, that we might be justified in going no further than his writings. We mean the judicious Hooker.

"Of honored names (says Dr. Hook) the Church of England holds none more highly in honor than that of the judicious Hooker." *

Adopting the language of Wordsworth's biography, the same writer proceeds :

* Call to Union, p. 70.

"Hooker may justly be regarded as the genuine lineal descendant of the most enlightened English Reformers : and possessing learning equal to any of them, with more opportunities of meditation and the accumulated advantage of their labors and experience, he may perhaps not improperly be considered as exhibiting in his writings a model of the true, settled, most approved, mature and Catholic principles of the English Reformation."

Now it is not pretended by these Divines that this most eminent authority was of the same mind with themselves, on the question of justifying righteousness, whether it be *inherent* or *imputed.* On this fundamental point of their whole system it is granted, in Mr. Keble's introduction to his late edition of Hooker's works, and by Mr. Newman, in the appendix to his Lectures on Justification, that Hooker's sentiments were wholly contrary to theirs. But this confession is worth a little attention. They quote from Hooker on Justification the passage :

"The Romanists profess that they seek salvation no other way than by the blood of Christ ; and that humbly they do use prayers, fastings, alms, faith, charity, sacrifice, Sacraments, priests, only as the means appointed by Christ, to apply the benefit of His holy blood unto them ; touching our good works, that in their own natures, they are not meritorious, nor answerable to the joys of heaven ; it cometh of the grace of Christ, and not of the work itself, that we have by well doing a right to heaven and deserve it worthily. If any man think that I seek to varnish their opinions, to set the better foot of a lame cause foremost, let him know that since I began thoroughly to understand their meaning, I have found their halting greater than perhaps it seemeth to them which know not the deepness of Satan, as the Blessed Divine speaketh."

"This passage," (Mr. Newman says) "it must be candidly confessed, is by implication contrary to the sentiments maintained in the foregoing pages," i. e. in his Lectures on Justification, the authentic voucher for this system on that subject. Now what is the scope of this passage of Hooker ? He had been all along charging the Church of Rome with perverting the truth of Christ, and overthrowing the foundations of the Faith, by making the justification of the sinner to rest upon the merits of his own works ; and this charge he grounded, not upon their express pretense of meritorious obedience, but upon their making justification to consist in a righteousness *within us,* and therefore our *own* as much as our souls are our own.* Then in the above passage, he adverts also to their strong professions of *not* considering their own works as meritorious, but of seeking all merit in Christ. But those professions did not in the least diminish the weight of Hooker's condemnation. Deny the ascription of merit to their own righteousness, as they pleased, he still regarded their system as founded on the basis of a meritorious obedience of their own. Therefore said he, "I have found their halting greater than perhaps it seemeth to them which know not the deepness of Satan. If there were no other leaven in the lump of their doctrine but this, this were sufficient to prove that their doctrine is not agreeable to the foundation of Christian faith." Renounce the idea of a self-meritorious obedience as they would, this leaven of our own righteousness for justification, he considered the same thing as acknowledging that "we have received *the power of meriting,* by the blood of Christ," and thus he regarded the Church of Rome as "*an adversary to the merits of Christ.*"

Now it is where Hooker is expressing such strong condemnation of Romanism, that he is confessed by Mr. N. to be contrary to the sentiments of his Lectures, which is no less than the acknowledgment that the whole stress of Hooker's Discourse on Justification is contrary to his Lectures, since it is all upon the same principle. Here then we have the confession that the words which Hooker wrote expressly against Romanism are applicable also to this system; that where he charges the doctrine of human merit upon the Romish system, in spite of the declarations of Romanists that they ascribe all merit to Christ, he would alike ascribe the same to the Oxford system, in spite of the similar protestations of Oxford Divines; inasmuch as in one system as well as the other, the basis of Justification is our own righteousness. Consequently it is acknowledged that what Hooker said of the Romish, he would equally say of the Oxford doctrine, that it "*perverts the truth of Christ;*" is "*an adversary to Christ's merits,*" and "*overthroweth the foundation of the Faith.*"

The mode by which Mr. Newman attempts to do away the effect of Hooker's opposition, is too curious not to be noticed. Having confessed the contrariety of Hooker's doctrine, he says:

"It does not avail in the least as authority against them (the

* Disc. of Justif. § 6.

doctrines of his own Lectures) for the following plain reason: because this great author, in the very treatise in which he so speaks, *confesses he is not acquiescing in the theology of the early Church.*"

Who would not suppose, from this bold assertion, that Hooker had indeed confessed that on the subject of justification, (which is the whole subject of his Discourse, and especially of the passage alluded to by Mr. N.) he is not in agreement with the ancient and universal Church? It is startling indeed to hear thus of a divine so praised by these same writers, for his Catholic doctrines; and when he is in the very act of defending the doctrines of a Church, which expressly claims the consent of "*all old and ancient doctors of Christ's Church, both Greeks and Latins.*" The reader will be amazed to see in what the confession consists. The passage extracted from Hooker, as containing it, is the following:

"The heresy of free-will was a mill-stone about the Pelagians' neck: shall we therefore give sentence of death inevitable against all those Fathers in the Greek Church, which, being misdirected, died in the error of free-will?"

But by what process does Mr. N. make out from this passage that Hooker *confessed* that his views of Justification were diverse from those of the early Church? Thus:

"The doctrines of grace and justification are too closely connected to allow of a treatise judging rightly of the importance of questions concerning the latter, which is not to be followed in its view of the former." *

The reasoning then is this: because Hooker considered *some* Fathers of the Greek Church to be infected with errors concerning *free-will;* therefore we are to consider him as *plainly confessing* that he differed with those Fathers concerning the *righteousness of Justification*. But Hooker speaks only of *some* Greek Fathers. Yes, but Mr. N. says: "To accuse a *number* of Greek Fathers of mistake, is to accuse *all*." Well, but should we grant even that, still he only accuses the *Greek* Fathers, not the whole Catholic Church. But, says Mr. N.: "To accuse the Greek Fathers is virtually to oppose the *whole Catholic Church.*" It comes to this; to accuse *some* of the Greek Fathers of error, is to accuse the whole Catholic Church of error. To confess that we differ from some

---

* Newman's Lectures, pp, 442, 443.

Greek Fathers on *free-will*, is a plain confession that we differ from the whole Catholic consent, both Latin and Greek, on *justification!* Thus the authority of Hooker, against Oxford doctrine, is made of no account! Let us see how such reasoning will answer! It is common for the Tract Divines to acknowledge some things to have been believed by *some* Fathers, and not by the whole Church; and therefore to be not of *Catholic* verity. Thus they accuse some Fathers of error. But to accuse some, according to Mr. N. is to accuse all; therefore their own opinions, where they are opposed to the *some*, are opposed to all, and of no manner of avail. This is a singular illustration of what the Oxford Doctrine of Tradition comes to, and what a nose of wax it is when they find it convenient to elongate or depress it, for the sake of ruling out of court an unacceptable witness.

Such then being Hooker's acknowledged doctrine, and such the acknowledged eminence of his authority, we will station our citations from him as a sort of center around which shall be assembled those of the age immediately before him, with such as we shall produce from the 17th Century; thus obtaining the evidence that, what Hooker so earnestly maintained as the doctrine of the Anglican Church, was universally received among the great lights of that Church, from the Reformation to his day, and for a long time after he had gone to his rest.

In all the passages to be produced in this Chapter, the reader will note the bearing on the following fundamental points.

1. That the righteousness by which we are Justified before God is no other than the Righteousness of Christ, *external* to us and *imputed*.

2. That the only means whereby we apply, embrace, or apprehend that righteousness, is a living faith; no external ordinance, no internal grace, having any part with faith in its office of justifying.

3. That in this office, faith acts, not as having in itself any justifying virtue or quality, nor as it stands for obedience and all religion, but only *relatively* and *instrumentally*, as the hand by which we put on the righteousness of Christ.

With these points in view, we will cite from Hooker's Ecclesiastical Polity, his Discourse on Justification, and his Sermons on St. Jude.

HOOKER.

"Thus we participate Christ, partly by imputation, as when those things which he did and suffered for us *are imputed unto us for righteousness;* partly by habitual and real infusion, as when grace is inwardly bestowed while we are on earth, and afterwards more fully, both our souls and bodies made like unto his in glory. * * * That wherein we are partakers of Jesus Christ by imputation agreeth equally unto all that have it. For it consisteth in such acts and deeds of his, as could not have longer continuance than while they were in doing, nor at that very time belong unto any other, but to him from whom they come; and therefore, how men, either then, or before, or since, should be made partakers of them, *there can be no way imagined, but only by imputation.*"—*Eccl. Pol. l. v.* § 56.

"Christ hath merited righteousness for as many as are found in him. In him God findeth us if we be faithful; for by faith we are incorporated into Christ. Then, although in ourselves we be altogether sinful and unrighteous, yet even the man which is impious in himself, full of iniquity, full of sin; him being found in Christ through faith, and having his sin remitted through repentance; him God beholdeth with a gracious eye, putteth away his sin by not imputing it, taketh quite away the punishment due thereunto, by pardoning it, and accepteth him in Jesus Christ, as perfectly righteous, as if he had fulfilled all that was commanded him in the Law; shall I say more perfectly righteous, than if himself had fulfilled the whole Law? I must take heed what I say: but the Apostle saith, '*God made him to be sin for us, who knew no sin, that we might be made the righteousness of God in him.*' Such we are in the sight of God the Father, as is the very Son of God himself. Let it be counted folly, or frenzy, or fury, whatsoever, it is our comfort and our wisdom; we care for no knowledge in the world but this, that man hath sinned and God hath suffered; that God hath made himself the Son of Man, and that men are made the righteousness of God. You see, therefore, that the Church of Rome, in teaching justification by inherent Grace, doth pervert the truth of Christ; and that by the hands of the Apostles we have received otherwise than she teacheth. Now concerning the righteousness of sanctification, we deny it not to be inherent; we grant that unless we work, we have it not; only we distinguish it as a thing different in nature from the righteousness of justification; we are righteous the one way by the faith of Abraham; the other way, except we do the works of Abraham, we are not righteous. Of the one, St. Paul, '*To him that worketh not, but believeth, faith is accounted for righteousness;*' of the other St. John, *Qui facit justitiam, justus est.* 'He is righteous which worketh righteousness.' Of the one, St. Paul doth prove by Abraham's example, that we have it of faith without works; of the other, St.

James by Abraham's example, that by works we have it, and not only by faith. St. Paul doth plainly sever these two parts of Christian righteousness one from the other. For in the sixth to the Romans, thus he writeth, '*Being freed from sin, and made servants to God, ye have your fruit in holiness, and the end everlasting life.*' '*Ye are made free from sin, and made servants unto God;*' this is the righteousness of justification; '*Ye have your fruit in holiness;*' this is the righteousness of sanctification. By the one we are interested in the right of inheriting; by the other we are brought to the actual possession of eternal bliss, and so the end of both is everlasting life." *Discourse on Justification*, § 6.

"We ourselves do not teach Christ alone, excluding our own faith, unto justification; Christ alone, excluding our own works, unto sanctification; Christ alone, excluding the one or the other unnecessary unto salvation. It is a childish cavil wherewith in the matter of justification our adversaries do so greatly please themselves, exclaiming, that we tread all Christian virtues under our feet, and require nothing in Christians but faith; because we teach that faith alone justifieth; whereas by this speech we never meant to exclude either Hope or Charity from being always joined as inseparable mates with faith in the man that is justified; or works from being added as necessary duties, required at the hands of every justified man; but to show that faith is the only hand which putteth on Christ unto justification; and Christ the only garment, which being so put on, covereth the shame of our defiled natures, hideth the imperfection of our works, preserveth us blameless in the sight of God, before whom otherwise the weakness of our faith were cause sufficient to make us culpable, yea, to shut us from the kingdom of heaven, where nothing that is not absolute can enter." § 31.

"*Imputation* of righteousness hath covered the sins of every soul which believeth; God by pardoning our sin hath taken it away: so that now although our transgressions be multiplied above the hairs of our head, yet being justified, we are as free and as clear as if there were no spot or stain of any uncleanness in us. For it is God that justifieth; '*And who shall lay any thing to the charge of God's chosen?*' saith the Apostle in Rom. viii. 33.

"Now sin being taken away, we are made the righteousness of God in Christ: for David, speaking of this righteousness, saith, '*Blessed is the man whose iniquities are forgiven.*' No man is blessed, but in the righteousness of God; every man whose sin is taken away is blessed: therefore every man, whose sin is covered, is made the righteousness of God in Christ. This righteousness doth make us to appear most holy, most pure, most unblamable before him.

"This then is the sum of that which I say; *faith doth justify;* justification washeth away sin; sin removed, we are clothed with the righteousness which is of God; the righteousness of God maketh us most holy. Every of these I have proved by the testimony of God's own mouth; therefore I conclude, that faith is that which maketh us most holy, in consideration whereof it is called in this place *our most holy faith.*

"To make a wicked and a sinful man most holy through *his believing* is more than to create a world of nothing. Our souls most holy! Surely, Solomon could not show the Queen of Sheba so much treasure in all his kingdom, as is lapt up in these words. O that our hearts were stretched out like tents, and that the eyes of our understanding were as bright as the sun, that we might thoroughly know the riches of the glorious inheritance of the saints, and what is the exceeding greatness of his power towards us, whom he accepteth for pure, and most holy, through our believing! O that the Spirit of the Lord would give this doctrine entrance into the stony and brazen heart of the Jew; which followeth the law of righteousness, but cannot attain unto the righteousness of the law! Wherefore, saith the Apostle, They seek righteousness, and not by faith; wherefore they stumble at Christ, they are bruised, shivered to pieces, as a ship that hath run herself upon a rock. O that God would cast down the eyes of the proud, and humble the souls of the high-minded! that they might at length abhor the garments of their own flesh, which cannot hide their nakedness, and put on the faith of Christ Jesus, as he did put it on which hath said, "*Doubtless I think all things but loss, for the excellent knowledge-sake of Christ Jesus my Lord, for whom I have counted all things loss, and do judge them to be dung, that I might win Christ, and might be found in him, not having my own righteousness which is of the law, but that which is through the faith of Christ, even the righteousness which is of God through faith.*" *Second Sermon St. Jude,* §§ 24—28.

We have said before, that the contrariety of Hooker's doctrine of justification to that of the Oxford School is granted by the leading men of that fraternity. But, as if his Discourse on Justification were the only work in which Hooker has bequeathed his doctrine on that subject, we find in Mr. Newman and Mr. Keble, an attempt to evade his testimony in that which cannot go unnoticed. "There is enough (says Mr. N.) in Hooker's writings and history to show that this valuable treatise, written before his views were fully matured, and published after his death, is not to be taken in all points as authority."* In the same strain, writes Mr. Keble in his Edition of Hooker's Work. "Hooker's compositions upon this subject" (justification,) "are mostly of an early date, when he hardly seems to have acquired that independence of thought which appears in the Polity."

Thus it is attempted to take away the strong testimony of "the glory of the English Priesthood," by the consideration that he delivered it in immaturity of mind. But let us hear another writer, whose assertions. if his name be not as well known as that of Mr. Newman or Mr. Keble, are too undeniable to need the weight of any name. Speaking of Hooker's Discourse on Justifcation, he says:

"It was written upon a most important occasion, under circumstances which rendered it necessary to bestow the most careful consideration upon every word, was elaborated with the utmost sedulity, and transcribed by the author himself, for the purpose of having it attentively examined by his friends. So far from betraying any symptoms of a *dependent* mind, it was composed in defense of what some of the greatest theologians of the time were startled at as a novel and dangerous paradox; (but having no reference to the present question) and it is inferior to none of his other writings in originality of conception, vigor of thought, and energy of diction. But suppose that this sermon actually was written before its author was quite out of leading strings, is there any evidence to show that in this particular his more robust judgment corrected the weak conclusions of the youth? Not a particle. On the contrary, in the very latest legacy which he bequeathed to the Church, the Fragment of a reply to 'The Christian Letter,' (vol. ii. p. 700 et seq. of Keble's Edition) *he has incorporated an abstract of this very sermon, and repeated almost in the same words, his former profession of belief in the imputation of Christ's righteousness and the justification of sinners by faith only.*" *

With the foregoing citations from Hooker, which might be greatly multiplied, we consider the question as to the conformity

* Lectures on Justif. p. 443.

* Episcopacy, Tradition and the Sacraments, by Rev. W. Fitzgerald, B. A.

of the Oxford views of justification and of faith, with those of the Anglican Church, to be really settled; for it is out of the question to suppose him to have been the divine they say he was, and yet to have been so egregiously mistaken upon the most important features of Church doctrine, as he must have been, if the doctrines of the above extracts were not those of the Church for which he was writing.

But we proceed to show how very prominently and earnestly and generally these same views were professed and urged by the Reformers before him.

TYNDALE, REFORMER AND MARTYR.

"In opening the Scriptures (says Foxe of Tyndale) what truth, what soundness can a man require more, or what more is to be said than is to be found in Tyndale? Not unrightly he might be then, as he is yet called, the Apostle of England, for as the Apostles in the primitive age first planted the Church in truth of the Gospel; so the same truth being again decayed and defaced by enemies in this our latter time, there was none that travailed more earnestly in restoring the same in this realm of England than did William Tyndale."

"When I say faith justifieth, the understanding is, that faith receiveth the justifying. God promiseth to forgive us our sins and to impute us for full righteous. And God justifieth us actively; that is to say, forgiveth us and reckoneth us for full righteous. And Christ's blood deserveth it, faith in the promise receiveth it, and certifieth the conscience thereof. Faith challengeth it for Christ's sake, which hath deserved all that is promised, and cleaveth ever to the promise and truth of the promiser, and pretendeth not the goodness of her work, but acknowledgeth that our works deserve it not, but are crowned and rewarded with the deservings of Christ. * * * Our works which God commendeth, and unto which he annexed his promises that he will reward them, are as it were very Sacraments, and visible and sensible signs, tokens, earnest obligations, witnesses, testimonies, and a sure certifying of our souls, that God hath and will do according to his promise, to strengthen our weak faith, and to keep the promise in mind. But they justify us not, no more than the visible works of the Sacraments do. As for example, the work of Baptism, that outward washing, which is the visible Sacrament or sign, justifieth us not. But God only justifieth us actively, as cause efficient or workman. God promiseth to justify whosoever is baptized to believe in Christ, and to keep the law of God, that is to say, to forgive them their fore-sins and to impute righteousness unto them, to take them for his sons and to love them as well as though they were full righteous. Christ hath deserved us that promise and that righteousness. And *faith doth receive it, and God doth give it and impute it to faith, and not to the washing.* And the washing doth testify it and certify us of it, as the Pope's letters do certify the believers of the Pope's pardons. Now the letters help not nor hinder, but that the pardons were as good without them as with them, save only to establish weak souls that could not believe, except they read the letters, looked on the seal, and saw the print of St. Peter's keys."—*Tyndale's Expositions*, pp. 90, 91.

"Hereof ye see that I cannot be justified without repentance, and yet repentance justifieth me not. And hereof ye see, that I cannot have a faith to be justified and saved except love spring thereof immediately; and yet love justifieth me not before God. * * * And when we say, faith only justifieth, that is to say, receiveth the mercy wherewith God justifieth us and forgiveth us, we mean not faith which hath no repentance, and faith which hath no love unto the laws of God again and unto good works, as wicked hypocrites falsely belie us. * * * Hereof ye see what faith it is that justifieth us.—The faith in Christ's blood, of a repenting heart towards the law doth justify us only, and not all manner of faiths. * * * We make good works sure tokens whereby we know that our faith is no feigned imagination and dead opinion, made with captivating our wits after the Pope's traditions, but a lively thing wrought by the Holy Ghost. * * * And when Paul saith '*faith only justifieth*,' and James, that '*a man is justified by works, and not by faith only*,' there is a great difference between Paul's *only* and James' *only*. For Paul's *only* is to be understood that faith justifieth in the heart and before God without help of works, yea, and ere I can work. For I must receive life, through faith, to work with, ere I can work. But James' *only* is this wise to be understood that faith doth not so justify that nothing justifieth save faith. *For deeds do justify also. But faith justifieth in the heart before God, and the deeds before the world only, and make the other seem.*"—*Tyndale's Answer to Sir Thomas More*, pp. 196—202.

ROBERT BARNES, D. D., REFORMER AND MARTYR.

This Reformer is one of the three, Tyndale and Frith being the others, whom Foxe calls "chief ringleaders" of the English

Reformation. They "sustained the first brunt, and gave the first onset against the enemies." Bishop Bale, a learned and zealous cotemporary Reformer, in his *Catalogus Scriptorum illustrium Britanniarum*, says of him that "with great firmness and sincerity, he maintained the justification of a sinner through faith alone, in the work of Christ our Saviour, against the ungodly preachers of human works." He was martyred by fire in 1541. In answer to the argument that "faith is a work, but works do not justify; therefore faith doth not justify," he says:

"Truth it is, that we do not mean, how that faith for his own dignity, and for his own perfection, doth justify us. But the Scripture doth say, that faith alone justifieth, because that it is that thing alone, whereby I do hang on Christ. And by my faith alone am I partaker of the merits and mercy purchased by Christ's blood: and faith it is alone that receiveth the promises made in Christ. Wherefore we say with blessed St. Paul, that faith *only* justifieth *imputatively;* that is, all the merits and goodness, grace and favor, and all that is in Christ to our salvation, *are imputed and reckoned unto us because we hang and believe on him,* and he can deceive no man that doth believe in him. And our justice is not (as the Schoolmen teach) a *formal justice* which is, by fulfilling of the law, deserved of us; for then our justification were not of grace and of mercy, but of deserving and of duty. But it is a justice that is reckoned and imputed unto us, for the faith in Christ Jesus, and it is not of our deserving, but clearly and fully of mercy imputed to us.

"Then cometh my Lord of Rochester (Fisher, Romish Bishop of Rochester) and he saith, that faith doth begin a Justification in us, but works do perform it and make it perfect. I will recite his own words: 'Justification is said to be begun only by faith, but not to be consummated, for consummate justification can no otherwise be attained than by works, wrought and brought forth to light.'"

This is precisely the Oxford doctrine, of Justification increasing according to the degrees of sanctification—or of Fides Formata, faith made perfect by love and other works, and, through them, justifying.

"What christened man (says Barnes) would think that a Bishop could thus trifle and play with God's holy word! God's word is so plain, that no man can avoid it, how that faith justifieth alone: and now cometh my Lord of Rochester, with a little and vain distinction invented of his own brain, without authority of Scripture, and will clearly avoid all Scripture. But, my Lord, say to me of your conscience, how do you reckon to avoid the vengeance of God since you thus trifle and despise God's holy word? Doth not St. Paul say that our Justification is alone of faith, and not of works? How can you avoid this same, *Non ex operibus?* (not of works: Eph. 2.) If that works do make justification perfect, then are not St. Paul's words true; also St. Paul saith, that 'we are the children of God by faith.' And if we are the children, we are also the heirs. Now what imperfection find you in children and in heirs? Christian men desire no more but this, and all this they have by faith only. And will you say that faith doth but begin a justification?"—*Treatise on Justification, entitled " Only Faith justifieth before God." Fathers of the English Church*, vol. v. pp. 577 and 587.

BISHOP HOOPER, REFORMER AND MARTYR.

"In his doctrine (says Foxe) he was earnest, in tongue eloquent, in the Scriptures perfect, in pains indefatigable." "Of all those qualities required of St. Paul in a good Bishop, I know not one in this good Bishop lacking." In citing from Hooper, we have the advantage of virtually citing the contemporaneous Reformer and Martyr, Bishop Ridley, inasmuch as while both were in prison, for the testimony of Jesus, the latter wrote to Hooper in these words: "Forasmuch as I understand by your works, that we *thoroughly agree and wholly consent together in those things which are the grounds and substantial points of our religion*, against the which the world doth so furiously rage in these our days," &c. Thus then writes Hooper, in his " Declaration of Christ," of Justification:—

"St. Paul when he saith that we be justified by faith, meaneth that we have remission of sin, reconciliation, and acceptance into the favor of God. * * * To be justified by faith in Christ, is as much as to say, we obtain remission of sin, and are accepted into the favor of God by the merits of Christ. To be justified by works, is as much as to say, to *deserve* remission of sin by works.* Faith doth not only show us Christ that died and now sitteth

---

* According to Oxford doctrine we are justified by our *obedience* or *works.* Hooper says, this is to say that we *deserve* remission of sin. So that while the Oxford system rejects merit in the *name*, it espouses it in the *thing.*

at the right hand of God, but also *applieth* the merits of this death unto us, and maketh Christ ours." (Oxford Divinity says Baptism, not faith, does this.) * * * "It disputeth not what virtues it bringeth to claim this promise of mercy; but forsaking her own justice, offereth Christ dead upon the cross, and sitting at God's right hand. It maketh nothing to be the *cause*, wherefore this mercy should be given, saving only the death of Christ, which is the only sufficient price and guage for sin. And although it be necessary that in the justification of a sinner, contrition be present, and that necessarily charity and virtuous life must *follow:* yet doth the Scripture attribute the only remission of sin unto the mercy of God, which is given only for the merits of Christ and *received solely by faith.* Paul doth not exclude these virtues to be present, but he excludeth the merit of those virtues, and deriveth the cause of our acceptation into the grace of God, only for Christ. And mark this manner of speech: '*Fide justificamur;*' hoc est, fiducia misericordiæ sumus justi. This word faith, doth comprehend as well persuasion and confidence, that the promise of God appertaineth unto us, for Christ's sake, as the knowledge of God. For faith, though it desire the company of contrition and sorrow for sin, yet contendeth it not in judgment upon the merits of any works, but only for the merits of Christ's death. We must therefore only trust to the merits of Christ, which satisfied the extreme jot and uttermost point of the law for us. *And this his justice and perfection, he imputeth and communicateth to us by faith.* Such as say that faith *only* justifieth not, because other virtues be present, they cannot tell what they say. Every man that will have his conscience appeased must mark these two things, *how* remission of sin is obtained, and *wherefore* it is obtained. Faith is the *means* whereby it is obtained, and the cause *wherefore* it is received is the merits of Christ. Although faith be the *means* whereby it is received, yet hath neither faith, nor charity, nor contrition, nor the word of God, nor all those knit together, sufficient merits *wherefore* we should obtain remission of sin. Let the man burst his heart with contrition, believe that God is good a thousand times, and burn in charity, yet shall not all these satisfy the law, nor deliver man from the ire of God, till such time as faith letteth fall all hope and confidence in the merits of such virtues as be in man, and say, 'Lord, behold thy unfruitful servant; only for the merits of Christ's blood give me remission of sins.'" * * * "As the fathers of the old Church used the serpent, so must those of our Church use the precious body of Christ. They looked upon him (the serpent) only with the eyes of faith, they kissed him not, they touched him not with their hands, they ate him not corporeally nor really, nor substantially; yet by their belief, they obtained health. So Christ himself teacheth us the use of his precious body; to believe and look upon the merits of his passion suffered upon the cross, and so to use his precious body against the sting of original and actual sin; not to eat his body transformed into the form of bread, or *in* the bread, *with* the bread, *under* the bread, *behind* the bread, or *before* the bread, corporally or bodily, substantially or really, invisible, or any such ways, as many men, to the great injury of Christ's body, do teach."

"They that will justify themselves any other way than by faith, do doubt always whether their sins be forgiven or not; and by reason of this doubt they can never pray unto God aright."—*Works*, vol. i. pp. 49—56.

BISHOP LATIMER, REFORMER AND MARTYR.

Christ was "a Lamb undefiled, and therefore suffered not for his own sake, and with his suffering hath taken away all our sins and wickedness, and hath made us, which were the children of the devil, the children of God, fulfilling the law for us to the uttermost, *giving us freely, as a gift, his fulfilling to be ours*. So that we are now fulfillers of the law by his fulfilling, so that the law may not condemn us. For he hath fulfilled it, so that we believing in him, are fulfillers of the law, and just before the face of God. Wherefore we must be justified, not through our good works, but through the passion of Christ, and so live by a free justification and righteousness in Christ Jesus. Whosoever thus believeth, mistrusting himself and his own doings, and trusting in the merits of Christ, he shall get the victory over death, the devil and hell. Therefore when thou art in sickness, and feelest that the end of thy bodily life approacheth, and that the devil with his assaults cometh to tempt thee—saying 'It is written in the law that all those which have not fulfilled the law to the uttermost shall be condemned. Now thou hast not fulfilled it, therefore thou art mine,' &c. Against such temptations and assaults of the devil, we must fight in this wise, and answer: 'I acknowledge myself to be a sinner most miserable and filthy in the sight of God, and therefore, of myself, I should be damned according to thy saying. But there is yet one thing behind; that is this, I know, and believe without all doubt that God hath sent his Son into the world, who suffered a most painful and shameful death for me, and fulfilled the law wherewith thou wouldst condemn me. Yea, he *hath given me, as a gift, his fulfilling,* so that I am *now reckoned a fulfiller of the law before God,* therefore avoid, thou most cruel enemy, avoid, for I know that my Redeemer liveth, who hath taken away all my sin and wickedness, and set me at unity with God, and made me a *lawful* inheritor of everlasting life."—*Fathers of English Church,* vol. ii. pp. 451—453.

"When we believe in Christ, it is like as if we had no sins. For he changeth with us; he taketh our sins and wickedness from us, and giveth unto us his holiness, righteousness, justice, fulfilling of the law, and so consequently, everlasting life. So that we be like as if we had done no sin at all; for his righteousness standeth us in good stead, as though we of our own selves had fulfilled the law to the uttermost."—*Sermons on the Lord's Prayer,* vol. ii. p. 485.

"The preacher hath a busy work to bring his parishioners to a right faith, as Paul calleth it—to a faith, that *embraceth* Christ and trusteth to his merits; a lively faith, a justifying faith, a faith that maketh a man righteous, without respect of works, as ye have it very well declared and set forth in the Homily.—*Sermon of the Plough,* p. 646.

"Faith is a great lady, and she hath ever a great company and train about her. First she hath a gentleman-usher that goeth before her, and where he is not there is not Lady Faith. This gentleman-usher is called knowledge of sin. Now as the gentleman-usher goeth before her, so she hath a train that cometh *behind,* they be all of faith's company, they are all with her—her whole household; and those be the works of our vocation, when every man considereth what vocation he is in, and doth the works of the same, as to be good to his neighbor, to obey God, &c. Faith is never without her train, she is no anchoress; she dwells not alone, she is never a private woman."—*Fourth Sermon before King Edward,* p. 652.

Of one of the above train of faith, viz., *love,* which Paul says is greater than faith and hope, Latimer says:

"Though love be the chieftest, yet we must not attribute unto her *the office which pertaineth unto faith only.* Like as I cannot say, The Mayor of Stamford must make me a pair of shoes, because he is a greater man than the shoemaker is! For the Mayor, though he be the greater man, *yet it is not his office to make shoes*: so though love be the greater, yet it is not her office to save."—*Sermon on the 3d Sunday in Advent*, p. 667.

The Homily on Justification, which is but the authorized exposition of the Article of Justification, was written in the reign of Edward VI. In the same brief reign appeared, by authority, a Catechism, now known as King Edward VI's. Catechism.

"In this (according to Archbishop Wake,) the complete 'model of our Church Catechism was laid.' It was published by the King's authority, having been examined (as the injunction of the Council, for its use, declares,) by 'certain bishops and learned men :' it was subscribed by Cranmer and Ridley, as well as others, and passed by the same Synod of London 1552, by which the Articles were framed and concluded."—*Strype's Memorials*.

CATECHISM OF EDWARD VI.

"As oft therefore, as we use to say that we are made righteous, and saved by only faith, it is meant thereby, that faith, or rather trust alone, doth lay hand upon, to understand, and perceive, our righteous making to be given us of God freely; that is to say, by no deserts of our own, but by the free grace of the Almighty Father. Moreover faith doth engender in us the love of our neighbor and such works as God is pleased withal. For, if it be a lively and true faith, quickened by the Holy Ghost, she is the mother of all good saying and doing. By this short tale, it is evident, whence, and by what means, we attain to be made righteous. For, not by the worthiness of our deservings were we either heretofore chosen or long ago saved; but by the only mercy of God and pure grace of Christ our Lord, whereby we are in him made to those good works that God hath appointed for us to walk in. And although good works cannot deserve to make us righteous before God ; yet do they so cleave unto faith, that neither can faith be formed without them, nor good works be any where without faith."

CONFESSION OF MARTYRS AND DIVINES IN PRISON.

"A brief confession has come down upon us, (says the historian, Strype,) drawn up by certain Bishops and Divines imprisoned for the faith under Queen Mary. It was signed by Robert Farrar, Bishop of St. David, Rowland Taylor, John Philpot, John Bradford, Lawrence Saunders, John Hooper, Bishop of Gloucester, Edward Crome, John Rogers, and Edward Lawrence. It is dated May 8th,

1554, and it has annexed the subsequent declaration. 'To these things aforesaid, do I, Miles Coverdale, late Bishop of Exeter, consent and agree, with these mine afflicted brethren being prisoners—*Mine own hand, Miles Coverdale.*'"

"We believe and confess concerning *justification*, that as it cometh only of God's mercy, through Christ, so it is perceived and had of none, which be of years of discretion, otherwise than by faith only; which faith is not an opinion, but a certain persuasion wrought by the Holy Ghost in the mind and heart of man, whereby as the mind is illuminated, so the heart is suppled to submit itself to the will of God unfeignedly, and so showeth forth an inherent righteousness which is to be discerned in the article of justification, from the righteousness which God endueth us withal in justifying us, although inseparably they go together.

This we do not for curiosity or contention sake, but for conscience sake; that it might be quiet, which it can never be, if we confound without distinction, forgiveness of sin, and *Christ's justice imputed to us, with regeneration and inherent righteousness.*"—*Strype's Memorials—Cat. of Originals,* No. 17.

NOWELL'S CATECHISM.

This Catechism was approved and allowed by the Convocation in the reign of Elizabeth; after laying sometime unpublished in the hands of Secretary Cecil, it was called for by both Archbishops, for publication, and was at length issued from the press in 1572, under a dedication to the Archbishops and all the Bishops of the Church of England. Such was the standard value set on this work, in that age, that "it was thought fit that Ministers should converse in this Catechism and learn true divinity from it." Archbishop Whitgift said of it: "I know no man so well learned, but it may become him to read and learn that sacred and necessary book." To these testimonies, Strype adds the following:

"Many years after, concerning this Catechism thus it was writ by a great Bishop, in answer to Martin Mar, Prelate: 'For a Catechism I refer them to that which was made by the learned and good man, Mr. Nowell, Dean of St. Paul's *received and allowed* by the Church of England, and very fully grounded and established upon the word of God. There may you see all the parts of true religion received, the difficulties expounded, the truth declared, the corruptions of the Church of Rome rejected.'"—*Annals of the Reformation,* p. 212

This Catechism may therefore be received as a most authentic voucher for the doctrines of the Church as understood in the reign of Elizabeth.

In answer to the question, what way we must take to be received into God's favor, the Catechism answers:

"We must flee to the mercy of God, whereby he freely embraceth us with love and good-will in Christ, without any our deserving or respect of works, both forgiving us our sins, and so giving us the righteousness of Christ by Faith in him, that for the same Christ's righteousness he so accepteth us, as if it were our own. To God's mercy therefore through Christ we ought to impute all our justification.

Master. How do we know it ought to be thus?

Scholar. By the Gospel, which containeth the promises of God by Christ, to the which when we adjoin faith, that is to say an assured persuasion of mind and steadfast confidence of God's good will, such as hath been set out in the whole Creed, we do, as it were, take state and possession of this justification that I speak of.

Ma. Dost not thou then say, that faith is the principal cause of this justification, so as by the merit of faith we are counted righteous before God?

Schol. No: for that were to set faith in the place of Christ. But the spring-head of this justification is the mercy of God, which is conveyed to us by Christ, and is offered to us by the Gospel, and received of us by faith as with a hand.

Ma. Thou sayest then that faith is not the cause, but the instrument of justification, for that it embraceth Christ, which is our justification, coupling us with so strait bond to him, that it maketh us partakers of all his good things?

Schol. Yea, forsooth.

Ma. But can this justification be so severed from good works, that he that hath it can want them?

Schol. No: for by faith we receive Christ such as he delivereth himself unto us. But he doth not only set us at liberty from sins and death, and make us at one with God, but also with the divine inspiration and virtue of the Holy Ghost doth regenerate and newly form us to the endeavor of innocency and holiness, which we call newness of life.

Ma. Thou sayest then that justice, (justification,) faith, and good works, do naturally cleave together, and therefore ought no more to be severed, than Christ, the author of them in us, can be severed from himself?

Schol. It is true.

Ma. Then this doctrine of faith doth not withdraw men's minds from godly works and duties?

Schol. Nothing less. For good works do stand upon faith as upon their root. So far, therefore, is faith from withdrawing our hearts from living uprightly, that, contrariwise, it doth most vehemently stir us up to the endeavor of a good life; yea, and so far, that he is not truly faithful that doth not to his power shun vices and embrace virtues, so living always as one that looketh to give an account.

Ma. What thinkest thou of those works which we, after that we be reconciled to God's favor, do by the instinct of the Holy Ghost?

Schol. The dutiful works of godliness, which proceed out of faith, working by charity, are indeed acceptable to God, yet not by their own deserving; but that for he, of his liberality, vouchsafed them his favor. For though they be derived of the Spirit of God, as little streams from the spring-head, yet of our flesh, that mingleth itself with them in the doing by the way, they receive corruption, as it were by infection; like as a river, otherwise pure and clear, is troubled and mudded with mire and slime, where through it runneth.

Ma. How then dost thou say that they please God?

Schol. It is faith that procureth God's favor to our works, while it is assured that he will not deal with us after extremity of law, nor call our doings to exact account, nor try them as it were by the square; that is, he will not, in valuing them and weighing them, use severity, but remitting and pardoning all their corruptness, for Christ's sake and his deservings, will account them for fully perfect.

Ma. Doth not this doctrine withdraw men's minds from the duties of godliness, and make them slacker and slower to good works, or at least less cheerful and ready to godly endeavors?

Schol. No: for we may not therefore say that good works are unprofitable or done in vain and without cause, for that we obtain not justification by them. For they serve both to the profit of our neighbor and to the glory of God; and they do, as by certain testimonies, assure us of God's good will towards us, and of our love again to God-ward, and of our faith, and so consequently of our salvation. And reason it is, that we being redeemed with the blood of Christ the Son of God, and having beside received innumerable and infinite benefits of God, should live and wholly frame ourselves after the will and appointment of our Redeemer, and so show ourselves thankful and mindful to the author of our Salvation, and by our example, procure and win others unto him. The man that calleth these thoughts to mind may sufficiently rejoice in his good endeavors and works."—*Nowell's Catechism*, pp. 179—182.

HADDON AND FOXE AGAINST OSORIUS.

In the latter part of the 16th Century, a Portuguese Divine, named Osorius, published a work against the English Reformation, by way of a letter to Queen Elizabeth. Her Secretary, Cecil, fixed on Dr. Walter Haddon, a man of great learning, for the answerer. Haddon's book is called by Strype, *"a State Book;' "a public vindication, the like to which he knew none, except Bishop Jewell's Apology."* To this, Osorius replied in a work of three books, transferring his attack to Luther and his associates. While answering this and defending the continental Reformers, Haddon died in Flanders, 1566. John Foxe, the celebrated author of the Martyrology, was chosen to complete his unfinished work, which he did in three additional parts, under the special directions of Secretary Cecil. This joint work, a large part of which is on Justification, must be considered a most accurate exhibition of the doctrines of the English Reformation and of those precise points on which the Anglican Church protested against the doctrine of Rome. Whoever will consult it, as given in Richmond's collection of the English Reformers, or in the "Fathers of the English Church" vol. viii.—will perceive two things very distinctly, viz.,—that the precise doctrines of Justification and Faith, in their several ramifications, as maintained by these Oxford writers, and exhibited in this volume, are precisely those against which, the sternest rebukes of Haddon and Foxe are leveled, as the essence of Romanism, and directly at war with the Gospel; and also that instead of the doctrine of the English Church being then in any important sense, a Via Media between that of Luther and the Continental Reformers generally, on the one side, and Romanism on the other, as to Justification, the doctrine of Luther and those other Reformers is entirely assumed by these English champions, as without a question their own and that of the Reformation universally; so that the defense of the doctrine of one is necessarily the defense of all the rest. It is difficult to make selections where a great part of the book is precisely in point. There is room only for the following. In answer to the Popish argument, that *lively faith is not alone without charity; ergo, not faith only, but faith as coupled with charity, doth justify,* we read:

"If all things that go commonly after a certain manner together, and be done together, must be coupled and applied to one and the self-same operation, by this reason it must come to pass, that he that hath feet, eyes, and ears, shall be supposed to go not upon his feet only, but to walk upon his eyes, and to see with his ears. For the matter goeth none otherwise in faith, hope, and charity; which three heavenly jewels, albeit they be instilled into us by the free liberality of God, with remission of sins, and cleave fast with one subject, yet every of them is distinguished by its several properties and functions notwithstanding.

"As for example, if a question be demanded, what thing it is that doth justify us in the sight of God? I do answer, that it is faith, yea, and faith *only*. If you demand by what *means?* I do answer, through Jesus Christ the Mediator. Again; if you ask what kind of faith that is? I do answer, not an idle, nor a dead faith, but a lively faith and a working faith. If you will demand further, by what marks you may be able to discern a true faith from a false faith? St. Paul will make answer unto you. 'The true faith is that which worketh by charity?' If you will demand further yet, what this faith worketh? I do answer, according to the several properties thereof, two manner of ways; faith worketh salvation through Christ, and it worketh obedience of the law, by charity. What! absolute obedience? I do not think so. What then? Imperfect obedience. But such a faith must needs be insufficient to the full measure of absolute righteousness and perfect felicity.

"And where is now that solemn decree of the Tridentine Council," (we add, that confident doctrine of this divinity of Oxford,) "which doth ascribe the only *beginning* of our justification to faith, but maketh the *formal cause* thereof only charity, as a certain *new kind of obedience,* (which they call a righteousness cleaving fast within us) whereby we are not only accounted righteous, but be both truly called righteous, and be also truly righteous in the sight of God?

"They do discourse and determine upon Justification, but none otherwise than as they might argue in Aristotle's school, about natural causes, or powers of the soul. Which consideration of doctrine, if it must be holden for an infallible foundation, then let us be bold, and blush not to root out withal the whole nature and essential substance of all mystical (spiritual) divinity, and *let us raze out the foundations of all our religion.*

"For if the state of our salvation be come to this pass, that it must be established by merits and not by free imputation only, where then is that righteousness, which is called the righteousness of faith? the force and power whereof is so highly and often advanced by Paul?* What shall become of the difference between the law and the Gospel? Moreover, what shall become of that antithesis of Paul betwixt the righteousness of the law and of faith, betwixt grace and merit? And what shall become of all that excluding of glorious boasting upon works? Where is that faith imputed to Abraham for righteousness? Moreover, how shall this saying of Paul agree with these Tridentine law-givers, to wit: 'Not to him that worketh, but unto him that believeth on Him that doth justify the ungodly, faith is imputed for righteousness? Moreover, what shall become of those exceptive and exclusive sentences of St. Paul, wherein all the consideration of our salvation being taken away from confidence in works, is ascribed wholly to *imputation?* Finally, what shall become of all those sweet and most amiable promises of God, if according to the rule of this doctrine, we shall be excluded from our assuredness of salvation and God's free imputation?

"We are made the righteousness of God through Christ by the very same reason whereby Christ was made sin for us.

"But Christ was not made sin but *by imputation* only; *ergo,* neither are we made righteous in the sight of God, but *by imputation only.*

"In the whole work, the mercy of the Lord doth bear the whole and full praise and palm, not our works, *which do but follow God's reconciliation as fruits,* and not make atonement with God.

"None otherwise than as Osorius, when he doth consecrate, when he doth wear his miter, he doth not these *to the end he would be made a Bishop,* but because he *was* made a Bishop *before*; therefore he doth execute the duties of appertaining to a Bishop; and as the servants of noblemen are known by their several badges, but do not wear noblemen's badges *because they shall become* those noblemen's servants. In semblance wise; Christian faith, albeit it work always by love, and doth show a special demonstration of pure and true

---

* The reader will observe that in all the writers we have cited, it is assumed that between Justification by a righteousness imputed, and by our own works or merits, there is no medium. A half-way plea of righteousness *in us* for justification, not involving the doctrine of human merit, they know nothing of.

faith, doth not therefore procure salvation *because it worketh*, but because it doth believe in Christ Jesus."—*Fathers of the English Ch.* vol. viii. pp. 777—784.

WILLIAM PERKINS, FELLOW OF CHRIST'S COLLEGE, CAMBRIDGE.

This eminent writer died in 1602. His works, in three volumes folio, have been deemed worthy to be translated into divers languages, as Latin, Dutch, Spanish, &c. He connnects the Reformers with the writers of the 17th Century. It was a high eulogium for such a man as the profoundly learned Joseph Mede, Fellow of the same College (Christ's College, Cambridge) of which Mr Perkins had been a member, to say of him concerning some matter connected with the satisfaction and intercession of Christ, as represented in the Eucharist:

"This a reverend and famous Divine of blessed memory, once of this society, and interred in this place, saw more clearly, and expressed more plainly, than any other Reformed writer I have yet seen."

From his "*Reformed Catholic, a Declaration showing how near we may come to the present Church of Rome, in sundry parts of religion; and wherein we must for ever depart from them,*" are taken the following extracts:

"Justification stands in two things—first, in the remission of sins by the merit of Christ's death; secondly, in the imputation of Christ's righteousness, which is another action of God whereby he accounteth and esteemeth that righteousness which is in Christ as the righteousness of that sinner which believeth in him. By Christ's righteousness, we are to understand two things, *first*, his sufferings, specially in his death and passion; *secondly*, his obedience in fulfilling the law; both which go together; for Christ in suffering obeyed; and obeying, suffered. And the very shedding of his blood, to which our salvation is ascribed, must not only be considered as it is *passive*, that is, a suffering; but also, as it is *active*, that is, an obedience; in which he showed his exceeding love both to his Father and us, and thus fulfilled the law for us.

"A man is justified by faith alone, because faith is that alone instrument, created in the heart by the Holy Ghost, whereby a sinner layeth hold of Christ's righteousness and applieth the same unto himself. There is neither hope, nor love, nor any other grace of God within man, that can do this, but faith alone.

"We grant that the habit of righteousness, which we call *sanctification*, is an excellent gift of God, and hath its reward of God, and is the matter of our Justification *before man*, because it serveth to declare us to be reconciled to God and to be justified; yet we deny it to be the thing which maketh us, of sinners, to become righteous before God. And this is the first point of our disagreement in the matter of Justification, (with Papists) which must be marked; because if there were no more points of difference between us, *this one alone were sufficient to keep us from uniting of our religions; for hereby the Church of Rome doth raze the very foundation.*

"All, both Papists and Protestants, agree that a sinner is justified by faith. This agreement is *only in word*, and the difference between us is great indeed, And it may be reduced to these three heads. First, the Papist, saying that a man is justified by faith, understandeth *a general or a Catholic faith*, whereby a man believeth the articles of religion to be true.* But we hold that the faith which justifieth is *a particular faith*, whereby we apply to ourselves the promises of righteousness and life everlasting by Christ. The second difference touching faith, is this: the Papist says we are justified by faith, because *it disposeth the sinner to his justification*."† We say otherwise; that faith justifieth because it is a *supernatural instrument* created by God in the heart of man, at his conversion, whereby he apprehendeth and receiveth Christ's righteousness for his justification. The *third* difference is this: the Papist saith that a man is justified by faith, yet not by faith alone, but also by other virtues, as hope, love, the fear of God. Faith (he says) is never alone, therefore it doth not justify alone. They might as well dispute thus: the eye is never alone from the head, and therefore it seeth not alone; which is absurd. And though in regard of substance, the eye is never alone; yet in regard of seeing, it is alone; and so though faith subsist not without love and hope, and other graces of God, yet in regard of the act of justification, it is alone without them all. Now the doctrine which we teach is, that *a sinner is justified before God by faith,* yea by faith alone. The meaning is, that nothing within man, and nothing that man can do, either by nature or by grace, *concurreth* to the act of

---

* This is the *dead* faith, until it be made alive in Baptism, as found in Oxford Divinity, see chap. vi.

† This is precisely the language of Dr. Pusey and Mr. Newman—see chap. vi.

justification before God, as any cause thereof, either efficient, material, formal, or final, but faith alone; all other gifts and graces, as hope, love, the fear of God, are necessary to salvation as consequents of faith. And faith itself is no *principal*, but only an *instrumental* cause, whereby we receive, apprehend and apply Christ's righteousness for our justification." *—*Perkins' Works*, vol. i. pp. 567—572.

We come now to the Divines of the 17th Century, beginning with Downame, whose learned Treatise of Justification, with special reference to the writings of Cardinal Bellarmine, in defense of Romanism, was published in 1633.

DOWNAME, BISHOP OF DERRY.

"Which doctrine" (viz., of imputed righteousness,) "is so inviolably and incorruptibly to be held, that if an Apostle, if an Angel from Heaven shall teach any other Gospel, that is, any other doctrine whereby to be justified and saved, than by the only merits of Christ apprehended by faith, he ought to be held *accursed*. But by how much the more necessary and comfortable this doctrine is, by so much the more it is oppugned by Satan;—who hath opposed it by all means, as namely by raising, not only other false teachers in the Apostles' times and since, but even Antichrist and his adherents in these later times, who have not only perverted this doctrine, but also subverted it, and have as it were taken away the subject of the question; for by confounding the law and the Gospel, the covenant of works and the covenant of grace, the benefits of justification and sanctification, and of two making but one; they have wholly abolished that great benefit of the *Messias* about our justification, whereby we are freed from hell, and entitled to the kingdom of Heaven; and consequently they are fallen from grace, having annulled the covenant of grace, and made the promise of none effect. For whosoever seeketh to be justified by inherent righteousness, he is under the curse, he is a debtor to the whole law, and therefore to him Christ has become of none effect." p. 2.

"The formal cause of justification is the *imputation of Christ's righteousness*, because by imputing it the Lord doth justify. * * *

---

* Not only does the "Reformed Catholic" of Perkins contain a very clear exhibition of the Romish doctrine of justification—but under several of its heads it is a singularly clear exhibition of Oxford Divinity, under the name of Romanism.

For it cannot be imagined how we should be justified by that righteousness of Christ which is out of us in him, otherwise than by imputation. For even as we were made sinners by *Adam's* personal obedience; so we are made righteous by the obedience of Christ. But how could we either be made sinners by Adam's disobedience, or justified by the obedience of Christ, whether active or passive, unless they were communicated unto us. How could they possibly be communicated unto us, being both transient and having now no being! For true is that saying of a learned Philosopher, *motus non est nisi dum fit; postquam factus est, non est:* A motion (whether it be action or passion) hath no being but while it is in doing or suffering; after it is done, it hath no being. Adam's transgression was transient, and is past and gone, so many thousand years past: the active obedience of Christ was transient, and so was his passive obedience, which had a being in *rerum natura,* no longer than they were in doing and in suffering. How then can either Adam's disobedience or Christ's obedience be communicated unto us? I answer, in respect of both, as Bellarmine answereth in respect of the former, *Communicatur eo modo, quo communicari potest, id quod transiit, nimirum per imputationem:* It is communicated after that manner, whereby that may be communicated which is transient and gone, to wit, *by imputation.*"—p. 21.

" And yet we deny not, but that as they, to whom the guilt of Adam's transgression is imputed, are also by sin inherent transfused from him by carnal generation formally made sinners; so they, to whom the obedience of Christ is imputed unto justification, are also made formally just by an inchoated righteousness received by influence from Christ, and infused by his Spirit in their spiritual regeneration."—p. 40.

" The first capital error of the Papists is, that they confound justification and sanctification, and by confounding of them, and of two benefits making but one, they utterly abolish, as shall be showed, the benefit of justification; which notwithstanding is the principal benefit which we have by Christ in this life, by which we are freed from hell, and entitled to the kingdom of Heaven. And this they do in two respects: for first, they hold that to justify in this question, signifieth to make righteous by righteousness inherent, or by infusion of righteousness; that is to sanctify. Secondly, they make remission of sin, not to be the pardoning and forgiving of sin, but the utter deletion or expulsion of sin by infusion of righteousness. Thus they make justification wholly to consist of the parts of sanctification."—p. 50.

"For if they should hold that justification consisteth partly in remission, that is the forgiveness or non-imputation of sin, and partly in renovation or sanctification, then they must confess, that there are two formal causes of justification, which Calvin objected against the Council of Trent, (and may truly be objected against such of the Fathers as held justification to consist, partly in remission, and partly in renovation) and consequently should be forced to acknowledge two ways of making men just, by one and the same act of justification; the one by imputation of that righteousness, by which, being without us, we have remission of sin; the other, by infusion of righteousness inherent, by which sin is expelled."—p. 82.

"The Papists, by remission of sin, understand the expulsion or extinction, the utter deletion or abolition of sin, which is not a distinct action (as they teach) from infusion of righteousness, but one and the same action, which is the infusion of righteousness expelling sin: and is an action of God, not without us as the other, but within us, working in us a real and positive change: and therefore remission of sin in the Popish sense, belongeth not to justification, but to perfect sanctification, as being a total mortification of sin, which none attain unto in this life; but of this point I have already treated in the second question of the first controversy. Secondly, the Fathers oftentimes use the word justification in the same sense that we do according to the Scriptures, as implying the forgiveness of sins, and acceptation unto life by the satisfaction and merits of Christ communicated unto us. As namely, when they teach, as very oft they do, that we are justified by faith alone; which they could not have taught, if by justifying they had meant sanctifying; for we are not sanctified by faith alone, as all confess. Thirdly, the Fathers did not look to be justified before God by any righteousness inherent in themselves or performed by them, but renounced it, as being unperfect and stained with the flesh. And therefore where they speak of justification by inherent righteousness, they meant sanctification, and not justification before God, whereof our question is. For they profess that by inherent righteousness, no man living can be justified in God's sight, as I have showed in this third controversy, and in the fifth and sixth."—p. 258.

"Whereas, they derive imputed justice, calling it *putativam*, as if it were an imaginary righteousness only; which also, they say, doth both derogate from the glory of God, to whom it were more honorable to make a man truly righteous, than to repute him righteous, who in himself is wicked, and also detract from the honor of Christ's Spouse, who is only arrayed with her Husband's righteousness, as it were a garment, being in herself deformed; I answer first, whom the Lord doth justify, he doth indeed and in truth, constitute and make them righteous by imputing unto them the righteousness of Christ, no less truly and really, than either Adam's sin was imputed to us, or our sins to Christ, for which he really suffered Secondly, whom God justifieth or maketh righteous by imputation, them also he sanctifieth, or maketh righteous by infusion of a righteousness begun in this life, and to be perfected when this mortal life is ended. And further, that it is much more for the glory both of God's justice and of his mercy, when he justifieth sinners, both to make them perfectly righteous by imputation of Christ's righteousness; and also having freed them from hell by the perfect satisfaction of his Son, and entitled them to the kingdom of Heaven by his perfect obedience; to prepare and to fit them for his own kingdom, by beginning a righteousness inherent in them, which by degrees groweth towards perfection in this life, and shall be fully perfected so soon as this life is ended, rather than to justify, or to speak more properly to sanctify them only by a righteousness which is imperfect and but begun, which in justice can neither satisfy for their sins, not merit eternal life."—p. 290.

"The Papists do not only hold that justifying faith may be without knowledge, but that also it may better be defined by ignorance than by knowledge. This faith, which is without knowledge, they call implicit faith; because they, believing some one common principle, as namely, *I believe the holy Catholic Church*, do thereby believe *implicitè*, whatever is to be believed, that is, whatsoever the Catholic Church believeth and propoundeth to be believed. And therefore this they call also an entire faith; because thereby, a man doth not only believe the written word, but also unwritten verities, which are the traditions of the Church of Rome, and both of them, not for themselves, but for the authority of the Church propounding them to be believed."—p. 315.

"The other question is, whether faith doth justify formally, as they speak, as being a part of inherent righteousness; or instrumentally only, as the hand to receive Christ who is our righteousness. The Roman Catholics hold the former; the true Catholics, the latter. But the former I have sufficiently disproved before, and proved the latter. For if we be not justified by any grace or righteousness inherent in ourselves, or performed by ourselves, which I have before by many undeniable arguments demonstrated; then it followeth necessarily, that we are not justified by faith, as it is a gift of grace, an act, or habit, or quality inherent in us, or performed by us. And if we be justified by the righteousness of Christ only, which being out of us in him is imputed to those who receive it by faith, which also before I invincibly proved; then also it followeth by necessary consequence, that we are justified by faith, only as it is the instrument or hand to apprehend or receive Christ, who is our righteousness. Wherefore where faith is said to justify, or to be imputed to righteousness, it must of necessity be understood relatively, and in respect of the object, to which purpose, justification and all other benefits which we receive by Christ, are attributed to faith, as I have showed before. Not that faith itself worketh these things, but because by it we receive Christ, and with him, all his merits and benefits. And for the same cause, the faith of all the faithful, though unequal in degrees, in some. greater, and in some less, is alike precious in the righteousness of God and our Saviour Jesus Christ, 2 Pet. i. 1, which is an evidence, that faith doth not justify in respect of its own dignity or worthiness, but in respect of the object, which it doth receive; which being the most perfect righteousness of Christ, unto which nothing can be added, is one and the same to all that receive it.

"Here now the Papists, because we deny faith to justify in respect of its own worthiness and merit, take occasion to inveigh against us, as if it made it *Titulum sine re*, and as it were a matter of nothing, which is a malicious, and yet but a frivolous cavil. For first in respect of justification; we acknowledge it to be the only instrument on hand to receive Christ, to be the condition of the Covenant of Grace, to which the promises of remission of sins and of salvation are made, without which the promises of the Gospel do not appertain unto us, and without which our blessed Saviour doth not save us. Secondly, in respect of Sanctification, we attribute all that and more, which the Papists ascribe unto it, in respect of their imaginary justification. That it is the beginning, foundation, and root of all inherent righteousness; the mother of all other sanctifying graces, which purifieth the heart, and worketh by love; without which it is impossible to please God; without which whatsoever is done is sin.

"Yet howsoever, here the Papists would seem to plead for faith, yet, the truth is, that as they have abolished the benefit of justification as it is taught in the holy Scriptures, so with it they have taken away the justifying faith. For though they retain the name, yet in their doctrine there is no such thing. For first, to faith they do not ascribe the power to justify, but only (make it) to be a disposition, one among seven, even such a one as servile fear is, of a man unto inherent righteousness, or to the grace of sanctification itself being not as yet a justifying or sanctifying grace. Secondly, that faith, being infused, becometh the beginning, and a part of formal inherent righteousness. But so small a part they assign unto it, that they say, that the habit of formal righteousness differeth not from the habit of charity; so that in justification it hath no use at all, and in sanctification, charity is all in all; which is a manifest evidence, that the Church of Rome is fallen away from the ancient doctrine of the faith. For both Scriptures and Fathers everywhere ascribe justification to faith and not to charity; to faith, and not to works; but the Papists ascribe the first justification to charity, which they make to be the only formal cause of justification, which as themselves teach, is but one; and the second justification they assign to works."—p. 369.

ANDREWS, BISHOP OF WINCHESTER.

This great divine is called in the Oxford Tracts, "*one of our wisest doctors and rulers.*" He was one of the Translators of our authorized version of the Bible. The following is from his Sermon on Justification, on the text "*Jehovah our righteousness.*"

"I know St. Paul saith much: That our Saviour Christ *shed his blood, to show his righteousness, that he might not only be just, but a justifier of those which are of his faith.* And much more again in that when he should have said, 'To him that believeth in God,' he chooseth thus to set it down, *to him that believeth in him* that justifieth the ungodly: making these two to be all one; God, and the Justifier of sinners. Though this be very much, yet certainly this is most forcible, that *he is made unto us, by God, very righteousness itself.* And that yet more: that he is made *righteousness* to us, *that we be made the righteousness of God in him,* which place St. Chrysostom, well weighing, this very word, (saith he) the Apostle useth to express the unspeakable bounty of that *gift;* that he hath not given us the *operation or effect of* righteousness, but this very righteousness, yea, his very self unto us. 'Mark (saith he) how every thing is lively, and as full as can be imagined. Christ, who not only had done no sin, but that had not so much as known any sin, hath God *made* (not a sinner, but) sin itself, as in another place (not accursed, but) a curse itself: *sin*, in respect of the guilt, a *curse*, in respect of the punishment. And why this? To the end that we might be made, (not *righteous persons;* that was not full enough, but) *righteousness itself*: and not every righteousness, but the very *righteousness of God Himself.* What can be further said; what can be conceived more comfortable? To have him ours, not to make us *righteous*, but to make us righteousness, and that not any other but the righteousness of God. The wit of man can devise no more. And all to this end: that we might see there belongeth a special *Ecce* to this *name;* that there is more than ordinary comfort in it: that therefore we should be careful to honor him with it, and to call him by it; *Jehovah our Righteousness.*" *

JOSEPH MEDE, B. D.

This profoundly learned and eminently pious divine of the 17th century, so well known for his works on the Prophecies, was an intimate friend of Dr. Jackson and Bishop Andrews. In the 31st of his published Discourses, on Matt. xi. 28, 29, we read:

"This *coming unto Christ*, is the *approaching unto him by faith;* which is manifested by those places of Scripture where *coming* and *believing* are interchangeably used as one and the same thing. '*He that cometh to me shall never hunger: he that believeth on me shall never thirst.*' Here *coming* is expounded by *believing.*

"Here therefore, observe, that a *saving faith*, a faith which makes Christ her own, and hath promise of *ease* by him, in a word that faith which gives us an interest in Christ Jesus, is more than a bare assent, or persuasion that the Gospel is true.—It is a *coming belief*, a *coming faith;* that is an assent inclining the soul to Christ, to be made partaker of the benefits through him—such an assent as not only believes the promises made in Christ, but goes unto him, *relies upon him, clings unto him for them.* Saving faith, though it begins with what is usually called *historical faith*, yet it stays not there. It stands not only gazing upon Christ, but is effectual and powerful upon the soul to make it apply and betake itself unto him.

"The motion or flight of the soul is *desire*. He that out of a true sense and feeling of his sin (for no other can do it in good

---

* See another extract from Bishop Andrews in chapter III.

earnest) *desires* Christ, he *goes* unto him. *And Christ requires no more*, but that all those who are weary and heavy laden, should thus come unto him, and he will ease them. And this is the first degree of a faith which is *justifying*, and gives interest in Christ Jesus; for this faith is not barely *historical* and in *speculation* but a *faith in motion*, and able to walk and to go unto Christ Jesus, whom it believeth; which, if cherished, will in time gather such further strength as will fill the soul with a full and steadfast confidence.

"Now follows the benefit, ease and rest to thy soul. '*I will give you rest;*' that is, I will ease you of your sin, I will acquit you. And this is what we call *justification* of a sinner, which is an absolution or remission of sins, by the only merits and satisfaction of Christ, *accepted for us and imputed to us;* an acquitting and canceling of all bonds and obligations of transgression for Christ's sake. For he that hath right to Christ, hath right in Christ, to be partaker of his righteousness and of whatsoever satisfaction he hath undergone for the sins of mankind; whereby he is *justified*, that is *acquit* before God of the guilt of sin, and of the punishment, according to the Law due for the same.

"As in coming unto Christ, you had faith in the *ease* by him, acquittal or *justification;* so *in the taking his yoke*, ye have *sanctification* or holiness of life. All which are so linked together, that neither must they, nor can they be put asunder. No man comes to Christ by faith, but shall be eased; but no man can ever truly and seriously come unto him to be eased by him, but he must take his *yoke* upon him. No man puts on Christ to be *justified*, but he takes on his *yoke* also to be *sanctified*. True it is, and nothing more true, that no works of ours in this life can abide the touch-stone of God's law, and therefore not able to justify us in the presence of God, but to condemn us. But it is true also that we are therefore justified through faith in the blood and righteousness of Christ, that in him we might do works pleasing and acceptable to Almighty God, which out of him we could not do. For as the blood and sufferings of Christ, *imputed to us*, through faith, cleanseth us and acquitteth us of all the sins whereof we stood guilty before we believed; so *the imputation of his righteousness*, when we believe, makes our works (though of themselves far short of what they ought to be, yet) to be acceptable and just in the eyes of the Almighty; Christ supplying out of his riches, our poverty, and by *communicating of his obedience;* continually perfecting ours where we fail, that so we might receive the reward of the righteous, of him that shall reward every man according to his works.

"Unto whomsoever Christ is given for justification, through the imputation of his merits and righteousness, in him God *creates a new heart and reneweth a right spirit.*"—*Mede's Works*, pp. 154—157.

No reader of the great divines of the Church of England, needs to be informed of the eminent learning, spiritual character, and doctrinal authority of Bishop Hall.

HALL, BISHOP OF NORWICH.

"That there is an inherent righteousness in us is no less certain, than that it is wrought in us by the Holy Ghost. For God doth not justify the wicked man, as such; but of wicked, makes him good, not by mere acceptation, but by a real change; while he justifies him whom he sanctifies. These two acts of mercy are inseparable; but this justice being wrought in us by the Holy Spirit is not so perfect that it can bear us out before the tribunal of God. It must be only under the garment of our elder Brother that we dare come in for a blessing: his righteousness made ours by faith is that whereby we are justified in the sight of God; this doctrine is that which is blasted with a Tridentine curse."

"It is not the logic of this point we strive for—it is not the grammar, it is the divinity: what that is whereby we stand acquitted before the Righteous Judge; whether our inherent justice or Christ's imputed justice apprehended by faith. The Divines of Trent are for the former: all antiquity with us for the latter. A just volume would scarce contain the pregnant testimonies of the Fathers to this purpose." *Works, 8vo. vol. IX.* pp. 238—240.

"Scripture every where teacheth as, on the one side, the imperfection of our inherent righteousness; so, on the other, our perfect justification by the imputed righteousness of our Saviour, brought home to us by faith.

"The latter is the sum of St. Paul's Sermon at Antioch: 'Be it known unto you, men and brethren, that through this man is preached to you forgiveness of sins; and, by him, all that believe are justified.' They are justified; but how? 'Freely, by his grace.' What grace? Inherent in us, and working by us? No; 'By grace ye are saved, through faith, and that not of yourselves, it is the gift of God.' 'Not of works, lest any man should boast.' Works are ours; but this is 'the *righteousness* of God, which is by the faith of Jesus Christ to all them that believe.' And how doth this become ours? By his gracious *imputation.* 'Not to him that worketh, but believeth on him who justifieth the wicked, is his faith imputed for righteousness.'

"Lo, it is not the act, nor the habit of faith, that justifieth: it is He that justifies the wicked, whom our faith makes ours, and our sin his. 'He was made sin for us, that we might be made righteousness of God in him.' Lo, so were we made his righteousness; as he was made our sin. Imputation doeth both. It is that which enfeoffs our sins upon Christ, and us in his righteousness; which both cures and redresses the imperfection of ours. That distinction is clear and full. 'That I may be found in him, not having mine own righteousness, which is of the law, but that which is through the faith of Christ, the righteousness which is of God by faith.' St. Paul was a great saint: he had a righteousness of his own; not as a Pharisee only, but as an Apostle; but that which he dares not trust to, but forsakes, and cleaves to God's— not that essential righteousness, which is in God, without all relation to us; nor that habit of justice, which was remaining in him; but that righteousness which is, of God, by faith made ours.

"Thus, 'being justified by faith, we have peace with God through our Lord Jesus Christ.' For what can break that peace, but our sins? And these are remitted; for 'who shall lay any thing to the charge of God's elect? It is God that justifieth.' And, in that remission, is grounded our reconciliation; 'for God was in Christ, reconciling the world to himself, not imputing their sins unto them;' but contrarily, imputing to them his own righteousness, and their faith for righteousness.

"Let the vain sophistry of carnal minds deceive itself with idle subtleties, and seek to elude the plain truth of God with shifts of wit. We bless God for so clear a light, and dare cast our souls upon this sure evidence of God, attended with the perpetual attestation of his ancient Church." pp. 242—244.

NICHOLSON, BISHOP OF GLOUCESTER.

This learned divine was made Bishop of Gloucester in 1660. While Archdeacon of Brecon, he published a series of discourses on the Apostles' Creed, from which the following extracts are made—a work of the soundest divinity, and of a vigorous style. During the storm under which the Church of England was so cast down in the earlier part of the century, he was one of her faithful defenders; and after it had passed, one of her brightest ornaments.

"His works (says Nelson in his life of Bishop Bull,) show him to have been a person of great learning, piety, and prudence, particularly his *Apology for the discipline of the Ancient Church, and his Eposition of the Apostles' Creed*. Not only for his knowledge of the Fathers and Schoolmen, but also for the great share of critical learning whereof he was master;" he was much consulted by Mr. Bull, afterwards Bishop Bull, who, while engaged on his *Harmonia*, was a Presbyter of the Diocese of Gloucester.

"By righteousness we are to understand, 1. That which is inherent. 2. Then that which is imputed. The inherent is imperfect, proportionable to our estate, consisting in true sanctification and holiness, enabling a man to mortify his sins and lusts, and to bring forth the fruits of repentance, and to beautify his soul with the virtues of faith, hope, and charity; so that there be none truly ἀπιστεις, but they who are ἀπειθεις; none unbelievers but the disobedient. And happy is the soul that hungers and thirsts after this righteousness.

"But because this righteousness, in what degree soever, is imperfect, necessary it is, that we hunger and thirst after another, which is the righteousness of Christ arising out of his obedience, whereby he fulfilled the law, and satisfied the punishment, in his life, and in his death for us; which obedience both merited the remission of our sins, and effectually wrought the righteousness of the law, and acceptation of our persons in Christ. For the deriving whereof to us, two things must be done, one in God's behalf, the other in ours.

"That which God doth is called *imputation*; that which we do, is called believing in Christ, and so receiving that which God offereth. And happy is that soul to whom this righteousness is imputed."

"That we may understand this point the better, and be practitioners in it, know we must, that there is a twofold purging; one that is made by the blood of Christ, this is perfect even now; for they to whom the merit of Christ is imputed, have instantly the guilt of their sin remitted, so that it hath no power to condemn.

"The other, purging away sin, is by the Spirit of Christ, which will never be brought to perfection while it works upon this our flesh. For his Spirit begins only this work in this life by the mortification of our earthly members, weakens and subdues the power of sin; so that, though it remain in motion and act, yet the dominion is removed; for not any one sin reigns in us to command as it was wont to do."—*Exposition of the Apostles' Creed, delivered in several Sermons, by William Nicholson, Archdeacon of Brecon,* pp. 40, and 607.

USHER, ARCHBISHOP OF ARMAGH, AND PRIMATE OF ALL IRELAND.

Early in life, this *acatholicorum doctissimus,* (as the Jesuit Fitzsymonds pronounced him, *the most learned person out of the Catholic Church*) commenced "to read the Fathers all over and trust none but his own eyes in the search of them." This stupendous undertaking he was spared to accomplish. He read a certain portion every day in chronological order, till at the end of *eighteen* years he had completed the task, beginning with the Fathers of the 1st century, and "observing the doctrine of the ancient Church." From this divine, thus thoroughly furnished, we have the following lucid statement of the doctrine of justification and faith.

"The word *justify* doth not signify in this place, (Rom. viii. 30, 33, 34,) to make just by *infusing* a perfect righteousness into our natures; (that comes under the head of sanctification begun here in this life, which being finished, is glorification in heaven); but here the word signifieth to pronounce just, to quit and to discharge from guilt and punishment; and so it is a judicial sentence opposed to condemnation. Rom. viii. 34, 35. *Who shall lay any thing* (saith Paul) *to the charge of God's elect? It is God that justifieth; who shall condemn?* Now, as to condemn is not the putting any evil into the nature of the party condemned, but the pronouncing of his person guilty, and the binding him over unto punishment: so justifying is the Judges' pronouncing the law to be satisfied, and the man discharged and quitted from guilt and judgment. Thus God imputing the righteousness of Christ to a sinner, doth not account his sins unto him; but interests him in a state of as full and perfect freedom and acceptance, as if he had never sinned or had himself fully satisfied. For though there is a power purging the corruption of sin, which followeth upon justification; yet it is carefully to be distinguished from it; as we shall further show hereafter.

"*This for the name of justification: but now for the thing itself; which is the matter first of our justification?*

"The matter of justification, or that righteousness whereby a sinner stands justified in God's sight, is not any righteousness inherent in his own person and performed by him; but a perfect righteousness inherent in Christ, and performed for him.

" *What righteousness of Christ is it whereby a sinner is justified?*

" Not the essential righteousness of his divine nature: but,

First, the absolute integrity of our human nature, which in him, our head, was without guile, Heb. vii. 26.

" Secondly, the perfect obedience which in that human nature of ours he performed unto the whole law of God; both by doing whatsoever was required of us;—and by suffering whatsoever was deserved by our sins.—For he was made sin and a curse for us; that we might be made the righteousness of God in him.

" *What is the form or being-cause of our justification, and that which makes this righteousness so really ours, that it doth justify us?*

" The gracious imputation of God the Father, accounting his Son's righteousness unto the sinner, and by that accounting, making it his, to all effects, as if he himself had performed it.

"*But how can Christ's righteousness be accounted ours? Is it not as absurd to say that we are justified by Christ's righteousness, as that a man should be fed with the meat another eats? Or be warmed with the clothes another weareth? Or be in life and health with the life and health of another?*

" No, doubtless, because this righteousness is to Christ, not as in a person severed from us, but as in the head of our common nature, the second Adam: from whom therefore it is communicated unto all, who being united, as members unto him, do claim thereunto, and apply it unto themselves, Rom. v. 19; x. 4. For if the sin of Adam, being a man, were of force to condemn us all, because we were in his loins, he being the head of our common nature: why then should it seem strange, that the righteousness of our Saviour Christ, both God and man, should be available to justify those that are interested in him, especially considering that we have a more strict conjunction in the Spirit with him, than ever we had in nature with Adam?

What gather you from the doctrine of justification by CHRIST'S *righteousness?*

" To condemn the proud opinion of Papists who seek justification by their own works and righteousness inherent in themselves; whereas though being accepted, we must in thankfulness do all we can for God; yet when all is done, we must acknowledge ourselves unprofitable servants: the only matter of our joy and triumph both in life and death, must be the imputation of Christ's righteousness. Not our persons, nor the best actions of the holiest men, dare appear in God's presence, but in his name and merit who consecrates all, the Lord Jesus.

"*But how is this great benefit of justification applied unto us, and apprehended by us?*

"This is done, on our part, by faith alone: and that, not considered as a *virtue* inherent in us, working by love; but only as an *instrument or hand of the soul* stretched forth to lay hold on the Lord our righteousness, Rom. v. 1; x. 10. Jer. xxiii. 6. So that faith justifieth only *relatively,* in respect of the object on which it fasteneth; to wit, the righteousness of Christ, by which we are justified: faith being only the *instrument* to convey so great a benefit unto the soul, as the hand of the beggar receives the alms.

"*What is that which you make the object of saving faith?*

"The general object of true saving faith is the whole truth of God revealed; but the special object of faith, as it justifieth, is the promise of remission of sins by the Lord Jesus. For as the Israelites, by the same eyes by which they looked upon the brazen serpent, saw other things; but they were not healed by looking upon any thing else, but only the brazen serpent; so, though by the same faith whereby I cleave to Christ for remission of sins, I believe every truth revealed; yet I am not justified by believing any truth but the promise of grace in the Gospel.

"*What gather we from hence?*

"First, the folly of Popish Doctors, who persuade the multitude to rest in a blind faith, which they call implicit and folded up; telling them that it is enough for them to believe as the Church believes, though they know not who the Church is, whereas the Scripture teacheth us that faith comes by hearing; that is, by hearing the blessed promise of grace offered to the people, *Rom.* x. 14, 17."—*Usher's Body of Divinity,* pp. 194, 198.

The Doctrine of imputed righteousness, expressed in the above extracts from Usher, is given in precisely the same substance, and with equal plainness, throughout his Sermons on Justification, preached at Oxford, where he says more than once of the doctrine: "*This is imputative righteousness,* AS IT IS IN THE ARTICLES OF THE CHURCH OF ENGLAND."

HOPKINS, BISHOP OF DERRY.

"It is very wonderful, that the Papists should so obstinately resolve not to understand this doctrine of imputed righteousness, but still cavil against it, as a contradiction. It being, say they, as utterly impossible to become righteous through the righteousness of another, as to become healthful through another's health. And some, besides this slander of a contradiction, give us this scoff into the bargain; that the Protestants in defending an imputative righteousness, show only an imputative modesty and learning. But they might do well to consider that some denominations are physical, others only legal or juridical. To be righteous may be taken, either in a physical sense, and so it denotes an inherent righteousness, which in the best is imperfect; or else in a forensic or juridical sense, and so the perfect righteousness of another who is our surety, may become ours, and be imputed for our justification. It is the righteousness of another *personally;* ours *juridically;* because by faith we have a right and title to it; which accrue to us by the promise of God, and our union to our surety."— *Works*, vol. ii. pp. 323, 324.

"Justification is a gracious act of God, whereby through the righteousness of Christ's satisfaction *imputed*, he freely remits to the believing sinner the guilt and punishment of his sins; and through the righteousness of Christ's perfect obedience *imputed*, he accounts him righteous, and accepts him into love and favor, and unto eternal life. This is justification, which is the very sum and pith of the whole Gospel and the only end of the Covenant of Grace."— *Doct. of the Two Covenants*, p. 382.

BEVERIDGE, BISHOP OF ST. ASAPH.

' Whatsoever we lost in the first, we gained in the second Adam. Are we accounted sinners by Adam's sin imputed to us? We are accounted righteous by Christ's righteousness laid upon us. Are we made sinners by Adam's sin, inherent in us? We are made righteous also by Christ's righteousness imparted to us; his Spirit being our's for the sanctification, as well as Adam's sin our's for the corruption of our nature; and his merit our's for the justification, as well as Adam's transgression our's for the condemnation of our persons.

"By this merit it is that we are accounted righteous before God; where we may take notice by the way, how our being justified is here expressed by our being *accounted* righteous, and not by our being *made* righteous. For it is not by the inhesion of grace in us, but by the imputation of righteousness to us, that we are justified; as it is not by the imputation of righteousness to us, but by the inhesion of grace in us, that we are sanctified. Thus we find the Apostle speaking of the justification of Abraham, saying, 'Abraham believed God, and it was counted to him for righteousness!' Rom. iv. 3; and again, 'but to him that worketh not, but believeth on him that justifieth the ungodly, his faith is counted for righteousness.' And if faith is accounted for righteousness, we must needs be accounted righteous by faith, and so we be justified by faith, that is, it is accounted for righteousness to us by grace, not as a principle of righteousness in us. Which also further appears in that justification is here said to be of the ungodly,—'who justifieth the ungodly.' For so long as a man is ungodly, he cannot be said to be justified by any inward and inherent, but only by an outward and imputed, righteousness; so that justification is properly opposed to accusation. So, St. Paul plainly, 'who shall lay anything to the charge of God's elect? It is God that justifieth, who is he that condemneth? It is Christ that died,' Rom. viii. 33, 34. Who shall accuse or lay any thing to the charge of God's elect? The devil, their own consciences? But it is God that will justify and pronounce them righteous. How? Because they are righteous in themselves? No; but because Christ's merits are imputed to them, who is therefore said, 'to be made sin for us, that we might be made the righteousness of God in him,' 2 Cor. v. 21. How was Christ made sin for us? Not by our sins inherent in him; that is horrid blasphemy; but by our sins imputed to him; that is true divinity. And as he was made sin for us, not by the inhesion of our sins in him, but by the imputation of our sins to him, so are we made the righteousness of God in him, by the imputation of his righteousness to us, not by the inhesion of his righteousness in us. He was accounted as a sinner, and therefore punished for us; we are accounted as righteous, and therefore glorified in him. Our sins were laid upon him, and therefore he died for us in time; his righteousness is laid upon us, and therefore we shall live with him to eternity. Thus was the innocent punished as if he were guilty, that the guilty might be rewarded as if they were innocent. And thus we are accounted as righteous in him, as he was accounted as a sinner for us.

"He was accounted as a sinner for us, and therefore he was condemned; we are accounted as righteous in him, and so we are justified. And this is the right notion of justification as distinguished from sanctification. Not as if these two were ever severed or divided in their subjects; no, every one that is justified, is also sanctified, and every one that is sanctified is also justified. But yet the acts of justification and sanctification are two distinct things: for the one denotes the imputation of righteousness to us; the other denotes the implantation of righteousness in us. And therefore, though they be both the acts of God, yet the one is the act of God towards us, the other is the act of God in us. Our justification is in God only, not in ourselves; our sanctification is in ourselves as well as God. By our sanctification we are made righteous in ourselves, but not accounted righteous by God; by our justification we are accounted righteous by God, but not made righteous in ourselves. And we are thus justified or accounted righteous before God, only for the merit of our Lord Christ, and not for our own works. As it is not by our own strength that we can be sanctified in ourselves, so it is not by our own works that we can be justified before God. But as it is only by the Spirit of Christ that our natures can be made holy, so it is only by the merit of Christ that our persons can be accounted righteous. And seeing this merit of Christ is made over unto us by our faith in him, we are therefore said 'to be justified by faith,' not as it is an act in us, but as it applies Christ to us. We are therefore said to be justified by faith in Christ, because we should not be justified by Christ without faith. Wherefore, that we are justified by faith only, is wholesome doctrine, and very full of comfort, as more largely is expressed in the Homily of Justification, whither I refer the reader for more satisfaction in that particular."—*On the Articles. Art. XI.*

We have now presented a chain of testimony to the great Protestant and Gospel doctrine of Justification by the *imputed* righteousness of Christ; that righteousness consisting in Christ's *active* obedience in fulfilling the law, as well as in his *passive* in suffering its penalty; that righteousness applied, embraced, or apprehended only by faith; and faith in this act, though necessarily a lively and working faith, and working by love, yet not effectual in this application of Christ's righteousness, *because* it is a virtue, or works by love, but simply because it is the empty hand of an unworthy beggar reached out unto and taking hold on Christ. We have presented a chain of testimony from Tyndale and Barnes, morning stars of the Anglican Reformation, down through some of the most distinguished of the Reformers, to the time of the admirable Beveridge, whose days reached into the eighteenth century. A few things must be noted as conspicuous in these extracts. *First*, they are from the most learned, conspicuous, influential, and eminently holy divines of their several ages, to whom especially the Church of England looks for her noblest sons, and the Church of succeeding ages will look for her most venerable Fathers. *Secondly*, they are too plain, pointed, reiterated, concurrent, unvaried and homogeneous to admit of a supposition that their *appearance* of doctrine, in this work, is owing to their being seen in a disconnected form. *Thirdly*, they all speak precisely the same language. Just what Tyndale and Hooper said in the early part of the 16th century; Andrews and Mede and Downame said in the early part of the 17th, and Hopkins and Beveridge in the latter part of the same. If there be an increase of precision in such men as Usher and Hall, over those of the early Reformers, there is no variety of doctrine. *Fourth*, there is, in all these writers, the most thorough conformity, and the most minute similarity of doctrine, to that of the Articles and Homilies of the Church of England, none either stretching beyond or falling short of those standards in any degree, as regards justification. *Fifth*, wherever any persons are mentioned by these great writers as opposing their doctrines on this head, they have no reference to any but Romanists, or Socinians; the idea not having arisen in their minds that the denial of justification by a righteousness *imputed*, and the substitution of a righteousness *inherent*, could spring from any other source than Popery, or Socinianism. *Sixth*, wherever the doctrine common to Popery and the divinity herein considered, as to justification and faith, is treated in the extracts above given, it is invariably regarded as a fundamental error, of the very first importance; a doctrine of *merits* in opposition to *grace;* of *works* in opposition, to *faith;* destructive of the sinner's peace; subversive of the foundations of the Gospel; by all means to be rooted out; unheard of in the Church, till "the spawn" of the Schoolmen, (as Usher says,) brought it forth, and the arts of the Jesuits nourished it up; a doctrine considered in England's Reformation, precisely as in that on the Continent, *articulus cadentis ecclesiæ*. Let this "abomination of desolation" be once admitted into the Temple of God, and instantly will be heard, therein, as before the destruction of the Temple of Jerusalem by the Romans, the voices of all the precious consolations of the Gospel, saying "*Let us remove hence.*"

CHAPTER XII.

CONCLUDING OBSERVATIONS.

AFTER all that has been developed in the preceding chapters, it seems hardly possible that any of our readers, whichever side they may sympathize with, can regard the difference between this system and the doctrine of the Anglican Church, and of her Reformers, and standard Divines, as little else than a difference of words, or as not, in sober and solemn verity, a difference of vital importance to the interests of Christian truth, a difference upon grand primary questions, involving all that was so nobly contended for by the martyrs of the Reformation, and all that is precious to the sinner in the Gospel of Christ.

One thing is certain. To the divines at Oxford, the difference seems of most radical and fundamental importance. On no one subject of all their voluminous writings, has so much labor care, learning, diligence been expended, as that of justification. Justly considering it as the corner-stone of their system, according to which every thing else must be conformed, Mr. Newman has devoted a whole volume of elaborate lectures to the establishment of the peculiar views of his school on that head. Dr. Pusey has done the same. The close and exceedingly earnest volume of this writer on Baptismal Regeneration, is substantially a treatise on Justification, these two, in this divinity, being one; "different aspects of the same divine gift." The entire engrossment of energy and zeal with which these writers have labored the proof of their doctrine of inherent righteousness for justification, communicated by the sole instrumenatlity of Baptism; the strong and unmitigated condemnation which they pronounce upon the doctrine of an external and imputed righteousness, apprehended only by faith; their declarations that such righteousness is unreal, except as a corruption, a bondage to shadows, a substitution of husks and shells for the bread of life, an arbitrary, tyrannical usurpation in place of the rich grace of the Gospel; the tone of contempt in which they cry "*away with it;*" their contrast between the effects of the preaching of justification through the accounted righteousness of Christ, by faith alone, upon men's consciences, to wean them from holiness, and the effects of the wretched system of indulgences, and "the stale dregs of the ancient medicine" in the Church of Rome, giving decidedly the preference, in point of moral influence, to the latter; their positive statement that the departure of Romanism from the ancient faith, is only "external and objective," while that of common Protestantism is "internal and radical;" their express declaration that the doctrine of justification by imputed righteousness is "*another Gospel;*" their very intelligible intimation that it brings its advocates under the anathema pronounced in Scripture upon whosoever should preach any Gospel than that preached by St. Paul—all this, so like the anathematizing language of the Council of Trent, in the same cause, for precisely the same doctrine, and against the same opposers, most impressively teaches that if it seem to any that the difference between their views and those exhibited in this work, as those of the Scripture and of the Anglican Church, is of subordinate importance, it is just the reverse with the divines of Oxford. With the Church of Rome, they consider their common doctrine of justification as of such fundamental importance, that if that be not established their cause fails, their restorations are null and void. They are perfectly right. The difference is at least as great as they represent it. Their teaching of the way of salvation is indeed "another Gospel" to us; another to the Scriptures. The whole ground-work on which they teach the sinner to rely for justification and acceptance before God, is the very reverse of that which we have learned from the word of God, and which our Fathers have declared unto us. The righteousness, on which their hope of acceptance is based, is their own, as much as their intellects are their own. That on which *we* rely for all hope of present mercy or final acceptance is exclusively the righteousness of Christ. To them justification consists in being made personally holy. To us, it consists in being accounted righteous through the obedience and death of our Redeemer. They satisfy the law by their own obedience; we have no hope of its fulfillment and satisfaction in our behalf, but as it received its full demand in the obedience of our Surety. While professing to have no idea of any merit but that of Christ, they look to it, not for direct acceptance with God, but for the power of divine grace to enable them so to work and walk, that in themselves they may be acceptable. We, entirely rejecting such a scheme, as equivalent to a righteousness of works, and believing it to be precisely that of the law in which St. Paul so earnestly desired that he might not be found, do look directly unto Jesus, the author and finisher of our faith, not only for the Holy Spirit to make us meet for the presence of God, but for all the righteousness on which the title to that presence must be founded. Thus, as to "the nature and essence of the medicine whereby Christ cureth our disease," we are as wide apart as two opposite descriptions of remedy can make us.

Complete as is the change required by this system in all our ideas of the sinner's only ground of reliance for acceptance with God, so also is the transformation it demands in all that we have been taught, by the standards of our Church, of the way of *applying* the only remedy in the Gospel, for the sinner's ruin. Justifying faith is literally nothing in this system but a *name*, a pretense to something which it is not. According to the old way of the Apostles, faith is every thing in the application of the righteousness of Christ; as faith was every thing in the coming of blind Bartimeus to have his eyes opened by the power of Christ. It was Christ the efficient cause that opened his eyes. But the blind man's faith was that which instrumentally brought down upon his dark eye-balls that wonder-working power. Such precisely is the agency of faith, in bringing the soul to Christ, and in obtaining that wedding garment of his perfect righteousness; an agency so essential, so peculiar, so solitary; not as if any but a living faith could thus avail, but that while, as a living faith, it contains within itself the whole essential life of all love and active obedience, it comes not to Christ pleading that love and obedience as a price, in part, of acceptance; but renouncing all thought of itself, and of the love it practically works by, holds out the empty hand of a poor, miserable, worthless beggar, crying, *mercy to unrighteousness, only through the meritorious obedience and death of Him* " *whom God set forth to be a propitiation through faith in his blood.*"

But no such peculiar office has faith in the application of the Gospel remedy, according to this divinity. When a sinner who was baptized in infancy, applies to know, "*what he must do to be saved*," he is told that he has been already spiritually and savingly regenerated and justified; that he has been made "the temple of the Holy Ghost;" has had "the indwelling of God," "the Shekinah" of the Holy One, abiding in him and investing his soul "with the only wedding garment;" that, in this Baptism, all original sin was taken away from him, and he received "an angel's nature," and was made pure and spotless before God. But, answers the inquirer, I have sinned. Ever since I became capable of knowing good from evil, I have had to confess, that I have *erred and strayed from God, as a lost sheep, and there is no health in me.* My inquiry is not, what I was when a baptized infant, but how I may become what a sinner must be before he can see God in peace. What must I do to be saved from the condemnation of my past and present sins? This divinity answers, by inquiring, whether his sins belong to the class of *mortal* or *venial.* They are "*sins after Baptism.*" It is an immense matter for the inquirer to settle in his mind, if he would drink of the consolations of this system, to which class his sins belong. If they have all been venial—that is, if they have not been mortal, then they say to him, "*go in peace, thy sins be forgiven thee.*" The virtue of your Infant Baptism remains. Faith which proceeded therefrom, whether you have ever been conscious of its operation or not,—faith, as the symbol and representative of Baptism, has not lost the life which it received in Baptism, since nothing but mortal sin can slay it. Therefore, the cleansing from all sin, as well actual as original, which Baptism conveys, still abides. You are still regenerate and justified; the cross is still erected within you; still have you "an indwelling God;" "the righteousness of the law is fulfilled" in you, and so are you accepted in God's sight. But, replies the inquirer, my conscience cannot be satisfied in this way. What is my faith? I am no infidel, indeed. I receive the Christian religion as true. But I have never considered why I receive it. It has come to me as a sort of inheritance. It is the faith of the Church in which I was baptized, and that is about all the reason I have known for retaining it. Experience of its power, internal evidence from its effects, I know of none. Besides, I am ignorant of its great and peculiar doctrines. There is the death of Christ, as set before me in the cross which is erected in the Church, and marked on my forehead. I really do not know any thing about it, except what that naked cross can tell me. I have heard of something called the atonement, as a great doctrine of the Gospel, but what it means I know not. Certain Protestants say, that I must look unto Jesus, embrace him as all my hope, put all my trust in what he did for me, or else I can have no peace with God; but this I have never done; I have attended Church, kneeled and bowed, and made the sign of the cross ; I have kept my eye very much upon the image of the cross, over the altar, and have regularly taken the Holy Supper, and led a good moral life ; I have not been profane, nor licentious, nor a bad neighbor: I have fasted when directed by the Church, and kept her feasts, and given alms to the poor; but still I have not been directing my mind, and heart, and trust, at all to what Christ did for me on the cross ; and for a very good reason, because I do not know what he did; and yet you tell me that because I have committed no *deadly sin*, I am still as entirely clear and justified before God, as I was when baptized in infancy, though I daily confess that I have erred and strayed like a lost sheep. Yes, answers this divinity. Your case is uncommon. We do not often meet with a person so ignorant of what Christ did for us on the cross. But that does not hinder you from having a true and living faith. "EXPLICIT *faith in the atonement*" is not necessary to justification. You believe the Church, and whatever the Church declares. In this way, you may be considered as believing in the atonement, not waiting to know what the Church teaches in regard to it, nor presuming to ask why she teaches it. Thus you have an *implicit* faith. And this knowledge is enough to enable that faith to act as the representative of your Baptism, and as sustaining the justification which your Baptism communicated. Distinct reference to the atoning sacrifice of Christ is not required of your faith. A cross was erected within you at your Baptism. Look to that, and all will be right. You have had a living faith ever since you were baptized, even in your unconscious infancy. All you have to do is just to go on in the course you have so well begun; not to destroy, by mortal sin, that 'divine gift,' that glorious 'Shekinah of the Word Incarnate,' that 'angelic nature' which you received in Baptism, and are now ennobled by. We must remind you, however, that all depends upon the accuracy of your knowledge of the difference between sins that *are mortal*, and sins that are *not mortal*. A mistake here is fatal. One mortal sin is death to all your baptismal blessings, and hopes, and dignities, and gifts. Consider well, then, whether you have ever committed a MORTAL sin.

But how shall I know? Give me some rule by which to judge.

A rule which shall so accurately guide you in all circumstances that you shall be at no loss to determine, in each particular case, whether the sin was mortal or not, and especially a rule as to all those sins *which it is now impossible for you to remember*, we cannot furnish you. Nothing but a general definition can be given, subject in its application to circumstances, which you must remember and weigh as you can.*

But I have now been living some sixty years. How can I call up all my sins, with all their circumstances, and bring them to the trial of a rule so general, and thus ascertain of each sin, out of those of every day and hour of my life, whether it was of one class, or the other? And yet on this all my consolation from my baptismal justification depends!

True, we do not pretend to any better consolation. To enable you so to estimate your state before God, that you may have anything better than a very *uncertain* hope, is beyond the promise of our doctrine.

Well then (says the inquirer,) my safest way is to believe the worst; that during my sixty years of sinning and confessing, in the midst of so much responsibility, required of God to love Him

* The following passage from Dr. Pusey contains a most painful showing of the impossibility of distinguishing between sins *venial* and *mortal*, and the consequent necessity of every baptized person, either concluding that he has committed *mortal* sin, since his Baptism, and has thus lost justification, or else of being in a state of uncertainty which cannot but destroy all confidence of peace with God. " A question will probably occur to many; What is that grievous sin after Baptism which involves the falling from grace? what the distinction between lesser and greater—VENIAL and MORTAL sins? or if MORTAL sins be 'sins against the decalogue,' as St. Augustine says, are they only the highest degrees of those sins, or are they the lower also? *This question, as it is a very distressing one, I would gladly answer if I could or dared*. But, as with regard to the sin against the Holy Ghost, so here also, *Scripture is silent*. I certainly, much as I have labored, have not yet been able to decide anything. Perhaps it is therefore concealed, lest men's anxiety to hold onward to the avoiding of all sin should wax cold. But now since the degree of VENIAL iniquity *(venial iniquity! !)* if persevered in, is unknown, the eagerness to make progress by more instant continuance in prayer is quickened, and the carefulness to make holy friends of the mammon of unrighteousness is not despised."

Some who were disposed to go to a considerable length with the school of Dr. Pusey, have been aroused into indignant opposition by these and kindred perversions and abominations. Of this class is the writer of "*Letters on the Kingdom of Heaven*," &c., who asks, "Where is the minister of Christ in London, Birmingham, or Manchester, whom such a doctrine, heartily and inwardly entertained, would not drive to madness? He is sent to preach the Gospel. What Gospel? Of all the thousands whom he addresses, he cannot venture to believe that there are ten who, in Dr. Pusey's sense, retain their baptismal purity. All he can do, therefore, is to tell wretched creatures, who spend eighteen hours out of the twenty-four in close factories and bitter toil, corrupting and being corrupted, that if they spend the remaining six in prayer—he need not add fasting—they may possibly be saved. How can we insult God and torment man with such mockery!"—*Letters on the Kingdom of Heaven*, &c., vol. 1.

with all my heart and strength, and my neighbor as myself, I have, by thought, word, or deed, by omission or commission, committed, at least, *one mortal sin,* one sin that deserves God's wrath and indignation. What then?

Your case is entirely and awfully changed. That one sin destroyed your faith, which is now dead. There remains no representative of Baptism to sustain its efficacy. Consequently your regeneration and justification have ceased. There is now no cross erected within you. 'The Shekinah of the Word Incarnate' has passed away. Your sin is condemning to the soul, and abideth on you.

O tell me then what must I do to be saved? I am old and grey-headed. The grave waits for me. The wrath of God is upon me. What can I do?

Repent of this thy wickedness! answers this system.

But how can I repent? I have been taught that there is no true repentance without love to God, and that the love of God is shed abroad in the heart only in Baptism, and as I cannot be baptized again, how shall I get the love of God, and how can I truly repent? Besides, what sort of repentance is necessary for this mortal sin, and of what avail will it be? Do help my aching heart.

Dr. Pusey answers: 'Who *truly* repent (for such a sin); what are helps towards true repentance; when a man who has been guilty of deadly sin willfully committed after Baptism may be satisfied that he is truly repentant for it; whether and to *what degree* he should all his life continue his repentance for it; whether he be altogether pardoned; wherein his penitence should consist; whether continued repentance would efface the traces of his sin in himself; whether he might ever in this life look upon himself as restored to the state in which he had been, had he not committed it; whether it affect the degree of his future bliss (*after being repented of*); whether it shall appear again at the day of judgment; these are questions upon which a modern popular theology has decided very peremptorily,'* but on which our better Divinity, the Catholic verity, does not presume to speak to you with any definitiveness.

Then, (answers the inquirer,) am I to be left here on the brink of the grave uninformed as to what is true repentance, what are its effects, and how I am to get it, for this one mortal sin after Baptism?

* Letter, to the Bp. of Oxford, p. 55.

'The bitterness of the ancient medicine' requires us to say we have no more light to give.

But, besides repentance, (says the inquirer,) I cannot be saved without a *living faith;* and now all the faith I ever had is dead, because of this one sin. How can it ever be made alive again?

Dr. Pusey answers, 'The Church has no second Baptism to give,' and therefore, as we know of no way for the regeneration of faith but in that Sacrament, the Eucharist being only for those whose faith is living, we must decline any further answer to that question.

Then what shall I do? I have lost my regeneration and justification; I cannot be saved unless I can regain them. Baptism is the only instrument of both. It cannot be repeated—what shall I do? To go to the grave in such uncertainty is intolerable.

Friend, be not surprised that we can give you no better consolation. 'Romanism, as well as Ultra Protestantism, would readily consult for this your feverish anxiety to be altogether at ease.' The special excellence of our system is that it leaves you in all this uncertainty. It 'sets you in the way in which God's peace MAY descend upon you, but forestalls not his sentence. It has no second Baptism to give, and so cannot pronounce you altogether free' from that mortal sin. 'There are but two periods of *absolute* cleansing—Baptism and the day of Judgment. We therefore teach you continually to repent that so your sins *may* be blotted out, though we have no commission to tell you absolutely that they are.' *

But is this the whole consolation the Gospel brings to me a

---

* Pusey's Letter, p. 62. This doctrine is kept up through the Tracts. It appears in Newman on Justification thus: "It is often said by way of reproach that we leave Dissenters to the '*uncovenanted* mercies of God;' nay in a sense we leave ourselves; there is *not one of us* but has exceeded by transgressions its revealed provisions and finds himself by consequence thrown upon those infinite resources of divine love which are stored in Christ, but have not been drawn out into form, in the appointments of the Gospel.—There is no other ordained method on earth for the *absolute* pardon of sin, but Baptism, and Baptism cannot be repeated." *Lectures,* p. 367.

Thus, according to this writer, there is not one of these divines themselves who has not committed mortal sin, the *sin after Baptism* which is so deadly, whose faith therefore has not lost its life, to whom there is no revealed method of absolute pardon, who have any hope based on any promise of the covenant of grace; whose sin has not exceeded the *known* provisions of divine grace. Such is the consolation of such a gospel as Tractarians and Romanists teach. '*Away with it,*' we say.

poor, dying sinner? Soon shall I be upon my death-bed. I have sinned *after Baptism*, and the provision of the Gospel is so limited that I must die in the awful uncertainty whether I have repented of it, as sin after Baptism requires, and whether it will not meet me, and return upon me, at the judgment, even if I have repented. Is there no better peace than this?"

"Friend, (answers Dr. Pusey,) should we endeavor to remove your trouble, it would be consulting for your 'feverish anxiety to be at ease.' This very uncertainty is part of the benefits of our system. This is 'the deep and searching agony, whereby God, as in a furnace of fire, is purifying your whole man, by the Spirit of judgment and the Spirit of burning.' There are two other ways indeed. The one is that of our Holy Mother, the Church of Rome, whose teaching as to the present matter is precisely ours, except that for sin after Baptism, she has invented the Sacrament of Penance, by means of which the soul is assured by the Church of forgiveness, but not without the necessity of the pains of Purgatory. This is *her* way of comforting troubled souls. We object to it because it is consulting 'man's feverish anxiety for ease' of mind. The other way is that of Ultra Protestants, which tells you that repentance for sin *after* Baptism is no other than that for sin *before* Baptism, nothing but a contrite heart; that a living faith can be obtained as well after Baptism, as by Baptism; and with such repentance and such faith, it directs you immediately to Christ, promising entire release from the bond of your sin, the moment you embrace Him with a true penitent heart and lively faith! Now if you are determined not to be content with such consolation as it is consistent with our system to offer you, and ask which of these two systems we advise, we have no hesitation in saying that the way of the Romish Church, even should you take up with her system of Indulgences, is the better. 'The abuse of the doctrine of Justification, in the other, sears men's consciences as much as the Indulgences of the Romish.' If the latter has 'but the dregs of the system of the ancient Church, stale and unprofitable as these often are, it has yet something of the strength or bitterness of the ancient medicine'—'Romanism in practice as well as in doctrine, is decayed'—'yet there is often reality in it, to those who would find it,'* while the way of peace proclaimed by the Ultra Protestant, that of the imputed righteousness of Christ,

---

* Letter to Bp. of Oxford, pp. 56 and 57.

embraced only by faith, is 'unreal'—'a real corruption' and 'another Gospel.'"

Alas! reader, what *shall* we do to be saved, so as to have any consolation in Christ, if this be all our refuge? The system, you see, is not a mere change of names from what we have learned of Christ; it is not a departure from the usual doctrine, by a few shades of difference only. It does not demand of us, a mere bending, and shortening, or lengthening of our accustomed views of truth, so as to make them fit their mould. It is a change of great fundamental doctrines; a new creation of our whole belief of the way of salvation; old things must pass away; all things concerning the nature of the Gospel remedy, and its application to the sinner, and the number and efficacy of the means of that application, must become new. The Atonement of Christ, lifted up on high for every soul to be ever looking at, as the single object of his faith, and foundation of his hope, must be borne away from its central position in the grand panorama of Gospel truth, and laid down almost out of sight, and Baptism set up in its stead, having for its virtue a cross within, which is but a name for self-mortification. Thus must we change our hopes, and desert our consolations, and bring a cloud of dark uncertainty over our eternal prospects, and refuse to rejoice in Christ, and fear, as presumption, a confidence of plenary justification through the blood of Jesus, except we can persuade ourselves, as never a mortal being could, with truth, that since our Baptism in infancy, we have never sinned.

We need go no further in showing how completely this pretended Via Media is an abandonment of all that we have been taught by our Church to believe as the true, the narrow, the happy way that leadeth unto life; how entirely it is the very soul and strength of all that is evil in the Romanism against which our Reformers protested to their last breath out of the furnace of fire. To whomsoever this system may seem to involve little else than a very tolerable difference of opinion, we call up the venerable Bishop Hall, who, himself, had to war with precisely such latitudinarian ideas of the importance of the question, to deliver his testimony. Hear him!

"The grossest of the Popish heresies and the most venomous opinions of Rome are conversant about justification, free will, the merit of our works, human satisfaction, indulgences, purgatory, and the differences of mortal and venial sins." * * *

"That point of justification of all other is exceeding important, insomuch that Calvin was fain to persuade that if this one might be yielded safe and entire, it would not quit the cost to make any great quarrel for the rest. But while the Tridentine Fathers take upon them to forge the formal cause of our justification, to be our own inherent justice, and *thrust faith out of office:* what good man can choose but presently address himself to an opposition? Who would not rather die than suffer the ancient faith of the Church to be depraved with these idle dreams? In the meantime we cannot but scorn to see the souls of men so shamefully deluded, while we hear the Spirit of God so often redoubling *"without works; not by works; but by faith; being justified freely by his grace."*

"But some perhaps may think this a mere strife of words, and not hard to be reconciled; for that which to the Papist is inherent justice is no other to the Protestants than sanctification; both sides hold this equally necessary. True, but do both require it in the same manner? Do both to the same end? I think not. Yea, what can be more contrary than these opinions to each other? The Papists make this inherent righteousness the cause of our justification; the Protestants the effect thereof. The Protestants require it as the companion or page. The Papists as the usher, yea, rather as the *parent* of justification.

"But what matters it (say they,) so both ascribe this whole work to God? As though it comes not all to one to pay a sum for me, and to give it me to pay for myself. I know not how these things seem so little dissonant to these men's ears, which the Spirit of God hath made utterly incompatible, *'To him that worketh is the reward not imputed of grace, but of debt. If by grace, then not of works: or else grace should be no more grace.'* 'For neither is it grace any way, if it be not free every way,' saith Augustine. But these men say, 'Therefore of grace because of works.' *'Not of works least any man should boast,'* saith the Spirit.

"To be *imputed* therefore, and to be *inherent*, differ no less than God and man, Trent and Heaven. Wherefore let our Romanists confess that which both Scriptures and Fathers and all their modester Doctors have both thought and reported to be the common voice of the former Church in all times, and we are agreed: otherwise what fellowship hath God with Belial, light with darkness?"*

Precisely the doctrine which this good and faithful witness thus declared to be as far asunder from the Protestant and Anglican

---

* "No Peace with Rome," §§ vi. and vii.

doctrine, of imputed righteousness, as *God and man*, as *Trent and Heaven*,—the learned Dr. Jackson calls the "unroofing the edifice and defacing the walls of Christian faith, leaving nothing thereof but loose altar stones for the idolatrous sacrifices of Romanists." Bishop Andrews granted that Romanists went so far as to allow imputation "in that part of Christ's righteousness which is satisfactory for punishment;" yet because they allowed it not "in that positive righteousness of Christ which is meritorious of reward," viz. his active obedience to the law for us, he said "they did shrink up the name of Christ as the Lord *our righteousness*," and "spoil him of half his name." What Hooker thought of the vital importance of the question, none can be ignorant of who has ever looked into his admirable discourse on this very subject. That the principle of justification by inherent righteousness—in other words, what he calls it, "*the attributing unto works a power of satisfying for sin*," as Rome and this Divinity do alike, while both declare that the power cometh only through the merits of Christ, because he doeth the works in and by us; that this principle "overthroweth the foundation of faith,"* though it is not "a *direct* denial thereof," it was the main object of Hooker in that discourse to show.

We have been aware, all the while of the preparation of this book, that it may be said, and probably will be, by some reader, that some of the features of doctrine which we have been ascribing to Romanism, are not peculiar to the Church of Rome, but have been always held by some Protestants, here and there, and are now to be found, in more or less development, in writers, or preachers, or divisions, of almost all Protestant Churches.

If by this, it be meant, that any bodies of Protestant Christians, united together under the sacramental seals of the Gospel, have made such doctrines the subjects of solemn confession, adopting them into creeds, or articles of faith, as Romanists have done; we deny. It has been the peculiarity of Rome to take the self-gratifying doctrines of man's self-righteous nature, and with their several ramifications, and defenses of man's unsanctified wisdom, to set them up on high, in the uppermost seat of her synagogue, as solemn Church-doctrine, to be received of all.

But if it be meant that such, in more or less development, have been the doctrines of *individuals* in all sections of the Protestant world, we have no disposition to deny it. On the contrary, it is precisely in evidence of what we desire earnestly to impress on all

* Disc. on Justification, § 32.

minds, that the essential principle of Romanism, justification by our own righteousness, so far from having the least resemblance to that of the doctrine of the Apostles, which was "*to the world foolishness,*" *and* "*an offense,*" is precisely the very principle most akin to man, most congenial to his natural mind, most likely to spring up and bear fruit after its kind, and only to be kept down by the positive over-bearing of the Gospel. There is unquestionably a powerful tendency in the human mind, feeling as it does, the want of some religion, but desiring a religion as little spiritual as possible, to take up with the essential principles of Romish divinity, even while the Church of Rome is execrated, her more *overt* corruptions abhorred, and the profession of Protestantism is loud and high. Ingredients of Romanism may be found under all Protestant confessions. Almost every form of error has affinity to some parts of that system. But this certain fact, instead of making the true and systematized and developed Romanism, as it has been exhibited in these pages, the less to be feared, only sets its dangerous presence in the more impressive light. If it be but the carrying out of the natural tendencies of the human mind; then the more we see of their power the more should we be afraid of that which by calling them out and giving them the dignity of religion, and the force of embodied association, (whether it take the name of Romanism or not,) does but strengthen the resistance of man to the power and wisdom of God in the cross of Christ. When physicians are alarmed at the appearance of a formidable disease coming forth in full array of complex symptoms, you will little diminish their anxiety by assuring them that, everywhere are there evidences of the atmosphere being genial to it, and of a partial operation of its latent principles. If they give it a distinctive name, and set themselves to alarm a careless community against it, it would be strange indeed should some one say, as a reason against their zeal, that certain partial features of that malady have long been known, and are now often seen, without being marked by a name so alarming. Call the evil what you will, it is the same. As long as the several parts are scattered, and threaten not to unite for associated influence, they are comparatively harmless, and may go unnamed. But when they come together, and the system is being set up, for united onset, then is the time to fear; and then, for the more distinct disclosure of the danger, and marking of the evil, we fix on it the distinctive name, that all may know it for what it is, and take the warning.

We are well aware of the efforts which apologists of this system have made, to stop the effect of the charge of Romanism, by saying that it is an old charge, which sundry advocates of truth, since the Reformation, whom none now suspect of Romanism, have had to be patient with. The inference they would have us draw is, that such will, by and by, be the clearing of this divinity, in the judgment of a better reasoning community. The premises are acknowledged. The desired inference is not. Hooker was charged with Popery, because he did go far enough in the condemnation of the Romish Church, for her doctrine of an inherent righteousness for justification, though he charged her with, therein, *overthrowing the foundations of faith*. And because he was innocent of the charge, it is desired that we should adjudge those also to be innocent who not only do not grant that the doctrine of Rome deserves the condemnation which Hooker has annexed to it, but entirely unite with and defend her in that very thing, as sustaining the truth of God! We cannot be so conciliatory as this. If men have cried "Popery!" when there was no danger, it does not follow that whenever the cry is raised, we should remain at ease. Many groundless alarms of fire are heard in our cities. Incendiaries would be glad to persuade us that therefore all future alarms are so likely to be groundless that we need not heed them. So would Satan rejoice in his work, and have free course to inflame the city of God with his fiery darts, could he only persuade us that because such men as Hooker and Whitgift, &c., were falsely accused of Popery, we need be under no apprehension of Popery from the men of Oxford. We are not put asleep by such opiates, nor blinded by such dust. Popery is on the alert. Satan is about his work. The Church of England is his strong antagonist. Her citadel, he longs to possess. Secret mines are to be expected under the very feet of her garrison. Wisdom is to fear, alway.

Let it not be supposed that this system of divinity, and its resulting practices, have now reached their full maturity either in the minds and plans of their teachers, or in the fullness of their visible ramifications. They must of necessity go onward, or retire from the ground they stand on. In its originating principle of Justification by a righteousness within, the tendency of the system is either to a cold and naked Socinianism, in which the cross of Christ is moved out of sight for a self-righteousness of unmystified morality; or else to a complex Romanism, in which the true cross is equally moved out of sight, to make room for a self-righteousness of mystic pseudo-spirituality, combined with a cumbrous system of external observances and works. To which of these, by no means *opposite* results, the radical principle will tend, depends altogether upon circumstances within and around the mind of its holder. In the atmosphere of Germany, its tendency is to a philosophic rationalism. In the circumstances of the early Quakers, it was to a spiritualized, but unitarian mysticism, resulting, in the present age, in a lamentable harvest of naked Deism. In other conditions it is to entire Popery. Circumstances determine to which gulf the same fountain shall send its streams. The direction of the stream which we have now been tracing, is well determined. Its bold tide is straight onward and downward, regardless of obstacles, proud of overleaping them, rejoicing in its bounds, constantly becoming capable of greater and bolder. It must go on and become, more and more, in overt manifestation, what it is at heart, downright, complete, Tridentine Popery. Further developments are continually to be expected. There is unquestionable evidence that when its present chief agents began their work, they had little idea of eventually arriving at their present attainments in, what they dignify as, Catholic restorations. The germ has been growing and expanding in their own minds, and they have been seeing further and further into "the depth and richness" of the Roman and Parisian Breviaries, and into the excellence of "the bitterness of the ancient medicine," and getting more and more knowledge of what ought to be restored in the "degraded" Church of England, in order to raise her to the condition of the King's daughter. Whoever will look back to the state of Dr. Pusey's mind in 1828, when he wrote his book on the Rationalism of Germany, in reference to the discourses of Mr. Rose on German Protestantism, will see that since then there has been a wonderful progress in his opinions from, what he would now call, Ultra Protestantism, towards its opposite. There we read of the "*endless straw-splittings of the Schoolmen,*" who are now so earnestly praised and studied. "Scholastic definitions (he says) buried the hardly won evangelical truth of the German Reformers."* The system which succeeded to that of Luther "could not endure, a re-action, he says, was unavoidable unless some one or some succession of men gifted with *Luther's pious and discriminating mind appeared.*" Luther's lesser Catechism was then in Dr. Pusey's view, "a full and clear exposition of the sum of Christian faith, in reference to Christian life, with well-selected Scripture proofs." †

* Pusey on the Theology of Germany, p. 16.   † Pages 50 and 75.

"Had the German Reformation been perfected in the spirit in which its great instrument might have completed it, if permitted tranquilly to finish his work, or supported by others acting on his own principles and surveying the whole system of Revelation, with the comprehensive and discriminating view of his master-mind, the history of the German Church had probably been altogether different. The fruitless attempts to satisfy an uneasy and active conscience by the meritorious performances of a Romish convent had opened his eyes to the right understanding of Scripture, in whose doctrines alone it could find rest; and the clear and discerning faith, which this correspondence of Scripture with his own experience strengthened in him, gave him that intuitive insight into the nature of Christianity, which enabled him for the most part unfailingly to discriminate between essentials and non-essentials, and raised him not only above the assumed authority of the Church, and above the might of tradition, but above the influence of hereditary scholastic opinions, the power of prejudices, and the dominion of the letter. Unfortunately, however, the further expansion of his views necessarily yielded to the then yet more important practical employments, to which this great apostle of evangelical truth dedicated the most of his exertions;—the instruction of the young, the care of all the churches, the necessary struggles with the Romish Church, or with those seceders from it, who maintained tenets inconsistent with the first principles of the Reformation, as in the opposed tenets of the Anabaptists and of Zuinglius.

"His successors in developing to the utmost, subordinate but contested points of his system, neglected the great views which lay beyond the sphere of their polemics. Few, comparatively, in the large mass of the active agents in the Reformation, were led to the rejection of the errors of the Church of Rome through the same school of experience, by which the master-mover had been conducted. Many had been merely theoretically convinced of its errors, others sought a freedom from intellectual tyranny, others political advantages, some finally followed, but half-consciously, the mighty impulse. The number of the noble band, who were actuated by the same spirit which impelled Luther, was diminished, and their agency disturbed by the troubles of the times; by which e. g. Melancthon and Chytræus became for some time wanderers in Germany; Bucer acquired among ourselves a new scene of evangelical exertion."*

* Pusey on the Theology of Germany, p. 8.

How perfect the opposition to this in all Dr. Pusey's present sentiments concerning Luther, his associates, the tendencies of his work and principles, and of all the Reformation! Now, the evil results in Germany are the direct consequence of Luther's system. In 1828, they were considered as the direct result of a departure from his system. Now, he is the Prince of Ultra-Protestants; then, he was the master-mind of a noble band who "set aside the impractical formulæ of the schools, for other language, but especially that which came *from the pure and rich fountain of Luther.*"* But let us proceed a little further.

Mr. Rose had ascribed the decline of theology in Germany, in a great degree, "to the neglect of a controlling superintendence, and of adherence to the letter of the symbolical books." Dr. Pusey, in 1828, "could not but think that this view involved *the abandonment of the fundamental principles of Protestantism, and derogated from the independence and the inherent power of the word of God.*"

" That Scripture needs no such adscititious means to preserve generally its healthful truths from such corruption as would neutralize their efficacy, appeared to result from the history of the early Church, in which for above two centuries no symbols were at all received, and even when heretical speculation did render such safe-guards necessary in individual cases, they were extended no further than the emergency of such cases required; the rest of the body of Christian doctrine was committed to the keeping of UNAUTHORITATIVE tradition, expounding the word of the Scripture. *That a recurrence to Scripture is sufficient to regenerate the system when corrupted, independent of, or in opposition to, existing symbols*, resulted from the various portions of the history of the Reformation. It must be repeated that it is not intended by the maintenance of these views to derogate from the value of articles generally, much less of such as are drawn up with so much judgment and moderation as our own; their value is certainly very great; both to individuals, as presenting a test by which to examine the character of their own faith, and to the Church, as enabling it to exclude those who depart from the principles upon which itself was founded. The view in which the author felt it impossible to participate, was not a supposed probability that the Church might suffer from individual deviations, but the supposition that the whole or the greater part of the body must *necessarily* decline, unless it were

* Pusey on Theology of Germany, p. 102.

voluntarily to bind its hands by the resolution *never to deviate from the letter of the faith of its earlier state.*" *

After this exhibition of the rapid progress which the views of the Oxford Divines have already made, having the boundless field of Tradition from which to gather their resources, and all the treasures of the Schoolmen, no longer regarded as so full of hair-splittings, (especially in distinguishing between a righteousness *in* us, and *within us*), at their command, it is natural to suppose that their system will continue to grow with greatly increased vigor. The seminal principal of the Invocation of Saints; the partially developed duty of praying for the dead; the half-way step to image-worship, in the present reverence to the image of the cross; the approach to a disuse of preaching, and to a service in an unknown tongue, found in the urgent inculcation of "Reserve in communicating religious knowledge;" the almost-doctrine of Transubstantiation, in the teaching of a real, substantial Presence of the Body of Christ in the Eucharist; the preparation for further restorations, in the adoption of the whole body of unwritten Tradition, as proceeding from the same fount of Inspiration as the Scriptures, and as the *authoritative* Interpreter of Holy Writ; the additional preparation, in the doctrine of Implicit Faith, viz., taking articles of faith implicitly from the Church, because the Church declares them; afford too much ground to the fear that this Divinity will soon make good our prediction of its future.

The facility of growth in the one doctrine of purgatory, may be judged of, from what Dr. Pusey tells us of its history among early Christians, situated, in regard to it, precisely as he is. In his account of the rise of that doctrine, we have the following statement.

"The very circumstance that no second instrument of a plenary and entire cleansing from sin was given after Baptism, such as Baptism, led Christians to expect that unknown means, when accorded, would be of a more painful nature than that which they had received so freely and instantaneously in infancy, and confirmed, not only the text already cited, ' He shall baptize you with the Holy Ghost and with fire,' but also St. Paul's announcement of the 'judgment and fiery indignation' which awaits those who sin after having been once 'enlightened,' and by *Christ's* warning to the impotent man, to sin no more, lest a worse thing come upon him.

* Pref. p. 10.

"Lastly, the universal and apparently apostolical custom of praying for the dead in *Christ*, called for some explanation, the reason for it not having come down to posterity with it. Various reasons may be supposed quite clear of this distressing doctrine, but it supplied an adequate and a most constraining motive for its observance, to those who were not content to practice it in ignorance.

"Should any one for a moment be startled by anything that is here said, as if investing the doctrine with some approach to plausibility, I would have him give God thanks for the safeguard of Catholic Tradition, which keeps us from immoderate speculation upon Scripture, or a vain indulgence of the imagination, by authoritatively declaring the contents and the limits of the Creed necessary to salvation, and profitable to ourselves." *

Let any one, after reading the above, just ask himself: if this be true, why not expect the same results from the same circumstances, now as well as then? The way is as well prepared, the need is as much felt, the dead are alike prayed for, and passages of Scripture are just as favorably interpreted. Where is the barrier against the doctrine of Purgatory? In Tradition it is answered. Scripture, they think, instead of furnishing any protection, must be interpreted, *on the other side*, unless defended from such conclusions by its Interpreter, Tradition. All the whole Church, learned and unlearned, after getting to precisely the same sense of the need of Purgatory, as the ancient Christians had, to comfort them under a sense of sin after Baptism, to make the Scriptures consistent, and to furnish a good reason why they should all be praying for the dead,—all of the present Church are to be held fast, where the ancient drifted upon a lee shore, by the single anchor of Tradition, let down into the shifting sands of men's whims and caprices and prejudices and corruptions, and assaulted on all sides by "the Prince of the Power of the Air." But had not the ancient Church that anchor better than we? Was not Tradition a stronger stay to them who were so much nearer its origin; more uncomplicated, easily ascertained and readily used? How then, if they drifted upon the dark reefs of Purgatory, are we ever to be held in safety by the same anchor? Oh, no! Prayers for the dead, and the denial of a plenary absolution for sin after Baptism, and the granting of a purification in another world, all of which are attained already in the race of this divinity, must soon cross the

* Tract No. 79, pp. 536 and 537.

invisible line that separates it from Popish Purgatory. Tradition will be carried with the current and made to raise its voice, as it will easily find the excuse for doing, as the bold preacher of the very doctrine, of which it was before the appointed antagonist.

A few lines more and we shall conclude this chapter and book. We hear much of the eminent holiness of the divines who are zealously urging on this system, and of the holy tendency of much of their writings; and much hope is entertained by some that, in spite of some serious errors of doctrine, the result of their labors will be a great increase of holy living in the Church.

Of the personal attainments of the divines alluded to, in the beauty of holiness, we have nothing to say. We trust it is all that it is said to be. God forbid that we should tread on such ground, with any but considerations of the highest Christian charity and kindness. But, of the system, as to its probable effects on the holiness of its future disciples, we must speak. If Romanism has any special tendency to the increase of holiness; if its history bears testimony to the efficacy of its shallow principles, its crowded observances, its reserve of preaching, its *opus operatum* of Sacraments, its penances, its unctions, its prayers for the dead, &c., to promote holiness of heart and life; if, where it is best tried, in its monasteries of old Papal States, men are most spiritually-minded, most pure in morals, most elevated in the worship of God, in spirit and in truth; if to "overthrow the foundations of faith;" to substitute our own righteousness for the righteousness of God; to keep out of view the atonement of our Lord; to preach a cross within, for men to glory in, instead of the atoning sacrifice of our crucified Redeemer; in a word, if the wisdom of man, instead of "the word of God;" if looking to Sacraments, instead of the direct looking unto Jesus, be the way to promote holiness in God's Church, and man's heart, then will this divinity fulfill its promises. But we must take heed. "What God hath joined, let no man put asunder." Holiness cannot abide but as the true doctrine of justifying faith abides. It draws life from Christ, the True Vine, through no other instrumentality than that of a justifying faith. The righteousness of Christ, accounted unto the sinner for justification, through the instrumental agency of a living faith, this is the foundation of all that ministry out of which grows the permanent blessing of true righteousness of life. Under any other system, there may be individual examples of elevated holiness in spite of adverse tendencies, and in virtue of a better education which planted seeds of truth not yet eradicated. Souls are converted and sanctified under modes of ministry which all of us would acknowledge to be eminently wrong, and, in their exhibitions of doctrine, exceedingly defective. We are speaking of permanent and general results—what is called in homely phrase, "the long-run." And in this view of the tendencies of this divinity, we cannot question, that its certain results, if time and room be allowed it, will be the driving of true godliness from God's house, and the surrounding of its altars and the crowding of its courts with the "wood, hay, and stubble" of a dead formality, which the Lord, when he cometh, will destroy with the breath of his mouth.

That the doctrine of Justification, as maintained in these pages, in contrast with that of this system and Romanism, when unreservedly preached, is liable to be abused by those who are ever ready to draw encouragements to continuance in impenitence, from the mercies of God, cannot be questioned. "It is impossible to preach the Gospel, but that a carnal and sinful heart may wrest it so as to suck poison, instead of honey from it; such being apt to take all occasions of turning the grace of God into wantonness. And therefore the Apostle himself, when he treated upon this subject, even our justification by faith in Christ, was still forced to prevent this objection by a peremptory denial of the consequence." Precisely the evils which by many are supposed to result from the unreserved exhibition of this doctrine, were laid to the charge of the same, as preached by St. Paul. He denied the charge, and continued to preach the doctrine. He denied that the accuser had rightly interpreted its proper inferences and effects. The abuses were of man's corruption; the doctrine was of God's wisdom, and grace, and holiness. He might as well have ceased to declare the plenteous goodness—the wonderful long-suffering—the infinite mercy of God; for out of all is extracted, by the subtle devices of human depravity, the very poison that makes men sleep securely in their sins. But while we must faithfully imitate the example of St. Paul in suffering no consideration to prevent us from assigning to this doctrine a most prominent place in our ministry, as emphatically "the word of reconciliation" which, as ambassadors of Christ, we are to proclaim to all people; we are bound, like him, to see to it, most anxiously, not only that it be so delivered as to be as much as possible protected from misunderstandings and perversions, but so also that it may be productive, through the Spirit of Christ, of true holiness of heart and life in those who profess to embrace it. We must take care that in our own hearts, in all our words, we do manifestly insist, as zealously, and with as much sense of necessity, upon personal holiness, to make us "*meet*," as upon a justifying righteousness, not personal, to give us a *title*, "to be partakers with the saints in light." Justification by faith without works, is no more to be preached than sanctification, which embraces faith and all good works. The righteousness of Christ, imputed, is one part of salvation. It delivers us from the *condemnation* of sin. The righteousness of Christ, dwelling in us, by His Spirit, is another, and equally important part of our salvation. It delivers us from the *dominion* of sin. "We are far from that libertinism to conclude, that because Christ hath obeyed the whole law for us, therefore we are exempted from obedience. He hath done for us whatever was required in order to *merit and satisfaction;* yet he hath not done for us whatever was required in order to *obedience and a holy conversation;* he hath done the work of a Mediator and Redeemer; yet he never did the work of a sinner, that stood in need of a Redeemer, so as to excuse him from it. And, therefore, though men may be justified by a surety, yet they cannot be sanctified by a surety; but still holiness, obedience, and good works, must be *personal* and not *imputative*."* Christ is become the Author of eternal salvation unto all them *that obey him.* His people must be "a peculiar people,—a holy nation,—purified unto himself—zealous of good works." St. Paul preached that we are saved "by *grace through faith, not of works*," but not without immediately adding that we are "created in Christ Jesus *unto good works,* which God hath ordained that we should walk in them." "Herein, is my Father glorified that ye bring forth *much fruit,* so shall ye be my disciples."

We come far short of the spirit of our ministry, if our hearts be not intently fixed upon the promotion of personal holiness in the lives of our people; we fail entirely in the effect of our ministry if our doctrine be not successful in securing it. But how is this blessed result to be secured? How shall we preach the way of a sinner's justification by faith, so as the most successfully to promote in him "the sanctification of the Spirit unto obedience?"

I answer, not by any *reserve,* on the subject of justification, exhibiting that doctrine only partially and fearfully, in reduced terms, and in a background position, as if afraid of the fullness in which the Scriptures declare it to all. Reserve here is reserve in preaching "Christ, and him crucified." Our grand message,

* Bp. Hopkins' Works, 8vo. English Edition, vol. ii. p. 394.

every where, is,—" Be it known unto you, men and brethren, that through this man is preached unto you the forgiveness of sin : and by him all that believe are justified from all things from which they could not be justified by the law of Moses." St. Paul waited not till men were well initiated into Christian mysteries, before he unveiled the grand subject of atonement and justification through the blood of Christ. No, the gospel plan of promoting sanctification is just the opposite of holding in obscurity any feature of the doctrine of justification. It is simply to preach that doctrine most fully, in all its principles and connections ; in all its grace, and all its works ; in its utmost plainness and simplicity ; so that whatever leads to it, whatever is contained in it, and whatever legitimately results from it, whether it be sin and condemnation, as needing an imputed righteousness ; the love of God, as providing that righteousness in his only begotten Son ; the blessed Redeemer, as offering up himself a sacrifice to obtain it; faith, as embracing it freely; hope, as resting upon it joyfully ; the promises, as assuring the believer perfectly ; the Sacraments, as signing and sealing them effectually to those who duly receive them ; a new heart, as the essential companion of a living faith ; unreserved obedience, as the necessary expression of a new heart ; obedience springing from the love of God in Christ, keeping its eye of faith, for motive, strength and acceptance, upon the cross, and embracing in its walk, all departments of duty ; all this, as coming legitimately within the embrace of the full preaching of justification by faith, is the way to promote, through the effectual working of the Spirit of God upon the conscience and heart of the sinner, *sanctification through the truth.*

We cannot preach the righteousness of Christ, for justification, with any propriety, unless, as the first thing, to show the sinner's need thereof, we preach the righteousness of the law in the condemnation of every soul that sinneth. No more can we preach the righteousness of Christ, for justification, with any justice, unless, beside its need and nature, we preach its fruits, and trace them out in all their branches, and show how they all spring out only and necessarily of a true and lively faith. Thus does the doctrine of faith embrace, on one hand, the righteousness of the law in the condemnation of the sinner, bringing him to Christ that he may be justified by faith ; and on the other, that same righteousness, in the sanctification of the believer, witnessing that he is in Christ, and is justified by faith.

Does St. Paul describe the blessedness of those " who are in

Christ Jesus",—witnessing that "to them there is no condemnation?" He adds immediately—"*who walk not after the flesh, but after the Spirit,*" thus insisting on the essential connexion between a justifying faith and a spiritual life. Let this text be carried out by the preacher. Let him show Christ, if ever "made unto us, of God, by imputation, *righteousness,*" must also be made unto us, by the indwelling of His Spirit, *sanctification;* both equally, though differently, necessary for final redemption ;—both equally, though differently, derived from Christ, through his obedience unto death ; both obtained by the same faith, at the same time; distinct in office, but, like the water and the blood from the side of the Lamb of God, inseparable ; so that by the blessed union of justification and holiness, peace and purity, in all the way of the believer, he may be complete in Christ. Let the preacher dwell minutely upon the *developments,* as well as the principle, of personal sanctification. The planting of the root of faith does not supersede the necessity of training and pruning the branches of obedience. It follows not in this husbandry, any more than in any other, that if the root be good, the branches will all take, of themselves, precisely the right direction. We must copy the ministry of the Apostles in the minute tracing out of the fruits of faith in all the ways of holy living—in the affections, desires, tempers, habits, conversation, and all relative duties. To expect the *issues* of life without seeing to the indwelling of the *principle* of life, is an error only next worse to that of being content with the latter, without attending carefully to all its processes in the former. Parental care is not satisfied when the child is evidently governed by a filial love. It brings line upon line, to guide, instruct, admonish, remind, and exhort that love. So is "the nurture and admonition" by which the minister must seek to lead out the great principle of "faith that worketh by love"—bringing the various and minute applications of that love, "seasonably to the remembrance" of the believer, holding up continually to an eye, prone to dullness, and a heart, prone to negligence, the *law ;* the *precept* of holiness, "as it is in Jesus," commended by his authority, illustrated in his example, expounded in his word, enforced by his love, and fulfilled in us by the indwelling of His Spirit. If we have it not to urge, as a motive to obedience, that it will obtain or promote the sinner's justification, what matters it? We have it to urge, that without obedience there can be neither the living faith that justifies, nor the true holiness that makes us meet for the presence of God; we have the *duty* also, as well as the necessity of unreserved obedience, to urge upon the heart and conscience, with just as much authority as if works, instead of faith, were the only way of justification; we have more; we have also the love of God in Christ, preparing for our ruined souls his only begotten Son to be the sacrifice for our sins; and the amazing love of Christ, bringing him to be obedient unto the death of the cross for us miserable sinners. And thence, from his agony and bloody sweat, his cross and passion, springs the constraining motive to a diligent, devoted, cheerful, filial, zealous obedience, in all things.—"The love of Christ constraineth us," said Christians of old, "because we thus judge, that if one died for all, then were all dead; and that he died for all, that they which live should live not unto themselves, but unto him that died for them and rose again." Here is love *fulfilling the law*, banishing the living unto ourselves; substituting devotedness to Christ; discerning its conclusive reason, obtaining its all-powerful motive by the eye of faith which beholds the love of Christ dying for the ungodly, and thence begins immediately to *work by love*, and keep his commandments.

Such is the inseparable connection between the *faith* which looks unto Jesus and justifies the soul, through a righteousness imputed, and the *love* that equally looks unto Jesus and bears witness to the living power of that faith, and glorifies God, by a righteousness, personal and inherent, doing whatsoever he hath commanded.

THE CHIEF DANGER OF THE CHURCH IN THESE TIMES.

A CHARGE DELIVERED TO THE CLERGY OF THE PROTESTANT EPISCOPAL CHURCH IN THE DIOCESE OF OHIO, AT THE TWENTY-SIXTH ANNUAL CONVENTION OF THE SAME, IN ROSSE CHAPEL, GAMBIER, SEPTEMBER 8TH, 1843, BY THE RT. REV. CHARLES PETTIT M'ILVAINE, D. D.

REVEREND BRETHREN,

It is now four years since I delivered my last charge to the Clergy of my diocese. Perhaps, if you have considered the specially engrossing nature of my late engagements, and all the burden and anxiety of mind necessarily connected with my effort to rescue our diocesan College and Theological Seminary from their most threatening pecuniary difficulties, you have hardly expected that, even now, I would be prepared to address you in that form again. But, though pressed in mind almost above measure, there are circumstances which forbid me to keep silence under such a stewardship as mine, and with so large an assemblage of the watchmen and shepherds of Christ's flock before me. Four years ago, my subject was that cardinal doctrine of Christianity, the plain preaching of which, in the sixteenth century, raised, almost from the dead, the whole testimony of the Gospel, after centuries of papal darkness had covered its light from the sight of men— *Justification before God, in the righteousness of Christ alone, accounted unto us through faith only.*

At that time, the system of doctrinal evil, whose name we now know to be Legion, and which is now so threatening to our Protestant Churches, mocking all restraint, had just come up out of the tomb of the schoolmen.* Its name was not then declared.

---

* It now calls Thomas Aquinas "the great prophet of the Church in all succeeding ages."—*Brit. Crit. for July,* 1843, p. 39.

Its distinct form and position were not as yet avowed. It boasted great things of its attachment to the doctrinal peculiarities of the Anglican Protestant Church, and of its antipathy to the opposing peculiarities of the Church of Rome. It was not *Protestant* doctrine it then professed to oppose, but only *Ultra*-Protestant. It was not the *unprotestantizing* of the Church of England it then professed to aim at, but the bringing of all, both Romanists and Protestants, to unite in precisely that form of doctrine which it professed to believe to be at once the glory of the Church of England, and the *Via Media* between the two extremes of Romish corruption and Lutheran extravagance. To "recede farther and farther from the principles of the Reformation," so far from being, as now, publicly avowed as a distinct feature of the plan, and necessary to the carrying out of the system, was then, whenever laid to its account, repudiated as slander. How great has been the advance in the developing of tendencies, and confession of principles and objects, within the last four years, I need not here point out. To myself that advance has been in no wise unexpected. I confidently predicted it. I have been surprised at nothing but its rapidity. In no step of the progress, however, has there been any *substantial* addition to what was really exhibited, though cautiously, in the early efforts of the movement. What we have now in open avowal, we have had ever since the Tracts began under disguised insinuations. Long ago the seeds of all the recent growths of Romish heresy were carefully planted, and it needed only a practiced eye to see them skilfully and widely mingled, for concealment and protection, with various materials of a better, and often adverse character. The doctrine of "*Reserve*," of "the *Secret*," of what they called "*Economy*," of what, considering its bearings and applications, is nothing but the old sin of "pious frauds" revived, was employed most thoroughly, in order that, while men slept, the tares might be getting strength enough to mock all efforts to eradicate them.

To minds skilled in the old contests of the truth against the corruptions of Rome, it was not difficult to see where they were making their main, though often masked, attack. To get away from the Church that palladium of her strength—the doctrine of justification by a righteousness *external* to us, and only in Christ—and to substitute the precise opposite—a justification by a righteousness *in* us, and not in Christ, implanted by Sacraments and increased by good works—this was the first and main object.

This gained, the citadel of Protestant faith was gained; their cause was gained; the Church was "*unprotestantized.*"

It seemed, therefore, that the first thing, in setting up our defense, was to secure the clear, well-defined understanding, and the decided holding and preaching of the doctrine of our Church, in her Articles and Homilies, on that subject. In aiming at that, by means of my last charge, there was little direct reference made to Tractarian publications. My next effort at the same object was the publication of a volume, inscribed to my reverend brethren of Ohio, in which the system of divinity attempted to be established among us, under the name of "Catholic Verity," was compared with the doctrines of the Church of which its chief advocates are presbyters, and with those of the apostate Church against which she protests at every angle and bastion of her fortress.* When that work appeared, many thought it had come too late; that the spirit of evil was laid, and the danger over. I believed, on the contrary, that it was then continually gaining strength, and would be gaining, till, with its parent Popery, the Lord shall destroy it, "with the brightness of his appearing," in the day when the cry shall be heard, "Babylon is fallen, is fallen!"

Since then, it has been continually enlarging its influence, multiplying disciples, infecting partially those whom it did not poison entirely, and enfeebling the hold of the truth upon those whom it did not wholly pervert. It is now fast preparing minds in which it has not yet effected a lodgment. Every new publication of its leading organs exhibits some new development of designs, of tendencies, of results. It displays a boldness in avowing its objects, and uncovering its principles and springs, which once would have been its death.

The concentration of almost all questions of religious interest upon the great points involved in this system; the standing aside of almost all other forms of theological controversy till the issues of this be determined; the room devoted to the subject in the charges of bishops of the Church of England; the excitement of the public mind with regard to it, as evinced in all the religious, and in so many of the merely literary or political publications of the day; yea, the whole aspect of the literature of the age, attests the truth of what the Lord's faithful watchman on the towers of the Church in India declares, that the controversy connected with the Tractarian movement is "the most momentous struggle in which our Church has been engaged since the period of the

---

* The preceding Work.

blessed Reformation."* It is precisely and avowedly the same struggle as that of the Reformation. The object of the one side is boastfully published, to "*unprotestantize*" the Church—to get back what the Reformation drove away. The main difference of circumstance is that the Reformers contended with Romanism in its dotage, with all its horrible corruption of morals around it, to shame it; with all Europe groaning under its oppression, and with all its poetic associations of antiquity drowned in the practical consciousness of its iniquity. The contest is now with Romanism revived in its early youthfulness. The great adversary of the Church would not lay aside an instrument so precisely to his mind, and for centuries so triumphant. He could transform the dry tree into the green as easily as his magicians did once change their dry rods into active serpents. The work has been done. The old root of Rome, dead at the top, has thrown up in the midst of us a youthful sapling, vigorous, aspiring, full of life, "heady, high minded." It is already a great tree. I believe most solemnly, that, under this new shape, we have a revival of anti-Christian heresy and opposition to "the truth as it is in Jesus," which cannot be dreaded too seriously, or resisted too earnestly. There is no controversy of these times comparable with this. We have important controversies about the polity of the Church; this is about the very life of the Gospel. We have questions about the walls and courts of the temple; this is for the possession of the ark and the mercy seat. We have differences of opinion about this or that particular doctrine, while essentially agreeing in the main system. Here we have a difference about the whole system of faith, from fundamental principle, to minutest inference. Should we yield the ground, nothing would be unchanged, either in its nature, its application, its relative position, or in the basis on which it would rest. Even the Atonemeut, though retained, would be put back from front to rear; from its bold exhibition, as a City of Refuge set on a hill, to that of its ancient type, the brazen serpent, after it had done its work, and was put out of sight as useless. Even the doctrine of the Trinity, though left as the Church of Rome has left it, untouched in substance, would be moved from its broad basis of proof in the Scriptures, and set upon the support of man's tradition.

In a word, the controversy is for Christianity. And with this most serious belief, dear brethren, I cannot but claim your attention while I endeavor, in this discourse to protect my diocese

---

* Bishop Daniel Wilson's Metropolitan Charge.

from the evils with which our whole Church is threatened. I know you are already sensible that there is great evil in the system of divinty alluded to. I wish to make you sensible that it is nothing but evil. I know you think it ought to be feared and opposed. I wish to make you duly sensible with what solemnity watchfulness, and prayerfulness, it should be feared, and with what uncompromising firmness, what patient zeal, what decided manifestation of the truth, it should be continually opposed.

Let us consider some of the main points in the doctrinal aspects of religion which are brought into the controversy, and how the two sides are divided in relation to them.

No question can be more fundamental than that of *the Rule of Faith*. It lies at the portal of the temple of truth. On this head there is entire disagreement between this system and the Protestant faith of our Church. The Reformation was erected on the distinct basis of the *single authority* and *entire sufficiency* of Scripture as a rule in matters of faith. The position of our Church in this respect is perfectly well defined. She maintains that Scripture "containeth all things necessary to salvation, so that whatever is not read therein, nor may be proved thereby, is not to be required of any man that it should be believed as an article of faith, or thought necessary to salvation."* The application of this to the two creeds illustrates her position. She declares that the Nicene and Apostles' Creed "*ought to be thoroughly received and believed, for they may be proved by most certain warrant of Holy Scripture.*" †

Now in the Apostles' and Nicene Creeds we have a summary of the most unquestionable articles of primitive tradition. They are the representatives of tradition in its most reverend and authoritative form. The doctrine of the Church concerning the Rule of Faith must stand or fall according to what she pronounces concerning the authority on which they are received. But she pronounces that they ought to be believed, not because the traditions of the Church assert them, but only because they *may be proved by most certain warrant of Scripture*. Thus, therefore, is the claim of all tradition to be settled. It must be tried by the warrant of Scripture—not Scripture tested by tradition, but tradition tested by Scripture—the Bible only being the ultimate arbiter of faith.

Such is the precise position of our Church. But precisely the reverse is that of the system before us. There, whether we must believe an asserted doctrine depends not in the least upon the

* Article 6th.   † Article 8th.

question whether *we* can see any glimpse of it in Scripture, but exclusively whether it is taught in the traditions of the Church; the Church, by her traditions, being (as is pretended) not only in possession of a collateral revelation, just as much derived from the Apostles, and just as much inspired, as that of the written Word, but also herself inspired to be, by means of her traditions, the *authoritative* interpreter of the written and inspired Word. Of Church tradition, it is declared that it is "parallel to Scripture, not derived from it, and fixes the interpretation of disputed texts, not simply by the judgment of the Church, but by authority of that Holy Spirit which inspired the oral teaching itself, of which such tradition is the record."* Tradition is described as "another great gift equally from God" with the Bible, and as affording a certainty with regard to high theological doctrines, "which supersedes the necessity of arguing from Scripture against those who oppose them." † "The primitive Church has *authority as the legitimate expositor* of Christ's meaning; she acts not from her own discretion, but from Christ and his Apostles." ‡

Thus, however this sound of doctrine may be made to seem a little less startling by such modified expressions as that "Scripture is *interpreted* by tradition, tradition *verified* by Scripture," the real meaning is, that, be the office of Scripture in verifying what it may, it is tradition alone that *judges* of the verification, and tradition is the "*authoritative interpreter* of Scripture." §

The question is not whether the writings of the fathers shall *help* us in ascertaining the meaning of Scripture, but whether they shall *authoritatively rule* us in the interpretation of Scripture. It is one thing to interpret, another to interpret authoritatively. Whatever does the latter is the rule. Allow the authority of tradition as the rule, under any form, and then, since but a small part of men can judge for themselves what is tradition, or what it teaches, and private judgment would be at least as much confounded amid the works of the fathers as the writings of the Apostles, you must have an authoritative interpreter of tradition to decide what are its catholic sources, and what are the catholic verities to be derived therefrom. That interpreter can be found only in the Church, which is therefore pronounced to be infallible. But who shall authoritatively interpret the Church? She cannot speak but by representatives. Where are they? General Councils are no

---

* Keble on Prim. Trad., p. 23. † Tract 71, p. 28.
‡ Newman on the Prophetical Office, p. 95.
§ Ibid, p. 327, and Tract 78, p. 2.

more. The ministry of the Church alone remains to be the *ecclesia docens*, the voice of the body of Christ interpreting the traditions which interpret the Word of God, which tells me what I must do to be saved. The authoritative Rule of Faith in this system, therefore, is really the word of the ministry of the Church as the teaching of the Spirit of God. To this, therefore, "*implicit submission*" is required as a duty, a privilege, a happiness. "Nature," they say, "gives sentence against a habit of inquiry." " Happiness is attached to a confiding, unreasoning faith." " Never to be troubled with a doubt of what has been taught us, is the happiest state of mind. *Implicit* belief is our duty." " Let us maintain before we have proved." *

Such is the substance of the doctrine of this system as to the Rule of Faith. You see, brethren, where the real question lies. It is simply whether we shall be guided, in the infinitely momentous interests of the soul, by the Word of God, or of man. It is whether we shall rest our hopes of salvation on a basis for which our most consoling warrant is that man prescribes it, or whether we shall build upon a rock, elect of God, and encompassed with the assurance of his own written, inspired Word. I beseech you, brethren, take into your minds the full, the boundless importance of this question. No words or thoughts can span the gulf it opens. No bridge of religious communion can unite the parties whom it separates. Beware of being beguiled into an idea that the difference is a mere question as to whether the Fathers of one set of centuries should be received as fair representatives of the primitive Church, or whether those of another succession of centuries should be added.† Beware of suffering your minds to be shaken out of a right sense of the infinite seriousness of the

---

* Tract 85.

† The tradition-doctrine of the system can take in whatever is convenient for proof. If it need the aid of the Apocrypha, it embraces it. If it need the writings of the schoolmen, it puts them on a footing with the early Fathers. The hardest canon to be settled is the canon of the books of authoritative tradition. Thus speaks the British Critic, No. lxiii. p. 215 :

" . . . . How far does the Mediæval Church [Church of the Middle (or, as they are generally called, the Dark) Ages] demand our *unqualified sympathy ?* How far may it be considered *as the very same in its claims upon us with the earlier Church,* as being the external exhibition of *the very same spirit,* changed only in that it is *in a farther stage of growth,* and that the external circumstances with which it has to cope are so widely different ? And, in speaking of the Mediæval Church's exhibition, we are far, of course, from confining our view to the mere formal statement of doctrine made at that period ; *we extend it to the whole system,* which virtually received the Church's sanction."

question by being led to suppose that it has any likeness to that of how far the Fathers should be esteemed as valuable *aids* in ascertaining the sense of Scripture. To speak of aid in the interpretation of Scripture is one thing, to speak of *authority* is quite another. We may differ among ourselves, and with brethren of other Churches, as to the amount of value to be set on the writings of the Fathers, as *contributors* to the varied apparatus by which we determine the meaning of the inspired Word. Such difference is not of principle, but of degree only: for all consent that some value, at least, is to be assigned the Fathers in that respect. It is a mere difference of more or less, among those whose principle is the same. But when you speak of the Fathers as men having *final authority* in interpretation, the question is wholly changed. It is then a matter of fundamental principle. The question of degree may be not only between differing Churches of essentially the same Protestant faith, but between different individuals of the same Protestant Church, while all are in the main consistent Protestants. But the question of final authority in the Fathers can be only between Protestants and Papists, and such as are drawing at the same broken cisterns with the latter.

Next to the Rule of Faith, comes the *Substance of the Faith*.

If I were asked what is the place to begin at for the purpose of attacking the Tractarian system, as a thing of *external* evidence, I should answer, the Rule of Faith. Settle the point that the Bible alone is to be the final arbiter of the controversy, and the work is done. But if I were asked what is the point whence to survey the Tractarian system, and try it to the heart, as a *doctrinal theory, professing to be the Gospel of Christ,* so as best to get all its bearings into one view, I should answer, *the great Scripture doctrine of justification by faith only, through the imputed, or accounted righteousness of Christ.* Take your stand at that central eminence. All the lines of Gospel truth meet therein. Let your eye trace them out. The whole map of this false pretense of truth, in the manifest opposition of its every course and bearing, will lie out before you.

As to the substance of the faith, you know, brethren, what the doctrine of this system is concerning the righteousness whereby a sinner must be justified before God. We say as our Church says,* as the Bible says, the righteousness of Christ's obedience unto death as our surety, whereby he fulfilled the law and paid our ransom; a righteousness external to us, and becoming ours only by being accounted of God unto us, when we put forth the hand

* See Article XI., and Homily on Salvation.

of a living faith to Christ. This, the system under consideration rejects with utter disdain and execration, and sets up in its place a righteousness in man, implanted by the Spirit in Baptism, and increased by good works. It distinctly asserts that "the righteousness in which we must stand at the last day is *not Christ's own imputed obedience,* but of *our good works.*" * Righteousness imparted and inherent in us, instead of righteousness accounted unto us and inherent only in Christ, is their whole basis of a sinner's hope." †

I know it was once positively denied, in the earlier writings of the school, that they held to the doctrine of "inherent righteousness." Then it sounded too much like Rome. They have lost the fear of such a sound. Romish sympathies are rather to be boasted at present than denied. The identity of their doctrine with that of Trent, in this particular, is now no more concealed. The only veil they were ever able to use, while as yet reserve was convenient, was an old scholastic invention which the Decrees of Trent allowed to remain unadopted and uncondemned, the alleged difference between a righteousness *within,* but not *in* us; indwelling, but not inwrought; indwelling as an inhabitant, but not inherent as a *quality,* of the man. The invention was too subtle to serve any purpose.

Take it, then, brethren, as a matter confessed, that the whole foundation on which this system directs the sinner to trust for justification before God is a righteousness within him, his own, as his soul is his own, implanted by the Holy Spirit, and that only in Baptism, but brightened in the Eucharist, good works also increasing it, venial sin diminishing it, mortal sin effacing it.

Need I say a word to make you sensible of the awful perversion of the Gospel which is contained in this? Sad is the state of any mind when such a doctrine can pass before it as a mere matter of opinion, or, at most, as a subordinate subject of condemnation.

---

* Newman on Justification, p. 59.

† It is of this doctrine, which these writers will not now deny to be the doctrine of our Homilies and Articles, and of such standard writers as Hooker, Beveridge, &c., not to speak of the Reformers, that the following is written in No. lxv., p. 227, of the British Critic:

" . . . . With regard to one statement very common among Protestants within our Church, for our humble part, we took the liberty in our last number of characterizing it (taken as a statement, however neutralized by the conscience, or, in many cases, personal religion of its advocates) as being *by so much worse than heathenism, by how much radical error is worse than partial truth.* Without, however, recurring to this sentiment *(which was both conceived and expressed by no means at random, but with perfect deliberation),* nor to the doctrine which gave it birth, let us look at other points of less awful importance now in controversy."

Low, indeed, is the spiritual condition of our Church, if controversies from without, as to matters of order, can seem to bear comparison in the sight of her Clergy with this within, as to our hope, our life, our all. It was precisely for the same doctrine that Hooker charged the Church of Rome with "overthrowing the foundations of faith."* Brethren, it is no light thing to take away from the contrite sinner that corner-stone, elect, precious, which God hath laid in Zion for his sure hope and refuge. That refuge is "a stone of stumbling and a rock of offense." The self-righteousness of the Jew stumbled over it. The wisdom of the Greek despised it. The whole Babel-tower of Romish invention has fallen upon it to crush it. Let us beware! It is "the foundation of God," and "standeth sure," sealed with the King's signet, precious to them that believe. "Whoever falleth on that stone shall be broken." "Wood, hay, and stubble" cannot fight with a rock. No system of faith can escape entire destruction and shame, sooner or later, that is not built on that corner-stone.

Hence, brethren, you may estimate the character of this system in regard to that other great division of the substance of the faith, *Sanctification*. What can you expect of holy fruits when the only tree on which the Scriptures bid us look for them is cut up by the roots? All the holiness of the Christian life is ascribed in the Word of God to the operation of justifying faith. But the whole existence, as well as operation, of such faith is destroyed, when you have not only removed the foundation of its trust, but substituted another of precisely an opposite character. In the Gospel plan, justifying faith is a *trusting* of the heart in Christ. In this, it is only *"the belief and acceptance of certain principles."* † In the

---

* Discourse on Justification.
† Tract 86, p. 94.
"Faith brings us to Baptism; by Baptism God saves us." "By faith we desire to be healed. By Baptism He healeth us."—*Pusey's Views of Baptism*, Am. ed, p. 49, 69, 70. Faith is "that which *earns Baptism.*"—*Newman's Sermons*, vol. iii. serm. 6, Eng. ed. "What does the Scripture say of faith before Baptism, *but as a necessary step* to Baptism? Its highest praise before Baptism is, that it *leads to it;* as its highest efficacy after it is, *that it comes from it.* Nothing is said of it before Baptism that is not said of repentance or of RESTITUTION, which are also necessary conditions; but before it, it is without availing power, without life in the sight of God, as regards our justification. *Upon* these, not in and through them, comes Gospel grace; *meeting*, not *co-operating* with them."—*Newman on Justification*, p. 277. Thus faith justifies no more than does the restitution of stolen goods. It is necessary to justification, because necessary to Baptism; and it is necessary to Baptism no more than restitution. It *meets* baptismal grace, but has no *co-operation* with it in our justification. And yet these writers, *teaching*

Gospel, faith brings the sinner directly to Christ; in this system, faith only brings him to the Church and its Sacraments. It need not know anything *explicitly* of Christ. In the Gospel, two things are continually united as those which make for our peace—Christ's righteousness, and faith embracing it, putting it on, taking refuge therein, and drawing therefrom the Spirit of God to carry on the work of God in the heart. These are always in the foreground. In this system they are utterly excluded; and the substitute is a righteousness in the sinner, and faith coming to Baptism to have it implanted, to the Eucharist to have it renewed, and to almsgiving and various works and sufferings of man for its increase, the sinner knowing no better refuge for peace with God.

The great motive by which the Gospel acts, and from which faith takes its chief and holiest incitement to obedience, is the love of God as manifested in the atoning sacrifice of Christ. The Atonement is always in the eye of Gospel faith. But here, to set the Atonement in any such prominence is pronounced "*unscriptural, uncatholic, unreal,*" to which the principle of this system is declared to be "*directly opposed, throughout, in tone and spirit, in tendencies and effects, in principles and practices.*" * We are taught that the doctrine of the Atonement should not be brought into "*prominent and explicit mention.*" † We are to preach it (we read) as John the Bapist preached it, by preaching repentance, alluding to the Atonement only, as they suppose he did, "*secretly, obscurely,* and, probably, only to a few chosen and favored disciples, to whom it must have been *a dark saying.*" ‡ We are to prepare the heart " for receiving the faith in its fullness," " by insisting, first of all, if need be, on natural piety, the necessity of common honesty; on repentance, judgment to come; by urging such assistances to poverty of spirit as fasting and alms, and the necessity of reverent and habitual prayer." § What less could a Platonic philosopher have said? We are to preach men into the acceptance of the Gospel without a word of Gospel in our preaching; we are to lead men to the cross of Christ without a word explicitly about Christ and his cross. Yes, they say, " explicit belief in the Atonement is not to be expected " in a believer any more than the explicit teaching of it is to characterize the preacher. It is "*hidden* in the

---

Economically, would have it appear as if they did really hold to faith as the "*internal* instrument" in justification, as Baptism is the *external*.

See their doctrine of Faith treated at large in my work entitled Righteousness by Faith, chap. vi.

* Tract 87, p. 48.   † Ib., p. 53.   ‡ Ib., p. 52, 53.   § Ib., p. 50, 51.

Sacraments."* "We hardly know what we speak of when we speak of the Atonement."† "The true knowledge of it is expressed in such words as these, '*the salvation of God is nigh unto them that fear him.*'"‡ The contrast drawn between the manner of exhibiting the Atonement in this system and in that which it opposes, is that, by the latter, it is *declared* by eloquence of speech;" by the former it is *held*, not declared; "held in its substance," "after a certain manner of reserve in the Sacraments."§ "He who has embraced the Atonement (we are told) with most affection will speak of it with most reserve." "Doubtless (they say) we are saved by faith in Christ alone; but to come to know this in all its power is the very perfection of the Christian. * * * But as for that assurance and sensible confidence with which it is thought necessary that it should be preached, it would seem as if there was scarcely anything against the subtle effect of which we are so much guarded in Holy Scripture as this."

What, brethren, must we do with our ministry, if this system shall make us its captives? Must we so unlearn all we know of the blessed Atonement of our Lord, that we shall feel that we hardly know what we mean when we speak of it? I trust, indeed, you all know now what it is. May God teach you more and more! Must we so preach Christ crucified, "that, instead of aiming anxiously to make the poor, penitent sinner know at least as much about his death, his Atonement, his full and perfect oblation and satisfaction for the sins of the whole world as we know, we shall aim at keeping him in utter ignorance; wrapping up, as "*a great secret,*" all that is blessed and comforting in the Gospel; hiding it under veils, instead of declaring it from the housetops: putting the light of life under the altar-cloth, instead of setting it in the golden candlestick of the sanctuary; coming down from the high and blessed station of ambassadors of Christ, charged with "the Word of reconciliation" to preach to every creature, and making the chief value of our office consist in the ministering of Sacraments, as curtains to keep out of sight the doctrines of Christ? Is it to be our great consolation, when we come to review our ministry from a deathbed, that, instead of being able to call our people to witness that we have "not shunned to declare unto them all the Gospel of God," we may bid them testify that we have told them nothing about their Saviour more explicitly than they could learn by looking at the unrent veils of Sacraments; that we have never alluded to the Atonement but "secretly and obscurely" to "a few chosen

---

* Tract 87, p. 88.   † Ib., p. 67.   ‡ Ib., p, 61.   § Ib., p. 88, 61, 53.

and favored disciples" among them, and even then only so as to leave but "*a dark saying*" in their minds? Begone, with shame such impudent grasping at priestly domination over the minds of men, by means of their ignorance, under pretense of Gospel wisdom and truth! The system that carries all this within it— the system that does not necessarily and instinctively revolt at all this as utterly false and vile, deserves itself to be utterly reprobated. No milder language becomes it. We have no right to speak more softly of what must be so abominable in the sight of Him whose last charge was, "*Go preach the Gospel to every creature.*"

In the Gospel, the great instrument of sanctification, of awakening and converting the sinner, of leading him to Christ, and promoting the whole work of God's grace within him, is the *Word* of God—the Word preached by his "ministry of reconciliation." The Saviour's great prayer on earth for the sanctification, of his people was, *Sanctify them through thy truth.*" But here, the free circulation and general reading of the Scriptures are discountenanced. Nothing is said in favor of the private reading of the Word of God as a means of grace. It is not *sacramental:* it is private, not priestly. The system, therefore, has nothing to do with it. But an image or sign of the *cross* is a great means of grace, for it is (they say) "*a sacramental sign,*" "a holy, *efficacious* emblem." Its use is "*half sacramental.*" That Bibles should be multiplied far and wide is no matter of zeal with them; but that crosses should be everywhere, this is their zeal. "Let us multiply the holy, efficacious emblem (their enthusiasm exclaims) far and wide. *There is no saying how many sins its awful form may avert.*" By that sign, we are told, the early Christians "put devils to flight, and drew to themselves the fuller blessings of Him who died on the cross." *

As for the *preaching* of the Word, they grant "it may be necessary *in a weak and languishing state*, but, to say the least, Scripture has never much recommended it as a mode of doing good." † The great tendency to sermons, since the Reformation, indicates a low and decayed state." "Such passionate appeals to the feelings, as they often are, would not be so objectionable in themselves, if they were given outside the Church, and not allowed to occupy the place of religious worship." ‡ Then, for countenance in this low estimate

---

* Ib., No. lxvii., p. 14. Tract 86, p. 58.

"With the cross should be associated (we are gravely instructed) other Catholic symbols, such as the Lamb with the Standard; the descending Dove; the Anchor; the Triangle; the Pelican; the Ιχθύς (fish), and others. These should be confined to the most sacred portion of the building."—*Brit. Crit.* No. liv., p. 271, 272.   † Tract 87, p, 75.   ‡ Tract 86. p. 18.

of preaching, they turn to heathen moralists, especially Pythagoras and Socrates: "the former (they tell us) being remarkable for his mysterious discipline and the silence he inspired; the latter, for a mode of questioning which may be considered as entirely an instance of the kind of reserve in teaching" which is advocated in the Tracts.*

In short, brethren, the direct presentation to the mind, and conscience, and heart, of the simple truth of God, as revealed in, and peculiar to the Gospel, by means either of private reading or public preaching of the Word; the direct, immediate contact of revealed truth, concerning the faith of Christ, with the sinner's understanding and affections, for his conviction, conversion, sanctification, is not in the least a feature of this system. On the contrary, the knowledge of Gospel doctrine, concerning Christ in his person and offices, is represented as lying at the end, rather than at the beginning, of a Christian life. The *explicit* knowledge of such matters has no connexion with the setting up of the kingdom of God in our hearts. It is enough to know them *implicitly*, that is, to know the Church, and to believe that the Church knows and holds whatever is true. A sinner becomes a Christian under the preaching of "*natural* piety," "of common honesty, repentance, judgment to come, fasting, alms, and prayer." † This sort of preaching will make him desire salvation, and, therefore, desire Baptism, as that power of grace by which "God saves us." This *desire of Baptism* is said to be the very essence of justifying faith. He comes and is baptized. Now he is a Christian, and without any knowledge of Christ. Truth is not taught him, but kept for him in the Church, behind the altar. It is his, because he is part of the Church. She gives him the benefit of its possession, without the necessity of his knowing what it is. It is enough that the Church knows. The more obedient he shall be to the Church, the more she will reward him with the knowledge of her secrets. By-and-by he may come "fully to know that we are saved by faith in Christ only" (in the sense of the Tracts), but his attaining eternal life has no connexion with any such knowledge. All things belonging to his salvation are to be sought and found in, to be begun and finished by, the Church; through her priesthood, as her *hand* by which, and through her Sacraments, as the *channels* through which, out of her own "*abiding,*" *inherent* treasure of grace, deposited in her as "a storehouse" at the beginning of the Gospel, she communicates regenerating and justifying grace to the

---

* Tract 87, p. 75. † Tract 87, p. 50, 51.

sinner. She is, to the sinner, *Christ*. The language is not too strong for the head writers of this system. She is all the Christ to which they teach the sinner to look *directly* for grace.

We are expressly told that the Church is "an abiding personification of the great sacramental principle of the consecration of matter" for the conveyance of grace; that "Christ is continually *incarnate* in his Church;" that "the priesthood may be called *the organs of the Spirit,* who dwells within the Church, whereby He grasps the several members, and unites them to the one body;" they are "the Church's functionaries, in dispensing to the people *her* varied blessings; by whose special agency the Church collective intercedes for, and applies *her* blessings to, her members, *one by one.*" They are "organs of that Body which is the fullness of Him who filleth all in all."* Christ is represented as having purchased the grace of eternal life for all alike, and as having left to the Church the office of going from one to another of his people, and *making the special dispensation* thereof out of *her* own abiding deposite, according as each has need. "She descends from her throne in the congregation, and comes to us, *one by one*, and knows us by name, and investigates our several needs, and prescribes for our private ills;" and this she does, we are told by the priest, *in auricular confession!* †

The whole system, you see, brethren, is one of Church, instead of Christ; priest, instead of Gospel; concealment of truth, instead of "manifestation of truth;" ignorant superstition, instead of enlightened faith; bondage, where we are promised liberty—all tending directly to load us with whatever is odious in the worst meaning of priestcraft, in place of the free, affectionate, enlarging, elevating, and cheerful liberty of a child of God.

From all this you see how different is the expression so current among us of the *Gospel in the Church,* when used by such writers, from its acceptation when used by ours. With us it means only the Gospel, *preached*, indeed, with all fullness and freeness, but preached in connexion with, and under the several provisions of Christ's Church, and not in exclusion of them. With them it means precisely the contrary—the Gospel not *preached*, but *hid*, in the Church; reserved under the robe of the priesthood, and the veils of Sacraments and sacramental signs; the Gospel, kept in the Church, as the Ark of the Covenant was kept under the curtains of the Tabernacle, and seen by the people only as they saw the coverings that concealed it.

* Brit. Critic, No. lxvii., p. 54, 55, 56.   † Ib., No. lxiv., p. 315, 316.

What more need I say, brethren, to show the wretchedness of this system—as one pretending to be the instrument of God for the promotion of holiness among men? I had thought to tell you something of the miserable work it makes of that great work of New Creation by the Holy Ghost, which lies at the basis of all spiritual character; how, under the most exalted and spiritual expressions concerning the greatness of that change, it really evaporates it into a mere figment of cloudy mysticism; how it dishonors the whole spiritual character of Christianity, by teaching a doctrine of baptismal regeneration, such as the most advanced in belief on that head whom we ever had in our Church, never held—the doctrine that all who were ever baptized, except simply those *adults* who placed the resistance of positive unbelief or hypocrisy in the way of the influence of Baptism, that the millions of the ungodly, but baptized of Papal lands, for example, who have never exhibited one least sign of the fruits of the Spirit, have all been the subjects of a great "moral change," by which, in the most *actual sense,* they were *joined unto Christ,* and made "*partakers of the Divine nature,*" "*created anew,*" as they can never be created again; "*transformed,*" "*renewed,*" "*regenerated,*" "*born again,*" "*spiritualized, glorified in the Divine nature,*" and that not *conditionally,* in any sense, but "*actually*" and "*really*" in the fullest sense.* In truth, a greater dishonor is not done to the dignity of the Gospel and the understandings of men, by the Popish fiction of transubstantiation, than by the doctrine of baptismal regeneration, as it is boasted by this system for its great central position and chief glory. In the former, we are required to believe that consecrated bread has been changed into the actual flesh of Christ, while all our senses testify that it is as much bread as any that is unconsecrated. In the latter, we are required to believe that millions upon millions of persons have been made new creatures, the subjects of a great moral change, wherein the old man was put off and the new put on, actually, fully, spiritually, in the strictest sense, while our senses testify that they are precisely the same

---

* All the above expressions are used by the Tract writers for the change wrought by Baptism in every baptized infant, and in every adult who does not place the impediments named above in the way.—See *Pusey's Views of Bapt.,* Am. ed., pp. 33, 96, 97. *Preface to same, and Tract* 76. *Tract* 82, p. 16. *Newman on Justif.,* pp. 251, 252.

It is a great mistake to suppose there is any essential likeness between the doctrine of baptismal regeneration which such as Bishop Hobart held and that taught in the Tracts. I may hereafter take occasion to show the essential difference.

wicked men, and always have been, as the unbaptized and ungodly around them.*

Either we must suppose that we are expected to put up with such a barefaced contradiction of the senses of all men, or else that, after all this heaping of the strongest and most spiritual terms of Scripture upon the moral and internal nature of this baptismal transformation, nothing still is meant more radical and spiritual than may exist in company with entire ungodliness of living. The latter I believe to be the true state of the case. Strip this wonderful regeneration of all the transcendental and mystic verbiage with which they hide its real nature, and you will find nothing left but a name, a fiction of ages of Papal darkness, wherein the Bible was almost an unused book; a change so purely external and relative, to say the best of it, that it may exist as really in the wicked as the righteous; and this represented as the great spiritual regeneration required in the Scriptures, by which alone a sinner becomes a child of God, and meet for heaven. But this empty doctrine of baptismal regeneration is called by these writers "the very keystone of all practical theology," "upon which the whole fabric of Catholic truth depends for its strength and solidity." What, then, must be the spirituality and holiness of a system of divinity which rests upon, and is conformed to, such a basis! †

I have now said enough to show that from such a system we can no more expect holy fruits, than "grapes of thorns, or figs of thistles." What its *disciples* are in point of holiness, is not the

---

* The latest expression of the nature of the change wrought in Baptism, though by no means surpassing in strength what has often been said before, is as follows : In infant Baptism the infant is "the recipient of the greatest blessings which it can enter into the heart of man to conceive, even the translation from the kingdom of Satan into the kingdom of Christ, and *the transfiguration of the whole nature from a state of moral and spiritual debasement and helplessness, into one capable of performing the achievements of saints, and inheriting the glory of angels.*—*Brit. Crit.*, No. lxvii., p. 75.

† Perhaps the reader may see some explanation of the above in the xxviiith canon of the decree of the Council of Trent on Justification : " If any man shall say that when grace is lost by sin, faith is lost together with it ; or that the faith which remains is *not a true faith, though it be not living ;* or that a man is *not a Christian who has faith without love,* let him be accursed."

These ungodly millions of the baptized are still renewed and partakers of the Divine nature, Christians really, having a true faith ; but, having fallen into mortal sin, their really Christian state, though remaining, is not *availing*. It must be righted and made efficacious by *attrition* (it need not be *contrition*), united to confession to a priest, with absolution and penance, *i. e.*, by the Sacrament of penance. Is not this the Tractarian doctrine essentially ?

question. Men may be pious in spite of a defective creed, from influences prior to its adoption, or extraneous to its provisions. We are speaking of *the system*, not of those who now profess it. Its direct working must be to produce, in fruit, what it is in substance; a form of godliness, and the denial of the power thereof. As a system of religion, it is but another form (an old form new dressed) of formality, animated, indeed, to a very great degree, but with the life of fanaticism, the peculiar fanaticism of formality; the worst fanaticism, because the most intrenched in attractive forms; the worst formality, because the most insidious counterfeit of spiritual life. The old Pharisees were full of precisely this most dangerous of all types of spurious religion; compassing sea and land for prosyletes, full of zeal for traditions, for ceremonies, for fastings, for the Temple, for garnishing the sepulchres of the righteous, for holy days and holy places, for "taking away the key of knowledge" and hiding it under the interpretations of the Fathers, for "shutting up the kingdom of heaven against men." This was their religion. It was all dead formality, and yet all alive with fanaticism, and, like a whited sepulchre, looked very beautiful and pious to those who looked only on the outward appearance. But the Saviour abhorred it as full of uncleanness, and the men who taught that system of self righteousness he likened unto "*graves which appear not, and the men that walk over them are not aware of them.*" *

Such precisely is the deceitfulness of the active, vigorous formality of this system; and such, by-and-by, more and more, will be the men who shall teach it, whatever its teachers are now. Because fanatical, it looks spiritual. Because zealous, it seems pious. Because all in motion with the spirit that possesses it, it would make us believe it is all alive with the Spirit of God. Beware! Try the spirits! Dead bodies seem wonderfully alive when galvanized. There is a spirit, mighty, crafty, full of wiles, insatiably bent on the destruction of the kingdom of Christ, entering into forms of religion and bodies of doctrine as he used to into bodies of flesh and blood, and who thus appears sometimes as an angel of light, only to be more effectually an angel of darkness and death.

And now, brethren, can we fail to see that the true question between us and the advocates of this system is simply whether we shall come under the anathema pronounced by St. Paul upon the preacher, angel or man, who should preach any other Gospel than that which he had preached? A question, not between two aspects

---

* Luke, xi. 44.

of the same Gospel, or two modes of presenting the same substantial truth, but really between *two Gospels*, the one according to man, the other according to God; the very question of the Reformation revived in all its chief particulars, and to be met by Protestant Christians now, as then, in that spirit of deep seriousness and faithfulness which carried our fathers to the stake rather than allow them to compromise, or impair in the least, what they believed to be the solemn and precious truth of God.

Be assured, if *you* do not regard the difference between the two sides of the controversy as of such momentous importance, our adversaries do. Their last publication declares that "*it cannot be too often repeated, that if Protestantism be Christianity, Catholicism* (meaning of course, their system) *is Antichristianism, and vice versa.*" Protestantism, as a system, is in that article denounced by name as "Antichrist," "the man of sin who opposeth and exalteth *himself* above God."

But, plain speaking as this is, it is by no means new.* There is, however, one thing connected with it of great consequence, and for which we are thankful. Hitherto there has been a sort of generality in their language, by which they concealed from many eyes their real aim. First, they spoke of Ultra-Protestantism as their aversion; next, of plain Protestantism. But to this they joined the name of *Lutheranism*, as if they did not mean *our* Protestantism, that of the Articles and Homilies of the Church of England. Many supposed it was some hyper-Protestantism they were execrating, some extravagant caricature of the doctrine of

---

* Many years ago, one of the standard-bearers of this movement pronounced the Gospel, as held by Protestants, "*a new Gospel*," a modern, private, arbitrary system, "with barren and dead ordinances," feeding men "on husks and shells;" "a visionary system," with "an unreal righteousness and a real corruption." * The language has recently become only more bold. A person is "warranted," we are now told, "in rejecting Lutheranism, on the very same grounds which would induce him to reject *atheism*, as being the contradiction of truths, which he feels, on the most certain grounds, to be the first and necessary principles." † The theological system of which the Protestant doctrine of justification is "the origin and representative," is called, in the same article, "a strange congeries of notions and practices." "Whether any heresy has ever infected the Church so hateful and unchristian" as that doctrine (acknowledged to be the doctrine of our Homilies, and of such men as Hooker, Beveridge, Usher, &c.), "it is, perhaps, not necessary to determine, says the Tractarian organ. None certainly has ever prevailed so subtle and exclusively poisonous. *A religious heathen*, were he really to accept it, so far from making any advance, would sustain a loss *in exchanging fundamental truth* for fundamental error." ‡

* Newman on Justification.   † No. lxiv. p. 282.   ‡ Ibid p. 390.

the Reformation, some abuse of the doctrines of the Church of England. But now they have most conveniently fixed and *personified* their meaning. They have selected a well-known living divine and prelate, whose writings are widely circulated and approved in the Church, as the full example of what they call Protestantism, the man of sin and Antichrist. And who is it? The present meek, learned, faithful, universally beloved Bishop of Chester.* You know, brethren, the eminently spiritual and valuable writings of that well-balanced and judicious mind. No example of Protestantism could have been chosen more in our favor. He is selected as the representative of the Protestant school in the Church of England, while Mr. Newman is put forth as the representative of the Catholic; and the great distinguishing features of the two schools, as shown in these writers, is given in these words: "The bishop considers the act of justification as wholly *extrinsic* and appropriated in each case by the sole instrumentality of faith, Mr. N. understanding justification to consist in the *inward* work of the Holy Spirit. The bishop would say that justified Christians are *accounted* righteous in consideration of a righteousness not their own; Mr. N. that they are accounted righteous inasmuch as they are *made* so, through Christ's righteousness inwrought into them." For this precise view, the Bishop of Chester is said to have embraced the *Lutheran* doctrine; and it is on account of this central point in his system of doctrine that we are boldly told, in the main publication of the Tractarian school, and in an article which comes from no under-workman, that "*the theology which the Bishop of Chester supports, and that to which the Tracts have contributed, are as opposite as light and darkness.*" † Thus it is settled once for all what they revile under the name of Protestantism—nothing foreign, nothing extravagant; simply the doctrine of our Articles and Homilies, in all its simplicity, purity, and moderation.

As to the great gulf between such Protestantism and the system of the Tractarians, these writers are perfectly right. Good Bishop Hall expressed it in a few words, when he said, "To be *imputed* and to be *inherent* differs no less than God and man, Trent and heaven."‡ We shall never meet this controversy aright till we see the question in that aspect of life and death. The words of our adversaries are quite just in reference to those who try to believe, and to

---

* J. Bird Sumner, now Arch. Bp. of Canterbury, 1862, whose works on "Apostolical Preaching," and on the Gospels, were published by the N.Y. *P.E.* Press.
† Br. Crit. for July, 1843, p. 64, 65, 74.   ‡ Hall's "No Peace with Rome."

make others believe, that the matters in dispute are not vital to the Gospel. "There never was," they say, "and never will be, charity in softening down real distinctions; open hostilities are ever a shorter road to eventual peace than hollow and suspicious alliances." *

I repeat and adopt their plain declaration of war, "that if Protestantism (such as they condemn in the writings of the Bishop of Chester) be Christianity, Catholicism (such as we condemn in their writings) is Antichristianism." This is the true issue, and the sooner it is univerally acted upon, the better. We cannot be at peace with this system. We must detest it, because we must love the Gospel of Christ.

And now, my dear brethren, I beseech you "have in remembrance to how weighty an office and charge ye are called—to be Messengers, Watchmen, and Stewards of the Lord." "It is required in stewards that a man be found faithful." The Gospel of Christ, the purity of his Church, the interests of the souls he died for, the glory of God, are committed to your care. You have promised to "give your faithful diligence always to minister the doctrine of Christ as the Lord hath commanded, and as this Church has received the same." You have promised to be "ready, with all faithful diligence, to banish and drive away from the Church all erroneous and strange doctrines contrary to God's Word." Never before were you called, as the dangers of the Church now call you, to fulfill these vows. Take care that you keep your minds exercised in the Word of God, so as to be quicksighted to discern between the good and the evil, lest ye be deceived with vain words, and your weapons be put to sleep with false pretenses, or dishonest concealment on the part of the adversary. Take care that you do not suffer yourselves to be lulled into a false security, by imagining the danger little, because it seems to be distant; not worthy of your watching, because its infection is not visibly spreading in your parishes; exaggerated, because you may not see nor hear of any in our Church so far deluded as to be actually carried captive into outward and visible Romanism.

I am alarmed for our Church; not that I fear for her ultimate purity and continued steadfastness, but that I apprehend a great trial is awaiting her, a great effort of Satan to sift her as wheat, during which her progress will be staid, her testimony enfeebled, her beauty defiled, her great good more evil spoken of than ever, through great evil in her professed lovers and advocates, though

* Br. Crit. No. lxvii., p. 64.

at last she will come forth as gold from the fire. Call me an alarmist? I had rather my trumpet should sound a hundred times in warning when danger is not, than be once silent when it is nigh, even at the door.

I see the praises lavished upon the writings which contain all this system of anti-Christian error. In almost every instance where they have been eulogized in this country, the only drawback is some feeble expression indicating that the eulogist is not to be considered as agreeing with all they contain, while scarcely an instance of eulogy has occurred wherein the points of disagreement have been stated. What can this mean? Is it that the productions praised have not been really read and pondered enough to know what they contain? Is it that they have not been read with eyes sufficiently accurate in the great points of Gospel doctrine to be able to detect their manifold errors? Is it that while their errors, such as that of a righteousness of works for justification, instead of the righteousness of Christ alone, have been really seen and acknowledged, there has not been enough appreciation of the importance of such errors, a sufficient sense of what is vital and precious in the Gospel, to make them seem worthy of being distinctly named and condemned? Or is it that, while these errors have been seen and privately confessed, and really lamented as serious, there has been such a preponderance of zeal for the outward structure of the Church over that for the inward life of the Gospel, that because these writings seemed most potent auxiliaries for the former, though really most injurious to the latter, they must be lauded to the skies for their usefulness, and circulated as lights in the Church? One or other of these modes of accounting for facts must be true. Take either, or take all, as applicable somewhere (and this is my view of the case), and then you have assuredly a state of things calling for alarm. In proportion as we may have ministers in our Church whose doctrinal discernment is too confused to perceive the errors of this system, or whose spiritual discernment is too feeble to perceive their vital importance, or who so hold the proportion of faith that vital errors as to the way of salvation can be overlooked, because there is connected with them what seems important and seasonable truth as to the outworks of the Church; I say, so far as we have such a ministry or laity, we have cause of alarm.

For myself, I know of no good these writings have done, or can do, except as God makes all things work together for good to his Church. If a man go into your house, and set to rights its furniture, and establish its rightful order, and then for bread leave your children a stone; or if he drop the seeds of a plague, and distribute death through your household, will you speak of his benefits? But I deny that, even in outward things, we have received any good. What they have taught in points of order or discipline, even when true in itself, has been rested upon such a basis, or urged by such motives, or placed in such a relative position, as to leave us nothing to be thankful for. Take, for example, the Apostolic succession. There is a part of their doctrine, on that head, which has always been held in our Church, viz., that the ordaining power has descended from the Apostles through the line of bishops. The Presbyterian doctrine is the same as to the reality of a succession, differing as to the line. In both these respects the Tractarian doctrine is the old one of our Church. But when they speak of a succession of saving grace, as well as of ordaining power—of saving grace inherent in the line, and sent down from hand to hand, precisely as the right of ordaining is inherent and descending: when all that is precious in Christ to sinners is made to come to us exclusively through that descent, so that not only does the validity of the Sacraments depend thereon, but the very being of a Church, and the whole regeneration and justification which the Gospel offers; when we are instructed that a sinner comes not to Christ but by coming to his vicars in that line of descent, and Christ comes not to the soul of a sinner, with grace to pardon and sanctify, but through that succession, and that the gate of life is unlocked only by its keys, and the bonds of sin are not unloosed but by its hands; when such awful pretensions are joined to the simple basis acknowledged of old, the doctrine is no longer the same; its whole form and visage are changed. It is the doctrine we have been used to, no more than their doctrine of sanctification or justification is that to which we have been used. In both we recognize some truth; but truth so changed by additions and new relations, that, like the Rule of Faith, when to Scripture is added tradition of men for joint authority, we know it no more, but utterly renounce it.

I have spoken, brethren, of my fears for the Church. It is not that I much apprehend the going over of our Clergy or laity to the Roman obedience. It is not that I suppose there will be any general setting up of this whole system, with all its parts, in the minds of our people. We may have Romanism in substance, without going to Rome. We may take enough of her cup of abomination to paralyze us, if it does not kill us. We may live as a Church of Apostolic order, and die as a Church of Christian spirit, and zeal, and energy, and usefulness. I fear there will be a spreading of these doctrines, whether in part or in whole, to such an extent as greatly to weaken and obscure the preaching of the Gospel, where it does not quite prevent it; to introduce a counterfeit spirituality—one of imagination and mysticism—for the spirituality which hath life and peace; to set up a machinery of "new measures," new to the Gospel, but old to the history of the Church, for the promotion of religion; measures of ceremonial and fanciful innovation taking off reliance from the simplicity of the doctrines of the cross and "the foolishness of preaching" Christ crucified, as "the power of God unto salvation." If such consequences ensue, especially if the coming in of these novelties be the means of encouraging unconverted men to seek the ministry, which, I have no question, is the direct tendency (for it is so much easier for the unconverted to labor in the ministry acceptably to man, when the stress of their office is the administration of Sacraments, instead of the preaching of the Word); I say, if such results ensue, then we shall have sinned and suffered enough to make us put on sackcloth, and weep, and cry, "Spare us, good Lord, and let not thine heritage be brought to confusion."

In the conclusion of this address, I must charge you, brethren, with a few particulars of caution and counsel.

Take care lest you allow an affectionate concern for the honor of our Church to blind your eyes to the reality of the present evil and the resulting danger; so that you will attempt to conceal it and extenuate it, instead of standing against it with watchfulness and prayer. I have no doubt that the accounts circulated in the prints of various denominations of Christians around us as to the spread of this heresy in England, and those so general as to its prevalence in our American Episcopal Church, are greatly exaggerated. In the estimate of many who contribute to those impressions, to be strict in adherence to the universally-acknowledged order of our Church; to be strongly attached, upon principle, to our liturgical worship; to follow faithfully the rubric; to hold Episcopacy on any higher ground than that of expediency; to hold that other and opposing forms of Church order and polity are not just as Apostolic, and consistent with the perfection of a Church, as our own, is to be a partaker of this heresy. Hence it is not surprising that nine tenths of the Clergy of the Church of England are said to be of that way. But the evil is great enough, and the spread of it is sorrowful enough, and the danger is threatening enough, whatever the current exaggerations. No good can come from concealing, denying, or extenuating it. To do so is calculated reasonably to produce the stronger conviction of the extensive working of its leaven. The best way of honoring the Church is to show in your own examples that she has Clergy of spiritual discernment enough to detect and rightly appreciate the evil, and of faithfulness enough to make them its uncompromising opponents.

Again: take care lest your sense of the evil of this system be unduly affected by the reputed piety of its advocates, and its own aspect and boast of spirituality.

What if all that is supposed of the personal piety of the leaders of this movement be true (and to deny it is not any business of mine), is there any evidence that it is the consequence of their present system; that they had it not before their minds were thus perverted from the simplicity of the Gospel; that it has not been deadened and formalized, instead of quickened and spiritualized, by their new sympathies and associations? Will not *they* acknowledge the great personal holiness of those who have carried the standards of Protestantism; and yet do they not denounce that same Protestantism as "another Gospel," and "Antichrist?" Learn, brethren, to separate the cause from its advocate, and to measure doctrine simply by the Word of God.

As to the spirituality of this system, what is it? A man substitutes his own righteousness for that of Christ, and then speaks of his foundation of hope in the highest spiritual language, and with the utmost complacency, and confidence, and thankfulness. Can there be any real spirituality while the basis of the Gospel plan of salvation is denied? A man speaks of eating the body of Christ in the Eucharist. He denies, it is true, the transubstantiation of the bread, but maintains the actual, "*corporal*" reality of the presence of the body of Christ therein, or therewith. He calls it a spiritual presence, but means thereby nothing less than a corporal presence still, a presence as real and substantial as that of the body of Christ in heaven. He tells you that it is by this receiving of the body of Christ—of that same body which rose from the dead, and is now at the right hand of God, and which is given to be eaten in the Eucharist, in a manner he pretends not to be able to explain, that he receives justification, and all the blessings of the Gospel. He receives them by *contact* with the actual body of Christ. All that he means by faith, in that act, is that it brings him to the Eucharist, and so to the body of Christ. The priest in the Sacrament gives him the

* See Tract No. 90.

real flesh of Christ, and thus he is justified. Now let him invest that doctrine with all the spiritual drapery that imagination and enthusiasm can invent. The counterfeit may be very plausible, but the reality is one of the grossest, most carnal corruptions of Christianity. Anything can be made to seem spiritual to those who are not spiritually discerning. The worship of the Virgin Mary, that most odious of all forms of idolatry, when seen under all the passionate expressions of love, and trust, and praise, and prayer, with which Romish superstition arrays it, appears just as spiritual as any of the main peculiarities of the system.* The truth is, nothing can be really spiritual but as it is made up of "the things of the Spirit of God." We may mount up on wings as eagles, but the wings may be only of imagination, or passion, or presumption, and yet may carry us so far into the clouds, that our flight may seem very heavenly, and our path bright with the light of God. But only take another way of reconciliation to God, and another way of holiness than that which God hath made known, and all the mists you can cloud it in, and all the poetic beauty you can cast around it, and all the exalted language of Scripture you can describe it by, cannot raise it one least step above the dead level of earth and of man's unsanctified nature.

Again: Take care lest you be so affected in your minds by the sight of all the sectarian strife and divisions for which our day and land are so remarkable, and by all the evils arising from defective Church-organization and principle, that you become too kindly disposed to a system which comes like our venders of new cures, promising to set in order all that is deranged, to unite all that is divided, to establish whatever is weak.

I grant the exceeding evil and injury arising out of the divisions and strifes of Protestant Churches. But there are greater evils even than these, and one of them is the very remedy proposed. Can we, my brethren, be attracted by a remedy which would give us peace by subverting the Gospel; by chaining down our minds to ignorance and superstition under the implicit faith of the Romish obedience; by locking us up, under what are called

---

* There is a peculiar leaning of all that is spiritual, in appearance, in this system, towards this very abomination. When these writers seem most to mount upon their high places, they seem nearest the express vindication of the Romish Mariolatry. "No one," says the British Critic, No. lxiv. p. 408, "who has not fully mastered this great doctrine, is entitled to any opinion on a subject which many, however, treat in an off-hand manner which is perfectly startling, the question, namely, what is the full and legitimate *development of the Catholic doctrine* on the exaltation and *intercessory power of the Blessed Virgin.*"

the keys of the Catholic discipline, to close fellowship with the worst form of anti-Christian corruptions? Oh! may we pass all our days in divisions, and confusions, and contentions "for the faith once delivered to the saints," rather than die unto God, as a Church, in the prison of such peace!

That the means now in our hands for the securing of unity and peace among all who call themselves Christians are not more successful, is no evidence that we need, or could find, any better. Especially is it no evidence that the faith of Rome could help our infirmities. There is a peace which Satan fears not, and is careful not to disturb. There is another which he has fought against with all his hosts and weapons ever since the Gospel began. That he has so far succeeded as to introduce divers sects and contentions among Protestants, is no proof that the Rule of Faith is not good and sufficient, but only that in the use of it they have not escaped the infirmities of man and "the wiles of the devil."

Finally, brethren, my counsel is, that when you study this evil doctrine, you be especially careful to do it with the lamp of the Scriptures trimmed and burning. It is when the mind gets away from the bright shining of God's own light, that mystical imaginings put on their attractions. Never do clouds seem so beautiful as when the sun is just below the horizon.

Keep your hearts imbued with the savor and unction of the Gospel. When the affections are faithfully exercised with the simple truth as it is in Jesus, there is acquired a spiritual discernment, which, like the apple of the eye, at once detects and resists such errors.

Cultivate simplicity and directness of faith in Christ. The strongest and most established state of the minister, as well as of every child of God, is when he is most sensible that every moment he is dependent upon Christ for wisdom, righteousness, sanctification, and redemption. Be exceedingly jealous lest anything get between your souls and Christ. Near, immediate, simple, affectionate, constant, childlike communion with Him in faith, is your life as Christians, your life as ministers.

Keep your aim fixed upon the great work of saving sinners, by the preaching of the Gospel. It is a great protection against this heresy. There is such a thing as great zeal to bring souls to the Church, not so much that they may be saved, as that the Church may be magnified. There is another zeal which looks first and last upon the saving of sinners by leading them to Christ, and which loves the Church because it is God's consecrated instrument of accomplishing that object *"through belief of the truth."* In this there is great protection. The minister of the Gospel whose heart is earnestly set upon the conversion of sinners to God simply for their salvation and the glory of Christ therein, has a strong breastplate against this danger. And the more he can, by God's blessing, fill the Church with decidedly *converted men*, men of experience in the reality of being made "new creatures in Christ Jesus," the more will he strengthen the Church to stand fast in this trial. The material which will ever be found the readiest to receive the mould of this form of doctrine, is that of the mind which has a serious sense of the need of religion, and little knowledge of what religion is; which understands enough to know that religion must be spiritual and elevated in its contemplations and desires, but has too litle discrimination to perceive the difference between the poetry of religion and its spirituality, between the mysticism of man's imaginings and the mysteries of God's revelation; between a zeal for the Church as a thing of external organization, and zeal for the Church's great Head and Life, as the Alpha and Omega of all saving religion. Make the seriousness of such minds more enlightened, more decidedly spiritual, more distinctly based upon the knowledge of the Scriptures, more specially the seriousness of a heart wholly fixed upon Christ as all its righteousness and hope, and you will proportionably remove them from the reach of this snare. Oh! brethren, above all means for us to use wherewith to protect our own hearts, and those of the people committed to our charge, against these wiles, none can be compared to the faithful study and manifestation of the Word of God, especially in those connexions which are most efficacious in leading sinners to see their guilt and utter condemnation under the law of God, and to take refuge by faith in Christ, as their "wisdom, righteousness, sanctification, and redemption."

Finally: Brethren, in your reliance for the protection of the Church against its present most serious dangers, put your trust only in God. As I have probably a much stronger impression of the greatness of the trial that is now fast increasing, and is yet to increase more and more, than many others who take substantially the same views of the present controversy, so I have, perhaps, a more serious impression of the necessity of calling away the minds of all who stand for the truth from reliance on any devices or labors of man, to a simple, prayerful appeal to, and reliance on, the strong interposition of the power of God. "When the enemy cometh in like a flood," then the Lord only can, and then "the Lord will lift up a standard against him." Nothing else will do in this contest. It is the flood coming upon us. The same which once nearly drowned the Gospel out of the earth, and drove the Bride of Christ into the wilderness. The Lord lifted up his standard against it at the Reformation, and "the waters were driven back." We need again that he should make bare his arm. True, we must not withhold our efforts. Books are good. Sermons, charges, warnings, instructions are good. But God alone can wage this war. Be much in prayer, dear brethren, for the interposition of God to "cleanse, and defend," and raise up with new beauty and power, his Church; that, instead of being torn with controversies within for the very essence of the faith, she may go forth united and mighty "as an army with banners," to do her great work among the nations. Keep yourselves in the cleft of the rock. "Be still" and steadfast, and "wait for the salvation of God."

"Now unto Him that is able to keep you from falling, and to present you faultless before the presence of His glory with exceeding joy, to the only wise God our Saviour, be glory and majesty, dominion and power, both now and ever. Amen."

NOTE.

The following account of the ordination of Rev. Arthur Carey is taken from Extracts from a Sermon by Rev. Mason Gallagher, Rector of the Church of the Evangelists, Oswego, N. Y.;" preached January 13th, 1861, after the decease of Rev. Dr Anthon, and published in the Protestant Churchman, March 2nd of same year.

The publisher adds it on his own responsibility, not having had an opportunity of consulting with Bishop M'Ilvaine, without occasioning too great loss of time.

"You know the history of the Tractarian system, which originated at Oxford. Its unsound teachings reached this country, and were embraced by Clergymen and laymen in great numbers.

"In July, 1843, a young man named Arthur Carey graduated at the General Theological Seminary, and sought orders in our Church. He was gentle and lovely in his character. I knew him well. He was suspected of unsoundness in the faith. The Seminary, it was well known, was largely leavened with the new theology. I can testify to the truth of this charge, as I was then a member of the institution. It was a hot-bed of unscriptural doctrine. The leaders of the new movement had more influence than its sound, able, and venerable Professors. Of my own class in the Seminary, *four* have since become Romanists. After a full conversation with Mr. Carey, Dr. Hugh Smith (with whose parish Mr. Carey was connected) refused, with the advice of Dr. Anthon, to sign the candidate's testimonials. A special examination of Mr. Carey took place, at which the Bishop and eight presbyters were present. At this examination, Mr. Carey avowed that he deemed the differences between us and Rome such as embraced no point of faith. He doubted whether the Church of Rome or the Anglican Church were the more pure; considered the Reformation unjustifiable, and followed by grievous and lamentable results, though not without others of an opposite character; faulted not the Church of Rome for reading the Apocrypha for proof of doctrine, and did not consider that we were bound to receive the Thirty-nine Articles in any close and rigid construction of the same; declared that he knew not how to answer the question which had been repeatedly asked, whether he considered the Church of Rome to be now in error in matters of faith; was not prepared to pronounce the doctrine of transubstantiation an absurd or impossible doctrine; did not object to the Romish doctrine of Purgatory, as taught by the Council of Trent. He believed that the state of the soul after death was one in which it could be benefited by the prayers of the faithful and the sacrifice of the altar; regarded the denial of the cup to the laity as a severe act of discipline only; justified the invocation of saints; in one instance, declared that he did not deny, but would not positively affirm the decrees of the Council of Trent; in another, that he received the articles of the creed of Pius IV., so far as they were repetitions of the decrees of that council."

"Incredible as it may seem, such was the madness of the hour, the Bishop and six of the presbyters decided to ordain this candidate; are we surprised that Drs. Smith and Anthon, as faithful Protestant Clergymen, refused to give their sanction to such an act? The day of the ordination arrived—a most eventful day in the history of our Church. I was present at the scene. I remember the question of the Bishop, whether any one present knew any impediment in the way of the ordination. I remember how those two undaunted men arose, and read their public protest. The ordination proceeded. The two protesters left the Church. I remember the loud Amen of Bishop Ives, at the conclusion of the form of ordination. He was present in the chancel. Mr. Carey died a few months after his ordination. Five years later, Dr. Smith rested from his labors. The ordaining Bishop was suspended for unworthiness, the year after the ordination; and Bishop Ives entered the Church of Rome."

REASONS FOR REFUSING TO CONSECRATE A CHURCH HAVING AN ALTAR INSTEAD OF A COMMUNION TABLE: OR, THE DOCTRINE OF SCRIPTURE, AND OF THE PROTESTANT EPISCOPAL CHURCH, AS TO A SACRIFICE IN THE LORD'S SUPPER AND A PRIESTHOOD IN THE CHRISTIAN MINISTRY, BY CHARLES PETTIT M'ILVAINE, D. D., BISHOP OF THE PROTESTANT EPISCOPAL CHURCH IN OHIO.

The following pages were addressed by the Author to the Convention of his Diocese in 1846, and made part of his annual communication to that body. The reader will thus account for some appearance of abruptness at the beginning—and other features as it proceeds:

IN times past, when nothing seemed less possible than that the Romish corruptions of Christianity should make head in the Protestant Churches of England and of this country; when a man would have been thought almost mad who should have predicted that, by this time, and as the work of about ten years, such changes as we are witnesses of, as well in attachment to the great principles of the Protestant Reformation, as in detestation of the antichristian doctrines of Popery, would take place at home and abroad; when for one minister of a Protestant Church to become a Romanist, was singular enough to excite universal astonishment; and when the fact that nearly one hundred clergyman of our mother Church in Great-Britain, and several from our own Church, have apostatized to the faith of Rome within some five or six years, had it been predicted would have been utterly ridiculed, as too impossible to be even dreamed of; it is not singular that some things then should have been looked upon as matters of indifference which such alarming changes have now compelled us to regard as of serious importance in connection with the growth of false doctrine among us.

Of that class, is *the form of the structure on which we celebrate the Supper of the Lord.* We have not been accustomed hitherto to take that matter into much account, except as a question of taste. It has always indeed been decidedly the usage of our Church to have a literal table, as distinguished from an altar-form structure. Until a very few years, the contrary was not seen. It is still an exception to the general custom. But as long as it seemed to be a mere matter of architectural preference; as long as there appeared among those who called themselves members of the Protestant Episcopal Church, no effort to "*unprotestantize*" the Church, to east dishonor upon the principles of the Reformation, and to bring back the outcast corruptions of the Church of Rome, especially her doctrine concerning a real and propitiatory sacrifice in the Eucharist, and a real, sacrificing, mediatorial priesthood in the Gospel minister, as if he stood between God and man at an altar of mediation, and as if your peace with God depended on his priestly intercession there; under such circumstances there was no sense of hazard in leaving people to follow their fancies in the particular article of Church furniture referred to; although then, just as much as now, to have any thing but a *literal table*, in the usual sense, for the communion of Christ's household of faith, was at variance with the directions of the Prayer-Book, the precedents of the Scriptures, and the practice of the early Church.

But wonderfully have matters changed within a very few years. What sort of language and of sympathy, in regard to the Reformation, and the peculiar doctrines of the Church of Rome, especially those most connected with our present subject, have we become so accustomed to, of late, among professed Protestant Episcopalians, that we almost cease to notice them; but which, a few years ago, would have seemed impossible to any but a real Romanist! It is now too late for any man of ordinary observation to question that there is in the bosom of the Church of England, and of our own, which shares so necessarily in all the influences that affect the doctrinal condition of the former, a decided and concerted effort to propagate among the Clergy and laity those very essential and central doctrines of Romish divinity against which our Church declares her strong protest on every fold of her banner. This effort is too systematic, too bold, too diligent, too artful, and is already too successful not to be alarming to any mind not already so drugged with its poisons as to be incapable of natural sight; or else so indifferent, or so inordinately anxious for peace, at almost all hazards, as to be unwilling to believe there is an enemy at the gate, until his standard is planted on the citadel.

No object is more essential to the unprotestantizing of our Church, and to the taking away of the great gulf that lies between the Gospel, as she teaches it, and its awful perversion and denial in the Church of Rome, than that of getting away the doctrine of our Articles and Homilies concerning the nature of the Lord's Supper, and substituting that of the decrees of the Council of Trent. Our Church, in the "*Homily concerning the Sacrament,*" having in her eye the very corruptions now sought to be propagated among us, exhorts us to "take heed lest of *the memory* (i. e. of the doctrine of a *remembrance* of the death of Christ in the Eucharist) be made a *sacrifice;*—lest applying it for the dead *we* lose the fruit that be alive." And she assures us that in the Lord's Supper we "need *no other* sacrifice or oblation" (than that of Christ on the cross:) "*no sacrificing priest*, no mass, no means established by man's invention."* But the revolutionary effort, which is best known as the Tractarian, directly contradicts this language of our Church, teaching that we do need another oblation and sacrifice; that the sacrifice of Christ on the cross cannot avail us, unless it be applied by what is called the "*unbloody*" sacrifice of his body and blood upon the altar of the Eucharist; that we must have the mediation of a "*sacrificing priest*" at that altar, or we cannot partake in the mediation of our Great High Priest before the mercy-seat in the sanctuary in the heavens; and consequently that the Lord's Supper is not a mere "*memory*" of a sacrifice, but is a real sacrifice for sin. This is Popery in the essence. This is one of the devices by which, under a mask of Gospel phrase, the Church of Rome evacuates the Gospel of all that makes it a Gospel. This is the hand by which she forges the chains of superstition and priestcraft, and riveting them around the reason and the consciences of men, fastens them down, under bondage, to whatever terms a despotic priesthood may employ.

Now where this doctrine, concerning a real sacrifice and priesthood in the Eucharist, exists, it must have a literal *altar* in the communion; because an altar expresses, and is part of, the very idea of the Sacrament which the doctrine maintains. And it must get rid of a literal *table;* because that declares the very truth concerning the Sacrament, as simply a *commemorative* feast, upon a sacrifice, once offered on the cross, and never in any form to be repeated, which, is most absolutely denied.

This view is so well expressed by Gregory Martin, a learned Romish divine of the sixteenth century, and one of the principal hands in the Rhemish translation of the New Testament, that I am content with his words. "The name of altar, both in the Hebrew and Greek, and by the consent of all peoples, both Jews and Pagans, implying and importing *sacrifice*, therefore we, in respect of the sacrifice of Christ's body and blood, say '*altar*,' rather than '*table*.' But the Protestants, because they make it only a communion of bread and wine, or a *a supper and no sacrifice*, therefore they called it a table only." "Understand their wily policy therein is this: to take away the holy sacrifice of the mass, they

* Homily concerning the Sacrament. Part I.

take away both altar and priest; because they know right well that these three, priest, sacrifice and altar, are dependents and consequents, one of another, *so that they cannot be separated.* If there be an external sacrifice, there must be an external priesthood to offer it and an altar to offer the same upon. So had the Gentiles their sacrifices, priests and altars; so had the Jews; so Christ himself, being a priest, according to the order of Melchizedec, had a sacrifice, his body, and an altar, his cross, upon the which he offered it. And because he instituted *this sacrifice* to continue in his Church for ever in commemoration and representation of his death, therefore did he withal ordain his Apostles *priests,* at his last supper, and there and then instituted the holy order of priesthood and priest (saying *hoc facite,* do this) to offer the *self same sacrifice,* in a mystical and unbloody manner, until the world's end." *

To the truth of the above, as to Protestants making the Eucharist only a communion of bread and wine, I do not agree. But as to the essentially Romish connexion of *altar,* sacrifice and priest, it is all most true. And hence you see that whether the Lord's Supper be celebrated on a table, or on an altar; on a structure the form of which shall express only a feast of communion; or on one which is ever associated with the idea of a proper priest and sacrifice, cannot with Romanists, or those who sympathize with their doctrine of the Eucharist, be a matter of indifference.

We have therefore seen that in proportion as the Tractarian type of Romish doctrine and sympathy has gained favor in England, or this country, there has grown up a marked fondness for altars, instead of tables. In some instances where this substitution is made, I doubt not it is, as it used to be, a mere matter of taste, unassociated with any doctrinal bearing. But I fear such is not generally the case. There is undoubtedly in many a decided charm in the form of an *altar,* because of its connexion with certain forms of doctrine; and for this it takes the place of the simple communion-table. Thus testifies a learned and most able champion of the truth in the Church of England, concerning the state of things there. "Of all the acts of these anti-Protestant agitators" (writes the Rev. W. Goode, author of "the Divine Rule of Faith and Practice") "none more demands our attention, at the present moment, than the attempt to substitute altars for communion-tables

---

* Fulke's Defense of the English Translations of the Bible against the cavils of Gregory Martin. Park. Soc. edit. pp. 515, 516, 240, and 241.

in our Churches. They are now notoriously set up for the furtherance of Tractarian views of the nature of the Sacrament of the Lord's Supper. The communion-table is thrust out of the old Churches to make way for them. They are studiously introduced whenever practicable, into our Churches. And thus the purity of our Church's doctrine on the subject is placed in jeopardy."*

I have not looked without serious consideration upon these things. For several years, I have not consecrated a Church, so far as I can remember, in which there was an altar-form structure, instead of a proper table. But this was rather because such a structure did not happen to be in the new Churches; than because I was prepared to make any serious objection to it. But the new condition of things to which I have already referred, has placed the subject in a very different light; so that I have been led to consider my duty with regard to it, as I had not done before. The conclusion to which I have come is this: that hereafter I must refuse to consecrate any Church in which there is an *altar-form* stucture for the Lord's Supper, and in which there is not a *proper table*, in the usual sense, as the permanent furniture. I must require, not only that there be not an altar, but that there be a *permanent* and *proper* table. Of this determination I take the present opportunity of giving notice to the diocese.

In taking a position which may seem somewhat over-scrupulous to some whose attention has not been much drawn in that direction, it is due, as well to you, as myself, that I should assign my reasons. This I now proceed to do. And, my brethren, if I should go more largely into the subject than the determination just declared would seem to require, you will not think the time misapplied when you see how the whole view brings out most conspicuously the doctrine of our Church concerning the Lord's Supper as containing no sacrifice but such as all believers offer in common with the minister, and as implying no officiating *Priest*, except as that name is used in its original signification of *Presbyter*, or in English—*Elder.* †

---

*Altars prohibited by the Church of England, *by the Rev. W. Goode, M. A., F. A. S.* London.

† The English Translations of the Bible were violently attacked by Romish writers, in the age of the Reformation, because the original word πρεσβυτερος (whence comes our word Presbyter) was never rendered Priest. The Reformers answered thus; "The word *priest*, by Popish abuse, is commonly spoken for a *sacrificer*, the same as *sarcerdos* in Latin. But the Holy Ghost never calleth the ministers of the word and Sacraments of the New Testaments ιερεις or *sacerdotes*. Therefore, the translators, to make a difference between the ministers of the Old Testament and them of the New, call the one according to the usual acceptation, *priests*, and the other according to the original derivation, *presbyters* or *elders*. The name

Let me first go to history. What was the primitive use?

None can deny that our Lord instituted and administered the Eucharist at a common *household table*. And when he says "the hand of him that betrayeth me is with me on the *table*," we necessarily contemplate the Saviour and the twelve as engaged in an act of family, spiritual communion simply; analogous to that of a household around the family table. Nothing can more perfectly exclude the idea of sacrifice, priest, and altar. It was the communion of the Passover. The Supper of our Lord took the place of the Jewish paschal feast. The latter was a feast *after,* and *upon,* a sacrifice which had been previously offered at the great altar of burnt-offerings at the temple. The work of the Jewish *priest* was finished when the paschal lamb had been sacrificed. Other altar a Jew could not have, than that of the temple, around which the blood of that lamb was sprinkled. Other sacrifice there remained none in connection with that feast, when once that lamb had been slain. But there did remain the feast of communion *upon* that lamb, thus offered. The lambs were many; the sacrifice, the feast, the type, was one. It was the communion of the whole household of the chosen people. They met in families, as we meet for our communion in congregations. They met, not at *the altar,* where the sacrifice was offered, but *at the table of the family fellowship;* as we meet

---

of priest, according to the original derivation from *presbyter,* we do not refuse; but according to the common acceptation for a sacrificer we cannot take it, when it is spoken of the ministry of the New Testament. But seeing your Popish sacrificing power, and blasphemous sacrifice of your mass hath no manner of ground in the holy Scriptures, either in the original Greek, or in your own Latin translation, you are driven to seek a silly shadow of it in the abusive acceptation and sounding of the English word *priest* and priesthood. And therefore you do, in great earnest, affirm, that priest, sacrifice, and altar are dependents and consequents, one of another, so that they cannot be separated. If you should say in Latin *sacerdos, sacrificium, altare,* be such consequents, we will subscribe to you; but if you will change the word, and say *presbyter, sacrificium, altare,* every learned man's ears will glow to hear you say they are dependents and consequents, inseparable. Therefore we must needs distinguish of the word *priest* in your corollary; for if you mean the *sacerdotium,* we grant the consequence of sacrifice and altar; but if you mean *presbyterium,* we deny that God ever joined those three in an inseparable band; or that *presbyter,* in that he is *presbyter,* hath any thing to do with sacrifices, or altar, more than *senior* or *ancient* or *elder.*" *Fulke's Defense of the English Translations of the Bible.* Parker Society Ed. pp. 109, 252, 253.

"Ambiguity," says Bishop White, "has arisen from the circumstance that the English language applies the same word 'Priest' to denote two words in the original ἱερεύς and πρεσβύτερος. Of the latter word, it is here affirmed that it never denotes an offerer of sacrifice; and as to the former word, no one alleges that it ever stands for a Christian minister in the scriptures"—*Bishop White's Dissertation on the Eucharist.*

not at the cross, where Christ our Passover was sacrificed for us, but at a table expressive of the family fellowship of all believers in the reconciliation effected by the blood of Jesus. They met without a priest; all that pertained to the office of priest having been finished at the Temple. We meet at the Lord's Supper without any mere human priest : * for all that pertaineth to the office of a priest on earth, in our reconciliation to God, was finished when Christ offered up himself, "*once for all*," on the altar of the cross. The Jews met at the table of the household to feed upon what had elsewhere been offered on an altar as a propitiatory sacrifice to God. Christians meet to feed, by *faith* with thanksgiving, *spiritually*, upon a propitiatory sacrifice, long since offered, even the flesh and blood of Jesus, by which we draw nigh to God. The Jewish Passover was of two parts—"the *sacrifice* of the Lord's Passover," and "the *feast* of the Lord's Passover;" the propitiatory offering at the temple, and the eucharistic supper on that offering, in the family dwelling. It was as much commanded that the feast should be in the house, and not at the temple, as that the sacrifice should be at the temple, and not in any private house. Our Passover is of like two parts, *the sacrifice* and *the feast;* the offering of the Lamb of God, and the eucharistic supper of the whole household of faith, partaken in spirit, by faith in that Lamb. In the beginning of the dispensation of the Gospel, the *sacrifice* of our Passover was slain, once for all. Jesus was priest and victim. The whole period, since then, and to the end of the world, is the feast of the Lord's Passover, during which each believer, every day, is living by faith, in the secret of his own heart, upon the sacrifice of Christ, as all his life and hope; and the whole Christian household of faith are, at stated periods, assembling together to *express and declare*, in the Sacrament of the breaking of bread, their common dependence on, and their common thankfulness for, that one perfect and sufficient oblation and satisfaction for the sins of the whole world. As the Jews were not allowed to unite the offering and the eating, the priestly sacrifice and the eucharistic feast, but were commanded to separate them in point of place and time; so we cannot, by any possibility, unite them, under the Gospel. The sacrifice for us was offered eighteen hundred years ago, "*once for all*." It cannot be repeated. The feast alone remains—a feast *commemorative of a sacrifice*, but not a *sacrifice of commemoration*, except as the offering of prayer and thanksgiving is *figuratively* a sacrifice and each communicant is in that sense a priest.

* Of course I mean priest in the sense of a *Sacrificer*.

All this illustrates how entirely it was as pertaining to the design and original institution of the Lord's Supper, that our Lord assembled the twelve around a common *household table,* for the first administration of that Sacrament; and how little connexion it had with any *sacrifice* as then being offered, or with any altar as then present.

Long after the first institution of the Lord's Supper, the Christian Church continued to keep aloof from any thing expressive of sacrifice, except as it commemorated that of Christ, and was accompanied, on the part of communicants, with the offering of their prayers and alms. Our venerable Bishop White expressed his belief that "the *term* 'altar,' did not supplant the original word 'table' for a considerable time after the Apostolic age."* Suicer says it is clearer than mid-day that altars were not in the primitive Church;" (*meridiana luce clarius.*)

Basnage says that the writings of men of the Apostolic age, such as Clement, Polycarp, Justin, never employed the words High Priest, Priest, &c., for the Christian minister; nor did they any more use the word altar to signify the table of the Eucharist." †

---

* *Dissertation on the Eucharist.*—On the occurrence of *altar* in the Epistles of Ignatius, Bishop White says: "If there be known any opposite testimony, it is in the Epistles of Ignatius, where he speaks of '*within the altar,*' as descriptive of being within the communion of the Church. But he probably spoke figuratively; as the literal construction of his words is inapplicable to the subject, and indeed conveys no clear sense. In the very many places in which he speaks of *presbyters,* he never designates them by the Greek word applied to Jewish *priests.* And yet *altar* in the Jewish sense, would also have required *priest* in the same; and both with the connection of sacrifice."—*Ibid.*

† Basnage Ann. v. xii. Mede, with all his learning in antiquity, could find no instance of the word altar, for table, earlier than Tertullian, who flourished in the beginning of the third century. His next instance is from Cyprian, in the middle of that century. How easy it is to be deceived as to the doctrine of the Church in the early centuries, by reading certain names and phrases, not reflecting on the different use they may have had from that which is now assigned them, is well illustrated in the following from Daille. We have the use of these words, *Pope, Mass, Oblation, Mortal Sins, Penance, Confession, Satisfaction, Merit, Indulgence,* as the ancients had, and make use of an infinite number of the like terms; but understand them all in a sense almost as far different from them, as our age is removed from theirs; just in like manner as of old, under the Roman emperors, the names of offices and of things, for a long time continued the same, that had been in use in the time of the old republic; but with a sense quite different from what they had formerly borne. Thus when we light upon any passage in the ancients, where the Bishop of Rome is called *Papa,* or *Pope,* we immediately begin to fancy him with all the glory at this day belonging to this name; not disallowing him so much as his guard of Swiss and his light horse: whereas they that are but indifferently versed in these books, know that the name *Papa,* or *Pope,* was given to every bishop. The word *Mass* likewise makes us prick up our

Bingham, our learned and standard author in ecclesiastical antiquities, says that as late as the time of Athanasius (4th century) "the Churches had *communion tables of wood;*" and of the churches of Africa and Egypt, particularly, he says : " There is no question to be made that about this time, *the altars were only tables of wood.*" In the year 509, a general decree was made in France " that no altars should be consecrated but such as should be made of stone only." And Bingham says, " This seems to be the first public act of that nature that we have upon authentic record in ancient history. And from the time of this change in the *matter* of them, the *form* or *fashion*, of them changed likewise. For whereas before they were in the form of *tables*, they now began to be erected more like *altars*." *

This comparatively modern use of the form of an altar, instead of that of a table, is strongly asserted by Bishop Jewell, in his Defense of his Apology for the Church of England against the Jesuit Harding.

" As for the altars (he says) which the Donatists brake down, (in tl e Churches of the 4th century) they were certainly *tables of wood, such as we have,* and not heaps of stones such as ye have. St. Augustine saith the Donatists, in their hurry, broke down the *altar-boards.* His words be these : *Lignis ejusdem altaris effractis.* Likewise saith Athanasius of the like fury of the Arians ; *Subsellia, thronum, mensam ligneam et tabulas ecclesiæ et cætera quæ*

cars, as if, even from those ancient times, the whole liturgy, and all the ceremonies used at the celebration of the eucharist, had been the very same that they are at this day. Whereas the learned of both parties acknowledge that these names have, since that time. lost very much of their old, and acquired new significations.—*Daille De Usu Patrum,* c. v.

But how great has been the harvest of evil from the seed of figurative language sown by the Fathers! Bishop Morton says : " The primitive antiquity (as hath been confessed) did abstain from the name of *priest*, and so consequently of *altars* and *sacrifice*, terming them according to the tenor of the New Testament, elders or bishops, *tables*, and eucharist. In the after times, the Church being established in the truth of doctrine, the Fathers might presume to take a greater liberty of speech, knowing that they should be understood of catholic hearers, catholicly. But because ages more degenerate did set, as it were, a bias upon the phrases *priest, altar, sacrifice,* (which had been used by the Fathers improperly,) to draw them to a proper (literal) signification, flat contrary to their first intention ; therefore did Protestants rather wish that those objected ancient Fathers had rather contained themselves within their more ancient restraints, than that the liberty of their speeches should have occasioned in the Romanists that prodigal error in doctrine, which we shall hereafter unfold."—*Bishop Morton's Catholic Appeal for Protestants.*

* Bingham's Antiquities, b. viii. c. vi. § 15.

poterunt, foris elata, combusserunt; they carried forth and burnt the seats, the pulpit, the wooden board, the Church tables, &c. Touching your stone altars, Beatus Rhenanus saith: *In nostris Basilicis, Ararum superaddititia structura novitatem præ se fert;* in our churches the building up of altars, added to the rest, declareth a *novelty.* This learned man telleth you, Mr. Harding, that your *stone altars* are but newly brought into the Church of God, and *that our communion tables are old and ancient, and have been used from the beginning.* We have such altars as Christ, his Apostles, St. Augustine, Optatus, and other catholic and holy Fathers had used."*

Bishop Babington, in his notes on Exodus, published in 1604, says: "The altars used in Popery are not warranted by this example, (i. e. of the Jewish altars.) But the primitive Churches used communion tables, as we do now, of boards and wood, not altars, *as they do,* of stone. Origen was about 200 after Christ, and he saith that Celsus objected it as a fault to Christians, *Quod nec imagines, nec templa, nec aras haberent:* that they had neither images, nor temples, nor altars. Ambrosius, after him, saith the same of the heathens: *Accusatis nos quod nec templa habeamus, nec aras, nec imagines.* Gerson saith that Sylvester first caused stone altars to be made—Upon this occasion, *in some* places, stone altars were used for steadiness and continuance, wooden tables having been before used; but, I say in *some places not in all.* For Saint Augustine saith that, in his time, in Africa, they were made of wood. For the Donatists, saith he, break *in sunder the altar-boards.* Again the Deacon's duty was to *remove the altar.* Chrysostom calleth it *the holy board.* St. Augustine, *the table of the Lord.* Athanasius, *Mensam ligneam,* the table of wood. Yet was the communion table called an altar; not that it was so, but only by allusion metaphorically, as Christ is called an altar; or our hearts be called altars, &c. Mark with yourselves therefore the newness of this point for stone altars in comparison of our ancient use of communion-tables, and let Popery and his parts fall, and truth and sound antiquity be regarded." †

The learned Perkins, one of the greater lights at Cambridge, in the latter part of the 16th century, says: "About this year, 400, the use of altars began; but not for sacrifice, but for the honor and memory of the martyrs. ‡

---

* Defense of Apol., &c. 111, ch. i. div. 3.
† Bishop Babington's Works. Ed. 1622, p. 307.
‡ Perkins' Works, II., p. 553.

It would be easy to show that the use of altars originated contemporaneously with that inordinate veneration for the relics of saints and martyrs which was very soon matured into that idolatrous adoration which is now one of the grievous crimes of the Church of Rome. It is little to the credit of altars, in the Christian Church, to look back to the various growths of astonishing superstition which grew up in company with their use. Mosheim, speaking of the fourth century, says: "An enormous train of different superstitions were gradually substituted in the place of true religion and genuine piety. This odious revolution was owing to a variety of causes. A ridiculous precipitation in receiving new opinions; a preposterous desire of imitating the Pagan rites and of blending them with the Christian worship, and that idle propensity which the generality of mankind have towards a gaudy and ostentatious religion, all contributed to establish the reign of superstition upon the ruins of Christianity. * * The virtues that had formerly been ascribed to the heathen temples, to their lustrations, to the statues of their gods and heroes, were now attributed to Christian Churches, to water consecrated by certain forms of prayer, and to the images of holy men. * * The worship of the *martyrs* was modeled, by degrees, according to the religious services that were paid to the gods before the coming of Christ." *

To such heights of superstition and imposture had the veneration of relics arrived in the latter part of the 4th century, that the 5th council of Carthage was obliged to resist its more odious extravagances. The following extract, from the 14th canon of that Council, will show in what connexion altars arose in the Church: "It is decreed that the *altars* which are set up every where in the fields, or in the ways, as monuments of martyrs, in which no bodies or relics of martyrs are proved to be buried; be overthrown by the bishops of those places, if it may be. But if, on account of tumults of the people, that cannot be done, yet let the people be admonished that they frequent not those places, &c. And let no memorial of martyrs be allowed and accepted, except the body, or some undoubted relics, be there, or that some original of their habitations or suffering be there delivered from a most faithful beginning. As for those altars that are set up, *in every place*, by dreams, and vain revelations of any men, let them by all means be disallowed."

* Mosheim's Eccl. His. Cent., iv., p. 11, § 2.

Faithful to this original connection between altars and tombs, the Sacrament of the Lord's Supper on the top, and dead men's bones within, is the present use of the altar in the Church of Rome. The Rhemish Annotators on the New Testament, commenting on Revelations vi. 9, where occurs the vision of *the souls under the altar,* say, " Christ, as man, (no doubt) is the altar under which the souls of all martyrs lie, in heaven, expecting their bodies, as Christ their head hath his body there already. And for correspondence to their place, or state, in heaven, the Church layeth commonly their bodies also, or relics, *near, or under the altars,* where our Saviour's body is offered in the holy Mass; and hath a *special proviso that no altars be erected, or consecrated, without some part of a saint's body or relics.*" And this " *special proviso* " is founded on the assumption that " the relics of the saints add not a little to the sanctity of the Sacrament *when they are contained in the altar;*" thus fully carrying out the abominable doctrine that we are assisted by the merits of the saints in obtaining justification through the merits of Christ.

Conformed to this tomb-like *use* of Romish altars, and their monumental origin, is their almost invariable *shape.* They are in the shape of *arks* or *chests,* resembling very closely, in general appearance, those oblong structures of stone or brick, surmounted with a marble slab, which from time immemorial have been erected over the dead, as monuments to their memory.*

This peculiar, chest-like form of the Romish altar is wholly unlike any thing under the name of altar of which we have any account. The altars which Moses was directed to make for the worship of Israel, and those which were afterwards set up, according to that model, in the temple at Jerusalem, had no such character. Bingham says, that " when such structures for altars began to be used in the sixth century, they were built *like a tomb,* as if it were some monument of a martyr;" and he quotes an eminent

* " The altar which has been erected " (under Tractarian auspices) " at the Round Church, Cambridge," (which has been condemned by an ecclesiastical court as illegal) " is a mass of stone work, rising as an erection from the ground, and attached to the fabric of the Church. The only point in which it differs from the *tomb-like* altars generally seen in Romish churches, is that it is not closed in front, (though it is on the sides,) the Romish altars being generally closed all round, the interior being devoted to the reception of relics, without which there is a very general feeling among Romanists that the eucharist cannot be properly celebrated upon them. But this *tomb-like* form is not reckoned essential to the being of an altar ; *occasionally,* I believe, a portion of the front is left open, that the relics may be seen, and protected only by a trellis work of brass or other metal.''—*Goode's Altars prohibited in the Church of England.*

authority (Bona) as saying that specimens of such ancient monuments to martyrs were still found, in his days, in the catacombs of Rome and other places.*

It is not difficult to trace the steps by which the martyr's tomb came to be so universally the Romish altar. It is well known that at an early period, Christians took great pleasure in honoring the memory of martyrs, by erecting monuments, over the place of their burial, and in assembling there, for worship, on the anniversary of their death. On these occasions, the martyr's monument served as *a table* on which they celebrated the eucharist.

But now the habit of calling the table an altar was fast driving out the true and primitive name, as Christians, out of a most degrading disposition to conciliate the heathen by adopting their names and conforming to their customs, were getting more fond of speaking of the Lord's Supper as a *sacrifice*, and of its minister as a priest. Thus Jerome is quoted by a Romish Annotator as "calling *the bodies or bones of St. Peter and St. Paul the altars of Christ, because of this sacrifice offered over and upon them.*"† Soon Churches were built over some of those venerated tombs, and the relics were removed from others into Churches, and of course were enshrined in tombs, as became the sepulture of the illustrious dead. And there, as before in the open fields, the eucharistic sacrifice was offered *over*, and *upon*, them; the doctrine having now grown up that "prayer was more acceptable to God when made before the relics of the saints." As the doctrine of the real, corporeal presence of Christ in the eucharist gained prevalence, so grew that of a real sacrifice and a literal altar; and as the idea of uniting the merits of Christ's sacrifice, with the supererogatory merits of saints, for the remission of sins, made progress, so

---

* Bingham's Antiquities, b. viii. c. vi. § 15.

† Gregory Martin, in Fulke's defense of English Translations. The doctrine of any sacrifice in the Lord's Supper, except as the commemoration of that on the cross was *metonymically* called a sacrifice, or as the prayers of communicants were called so, did not get place in the Church till long after; but there was now a dangerous use of figurative terms and a dangerous fondness for the introduction of heathen rites into Christian worship, out of which very naturally grew, by and by, the full doctrine of a literal sacrifice, altar and priesthood. Bishop White says, "there were no *sentiments* for three hundred years, in the Christian Church, which threatened to lead, *even by remote consequences*, to such an extreme," as the Romish errors on this subject.—*Lecture on the Sacraments.* In the fourth century, Eusebius said that the "unbloody and reasonable sacrifices which our blessed Saviour taught his followers to offer, were such as were to be performed by *prayer* and the *mystical service of blessing and praising God.*" *In Laudibus Constantini,* quoted by Mede.

seemed it the more appropriate that in the so-called "Sacrament of the altar," the relics of the saints and the body of Christ should be associated together, the one *upon*, the one *under*, the altar. Thus it came to pass that the only form with which the Church of Rome learned to connect the idea of a Christian altar was that of a Christian martyr's tomb. Such was the form which she handed down to the age of the Reformation and to the present; sacred now in the eyes of her children, as identified with the whole history of her missal solemnities and her miracle-working relics. And now, even among Protestant Christians, so is the association of ideas affected by the outward forms which the pompous ceremonial of Romish worship exhibits, especially when they appear under the garb of antiquity, and are identified with a favorite style of ecclesiastical architecture, that when under the influence of a false architectural taste, or a wrong doctrinal sympathy, our people attempt to erect altars, instead of tables, in their Churches, none ever think of copying the models which God gave to Moses for the worship of Israel, and which are hallowed in our thoughts by all the sacred solemnities of the Jewish Church, as divinely ordained types of the sacrifice of Christ. To imitate the brazen altar of burnt offering—or the golden altar of incense, the only real altar forms that we know of, except those of heathen worship, would at once seem too Jewish. To have something more Christian, we go to the altar of the Church of Rome, for a model; which is Christian, just so far as the idolatrous worship of the wafer in the Mass, and of dead men's bones beneath, is Christian, and no more. When one sees in a Protestant Episcopal Church, instead of a proper table such as he has a right to find, for the holy Supper, what is now called *an altar*, an oblong chest or ark, of stone or wood, closed in on all sides, as if some sacred mysteries were concealed therein; what edifying thoughts is it calculated to awaken in his mind? Is he reminded of the *institution* of the Lord's Supper? But then there was only a common table. Does it symbolize, to his eye, the *nature* of the Lord's Supper? He knows of no sacrifice therein and therefore nothing of which an altar is the proper expression. Does it teach him his *privilege and duty*, as a believer, spiritually to feed by faith, upon the sacrifice of Christ once offered on the cross? He wants a table, not an altar, to suggest that lessson. Does it stand before him surrounded with edifying and inspiring associations arising out of the recollections of the primitive and pure ages of the Gospel? Those ages had no such device. Is it even connected, in his mind, with the venerable usages of the Protestant Episcopal Church? It is a novelty among them! What then? It is fitted only to remind him of its own original, in the midst of the rankest growths of spiritual deformity, when it was a mere martyr's tomb: its top the birth-place of the idolatry of the Mass; its interior a depository of worshiped bones; a most fit symbol of that whole system of spiritual bondage and death, (all centering in the so called "Sacrament of the altar,") under which the Church of Rome has always, since she became what she is, buried the Gospel and imprisoned the minds of men. If there be any thing edifying to a communicant at the Lord's board in contemplating what suggests nothing but the remembrance of all that is false and superstitious in Popery, then indeed is such an altar edifying. The primitive table is just the opposite.

To return to our history—I need not tell you that such was the altar, found in the Churches of England at the period of the Reformation. But it did not remain long undisturbed. With the revival of Gospel truth concerning the nature of our Lord's Supper came the restoration of the primitive table for its celebration. In 1550, Ridley, Bishop of London, issued injunctions to the Churches of his diocese, exhorting that *all altars should be taken down* and that they should "set up *the Lord's board*, after the form of *an honest table*." And one of his reasons was that "the form of a table may more turn away the people from the old superstitious opinions of the Popish Mass, and to the right use of the Lord's Supper." *

An *order* to the same effect, was issued the same year, under date of November 19. We read in King Edward's journal, the following entry: "*There were letters sent to every Bishop to pluck down the altars.*" † Day, Bishop of Chichester, having refused compliance, was imprisoned. When Mary succeeded to the throne, Romanism was re-enthroned, and of course tables were cast out of the Churches, and altars restored. It was then made a serious charge against the Reformers that they had taken away the altars; to which Bishop Ridley, on the eve of his martyrdom, answered: "As for the taking down of the altars, it was done upon most just considerations; for that they seemed to come too nigh the Jews' use; neither was the Supper of the Lord at any time better ministered or more duly received than in those latter days," (the reign of Edward)

---

* Ridley's work's, P—S. Ed. pp. 319—324.
† Burnet's Hist. of Ref., vol. ii. fol.

"when all things were brought to the rites and usages of the primitive Church."*

On the return of the Reformation, under Elizabeth, altars were again cast out by authority, and tables again restored. In 1564-5, certain "*Advertisements for due order in the using of the Lord's Supper*" were "set forth by public authority," in which it was ordained that each parish should provide "*a decent table standing on a frame*, for the communion table." †

In 1569, Archbishop Parker issued to his diocese certain visitation articles; one of which was thus: "Whether you have in your parish Churches all things necessary for common prayer and administration of the Sacraments, especially, * * * the Homilies, a convenient pulpit, well placed; a *comely and decent table* for the holy communion: * * * And *whether your altars be taken down according to the commandment in that behalf given*." ‡

In 1571, were issued the Canons of the Synod of that year, which enjoined that the Church-warden should "provide *a table of joiners' work for the administration of the holy communion*." §

In the same year, Grindal, while Archbishop of York, and afterwards, when in the See of Canterbury, set forth injunctions directing the Church-wardens to "provide in every parish, a *comely and decent table standing on a frame, and to see that all altars be utterly taken down*." ‖

Now it was with this well understood character of *a table* for the communion, as distinguished from an *altar* of sacrifice, "an *honest table*," "a *table of joiners' work*," "a *table of wood standing on a frame*," that in 1603, the present Canon of the Church of England, (the 82d) was enacted; which requires that "there shall be a *decent communion table in every Church*." What the Canon means by "a *table*" the injunctions I have cited perfectly determines.

Cotemporaneously with the injunctions, published in the reign of Elizabeth, was issued our second Book of Homilies, in one of which we are told that "God's house is well adorned, with places convenient to sit in, with the pulpit for the preacher, with the Lord's *table* for the ministration of his holy Supper, with the font to Christen in," &c.¶—In those days it would have been as

* Ridley's works, P. S. Ed. p. 281.
† Quoted from Goode's "Altars Prohibited," who cites Sparrow and Cardwell as his authorities.
‡ Strype's "Life of Parker." App. b. ii., No. xi.
§ Quoted by Goode from Wilk. iv. 266.
‖ Grindal's Works. P—S. E—D. 133, 134.
¶ Homily on Repairing of Churches.

impossible to mistake what, in the laws of the Church of England, was meant by a table, in distinction from an altar, as to confound a pulpit for the preacher, with a font for Baptism.

It is an impressive fact, in this connexion, that whereas in the first Prayer Book of Edward VI., 1548, the word *altar* was retained in some places, where a literal table was meant; when that book was revised in 1552, and the second Book of Edward VI. was set forth, that word was, in every case, erased, and *table* was put in its place. Thus has the Prayer Book of the Church of England remained to this day. The word *altar* is not there, in any connection with the Lord's Supper. It was struck out when it *was* there, as not according to the doctrine of the Church. Every where now the word is *table*. Thus, what is the law of that Church according to her rubrics and canons, as expounded by the visitation articles and injunctions of her Bishops and Archbishops, by the decrees of Synods, and the declarations of her greatest divines, is manifest beyond a rational question. A learned writer states it thus: "The only thing which properly answers the legal requisition of our Church, must have the three following characteristics:

First,—As to *material*, that it be made of wood.

Secondly,—As to *form*, that it be a table in the ordinary sense, of the word, that is, a horizontal plane resting upon a frame or feet

Thirdly —That it be unattached, in any part, to the Church, so as to be a *moveable* table." *

The recent decision of the highest ecclesiastical and judicial authority in England, commanding the altar lately erected in the Round Church in Cambridge to be removed, as illegal, fully, confirms all that we have now said as to the law of the Church of England on this subject.

Before leaving this historical view, it will be edifying to reflect upon the alternate rise and fall of altars and tables, in the history of the English Church, according as Romish or Protestant principles prevailed. With the prevalence of the Reformation under Edward, the symbol of a priestly sacrifice and a priestly mediation, fell down before the ark of Christ's holy Gospel, and the primitive symbol of the *communion feast*, at which all believers have equal rights of fellowship with their Lord and Saviour, was set up again as Christ and his Apostles left it. But with the return of the dominion of Popery under Mary, came back the priests and their altars—and the casting out of the Lord's table. The restoration again of the Gospel to the pulpits, under Elizabeth

* Goode's Altars Prohibited.

was the signal for the restoration of the symbol of its blessed feast of grace, in Jesus Christ. When, afterwards, in the times of Archbishop Laud, there was a revival of Romish sympathies and doctrines, corresponding perfectly, in spirit and principle, with what we now see, in a more mature development, under the name of Tractarianism, there was an equal revival of zeal for altars; and there were those who took advantage of the favor known to be secretly felt in high quarters towards such things, and erected altars in the Churches. A Bishop (Montague of Chichester) went so far as to insert in his visitation articles, questions which were intended to suggest and promote their erection. And this same Bishop, while professedly of the Protestant Church of England, was in his heart an apostate to the Church of Rome, and was at that time holding secret interviews with the Pope's emissary, then in England, for the purpose of bringing about a union of the Churches of England and Rome. His zeal for altars was fitly united with a zeal to assure Panzani *"that he was continually employed in disposing men's minds, both by word and writing, for a re-union with Rome;"* and that both he and many of his brethren were prepared to conform themselves to the method and discipline of the Gallican Church, where the civil rights were well guarded; *"as for the aversion (said he) we discover in sermons and printed books, they are things of form, chiefly to humor the populace and not to be much regarded."* * We cannot but be reminded by these sad words of certain strong expressions against Rome put out in the earlier writings of certain leading Tractarian authors, and which had the effect, as was intended, of convincing many that those men were strong opposers of Romanism; which expressions having done their work, *have been taken back,* with the not unintelligible intimation that they were not sincere, only words *for the times,* while some of their authors have apostatized to the Church of Rome, in form, and others evidently in heart.†

By such men, altars were revived in the days of Laud. When,

* Memoirs of Gregorio Panzani, quoted by Goode in his Introduction to Jackson on the Church.

† The acknowledgment in Laud's time that the opposition professed to the Church of Rome, in the sermons and books of certain so called Protestants was *a thing of form, to humor the populace and not to be regarded* elsewhere, reminds us of what Mr. Newman, now a Priest of Rome, used to say of that Church, when it would serve his purpose in the Church of England, and what account he gave of it afterward. In 1833, he said of the Church of Rome. "Their communion is infected with heresy, we are bound to flee it as a pestilence. They have established a lie in the place of God's truth, and by their claim of immutability in doctrine, cannot undo the sin they have committed." Tract xx.

those days were passed, and the Church of England had weathered the storm which by a fierce and desolating re-action they had raised, no more was heard of altars; except as a lingering survivor of the nonjuring divines kept up the taste for sacrifice and priests. From that time, until the recent revival of Romish doctrine and feeling in some members of the English Church, it is not known that any thing but "*an honest table*" was placed in the Churches of that land. But now, just so far as Tractarianism has extended its virus through our mother Church, producing its legitimate fruits in a real, though partially masked, Romanism, has there appeared a solemn zeal for a real sacrifice in the Lord's Supper, for a sacrificing priesthood in the Christian ministry; for a confinement of the dispensation of Gospel grace to the ministrations of a priest in the sacrifice of the Eucharist; and, by necessary consequence, *an altar* in the Church as the only thing at which a priest can appropriately stand, in his mediatorial office, and offer the body of Christ as a propitiation for the sins of the faithful.

This history of the alternate revival and declension of zeal for altars and tables makes it so evident with what kind of sympathy, Romish or Protestant, each is doctrinally connected, and how far it is from being a matter of indifference whether we have one or the other, that he who runs may read.

I am now prepared to state *four* reasons for the determination of which I have notified you, viz. that I will not consecrate any Church hereafter in which the structure for the ministration of the Lord's supper is of an *altar form;* or in which there is not, for that use a table, in the ordinary sense, as the permanent furniture.

1 *The Rubric of our Communion office requires such a Table.*

Our prayer Book, like that of the Church of England, no where uses the word *altar*, with reference to the Lord's Supper. It was

---

In 1834, he said in a Magazine. "The spirit of old Rome has risen again in its former place, it has possessed the Church there planted as an evil spirit might seize the demoniac of primitive times."—Popish Rome has succeeded to Rome Pagan; and would that we had not reasons to expect still more crafty developments of Antichrist, and the wreck of institutions which will attend the fall of the Papacy. In 1837, he said in a Review. "She is her real self only in name, and till God vouchsafe to restore her, we must treat her as if she were the evil one which governs her." These are only specimens.

In 1845, Mr. Newman openly avowed himself a member of that very Church of Rome. His friend Mr. Palmer, acknowledged that he had been a Romanist in heart, and intention *four years previous.* In Dec. 1842, while thus a secret Romanist, he published a sort of apology for those hard sayings, in which he said they were "to be ascribed in no small measure to a hope of approving myself to persons' respect *and a wish to repel the charge of Romanism.*"

not until the office for the Institution of Ministers, was annexed that the word *altar* obtained admission, even in a figurative sense.* Of this more by and by. Only in that office is that word now found. In the Rubric at the head of the Communion office it is directed that *"the table,* at the communion, having a fair, linen cloth upon it, shall stand in the body of the Church, or chancel."

It would therefore be perfectly consistent with the order of the Church, as thus set forth, were the communion-table placed in the middle of one of the aisles; if the space around were large enough to be convenient for communicants; and then it might be entirely *open, unprotected by rails,* as it was for some hundreds of years in the beginning, and as it often was in the Churches of England, after the Reformation; instead of being enclosed within the barrier of the chancel. However inexpedient this might be, it would not be inconsistent with the provisions of our Church. Consistently with these provisions the table might be sometimes in one part of the body of the Church, sometimes in another. And while we think of it as a table only, the symbol of the spiritual feast of the Lord's family, there is nothing *intrinsically*, objectionable in this. But what would it be were it a real *altar*, with the sacrifice of the Lord's body offered thereon, and a minister in the special sacredness of a mediating, sacrificing Priest, officiating thereat? The very idea of such a structure implies separation, a privileged place, ground specially holy, as the Court of the Priests, in the temple, having in it the altar of sacrifice, was separated from the Court of Israel.

The Rubric says, *" the table."* It no where goes into any account of what it means by a table. Of course then we are to understand a table in the usual sense.

To say that because an altar may in a certain accommodated sense be called a table, it is therefore consistent with the Rubric to have a literal altar in our Churches, is just as much as to say that whatever may in any figurative, accommodated, or unusual sense be termed a table, however perfectly unlike what all are accustomed to understand by that name, is contemplated by the Rubric. You may go out into a graveyard and serve up your family meal upon a tombstone, and call it a table, because you have used it for a table. But is it a table in any ordinary or proper sense? And would it be rubrical to place it in the Church for the feast of the Lord's Supper? But why not, as much as a Romish altar?

But what our Rubric means by *the table* is easily and perfectly

---

* The office for the Institution of Ministers, though bound up like the Metrical Psalms and Hymns with the Prayer Book, is not a part of it, any more than they are, nor is it of any more authority in questions of doctrine.

settled by the sense of the Church of England. Our Rubric is precisely hers. Her doctrine and practice, as to the ministration of the eucharist is by universal acknowledgment ours. All that we have, in these respects, came through her. Consequently the whole history of the removal of altars and substitution of "*honest tables of wood standing in a frame;*" all the government orders, episcopal injunctions and judicial decisions by which the law of the Church of England is so clearly interpreted, apply with equal conclusiveness to the interpretation of ours, and prove that what is meant by a table for the communion cannot admit of any thing but a table in the ordinary sense, requiring no ingenious eye to see how it can be a table, but intelligible in this respect to all descriptions of men. I know it is pleaded that in the Office for the Institution of Ministers, the table is called "the altar." That office was not annexed to our Prayer Book till about fifteen years after the final ratification of the latter. It has already been said that it is not part of the Prayer Book and has none of its authority. It speaks of "*the altar*" some six or seven times. But, was there such a thing known in our Churches at the time of its adoption, as an altar in the literal sense? We answer No, except possibly as a very rare departure from a general custom. What then could the Office have meant by altar, but the Table; and inasmuch as the table then was no figurative table, but the literal thing, in the ordinary sense, how could it be called an altar, but figuratively, as we speak of "the family altar;" and why should we any more infer from such use that it is consistent with good taste or Church-propriety to have a literal altar in our houses of worship, than we should infer from the common expression *family altar*, that people really erect altars in their houses of residence; or why, if the Prayer Book speaks literally when it mentions *the table*, and figuratively when it speaks of the altar, should we have, as our article of furniture for the communion, *literally* an altar, and only *figuratively* a table?*

We have no disposition to deny that the communion table may, in some sense, be unobjectionably called an altar, though in these days the writer will not use the word in such connexion. When

---

* Seeing the peculiar fondness of some for always calling the table "*the altar,*" as if the other name were less *Churchlike* and *reverential*, I have taken the pains to look out the striking contrast between our Church and them in this particular. In the communion office we read of "*the table*," or "*the Lord's table*," or "*the holy table*" thirteen times, and of *the altar* not once. In the Homilies, we read "*the table*" twenty-three times, and *altar*, in any connexion with the Lord's Supper, not once.

Romish writers, in controversy with our Reformers, adduced the use of the term among the Fathers, they were answered by Dean Nowell as follows; "If St. Basil and some other old writers call it an altar, that is no proper but a *figurative* name; for that as in the old law, these burnt-offerings and sacrifices were offered upon the altar, so are our sacrifices of prayer and thanksgiving, &c., offered up to God at the Lord's table, *as if it were an* altar. But such kind of figurative speech can be no just cause to set up altars, rather than tables; unless they think that their crosses also should be turned into altars, for that like phrase is used of them, where it is said Christ offered up himself upon the altar of the cross." *

2. My second reason is that the form of a table is according to the institution of Christ, the practice of the primitive Church, the practice of the Church of England, and until recently the almost unvaried practice of the Protestant Episcopal Church in these United States; while on the other hand, the form of an altar is no older in the Church than those grievous corruptions of Christianity, which became prevalent in the 4th and 5th Centuries, and is identified with the whole history of the Romish apostasy.

3. My third reason is that the form of a table is according to the nature of the Sacrament of the Lord's Supper, while that of an altar is not. This was one of the reasons given by Bishop Ridley when he issued the Injunctions for the placing of tables in the Churches of his diocese, and I am content to use his words. "The use of an altar (he says) is to make sacrifice upon it: the use of a table is to serve for men to eat upon. Now when we come to the Lord's board, what do we come for? To sacrifice Christ again, or *to feed upon him that was once only crucified and offered for* us? If we come to feed upon him, *spiritually* to eat his body and *spiritually* to drink his blood, which is the true use of the Lord's Supper, then no man can deny but the form of a table *is* more meet for the Lord's board than the form of an altar.†

---

* Nowell's Reproof of Dorman's Proof.

† On the passages of Scripture which are pleaded as affording some warrant for an altar in the Christian Church, see Bishop White's Diss. on the Eucharist, particularly on Heb. xiii. 10, "*we have an altar whereof they have no right to eat which serve the tabernacle.*" As this is a favorite text with Tractarians, and such like, it may be well to remind them that even many of the chief Romish divines have given it up. Thomas Aquinas expounds the place to signify *Christ's altar on the cross,* or else *his body as his altar in heaven,* mentioned in Rev. viii. and called *the golden altar.* The same text was expounded in the "Anti-Didagma of the Divines of Cologne," as the body of Christ in heaven, upon which, and by which, all Christians are to offer up their spiritual sacrifices of faith. Cardinal

4. My fourth reason is that the due guardianship of the Scripture doctrine of the Lord's Supper, against those errors and corruptions which the great adversary of Christ is ever seeking to insinuate among us, requires that we carefully keep up the form of a table and reject that of an altar.

And here I am content to take the language of the leading divines of the Reformation, in the reign of Elizabeth, as found in a list of reasons for the removal of altars, supposed to have been written by Archbishop Parker. "An altar (they say) hath reference to a sacrifice: for they be correlative, so that, of necessity, if we allow an altar, we must grant a sacrifice; like as if there be a father, there is also a son, and if there be a master, there is also a servant. Whereupon" (this sentence I would particularly ask the reader to mark) "divers of the learned adversaries have spoken, of late, that there is no reason to *take away the sacrifice of the cross, and to leave the altars standing seeing the one was ordained for the other.*" *

I will now conclude by reminding you of the earnestness with which that late venerable Father of our American Episcopal Church, Bishop White, contended against whatever had a tendency to introduce among us that doctrine of a real sacrifice and priesthood in the eucharist, with which the altar is so essentially connected. One of the legacies left us by that far-seeing divine is a Dissertation on the eucharist, written throughout, for the purpose of showing that in the Christian Church there is no such thing as a material sacrifice, since that of Christ on the cross; no priest, in the sense of an offerer of sacrifice, but Christ himself: therefore no altar but that of his cross. Allow me to quote from that, and another of his Works, a few passages. "I conceive (he says) so unfavorably of whatever may lead, by *remote consequence*, to creature-worship, as to give a caution against a notion which sometimes appears in writers, who were sincere, though inconsistent Protestants. The notion is then that there is in the eucharist a *real sacrifice*, that it is offered upon an *altar;* and that the officiating minister is a *priest,* in the sense of an offerer of sacrifice. Under the economy of the Gospel, there is nothing under the names referred to, except the fulfillment of them in the person of high-Priest of our profession. As to our

---

Bellarmine admits that thus many Romish divines interpreted the passage. The Jesuit Estius explained it as meaning "*the cross of Christ's sufferings.*"

Not having the original authorities, I take the above from *Bishop Morton on the Lord's Supper,* b. vi. c. 3, § 8.

* Strype's Annals vol. 1. p. 1. p. 160.

Church, although she *commemorates* a great sacrifice in the eucharist, yet she knows of no offering of any thing of this description, except in the *figurative* sense in which prayers and alms are sacrifices. She calls the place on which her oblation is made, not 'an altar' but 'a table;' although there is no impropriety in calling it an altar also, the word being understood *figuratively*. And as to the minister in the ordinance, although she retains the word priest, yet she considers it synonymous with Presbyter."* Bishop White said that the Romish error on these heads, "makes an irreconcileable division between us and the Church of Rome;" that the intercommunity of the names altar and table is only justifiable in an accommodated, or figurative sense; for "although an altar may be called a table because of some common properties which they serve, it does not follow that any table, not possessed of the discriminating property of the altar, may be so called. It is like the occasional calling of a Church a house. Such it is, without its being right to call every house a Church. In short an altar is a place of sacrifice: and the taking of its name carries by implication an assumption of its distinguishing property.†" He said that the errors concerning priest, sacrifice and altar, against which he was contending, and which were precisely those which are now striving so powerfully to gain prevalence in our Church, and have already gained such alarming accessions, "appeared at first in the closet-lucubrations of the few writers (of antiquity) whose works have been handed down; crept in gradually; and began in the *literal* application of language which had been all along, and may be now, *figuratively*, used on the respective points.

"In England (he continues) the doctrine was completely put down at the Reformation. If in later times, the notion has been entertained by some of the Clergy of the Church of England, it has not crept into her public institutions." The venerable author closed his Dissertation on the Eucharist, from which I have just quoted, with these almost prophetic words: "*The author would lament an approach to the opposite theory,* (opposite to that which he was advocating) *among the Clergy and other members of this Church, as having a threatening aspect on her peace.*" An *approach* even to the doctrine of a real sacrifice, and priest, and altar in the eucharist, Bishop White thus deprecated as dangerous to the peace of the Church. How like he was, in this, to the views of the English Reformers! when with Archbishop Parker at their head,

---

* Bishop White's Lectures on the Catechism. Lec. iv.
† Dissertation on the Eucharist.

they addressed themselves to Queen Elizabeth, giving certain reasons why it was not convenient that the communion should be ministered at an altar. One was that "the consciences of many thousands, which from their hearts embrace the Gospel, would be wounded by continuance of altars; and great numbers would abstain from receiving the communion at an altar; which, in the end, might grow to occasion a *great schism and division* among the people." *

Alas! if Bishop White would have lamented even an "*approach*" to the theory which he wrote against, what would he feel were it his cross to live in these days of the boasted revival of the misnamed "Catholic system," when one may forfeit his good name, as a Churchman, if he profess the simple Gospel truth concerning the eucharist which that good man taught; and when the bold teaching in a Protestant Episcopal Church of the precise form of error which he opposed, has become so frequent, that we have lost the sense of it as being strange sound of doctrine, and scarcely notice it. Did that wise and watchful Father conceive it his duty to raise his voice against the *least beginnings* of a tendency to Romish error, at a period when the prospect of its ever spreading among us was not even as a little cloud upon the horizon, of the bigness of a man's hand; and is it a gratuitous and needless work to take precautions against the same errors now, when the storm has shrouded the sky and the winds of that evil doctrine have already caused so many to lose their anchorage and drive towards those dark shores of superstition and idolatry where others have already made shipwreck of the faith?

I fully agree with Bishop White that any approach towards the theory which he opposed, of a real sacrifice, priest, and altar, would endanger the peace of the Church. That peace is now endangered precisely as he feared—but where lies the blame? On those who like himself have endeavored to protect and maintain the integrity of our Church's doctrine against all innovations, contending "earnestly for the faith once delivered to the saints," and subsequently received at the Reformation, and now professed in our Articles, and Liturgy, and Homilies? Or does it lie on all such as attempt to break in upon the established standards and the well-known teaching and usages of our Church, with novelties which our Fathers knew not of and could not bear?

I trust, my brethren, I have now said enough to show, that in the determination I have taken, and announced in the earlier part

* Strype's Annals, as before cited.

of this address, I have not acted without consideration, without precedent, without reason. Viewed in one aspect, as the world would view it, I may seem to have made a great deal out of a trifling matter. So it seemed to the world when Epiphanius, a Bishop in the 4th century, image worship being then in the seed, tore away from the door of a Church a picture of Christ, and to pour condemnation upon the admission of such things into Churches, ordered the painted cloth to be used for a shroud to bury a dead man in."* The subsequent history of the worship of images and pictures in the Churches, teaches us how well it would have been had all men seen with the same eyes as that faithful bishop. God grant that the progress of events, within a few years to come, may not speak a language quite as strong in vindication of those who plant their protests against an invading Romanism beside things unimportant, to some eyes, as altars and crosses, and who strive to escape the final and full issues of evil, by thus resisting the beginning. *Obsta principiis.*

I have now finished what I wished to say on this subject. Had there been nothing in view but the mere justification of the position I have taken as to the consecration of Churches, I should have been well satisfied with saying much less. But considering the subject as bearing very strikingly upon the exposition of the doctrine of our Church and of the Scriptures on the nature of the Lord's Supper, and of the Christian ministry, against the claims of Popery and of those who emulate its priestly and sacrificial pomp and dignities, I have taken advantage of an occasion to go into it the more largely. In doing so, I have endeavored to cast in my mite towards the prosecution of that great war for the saving truth of the Gospel against the strong array of the Romish Antichrist, which is not to cease, but is probably to grow in the formidable marshalling of its powers, until *He* shall come "whose kingdom shall have no end."

* Homily on Peril of Idolatry.

THE
WORK OF PREACHING CHRIST.

A CHARGE: DELIVERED TO THE CLERGY OF THE DIOCESE OF OHIO, AT ITS FORTY-SIXTH ANNUAL CONVENTION, IN ST. PAUL'S CHURCH, AKRON, ON THE 3D OF JUNE, 1863. BY CHARLES PETTIT M'ILVAINE, D. D., D. C. L., BISHOP OF THE DIOCESE.

BRETHREN:—It is a long time since I addressed you in the form of a Charge. Various have been the causes; the chief of them, as you well know, having been connected with the state of my health. Addressing you again in that mode, and with exclusive reference to matters peculiar to our office as Ministers of Christ, realizing how near my time is to lay it down, I choose a subject with which a Bishop may well desire to close his ministry; with which indeed all our work should be identified, and which, I am thankful to say, has been obtaining, ever since mine began, a deeper and stronger possession of my mind, my affections, and my ministry—I mean *the work of preaching Christ*, according to the Scriptures, and the example of the Apostles.

"Go preach the Gospel," were the words of our Lord to his Apostles, which conveyed to them and to us the whole weight and substance of the commission of his Ministers and Ambassadors. It was the unquestioning obedience of a simple and unhesitating faith to that one command, animated by an unquenchable love to its divine Author and to the souls he died to save, enlightened by the teaching and made mighty by the power of the Holy Ghost, that constituted all the vigor and efficacy of the ministry of the Apostles. It was thus that their weapons of warfare became "mighty through God," and achieved those stupendous victories of the truth over "the spirit that ruleth in the children of disobedience," which the weaker faith and more timid obedience of the Church in later days have so poorly imitated. And, as in the beginning, so also in all times of the Christian dispensation, it has pleased God that sinners shall be brought "into captivity to the obedience of Christ" and made partakers of his salvation, by the obedience of his ministers to that one original charge and command—"*preach the Gospel*." Faith by hearing; Gospel faith, by hearing Gospel truth;

and such hearing, by the preaching of the Word of God, is His standing rule according to which He bestows His Spirit for the conviction, conversion, and sanctification of men.

But it is manifest from the Scriptures that the Apostles identified the Gospel *with Christ;* so that, in their view and practice, to preach the Gospel was neither more nor less than to preach Christ. The record which, in a few words describes their ministry, is that, " daily in the temple and in every house, they ceased not to teach and preach Jesus Christ." St. Paul to the Romans defines the whole Gospel by saying that it is " concerning Jesus Christ."* The employment of his two years' imprisonment at Rome was all comprehended in " teaching those things which concern the Lord Jesus." And his whole ministry was given unto him, he testifies, that he " might preach the unsearchable riches of Christ." As he could say, " For me to live is Christ ;" so for him to preach was Christ. To him Christ and the Gospel were one.

But we must here note the chief feature in their preaching of Christ. They omitted nothing pertaining to him ; but there was one thing on which, more than any thing else, they very particularly and emphatically dwelled. They took great pains to set forth the Lord Jesus in all that he was and is, in person and office, as once on earth and now in heaven, his pre-existent glory with the Father, his incarnation and humiliation in our nature, his death, resurrection, and intercession ; all his love, all his promises, all his commandments ; so that there was no part of the whole counsel of God, " concerning His Son Jesus Christ," which they kept back. But manifestly there was one event in his history, one work amidst all his works, which stood in their view as the great event and work, around which they gathered the force of their testimony, as its central light and power—to which they made all that went before it look forward for consummation, and all that succeeded look back as to its foundation, and on the faithful declaration of which, with its immediate connections, they very especially rested the faithfulness of their work as preachers of the Gospel. No doubt you anticipate me. Such passages of the Apostles arise to your minds, as, " we preach Christ *crucified;*" " I am determined not to know any thing among you (while declaring unto you the testimony of God) save Jesus Christ and *him crucified;*" " God forbid that I should glory save in the *cross* of our Lord Jesus Christ ;" " For the preaching of the *cross* is to them that perish foolishness, but unto us which are saved it is the power of God."

* Rom. i. 3.

They preached Christ—but as Christ *crucified*. They said continually, like John the Baptist, "Behold the Lamb of God which taketh away the sin of the world," but it was the "Lamb *slain*"—Christ *in his death*—bearing "our sins in his own body on the tree," to whom they pointed. They rejoiced in every thing pertaining to their Lord, from his birth at Bethlehem to his present glory at the Father's right hand; but the one thing in which they rejoiced so supremely, that every thing else was lost in comparison, was his cross. Of the two Sacraments ordained of Christ for his Church, that which alone goes with the believer to be renewed and repeated all along the way of his earthly life, has for its great object to "show the Lord's *death* until he come." It was a great lesson which the Lord thus taught us as to how we must preach him. His Apostles therefore became in speech, what that Sacrament is in symbol; constantly showing the Lord's death as the sinner's life. Thus, when they spoke of the Christian's race for "the prize of the high calling of God in Christ Jesus"—and when they exhorted us while in that contest to be always "looking unto Jesus"—the special aspect in which they presented him, was as *enduring the cross*. And I need not here say that their sense of the supreme importance in their ministry of the death of Christ was because they beheld therein the one only and the one all-sufficient sacrifice and propitiation, the *vicarious* atonement, for the sins of the whole world; that great work of God wherein he laid in Zion, for a sure foundation, the precious cornerstone, on which the sinner believing shall not be confounded. It is all contained in one verse—"Christ hath once suffered for sins, the just for the unjust to bring us to God."* And again, "Christ hath redeemed us from the curse of the law, being made a curse for us."†

Thus, brethren, we have our lesson and example. In the way the Apostles preached the Gospel we must try to preach it. As they preached Christ, so must we. God forbid that we should glory in any thing else as ministers of the word. Preachers of Christ, according to the mind of Christ—ah, how all honors, all satisfaction in our work will perish but that! When our stewardship is to be accounted for, and we are just departing, and the veil, half drawn aside, discloses what we are to meet and what to be forever, how then shall we care for praise of learning or praise of speech or any vapors of men's applause? But then, to have "the testimony of our conscience that in simplicity and godly sincerity,—not with enticing words of man's wisdom," we have

* 1 Pet. iii. 18. † Gal. iii. 13.

made it our life-business and our heart-pleasure to "teach and preach Jesus Christ," as they did whom he gave to be our examples, having ourselves first learned his preciousness to our own souls; oh, what consolation and thankfulness with which to die.

Evidently then, my brethren, it is a most serious question to be always studying, how we may so proclaim the truth committed to us in Holy Scripture, that in the sense of the Apostles it may be said of us in our whole ministry that "we preach Christ crucified." To this we devote this address. It is a great question indeed. Many are the failures—many the egregious failures. Sometimes it seems as if the preacher could preach just as he does if Christ and his work were a mere incident in religion, a name, and little more—answering now and then as a convenience to a sentence; introduced occasionally, because, under some texts, not easily avoided, but never as the root and foundation out of which our whole ministry proceeds. But what awful condemnation to be thus essentially defective at the very heart of the great work committed to us! Nothing can in the least atone for its absence. You might as well attempt to turn night into day, by lighting a candle as a substitute for the sun. Our ministry is all darkness, emptiness, and impotence; all condemnation to us, all delusion to those who hear us, all dishonor to the grace of God, whatever the breath of man may say of it, except as it is pervaded, illumined, filled with the testimony of Christ as once the sacrifice for sin, crucified and slain; now the glorified and ever-living intercessor for all that come unto God by him.

There are many ways of approaching more or less to that attainment without ever reaching it. Some of the most common we will endeavor to state:

It is very possible to preach a great deal of important religious truth, and so that there shall be no admixture of important error in doctrine or precept—yea, truth having an important relation to Christ and his office, and yet not to preach Christ. The defect will be not in the presence of what should not be there, but in the absence of what should be, of that which is necessary to give all the truth delivered, the character of *"truth as in Jesus."* Such absence, when nevertheless all is true, may be more destructive to the Gospel character of the preaching, than even the introduction of some positive error. The preaching may be very earnest. It may contain much that is affecting and deeply impressive—strong emotions may be stirred in the hearers. The earnest inquiry may be excited—what must we do? And yet, the preaching may wholly fail in giving any such distinct answer to that question as will turn the attention of the inquirer to Christ as all his refuge. We may say a great deal about and around the Gospel and never preach the Gospel. Religious truths are not the Gospel, except in proportion as, like John the Baptist, they point to the Lamb of God. For example—suppose you preach on the vanity of the world; the uncertainty of life; the awfulness of death unprepared for; the tremendous events of the judgment-day; the little profit of gaining the whole world and losing the soul; suppose you enlarge on the necessity and blessedness of a religious life, and the happiness of the saved. Does it follow that you have preached the Gospel, or any part of it? If deep impressions are made, and serious inquiries excited, does it follow that Christ is preached? Such topics unquestionably belong most legitimately to our ministry; they are important parts of the truth given us to enforce; but they are entirely subordinate and preliminary. They are not the distinctive *seed* of the word from which God has ordained that newness of life shall spring. They are rather the plough and the harrow to open and stir the ground, that it may receive the seed of life. You may spend all your time in such work—not omitting to sprinkle your discourses with the oft-repeated name of Christ and with much Gospel language; and just because there is no pervading exhibition of Christ, in his work of Justification by his righteousness and of Sanctification by his Spirit, given so pointedly and plainly that whosoever will may understand, you may never attain to the honor, in the sight of God, of teaching and preaching Jesus Christ, whatever the estimate of those who have not learned to discriminate between truth that is *religious*, and truth that is not only religious, but distinctively *Gospel*-truth; who know not the difference between such preaching as makes the hearer feel some spiritual want, and that which tells him what he wants and where and how he is to find it. The hearer who has learned Christ, as his lesson of heart and life, of hope and peace, and knows nothing as precious to his soul, but as it leads him to Jesus, on the cross of sacrifice and on the throne of intercession, Jesus in his invitations and promises, Jesus in his grace to help, his righteousness to clothe, and his power to sanctify, will feel that in all that ministry "*one thing is needful*"—and that one thing, the very thing on which all its character hinges,—CHRIST.

But let us advance a little further. You may preach with faithfulness and plainness the strictness and holiness of the law, how it enters with its requirements into all the thoughts and affections of the heart, pronouncing condemnation on the sinner, and bringing us all in guilty before God. There may be no shrinking from the fullest exposition of the Scriptures concerning the end of the impenitent. Still more: the office of Christ as the only Saviour, and his merits as the only plea, may be introduced not unfrequently, and yet may there be a great lack of such distinct setting forth of Christ—such holding up of Christ crucified, as Moses lifted up the serpent in the wilderness before the dying Israelites for all to see and live—such presentation of God's great remedy for every man's necessities, as belongs to the consistency, simplicity and fullness of the work committed to the minister of the Gospel. While speaking much of duty, the grace to enable us to do it may not be proportionably presented. While the penalties of sin may be kept in full view, the fullness and tenderness and earnestness of the invitations and promises of Christ to the sinner turning unto God, may be very dimly exhibited. That great lesson, which we have need to be always studying, may have been but little learned, how to preach the law as showing our need of the righteousness of Christ, and how to preach the Gospel as establishing and honoring the law; the one to convince of sin and condemnation, the other as providing a deliverance so complete that to the believer there is no condemnation; the one as taking away all pleas derived from ourselves, the other as furnishing a most perfect and prevailing plea in the mediation of Christ; the law as giving the rule of life, the Gospel as giving the power of life, yea, life from death, in Jesus Christ; the law to humble us under a consciousness of an utter beggary before God; the Gospel as directing us to him in whom it pleased the Father that all fulness should dwell.

Again. It may be that doctrine immediately concerning the Lord Jesus, and bringing his person and office into view, may be much introduced. We may take opportunity to speak of his infinite dignity of being; the mystery of his incarnation; the humiliation and love and grace of his coming in our nature; his tenderness and compassion, and power to save; the perfectness of his example and the depth of his sufferings. Indeed, every thing revealed concerning him may at times be found in our teaching, without error, and in each particular, as it stands by itself, without serious defect. But there may be still an important deficiency. The *proportion of truth* may not be kept. There is a proportion of parts in the whole body of Gospel truth just as there is the same in our own bodies. We must omit none of the parts, but put each in its right relation to all the rest. To fail in this, so that while we embrace all we deform all, by a disproportionate exaltation of some, and depression of others, may be just as destructive of the Gospel character of our ministry, just as confusing and misleading, as if we omitted some truths, and perverted others. For example, you may preach Christ in various aspects; but Christ *crucified*, the great sacrifice of propitiation, though not omitted, may not have that high-place, that central place, that all-controlling place, that place of the head-stone of the corner, which is necessary to its right adjustment to all parts of the system of faith. You may preach the Incarnation of Christ in all its truth as a separate event, and yet in great error as regards its relations to other events, making it so unduly prominent that his death shall be made to appear comparatively subordinate and unessential—the means exalted above the end—the preparation of the body of Christ for sacrifice, being made of more importance and more effective in our salvation than his offering of that body on the cross. But the great Sacrament which we carry with us all the way of our journey, as our great confession and joy and glory, is to show, as oft as we eat that bread, and drink that cup, not the Lord's *birth*, but " the Lord's *death* until he come."

You may preach all of Christ's work as well as person, and all in due proportion of parts, and yet some other vital truth essentially connected may be so disproportionately presented as to create in the whole a most important defect. You have exhibited the foundation which God hath laid in Zion. The question remains, how the sinner is to avail himself of that foundation. He is to build thereon. But how? The Apostle answers, "*He that believeth* on him shall not be confounded." We build by faith. We cannot preach Christ without preaching on that by which we become partakers of Christ. Evidently confusion, indistinctness, feebleness, deficiency there, must produce the same effect throughout the whole Gospel. If faith, in its nature, office, efficacy and distinctive operation and fruits, be kept in a place so obscure, so subordinate, or taught so confusedly that either it is wholly out of sight or hid in a crowd of other things; placed in the outer court of the temple instead of immediately by the altar of sacrifice, as the one instrumental grace by which the sinner partakes of the "Lamb of God;" if the works which are its fruits be so confounded with itself that the grace by which we are "rooted and grounded" in Christ, is made of no more influence in our participation of him than the several works of righteousness which grow out of its life, and follow upon the participation of Christ through its agency, then is the relative adjustment of truth most seriously spoiled and deformed.

Lastly, under this head of our inquiry; it may be that occasionally in a discourse, now and then, the setting forth of Christ is satisfactory in point of doctrine and the proportion of truth. But it may be only occasionally thus, when the text obliges, according to rhetorical propriety, so that we cannot avoid it. But such texts may not be chosen very often. Passing from subject to subject, the preacher comes, from time to time, to one which necessarily leads to the manifestation of Christ, in some leading feature of his grace and salvation, and then all may be well done and calculated to enlighten a mind hungering for the truth. But, meanwhile, you may hear many a discourse which contains scarcely more of any thing distinctive of the Gospel, or pertaining to Christ, except perhaps his name sometimes introduced, than if it were some other religion than Christ's of which the preacher is the minister. And in the general course of his work we may look in vain after that evident fondness of heart for views which most intimately and directly look *unto Jesus;* that habitual feeding of the flock in pastures watered by the river that proceedeth out of the throne of God and the Lamb; that strong tendency, when subjects not directly testifying of Christ must be handled, to keep them as near to him as possible, and to return from them as soon as possible to others of a nearer neighborhood to the cross; that desire to illuminate all subjects with light from "the face of Jesus Christ," which proves the preacher's determination "to know nothing among men, but Jesus Christ and him crucified." We miss that *habitualness* of the testimony of Christ, that special love for all the region round about Gethsemane and Calvary, the atonement and the intercession, and the great gifts of the Spirit purchased thereby; we miss that constant tracing of all spiritual life and consolation, in its every influence and fruit, to Christ as the life, and that careful binding of all spiritual affections and duties upon him for support and strength, as the vine-dresser trains his vine upon its trellis, which appears so remarkably in the teaching of the Apostles.

We have thus endeavored to indicate some of the paths by which, without delivering any thing untrue, and while delivering much important truth, we may come short of the duty under consideration, We proceed to consider how we may fulfill it. *What is it to preach Christ?*

We have a great example in our Lord's own teaching. When after his resurrection, he met the two disciples on the way to Emmaus, and found them in such darkness and doubt concerning himself, it is written that, "beginning at Moses, and all the prophets, he expounded unto them, in all the Scriptures, the things concerning himself:" *the things concerning Himself*. Our office as Christian ministers, expounding the Scriptures, is to bring forth all their teaching concerning that glorious One, *Himself*. St. Paul therefore said that he was "separated unto the Gospel of God *concerning his Son Jesus Christ*."* To teach sinners to know Christ, and to "count all things but loss for the excellency of the knowledge of Him," looking to the power of the Holy Ghost to communicate, through the truth which we give only in the letter, that spiritual and saving knowledge which only God giveth, is the general expression of our duty.

But in the Gospel "concerning our Lord Jesus Christ," that is, in the circle of doctrines and duties and promises and blessings which constitute the message of great salvation in him, there is, as we have already hinted, a system of parts mutually related and dependent, all in perfect harmony, none so obscure or remote as to be of no importance to the right representation of the whole. That system, like that of our sun, has a center, by which all the parts are held in place, from which all their light and life proceed, and around which all revolve. You cannot exhibit the system of truth and duty till you have made known that central light and power; nor can you make known that power in all its truth, without exhibiting those surrounding and dependent parts of doctrine and precept. That central sun of light and life is Christ. All of Gospel truth and duty, of consolation and strength, abides in Christ—derives from Christ, and glorifies Christ—and must be so presented or it is divorced from its only life and loses its Gospel character. He is the True Vine, and all parts of Gospel truth are branches in him. Let such truth be presented without that connection, then its character as truth may remain, but its character for "*truth as in Jesus*" is lost. Its vitality is gone. Fruit of life in Christ Jesus, it cannot produce. It is just as true and important concerning truth as concerning men, that "the branch cannot bring forth fruit except it abide in the vine."

Now what is the best mode of setting forth this system of grace? Where shall we begin? Shall we first take up the elements of religion, the outsides of the circle; reasoning upward from general truths to the more particular; explaining and enforcing ordinances and institutions of the Church, as our road of approach to the Head and Life of the Church; confining attention to means of grace before we have directed our hearers to the grace itself in the great

*Rom. i. 1–3.

fountain head; and thus gradually, and after a long process of preparatory work, arriving at last at the person and mission and sacrifice of Christ? But we must remember who they are whom we are thus keeping so long in the cold and in the dark. They are sinners under the condemnation of the law of God. They are dying sinners. How brief the time of some of them to learn, you know not. You have no time to spend on preliminaries before you have introduced them to the great salvation. What they have most need to know is, Him who came to seek and to save the lost —how they may find him, and what are the terms of his salvation. Begin at once with Christ—"Behold the Lamb of God"—is the voice. There is no light till that light appears. The icy-bondage of the sinner's heart yields not till that sun is risen. Astronomers when they teach the solar system, begin with the sun. Thence, to the related and dependent orbs, is easy. So the Apostles taught. See how, when they had the whole system of the Gospel, as distinguished from that of the law, to teach the Jews—the whole outward and visible of the Christian Church, as well as all the inward and spiritual of the Christian life, all so new and strange and unpalatable to a people so unprepared, so entangled with traditionary aversions and deep-seated perversions, see how they leaped over all preliminaries, and began at once with Christ and him crucified, the sacrifice of his death, "and the power of his resurrection." At once they broke ground and set up the banner of their ministry there. Just at the point where the pride of the sinner would most revolt, and the wisdom of man was most at fault, and the ignorance of Jew and Gentile was most complete, where the Jew saw only a stumbling block and the Greek only foolishness, *there* they opened their message. "I delivered unto you, *first of all* (said St. Paul), that which I also received, how that Christ died for our sins according to the Scriptures."* They could not wait to root out prejudice, plant first principles, approach the entrenched power "that ruleth in the children of disobedience," by the strategy of man's wisdom, when they knew that Christ was the great "power of God unto salvation." At once to open the windows and let in the sun was their way of giving light to them that sat in darkness. At once to show the amazing love of God to sinners in not sparing His own Son, but delivering him up for us all, was their way to draw the sinner's heart to God. Human device would have said, as it has often said, in substance, Make philosophy prepare the way. Clothe your teaching in robes of man's wisdom. Keep back the offense of the

* 1 Cor. xv. 3.

cross till you have first conciliated the respect of your hearers by a show of human learning and reasoning. And when your master must be preached directly, don't begin at his death. Speak of his life, its benevolence, its beauty. Compare his moral precepts with those of heathen sages. Christ as the example and the teacher, is your great theme. "No," (said St. Paul), "lest the cross should be of none effect," "that your faith should not stand in the wisdom of men, but in the power of God." They remembered the words of their Lord, "I, if I be lifted up, will draw all men unto me." Lifted up on the cross he had now been. Lifted up as Christ crucified for us, in the sight of the whole world, by the ministry of the Gospel he was next to be. Such was God's argument with sinful men.

They believed and therefore preached. God gave the increase, and wonderful was the harvest.

Thus, dear brethren, we have our lesson. We must begin as well as end with Christ, and always abide in him, for the life and power of our ministry, just as for the peace and joy of our own souls. But having thus begun, what remains? It is the revealed office of the Holy Ghost, as the Sanctifier and the Comforter, to *glorify Christ.* "He shall glorify me," said the Lord. But how? "*He shall take of mine, and show it unto you.*" It is *our* office also, under the power of the Holy Ghost, to glorify Christ in all his person and relations to us, and by the same method, namely, to *take of what pertains to him and show it unto men.* Whatever pertains to him, we are to show. We must "expound in all the Scriptures the things concerning himself." Of those things we will attempt a brief sketch and outline, but it must be only the merest outline, and that very imperfect.

We must preach Christ in regard to the glory of the Godhead which he had with the Father before the world was. We cannot exhibit the death of the cross to which he became obedient, without considering the infinite majesty of the throne from which he descended. We must keep the connection which the Apostle has given us between the glory of our Lord before he came in the flesh, and his humiliation in the flesh. You remember that "*he became obedient unto death, even the death of the cross,*" is introduced by "*being in the form of God, he thought it not robbery to be equal with God.*"*

In the same connection is the Incarnation and Birth of our Lord. Very near are the mysteries of Bethlehem to those of Calvary. We cannot tell how Jesus bore our sins, without telling how he took

* Phil. ii. 6-8.

our nature. To show that he *could* stand in man's place under the law, we must show that he was made very man. Hence, in the Apostle's account, between the form of God from all eternity, and the obedience unto death, the connecting event is, *"he was made in the likeness of men."* We must take care that in a just zeal for his divinity we do not impair or put in a place of comparative unimportance his humanity. The one is as essential to the Gospel as the other—the perfect man as the perfect God. Our confession glories as much in the Word "made flesh," as in the truth that the same Word "was God." In beholding and showing the great salvation, we are to consider as of equal necessity thereto, "the *Man*, Christ Jesus," and that he was, and is, "Jehovah our Righteousness." In the earliest ages of Satan's attack upon the integrity of the Gospel, the heresies did not more assail the essential divinity than the real humanity of Christ; knowing that if he were not perfect man, the sacrifice for man's sins were as unavailing as if he had been only man. The assaults of these present times are indicative, we think, of the same strategy. How carefully and minutely do the Scriptures exhibit our Lord as man in all that is of man; while at the same time we are made to behold his glory, "as of the only begotten of the Father, full of grace and truth." "In the fullness of time, God sent forth His Son, made of a woman," that in all time and to all eternity he might be "made unto us of God," through his death, "wisdom, and righteousness, and sanctification and redemption."

In setting forth our Lord's atoning death, we must keep in full view his perfect life—that suffering life between the cradle and the cross, in which his obedience to the law, completed by the endurance of its curse for us, was all wrought out. He was the Lamb *without spot*, that he might be the sacrifice all-sufficient. It was his meetness as the purchase-price of our redemption, and at the same time the pattern of the mind which must be in us to make us meet to be partakers of that redemption. Christ our example of holiness is a most important part of the setting forth of Christ as our foundation of hope. There was one hour in his life for which he came into this world;* but every hour while he was in this world, as leading to that, exhibited the mind that was in Christ Jesus, and which must be also in us. In preaching Christ crucified, let us take care that we avoid the mistake, not unfrequently made, of terminating our representation almost entirely with the crucifixion—as if the slaying of the sacrifice completed the *oblation* of the sacri-

* John xii. 23, and xvii. 1.

fice; forgetting the office of the High Priest to enter within the vail with the blood of sprinkling, carrying the sacrifice before the mercy-seat, there to appear in the presence of God for us, and thus to "obtain eternal redemption for us." "Christ crucified" is not merely Christ on the cross, but Christ also "on the right hand of the throne of God," as having "endured the cross." That throne is called "the throne of the Lamb," and the redeemed in heaven are represented as praising "the Lamb *that was slain.*" The preaching of Christ *crucified* goes necessarily into all that Christ did and obtained for us after, and in consequence of, his crucifixion. The Resurrection, Ascension, and Exaltation to head-ship over all things, are great themes, vitally associated with what immediately preceded them, forming the essential connection between what was finished "once for all" when Jesus died, and what is yet to be finished "for all that come unto God by him," now that he "ever liveth." We must preach Christ in his ever living intercession— Christ the High Priest above with the incense and the blood, or we leave incomplete the view of Christ crucified. When he cried, *"It is finished,"* and "gave up the ghost," it was the slaying of the sacrifice; it was the suffering of the Lamb of God for us; it was the being "made a curse for us," that was then finished. "There remaineth no more sacrifice for sin;" but there does remain the perpetual oblation of the one finished sacrifice. Our hope stops not at the cross, but "entereth into that within the vail; whither the forerunner is for us entered, even Jesus, made an High Priest forever after the order of Melchizedek."* Thither, therefore, our ministry must also enter. Too often does what otherwise is well, as Gospel preaching, come short of that mark. Our preaching follows Christ in his resurrection, and perhaps in his ascension; but do we sufficiently place before the faith of the sinner, for his prayers and his hopes to rest on, for his consolation and peace to drink of when he strives to come unto God, Jesus as now the glorious Intercessor—showing in his hands the print of the nails of the crucifixion, and bearing in his heart all the necessities of every believer? When we exhort to the running the race with patience *"looking unto Jesus,"* do we sufficiently direct the eye of the hearer to Jesus, *the glorified,* in his present office and work for us? Remember, that when the Apostle said, "He is able to save to the uttermost," he added, as the essential evidence, *"seeing he ever liveth to make intercession for us."*

I must not pass from this immediate neighborhood of the great sacrifice, without a few words about its nature. To speak of it as

* Heb. vi. 19–20.

a sacrifice for sin in such general terms only as leave room for the most unreal, figurative and accommodated sense, is to come far short of our duty and of what the special tendency of error in these days demands. When we administer the Sacrament of the Lord's Supper, we "show the Lord's *death*." Let us take care that when we show the same in words, we do not come short of the teaching of the Sacrament. Our Church interprets that teaching with studied precision, in her communion office, in reference to errors prevalent when that office was framed. She calls the sacrifice "a full, perfect and sufficient sacrifice, oblation and satisfaction for the sins of the whole world." She teaches us to pray for remission of sins *through faith in the blood* of Christ. We must imitate that precision in reference to errors now propagated. Besides the perfectness and sufficiency of the sacrifice, in opposition to those who would add to it, we must insist strongly and pointedly on its strictly *propitiatory* and *vicarious* nature, in opposition to those who would destroy it. Under such strong texts as "Christ hath redeemed us from the curse of the law, being made a curse for us;"* "He hath made him to be sin for us, who knew no sin,"† we must teach Christ as standing literally in our stead under the condemnation of our sins; all our guilt laid upon him; he, the condemned one for us, that we might be accounted the righteous in him. I see not how we can come short of such a sacrifice and yet preach Christ crucified, according to the Scriptures.‡

Closely allied to our Lord's priesthood, offering the perpetual oblation of his sacrifice, is his office as the great Prophet and Teacher of his Church. "In him are hid all the treasures of wisdom and knowledge." He is "made unto us of God, *wisdom*," as well as "righteousness." Christ crucified is Christ the Light as well as the Life. To his invitation, "Come unto me and I will give you rest," is joined the precept, "*learn of me*." The great *subject* of saving learning is Christ himself, and he is the only effectual teacher of that learning. They that have "learned Christ," so as truly to know him, are declared to have "*been taught by him the truth as in Jesus*." Whatever our advantages of human teaching, even of the truest exposition of God's inspired word, all is powerless spiritually

---

* Gal. iii. 13. † 2 Cor. v. 21.

‡ The strictly *substitutionary* character of Christ's sacrifice for our sins I consider of the most vital importance to be clearly taught, if we would satisfy the language of Scripture, or do our duty to God and man. "*He was made sin for us;*" by which I understand that he stood for us under the law, by imputation of our sins, bearing all our sins, and as perfectly identified and charged with them as it was possible for one "who knew no sin" in himself to be.

to enlighten us in the knowledge of God and of Christ, till he who speaks as never man spake shall add to it the teaching of his Spirit, so that we shall learn, not merely by the Scriptures, but in them *from* and *of Him*. Christ as "*the truth*" as well as "*the way*," "the wisdom" as well as "the righteousness of God," the living "Word," as well as the ever-living Priest and Intercessor, must be showed in our ministry, if we preach Christ crucified, not merely as once on the cross, but as now in his glory.

But Christ crucified is not only "the righteousness of God" and "the wisdom of God," but "*the power of God* unto salvation." "Him hath God exalted to be a *Prince*," that he may be a Saviour, "*mighty to save*." "Unto the Son, He saith, Thy throne, O God, is forever and ever, a scepter of righteousness is the scepter of thy kingdom." Christ as King, in a glorious sovereignty over all things in heaven and earth, we must declare. It is the crowning aspect of Christ, the crucified. It is "the THRONE *of the Lamb that was slain*," before which the multitudes without number, of the saved in heaven are represented as ascribing "power and riches and strength and glory and honor and blessing." By his death he purchased, as Mediator, a glorious kingdom of redemption. At his ascension, he went to receive it. There now he reigns over all his people in earth and heaven, and over all else, for his people. When he shall come again, it will be in the glory of that kingdom. It was a grand introduction to that precious invitation, "Come unto me all ye that labor and are heavy laden," and that attending precept, "take my yoke and learn of me," when he said (in the verse next before), "*All things are delivered unto me of my Father.*"*

It was when he was in the humiliation and sufferings of the cross that, as the great King, he stretched forth the scepter of his power to the malefactor at his side, and gave him repentance and remission of sins, and opened unto him the kingdom of heaven. And now that, having endured the cross, he is set down at the right hand of the throne of God, to reign forever and ever, he hath all power to make good all his promises to those who receive him and to punish with everlasting destruction those who reject him. There is no part of our *Te Deum* that more animates the worship of my heart than these two sentences, "Thou art the King of Glory, O Christ!" "When thou hadst overcome the sharpness of death, thou didst open the kingdom of heaven to all believers." It is as King of Saints that he freely receives every sinner who seeks his salvation, writing the law of his kingdom in his heart, giving him

* Matt. xi. 27.

victory over the enemies of his soul, making him triumphant in death, and finally saying unto him from his throne, "Enter thou into the joy of thy Lord." It is as Christ crucified and glorified and "King of Saints" that he utters that promise of royal authority and power, "To him that overcometh will I grant to sit with me in my throne, even as I also overcame and am set down with my Father in His throne."*

Here then is another aspect in which we must lift up the Lord Jesus in our ministry. We must not let it be forgotten that, in all the tenderness of his invitations and promises, he speaks "as one that hath authority," not only to make them good, but to punish their rejection. The invitations of his grace are the commandments of his throne, to be answered for at his bar. Hence, the preaching of Christ crucified ceases not till it has exhibited "the judgment-seat of Christ." It must be noted that, when the Apostle says, "Knowing *the terror of the Lord* we persuade men," he is speaking of the terror of our Lord Jesus in his day of judgment.† That day is called "the great day of *the wrath of the Lamb*."‡ Why the wrath of the Lamb? Why but to keep still in view the great sacrifice of atonement; to teach that Christ on the throne of judgment is Christ that was crucified; that the chief question of that day will be, whether we have accepted or neglected the great salvation purchased by his blood; and the chief terror of that day will be the vengeance of that blood upon its rejection? While we love to speak of the blessedness of "the saints in light" as "joint heirs with Christ," we can not discharge our whole duty as preachers of Christ, unless we speak of the heritage of those who "receive his grace in vain." We have a most impressive example in St. Paul, who, knowing nothing in his ministry "but Jesus Christ and him crucified," pictured so solemnly that day when, coming "to be glorified in his saints and to be admired in all them that believe," the Lord Jesus "shall be revealed from heaven, in flaming fire, taking vengeance on them that obey not the Gospel, and who shall be punished with everlasting destruction from the presence of the Lord and from the glory of his power."§

But the preaching of Christ as the crucified extends through all the inheritance of his people forever and ever. It deserves your particular remark how carefully, in many places, the Scriptures, in speaking of the actual condition of the redeemed in heaven, and its connection with the Lord Jesus as its author, source, and substance, so speak of it as to keep not only Christ on the throne, but

* Rev. iii. 21. † 2 Cor. v. 10, 11. ‡ Rev. vi. 17. § 2 Thess. i. 7–10.

Christ *crucified,* Christ *the sacrifice,* in most conspicuous view. This is especially seen wherever he is spoken of in his glory as *"the Lamb,"* which of course means the Lamb of *sacrifice*—the antitype of the paschal lamb and of the daily sacrifice of the law; the fulfillment of Isaiah's prophecy, " He is led as a lamb to the slaughter," wounded for our transgressions. Thus the multitude which no man can number, who stand in white raiment and with palms of victory before the throne, are represented as *"before the Lamb,"* and their adoration is in ascribing *"salvation to the Lamb,"* and notice is carefully drawn to their having "washed their robes in the blood of *the Lamb,"* and all that high communion and blessedness is called *" the marriage-supper of the Lamb,"* and in all that dwelling-place *" the Lamb is the light thereof,"* and he that "feeds them and leads them to living fountains of water" is *" the Lamb* which is in the midst of the throne," and " the river of the water of life," representing their whole felicity, proceeds *"out of the throne of the Lamb,"* and the book of citizenship of the New Jerusalem, in which are written the names of all that are to inhabit there, is "the book of life of *the Lamb slain from the foundation of the world."** Most evidently the intent of all this is to carry adoring thoughts of the sacrifice of the cross into our every thought of heavenly happiness, and to represent the heir of that felicity as never forgetting that great price; never seeing the Lord in his glory without seeing him as once " crucified and slain;" never ascending any height of " the heavenly places," or drinking at any stream of their blessedness, without seeing in Christ not only "the Author and the Finisher," but all in him as "the *Lamb slain,"* as he that *" liveth and was dead,"* Christ the propitiation, Christ crucified. Atonement by sacrifice is written all over the heritage of the righteous. It is the chorus of every song of the saints in light. All heaven echoes with *"Unto him that washed us from our sins in his own blood."* So must it be in all our preaching concerning the happiness of the saved—Christ the purchaser and dispenser, but the glory of his cross never separated from the glory of his throne. When we " shall see him as he is," we shall not cease to think of him as he was.

Here a word about our representations of what is the happiness of the redeemed in heaven—what constitutes it. There is a chilling effect of many books and sermons on that subject—so much generality, so little about what the Scriptures place so above all; so much made of the subordinate and accessory features, the pastures

* Rev. xiii. 8 and xx. 12, 14.

and the flowers of the heavenly land, and so little of the Sun that gives them all their beauty and life; as if you should speak of the garden of Eden, and make more of what God planted than of the presence and communion of God therein—not remembering what Paradise in all its beauty became to man when that communion was withdrawn. Christ is carefully to be preached, as being, himself, in his glory and communion, the heaven of his people; as well as, in his humiliation and sacrifice, its purchase-price. How striking is the testimony of the Scriptures to this point. Has Jesus gone away to prepare a place for us in his Father's house? His promise is, "I will come again, and receive you unto myself, that where I am there ye may be also." Does he pray his Father in behalf of the happiness of his people? The prayer is, "that they may be with me where I am and behold my glory." While it doth not appear what we shall be "as sons of God" and "joint heirs with Christ," does St. John speak of one thing that we do know? It is that "we shall be like and see him as he is." Does Jesus promise to them that overcome, that they "shall eat of the hidden manna?" That manna is himself. "I am that bread of life." Is heaven described as a glorious city of habitation? "The Lamb is the temple" and "the light thereof." Hath it a river of water of life, and on either side the tree of life? All that river comes forth from "the throne of the Lamb." Christ is "the finisher of our faith" in this, that he is, in himself, the consummation of our hope; his presence, his communion, his everlasting love being the prize of our high calling, and the goal of our race. We come to him now, and he is our peace. We go to be with him forever, and he is our glory. Ask the way to heaven; we say, *Christ.* Ask where heaven is; we say, *where Christ is.* Ask what heaven is; we answer, *what Christ is.* Thus preach we Christ crucified, whenever we speak according to the Scriptures of what constitutes the life eternal of the sinner "redeemed by the blood of the Lamb."

But we must take good heed, that we do not so speak of our Lord in his heavenly power and glory as not to give due place to his ever present personal ministry, in and to, his Church on earth. The impression is too prevalent that here in our duties and wants and prayers we have only a Saviour and helper afar off.

The precious assurance of the Scriptures is, that we have a Saviour so near to every one of us, that he is "a very present help"—so present that nothing can separate us from him; that nothing but unbelief ever intervenes between our wants and his fullness, neither space nor time, nor unworthiness nor weakness—so present that he is ever at the door,—waiting to be received, or beneath our weakness ready to be leaned on. No presence is so "*very* present" as that of Christ, in the power of his Spirit to every heart that seeks him—enlightening, guiding, comforting, upholding, drawing sinners to himself, making himself known to them, giving efficacy to means of grace; whatever the instruments, He the only power. "I am the good shepherd." All is comprehended in that declaration. As the good shepherd, he is the *present* shepherd, so present to each of the flock that he "calleth every one by name and leadeth him out." Oh, what a help and comfort it is when we get a full comprehension and an abiding impression of *that presence*. How it strengthens the Minister of the Gospel! How it lifts up the heart of the Christian!

In this connection, the faithful preaching of Christ will keep in great prominence, that aspect of himself which he taught with such emphasis, when he spake of himself as "*the living bread—the bread of God*" of whom the manna in the wilderness was the type and the bread of our Eucharist is the Sacrament; Christ the present daily life of his people—they abiding in him by faith, he in them by his Spirit; all their life as children of God now—all their hopes of life forever, depending on that habitual communion—the vine and the branches. The more we ourselves enjoy of that *abiding*, the better shall we know how to teach it. Nowhere does mere book-knowledge of what is given us to preach assist us less.

When we speak of Christ as "*the life*," fulfilling the type of the manna, let us take care that we set in clear view, not only our dependence, but His *freeness*. It was one prominent aspect of that "spiritual meat" of which "all our fathers" of the Church in the wilderness ate, that all classes and conditions of people partook of it alike, and all with equal and perfect freeness. It lay all around the camp, as accessible to one as another. Moses, nor Aaron, nor any priest or ruler had any privilege at that table which the humblest Israelite had not. The priesthood had no office of intervention between the hungry and that bread. *Whosoever will, let him take and eat*, was the proclamation. Let us take good heed that what we cannot deny in the type be not narrowed or concealed in the antitype. Our text is, "*Him that cometh to me, I will in no wise cast out.*"* And I do not know a text that contains more of the essence of the preaching of Christ in the richness and freeness of his salvation. Oh, let us take care that our ministry shall keep full in the sight of men that open way, that free access, that direct-

* John vi. 37.

ness of coming, not to some mere symbolical representation, but to the *very present* Christ, in all his tenderness of love and power to save. Ordinances, ministers, are sadly out of place, no matter how divinely appointed for certain uses, when instead of mere helps in coming to Christ, they are made, in any sense, conditions or terms of approach, so that the sinner gets to Christ only, or in any degree, by them. The light of the sun is not more free to every man that cometh into the world, than is the salvation of Jesus to every believing sinner. It is our business to be continually showing that precious truth; coming by faith, all the condition;—Christ, the full and perfect salvation of all that come.

But in the range of Gospel truth, there are subjects of instruction, which though not directly concerning his person and office, are so connected with all right appreciation of his saving grace that we cannot keep them out of view, without affecting most injuriously our whole ministry. Be it remembered that while the cross with its immediate neighborhood is the metropolis of Christianity—all the region round about is Holy Land, more or less holy according to the nearness to that "city of our God;" "a land of milk and honey," "of brooks and fountains of water," intersected in all directions with highways by which pilgrims to Zion approach the desire of their hearts. It is the office of the Gospel preacher to map out that land; to trace those converging roads—to set up the way-marks to the city of Refuge. Christ is not fully preached when any truth which teaches the sinner's need of such a Saviour—illustrating his preciousness by showing our ruin and beggary through sin dwelling in us and bringing condemnation upon us, is kept in obscurity. The wisdom of "the scribe, instructed unto the kingdom of God, to bring out of his treasure things new and old," is found in his omitting nothing connected with the Gospel, however remote from the great central truths and duties; and in his giving to each its portion in due season, as well as its place in due relation.

For example: Christ is "our *righteousness*" unto justification to every one that believeth, so that in him there is no condemnation.*
But we shall preach him in vain, in that light, unless we show the sinner's absolute need of such righteousness. We must seek, under the power of the Holy Ghost, so to convince him of sin that he shall see himself to be under the condemnation of God's law, without excuse and without hope, till he flees to that refuge. Blessed is he whose ministry the Spirit employs to teach that lesson of ruin and beggary. It is the threshold of the way of life. The text-book

* Romans viii. 1.

in that teaching is the law—God's will, however and wherever expressed. Preached in a spiritual application to the secrets of the heart, not only as the rule of obedience but as the condition of peace with God to every one that is not in Christ Jesus, and on the perfect keeping of which all his hope depends; preached in view of the salvation of Jesus as only increasing the condemnation so long as it is salvation neglected; it is the instrument of the Holy Ghost to strip the sinner of self-reliance and self-justification, to humble him before God under a sense of guilt and ruin,—and as a " schoolmaster to lead him to Christ that he may be justified by faith." He that would preach a full justification in Christ, without works, must preach entire condemnation under the law, by works. By the law is the knowledge of sin and hence the knowledge in part of Christ. Clear, unequivocal statements of the divine law; the full exhibition of the text, *"Cursed is every one that continueth not in all things written in the book of the law to do them"* (that continueth not in all things from first to last of life), thus carrying the sword of the Spirit into the discerning of the thoughts and intents of the heart, is the special basis of and preparation for all saving knowledge of Christ. The way of the Lord is prepared by that fore-runner. How many more consciences would cry out for relief under the load of sin; how much oftener would the careless heart be awakened to seek mercy through Christ, were there only a more searching comparison of all that is in man with all the holiness of the will of God.

Again: Christ is " made unto us *sanctification*."* But how can we do justice to so cardinal a truth of God's grace, unless we do ample justice to that other great truth of man's nature out of which arises all the need of a sanctifier—the entire " corruption of the nature of every man that is naturally engendered of the offspring of Adam?"† The beginning of sanctification is to be born again of the Holy Ghost. According to men's views of the extent to which by nature they are corrupt and alienated from God, will be their views of the spiritual nature, necessity and extent of that great change. Hence to preach Christ in sanctification, we must preach man in his natural corruption. The *" carnal mind"* is *" enmity against God* and is *not subject to the law of God, neither indeed can be."*‡ Let us faithfully expound those words of St. Paul. We need no stronger declaration as the basis of the whole superstructure of the need of an entire inward regeneration, making the sinner a new creature in Christ Jesus—new in heart, new in life and hope. That this preach-

* 1 Cor. i. 30.   † Article IX.   ‡ Rom. viii. 7.

ing of the necessity of such new creature is eminently the preaching of Christ, we have a striking testimony in these words of the Epistle of the Ephesians (chap. iv. 20-24), "Ye have not so learned Christ; if so be ye have heard him and been taught by him the truth as in Jesus; that ye put off the old man which is corrupt according to the deceitful lusts, and be renewed in the spirit of your mind and that ye put on the new man which after God is created in righteousness and true holiness."

But how shall we speak of so great spiritual transformation without speaking with equal stress of Him who produces it? What sanctification is to salvation, such is the right teaching of the power and office of the Holy Ghost, the Sanctifier, the Spirit of Christ, and all comprehending gift of God. What is there in the Christian life, from first to last, that is not the work of the Holy Ghost? Is the sinner convinced of sin? Jesus sent the Spirit to do that work. Is he quickened from spiritual death? "*It is the Spirit that quickeneth.*" Is he born again? He is "*born of the Spirit.*" Is he spiritually minded? It is because he "*minds the things of the Spirit.*" Is he "a follower of God," as a dear child? It is because he is "*led by the Spirit of God.*" Hath he an internal evidence of that sonship? It is because *the Spirit beareth witness with his spirit.* Is the love of God "shed abroad in our hearts?" It is "by *the Holy Ghost given unto us.*" Do we learn how to pray as we ought? It is because "*the Spirit helpeth our infirmities.*" Are we comforted with the consolation of Christ? The Spirit is "*the Comforter.*" Are we strengthened in our duty? It is "by *the Spirit in the inner man.*" Do we grow in the knowledge of Christ? Jesus said of the Holy Ghost: "*He shall take of mine and show it unto you.*" And beside the spiritual resurrection and sanctification, will these vile bodies also rise; will they also be sanctified and made glorious according to the glory of our risen Lord? It is written that "He shall quicken your mortal bodies by *His Spirit that dwelleth in you.*"*

Rightly to honor the Holy Ghost as He is thus revealed in His own inspired word, how important to the faithfulness, the fruitfulness of our ministry. We may so come short of it—we may so contradict it, that while bearing a very reputable character before men, we may all the while be "grieving the Holy Ghost," yea, even "resisting the Holy Ghost." How much barrenness in the work of the ministry, in making not Church-members, but spiritually enlightened and spiritually-minded followers of Christ, may be

* Romans viii. 11.

ascribed to deficiency—negativeness at least, in this great department of our teaching! In no part of his work does a minister more need to be taught of God or to sit humbly at the feet of Jesus to learn of him; nowhere does a decline of spirituality of mind so soon show itself as here. In no part of our work do we depend more upon a decided, habitual, personal experience in our own souls of God's gracious operation. It is here that great departures from the truth which go on to carry away eventually whole communities of professing Christians into manifold and essential errors, almost always secretly or overtly begin; as it is the final construction of a system from which the personal office of the Holy Ghost is virtually if not professedly excluded, in which they culminate. The Scriptural description of a spiritual mind is, that it "minds the things of the Spirit." It is equally the test of a spiritual and evangelical ministry. That which specially tries our spiritual discernment and skill in rightly dividing the word of truth is the right adjustment of means of grace in their relation to the power of grace, of instruments of blessing to the hand that employs them and that gives them all their efficacy. The Spirit hath His instruments. His grace hath its means. His great instrument in our sanctification, is His own revealed Truth, by which he testifies of and glorifies the Lord Jesus in our eyes. Sacraments are that same essential truth, taught under other signs, and sealed with a special impressiveness. The preaching of that same truth by an ordained Ministry, is the great instrumentality of the Spirit. The point of caution is, that while giving all due place to the instrument we keep it exclusively in the place of a mere instrument—of no avail in itself; that we treat it as we treat the glass by which we seek to see some distant star—not as an object to be looked at—but only as a help to look immeasurably beyond and above it; that as the glass is nothing without the light, so the means of grace are nothing without "the Spirit of grace;" that all the power is of the Holy Ghost, and *that* power not deposited in the means, as we put bread into the hand of a distributor, so that whosoever receives the latter receives the bread; that power never divorced from the personal ministry of the Spirit, but applied directly by himself to each heart that receives His grace; He "dividing to every man severally as He will." To speak of an ordinance, a Sacrament, any means of grace, even the Holy Scriptures of truth, as if they were in any sense the *power* unto salvation, or as if they contained, whatever its original source, the grace by which we live unto God, thus leading men to look to them, instead of only, by their help, to Christ and His Spirit, is to "do despite to the Spirit of grace."

The whole truth in this connection is found where the Apostle says: "Who is Paul and who is Apollos, but ministers by whom ye believed, *even as the Lord gave to every man.*"* Instead of Paul and Apollos, read any ordinance or means of grace. What are they but ministrations of man by help of which ye believe, even as the Lord giveth to every man.

There is a text which the full and explicit preaching of Christ, will be always directly or indirectly, consciously or unconsciously, illustrating. It is those verses in the second chapter of the Epistle to the Ephesians, "By grace are ye saved, through faith, and that not of yourselves it is the gift of God: Not of works, lest any man should boast. For we are his workmanship, created in Christ Jesus unto good works." Salvation all of grace only; in its origin in the love of God; in its purchase by the blood of Christ; in the first quickening of the sinner from the death of sin; in all the renewal of his nature; in his acceptance through Christ, to the peace of God; in his whole ability to live as a child of God; and in his final admission to the glory of God—*all of grace only*—wonderful grace;—but *through faith alone*—and that faith itself a gift of grace; our works in every degree and aspect wholly excluded from the work of saving us, though necessarily included *as fruits* of the grace that does save us—we being created anew in Christ Jesus unto good works and not in any degree *by* good works—first God's workmanship making us new creatures, then our working as so created "unto good works which God hath ordained that we should walk in them." We preach such works, *first*, as absolutely excluded from having any part in procuring our Justification before God; *secondly*, as essential fruits and evidences of our having obtained such Justification. We preach the office of Faith as so vital that only by it are we united to Christ, as living stones built upon the living head of the corner; and the necessity of good works as so absolute, that only in them can we walk as God hath ordained and have evidence that we are true believers in Jesus; and at the same time both faith and works deriving all being from the Spirit of God and all value and efficacy to salvation from the Righteousness of Christ.

Here let me add some few *miscellaneous observations*. We are bound to instruct the believer in all the privileges and consolations that are in Christ that his joy may be full. But we must lay equal

* 1 Cor. iii. 5.

stress on all his obligations, that Christ may be glorified. Out of the same wounds of the cross come privilege and duty, promise and commandment, the consolation of faith and the duty of obedience; and the same preaching that leads to the one must alike insist on the other, and on both as necessary to our having that rest which Jesus promises. It is a great matter so to preach the precepts of Christ as to lead men to embrace his promises; and so the promises as to draw the disobedient to the love of his precepts. In all our work we have two great sources of persuasion, according to the example of St. Paul, namely, "We beseech you by *the mercies* of God," and again, "Knowing *the terror of the Lord*, we persuade men;" the love of God in Christ as a Saviour, and the wrath of God in Christ as Judge of quick and dead; a cloud of light and a cloud of darkness, each proceeding from the cross as accepted or rejected. We must do all in tenderness, but all in faithfulness. The whole counsel of God embraces the fearful penalty of unpardoned sin as well as the glorious inheritance of the reconciled in Christ. The faithful preacher of Christ keeps back none of it. While he delights in the loving aspects of his grace, he is not ashamed of the severities of his justice. He does not indeed denounce or judge. It is not for him to command or condemn. His work is always to entreat and persuade; tenderly, lovingly, patiently, in the mind of Christ. But persuasion has the alarming truths to use as well as the encouraging. That, "*God is a consuming fire*," out of Christ, is as much an argument of persuasion and tenderness, as that in Christ, "God is Love." We read of "*the goodness and severity of God.*"* We must exhibit both. They interpret and enforce one another. But how to balance aright judgment and mercy, invitation and warning, precepts of obedience, and promises of consolation, the tender "*Come unto me and I will give you rest,*" with the stern "*Depart ye cursed into everlasting fire,*" the darkness and the light—the loving voice from the Mercy-seat and the dreadful sentence from the Judgment-seat—all under the duty of teaching and preaching Jesus Christ, is not learned from books only, is not given by specific rule, comes chiefly out of the state of the heart, under the general light of the Scriptures, and by a careful endeavor to learn of, and be like, him of whom it is beautifully written that he hath "the tongue of the learned to know how to speak a word in season to him that is weary."†

From all that has now been said, it appears how mistaken is the idea that by conforming our preaching to Christ and him crucified

* Rom. xi. 22. † Isaiah l. 4.

we have a very narrow range of truth to expatiate in. In reality we have the whole vast range of natural and revealed religion. A wider field no preacher can find who does not seek it beyond the confines of religious truth. The difference between the man who confines himself to the preaching of Christ and him who does not, need not be that the latter embraces any portion of divine truth—of doctrine or duty, of history or prophecy or precept which enters not into the range of the former. It may be wholly a difference in the mode of presenting precisely the same truth—a difference in the bearings; in the relations assigned to every part; in the cardinal points to which all is adjusted, in the *polarity*, so to speak, which governs such manifestation of truth as deserves the name and praise of the preaching of Christ. You may take truth from the immediate neighborhood of the cross, or from the farthest boundaries of the domain of Christianity, and when its just relation to Christ and his redemption is exhibited Christ is preached. Thus there is no reason why, in the most faithful ministry, there may not be abundant variety of topic and of instruction. The sermon may be always shining in the light of our glorious Lord, while receiving it either by direct looking unto him, or indirectly from secondary objects which, as satellites of the sun, revolve around him and shine in his glory. The sermon, in all its spirit and tendency, may say, *"Behold the Lamb of God,"* and yet the view may be as changing as the positions from which it is taken, the circumstances which influence it, the lights and shadows of the several conditions and necessities of the minds before which it is placed. In general we may say that, as no subject is legitimate in the preaching of a minister of Christ that does not admit of being presented in some important relation to Christ; so no sermon is evangelical that does not truly exhibit such relation, giving him the same position to the whole discourse that he holds in the Scriptures to the whole body of truth therein. As some subjects have a much nearer and more vital relation to him than others, they will be much the most frequent and engrossing in the preaching of a faithful Christian minister. The great truths, the great facts, the great duties and privileges and interests and consolations which proceed the most directly from the person and office—the death and intercession of Christ and the work of the Holy Spirit—as well as those which lead the most immediately thereto, will be so habitually the subjects of his preaching, that the more remote and indirect will be only occasional exceptions to the standing rule and habit. And which of these classes of subjects his mind and heart most delight in, and which draw forth the deepest earnestness and the strongest emotions of his soul, will not be doubtful.

We have now exhibited as much of our great and wide subject as we could with any propriety occupy your time with. You will, of course, understand that we have not attempted to embrace the whole field. What has been attempted, we are deeply conscious is most imperfect and inadequate. Still, we have not withheld our best endeavors, where even St. Paul exclaimed, "*Who is sufficient for these things!*" We conclude with a brief view of the state of mind and spirit which qualifies a minister to be a faithful preacher of Christ.

1. *A spirit of Faith.* I mean Faith not merely in such of its exercises as make the minister a living Christian, and a growing, vigorous Christian; but in that special exercise which enables him to go on patiently, persistently, hopefully, immovably, preaching the Gospel as we have seen the Apostles preached it, in like simplicity and spirituality—with as little of the devices and mixtures and dilutions and subterfuges of man's wisdom, no matter what the obstacles or what the apparent fruitlessness—believing it is God's own way, to which alone His blessing is promised and which He *will* bless as his own "wisdom and power unto salvation." It was precisely with such meaning that St. Paul, just after he had pronounced, "We preach not ourselves, but Christ Jesus the Lord"—and just after he had adverted to the fact that such preaching failed to open the eyes of many that heard, saying, "If our Gospel be hid, it is hid to them that are lost, in whom the god of this world had blinded the minds of them which believe not;"* it was in full view of all whom their preaching did not succeed in convincing, but only made the more hardened and hopeless, that he said, "*We believe and therefore speak,*"† meaning not only that they believed what they spoke, but that they believed it was just what God commanded them to speak. And no rejection of it by man could shake that confidence or lead them to speak any thing else or in any other way. Well they knew what a "stumbling-block to the Jew," and what utter "foolishness to the Greek," was their testimony concerning Christ crucified; but not a word would they change—"*We believe and therefore speak.*" It was this lesson of faith that Paul gave to Timothy. He warned him of a time of apostasy approaching—"The time will come when they will not endure sound doctrine—and they shall turn away their ears from the truth and be turned

* 2 Cor. iv. 3, 4. † v. 13.

unto fables."‡ How then was Timothy to do in such times? What "*sound doctrine*" meant in the mind of St. Paul, we well know—all that way of justification by the righteousness of Christ imputed and of sanctification by the Spirit of God imparted to the believer; that whole way of life of which the *vicarious* propitiation by the sacrifice of Christ was the central power and life. It was all that doctrine which men would not endure. And what was Timothy to do? Conclude that he, and other preachers of Christ, had taken the wrong method because thus unsuccessful? That they must find out some other sort of preaching because that was so rejected? Since men would not endure sound doctrine, must he try to get them into the Church, or if in the Church already, to make them satisfied to stay there, by giving them unsound doctrine? If the truth caused them to turn away from it, must *he* turn away from it also and give them something else to correct the evil? What said the faith of an Apostle?—No compromise—no accommodation —only so much more earnestly and continually that same rejected doctrine. Hear Paul's remedy! "I charge thee before God and the Lord Jesus Christ who will judge the quick and the dead at his appearing and his kingdom—preach the *word* (the same offensive word), be instant in season, out of season—reprove, rebuke, exhort, with all long suffering and doctrine."* The more the truth is turned away from, so much the more proclaim it. God will see to the issue: "So we preach, not as pleasing men, but God, which trieth the heart." Such is the faith of which we are speaking, as of such importance in our ministry.

The *times* which St. Paul predicted, and which began before Timothy had ended his labors, are yet in being. We all know how they have been exhibited since the beginning of this century; in this country, under the name of Unitarianism, and in the continent of Europe, under that of Rationalism. And we have heard with amazement and grief how they have appeared of late in the venerable Church of England, among some of her clergy, in her high places of college and pulpit teaching, and how even a Bishop takes the lead; and how while it is manifest that he cannot endure the sound doctrine of the Scriptures, and therefore labors to destroy their authority, he dares, with a dishonesty most astonishing, and an effrontery unexampled, to persist in holding the office of a Bishop in the Church of Christ against the remonstrance of all his peers, and to the great disgust of right-minded people. The case

* 2 Tim. iv. 3, 4. † 2 Tim. iv. 1, 2.

is singular. There were Bishops of the Romish Church who under the reign of infidelity in France during the Revolution, renounced the faith; but they renounced also their office in the Church. We have a more primitive example. Judas Iscariot, when he had betrayed his Lord, having been "guide to them that took Jesus," had too much conscience left to continue in his "apostleship." "His Bishopric" another took.

But perhaps we have adverted with more point to the case of this English Bishop than his importance deserved. We were speaking of the new aspect of affairs among certain of the Church of England. True, the most prominent manifestation is in attacks on the Inspiration of the Scriptures. But let not any suppose the ultimate or inspiring object to be there. The citadel of truth and life can not be reached till that outwork is reduced. *Atonement* is the final object. Atonement for sin by the precious blood of Christ, with all the precious doctrines of salvation which reside therein, as branches in the vine, and which are dead and only fit to be cast away as rubbish the moment such atonement is taken away—that is the doctrine they cannot endure. That is the truth from which they turn away, but which they know is safe so long as the Scriptures are the final Rule of Faith. Meanwhile they would counsel us to give up the old way of preaching Christ, as no doubt the best way for the old times, but unfit for these times when through mature growth of man's wisdom such doctrine is counted, just indeed as it was by similar minds in the old times, *"foolishness."* They would have us lay aside creeds and confessions, in order that they who cannot endure the doctrine of Apostles and Prophets may be accounted Christians no less than those who believe and love it. They would make the Church so broad that any varieties or oppositions of belief may be embraced in its communion and even in its ministry, thus strangely sacrificing Gospel-truth to Church comprehensiveness.

Now suppose such evil times should visit us in our Church— what must we do? I ask it to illustrate what I mean by the faith of which I am speaking. Must we preach the word, as St. Paul understood it, any the less? Shall we suppose that to preach Christ crucified is not as much "the wisdom and power of God," as when apostles set us the example? Or shall we believe as they believed, and therefore continue to speak as they spoke, even though the whole earth should be covered with a flood of apostasy, and men everywhere should be turned unto fables? What says a true faith in God? No change, but in more earnestness with the unchanged. "Preach the word"—the same word—"Instant in season, out of season," "with all long suffering and doctrine." Let patience have her perfect work. Be not faithless—but believing—God's hand is not shortened that it cannot save by that same word now as in the ancient times.

These observations are not applicable only to circumstances which may hereafter exist among us. Always, everywhere in our ministry we find those calling themselves Christians, or at least numbered in Christian congregations, to whom what St. Paul meant by "sound doctrine" is an aversion. They do not like to hear, they turn away from hearing so much about atonement and justification, and a new heart, and faith, and all the inward work of the Holy Ghost. A less spiritual religion would be far more to their taste—and they think if we would preach much less about the great distinctive features of the Gospel and more about mere moral duties—that is, less religion and more of something else, many ears, now turned away, would hear. Very likely. And under the influence of such views, the testimony of the pulpit is sometimes grievously deformed. The minister seeks to commend himself more to the people's preferences than their consciences; and hence, of course, not by manifestations of the truth in its simplicity, directness spirituality and completeness. He enlarges the list of communicants by reducing the spiritual qualifications for the communion. He makes the narrow gate wider; invites a condition of mind which the Lord invites not. The middle wall of partition between the Church and the world is broken down, the more to please the world, the more to enlarge the Church. Such compliances we have no right to make. They spring out of unbelief. They poison the life of the Church. If men will not endure sound doctrine *we* cannot help it, we have no unsound to give. If the ground will not receive the good seed given us to sow, we cannot mend the matter by sowing bad seed. To the end of the world, come what may, that seed and that only must we sow. "God (that giveth the seed) giveth the increase," and *will* give it. Our strength is *to believe*.

2. A spirit of Love. To preach Christ is not only "a work of faith," it is "a labor of love." I will not say that no man can do it in a certain sense, that is, with doctrinal correctness, without the love of Christ in his heart; for St. Paul speaks of some in his day who preached Christ, "even of envy and strife, not sincerely," from selfish and evil motives. I will not prolong this discourse

in enlarging on the elementary truth that without a personal experience of the preciousness of Christ to our own souls, by each one's individual participation in the hope that rests on his justifying righteousness, and is witnessed by the sanctifying power of His Spirit dwelling in us, we cannot preach Christ, according to his will, in his mind, in the tenderness and earnestness and patience and godly wisdom which alone become our office, however correct our teaching in a mere doctrinal aspect. What I wish, in these concluding words to insist on is, the importance of a very earnest, tender and overcoming love, to give spirituality to our theology, and the mind of Christ to our teachings concerning him. Two preachers, alike in accurate and full statement of all that is revealed concerning our blessed Lord and his salvation, may be very different in the spiritual power of their ministry, and the difference will not depend so much on the superiority of talent or of eloquence, or even of diligence in one over the other, as on their comparison in point of love. He will preach best who loves most. His preaching will go most to the heart, and will be attended with most of "the demonstration of the Spirit," who, in all he says and does, is most constrained by the love of Christ, dictating, animating, sanctifying, with the tenderness and patient earnestness of his Master's mind, his whole discourse. Oh, brethren, that we were more earnest to grow in this grace! What ought we to value in personal attainment, compared with it? If your ministry fail in spiritual efficacy, inquire into the cause by searching the state of your hearts in regard to the love of Christ therein, to what extent the aim, the zeal, the topics, the temper of your work, and the whole character of your personal example are under the dominion of that love.

I have already occupied too much of your time, and yet I feel that I have come very far short of the height and breadth of what I have sought to exhibit. "We have this treasure in earthen vessels, that the excellency of the power may be of God and not of us." Blessed be God, that in our weakness we have His power to lean on. I humbly pray that power of God to bless to you, dear brethren, what in so much weakness and imperfectness and unworthiness I have now addressed to you. Nothing in this world could I rejoice in so much as to be instrumental, under God's grace, in promoting the spiritual excellency and efficacy of your work and your personal growth in the faith and love of Christ. The time is at hand when nothing else will seem of the smallest value. I commend you to God and the word of His grace, which is able to build you up and make you good stewards of the unsearchable riches of Christ. "The God of peace who brought again from the dead our Lord Jesus, that great Shepherd of the sheep, through the blood of the everlasting covenant, make you perfect in every good work to do his will, working in you that which is well pleasing in his sight, through Jesus Christ, to whom be glory and dominion forever and ever." Amen.

INDEX OF SUBJECTS.

[The following indexes of Subjects and Authors were prepared by the REV. CHAS. W. QUICK.]

Account and impute, in the language of the articles and homilies and their compilers, mean the same when joined to *righteousness and to sin*, 246, 247.

Adult, every, if duly prepared for Baptism, enjoys spiritual regeneration and remission of sins before the rite is administered, 324.

Altar requires a priest and a sacrifice, 427, 428—none in the primitive Church, 432—none before the 4th or 5th century, 433—originated at the same time with veneration for relics, 435—(See *Structure*.)

Altars, first were tombs of martyrs, 435—in Romish Churches cover bodies, bones, or relics of saints, 436—all Romish errors and superstitions cluster around them, 438—suggestive of nothing edifying to a Protestant communicant, 438, 439.

Argument of this work stated, 57.

Article, XXVIIth oppugned by Dr. Pusey, 170—IXth directly opposed to Romish and Oxford views of original sin, 183—XIth, XIIth, and XIIIth on Justification, 238, 245—the precision of the XIth remarkable, 245—especially in the Latin form, 245, *note*—the device by which it is made not to state in what our justification consists, 246.

Auricular Confession advocated by Bp. Goodman, and such advocacy approved by the British Critic, 208.

Baptism, the only instrument of justification in Romish and Oxford systems; 143—of Cornelius and his friends, Frith's declaration thereon, 319—Hooper's views concerning, 320—directly opposed to those of Tractarians, 321—maintain the *precedence* of spiritual life before water Baptism; 322—infant, best understood by considering the nature and benefits of adult Baptism, 325—its value acknowledged, 325—its use and improvement urged; 325—Tractarian exaltation of, super-superlative, 410, 411, *note*.

Boasting pretensions of the Oxford system, 95 — to be guarded against, and sifted, 419.

Buds of Romanism, 188, 199, 211, 213, 218.

Burnet and Jackson, their concurrence in regard to the Romanism of the Tractarian doctrines of original sin and righteousness, 184.

By faith in the language of the Reformers always means *through* faith, never *on account of* faith, 247.

Carey, Arthur, account of his ordination, 423.

Catechism, Nowell's, its authority in the age of the Reformers, 312

(483)

—two sets of expressions in it, respecting Baptism, 312—the apparent contradiction explained, 313—the assigned meaning sustained by quotations from, 313–315.

Charge of Bp. Wilson warning his clergy against the doctrines and usages of Tractarianism; 230–236—of the author on "the chief danger of the Church in these times;" 395—on "the work of preaching Christ," 451.

Christ, "*our righteousness*," fully preached requires the exhibition of the sinner's entire departure from the righteousness of the law; 470—"*our sanctification*," requires the statement of our entire depravity, 471—and of the Holy Ghost who sanctifies, 472.

Christ's merits, in what sense Oxford Divinity assigns to them any share in justification, 82.

Church substituted for Christ, 409—her real danger from Tractarianism, 415, 417—corruption of, by spread of Tractarian heresy, exaggerated, 418.

Comparison of the Brazen serpent and the body of Christ, in respect to the use of each, 340, 341.

Confession of faith, singular assertion in Dr. Pusey's, 243—its incredibility and absurdity proved; 243, 244—of Tractarians in regard to Hooker's views, 328, 329.

Communion Table, (see *Structure*.)

Controversy about Tractarian doctrines and restorations is the struggle of the Reformation repeated, 398—is for Christianity, 398.

Conversation, a supposed one, between an anxious inquirer and a Tractarian Teacher, 372–379.

Cross, as a sign and symbol, put on a level with Baptism and the Lord's Supper, according to Tractarians, 209—and should be joined with other Catholic symbols, 209.

Cross of Christ, or atonement, position of, in Oxford Scheme, 80–83, 379—preaching of and glorying in, 82.

Curiosities of Tractarian literature, 269, 329–331.

Developments, past, present and future of Tractarianism, 383, 384—in the views of Dr. Pusey between 1828 and the present time, 384–387—resources for, abundant in the Tractarian system, 387—of Tractarianism, 396.

Difference between Tractarians and their opponents clearly stated by the former, 413, 414—not a new statement, 413, note.

Difficulties of Tractarianism in its interpretation and use of homilies; 262–270—of the doctrine of Baptismal Regeneration as great as those of Transubstantiation, 410.

Disparagement of Mosaic Sacraments; 172, 173—of Anglican Christian holiness; 219—of the Homilies. 267, 268.

Divines, Oxford, their singular agreement with the schoolmen, 106—their defense against the charge of tendency to Romanism stated and proved inadequate, 125–131—abhor an imputed righteousness which is *external*, 129—careful to use the terms of Ultra-Protestants through perverting them, 129—the use of the word *impute*, in their *sense* of it, never opposed by Romanists; 131—esteem their system of fundamental importance. 371—*Anglican*, principle of selection from works of, 327—three fundamental points upon which citations from, bear, 331.

Divinity, Oxford, meaning of the term, 37—strenuously controverted, 37—essentially Romish; 41—three propositions relating to, stated and established; 108–112—difference between it and that for which the Reformers died is fundamental, if one is the Gospel, the other is not; 142—compared with Tridentine Romanism in relation to the Sacraments, 164—contains the Romish doctrine

INDEX OF SUBJECTS. 485

called the OPUS OPERATUM in all its offensive substance ; 165 —though Romish, claims to be Anglican ; 237—the " great gulf fixed" between it and the Scriptures and Church standards plainly displayed ; 290 et Ant.— as to Baptismal Regeneration and justification branded by Latimer as that of the reformers' and our Romish antagonists. 324.

Doctrine, true, of the Church of England on Baptism ; the author finds it stated in extracts from Hooper, Beveridge, and Taylor, 299, 300.

" Doubtful disputations," the penitent received to, 186–189.

Faith, explicit and implicit, explained, 85—the distinction held in Oxford Divinity ; 84—*justifying*, nature and office of, 143—*before* and *after* Baptism, a distinction which is the key to the doctrine of faith in Romanism and Oxfordism, 143—*before* Baptism, teaching of Rome on, 143-145—six main points in that teaching selected for comparison with Oxfordism, 145—1st. that faith before Baptism is not *living*, 146—2d, is only a necessary *preparation* for Baptism, 148—3d, this dead faith is still a Divine, *supernatural gift*, 150—4th, it is itself first justified and *made alive* in Baptism, 153—5th, that when thus justified it is not such a *trust* in the Divine mercy as lays hold of Christ's righteousness for justification, 154—and 6th, this faith only *continues* and *sustains* the justification received in Baptism ; 155—*after* Baptism the *representative*, the *symbol*, the *preacher* of justification, 160—a *sole instrument* only in name ; 160—*only*, justification by, the doctrine whereby the Reformation was effected, 218—and all Romish corruptions abolished, 218—to restore them it must first be overthrown ; 218—distinctions, definitions and deductions concerning ; 241, 242, *notes—the rule of,* one main point of dispute between Oxford writers and their opponents ; 399—*substance of*, another principal matter of controversy. 402.

Fears of the Romish tendency of Oxfordism justified by recent events, 141, *note ;* 229, *note ;* 423, 424, 425.

Feature, the chief in the Apostles' preaching of Christ, 452.

Gospel truths connected with a right understanding of the saving grace of Christ should be fully preached, 470.

Historical matters relating to the construction of the articles and homilies, 239.

Holy Ghost, to honor and exalt him in preaching highly important to the faithfulness and fruitfulness of the ministry, 472.

Holiness, on the *necessity* of, Protestants and Romanists agree, 121—on the *relation* of, to justification they differ ; 121—Christian attained by members of the English Church, disparaged when compared with that attained under Romish discipline, 220— what kind lauded by Tractarians, 221—eminently superior asserted by a Jesuit, of the Church of Rome, 224—Stillingfleet's heroic reply ; 224, 225—of the Divines who urge the Oxford system spoken of hopefully and charitably, 389—of the future adherents and disciples judged from the necessary tendencies of the system ; 389—fruits of cannot grow when the only tree on which they grow is eradicated, 404-408.

Happiness of the redeemed in heaven, direction concerning representations of it, 467.

Homily on faith, emphatic language of, on Old Testament Saints, 175 —quotation from garbled ; 176 —used for larger exposition of the articles, 238.

Hooker's views of Romish distinctions in regard to justification in three particulars, 136, 137—his rejection and denunciation of such distinctions apply fully to the Tractarian system; 137—*testimony*, value of it as authority, 326, 327—attempt of Tractarians to evade it, 335—settles the question as to the conformity of Oxford views of justification and faith, with those of the Anglican Church, 336.

Hope of the sinner rendered uncertain and his peace unsettled by Oxford view of justification; 85, 86—charitable in regard to Romish and Tractarian leaders, 138.

Illustrations of Oxford views of imputed righteousness; 75 *note*, 76-79—of the instrumentality of faith; 259, 260—of Bernard in regard to Baptism; 287, 288—of the author in regard to Sacraments, 310—in regard to the danger of Tractarianism, 382, 383.

Image worship, tenderness and tendency towards, manifested by Tractarians, 213-215—example of the abomination, 214—delicately called "honor paid to images," 213—called "devilish idolatry" by Cranmer, 215—in the estimation of Tractarians only an *incidental* corruption, not a legitimate result of Romanism; 215—Jackson's strong condemnation of, 218, *note*.

Imputation, and *counting righteous*, free use of such terms by Oxford writers misleads the reader, 73.

Inferences from Faber's comparison of Mr. Knox's views and those of the Oxford School on justification, 65.

Inherent righteousness for justification, the doctrine of, leads to full Romanism; 97—and *imputed* differ no less than God and man, Trent and Heaven, 380.

Instrument, internal and external, a distinction made by Tractarians, 259—a refuge invented by them to escape the condemnation of our Church standards, 258—the hail sweeps it away, 260—faith claimed to be a *sustaining* not an *originating*, 261—the homilies invoked to establish it, 261—crushed by its difficulties and absurdities, 263-266.

Instrumental character of justifying faith explained and enforced, 250, 251—and *only* so, 252, 253.

Interpretation of Scripture, comparison between Newman's and Romish, 124.

Justification by *inherent Righteousness*, the cornerstone of Romanism; 45—*before God*, precise doctrine of Oxford Divinity on, set forth, 67—Scriptural use of the word; 67, 68—*and sanctification*, essential difference between them; 69—forensic sense of, what the Oxford system means by it; 75—progressive according to Oxford divinity; 79—a distinction between justification and sanctification attempted by Oxford writers; 90, 91—Romish error of, origin of very ancient, 98—has had various dispensations, 98-100—Schoolmen gave fresh impetus to it; 100—*formal cause* of, distinction of *proper* and *improper* held alike by Rome and Oxford baseless; 126—*first* and *second*, an unscriptural distinction; 134—by faith only, "*a saying*," 160—doctrinal confession of our Church full on, 237—treatise of the Church on, 238.

Justification Baptismal, two propositions relating to stated and discussed, 271—effect of, in regard to original and actual sin, 272—agreement of Rome and Oxford, and the Anglican Church in their expressions; difference in the *sense* of those expressions, 272—limited to Baptism, as its only instrument, no hint of this in articles, catechism, or homilies, 275-277—expressly limited to faith only, 277, 278.

Key to the explanation of the language of the Fathers and our Church standards on the Sacraments, 305.

Knox, Alexander his views of justification stated, and adopted by the Oxford school, 58–60—his divinity compared with that of Rome, by Faber and found to be identical, 61, 62.

Language of Augustine applied to Baptism, 306—illustrated by reference to other matters in religion, viz.: the Lord's Supper, 307—orders, 309—also by reference to secular affairs; 309, 310—of *reformers and English divines* on Baptism explained, 279—how to be interpreted, 279 et seq.—viewed in connection with the premise, that there was no difference of opinion among them, on the subject, 279–282—if taken *literally* will prove too much for Oxfordism, 282—and are in direct contradiction to their cotemporaries; 283—of Hooker on Baptism, cited, explained, and compared with other language of his; 285, 286—of Barrow on Baptism treated similarly; 292, 293—also Jewell's; 294—Augustine's; 294–296—Cyprian's; 296—Jerome's; 297—Cyril's, 298.

Leaders in the Oxford movement, their motives not impeached, 46, 51—eminent learning of, no safe protection against their falling into serious error, 47—weight to be allowed to the writings of, against Romanism, 48–50.

Limbus Patrum, Romish doctrine of, 177, 178—necessary for consistency in Oxford views, 178.

Majority no criterion in matters of doctrine or history, 326.

Merit of our works necessarily follows if righteousness IN US is the *justifying principle*; 137—of Christ's works, strong language of a Romish writer on, 257—not exceeded by Oxford divines, 257—of our works maintained by the Council of Trent, 258—*equivalent* language used by Oxford writers; 258—rejected by the Oxford system in *name*, espoused by it in the *thing*, 339, *note*.

Miracles, age of, asserted by Rome to exist still, and claimed also by Oxford writers, 207.

Mistiness of Oxford writers' views, 93, 130, 134.

Monastic institutions, extravagant praise of, by the British critic, 227, *note*.

Opus operans and opus operatum explained; 166—*operatum* doctrine of, is that of Oxford and Rome, but not of the Anglican Church, 324.

Oxford and Tridentine writers compared; 122—both use the *language* of our Articles and Gospel standards, but their *meaning* is entirely different, 256.

Particulars, four important, derived from Vega, 107.

Pelagians and *Papists* compared, 122, 123.

Penance, doctrine of, necessary to the Oxford divinity, 188—Aquinas, Gandolphy, and Pusey compared in regard to views of, 190–192.

Per and *propter*, the clearness, force, and carefulness of their use in the Latin form of the XIth Art., 247, *note*.

Philosophy, its relation to theology, 95—"falsely so called" too much to do with Oxford divinity, 95.

Place to begin an attack upon Tractarianism as a thing of *external* evidence, 402—as a *doctrinal* theory, 402.

Prayers for the dead, injunction of Trent concerning, 201—encouragement of, given by Oxford writers, 202—decisively discouraged by the Church, 202—advocates of, condemned by the Bp. of Exeter.; 202—*and fastings* relinquished by Protestants happily discontinued, 222—Jackson's and Beveridge's denunciation of them, 222, 223.

Preaching Christ and Salvation, that way of, with which the author identifies himself; 56, 57—little use for frequent, in Oxford system; 212—of the word of God, the sole means of spiritual regeneration, 323, 324—urged as of prime importance, and directions given to promote due proportion in doctrinal teaching ; 392-394—decried by Tractarians, 407—heathen quoted as authority for such a course ; 408—of the Gospel, sinners saved thereby, 421—"*Christ crucified,*" how to challenge it as a characteristic of one's ministry, a most serious question ; 454—five methods in which preaching may approximate the Apostolic standard, yet fall short and prove defective, 454-458—*first,* by the *absence* of important truths relating to Christ, 454—*second,* by a want of *distinctness* commensurate with clearness on all points of law and duty, 456—*third,* by not keeping the *proportion of truth,* 456—*fourth,* by presenting some *essentially connected* truth disproportionately, 457—*fifth,* by a want of *habitualness* in the testimony of Christ ; 458—Christ, what it is positively, 458—examples of, drawn from our Lord's own teaching, 458—means to set forth all doctrines and duties of the Gospel system of truth in relation to Jesus, 459—illustration of, drawn from astronomy ; 459—miscellaneous observations on the work of, 474.

Propositions, three, in relation to Oxford Divinity submitted, 108.

Prominent features, four, of Oxfordism, 117—precisely those of Tridentine Romanism against which the Reformation was directed, 118-123.

Protestant, how far, according to Oxford writers, a person may advocate Romish errors, yet be a *sound* and *consistent,* 208.

Purgatory suggested and insinuated by Oxford Divinity ; 189—Tridentine and Oxford teachings in regard to, 199, 200—their close approximation, 200—their only difference ; 199—doctrine of, facility of its growth shown by Dr. Pusey, 387, 388—has the same stimulus now, 388.

Pusey's caricature of the views of the Evangelical Clergy of England, 54—his preference of the Romish system to such views, 55.

Quakerism and *Oxfordism,* likeness between them, 114-116.

Question, the fundamental one which serves as a position whence to command the whole field of inquiry in this work, stated ; 43—again stated and divided into *two main questions* in order to ascertain the doctrine of the Church formularies, 240—subdivision of each, 241.

Reasons for refusing to consecrate a Church having Tractarian restorations, 425, 443-447.

Regeneration and *Renovation,* a distinction not employed by the author, 301—rejected, 303, 304—its use shows the extreme difficulties of the system adopting it, 305—the distinction discarded by Hammond ; 323—Baptismal does as great violence to the Gospel as transubstantiation, 410—an empty doctrine, 411—only external, 411.

Reserve in preaching the Atonement ; 83—of Tractarians in expressing their own views ; 150—none observed in denouncing the Reformation and the Reformers ; 217—of Dr. Pusey in regard to his tenets, 221—drawn out by the British Critic ; 221—in preaching the righteousness and blood of Christ adverse to the promotion of holiness, 391—Tractarian doctrine of, only a revival of the old sin of "pious frauds," 396.

Restorations in doctrine similar to those in architecture ; 65—of what is old, may be restorations of old error ; 96—*and reformations* of Oxford solemnly rebuked ; 139-141—example of an edifying one, 204—flowers, altar-cloths, ringing of bells, lights on the altar, ecclesiastical dress, bowings when passing the altar,

INDEX OF SUBJECTS. 489

kneeling when offering alms; 210, 211—examples of such restorations seen in certain American Churches, 211, *note*.

Righteousness, Christian, two kinds of, 70—Inherent and implanted, for justification, a doctrine of self-righteousness, 105.

Righteousnesses for justification, *two* spoken of by Oxford writers, but *both inherent*, 128, 129.

Rome not to be reformed but destroyed, 217.

Romanism, agreement of Tractarians with, in prominent features, has an effect on their tastes and sympathies, in reference to the whole Christian walk and character; 219—the leading abominations of, termed only *external* changes in religion, by Tractarians; 226—contains the only formal confession of self-righteous doctrines; 381—congenial to the carnal mind; 382—essence of, found in the Tractarian teaching concerning the Lord's Supper; 427—the earlier denunciations of, by the Tractarians, only *for the times*, 442.

Sacramental justification, the most mischievous of practical errors of Rome; 179—signs and symbols, their increase advocated by Oxford writers, 209—will do away with the need of preaching, 209.

Sacrifice of Christ, how it should be preached, 464—its *substitutionary* character of vital importance in all teaching concerning it, 464, *note*.

Sacraments, office and efficiency of, unduly magnified, 164—as *signs* of grace kept out of view; 168—of the Old and New Testaments, difference made between them in regard to efficacy; 171—Whitgift's views concerning, 316, 317—his opinions not such as Tractarians would hold; 317—Haddon's statements concerning, in vindication of the Reformers, 318.

Saints, Old Testament, not justified till Christ came, 172—inferior to baptized reprobates and Atheists; 174—invocation of, faint and tender condemnation of by the Tractarians, 202—strong contrast of Bp. Hall's denunciation of, 203—days, new, recommended by Tractarians, 203—their argument for them, 204—a development too fast for the times, 205.

Schoolmen, age of the, that in which most of the latent errors and heresies of Romanism were developed, 102—such as, the seven Sacraments, Sacramental confession, transubstantiation, half communion, image worship, purgatory, indulgences, and disuse of the Scriptures, 102-104.

Simon Magus, Tractarian view of his case, 157, 173.

Sin after Baptism, how only forgiven according to Romish teaching, 185—consistency of this teaching with other parts of that system, 185.

Sin, original, Jackson's statement of Romish views on, 180—similar to those of the Schoolmen, 181—two deductions from them, 181, 182—the views of Tractarians precisely the same; 183—and *actual*, remain in the justified and regenerate according to our standard; annihilated in such according to Oxford teachings, 273—Jackson opposes such teachings, 273.

Sinner accounted righteous, as Christ was accounted a sinner, 73.

Sins, mortal and venial, defined, 193—*venial*, Romish doctrine of, 194-196—grows out of, and essentially connected with Rome's doctrine of original sin and justification, 195, 196—the distinction logically fastened upon the Tractarian system, 197, 198.

Spirit and mind, state of, which qualifies to be a faithful minister of Christ, 477—a *spirit of faith*, 477—*a spirit of love*, 480.

Statement of the present controversy by Newman, 72.

Structure on which we celebrate the Lord's Supper, *form* of, a matter of indifference in itself, 425—while a thing of preference and taste, not calling for serious discussion, 425—when designed to teach false doctrine, of great importance; 426—history of primitive use, and subsequent changes in, 430–434, 439–443.

Substance of doctrine may be unscriptural, while the *words* are orthodox, 135.

Summary of Oxford views on faith; 162—of points made from the articles and homilies in respect to righteousness and faith; 255—of Tractarian extracts from the homilies; 269—of extracts from Reformers and Anglican Divines, 368, 369.

System of the New Oxford Divinity represented in the writings of various authors, 39—is an abandonment of the vital principles of the Protestant faith, 40, 379—Letter of Dr. Pusey to the Bishop of Oxford, leads to a knowledge of, 40—claimed to be the *via media* of the Church of England between Romanism and Ultra-Protestantism; 53—makes words as well as doctrines; 174—difference between it and the doctrine of our Church, radical and fundamental; 370—apologists for, their efforts, 383—not successful, 383 and its resulting practices not yet fully matured, 383—probabilities of its abuse to unrighteousness extreme; 389—an awful perversion of the Gospel; 403, 405—its plain declaration of war; 415—boasting pretensions of; 95—to be guarded against, and sifted, 419.

System of grace, best mode of setting it forth, 459—completeness requires to preach Christ's Godhead, 461—his manhood, 462—his perfect life and obedience, 462—his continued intercession, 463—his priesthood, 464—his office as Prophet and Teacher of his Church, 464—his sovereign power, 465—his resistless authority, 466—his ever present personal ministry in the Church, 468—his freeness, 469.

Tendency of the Oxford doctrine to Romanism, 113—in its followers to develop the errors of the system; 114—of a system that rests in works to make its holders rely mainly on *external* works, 164.

Test, the essential one of the Romanism of any system of Divinity, 46.

Testimony of Bp. Beveridge against Oxford views of faith, 361—of Hooker against the same views, 331–336—of Barnes on justification and faith, 338, 339—of Hooper and Latimer on the same points, 339–343—of Nowell, do, 344–347—of Haddon and Foxe, do., 347–350—of Perkins, do., 350–352—of Downame, do., 352–357—of Andrews, do., 357—of Mede, do., 358–360—of Hall, do., 360, 361—of Nicholson, do., 362—of Usher, do., 363–365—of Hopkins, do., 365—of Beveridge, do., 366–368—chain of, to the great Protestant and Gospel doctrine of justification, 331–368—*six things* to be noticed as conspicuous in the extracts forming the testimony; 368, 369—of Bishop White against the doctrine of a real sacrifice and priesthood in the Eucharist, 447–449—an *approach* to it deprecated, 448.

Tertium quid? claimed by Tractarians for the presence of Christ in the Sacrament, 168, 205.

Tracts for the Times not a full development of the Oxford Divinity, 38.

Tradition used mainly by Rome and Oxford to defend their errors against Scripture, 230—and the Fathers, Latimer's opinion of them; 230—set above Scripture as a judge, 400—set up not to *help* us, but to *rule* us, 400.

Transubstantiation, Oxford tract writers reluctant to oppose it,

205—anxious to avoid discussion of it, 205—controversy on, to be settled only by reference to tradition, 206—lament of the Bp. of Exeter over such a course, 206—while discouraging *discussion*, they make *advance* towards it; 207—no more unreasonable and unscriptural than Baptismal regeneration, 410.

Trust in God only a sure reliance amid the perils of Tractarianism, 422.

Truth like Abner's spear fatal to its pursuers, 270.

Tyndale, Foxe's praise of, 336—his testimony on faith and justification, 336, 337.

Ultra-Protestantism, frequently used by Oxford writers, 53—what is meant by the term; 53—what is good in its adherents asserted by Oxford divines to be *in spite of the system;* 89—retorted upon them, 89—no kind apologies for it and its advocates, as are often made for the worst corruptions of Popery; 215—pointedly ridiculed by Oxford Divines, though exactly agreeing with our church standards, 289, 290.

Uncertainty about our peace with God inculcated as a duty by Oxford writers, 87.

Unction, extreme, according to Oxford writers, Scripture is in favor of it, 208—the *only* reason against it, is want of *Catholic consent*, 208—disuse of, at Baptism and confirmation lamented by Tractarians; 208—of the Gospel, a protection against error, 421.

Unity among Christian denominations not to be secured by adopting Tractarianism, 420.

Unprotestantize the Church, to, the avowed object of Tractarians; 398—the removal of the doctrines of our standards concerning the Lord's Supper, and the substitution of those of Trent essential, 426.

Usher and Jackson compared, 120, 127.

"*Vain jangling,*" examples of, by comparison of Knox's and Newman's views, 75, note.

Views of Tractarians, and, of the author and those with whom he agrees, contrasted, 371.

Worship promoted over preaching by Oxford writers and their sympathizers, 407.

Writings of Tractarians, eulogies of, causes of their production and acceptableness, 416—have done no good and can do none, 416, 417.

"*Yea and Nay,*" of Oxfordism illustrated, 147.

INDEX OF AUTHORS QUOTED,

OR TO WHOSE WORKS REFERENCE IS MADE.

Andrews, 69, 70, 95, 111, 154, 155, 281, 357, 358.
Annati, 110.
Aquinas, 79, 85, 103, 109, 111, 147, 159, 165, 167, 177, 178, 181, 194, 287.
Articles, 183, 187, 245, 276, 277, 304, 309, 311, 399, 402.
Augustine, 294, 295, 298, 305, 307.
Babington, 434.
Barclay, 114.
Barnes, 338, 339.
Barrow, 94, 146, 292.
Bellarmine, 102, 122.
Bennet, 115.
Bernard, 286, 287, 288.
Bethell, 186, 301, 302.
Beveridge, 69, 73, 161, 187, 198, 216, 223, 224, 281, 283, 290, 291, 299, 304, 366–368.
Bingham, 433, 437.
Blunt, 240.
Bradford, 278.
British Critic, 59, 62, 63, 64, 80, 83, 96, 106, 107, 153, 205, 207, 208, 209, 211, 212, 213, 215, 225, 227, 395, 401, 407, 409, 411, 413, 414, 415, 420.
Burnet, 179, 184, 439.
Calvin, 45.
Canons of Trent, 118, 121, 122, 123, 127, 131, 133, 138, 164.
Cassander, 102.
Catechism of Edward VI., 343.
Catechism of the English Church, 146.
Catechism of Trent, 166, 168, 195, 274.
Chemnitz, 67, 103, 105, 119, 125, 132, 177.
Clement of Alexandria, 95.

Cranmer, 215, 246, 278.
Cyprian, 296.
Cyril, 297.
Daille, 432, 433.
Downame, 122, 123, 258, 352–357.
Dupin, 103.
Enfield, 100, 101.
Exeter, Bp., 192, 193, 198, 201, 202, 203, 213.
Faber, 61, 87, 88, 108, 247, 267.
Fisher, 103, 326.
Fitzgerald, 335.
Foxe, 339.
Frith, 319.
Froude, 216, 217, 294.
Fulke, 428–430, 437.
Gandolphy, 144, 185, 190, 191.
Goode, 325, 429, 436, 440, 441, 442.
Grindal, 440.
Guibert, 103.
Haddon, 318, 348, 349.
Hall, Bp., 45, 120, 198, 217, 218, 289, 360, 380, 414.
Hammond, 323.
Homilies, 80, 175, 187, 188, 215, 216, 238, 248–256, 263, 272, 289, 290, 402, 427, 440, 450.
Hook, 302, 327.
Hooker, 43, 57, 67, 69, 70, 71, 80, 95, 112, 123, 131, 134, 135, 138, 279, 280, 283–286, 290, 306, 328, 330, 331–334, 381, 404.
Hooper, 280, 284, 299, 320–323, 339–341.
Hopkins, 273, 365, 366, 391.
Jackson, 101, 102, 119, 126, 127, 168–170, 180–182, 218, 222, 273, 307.
Jerome, 297, 307.
Jewell, 289, 293, 306, 311, 433, 434.

INDEX OF AUTHORS.

Keble, 112, 335, 400.
Knox, Alexander, 58, 59, 81, 92, 95, 266.
Latimer, 230, 298, 323, 341, 342.
Laud, 323.
Lawrence, 239, 240.
Le Bas, 240.
Leighton, 154.
Lewis of Granada, 257.
Luther, 45.
Mede, Joseph, 358, 359
Melancthon, 45, 94.
Morton, 433, 447.
Mosheim, 100, 101, 435.
Newman, 52, 56, 67, 71, 72, 74, 76–78, 81, 86, 93, 109, 122, 124, 126, 127, 131, 146–149, 151, 152, 154–157, 160, 172, 183, 196, 249, 258–262, 266, 268, 269, 282, 328–330, 335, 400, 404, 410, 413.
Nicholson, 361.
Nowell, 312–315, 345–347, 446.
Osiander, 93, 94.
Owen, 134.
Palmer, 158.
Paul's Hist. of Trent, 45, 132, 133, 218.
Penn, 115.
Perkins, 350–352, 434.
Pighius, 105.
Pusey, E. B., Rev. Dr., 39, 53–55, 79, 85, 87, 96, 114, 131, 133, 146, 148, 150, 155, 158, 160, 162, 171, 173, 185, 188, 189, 204, 243, 256, 259, 290, 297, 326, 375–378, 384–388, 404.
Ridley, 439, 440.
Scotus, 102.
Soames, 239.
Stillingfleet, 224.
Strype, 239, 343, 344, 440, 447, 449.
Taylor, 174, 300
Tertullian, 95.
Todd, 239.
Tomline, 239.
Tracts for the Times, 83, 104, 152, 158, 173, 183, 192, 193, 199, 206, 211, 219, 225, 327, 400, 401, 404–408, 419, 442, 443.
Tyndale, 336, 337.
Usher, 49, 103, 120, 177, 290, 306, 363–365.
Vasquez, 102.
Vega, 105.
White, 430, 448.
Whitgift, 316, 317.
Wilson, 230–236, 398.

www.ingramcontent.com/pod-product-compliance
Lightning Source LLC
Chambersburg PA
CBHW071135300426
44113CB00009B/978